Adolescents in
the Internet Age

A volume in
Lifespan Learning

Series Editors:
Paris S. Strom, *Auburn University*
Robert D. Strom, *Arizona State University*

Adolescents in the Internet Age

Paris S. Strom and Robert D. Strom, Series Editors

Adolescents in the Internet Age (2009)
by Paris S. Strom and Robert D. Strom

Adolescents in the Internet Age

by

Paris S. Strom
Auburn University

and

Robert D. Strom
Arizona State University

ST. RITA'S SCHOOL BABINDA LIBRARY

Information Age Publishing, Inc.
Charlotte, North Carolina • www.infoagepub.com

Library of Congress Cataloging-in-Publication Data

Strom, Paris.
 Adolescents in the Internet age / by Paris Strom and Robert D. Strom.
  p. cm. -- (Lifespan learning)
 Includes bibliographical references.
 ISBN 978-1-60752-118-1 (pbk.) -- ISBN 978-1-60752-119-8 (hardcover)
 1. Internet in education--United States. 2. Computer-assisted
instruction--United States. 3. Teacher-student relationships--United
States. 4. Internet and children--United States. 5. Internet and
teenagers--United States. I. Strom, Robert D. II. Title.
 LB1044.87.S847 2009
 373.133'44678--dc22

                                                        2009014749

Printed in the United States of America

CONTENTS

Preface   *xv*

PART I: IDENTITY EXPECTATIONS

1. Perspectives on Adolescence   *3*
   Historical Interpretations   *4*
       Biological Assumptions   *4*
       Cultural Assumptions   *5*
       Cultural Diversity   *7*
       Generation as Culture   *8*
   Adolescents In Social Context   *9*
       Roles and Identity   *9*
       Developmental Tasks   *12*
       Family Accountability   *18*
       Positive Psychology   *20*
   Teacher Action Research   *21*
       Autobiographical Reports   *22*
       Polling Students In Schools   *23*
       Guidelines for Interviews   *24*
   Empirical Research   *26*
       Cross-Sectional Studies   *26*
       Longitudinal Investigations   *27*
       Experimental Procedures   *28*
       Clinical Collaboration   *29*
   Summary   *29*
   Key Terms   *31*
   Visit These Web Sites   *31*
   Recommendations for Using This Book   *32*

Expectations for Adolescents   *32*
Collaboration Integration Theory   *33*
Definitions of Teamwork Roles   *34*
Students as Teamwork Evaluators   *40*

2. Cultural Change and Education   *43*
Stages of Cultural Change   *44*
        Change in a Past-Oriented Culture   *45*
        Change in a Present-Oriented Culture   *47*
        Change in a Future-Oriented Culture   *49*
Cultural Diversity and Cohesion   *50*
        Experiences Shared by Families   *51*
        Generational Differences   *52*
        Peers as Confidants and Advisors   *55*
Cultural Preservation and Adaptation   *57*
        Preoccupation With the Future   *57*
        Balance of Time Perspective   *58*
        Equality of Attention and Listening   *60*
Schooling in the Past   *61*
        Faculty Theory and Memorization   *61*
        Curriculum and Transfer of Training   *62*
        Students and Analytic Thinking   *63*
Schooling in the Present   *65*
        Over-Choice and Decision Making   *65*
        Students and Critical Thinking   *66*
        Voices of Adolescents   *67*
Schooling in the Future   *67*
        Creative and Critical Thinking   *68*
        Adjustment to Change   *69*
        Integration of Technology   *70*
Summary   *72*
Classroom Applications   *74*
For Reflection   *76*
Key Terms   *77*
Visit These Web Sites   *78*
Exercises and Roles   *79*
        Tutoring Poll 2.01   *79*
        Exercises 2.02–2.10   *82–85*

3. Goals, Identity, and Motivation   *87*
Adolescent Identity and Goals   *88*
        Contemporary Developmental Tasks   *88*
        Goal Exploration and Commitment   *88*
        Personality Goals and Achievement   *94*
        Instrumental and Expressive Cultures   *98*

Motivation of Self-Directed Learning   101
    Achievement Motivation Elements   102
    Origins of Achievement Motivation   103
    Attribution of Success and Failure   105
    Amendment of Goals   107
Teacher and Parent Guidance   109
    Influence of Teacher Expectations   109
    Family Access to Student Records   112
    Exploration of Career Options   112
    Voices of Adolescents   114
Interpretation of Progress Toward Goals   115
    Blind Collaborative Grading   115
    Innovative Reporting Practices   116
    Portfolios and Self-Evaluation   117
    Guidelines for Use of Criticism   119
Summary   120
Classroom Applications   121
For Reflection   124
Key Terms   124
Visit These Web Sites   125
Exercises and Roles   126
    Career Exploration Poll 3.01   126
    Exercises 3.02–3.10   129–133

PART II: COGNITIVE EXPECTATIONS

4. Mental Abilities and Achievement   137
Perspectives of Intelligence   138
    Quantitative Assessment of Intelligence   138
    Qualitative Differences in Thinking   139
    Social Constructivist Theory   145
    Emergence of Cyber Constructivism   147
    Multiple Intelligence Theories   150
    Voices of Adolescents   153
Functions of the Mind   154
    Information Processing Theory   154
    Teaching for Comprehension   158
    Memory for Visual Information   161
Insights From Neuroscience   162
    Brain Functioning in Adolescence   163
    Family and School Support for Sleep   165
    Sleep and Memory Consolidation   167
Summary   169
Classroom Applications   171
For Reflection   172

Key Terms   *173*
Visit These Web Sites   *174*
Exercises and Roles   *175*
    Time Management Poll 4.01   *175*
    Exercises 4.02–4.10   *178–181*

5. The Internet and Media Literacy   *183*
    Schools and the Internet   *184*
        Technology and Instruction   *185*
        Internet Learning Paradigm   *186*
        The Inversion of Authority   *191*
        Adolescents as Teachers   *193*
    Adolescents as Researchers   *194*
        New and Old Media   *194*
        Voices of Adolescents   *198*
        Criteria for Internet Research   *199*
    Future of Learning and the Internet   *201*
        Internet Assignment Guidelines   *202*
        Virtual Secondary Schools   *204*
        Families and The Digital Divide   *206*
    Visual Intelligence and Media Literacy   *210*
        Preparation for an Image-Driven Society   *211*
        Differences in Visual and Verbal Intelligence *214*
        Digital Images and Curriculum Enrichment   *215*
        Media Interpretation and Critical Thinking   *217*
    Summary   *219*
    Classroom Applications   *221*
    For Reflection   *223*
    Key Terms   *224*
    Visit These Web Sites   *225*
    Exercises and Roles   *226*
        Learning on the Internet Poll Exercise 5.01   *226*
        Exercises 5.02–5.10   *230–233*

6. Creative Thinking and Problem Solving   *235*
    Characteristics of Creativity   *236*
        Creativity and Intelligence   *237*
        Creative Thinking Abilities   *240*
        The Creative Process   *243*
        Psychology of Thinking   *250*
    Conditions for Problem Solving   *252*
        Assign High Priority to Creative Thinking   *252*
        Student Leadership and Problem Solving   *255*
        Self-Directedness and Divergent Thinking   *256*
        Novel and Stimulating Learning Activities   *257*

Scheduling and Resources   258
   Constructive Use of Unscheduled Time   258
   Chances to Practice Creative Abilities   259
   Solitude, Reflection, and Deliberation   260
   Family and School Support for Curiosity   262
Responsibilities of Students   264
   Mutual Support for Creativity   264
   Peer Criticism and Brainstorming   265
   Overcoming Boredom Together   267
   Families and Home Schooling   268
   Voices of Adolescents   270
Summary   270
Classroom Applications   272
For Reflection   274
Key Terms   275
Visit These Web Sites   275
Exercises and Roles   276
   Boredom Poll Exercise 6.01   276
   Exercises 6.02–6.10   279–283

PART III: SOCIAL EXPECTATIONS

7. Social Maturity and Teamwork   287
Peers and Social Development   288
   Voices of Adolescents   288
   Lessons From Peers   289
   Belonging and Rejection   290
   Peer Pressure Protectors   292
Friendship and Dating   294
   Sexual Harassment of Students   295
   Dating Abuse Among Teenagers   296
   Dating Rights and Responsibilities   297
   Family Dialogue on Relationships   300
Technology and Social Interaction   301
   The Internet and Multiple Selves   301
   Blogs and Social Networks   303
   Prevention of Exploitation   307
Cooperative Learning Classrooms   309
   Social Interdependence Theory   309
   Cooperative Models of Instruction   311
   Social Skills and Team Assessment   314
   Importance of Inclusion Practices   316
Summary   321
Classroom Applications   323
For Reflection   324

Key Terms   325
Visit These Web Sites   326
Exercises and Roles   327
    Peer Support Poll Exercise 7.01   327
    Exercises 7.02–7.10   330–334

8. Risks for Adolescents and Schools   335
Factors in Risk Taking   336
    Families and Students at Risk   336
    Demographics and Destiny   337
    Families and Truancy   338
Risk Assessment Practices   339
    Origins of Risk Analysis   340
    Retention and Promotion   342
    The Medical Risk Model   344
Risk Reduction Strategies   346
    Hurry and Over-Scheduling   347
    Protecting Teacher Time   350
    Voices of Adolescents   351
    Cyber Risk Taking   351
Instructional Risks   352
    Fast and Slow Learners   352
    Testing and Progress Reports   354
    Observations of Dropouts   356
    Taxonomy of Educational Objectives   362
Summary   364
Classroom Applications   366
For Reflection   368
Key Terms   368
Visit These Web Sites   369
Exercises and Roles   370
    School Frustration Poll Exercise 8.01 370
    Exercises 8.02–8.10   374–377

9. Values and Ethical Character   379
Cheating in School   380
    Prevalence of Dishonesty   380
    Motivation for Cheating   382
    Technology and Test Monitoring   383
Internet Ethics   385
    Prevention of Plagiarism   386
    Student Integrity and Maturity   388
    Voices of Adolescents   389
Expression and Tolerance of Differences   390
    Normative Family Conflict   390

Models of Disagreement   *391*
Generational Differences at Work   *392*
Character Building   *394*
Religion and Citizenship   *394*
Moral Development Theories   *396*
Curriculum and Community Service   *403*
Values as a Predictor Of Success   *405*
Values and Delinquent Behavior   *408*
Summary   *409*
Classroom Applications   *411*
For Reflection   *413*
Key Terms   *414*
Visit These Web Sites   *415*
Exercises and Roles   *415*
Exercise 9.01 Cheating Poll   *415*
Exercises 9.02–9.10   *419–423*

PART IV: HEALTH EXPECTATIONS

10. Physical Health and Lifestyle   *427*
Growth and Development   *427*
Height and Weight   *428*
Sexual Maturation   *429*
Vision and Hearing   *430*
Body Image Concerns   *432*
Nutrition and Diet   *433*
Nutrition Deficiencies   *434*
Family Dietary Guidelines   *435*
Families and Eating Disorders   *436*
Families and Obesity   *437*
Exercise and Fitness   *440*
Benefits of Exercise   *440*
Schools and Exercise   *441*
Voices of Adolescents   *442*
Sexual Behavior and Knowledge   *443*
Sexual Activity and Diseases   *444*
Contraception and Pregnancy   *446*
Involvement With Oral Sex   *450*
Comprehensive Sex Education   *451*
Substance Abuse   *453*
Marijuana and Cocaine   *453*
Methamphetamine   *454*
Inhalants   *456*
Alcohol   *457*
Tobacco   *458*

Summary   460
Classroom Applications   462
For Reflection   463
Key Terms   464
Visit These Web Sites   465
Exercises and Roles   466
    School Dress Code Poll 10.01   466
    Exercises 10.2–10.10   468–470

11. Self Control and Safe Schools   471
Theories of Civil Behavior   472
    Behavior Conditioning Theory   472
    Social Cognitive Theory   475
    Hierarchy of Needs Theory   476
Characteristics of Bullies   477
    Misconceptions About Bullies   478
    Family Relationships   480
    Influence on Peers   481
    Formation of Gangs   483
Virtual World Harassment   485
    Uniqueness of Digital Abuse   485
    Examples of Cyberbullying   487
    Teasing and Cyberbullying   489
    Solutions for Cyberbullying   491
School Initiatives   493
    Guided Student Discussions   493
    Anger Management Curriculum   495
    Voices of Adolescents   497
Families and Corrective Guidance   498
    Families and School Discipline   499
    Families and Student Misconduct   500
    Good Behavior Reports to Families   501
Summary   502
Classroom Applications   506
For Reflection   508
Key Terms   509
Visit These Web Sites   510
Exercises and Roles   511
    Cyberbully Poll Exercise 11.01   511
    Exercises 11.02–11.10   515–518

12. Emotions and Resilience   519
Influence of Stress   520
    Resilience—The Hardiness Asset   520
    Anxiety and Uncertainty   522
    Stress and Status Hierarchy   523

Worries of Adolescents   524
Stress and Depression   527
Emotional Intelligence   531
Patience and Learning to Wait   532
Impact of Hope and Optimism   534
Meditation and Relaxation   536
Voices of Adolescents   538
Family and School Challenges   539
Developmental Assets   540
Self-Esteem and Confidence   546
Inflated Self-Esteem   549
Staying Home for College   550
Summary   554
Classroom Applications   556
For Reflection   557
Key Terms   558
Visit These Web Sites   559
Exercises and Roles   559
Stress Poll Exercise 12.01   559
Exercises 12.02–12.10   563–566
References   567

PREFACE

This book introduces a new set of core topics for the study of adolescents who are growing up in post-9/11 and experiencing the nation's first Black President Barack Obama. The socialization, learning, health, and lifestyle of today's teenagers are distinctive because of their access to the Internet, cell phones, computers, wireless organizers, iPods, and satellite television. The potential of these tools to improve education is generally recognized but also requires changes in the teacher-student relationship. Teaching adolescents and learning from them is a goal that can benefit both parties.

SCOPE OF COVERAGE

Practical concerns that middle school and high school teachers have about students influenced the selection of topics. Some of these issues include Internet learning, critical thinking, visual intelligence, creative behavior, problem solving, evaluating achievement, discipline, values, cheating, risk taking, cyberbullying, media literacy, nutrition, exercise, stress, resilience, friendships, dating, sexuality, substance abuse, and parent involvement. In addition, much of what every teacher has to learn comes from getting to know students as individuals. Acquiring this knowledge from dialogue and observation is supported by guidelines and agenda for interviewing and polling students and their parents.

Importance of Identity

Books describing adolescents should explain how powerful forces like MySpace, Facebook and other social network sites influence identity. One chapter is devoted to exploring impact of the Internet on motivation, learning, and status. Other chapters consider how technology relates to cyber ethics, cheating, plagiarism, teen blogs, health, electronic bullying, the digital divide, virtual schooling, and online expression of multiple selves.

Teenagers enjoy using tools of technology. Schools can become more effective when this intrinsic motivation is respected. Guidelines for homework assignments on the Internet are presented. Possibilities for learning depend on what students are expected to read. Students at all levels should be expected to search for, locate, read, and reflect on materials beyond their textbook. This shift toward greater responsibility for active learning is motivated by providing opportunities to practice research skills, self-directed inquiry, and team learning.

Teachers should encourage students in constructing some of their knowledge. This goal was less important in the past when the teacher role focused on planning lessons and making presentations. Being a teacher no longer means serving as the main source of student learning. Today educators should spend more of their time preparing reflective tasks that allow students to engage in active learning and work together in cooperative teams. Each chapter includes exercises designed to motivate idea sharing and practice mutual accountability.

Families and Instruction

The life lessons that students receive at home differ from the curriculum provided in classrooms. Most parents are influential and have the potential to motivate persistence, model a work ethic, convey attitudes of civil behavior, and exemplify the importance of continuous learning. Society expects parents to be the main source of correction for student misconduct, provide examples for resolving disagreements, and offer guidance about friendship, healthy lifestyle, and religious beliefs. Teachers should be able to detect situations that are appropriate for enlisting parent involvement and recognize contexts where families can assume leadership for education. The prospect of student success is increased when teachers and parents value the efforts of one another and try to compliment their mutually understood roles. Each chapter discusses parent concerns, such as sex education, peer abuse, Internet safety, career exploration, dating advice, and how united efforts with the school can facilitate success and well-being.

Appreciation of Cultural Diversity

The workplace requires interdependence and cooperation as keys to individual and group success. This process can begin by acknowledging that most students have relatives who know customs, beliefs, and rituals associated with their cultural heritage. These out-of-school informants should be recruited to become part of the instructional equation. We provide interview questions that students can use for homework conversations with family and neighbors to explore perceptions about their culture. The cultural reporter provides insights that contribute to personal identity and motivates the pursuit of attributes that help people get along in a complex social environment.

Theories to Guide Teaching

Teachers make decisions about theories to rely on when providing instruction, fostering social-emotional intelligence, stimulating creative thought, building teamwork skills, supporting self-esteem, and monitoring student progress. Attainment of these goals is becoming more complex because of a need to broaden applications to include technology, expand school accountability, and be aware of emerging concepts. Social science theories are time-bound so it is important that educators recognize when a specific theory should be amended or replaced. Theories of development, learning, motivation, identity, and assessment are presented in relation to chapter themes where they are relevant instead of placing all theories in one chapter without linking to a context for application.

Exercises and Roles to Promote Teamwork

Teachers can be more effective if they collaborate with faculty, parents, and community organizations than when they act as isolated professionals. College students using this book have opportunities to practice the same teamwork skills they are expected to nurture in their classrooms. Each chapter concludes with 10 Cooperative Learning Exercises and Roles (CLEAR). The goals of CLEAR are to ensure a shift in the student role from being passive to active learners, make teamwork skills the focus for student collaboration, and encourage each individual to make a unique contribution to group learning.

Balancing Historical and Current Research

Seminal studies of adolescence are described along with discussion of emerging research. The coverage is up-to-date with 200 Web site references appearing in the narrative where they relate to a specific topic under consideration. Web sites can provide elaboration for issues of interest, present opposing points of view, and checked for data subject to periodic change. For example, some demographic statistics shift annually. Instead of limiting readers to the data available at the time of book production, we identify Web sites to retrieve current information. In addition, Web sites are provided that teachers can suggest to parents for family discussion at home regarding dating, goal setting, discipline, social interaction, substance abuse, friendships, sexuality, nutrition, sleep, cheating, and peer abuse.

Learning From Adolescents

The best way to know adolescents is by listening to them. Students are an essential source of learning for teachers. When teachers know how teenagers see the world, they can better fulfill their guidance role. Polling is a powerful method for teachers to discover how students perceive conditions of learning at school. Computers are in every school, public library, and most homes. Electronic polling allows students to express views anonymously. Inviting adolescent opinion reveals interpretations, promotes reciprocal learning, and allows practice in democratic decision-making. Polls help teachers better understand the teenagers that concern them the most, students in their own classes. There is a poll to assess student views about the theme of each chapter.

ORGANIZATION OF THE BOOK

Expectations are the common chapter theme for *Adolescents in the Internet Age*. Expectations shape goals, determine priorities, and evaluate the progress of individuals as well as institutions. When teacher expectations match student abilities and interests, the outcomes are achievement and satisfaction. However, when teacher expect too little of students, attainment of potential is undermined. There should also be concern when student expectations surpass their abilities. This occurs when individuals do not know their limitations or suppose they are capable of carrying out more goals than is possible. The decision to over-load or over-schedule is bound to restrict success. Sharing accountability involves setting complimentary and attainable expectations that are met by students, teachers, and parents. To support appropriate expectations, this book is organized in four sections that emphasize separate aspects of learning and development in adolescence.

1. *Identity Expectations* introduce traditional perspectives about adolescence, cultural change in learning sources and focus of schooling, and ways to facilitate intrinsic student motivation, goal setting, and formation of identity.
2. *Cognitive Expectations* examine mental abilities of youth, academic standards, reliance on Internet tools and media literacy, creative problem solving, and ways to support higher order thinking skills.
3. *Social Expectations* explore the broad scope of social development, acquiring teamwork skills, inclusion of exceptional students and risk assessment strategies that can apply to individual teenagers and the schools they attend.
4. *Health Expectations* center on issues that influence physical and mental health, lifestyle choices, stress and emotional intelligence, adoption of civil behavior, and student safety.

Features of Each Chapter That Support Learning

Chapter-opening outline. The goals and topics to be presented are introduced.

Polls. Student perceptions about conditions of learning are assessed by polls.

Summary. A sequential summary of the topic sections are placed in perspective.

Classroom Applications. Translating research into classroom practice is described.

For Reflection. Reflection questions urge readers to further explore some topics.

Key Terms. Basic terms are *bolded*, defined, and listed for review of comprehension.

Visit Web Sites. The perspective of this book is more comprehensive when Web sites referred to in the narrative are viewed to elaborate or challenge presentationof topics. You can link to these Web sites at http://www.infoagepub.com/strom-adolescents.

Exercises and Roles. Tasks and cooperative roles support problem solving in teams.

Authors

Teachers want to know their students. Similarly, students are interested in the background of the authors whose text they read for their course. Paris and Robert Strom are a son and father team whose dialogue always leads to their reciprocal learning. Both aspire to discover ways for improving the learning and maturity of adolescents.

Paris Strom (PhD, Arizona State University) is an associate professor of educational psychology at Auburn University in Auburn, Alabama. He began his teaching career in the public high schools of Scottsdale and Peoria, Arizona. Courses on human development that Paris teaches include students in the studio and online students in the region. The electronic polls he codesigned enable schools to become informed about the views of adolescents when making decisions about reforms. He is coauthor of the Teamwork Skills Inventory providing anonymous feedback from peers, and the Parent Success Indicator by which adolescents detect assets and learning needs of their parents. Paris is the author of 80 journal articles about lifespan learning and recipient of the Leischuck Award for Outstanding Undergraduate teaching at Auburn University.

Robert Strom (PhD, University of Michigan) is professor of educational psychology at Arizona State University. His teaching began in the public schools of St. Paul, Minnesota and Detroit, Michigan. Robert teaches courses on adolescence for secondary educators and counselors. He is the author of 400 articles, 20 books on lifespan development, and several measurement tools for teachers and parents. His scholarship is reflected by three Fulbright Senior Research Scholar Awards at the University of Stockholm, Sweden, University of Manila, Philippines, and University of Canberra, Australia. Robert has served as a Japan Society for the Promotion of Science Scholar in Tokyo, NATO Scholar at the University of Ankara, Turkey and recipient of the Danforth Foundation National Award for College Teaching.

ACKNOWLEDGMENTS

Having someone who can be relied on to detect your mistakes, improve the clarity of explanations, suggest practical examples that better connect with the experience of readers, challenge assumptions and logic, order better sequencing of ideas, sustain a healthy sense of humor, stimulate creative thinking, and encourage persistence is a wonderful asset. We are grateful to Shirley Strom for sharing these qualities with us. She has helped to make the writing process more satisfying and improve the quality of our work. We also want to thank Benjamin Gonzalez, the Information Age Publishing editor and cover designer for this book.

Paris S. Strom and Robert D. Strom

PART I

IDENTITY EXPECTATIONS

CHAPTER 1

PERSPECTIVES ON ADOLESCENCE

Dramatic changes are transforming the adolescent experience. Many situations that adults remember when they look back on their years of growing up are no longer the same. Teachers, parents, and other adults responsible for the guidance of middle school and high school students should become familiar with current conditions to avoid acting on out-dated impressions. Today's adolescents are the first generation to be educated in an environment permeated by digital media (Trier, 2007).

The goals for this chapter are to provide an overview of historical and current beliefs about how biology and culture influence adolescent behavior and status of youth in society. Ways to overcome some common obstacles that prevent attainment of identity are discussed. The developmental tasks of teenagers are explored in connection with the growing emphasis on positive psychology that seeks to support acquisition of ordinary strengths and resilience. *Reciprocal learning*, defined as adolescents and adults learning from each other, in the classroom and at home is considered. Action research methods are examined that teachers can rely on to gain insights about their students. Empirical procedures applied in the study of adolescence are described with implications for educators. Recommendations for using this book suggest expectations of students and faculty.

Adolescents in the Internet Age, pp. 3–41
Copyright © 2009 by Information Age Publishing
All rights of reproduction in any form reserved.

HISTORICAL INTERPRETATIONS

The portrayal of adolescence has evolved from an exclusive biological explanation to a broader view that also acknowledges the contribution of culture. This more comprehensive perspective urges educators to realize that development requires planning and arranging supportive aspects of environment that students experience in the classroom and at home.

Biological Assumptions

G. Stanley Hall (1844–1924) introduced the concept of adolescence. Hall was the first student to earn a doctoral degree in psychology from an American university. Following his graduation from Harvard University, Hall joined the faculty of Johns Hopkins University where he established the first psychological laboratory in 1883. Four years later, along with others, he founded the American Psychological Association (APA). Hall was critical of education practices and believed that teachers could become more effective if their training included some understanding of child and adolescent development (Munger, 2003).

Hall's (1904) ambitious goal was to write a text that would help explain the nature of adolescence. His two-volume work was called *Adolescence: Its Psychology and Relationship to Physiology, Anthropology, Sociology, Sex, Crime, Religion, and Education*. Hall defined *adolescence* as "the period beginning with puberty, referring to the timing and the processes involved with marked enlarging of the reproductive organs, and continuing until adulthood" (p. 6). He acknowledged that, while the particular ages when puberty and adulthood occur vary in individuals, distinctive markers are usually evident between age 14 and 24. Scholars today identify adolescence as the period from ages 10 to 20 or later (Epstein, 2007).

Hall (1904) saw adolescence as a stormy and stressful period, reflected by increased conflict with relatives, emotional instability shown by polar mood swings, and a tendency to take unreasonable risks. These signs of internal turmoil, depression, and rebellion were thought to be natural and inevitable. The assumption was that such behavior represented a biological stage everyone passes through in a normal transition from childhood to adulthood. In his recapitulation theory, the French zoologist Jean Lamarck (1830) hypothesized that each generation was destined to repeat evolutionary history as it progressed through successive stages characterizing human development. He speculated that the cumulative memories of mankind must somehow be genetically conveyed. These second-hand recollections triggered the mechanism that activated universal recapitulation (Kandel, 2006). Proponents agreed that there must have been a particularly turbulent period in ancient history which was perpetually repeated in the delinquent habits of adolescents. In this manner, development recapitulated evolution as young people reenacted the troublesome time period when primitive responses were predominant and patterns of civilized behavior had yet to emerge (Munger, 2003). G. Stanley Hall's contributions to psychology and education are discussed on the Muskingum College Web site archives at http://muskingum.edu/~psych/psycweb/history/hall.htm.

Hall's (1904) observations led him to conclude that sexual development could be a factor contributing to the stress experienced in adolescence. Overly active hormones might stimulate youngsters to behave in certain situations as though they are emotionally unstable. Twenty years later Sigmund Freud (1923) added psychoanalytic concepts such as repression, aggression, and defense mechanisms to a lengthy list of biological causes that were cited as explanations for the worrisome conduct of teenagers. This line of reasoning urged the public to tolerate outlandish and frustrating actions instead of trying to determine the reasons that motivate mysterious behavior in adolescence. The resulting misconception was to consider adolescence a stage that is inevitably reflected by stress, anxiety, confusion, mood swings, alienation, and rebellion (Hines & Paulson, 2006). Psychotherapist Anna Freud (1895-1982), daughter of Sigmund Freud, maintained that adolescents who deny experiencing the predictable 'storm and stress' syndrome probably need professional treatment (A. Freud, 1969).

Cultural Assumptions

The nation's first educational psychologist was Edward Thorndike (1913). He argued against Hall's (1904) thesis about biological determinism and universal prevalence of storm and stress during adolescence. However, most scholars considered the biological explanation appealing and dismissed contrary opinions. Someone from outside psychology presented the most powerful challenge. Margaret Mead (1901–1978), a doctoral candidate in anthropology at Columbia University, disagreed with Hall's assumptions that conflict and emotional instability during adolescence are caused by recapitulation and that rebellion is an accurate portrayal of how young people act in every culture.

Mead hypothesized that, if some culture could be found where youth did not exhibit delinquent behaviors, another explanation of adolescence would be warranted. Mead selected Western Samoa as the place to carry out an extensive field study. The 50 girls that she observed were divided into three groups representing prepuberty, puberty, and postpuberty.

Mead (1928) reported in *The Coming of Age in Samoa* that she found no significant differences in the behavior of girls going through adolescence from other girls who would become adolescents in 2 years or the group that had entered adolescence 2 years earlier.

Mead's (1928) findings were seen as revolutionary because they implied that culture instead of physiological or cognitive change could be the cause of adolescence. This meant that while puberty is universal, the storm and stress attributed to adolescence is not universal. In declaring adolescence to be a cultural invention, Mead suggested that industrial conditions might explain the stresses encountered by young people in societies like the United States. In less sophisticated societies where initiation rites immediately transform children to the status of an adult, there was no adolescence, no instability, no depression, and no visible evidence of behavioral disturbance. Biological processes related to adolescence are the same in every culture. Therefore, the fact that Samoan females did not encounter the same difficulties that were reported by American girls must attribute to cultural experiences in the United States that were not present in the Samoan society.

According to Mead (1928), the problems associated with adolescence for American females during the 1920s were an outcome of conflicting standards and the emerging belief that individuals ought to make personal choices without much guidance. Her contention was

> A society that is clamoring for choice, filled with many articulate groups, each urging its own salvation and variety of economic philosophy, will give each new generation no peace until all have chosen or gone under, unable to bear the conditions of choice. The stress is in our civilization, not in the physical changes through which children pass, but it is none the less real nor less inevitable in twentieth century America. (Mead, 2001, p. 162)

On the other hand, the dilemma confronting Samoan girls was on a smaller scale because the differences between parent and child experiences in that society were more narrow and painless, showing few among the unfortunate aspects ordinarily present in times of rapid transition. Essentially, the Samoan girls were growing up in a homogenous culture that consisted of uniform ideals and aspirations (Francis, 2006). The American Museum of Natural History presents Margaret Mead's video interview at http://www.amnh.org/exhibitions/mead.html.

Mead's (1928, 1930, 1978) hunch was that the need to make personal choices could be the source of most internal conflict and, with the introduction of a broader set of options, adolescents in Samoa would find themselves exposed to a greater amount of stress. In the meanwhile, so long as choices of Samoans' were restricted, their world would continue to be relatively simple and lack turmoil. It would be many years before there was consensus that a universal adolescent experience does not exist and many teenagers make their way through this developmental stage without outward signs of disturbance (Hines & Paulson, 2006). The shift came about when Larry Rutter and his colleagues determined that three-fourths of the adolescent participants in a large-scale survey reported satisfying and beneficial relationships with their parents (Rutter, Graham, & Chadwick, 1976). Further, among adolescents whose experience matched the "storm and stress category," most had communication problems with relatives preceding adolescence. These findings allowed Rutter (1980) to confidently reinforce Margaret Mead's conclusions by stating, "Young people tend to share their parents' values on major issues of life and turn to them for guidance on major concerns. The notion of parent-child alienation as being a common feature of adolescence is a myth" (p. 19).

Cultural Diversity

Some differences among adolescents may attribute to growing up in an Asian, Black, Hispanic, Native-American, or White household (French, Seidman, Allen, & Aber, 2006). Research has documented that culture can have a powerful effect on student perceptions of their identity, work ethic, self-assessment, failure, perseverance, gender expectations, and career aspirations (Chiu & Hong, 2006; Wineburg, Mosborg, Porat, & Duncan, 2007). Most teachers are responsible for students from varied backgrounds so they need to know how cultures differ in their support for adolescents and implications for improving home-school relationships. The following cultural diversity concerns are discussed in relation to themes in chapters where they appear most relevant: family demographics and at-risk behavior; parent expectations for academic achievement; support for tutoring; computers and the digital divide; adoption of values, motivation for learning; access to sex education; school-home communication; special education; nutrition, diet, and exercise; family configuration and challenges; differences in home learning environments; family corrective discipline; and adjustment of immigrant students.

Teachers can help all students recognize that evolution of culture and preservation of cultural harmony requires careful evaluation of the customs passed on from one generation to another (Kim, Sherman, Ko, & Taylor, 2006). For example, the American goal of achieving gender equity is experienced less often in certain subcultures than in others. When outsiders identify some absence of opportunity and recommend greater gender equity, the observations could be misinterpreted as ethnic prejudice or insensitivity (Chiu & Hong, 2006). Cultural evolution is also arrested when no longer appropriate traditions continue to be portrayed as necessary to preserve group identity, pride, and show respect to ancestors (French, Seidman, Allen, & Aber, 2006). An inflexible orientation can prevent the objective thinking each of us needs to be constructively critical of our subculture or recognize when changes and improvements are needed. Subculture insiders that propose new ways of doing things must often have courage and accept rejection because their suggestions may be misinterpreted as a lack of loyalty to the group (Hutchinson, Jetten, Christian, & Haycraft, 2006).

Generation as Culture

Teachers are in a unique position to help students think critically so they can maintain cultural cohesion while also stimulating needed change. Culture is often defined as a lifestyle reflecting the ethnicity and language for a particular group. Most children adopt elements of the culture they are oriented to by their parents and surrogates (Swann, Chang-Schneider, & McClarty, 2007). However, because growing up differs for successive generations, peers are bound to greatly influence adolescent choice of lifestyle. Peer norms are communicated and reinforced on a broader scale than ever before by social network Web sites and global media (Adams & Hamm, 2006). This partially explains why teenagers from Tokyo, Atlanta, and Moscow often share more similar views with each another than they do with their parents. These conditions reflect the observation that, generally people resemble their times more than they resemble their parents. Generational differences within cultures are often referred to in this book because teachers must keep them in mind as they try to motivate both students and their parents (Buckingham & Willett, 2006).

When generation is recognized as an important even though often overlooked factor in defining culture, the impressions of adolescents are viewed as deserving more attention (Goleman, 2006). In addition, adults become less inclined to assume an advocate role for youth in favor of encouraging teenagers to speak for themselves. In hierarchical cultures adolescents have always been discouraged from stating personal opinions that may contradict the views of older relatives, educators or others in positions of authority (Galinsky, Magee, Inesi, & Gruenfeld, 2006). In these environments teenagers who express ideas contrary to those of adults are usually characterized as lacking respect (Shek, 2007). Because of such constraints to authentic dialogue, some teenagers choose to remain silent. In turn, this leads adults to mistakenly suppose that the absence of opposition must mean that there is agreement across the generations (Asher, 2007).

A more promising outlook is to understand that when adults listen to the adolescent culture, youth may be less inclined to devalue their legacy or abandon customs that could otherwise be revised and retained. Teachers should act as models for other adults by demonstrating that listening to adolescents is essential for attaining the goals of cultural preservation, cultural evolution, and cultural adjustment (Black, 2005).

ADOLESCENTS IN SOCIAL CONTEXT

Another key to understanding adolescence is the changing social order that assigns purpose and status to segments of the population. There is agreement that having a well-defined role helps establish a favorable sense of identity. This is especially important during adolescence when pursuit of identity is the most common goal. Nevertheless, allowing youth to have a significant place in society seems more difficult to arrange within a technological environment than it was in previous eras. Teenagers commonly observe that, although they are no longer children, grown-ups are unwilling to recognize them as adults.

Roles and Identity

Roles

The term "teenager" first appeared during the 1940s in *Popular Mechanics*. Editors of this still published magazine speculated that, because youth would eventually become a lucrative consumer market, businesses should begin advertising to them. The same message was conveyed at the launch of *Seventeen Magazine* that began in 1944 (Savage, 2007). Another change in the way teenagers were perceived implicated efforts of the government to remove them from the work force. The purpose was to make sure that returning veterans from World War II, in 1945, would be able to find a job. To mobilize support for this shift in public policy, the United States Department of Labor widely disseminated forecasts that automation would soon require that all workers possess a high school diploma for entry-level positions. This message included the recommendation that adolescents should remain in school until graduation. Local boards of education supported the federal initiative by establishing compulsory attendance and starting remedial programs to help students who might otherwise decide to quit school (O'Toole & Lawler, 2006).

Hollywood filmmakers reinforced the change of image for teenagers, from considering them capable of working effectively along side adults to the impression that they are not ready to fully participate in adult activities. A popular teenage movie star, Mickey Rooney, appeared in numerous films where he portrayed roles demonstrating that adolescents are immature and need more education to prepare them for the workforce. The same message was conveyed by television in the 1960s and 1970s by programs such as *Leave it to Beaver* and *Happy Days* depicting teen dependence on parents (Coontz, 2000). Currently, adolescents are recognized as prominent customers of the music, fast food, fashion, cell phone, and footwear industries (Cappo, 2005).

In retrospect, since Stanley Hall (1904) introduced the concept of adolescence, this stage of life has appreciably improved. A balanced view of how teenagers are seen should include ways society has taken corrective measures to enrich quality of life for adolescents There have been benefits from the abolition of child labor, compulsory education policies, and ensuring learning opportunities for students from all backgrounds. Everyone has gained from a progressive increase in the mandatory age for schooling, providing special education for youth with disabilities, offering government health care for poor and immigrant students, establishing juvenile courts to support individual rights and access to rehabilitation programs. These shifts reflect the public goal to make an officially approved period of youth possible for every adolescent (Garrett, 2007).

Despite these improvements to support their development, many adolescents believe that arbitrary barriers have been erected to delay their identity as adults. Specifically, the following obstacles are frequently mentioned.

1. Extended education. Spending more years in school leads to better paying jobs and greater opportunities for advancement. However, this extended learning time delays financial independence, autonomy, and social identity (O'Toole & Lawler, 2006).

2. Objections to early marriage. There is general public objection to marriage for adolescents even though males reach the height of sexual urge and power during late adolescence, and females are fully responsive at this age. Statistics, however, underscore the wisdom of waiting to marry (Parks, 2007).

A daunting threat our society faces is coping with rapid change (Toffler & Toffler, 2006). Difficulties of adjustment and sustaining a sense of stability in the face of constant flux are a continuing challenge. Adolescents are particularly hard hit because they are starting to think about a job, getting married, deciding on a career, pursuing higher education, accepting community obligations, and determining personal identity.

The impression of some teenagers that they are unfairly denied adult status is shared by Robert Epstein. In *The Case Against Adolescence*, Epstein

(2007) explores fallacies in how adults perceive youth as inherently irresponsible, to be shielded from the challenges of adulthood, and incapable of making reasoned decisions about their health. Epstein describes the "artificial extension of childhood." by which adolescents are isolated from the people they are about to become and traps them in a meaningless world controlled by peers and the media. Epstein argues that society has forgotten how capable young people are even though adolescents know it and feel frustration. He describes contexts for competency testing that could be used as criteria to achieve adult status and points out some grown-ups would be unable to pass these tests.

Identity

The main goal of adolescents is formation of identity, working toward acceptance as an adult with an individual sense of meaning, purpose, and direction (Bergh & Erling, 2005; Temple, 2006). The customary criteria for granting identity must be revised because getting ready for a job, leaving home, working full-time, and perhaps getting married are necessarily delayed until later ages today (Maras, 2007). The current environment should be carefully examined to see how it could support a more significant identity for adolescents.

Technology skills, the tools that are needed for learning in the future, represent a credible criterion for identity. In this context, youth often possess greater competence than the adults supervising them, enabling teenagers to feel confident and able to provide reciprocal learning for adults (Zimmer-Gembeck, & Mortimer, 2006). Web sites like Facebook http://www.facebook.com and MySpace http://myspace.com are powerful resources for creating adolescent norms that challenge the status quo of withholding identity until students complete education and have full time employment.

The Internet offers opportunities for adolescents to experiment with multiple selves using alias screen names, present opinions on blogs, obtain feedback on their thinking, try out unfamiliar roles, and practice communication skills. These activities can contribute to the formation of identity. Because of age-segregation norms, adults rarely communicate online with adolescents—an aspect of life that teenagers find most appealing and where they prefer to spend significant time. Consequently, parents and teachers often underestimate the impact that technology can have on formation of identity (Buckingham & Willett, 2006; Eastin, 2005).

Adolescents rely on technology mainly for conversation with friends but these same tools could be used to expand the social context for identity through interaction with mentors, relatives, community leaders, elders, and persons from different cultures (Parks, 2007). Such efforts to enlarge the contextual basis of adolescent identity acknowledges that the emerging social self can be too narrow when defined exclusively by interaction with peers online or dialogue with members of one's own generation. In general, it seems appropriate to credit adolescents for acquiring the skills of technology they need for the future and accept this asset as a criterion for identity status in the emerging society (Cushman, 2006).

The concept of identity should include recognition of personal responsibility to improve the society. Adolescents need encouragement to reach beyond important personal concerns like—What will I do to earn money? What kind of person do I want to date and marry? Do I want to have children? In addition, from a self-actualization perspective, the quest should include—What needs of society could I respond to that will help others and provide a sense of purpose? (Hart, Donnelly, Youniss, & Atkins, 2007). Roles in relation to the community are essential so identity is not just an amalgam of personal ambitions but an outcome based, ongoing personal set of expectations for changing the world in a constructive way. Identity can be restricted when the emphasis is only on exploration of how to fit into a person's own age group, race, or religious institution. There should also be questions representing a higher level that implicate a longer time frame like—How do I favorably interact with others who are not like me in age, religion, region or race? What is a reasonable amount of community service for me? What personality goals should I pursue so my influence is more beneficial?

Efforts to nurture identity in this broader context require experience as a volunteer, interviewing relatives and community figures, using polls, blogs, and other procedures to foster broader data gathering and more critical introspection at both the personal and cultural level (DiMaria, 2006). Helping adolescents attain identity that leads toward maturity is discussed in most chapters of this book. Some relevant contexts include friendship, dating, goal setting, body image, career orientation, treatment of classmates, effects of gender and culture, honesty and cheating, values, self-esteem, peer pressure, cyberbullying, health care, developmental tasks, managing stress, and working in teams. Teachers have daily opportunities to promote the formation of healthy identity within these contexts.

Developmental Tasks

The goal of educating adolescents has been to prepare them for certain roles that do not begin until adulthood. Therefore, it is reasonable to identify the learning focus for this stage of development. Robert Havighurst (1900–1991), Professor of education at University of Chicago, sought to reconcile individuals needs with the demands of society. He referred to *developmental tasks* as the attitudes, skills, and understandings that people should acquire at particular ages through physical maturity, social expectation, or personal effort (Havighurst, 1972). By mastering developmental tasks for their place in the life cycle, people adjust, are recognized as competent, and prepare themselves for challenges to occur in the next stage.

Havighurst (1972) maintained that there are teachable moments when lessons can facilitate the accomplishment of developmental tasks. He acknowledged that arranging appropriate education could be complicated because tasks may be seen differently across cultures and distinctions exist within cultures. Table 1.1 presents tasks that require attention of all adolescents. Each task is discussed here in the 1970s context

Table 1.1.   A Comparison of Then and Now:
Havighurst's Eight Developmental Tasks for Adolescents

Havighurst's (1972) Developmental Tasks* For Adolescents	Contemporary Interpretations and Implications How is This Different Today?
Task 1. Achieving new and more mature relationships with age mates of both sexes.	Students practice social skills in cooperative learning groups to acquire teamwork attributes that will be necessary for success in the family, workplace, and community.
Task 2. Achieving a masculine or feminine social role.	Uniform expectations for gender roles no longer imposed in favor of more acceptance toward individuals choosing not to marry, not to have children, or enter civil unions.
Task 3. Accepting one's physique and using the body effectively.	Body image remains a prominent criterion to be judged as acceptable by classmates. There is increasing emphasis on exercise, nutrition and fitness for a longevity society.
Task 4. Achieving emotional independence from parents and other adults.	A more lengthy period of required education results in extended financial dependence on parents. In addition, students must prepare for interdependence, not just independence.
Task 5. Preparing for marriage and family life.	Need to accept new expectations for equality in sharing domestic tasks with spouses/partners, or define alternative lifestyle purposes when building a family is not chosen.
Task 6. Preparation for an economic career.	Overcoming feelings of anxiety and uncertainty about joining the workforce as a later age than prior generations by participation in career exploration and education planning.
Task 7. Acquiring values and an ethical system to guide behavior.	Youth are less inclined to adopt values of parents that do not fit emerging conditions and demonstrate greater reliance on interaction with peers in deciding on lifestyle.
Task 8. Desiring and achieving socially responsible behavior.	Recognition that extended education and later work entry require involvement with nonacademic socially maturing experiences to be gained through community service.

Source: *Havighurst's Eight Developmental Tasks originally appeared in R. Havighurst, 1972, *Developmental tasks and education* (New York: David McKay).
Contemporary Interpretations and Implications: How is this different today? have been developed by R. Strom, 2009.

when proposed as well as the current scene. The reason for this dual explanation is because social science theories are time bound. They usually match the period when proposed more closely than conditions of a later era. Educators who apply theories years after they were initially proposed can benefit most from taking two interpretations into account. The explanation of the theorist is central and can be juxtaposed with the interpretation of an observer reflecting on relevance of a theory in relation to contemporary conditions.

Task 1. Achieving new and more mature relationships with age mates of both sexes. The essence of this developmental task is learning to work with others for a common purpose and share leadership without domination. Havighurst recommended that middle school and high school teachers should get used to the situation that adolescents are intensely interested in their relationships with peers (Ladd, 2005). Therefore, this situation should be viewed as a teachable moment to develop social skills. He believed that, to become good citizens, students need experience with managing as much of their own affairs as possible. This view accords with recent findings that students find satisfaction in cooperative learning groups where they practice social skills to get along with others and work effectively in teams (Roseth, Johnson, & Johnson, 2008). Havighurst (1972) maintained that the most potent force in adolescence is peer group approval, and educators should capitalize on this motivation by helping students build constructive group norms to guide healthy behavior. In today's context, teachers can begin by asking these questions: Do I trust students to work together in teams? Can I arrange cooperative tasks that will support academic achievement while also contributing to development of mature relationships?

Task 2. Achieving a masculine or feminine social role. Puberty provides the biological basis for accepting and learning a socially approved adult role. However, there are no longer a uniform set of gender goals as there were in the 1970s that adolescents should adopt as they look forward to their identity as women and men. There has been a steady movement toward equity in schools and the workplace. Consequently, most women include employment as one of their roles. There is greater acceptance now of individuals who choose to either not marry or get married but not have children. Public opinion regarding same sex unions remains contentious but gaining in support as shown by challenges to marriage laws in many states (Fine & Harvey, 2005). While the numbers of roles that women perform have greatly expanded, there has been less of a corresponding increase for men (Kindlon, 2006). Sharing household tasks and offering childcare continues to be less common among husbands than is needed to support healthy and harmonious relationships. Socialization of adolescent boys should include awareness of what will be expected of them to attain gender equity (Gurian & Stevens, 2005).

Task 3. Accepting one's physique and using the body effectively. This task calls for accepting one's body and taking steps to protect it. Many studies have concluded that adolescents perceive body image as the most important criterion for acceptance by classmates (Jones, 2004). Therefore, appearance has a significant influence on self-impression. The resulting desire of many girls to appear as if they were thin, have a figure like fashion models or celebrities from the entertainment world can lead to unhealthy diets and provocative forms of dress (Durkin, Paxton, & Wertheim, 2005). Boys also want to look like their heroes in the sports world and sometimes suppose that taking vitamin supplements or steroids can provide them an edge over competitors (Shirma, 2005).

The wide variance in physical growth creates anxiety for adolescents who deviate from their age group norm in being shorter, taller, less or more developed. Early adolescent girls are usually much taller than boys of their age. Instead of ignoring the stress related to physical changes, teachers and parents should provide students with reasonable criteria to apply for evaluating themselves and their peers. Avoidance of tobacco, illegal drugs, unprotected sex, peer rejection and stereotyping based on body size or build, and a focus on ways to protect the body deserve more attention as topics for student discussion at school. Action for Healthy Kids (2006) provides information to start taking action—from initiating an after-school program to instituting a school wellness policy at http://www.actionforhealthykids.org/about.php.

Task 4. Achieving emotional independence from parents and other adults. Support for autonomy is essential so adolescents are able to make their own plans and, to the extent possible, feel some control over their future. What makes this task more difficult now than when Havighurst offered his observations is the need for extensive schooling. Many adolescents must remain in the home of their parents for a longer time. The consequent economic dependence can be a pretext for parents to treat adolescents as if they were still children and thereby delay emotional independence (Strom & Strom, 2005). Then too, as adults become aware of potential for dangers to children, some try to minimize hazards by making decisions that adolescents should make for themselves. Adults help teenagers attain emotional independence by trusting them to make certain decisions, being accessible to listen, and willing to provide feedback on quality of logic. In addition, adults should more often model concepts such as interdependence and emotional intelligence (Goleman, 2006; Goleman, Boyatzis & McKee, 2004).

Task 5. Preparing for marriage and family life. Most adults will eventually marry and some will have children. There is agreement that the best preparation comes from parents who model how to treat a spouse with respect, share household obligations, care for each another, and provide the time, affection, and guidance that all children need. This task involves parents but adolescents who witness dysfunctional behavior at home must find help elsewhere. Because of high rates of divorce, adolescent abuse of dating partners, spousal abuse, lack of parent supervision, and a variety of family configurations, schools should offer lessons that many youth cannot obtain at home (Fine & Harvey, 2005).

Adolescents need to learn how to build durable friendships, respect a dating partner, adopt suitable criteria for selection of a mate, and use methods to resolve common marital difficulties. Teenagers should accept expectations for the role of husbands and fathers that match the needs of the current environment, ensure that mothers and fathers have sufficient leisure time, and comprehend the effects that divorce can have on youth (Fine & Harvey, 2005). They should understand the importance of meeting the needs of a partner and know where to turn for assistance if problems are overwhelming and cannot be managed safely and effectively. These are practical issues that states throughout the nation have begun to consider and require of adolescents (Apter, 2006; Martin, 2005).

Task 6. Preparation for an economic career. Students will become full-time workers at an older age than in previous generations. The need to discover an occupation that matches their abilities and aspirations is often unmet and presents continuous uncertainty (O'Toole & Lawler, 2006). Some countries narrow the scope of career possibilities at an early age by decisions based on test scores. In contrast, education in the United States allows students to make career choices when they are older. This benefit can also reduce anxiety and stress if career exploration is part of the curriculum (Baker & LeTendre, 2005).

A growing number of adolescents are worried about financial borrowing to cover college tuition costs (Strom & Strom, 2004). One important source to consider for making occupational choices is *The Occupational Outlook Handbook* (United States Department of Labor, 2006a, 2006b). This guide describes the nature of most jobs, qualifications, training needed, number of positions and locations by state, earnings, working conditions, and projected prospects to the year 2014. If parents are made aware of this source by the high school Web site, they can help more than by just encouraging hard work, good grades, and graduation. The main purpose of public schools is to prepare students for work so career exploration should be part of the curriculum (Drucker, 2006).

Task 7. Acquiring values and an ethical system to guide behavior, developing an ideology. Havighurst (1972) asserted that the central task of adolescence is achieving identity and this depends primarily on preparing for an occupation and adopting an ideology by which to live. In the past the customary pattern was for adolescents to accept most of their parent's values (Baldwin, Falkner, Hecht, & Lindsley, 2006). However, the current rate of change is more rapid so the proportion of adult ideology embraced by adolescents is diminishing (Toffler & Toffler, 2006). As a result, the uncertainty that teenagers often feel when in the presence of adults is diminished when they are with peers. Group activities and acceptance of peer group values allows teenagers to evade a certain amount of uncertainty (Harris, 1998; Ladd, 2005).

Reliance on the standards of peers as a guide for behavior increases when adolescents spend excessive time with agemates and insufficient time with grown-ups. In many families a more favorable balance is needed. Historically, the transmission of values has been unilateral with adults passing on their heritage to younger people. While this practice should continue in some realms of activity, the reciprocal transmission of values also seems necessary (Rimm, 2005). In this way, adults can adopt some values of younger people that facilitate adjustment. For example, adolescents are more likely than adults to acquire technology skills, shun discrimination based upon race, gender, religion, or sexual preference, protect the natural environment, and recognize the need for teamwork to accomplish personal and group goals (Epstein, 2007).

Task 8. Desiring and achieving socially responsible behavior. The benefits of extended education are less when expectations are limited to performance in the classroom. This narrow scope can lead to emotional detachment from the welfare of others (Apter, 2006). On the other hand, the maturity that society seeks to nurture in schools can often be met by nonacademic experiences that promote a sense of obligation toward the community (DiMaria, 2006). The most common way to pursue this goal in middle school and high school is to become a volunteer for the mission of nonprofit organizations or government agencies.

Guidance in this context of development implicates families and schools. When adolescents are expected to demonstrate obligation toward loved ones, they are more likely to acquire caring attitudes. Some appropriate responsibilities for teenagers include sharing household chores with parents, helping older relatives and friends, responding to the social and physical needs of neighbors, and performing community service (Rimm, 2005).

The developmental tasks of adolescence are more complicated than when Havighurst (1972) first described them. The tasks will be reexamined within the contemporary setting as goal setting is discussed in chapter 3. Today's developmental tasks present students with greater uncertainty, anxiety, and stress than is usually recognized by teachers and parents. Understanding the complexity of these challenges and realizing that several could be faced simultaneously should motivate adults to become more accessible listeners and companions. Schools can contribute to achieving developmental tasks by reforms that help adolescents attain more mature relationships with peers and facilitate the unprecedented masculine and feminine roles that support equity. Students need to apply reasonable criteria for peer and self-evaluation and know the emerging expectations for possible roles in adulthood as husbands, wives, partners, and parents. They need opportunities to speak with employees to discover a suitable career, and encouragement to gain maturity by community service (Zimmer-Gembeck & Mortimer, 2006).

Family Accountability

Society expects families to provide suitable education for daughters and sons from infancy through adolescence. Parents should teach children how to manage stress, convey time management attitudes and skills, model a productive work ethic, urge resilience during times of difficulty, hold high standards of morality, show independence and interdependence, and encourage self-criticism that motivates personal improvement (Rubin, 2006). Parents can be powerful models of good character that motivate students to choose honesty and avoid cheating. Parents should respond to student misconduct by providing corrective discipline. They are also the primary source of guidance about nutrition, diet, and exercise. Being a parent and being a teacher must go together (Levine, 2006). Family learning for students should include lessons about coping with frustration, developing patience, responding to the needs of others, and adopting healthy values and beliefs that govern daily behavior. Students have two environments for their important learning from adults, the home and school. This book examines how parents and teachers can meet their separate challenges while pursuing united efforts.

The influence of parents is reflected by student attitudes, behavior, and performance in the classroom. Therefore, building a relationship with families has always been a goal for educators. In an ideal arrangement, parents and teachers provide their different but essential lessons, share observations of how students behave at school and at home, identify individual needs that may go undetected, and support one another in carrying out their complimentary roles (Savage, 2007). The importance of these tasks is reinforced by family related topics in each chapter. Strategies to yield collaboration are examined, perspectives of parents are explained, and the benefits for students that can accompany home-school collaboration are identified.

There are 25 million American parents who have children in high schools. Research has found that, regardless of family income or background, student rates of grade retention, suspension, expulsion, and dropout are lower when parents regularly monitor academic progress. When parents are involved with school, their students are likely to earn higher grades and test scores, pass courses, enroll in advanced classes, develop better social skills, graduate, attend college and find work. The opposite is true for students whose parents fail to assume their important function of encouragement, guidance, instruction, and correction (Benson, 2007). Parent readiness to establish a home-school relationship that will support their child's achievement is portrayed in *One Dream, Two Realities: Perspectives of Parents on America's High Schools* (Bridgeland, Dilulio, Streeter, & Mason, 2008). This national survey of 1,000 parents of high school students included an over sampling of minorities.

Before considering the survey findings, it is relevant to point out that every public school receives an annual report card required by the No Child Left Behind Act (NCLB) of 2001 that describes institutional progress toward fulfilling federal and state standards. NCLB guidelines require a status designation such as underperforming or excelling be assigned to the schools indicating whether adequate yearly progress has taken place. School evaluations are based upon student performance by grade, specific constituent groups including gender, ethnicity, students with disabilities, English language learners, economically disadvantaged, and whether 95% of students take required assessments. An additional factor is the graduation rate of high schools (Jennings & Rentner, 2006).

The *One Dream, Two Realities* (Bridgeland, Dilulio, Streeter, & Mason, 2008) results show that only 15% of parents with students in underperforming high schools feel that teachers challenge them to learn, compared with 58% of parents with students in excelling schools. Half of the parents with students in excelling schools believe their child is gaining the abilities and confidence needed for college or work, but less than 20% of parents of students in underperforming schools share that view.

According to parent reports, underperforming schools are half as likely as high-performing schools to communicate with parents regarding their child's performance or inform them about requirements for graduation and college admission. A majority of families with children attending underperforming schools want to be involved as educational advocates while 70% of the parents of children in excelling schools report that they actively participate as partners with faculty (Bridgeland, Dilulio, Streeter, & Mason, 2008). Teachers in underperforming schools dispute the interest level reported by parents, pointing to poor attendance at parent-teacher conferences and unwillingness to respond to messages that are sent home (Raymond & Raymond, 2008).

The conclusion of *One Dream, Two Realities* is that there appears to be two kinds of schools, one that helps students prepare for college and the workplace and another that does not; one that engages parents in fostering educational achievement of their children and another that does not. This disparity does not match the national promise of equal opportunity and need for an educated workforce. The imperative for all schools is to create ways that will increase and sustain parent involvement (Bridgeland, Dilulio, Streeter, & Mason, 2008).

Positive Psychology

The identification of roles for adolescents is contentious but there are changes underway that promise to make this goal more attainable. At the beginning of the 21st century some scholars began to challenge the direction of psychology and propose the adoption of positive psychology, a more optimistic perspective about the capacities, motives, and potentials for every segment of the population (Peterson, 2006). This reform movement appears likely to prevail because it originated within the leadership for the American Psychological Association. Reformers contend that a favorable theoretical outlook on development has become difficult to acquire because the training of professionals often orients them to perceive optimism with suspicion, as an expression of wishful thinking, denial, or gullibility. There may be times when misperceptions dominate behavior. In such cases, the role of professionals is to help students or clients see a more accurate picture of reality. However, there is widespread agreement that, over the past generation, the level of skepticism in psychology became excessive and in need of revision to recognize that human behavior cannot be understood by using primarily negative frames of reference (Cacioppo, Visser, & Pickett, 2006; Seligman, 2004, 2006; Sheldon & King, 2001).

Every specialty within psychology is implicated. The negative bias in clinical psychology is evident by pathologies that have received much greater attention than initiatives to understand psychological health. Social psychologists have shown more concern about individual and group rejection than for discovering how to help people acquire skills needed to get along with others. Evolutionary and economic psychology regards selfishness and greed as primary motivations so little research has been conducted on ways to develop altruism. Educational psychologists focus greater attention on student failure than on finding out why students from certain subcultures uniformly succeed. Counseling psychology has contributed less to what is known about people who are happy, in love, well adjusted, wise, or creative than about those who experience eating disorders or difficulties associated with divorce, stress, and abuse. Developmental psychologists strive to act as a resource for families about ways to reduce misconduct but have provided few insights on ways to nurture good behavior and self-discipline (Linley & Joseph, 2004).

Supporters of positive psychology believe that most people are satisfied with their lives despite the objective difficulties that they may experience. Therefore, the research thrust of positive psychology involves ordinary human strengths and virtues like optimism and resilience with more emphasis on positive emotions such as joy, contentment, pride, and love. Martin Seligman, clinical psychologist at the University of Pennsylvania and past President for the American Psychological Association defines *positive psychology* as "the study of positive subjective experiences, positive character traits, and positive institutions" (Peterson & Seligman, 2004). This transformation of psychology from excessive concern for healing damage and repairing weakness toward a more comprehensive outlook about life that includes building strengths is helpful to teachers of all grades (Linley & Joseph, 2004; Snyder & Lopez, 2007). To illustrate, studies in varied environments have found that optimists perceive obstacles and setbacks as temporary events that can be overcome. In contrast, pessimists take setbacks personally and look at obstacles as being pervasive and permanent. These differences impact performance in that optimists achieve more, bounce back from defeat more readily, recover better from rejection, and, from middle age until the end of life, have better physical health than peers that are pessimistic (Peterson, 2006). A salient factor is that the skills of optimism can be learned by teenagers and lead to resilience that safeguards them against depression as well as improve academic performance (Gilman, Hueber, & Furlong, 2009).

The George Lucas Educational Foundation disseminates information on innovation in schools, contributions of skillful educators, and projects that bring community improvement. This positive psychology resource was established by the Hollywood icon, George Lucas, to support the renewal of public education and guide the direction of reform by making known learning and teaching strategies that are successful and warrant replication. The continually updated presentations support school pride, bolster faculty morale, recognize teacher success, and encourages optimism. The Lucas Educational Foundation Web site is available at http://www.edutopia.org.

TEACHER ACTION RESEARCH

Much of what is understood about adolescence has come from research. *Action research* is a collaborative effort by teachers to find out more about the students at their school (A. Johnson, 2005). These studies are seldom presented in the literature on development but they produce insights that the researchers (teachers) can implement themselves. The key elements of action research that you can become involved with are discussed along with implications.

Autobiographical Reports

One way to learn about adolescents is by asking them to write about aspects of their lives. Autobiographical confessions have contributed much to teacher awareness of the unique mental and emotional challenges presented in adolescence. A well-known example is Anne Frank (1986) who wrote *The Diary of a Young Girl*. Anne's book was the first to show how teenagers perceive the world differently from adults. Anne wrote during World War II while she, her sister, parents, and four other Jews hid for 2 years in the rear secret annex of an office building in Amsterdam during the Nazi occupation. Her literary efforts began in response to a radio broadcast which promised that the diaries written by Jewish people in hiding would be collected and made public following victory by the allied forces. The possibility of recognition as a writer, published as one of the "hiding people," motivated Anne to start recording her thoughts. Her first entry reflects the privacy usually associated with diaries, "I hope I shall be able to confide in you completely as I have never been able to do in anyone before and I hope you will be a great support and comfort to me" (A. Frank, 1986, p. 1).

Some unknown individual(s) betrayed the Franks and companions by informing the Gestapo of their whereabouts. Everyone was arrested and sent to different concentration camps. The secret police ransacked their hideout looking for jewelry or other valuables. When they found Anne's diary it was judged to have no value and left on the attic floor. Anne died from typhus in the Bergen-Belsen camp shortly before her 16th birthday. One of the questions she posed in her diary was "Will I ever be able to write well?" (A. Frank, 1986, p. 14). Anne would never know the powerful impact that her writing would have on subsequent generations.

A friend found Anne's diary and kept it until the war ended. Then she gave it to Otto Frank, Anne's father, the only survivor in his family. When Otto finished reading the little book, he reflected, "I didn't know Anne until I read her diary" (A. Frank, 1986). He was so inspired by her thinking and wit that he tried to find a publisher. A Dutch company released a small printing in 1947 but the aspiration for a larger audience would prove difficult. One book editor from the United States wrote Otto that he doubted whether there would be enough interest in this topic to make a profit. Fortunately, in 1952, Eleanor Roosevelt, wife of the former president, wrote an introduction to the diary and the tide was changed.

Since then over 30 million copies of the book have been sold. A majority of American high school students have read it, and the movie (1959) received an academy award (Covington, 2001; A. Frank, 1986). The Anne Frank Center USA is located in New York City—see http://www.annefrank.com/.

During the 1990s so-called "voice books" exposed the inner life of adolescent females who, in the past, typically kept silent to avoid conflict and maintain harmonious relationships. Carol Gilligan (Gilligan & Brown, 1993) of Harvard University presented the outcome of her interviews with girls. These interviews led Gilligan to speculate that the confidence of girls is diminished as they internalize the cultural message that females should be passive and quiet following the elementary school years. Mary Pipher (2005), a clinical psychologist, presented the anguish of girls who feel they must define themselves mostly by physical appearance. Joan Brumberg (1997) at Cornell University offered a history of American girl experiences by compiling the messages of diverse voices from personal diaries of teenagers since the mid-nineteenth century. Pamela Haag (2000) researcher at the American Association of University Women, assembled the ideas and feelings of 2,000 girls, ages 11 to 17, recorded in their diaries or recalled in response to interviews.

The impression that girls are relatively disadvantaged compared to boys is challenged by Dan Kindlon (2006) of Harvard who offers a far more optimistic outlook expressed by the new American girl in her diaries, blogs, and interviews. He documents how girls generally perform better than boys in academics, experience greater self-esteem, and seem better equipped for the adjustments required to be successful and chosen as leaders. Electronic diaries of boys and interviews reveal a corresponding need to revise the narrow definition of masculinity as toughness in favor of such criteria as nurturing communication skills and empathy without being transformed into girls (Gurian & Stevens, 2005; Kindlon & Thompson, 2000). The best selling science fiction writer, Stephen King (2000), acknowledges reliance on his detailed diary entries that he wrote during adolescence as the source for many of the compelling descriptions in his books about how teenagers interpret and react to situations they find uncomfortable or frightening.

Polling Students in Schools

Polling is the survey of a population or representative sample to find out how they feel about particular issues. George Gallup is credited with making polling an acceptable form of inquiry. In *The Pulse of Democracy*, Gallup (1940) speculated that polling could become a national equivalent of New England town meetings by giving the public a voice in determination of government affairs. He believed polls could support democracy by reducing the political power held by corporate lobbyists in favor of permitting the common man to participate in dialogue regarding policy. The Gallup, Harris, and Roper organizations assess public opinion across a broad range of issues that confront the nation (Erikson & Tedin, 2004).

Polls for adolescents are usually sponsored by businesses that view them as potential consumers. Television programs also feature polling so viewers can have a role in deciding the winners of competitions and contestants for elimination. Outlets like VH1, Nickelodeon, and American Idol invite viewers to phone in or log on and cast their vote using specified criteria. Within a short time votes are tallied and the results are announced. The opportunity to vote on issues that interest them motivates viewers to become more involved than when their role is limited to being passive observers (Gewertz, 2004; Liu, 2005). We seem to be at the beginning of an entirely new era, an "age of personal or participatory media in which boundaries between audiences and creators become blurred and often invisible" (Trier, 2007).

Educators should consider Internet polling to systematically assess perceptions of students about their conditions of learning (Best & Radcliff, 2005; Girod, Pardales, Cavanaugh, & Wadsworth, 2005). Even though society acknowledges that growing up has dramatically changed, adults still rely exclusively on their observations as the sole source of judgment about school reform. Each of the subsequent chapters (2–12) includes a poll that can be completed by adolescents at the school where you work. These polls, described in Voices of Adolescents, allow students to anonymously express opinions about their school.

Guidelines for Interviews

Newspaper and television reporters as well as talk show hosts rely on interviews to determine the experiences of eyewitnesses to incidents, experts about special topics, and ordinary people to find out how they interpret particular events. Certainly the ideas expressed by one individual cannot be assumed to represent the way others from a similar background see things. This is why action research in schools should include interviews with student informants representing different cultural backgrounds (Rubin & Rubin, 2005).

This book provides questions for cultural reporters and for generational reporters. We have found that interviews are more successful when these guidelines are considered.

1. Give informants, whether students, fellow teachers, parents or other adults the prepared questions to read in advance and reflect on a few minutes before an interview begins. This strategy often reduces anxiety, provides a more well defined orientation to the scope of anticipated conversation, and allows for more focused responses. Sometimes additional questions might arise triggered by responses (Morrison & Anders, 2001).

2. Let the individual or group know the amount of time that is scheduled for the interview. Being informed of a schedule enables participants to gauge how little or much they should elaborate. If events proceed well and the interviewee agrees, the timeline could be extended.

3. Make sure that each informant is asked the same questions so that it is possible to compare their perceptions regarding a situation or event.

4. Unless the questions are progressive, let the informant choose the order in which to answer them based on their own sense of the priorities.

5. Make it clear that, if an individual feels uncomfortable with any of the questions and prefers not to talk about some particular issue, the suggested response should simply be "I pass on that one."

6. If someone chooses to respond in a language other than English, arrange for an interpreter to be present to help with the interview.

7. Thank the participant for cooperation, state that you intend to take notes and obtain their permission to use a recorder. Using a recording device is often easier and can produce a more accurate record. The downside is that some people may be less willing to self-disclose if their comments are recorded.

8. Assure the individual that names of persons interviewed will not be revealed in summaries.

9. If statements are difficult to comprehend and call for some inference, ask the person for an example that illustrates the intended meaning.

10. After presenting a question, allow enough time for reflection before expecting the answer. Avoid rushing people and you will find their responses to be more worthwhile.

11. Following the interview, ask if there is anything else s/he would like to share on the topic. Sometimes informants will appreciate hearing your own responses to the same questions they have just answered.

12.   Soon after the interview, review your notes and summarize what you will present to teammates, the teacher, school administrators, and informants.

EMPIRICAL RESEARCH

Much of the literature on adolescent development is based on work of scholars who seek to learn about specific groups of youth, typically involving samples larger than a single school. This broad frame of reference requires more rigorous methods than used for action research. This discussion focuses on *empirical research*, investigations based on trial and experimentation as the only accepted representation of experience (Teti, 2004). The selected strategies include cross-sectional studies, longitudinal investigations, experimental procedures, and clinical team collaboration.

Cross-Sectional Studies

Many formal studies on adolescent development rely on cross-sectional methodology. *Cross-sectional studies* take measurements or they make observations of many individuals within a particular age cohort or group representing another specific category such as gender, grade in school, socioeconomic status, or subculture (Cohen, 2000). Averages for a cohort (group born in the same year, similar historical period or undergoing similar influences) can be obtained from the results.

Lewis Terman (1916) used a cross-sectional strategy when he devised the Stanford-Binet Intelligence Test. Establishing trends permit comparison of individual performance with a hypothetical average for a chronological age, grade level or social status. However, such norms tend to obscure individual differences and can lead to undue concern when a person deviates slightly from the norm of their specific group. Consequently, tables depicting average height and weight for students of different ages that appeared in textbooks during the 1990s are no longer presented. Because individual differences are common, uniqueness is to be expected, and the cautious interpretation of central tendencies (averages) is necessary. Cross-sectional investigations are considered convenient and relied on for short-term investigations. They yield hypotheses regarding variation and, when applied carefully, create awareness of abnormality (Thorndike, 2005).

Assume that researchers want to determine how the body image perceptions of 10-year-old girls differ from the body image perceptions of women who are 30 years old. It is more reasonable to select a representative group from both age levels rather than having to wait 20 years to find out how perceptions of the 10-year-olds changed during that time frame. The time factor also means that cross-sectional studies are less likely to be compromised by such difficulties as loss of subjects because of attrition, repeated testing or outdated measures. Cross-sectional investigations also pose disadvantages like the cohort effect that can occur when subjects from a particular age group are influenced by factors that are unique to experiences of their generation. Thus, when today's 30-year-old women were 10 years old, they were less subject to pressure to appear thin as in the current environment (Durkin, Paxton, & Wertheim, 2005).

Longitudinal Investigations

Longitudinal studies record observations or measurements of the same persons (as far as possible in terms of death and geographic dispersal) over a period of many years. The tasks of planning and implementing longitudinal investigations are time-consuming and difficult for one person to manage. Accordingly, most of these studies become institutionalized and are continued by successive teams after the original investigator is no longer involved (Menard, 2002). Studies at Harvard University and Stanford have involved numerous waves of assessments conducted by successive investigators (Glueck & Glueck, 1968; Halloran & Sears, 1995; Terman, 1925; Terman & Oden, 1947, 1959; Valliant, 2003). To examine Terman's initiative, see http://www.cpc.unc.edu/projects/lifecourse.

Paul Torrance (1925–2003) started his longitudinal studies of creative students at the University of Minnesota Laboratory School in 1958. Students initially completed Torrance's Verbal and Figural Creative Thinking tests. Since then there have been two extensive follow-up studies conducted at 20-year intervals (Millar, 2001). The most recent investigation describes a 40-year overview of how the 101 children struggled to develop their creativity into adulthood (Torrance, 2006a). Stories by participants can inspire teachers, researchers, and parents to evaluate their own beliefs about the best ways to support divergent thinking. The Torrance (2006b) Center for Creativity and Talent Development at University of Georgia includes hundreds of cross-cultural reports and experiments related to the development of imagination—see http://www.coe.uga.edu/torrance.

One contemporary example of long-term inquiry involves the National Longitudinal Study of Adolescent Health. The purposes of this investigation are to identify key influences on resilience and vulnerability during adolescence and adulthood. Richard Udry (2008), principal investigator from the Carolina Population Center, began this investigation of 90,000 students in 1994 when they were in Grades 7–12. The sites involved were

140 schools throughout the country representing a full range of racial and socioeconomic backgrounds. Follow up assessments were completed in 1995 and 2000 when the subjects were 18–24 years of age. See http://www.cpc.unc.edu/projects/lifecourse/addhealth.

Longitudinal studies are of interest mainly to professionals but there has been one exception that fascinates the public. In 1964 film director Michael Apted (2007) brought together about a dozen 7-year-olds, boys and girls from all over England. The purpose was to explore the impact of the British class system. The documentary was introduced by urging television viewers to reflect on the assertion of Jesuit leader St. Ignatius Loyola who declared, "Show me the child until he is seven and I will show you the man." Some of the White and Black participants came from upper-class households, others were raised in orphanages, and some were growing up in working class neighborhoods. Apted's intention was to ask them about their lives and dreams for the future. However, viewer response to the documentary was so positive and broad that Apted continued to interview the "children" at 7-year intervals, when they were 7, 14, 21, 28, 35, 42, and 49 years of age. During their most recent interviews, in 2005, the middle-age subjects discussed some of the life-changing decisions and challenges they have faced concerning love, marriage, career, happiness, disappointment, health, educational opportunity, and prejudice. Viewers are captivated by the storyline as it moves back and forth across different ages to reveal how particular individuals have changed their minds and remained consistent. A detailed description of this film, titled *49 Up*, is available from Public Broadcasting System at http://www.pbs.org/pov/pov2007/49up/about.html.

Experimental Procedures

The basic ingredients for a broad range of classroom interventions implicate *experimental procedures* that include a hypothesis, an experimental group, a control group, a dependent variable, and an independent variable. An experimental group is one to which a specific set of conditions, in accord with a hypothesis, is applied (e.g., praise, rewards, drugs, environmental setting) in pursuit of a stated goal (Phye, Robinson, & Levin, 2005). The control group (composed of persons from the same age group, socioeconomic level, health status, school grades) is not involved with conditions of the experiment but complete the same set of measures to assess attainment of the goal. The special conditions applied in an experiment are the independent variables (praise, rewards, drugs). The outcomes for an experiment (improvement in scores or some other dimension of performance) are dependent variables. Comparative results for experimental and control groups may be subject to correlation or some other statistical treatment (Thorndike, 2005).

Clinical Collaboration

Clinical collaboration is another strategy for gathering data on teens (Hecker & Thorpe, 2005). This approach recognizes a need to explore beneath or beyond averages, trends, and probabilities (gathered by methods already described) to specifics that are related to a particular person or set of cases. Some observers claim, with considerable justification, that there is no average or even typical adolescent. It is necessary to know why a given individual behaves the way s/he does. The individuals participating as subjects in a clinical study for medicine might be administered various physical tests, questionnaires, and surveys. Then physicians representing relevant specialties come together to share knowledge and attempt to reach consensus regarding the most appropriate treatment (Schwartz-Shea & Yanow, 2006).

A similar approach occurs in schools when students are identified as having an academic or behavioral difficulty. In *clinical collaboration*, diagnostic tests are administered, observations are made, interviews carried out, and records are examined to detect, explain, and determine recommendations. Nearly 15% of American middle school and high school students are enrolled in special education (Osgood, 2007; Turnbull, Turnbull, Shank, & Smith, 2004). The clinical collaboration process of identification for student placement in special education implicates teachers, school psychologists, special educators, counselors, and social workers. Together they determine an *Individual Education Plan* (IEP) to guide instruction and monitor the effectiveness of support. Clinical research represents a team approach to understanding students as individuals.

SUMMARY

Historical Interpretations

The adolescent experience, beginning with puberty and concluding with adult status has historically been explained in contradictory ways. Stanley Hall reported that this stage of development consists of storm and stress triggered by memories of an ancient past conveyed by heredity. In contrast, Margaret Mead contended that cultural differences clarify variance in the behavior of teenagers. Recognition that the environment is a significant influence on development has motivated greater support for teachers in their important guidance role.

Adolescents in Social Context

To ensure that veterans of World War II came home to employment opportunities, teenage competitors for jobs were directed to stay in school and gain the skills they would need for a workplace characterized by automation. The identification of developmental tasks offered a comprehensive emphasis for education of teenagers in school and the family. Many adolescents regret that the need for more lengthy education represents an artificial barrier delaying their acceptance for adult status and urge that technology skills be recognized as a criterion for identity. The positive psychology movement is making progress toward a more balanced impression of adolescent potential along with ways to enhance their identity with appropriate roles.

Teacher Action Research

Educators should work together to better understand adolescents in their school by using action research methods. One strategy comes from anecdotal descriptions in student autobiographical reports. Polling is a seldom chosen method even though it may be the best way to tap into student views and find clues to improve the learning environment at school. Interviews can reveal much about how students feel provided that informants see the questions ahead of time, receive assurances that names will not be identified with responses, and are given time to reflect before providing answers.

Empirical Research

Cross-sectional research is a common technique for gathering data because the outcomes enable comparison of individuals with norms of their cohort group. Longitudinal investigations present evidence of how people change over an extended period and reveal durability of particular attributes or abilities. These studies are uncommon because of the sustained effort required, geographic dispersal of subjects, access to long-term funding, and need for collaborators. Experimental methods can produce evidence on effects of intervention efforts and whether field-tested educational reforms should continue or be rejected. Clinical collaborations merge perceptions of specialists from various fields who decide ways to assist individual learners. This strategy is used in special education to develop an IEP. Multiple data gathering procedures are recommended to yield the most comprehensive and balanced perspective.

KEY TERMS

Action Research
Adolescence
Clinical Collaboration
Collaboration Integration Theory (CIT)
Cooperative Learning Exercises and Roles (CLEAR)
Cross-Sectional Studies
Developmental Tasks
Empirical Research
Experimental Procedures
Introspection
Longitudinal Studies
Polling
Positive Psychology
Recapitulation Theory
Reciprocal Learning

VISIT THESE WEB SITES

Link to these sites at http://www.infoagepub.com/strom-adolescents

49 Up http://www.pbs.org/pov/pov2007/49up/about.html

Action for Healthy Kids
http://www.actionforhealthykids.org/about.php

Carolina Population Center
http://www.cpc.unc.edu/projects/addhealth

FaceBook http://www.facebook.com

Anne Frank Center USA http://www.annefrank.com/

G. Stanley Hall
http://muskingum.edu/~psych/psycweb/history/hall.htm

George Lucas Educational Foundation, Edutopia
http://www.edutopia.org

Margaret Mead, American Museum of Natural History
http://www.amnh.org/exhibitions/expeditions/treasure_fossil/Treasures/
Margaret_Mead/mead.html

MySpace http://www.myspace.com

Lewis Terman http://www.cpc.unc.edu/projects/lifecourse/

Torrance Center for Creativity and Talent Development
http://www.coe.uga.edu/torrance

RECOMMENDATIONS FOR USING THIS BOOK

This section describes the readiness of middle school and high schools students to practice teamwork skills that they need for success in the workplace, at home, and the community. The rationale for an innovative instructional strategy, known as collaboration integration theory, is presented along with well-defined roles students are expected to perform as they work together in cooperative learning teams.

Expectations for Adolescents

Teamwork and group evaluation of individual performance is common in the workplace. Therefore, adolescents need to acquire the collaboration skills employers will expect of them (O'Toole & Lawler, 2006). During early adolescence, around 10 or 11 years of age, students become capable of examining events as seen from perspectives other than their own. This ability to act objectively and think critically is accompanied by a decline in egocentrism. Adolescents also become capable of *introspection*, looking at themselves to improve behavior based on self-examination. They enjoy conversations with their classmates and often turn to peers for approval as well as advice. In an information-driven society, certain lessons at school may be applicable for only a short time. In contrast, teamwork skills can be relied on as valuable assets throughout life (Roseth, Johnson, & Johnson, 2008).

Collaboration Integration Theory

Direct instruction has been the traditional method of teachers to promote learning. In this approach teachers are considered to be experts who convey ideas students need to understand. A corresponding set of obligations for students is to pay close attention to the teacher, take notes, and memorize data for later testing. This paradigm is no longer appropriate because technology has produced new tools that transform the learning process. A consequent challenge for teachers is to enable students to become self-directed learners (Adams & Hamm, 2006; Trier, 2007).

Some observers suggest a simple solution, reduce teacher talk and give more time for student discussion. However, more comprehensive changes are necessary because new forms of learning and instruction must make room for appealing and powerful influences such as computers, the Internet, satellite television, personal digital assistants, films, videotapes, DVDs, and gaming simulation. In addition, ways must be found to incorporate the cultural, ethnic, and generational resources that most students rely on outside of school. Structured interviews and conversations with parents, relatives, and adults at work and in the community seem essential so students can integrate insights and opinions of these groups that been left out of the educational process (Diller, 2007).

No one knows how to include or connect the vast resources for learning that are available in the present environment. Bold and creative alternatives should be encouraged, described, implemented, and evaluated to find out their effect. Toward this goal, *collaboration integration theory* (CIT) is described along with expectations for using this book. By exposure to CIT, prospective teachers can decide whether the potential it offers to support teamwork is suitable for their own students (Wehlburg, 2008). CIT is based on these assumptions:

- Students need to practice teamwork skills that are required in the workplace.
- Incorporating the perspective of sources outside school can enrich learning.
- Cultural and generational diversity in outlook require more consideration.
- Allowing separate roles for individuals can increase scope of team learning.
- Accountability can be assessed by how well students perform specific roles.

- Observations of peer and self-contributions to a team improves evaluation.

The operational strategies for uniting CIT with classroom practices are referred to as CLEAR, the acronym for *Cooperative Learning Exercises and Roles* (Strom & Strom, 2002a). The CLEAR goals are to:

1. Shift the role of students from passive to active learners.
2. Make the collaboration process the focus for group work.
3. Enable every teammate to provide a unique contribution.
4. Reduce boredom by differentiating roles for individuals.
5. Ensure enough time in groups to support peer evaluation.

CLEAR provides the greatest benefit when all team members have some roles in common and individuals choose other roles for which they will be solely accountable. As each student takes on the responsibility for a separate exercise and then shares what is learned, team learning is much greater than if everyone has the same assignment. Each of the subsequent chapters in this text contains ten exercises along with classroom applications as well as questions for reflection. This approach makes it easier to establish individual accountability, support self-direction, increase sources of data, and expand the scope of group learning.

Definitions of Teamwork Roles

The 12 CLEAR roles are: Discussant, Organizer, Summarizer, Cultural Reporter, Generational Reporter, Challenger, Voter, Evaluator, Improviser, Storyteller, Reader, and Review Guide. These roles, shown in Figure 1.1 are defined in greater detail below as a guide for assumption of the roles.

Discussant. The benefits of conversation increase when students are provided their agenda ahead of time. Having advance notice allows them to act as teachers do when preparing for dialogue by referring to previously read material and bringing resources to the team. Listening carefully to what peers have to say makes it possible to acquire new insight, combine and build on ideas expressed by others, monitor the logic of peer thinking, and provide feedback. The quality of group dialogue is impacted by good attendance, being on time, allowing peers to speak without interruption, limiting the length of remarks, and avoiding put down remarks as a reaction to opposing viewpoints.

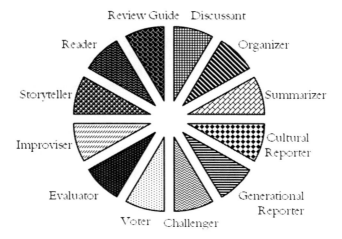

Source: From: Overcoming limitations of cooperative learning among community college students, by Paris Strom & Robert Strom. *Community College Journal of Research and Practice, 26*(4), 2002, 315-331. Reprinted with permission.

Figure 1.1.   CLEAR Roles for Students.

Students usually spend more time in the discussant role than in other roles. Nevertheless, the personal initiative necessary to fulfill this shared task is underestimated. If some students prepare for discussions and others fail to do so, there is bound to be disappointment and some reduction in learning. Besides having many opportunities to learn from conversations with teammates, students can benefit by being an audience for other teams that present their work to the class.

Organizer. Teams are more productive when their efforts are organized. One person should be responsible to lead discussions, identify group goals, assign tasks, keep time, monitor progress, and interact with the teacher as the group representative. The organizer is expected to ensure that conversations remain focused on assigned topics, everyone is allowed a chance to speak, length of participant remarks are limited to ensure a balance of views, and the amount of effort spent on issues is carefully monitored so that group work is completed on schedule.

The cooperative learning emphasis on equality can lead to occasional conflict. Students are usually able to rely on compromise and persuasion as the means to reconcile differences of opinion. However, when a group cannot achieve consensus, someone must break the deadlock and make a decision regarding next steps. As a last resort, the organizer serves as a judge who resolves disputes that could jeopardize productivity of the team.

Summarizer. Most of us summarize everyday as we share experiences with family and friends. We want them to be familiar with what pleases or bothers us, know some of the things we find hard to comprehend, and be aware of circumstances that cause our disagreement or disappointment. It is more difficult to summarize reactions and reflections of a team because collective experience is more complex than the experience of one person. Some common problems in summarizing for a group attribute to the summarizer being self-centered, not providing enough detail or leaving out information that is disliked or considered irrelevant. Summarizing can save time but also poses the possible danger of reporting a distorted impression of team interaction.

The summarizer, a role assigned to only one person, is expected to provide a coherent glimpse of the considerations, conclusions, and recommendations of a team. It is essential to state important points presented during dialogues, identify main themes, and describe elements of agreement and frame differences of opinion. A summarizer writes down ideas expressed by every speaker, no matter how teammates react to the comments. If someone's remarks are unclear, the summarizer urges clarification so the speaker is better understood and represented fairly. Following a discussion, the summarizer prepares a written report that teammates may be asked to read and perhaps initial signifying agreement that it is accurate. These reports are submitted to the instructor, perhaps for group points, and may be heard during an oral report.

Sometimes a summarizer may be asked by the instructor to monitor input of individual teammates. This task can be achieved by placing a tally mark beside the name of each person on the team every time they speak, thus producing a frequency of speech indicator. These records yield participation ratios. For example, in a discussion John spoke twice, Mary once, Ellen did not say anything, and Brian commented five times. Using such indicators of inclusion can help detect the persons who dominate, identify non-participants, and reveal whether students from minority groups or special education are integrated or left out of the group process.

Cultural Reporter. The appreciation of diversity requires consideration of events and situations from the vantage of other cultures. Unfortunately, many students have little knowledge about their heritage. Therefore, they are unable to acquaint outsiders with the uniqueness of their culture. However, they can talk to relatives and friends who may be more aware of customs and beliefs. Interviewing such people is one way to become better informed, promote reciprocal learning, and compare personal background with classmates representing other cultures.

There is also benefit in listening to people with direct experience of living in another society, reading opinions of authors that reflect other cultural orientations, and watching films that present unfamiliar ways to cope with common difficulties. These activities create awareness and empathy to get along in a complex social environment. Then too, when cultural pride is joined by the capacity to think critically about one's own group, the best elements of culture can be preserved while other aspects that have become inappropriate are altered or left behind. Instead of limiting cultural awareness to knowledge of the teacher, more variance can be portrayed by students who represent multiple cultures. Acting as a cultural reporter can support personal identity while also encouraging inclusion in cooperative groups.

Generational Reporter. The purpose of generational reporting is to obtain a broader outlook about events, ideas, and life than can be gained from classmates. Some homework in middle school, high school, and college should implicate relatives as primary sources of ideas and opinions. Ignoring the out-of-school advisors who students rely on prevents the formation of a school-home teaching partnership. Much can be learned from interviewing parents, other relatives, friends and neighbors. An agenda that corresponds to topics covered in class allows interviewers to pose questions and discover the impressions of individuals from other age groups. This role offers a more comprehensive perspective than is presented when student discussions are restricted to the views of their peers.

Challenger. During polite conversation people may announce that they will act as the devil's advocate. By warning ahead of time that an opposing view is about to be expressed, a challenger also makes known that the comments may not reflect his or her own opinions. Instead, the purpose is to increase the factors that receive consideration in a dialogue. This is an established strategy that can benefit everyone. First, the individuals whose viewpoints are challenged have to address concerns that they might otherwise overlook in the presence of a less critical audience. Comfort is provided for the challengers who want to avoid conveying the impression that friendships or motives are in question. They are seen as just playing a role assigned to them. The practice of demonstrating support for friends by only agreeing with their ideas is common at all ages and in certain settings is viewed as a critical factor to remain in good standing with the group.

The benefits of loyalty are enhanced by legitimizing the challenger role so that teammates recognize a mutual responsibility to help one another with the task of monitoring the quality of their thinking. Are people who constantly agree with us trustworthy or could they have other goals? Challengers assume the responsibility to identify concerns that are overlooked, question assumptions, seek examination of the implications that flow from decisions, and urge caution in reaching generalizations based on singular events or situations. Adolescents are often reluctant to assume the challenger role because they fear that it may result in their rejection by peers. However, when this role is recognized as beneficial for the team, students feel more comfortable because they can pursue it without risking their social status.

Voter. The practice of voting compliments cooperative learning. It gives opportunities for students to make known their feelings and opinions that deserve attention in improving school practices. Many adults presume to speak for adolescents, wanting to persuasively assert their needs and rights. Still, some perceptions can become known only by hearing from students themselves. They can be polled about conditions of learning such as the Internet, tutoring, time management, stress, boredom and react to other aspects of environment. To illustrate, school boards often establish dress code policies without soliciting input from students. More than any other method, polling demonstrates to adolescents that the community and its schools care about how they feel and want to take their opinions into account.

Besides detecting normative attitudes and beliefs, polling identifies problems that may require faculty attention. Polls to assess adolescent perceptions about conditions of learning are presented in the exercises for chapters 2–12. Teenagers can complete polls online using the Web site maintained by the authors at http://learningpolls.org. Alternately, any poll can be copied and administered to the person(s) interviewed in a class. After gathering data, summarizers from each team can collaborate in tallying class results. These findings can be read aloud so every member of the class can write the outcomes on their poll before discussing the implications.

Evaluator. Students can benefit from opportunities to evaluate decision making. Specifically, skills that require practice include exploring views that may not be liked at first, using logic to assess thinking and work methods of the team, and taking time for reflection to avoid reaching hasty conclusions. In addition, evaluators should learn to build on ideas expressed by others, discover different ways of looking at things and solving problems, and give helpful feedback that increases student receptivity to constructive criticism.

Teachers should share some aspects of evaluation with students. There is a need to consider the team observations regarding peer and self-performance during group work. Students are the best source to identify teammates who influence their thinking and ways in which help is given. Based on collective observations that are kept anonymous, each student is provided a personal profile containing confidential feedback on personal strengths and limitations. Every student can fulfill this role when it is time to record formative or summative observations about group interaction by using the online *Teamwork Skills Inventory* (Strom & Strom, 2009).

Improviser. The ability to improvise, to make the best of a situation is a special quality that can support personal adjustment, mental health, and success through life. Some aspects of creative thinking calling for improvisation include looking at things in novel ways with an eye to detect favorable possibilities, asking questions about how specific conditions could be modified, and generating alternatives to minimize the disadvantages associated with a particular arrangement or event. During brainstorming students can share the improviser role. Individuals could be assigned improvisation tasks to complete outside class and report the results to teammates. Scenarios drawn from student experiences are powerful motivators to practice skills needed to be effective improvisers.

Storyteller. The purposes of a storyteller are to present imaginary or real life examples that illustrate how some concept or method applies for a particular situation. Students like to listen to stories, pay close attention to the procession of events, and often remember key elements of a tale longer than factual information. Whether storytellers read from a book, describe a videotape or movie, convey an incident another person shared with them, or relate a personal recollection, their stories can enable teammates to make connections that increase the value of a lesson, grasp concepts which previously seemed abstract, and realize why specific issues deserve greater attention. The potential impact that stories can have on motivation, comprehension, and relationships is difficult to gauge but the magic is there for those who experience it.

Reader. Educators need to acknowledge and encourage learning they do not provide. One way to ensure that this happens is for students to participate in the reader role. The purpose of a reader is to help students bring more to team discussions than just personal opinion. Reading is a way to go beyond the collective experiences of the team. By searching the Internet, journals, and books, students can locate materials that add meaning to the lessons. Being able to find suitable sources is an undervalued aspect of reading that can do much to support team research.

Sometimes the views of an author can be reported to support personal views of a student. Another way to share the impressions of outsiders is by bringing documents to class and read selected passages aloud before giving teammates an opportunity to examine them. This self-directed activity sustains curiosity and promotes productive dialogue. For each lesson, students are expected to share additional sources that reinforce, clarify, or provide alternate perspectives. This strategy reveals how much more can be gained when everyone regularly takes the initiative of bringing relevant materials to class without being told to do so by their teacher.

Review Guide. Team reviews of each chapter can contribute to individual learning. The process begins outside class as each student underlines interesting as well as important comments from their text and class notes. Preparing for the group review means students ask themselves these kinds of questions:

1. What are the main points and key issues presented in this unit?
2. Which ideas made a difference in how I think about this topic?
3. What insights from this lesson can I apply in teaching situations?
4. What aspects of a lesson are confusing or require more explanation?

The review guide takes the lead by telling the page and paragraph from the text s/he will read from in response to the first question or reference to other sources relied on. In turn, each teammate answers that same question. This process is repeated for all review questions. The review guide may be called on to meet with the teacher to discuss outcomes, obtain feedback for teammates, and identify confusing aspects of a lesson.

Students as Teamwork Evaluators

How can teachers evaluate the performance of students as they work in teams? Impressions about what takes place in groups can be more accurate when student observations are considered. They are able to identify the teammates who influence their thinking and describe the help given. Sharing responsibility for evaluation of learning in groups is a departure from tradition in the classroom and requires a greater degree of faculty trust. Until now, external evaluation has been the only way to evaluate student achievement. Prevailing practices of evaluation are also based on a premise that assessing social skills can be ignored. The collaborative skills that employers want new workers to possess are not measured by the state examinations required for high school graduation.

Faculty who use cooperative learning typically acknowledge their frustration in evaluating student teamwork skills. The students are also frustrated because they know the teacher cannot fairly evaluate what happens in their team. Failure to credit individuals for team skills undermines effectiveness of group work. In settings such as sporting events, academic tournaments, and artistic exhibits, educators routinely acknowledge things that individuals do well. Similar recognition is necessary for students who demonstrate the social skills required for success in cooperative teams. In chapter 7 the authors describe the *Teamwork Skills Inventory* (Strom & Strom, 2009) they have devised for adolescent and adult students in cooperative learning teams.

CHAPTER 2

CULTURAL CHANGE AND EDUCATION

Some situations can be seen more clearly when observed from several points in time. As people look back, at the current scene, and ahead toward the future, a more complete picture often comes into view. Gaining a sense of historical perspective on ways in which cultural change has influenced schooling for adolescents enables teachers to consider how their role resembles and differs from previous generations of educators. This expansive outlook also informs the personal choice of *paradigm*, a model which unites the principles that shape the conceptual framework used to guide teaching (Barker & Erickson, 2005).

Choosing a paradigm is important because it establishes expectations, clarifies direction, and identifies the criteria to use for evaluation (Murray, 2006). Teaching adolescents while learning from them is the paradigm that is elaborated in this book. Our rationale is based on four assumptions: (1) Adolescents have unique experiences that qualify them as the most credible source about what growing up is like now; (2) Adolescents are more competent than many adults in using tools of technology that are needed for learning in the future; (3) Adolescents and teachers can support mutual growth through reciprocal learning; and (4) the adolescent quest for identity could be attained well before their full-time entry to the workforce. Our paradigm is consistent with a panel asked to describe their view of

Adolescents in the Internet Age, pp. 43–85

future schooling. Check it out on http://teachertube.com type in Learning to Change, Changing to Learn.

The goals for this chapter are to describe how education for adolescents has evolved in the United States. Changes in expectations of students and teachers are examined along with a shift in their relationship. The potential for adolescents to influence the learning of classmates is considered along with methods for integrating technology and curriculum. Ways schooling has changed are presented with an explanation of why reciprocal learning among generations is essential. A balanced perspective of the past, present, and future is emphasized as vital to support adjustment and development.

STAGES OF CULTURAL CHANGE

Culture is the way of life that reflects the customs, civilization, and achievements of a particular society or group of people. Margaret Mead (1978), Professor of anthropology at Columbia University, identified three stages of cultural evolution with their emphasis on the past, present, and future. The significance of these stages is that they determine the sources for education, kinds of thinking that are given priority, content of the curriculum, and methods of instruction (Wineburg, Mosborg, Porat, & Duncan, 2007).

In past-oriented cultures teenagers can see their future as they observe day-to-day activities of parents and other adults. When the environment is stabile and the pace of change is slow, parents are expected to socialize their children by communicating firm definitions about how to live. In contrast, the future in present-oriented cultures is less certain and requires consideration of trends, shifting events, and educated guesses about the world of tomorrow. There is a realization that certain aspects of the past should be retained while others must make way for innovation based on new ways of looking at ideas and situations (Davila, Epstein, & Shelton, 2006). A predictable change is that, in present-oriented cultures, adults are not the only source of learning about adjustment, problem solving, and planning. Instead, people of the same age that have a similar history of experiences assume greater prominence as agents of socialization (Ratner, 2006).

In future-oriented cultures where rapid adaptation is needed to keep up with social transformation, parents are regarded as having less wisdom to convey to youth because their recollections about growing up do not match the current environment. For this reason, adults have to learn vicariously from teenagers about the experiences they were not exposed to during their youth. Grownups are still recognized as having important lessons to teach while adolescents are also seen as possessing valuable assets that they can share. For example, teenagers are increasingly granted authority because of their greater competence in using the tools of technology (Burns, 2006). Even though the United States is a future-oriented culture, some of the adult population grew up in more present-oriented or past-oriented environments. Consequently, successive generations often have a different point of view about adolescence, appropriate sources of learning, and definitions of achievement (Baldwin, Falkner, Hecht, & Lindsley, 2006).

Change in a Past-Oriented Culture

The nature of relationships in a past-oriented culture becomes better understood when certain factors can be visualized. Figure 2.1A represents conditions of a past-oriented society. Notice that much of the sphere which encompasses adult experience is still unfamiliar to the youth population who have yet to encounter certain situations. In contrast, the child sphere shows that much of what happens during this stage of life is already known by the adults. A gradual rate of cultural change allows parents and surrogates to recall most of the events that characterize a relatively constant set of conditions. Adults and youth in such settings have much in common as illustrated by the large shared activity sector in Figure 2.1A (E. Schultz, 2004).

Past-oriented cultures still exist, places in which adults remain the only significant source of learning for children and adolescents. Visitors to Bali, an island in Indonesia, can see parents as they pass on woodcarving and painting techniques to children who anticipate making their living in the same way. The hands of time seem to have stopped for some aboriginal tribes in Australia and New Guinea where people commit to perpetuating the customs of ancestral communities (Peterson, 2005). Religious groups in America like the Amish in Ohio and Pennsylvania maintain a lifestyle that is remarkably similar to that of their predecessors (Davidson, 2005). An overview of life in a present day Amish community can be examined at http://www.800padutch.com/amish.shtml.

One common characteristic of past-oriented societies is that the community, composed of three generations, take their environment for granted. As children grow up, they do not challenge authority nor express doubt about the relevance of longstanding traditions. Instead, they accept prevailing conditions without question. In contrast, some Native American tribes aspire to retain selected aspects of their heritage while also embracing technology to support casino gambling that provides newfound

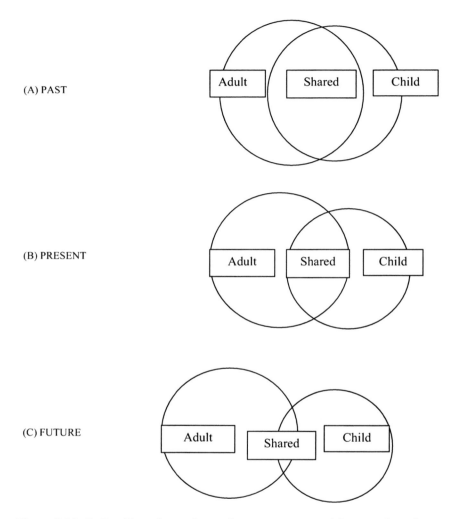

(A) PAST

Adult   Shared   Child

(B) PRESENT

Adult   Shared   Child

(C) FUTURE

Adult   Shared   Child

Figure 2.1A, B, C.   Shared experiences in past, present and future-oriented cultures.

affluence (Benedict, 2001). Information on Native American gambling history is available at http.//www.santaynezchumash.org/gaming_history.html.

Past-oriented societies typically do not recognize adolescence as being a separate stage of life. Instead, they celebrate *initiation rites,* called rites of passage that recognize the transformation from being a child to becoming an adult. These rites might seem cruel in the estimate of outsiders. However, the outcome always is an elevation from childhood status and identity to assumption of adult rights and responsibilities (Savage, 2007) Initiation experiences are no longer a part of technological societies where youth generally remain uncertain and anxious about their role in the culture and identity continues to be a major concern for a much longer period of time. Reliance on identity rites and rituals is most suitable in cultures where (a) children can reasonably expect to have an adult lifestyle that closely resembles their parents; (b) clearly defined gender roles define the family division of labor; (c) cultural homogeneity is in place; (d) there is a uniform structure to socialize youth; and (e) life is relatively short with everyone fulfilling predictable roles. None of these conditions are common in most of modern America (Campbell, 2004).

Adolescents in a slow changing environment look at the future as a repetition of the past. When life is so predictable and free of uncertainty, anxiety is uncommon. Freedom from anxiety has considerable appeal for many people today suffering from continuous stress. Because adults in past-oriented cultures suppose that things are bound to remain the same, they are often unable to conceive of change. Therefore, they feel justified in teaching youth that they should adopt the lifestyle of ancestors and the community reinforces this orientation. Accordingly, one common characteristic of slow-changing societies is that the oldest people, grandparents, are revered as wise authorities, models who everyone should look up to for guidance and aspire to resemble. Meanwhile, the youngest members of society are expected to listen and observe, to be seen but not heard (Ratner, 2006).

Change in a Present-Oriented Culture

Something happens when technology is introduced and the pace of life quickens. There is a corresponding increase in the pace of change. Many of the customary ways of doing things, familiar attitudes, and behavior norms become permanently modified. In addition, adults and children come to have fewer experiences in common. Figure 2.1B shows that young people are exposed to more situations that are new for their age group in times of rapid social transformation. They have experiences that were not part of their parents' upbringing. Compare the child spheres in Figure 2.1A (Past) and Figure 2.1B (Present). Notice that the realm depicting new experiences for children in a present-oriented culture is larger than it is in a past-oriented setting. Consequently, the scope of experience that adults and children share in a present-oriented culture is less than in a past-oriented setting. These configuration shifts which reflect changes in lifestyle confirm that adults are too old to know certain things about youth simply because they are not growing up now. This is a very different message from the one that children in the past heard, "You're too young to understand" (Rotberg, 2004). This common void should motivate greater efforts for generations to share their experiences. Such a goal will require an emphasis on reciprocal learning with more adults becoming listeners who learn about current aspects of the growing up process.

Teenagers encounter certain conditions that are unique. A generation ago people communicated primarily by telephone, most homework was handwritten, research required going to a library where bound volumes could be examined, and student grades were sent home to parents by postal mail. All of these functions have since become computerized. Adolescents everywhere rely upon satellite television, the Internet, and have awareness of global events while they happen. Many of them own computers, cell phones with photo capability, PDAs, iPods, MP3s and video games. Some take classes online, shop online, and make use of credit cards (Lenhart, Madden, & Hitlin, 2005). A much larger proportion than the past live in single or blended families, spend greater time with peers, and feel pressured to experiment with sex and drugs. Generally, they believe that their future depends on finishing college so they worry about grades and test scores (Altbach, Berdahl, & Gumport, 2005). Since 9/11/ 2001 there have been continuous threats from terrorists vowing to harm them (Marshall, Bryant, Amsel, Suh, Cook, & Neria, 2007). Many teens lack supervision after school. They observe intimate relationships and violence at the movies, on television or the Internet. The fear of becoming victims of a sexually-transmitted disease is common (McGue, Elkins, Walden, & Iacono, 2005).

Grownups cannot remember how they dealt with such challenges. Either these situations were less prevalent or did not exist during their adolescence. This awareness should cause grownups to abandon their impression that, because they were once teenagers, personal memories can provide sufficient information to understand what growing up is like now. A more respectful orientation is to acknowledge that the unique experiences of teenagers qualifies them as the best source to report on their experience. To fully appreciate perspective of adolescents, adults should listen to their concerns, feelings, and interpretations of events and situations (Girod, Pardales, Cavanaugh, & Wadsworth, 2005).

The need for reciprocal learning between generations is comically demonstrated in the film called *Freaky Friday* (Waters, 2003). Dr. Tess Coleman (Jamie Lee Curtis) and her adolescent daughter Anna (Lindsay Lohan) disagree about almost everything including fashion, men, and Anna's passion to join a rock band. One night the biggest freakout ever happens when mother and daughter are somehow mystically transformed and find themselves trapped in each other's body. Tess's wedding is scheduled for Saturday so the two must find a way to switch back in a hurry. Literally forced to walk in each other's shoes, both parties find it necessary to learn a lot about one another in a short time. An earlier version of the film that dealt with a male switch was *Like Father, Like Son* (Daniel, 1987). After taking a mysterious potion, a surgeon (Dudley Moore) and his son (Kirk Cameron) accidentally switch bodies. Both face unexpected adjustments and difficult lessons. Neither story could happen in real life but adults can become aware of teenager experiences by listening and looking at life from their perspective (K. Schultz, 2003).

Change in a Future-Oriented Culture

Some things about the future are already known. The United States Bureau of the Census forecasts significant demographic changes by 2050. During this period, the Hispanic segment of the national population is forecast to double, from 12% to 24%, while Asians are expected to increase from 3% to 8%, and Blacks increase from 12.7% to 14.6% (United States Bureau of the Census, 2008). This demographic shift urges that teachers understand and help students from a broader range of cultural backgrounds than ever before (Donlevy, 2006).

The current stage of civilization illustrates growing reliance on the Internet, e-mail, cell phones, PDAs, iPods, and other electronic devices (Buckingham & Willett, 2006). In this kind of an environment, formal education begins earlier, continues longer, and includes considerable information that was unavailable to previous generations of students. As a result, most adolescents are bound to view the world differently than their parents or teachers. The World Future Society Web site presents abstracts of articles about the future including forecasts of how social and technological developments are likely to impact life—http://www.wfs.org.

An unintended but frequent outcome of the knowledge explosion is lack of respect for differences in the experience of successive generations (Dunning, Heath, & Suls, 2004). Fortunately, there are ways to overcome this obstacle. Figure 2.1C implies that adults and adolescents should learn from each other to become aware of one another's needs and respond with appropriate support. This might seem to be a simple solution but there is no historical precedent for adults to learn from youth.

Another complicating factor is that global economic competition requires that nations pay less attention to the past and give greater consideration to the present and future. One predictable consequence is that in future-oriented cultures older adults will lose their prominence as models. All countries where the economy depends on technology have reported a decline in reliance on older adults as exemplars of lifestyle. Instead, people identify most with well-known individuals of their age or next older group, resulting in more age-segregation. Adults and youth in future oriented societies have less in common than do families in past-oriented or present-oriented cultures (Rimm, 2005). A steady decline in mutual experience is illustrated by the shared dimensions that are portrayed in Figure 2.1A (Past), B (Present), C (Future). An emerging challenge is finding ways to expand intergenerational sharing so mutual understanding and harmony can be preserved (Ball, 2006).

CULTURAL DIVERSITY AND COHESION

Culture is usually discussed from a tribal perspective. Nevertheless, members of the same racial and ethnic group often hold dissimilar views about many things because of the different period of time in which they grow up. Prior to Internet and global awareness, cultures were portrayed as being homogenous, with the members of all age groups sharing similar beliefs and values that allowed a common identity and ensured harmony (Lehman, Chiu, & Schaller, 2004). However, the significant changes in societies throughout the world urge observers to recognize ways in which the era of growing up influences how successive generations differ in their interpretation of events, relationships, and view of the future. The generation differences are further pronounced because adolescents are most interested in novel stimuli, accounting for why they become the first age group choosing exposure to new forms of technology. There are new experiences that young and old could acquire at the same time but, as a rule, adults tend to lag behind (Diller, 2007).

The elements of culture given the most attention are race, ethnicity, language, and tradition. This picture ignores the powerful effect of *schema*, the way that people process and organize information. Because of a common exposure to tools of technology and media, youth tend to be alike in their interpretation of many things but differ from adults in general as well as within their culture. Still, adults have been slow to realize that adolescents have a culture of their own which transcends place of birth or nationality. The schema that teenagers share translates into their holding similar values, a strong commitment to technology, more frequent and extended interaction, and an appreciation for the opinion of peers about fashion, music, and lifestyle (Twenge, 2006).

Generation differences within cultures should be determined and respected. For example, adults may be polled regarding their opinions about possible military action against other nations. However, adolescents are not consulted even though people of their age are the ones most likely to be recruited for military service. Dialogue among the generations can identify societal expectations that younger people disagree with and have reasons to revise. In the future, preservation of culture will necessitate a better balance of group identity, rooted in pride but also including due consideration for criticism expressed by younger members. In a new paradigm, adolescents would no longer be told to withhold criticism of customs because adults interpret discontent as a sign of disrespect. Similarly, middle age cultural leaders who presume to speak for youth but never assess their views will need to change by modeling respect for others.

Experiences Shared by Families

Even though different generations are bound to view some things from a different perspective, modern life also includes experiences that are relatively common across generations. For example, in many families, parents as well as their adolescents are going to school. Parents may be attending courses to qualify for a promotion or shift career paths at the same time sons and daughters begin to reflect on possible occupations. Some class assignments such as having to locate Internet resources, study for examinations, write reports, and suitably divide time to meet demands of work, school, and family can increase greater awareness, empathy, and yield greater closeness between parents and adolescents. In a similar way, a high rate of family dissolution means many single parents are returning to the dating scene at the same time their adolescents are starting to date. These situations provide opportunities to share concerns and satisfactions related to getting to know a boyfriend or girlfriend.

Adults and adolescents share a vast and often overwhelming array of choices that could motivate family dialogue about individual decision-making. Most households have adjusted to having husbands and wives in the workforce by adopting a less hierarchical structure which supports more communication and willingness to confide in one another (Rimm, 2005). Blurring of gender roles means that parents of their opposite sex children have common experiences such as when women are employed in high-pressure occupations similar to their fathers. In general, adolescents and parents share many stresses including over-choice, insufficient time to finish tasks, uncertainty about the future, and concerns for safety. There are other first-of-a-kind situations in the current setting that can enlarge the scope of intergenerational sharing (Elliot & Dweck, 2005).

Generational Differences

Some cultural transformation ensures that successive generations differ in outlook on life. In addition, changes within cultures can be more profound than are experienced by the general population. As a result, recognition of variance within cultures is needed to replace stereotypic thinking which assumes people from the same ethnic group are mostly alike. Figure 2.2 illustrates how living conditions for Blacks have changed in ways not experienced by persons from other ethnicities. When Black older adults were adolescents, they did not have career role models. Self-esteem was often low since they were led to see themselves as being inferior (Steele, 2006). In contrast, Black children today typically have favorable self-concepts and exhibit confidence (Fashola, 2005). Black elders more often grew up in households with two parents. In 1965, when civil rights legislation was enacted, 72% of Black children lived with two married parents. In 2006, 35% of Black children under age 18 lived with two married parents compared with 77% of White, and 65% of Hispanic children (Hollinger, 2006). Families and child well-being figures can be found at the Web site for Federal Interagency Forum on Child and Family Statistics (2008) available at http://www.childstats.gov.

Opportunities for education were restricted for older Black adults. Therefore, many of them did not experience pressure to achieve at school. Conditions have dramatically changed. The current stress level is high for Black adolescents whose relatives expect them to make up for possibilities unavailable in the past. Black elders attended schools separated by race and suffered other forms of segregation such as denial of access to public facilities (Boyle-Baise & Binford, 2005; Steele, 2006). There were no affirmative action policies and getting a good job was uncommon. In retrospect, the 'good old days' were not so good for Blacks (Donlevy, 2006).

People of every background can benefit from examining generational differences within their culture. One prominent example involves the Martin Luther King, Jr. Papers Project located at Stanford University. These documents help adolescents understand the struggle of Blacks in an earlier era, describe strategies of the civil rights movement, and chronicle achievements of this Nobel Peace Prize winner—see http://mlk-kpp01.stanford.edu

Figure 2.3 portrays distinctions that exist for some Mexican families (Berry, Phinney, Sam, & Vedder, 2006; Mahalingam, 2006). Certain of these differences are elaborated by a dialogue between a Mexican American mother and her daughter who work at the same restaurant. Carmen, the mother, immigrated to the United States 20 years ago. Her 17-year-old daughter, Lucia, has grown up in the United States. The two women

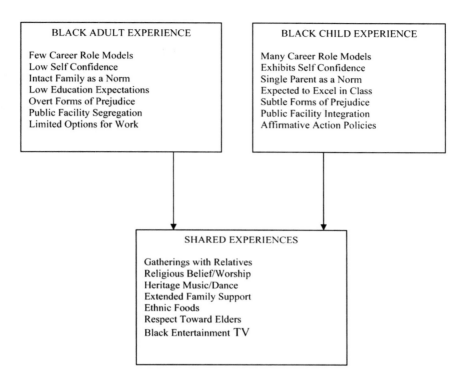

Figure 2.2.   An example of generational differences of experiences within Black groups.

were interviewed separately about issues that often produce conflict between them. The contrasting views of Lucia and her mother across a range of topics underscore a need for teachers to take into account generational differences in the families of their students (French, Seidman, Allen, & Aber, 2006; Rubinstein-Avila, 2006).

Dating. Mother and daughter disagreed on suitable practices. Lucia recently broke up with a boyfriend of 2 years. Carmen liked the young man and cannot understand why Lucia wants to date others. Lucia says that she wants to get to know more than just one guy. Carmen says that it is not good to date too many men.

Money. Lucia gives some of her earnings to relatives but objects to this practice. Carmen reports that the money is sent to family in Mexico. Carmen thinks Lucia should contribute to the financial needs of loved ones on a regular basis. Lucia feels that money she earns should be hers and she is not responsible to support others who should take care of themselves.

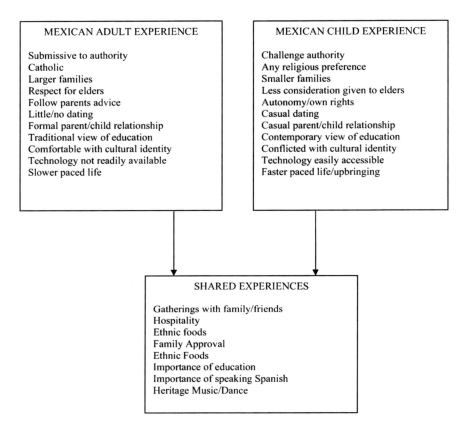

MEXICAN ADULT EXPERIENCE	MEXICAN CHILD EXPERIENCE
Submissive to authority	Challenge authority
Catholic	Any religious preference
Larger families	Smaller families
Respect for elders	Less consideration given to elders
Follow parents advice	Autonomy/own rights
Little/no dating	Casual dating
Formal parent/child relationship	Casual parent/child relationship
Traditional view of education	Contemporary view of education
Comfortable with cultural identity	Conflicted with cultural identity
Technology not readily available	Technology easily accessible
Slower paced life	Faster paced life/upbringing

SHARED EXPERIENCES

Gatherings with family/friends
Hospitality
Ethnic foods
Family Approval
Ethnic Foods
Importance of education
Importance of speaking Spanish
Heritage Music/Dance

Figure 2.3.   An example of generational differences of experiences within Mexican groups.

Language. There is a huge difference in language. Lucia is bilingual; Carmen speaks Spanish and understands limited English. Carmen does not see a need to learn English because she can shop and watch television in Spanish. Lucia says that sooner or later her mother should learn English.

Country of loyalty. Carmen likes to reminisce about Mexico and she talks about going back on vacation. Lucia has visited Mexico and has no desire to live or vacation there.

Fashion. Lucia likes name brand fashions that are sometimes expensive. Carmen likes to look for bargains in order to save money.

Responsibilities. Lucia thinks she has too many responsibilities at home including cleaning and watching her younger brother. Carmen believes that her daughter should be involved in housework and helping with the needs of others in the family.

Eating. Mother and daughter disagree on how often to eat out. Lucia enjoys fast food once in a while. Carmen insists on having home cooked meals because they taste better and cost less.

Relationship with extended family. Carmen insists on her daughter being involved in extended family gatherings and parties on weekends. She also thinks Lucia should get along with the rest of her family. Lucia accepts the schedule but does not like it.

Computer use. Lucia uses the computer at the library to e-mail friends, work on school projects, and play games. Carmen sees no use for computers in her life.

Work ethic. Carmen wants to work as many hours as possible. Lucia often needs and wants time off from work.

Differences within cultures also arise when families migrate. The youngest members usually adjust more readily because schools teach them the skills that are necessary for survival in the new setting. Peer pressure is also a powerful motivator to adopt unfamiliar customs and norms. In contrast, some adults resist social transition to the host culture in favor of retaining familiar traditions of their homeland. They may also avoid learning new ways of functioning (Buki, Ma, Strom, & Strom, 2003; Harriott & Martin, 2004).

Peers as Confidants and Advisors

Reliance on memories of youth as the basis for offering advice to adolescents lacks credibility in a cyber era. Parents who preface their advice by saying, "When I was your age ..." cannot reasonably expect the teenagers to pay attention. As the experiences of adolescents begin to diverge significantly from parents and both generations spend a declining amount of time together, the tendency is to more often consult with peers as advisors (Chu, 2005; Suzuki, 2004). Judith Harris (1998), in *The Nurture Assumption*, described a growing reliance of youth on peers throughout society. Harris provided evidence that the influence peers have on socialization is underestimated by scholars who inflate the contribution of parents, even those whose schedules seldom makes them available to their children.

Most mothers are employed so young children spend lots of time supervised in daycare or preschool where interaction is mainly with immature companions. During the elementary grades many students participate in after-school programs with classmates until their parents return home from work (National Institute on Out-of-School Time, 2005). The After

School Alliance is dedicated to raising awareness about after-school programs, research, and ensuring that all children have access by 2010—http://www.afterschoolalliance.org/. These age-segregated conditions covering extended periods of time guarantee that the opinions of peers become a more powerful factor in shaping adolescent thinking (Desetta, 2005; Gardner & Steinberg, 2005).

It should be acknowledged that turning to peers for advice is common among all age groups. Many adults suppose that the only persons able to understand them are of their same age or facing similar challenges. This impression has motivated formation of many *support groups,* people with a concern in common who meet on a regular basis to talk about their circumstance. Extraordinary benefits are claimed for spending time with people whose comparable circumstance must somehow enable them to comprehend what it takes to contend with a particular set of problems. To illustrate, many teenagers need a support group in school, convened by a counselor, because they experience trouble at home with family conflict, parental divorce, and other difficult to manage situations. Because peers are expected to understand and to provide nonjudgmental support, it is natural for them to be seen as a preferred source of advice. There is anecdotal evidence that support groups give comfort to those who realize they are not alone in coping with specific problems, and steps can be taken to improve their emotional status (Dimitriadis, 2003).

The limitations of support groups should be recognized too (Sommers & Satel, 2005). Having the same sense of history presents some disadvantages along with benefits. When peer norms condone inappropriate behavior, those outside the group who suggest change are dismissed by claiming, "They don't understand us." These arrangements encourage further isolation instead of trying to communicate with those who cannot understand us until we consider them capable of doing so and share our feelings with them. It is a mistake to choose peers as the only audience to listen to personal concerns simply because it is easier to talk with them. Everyone should interact with people of different backgrounds and ages than their own. In this way we learn about them and can make ourselves better known. Individuals who limit conversations to their *cohorts* (people sharing a common factor like growing up at the same time or being from the same income group) forfeit the communication skills and awareness needed to maintain generational harmony (E. Schultz, 2004). To achieve better dialogue, the Kaiser Family Foundation and Children Now support a Web site that encourages parents to talk with adolescents about issues like HIV, sex, terrorism, television news, violence, drugs, and alcohol—http://www.talkingwithkids.org.

CULTURAL PRESERVATION AND ADAPTATION

The average lifespan is longer today than ever before. Yet, many adults report a sense of urgency about having enough time for all of the activities they want to engage in and need to more effectively follow through on priorities they have chosen. A corresponding intention is to pass on planning and time management skills that can help adolescents to enjoy life and improve their culture. Understanding common obstacles to these goals and recognizing how to overcome them warrants reflection.

Preoccupation With the Future

A fundamental change that accompanies technology is greater concern about the future, especially the prevention of nuclear warfare, preservation of environment, and preparation for retirement (Locke & Latham, 2002; Rader, 2005). It is wise to look ahead, to set goals and make plans, so long as we also attend to current affairs. For some persons who become preoccupied with the future, there is no longer any spontaneity; everything must be planned. In contrast, when older adults were growing up, families often went to visit relatives and friends without advance notice. Currently, most people believe that a spontaneous visit to someone's home shows a lack of consideration. They expect an e-mail or phone call first to allow a calendar check, arrange a convenient time, and have sufficient notice to clean the house before visitors arrive (Honore, 2004).

The fascination with planning is also seen in classrooms where lengthy lists of course objectives can restrict the expression of spontaneity. The usual justification is that a mandated curriculum must be covered on time or the class will fall behind schedule (Barth, 2006). However, spontaneity must be allowed if teachers are to honor student motivation, show them how to cope with uncertainty, and live for the present as well as the future. When students lack the chance to depart from what adults plan for them, creative learning becomes off-limits. By over-scheduling adolescents, teachers deny themselves and youth the opportunities to do some things that are unplanned. A reminder is that planned activities are not always more worthwhile than spontaneous ones.

People who are strictly future-oriented constantly look forward to when they graduate, get a job, become parents, gain a promotion, or save enough money to travel. They avoid living in the present. Instead they wait, they save, they are going to do so many things, have such good times someday—and life goes by. All of us know people who live essentially for tomorrow. They look ahead to the freedom and economic security that will come after their children grow up. But in their anticipation of the future, they fail to enjoy their children now, their jobs now, and their lives together now. It seems that some people can become stuck in the future just as others find themselves stuck in the past or the present.

Balance of Time Perspective

The way to avoid living too much in the past, present, or future is by choosing a pattern of balance (Baumeister, 2005). For some aspects of life it could be wise to identify with the past, to emphasize cultural preservation. Many people feel this way about their religious faith rooted in distant history because this provides them with a source of hope for the future. Individuals often decide that the spiritual realm is one aspect of life in which it is preferable to be old-fashioned. In other sectors, however, it may be necessary to leave some aspects of the past behind to accommodate challenges of the present. Practices in medicine, manufacturing, and business are usually abandoned when research and invention reveal more promising ways of doing things. This shift is defined as progress or cultural evolution. In a similar way, schools and families should periodically evaluate whether their methods of interaction reflect a past orientation and make sense in the present (Evans & Wolfe, 2005).

Every generation must guard against getting stuck in one time frame or another. Because the past is where most of their achievements lie, older adults often engage in nostalgia, look back more than is good for their mental health. By bringing them into public schools as volunteers who help teachers, elders can become motivated to transition from a past orientation to one that also includes a healthy focus on the present. This is essential because persons fixed in the past have greater difficulty accepting contemporary goals such as racial equality, work opportunities for women, gender sharing of domestic chores, respect for the opinions of children, and personal involvement with technology. Resisting progressive attitudes can have the unintended effect of bringing social isolation. This is not a lost cause. Comparative studies of attitude shifts have shown that older adults are more capable of changing their minds than commonly supposed (McGuire, Klein, & Couper, 2005).

Parents can also get stuck in the past when they attempt to control sons and daughters using old-fashioned discipline like corporal punishment. Instead of requiring obedience in every instance, youth should be taught to think critically, make decisions on their own, and practice self-evaluation. Parents of adolescents reveal they are stuck in the past when they look back on their child's earlier years as the best of times. The fact is every age presents different opportunities and parents must discover the joys of interacting with daughters and sons throughout the process of growing up (Patrikakou, Weissberg, Redding, & Walberg, 2005). Some parents are stuck in the present by being preoccupied with a career and investing too little of themselves in their marriage or child guidance responsibilities. Other parents demonstrate excessive concern for the present by spending too much family income on current wishes while failing to set aside funds needed for college tuition of children and their own retirement (Rimm, 2005),

Adolescents sometimes become stuck, particularly when they are led to believe their identity should be based mainly on events in which they were not participants. It is important to recognize that ethnicity is a coincidence of birth making some people Irish, German, Hispanic, or Black. Heritage is not a matter of choice nor is any ancestry better than others. In a global environment, it seems that pride should relate primarily to the present instead of the past and reflect personal behavior, decisions, and achievements rather than what ancestors accomplished (Friedman, 2005).

People throughout the world have begun to reconsider whether the traditional bases used to define identity are too narrow (Harris, 2006). Increasing technology, aspirations for equality, and interdependence impact the identity of individuals from all nations. This means identity cannot continue to be as closely tied to power, rank, status, money, religion, color, or ethnicity as in the past. People with low incomes believe their lives are as important as the lives of persons who possess wealth and influence. This is a nontraditional way of looking at humanity and status. In effect, personal growth requires people to transcend their cultural identity, to care about people from other origins and cohorts. In the past a sense of belonging was often limited to subculture. Today, in many countries, there is a readiness to welcome people previously perceived as outsiders, as different and thus less valuable than ourselves—the disabled, immigrants, minorities. These fundamental changes are signs of cultural progress (Ball, 2006).

Some adolescents get stuck in the present because they have no sense of vision, lack important dreams to motivate them, and have no aspirations to stimulate or guide their efforts. Instead of being encouraged to set some goals on their own, they may be expected to follow plans laid out for them by parents, teachers and other adults (Locke & Latham, 2002). An over-scheduled life is frequently reflected by lack of self-direction. Another reason some adolescents are stuck in the present is that they have not learned to wait for anything. They want their wishes met immediately and fail to develop the patience needed to succeed in complex and significant tasks. Growing up and continuing to learn should be a common aspiration in a longevity society. For the immediate future, however, it appears that every generation will experience difficulty choosing a path that represents a healthy balance of living in the past, present, and future (Rader, 2005).

Equality of Attention and Listening

Teachers should make themselves available for listening so they can be seen as a source of guidance. At every age, the persons willing to listen to us are the ones we respect most. This view is reinforced when adolescents have made known their "ease of communication" with significant people in daily life. Schools in all socioeconomic strata have consistently found that teenagers find it easiest to communicate with friends of their age (Rosen, 2007). The next most preferred listener is mother. Ironically, the people that students find most difficult to communicate with are teachers and principals, the surrogates entrusted to teach them communication skills (Black, 2005).

Access to patient listeners and its effect on ability to cope with stress does not seem to improve during later adolescence. The University of Minnesota Medical Center surveyed 3,600 teenagers, asking them to rank order 54 options for how they cope with their daily stress (Lewis, 2000). Listening to music, watching television, and daydreaming topped the list of preferences. Talking with parents was more than halfway down the list. Tied for 54th in last place was talking with teachers and school administrators. Teachers and other faculty members should strive to be good listeners because this way of acting confirms that what youngsters have to say is important. Students feel few adults listen to carefully consider their ideas and feelings (Black, 2005).

The divided attention of teachers is becoming a greater concern. Many students who score at grade level or above observe that teachers spend most of their time working with and listening to low achievers. Parents are alarmed by such reports and often react by transferring sons and daughters to private schools so their learning needs will get more attention. Some educators believe that, unless incentives are put in place that ensure greater equality of teacher attention, public schools may experience an exodus of high achievers. Such a possibility is indicated by state reports for performance on the National Assessment of Educational Progress tests in the era of No Child Left Behind (Duffett, Farkas, & Loveless, 2008). From 2000-2007, the lowest scoring students (bottom 10%) made large gains in reading and mathematics while the highest achievers (top 10%) made minimal gains.

To probe why the high achievers made less progress, 900 teachers in grades 3-12 from throughout the nation were surveyed (Duffett, Farkas, & Loveless, 2008). A majority (81%) reported that struggling students are their top priority and receive more one-on-one attention whereas only 5% reported high achievers were their top priority. That the teachers believe all students deserve equal attention is clear from their response to this scenario:

> For the public schools to help the U.S. live up to its ideals of justice and equality, do you think it is more important that they (a) focus on raising the achievement of disadvantaged students who are struggling, or (b) focus equally on all students regardless of their background or achievement level?

Only 11% of the teachers favored focusing on the disadvantaged while 86% chose equal focus on all students. Teachers seem conflicted about the differences between what is expected of them and what they expect of themselves. Thomas B. Fordham Institute's Report on High Achieving Students in the Era of No Child Left Behind is available at http://www.edexcellence.net/detail/news.cfm?news_id=732&id.

SCHOOLING IN THE PAST

The education that students get at school shapes their attitudes toward others, determines how they approach problems, and sets a perspective for interpretation of events. As society undergoes rapid change, the public usually reacts by expecting schools to adapt so students are prepared for predictable challenges. From a distance we can look back on schooling and recognize certain residual influences on the contemporary classroom.

Faculty Theory and Memorization

Teaching in the first half of the twentieth-century was dominated by a single theory of learning (Spurzheim, 1883). *Faculty theory* suggested that the mind is made up of separate compartments containing attributes such as memory, judgment, and calculation known as faculties. Just as physical exercise strengthens the body, mental faculties could grow by academic tasks involving practice and drill. Teachers were expected to monitor the exercise of faculties like memory and language in which strength was desired while discouraging faculties such as anger and jealousy. Latin and Mathematics were viewed as being the best exercisers because they were more difficult (National Education Association, 1895).

Each of the mental faculties, depicted by a *phrenological chart* of the head, supposedly developed according to their unique schedules. For example, memory was seen as operational at a younger age than reason.

Early memory training would supply the raw material needed later by the faculty of reasoning when reason became accessible during adolescence. Faculty psychologists maintained that learning called for exercising the specific compartments in the mind. Students were expected to memorize names, dates and places (Aikin, 1942). The phrenological head illustrates what the public was told about mental assets and personality traits based on shape of the skull. You can examine the Phrenological Chart at http://www.cerebromente.org.br/n01/frenolog/frenmap.htm.

Because understanding was ignored as a main goal for instruction, and support for understanding was delayed until students were older, educators underestimated the potential of teachers to aid comprehension. Students would not benefit if their lessons were readily understood. In fact, giving assignments that could be mastered quickly and without some discomfort was thought to be an injustice because it took away the chance to experience the struggle of learning. Examination of supervisor reports during this era suggests that observing a classroom of frustrated students confirmed teacher success in requiring hard work (Murphy, 1949).

Curriculum and Transfer of Training

Edward Thorndike (1874–1949) of Columbia University was the first American educational psychologist. His research indicated that much of schooling had only a negligible effect. The slight carryover that occurred was attributed to the presence of "identical elements" in the tasks students practiced and an applied setting. Thorndike concluded that *transfer of training* requires identical elements in two situations as a condition for learning in one circumstance to carry over to the other. This result meant that faculty theory which claimed that difficulty of subject matter is important to ensure greater learning would be challenged by those advocating for placing greater priority on relevance of the curriculum for the workplace. If, as Thorndike proposed, a student is able to apply in a new situation what has been learned in a previous one only to the extent that there is similarity or 'identical elements' in the two settings, then schools have to offer studies that include practical application (Thorndike, 1924, 1932).

Thorndike contended that school assignments were sometimes absurd. For example, problems of this sort were common in mathematics, "Alice has three-eighths of a dollar, Bertha eleven-sixteenths, Mary three-fourths and Nancy two-thirds. How much do they have together?" Thorndike (1924) said this question would appear in real life only in an insane asylum. He maintained the same was true for studying Greek, poetry, and courses on logic. He asserted there was a lack of evidence that training a student in geometry would strengthen powers of comparison, mathematics would equip someone with reason in all situations; or that history can cultivate powers of good judgment for all of life's demands (Dallam, 1917). Instead, Thorndike recommended teaching arithmetic related to the likely adult use of numbers, assigning spelling words expected for writing letters, and master reading material that adults are likely to encounter. School critics supported Thorndike's view that, unless certain things are accomplished by a curriculum, it fails to provide applicability or transfer, and transfer of training must become the main concern of educators (Aikin, 1942; Mayer, 2003).

To demonstrate that no subjects in the curriculum have a special effect on mental ability, Thorndike (1924) studied 8,000 high school students. All of them, engaged in taking various courses, were administered a pretest of general mental ability. The following year another form of the same test was given after which scores were analyzed for groups that had selected different subject combinations to assess if larger gains related to unique benefits offered by particular subjects. Taking into account the normally expected growth in a year, it was found that students enrolled in practical courses like Bookkeeping, Home Economics, and English made similar gains as classmates who chose subjects thought to support greater mental improvement such as Latin, Geometry, and History. All courses seemed to be similar in improving performance on general mental ability tests. The transfer of training and identical elements studies led educators to view relevance as a priority for education (Morrison, 1926).

Students and Analytic Thinking

When older Americans (age 60+) attended high school, their school curriculum placed an emphasis on *analytic thinking*, the ability to separate things into constituent elements to study and examine, draw conclusions or solve problems. Figure 2.4 illustrates Past (A), Present (B) and Future (C) Changes in Education, Learning and Thinking. During the past (Figure 2.4A) students memorized notable events in national and world history and were expected to locate on a map where they happened. In addition, students were encouraged to reflect on how prior generations acted in ways that caused conflict and, in hindsight, judge how certain situations might have been avoided. Adolescents were warned that those who fail to understand the mistakes of the past are destined to repeat them (Anfara, 2006). Reliance on this premise meant that learning as much as possible about the past was the best preparation for the future. By studying popular personalities along with happenings of bygone days, Americans could find out who they were, become aware of their national identity, and appreciate the democratic principles the country stood for. History and literature were given most attention because these subjects

(A) PAST ORIENTED SOCIETY

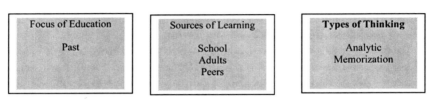

(B) PRESENT ORIENTED SOCIETY

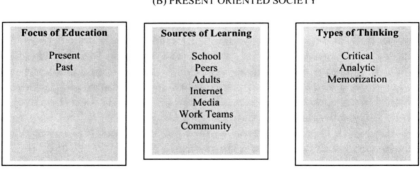

(C) FUTURE ORIENTED SOCIETY

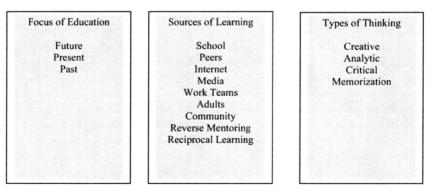

Figure 2.4A, B, C.   Past, present, and future changes in education, learning, and thinking.

were seen as offering the best possibility to instill patriotism needed for building a cohesive society (Reese, 2007).

Students were directed by parents to listen to teachers whose direct instruction was the main source of learning along with texts. Assignments required working alone, in competition with others. The emphasis on individual achievement reflected a view that independence is the key to success. Acquiring the ability to take care of oneself without asking for help, making it on your own, was the approved path. Interdependence was discouraged and working together was considered cheating and as a weakness of character. Therefore, students were rarely engaged in group work or learned team skills. Getting a job after high school or dropping out to enter the labor market early were common choices. Less than 20% of the students went on to vocational training or attend college (Lucas, 2006).

SCHOOLING IN THE PRESENT

Basic skills remain the highest priority for school curriculum. In addition, the learning focus has expanded to include critical thinking, decision making, self-esteem, and accepting differences among classmates. These more comprehensive goals are seen as an appropriate response to changing demands for personal and institutional adjustment in current society.

Over-Choice and Decision Making

Alvin Toffler (1970) invented the term, *future shock*, defined as the disorientation people feel when overwhelmed by continued social and technological change. The impermanence of society as reflected by high mobility, decline of nuclear families, appeal of throwaway goods, disparities in basic values among citizens, and extensive training which quickly becomes obsolete all contribute to future shock. For this reason, Toffler and Toffler (2000) recommended that, besides basic academic skills and computer literacy, students must also adjust to *over-choice*, living with more options than are easily managed. Satellite television is a familiar example of over-choice offering viewers a menu that can include hundreds of channels. Similarly, the Internet provides more choices than individuals are able to explore. There are also more cereals, automobiles, movies, credit cards, books, clothing, and leisure pursuits. Adolescents will be exposed to over-choice on a larger scale than currently faced by adults. Although options enable people to improve their lives, having to frequently choose from alternatives can also produce stress. Accordingly, students need preparation to cope with over-choice (Canton, 2006; Schwartz, 2004).

Students and Critical Thinking

As the nation's economy shifts from producing goods to information processing, knowledge is generated more rapidly than could be taught in the classroom. Therefore, thinking skills have higher priority than in the past. To achieve this goal, school boards have identified critical thinking as an essential outcome of schooling. Figure 2.4B (Present) illustrates current changes in education, learning, and thinking. *Critical thinking* is the process of considering a subject, content, or problem where judgment can be improved by skillfully analyzing, assessing and reconstructing it. Critical thinking includes skills that are needed to investigate and interpret data, evaluate options, and reflect on decisions before responding. Critical thinking is self-directed, self-disciplined, self-monitored, self-corrective and includes problem-solving abilities (Dozier, Johnston, & Rogers, 2006).

Increased support for critical thinking has brought about a gradual shift in what is expected of students at all grade levels. The importance once attached to memorization is waning in favor of more attention to problem solving. It is recognized that much of the information students memorize may be relevant for only a brief time. Because new knowledge is increasing so fast, some data is soon obsolescent. Therefore, achievement tests that feature memorization have been replaced with more balanced indicators that also assess problem solving and critical thinking (Dozier, Johnston, & Rogers, 2006).

Two shifts characterize the transition from education in the past and the present. Both involve sources of learning. In the past, students learned mostly from adults, reflecting the accepted hierarchical social structure where learning flowed in one direction, older to young people. In the present more horizontal social structure, students recognize their peers as important sources of learning. Accordingly, teachers should use this support system to create indigenous, constructive norms based on interaction in cooperative learning teams. And, instead of peer learning only, educators should assign generational reporter and cultural reporter tasks enabling learning from adults in the out-of-school environment.

Voices of Adolescents

When students fall behind, tutoring is the best form of remediation. However, although students from every income level sometimes need this assistance, the Supplemental Education Services (SES) provision of the No Child Left Behind Act restricts free tutoring to students from low-income families (Spellings, 2007). Consequently, private tutoring has become big business, catering to the middle class and affluent who complain that the cost of this service, an integral aspect of instruction, should be covered by the school for every student regardless of their economic circumstance.

Growing Stars is a nontraditional online tutoring option. The tutors are all well qualified, most possessing a masters degree in mathematics or science. Because most of these tutors live in India, their assistance costs about one-third the price of domestic tutors. The tutor in India and the student in the United States have two-way audio dialogues using special hands-free headsets with microphones, hooked up to their computers. Tutor and tutee share an electronic whiteboard with a pen mouse and keyboard input. The student scans worksheets to the tutor. They interact with questions and answers in writing which are displayed on both computer screens. Even though they are thousands of miles apart, the cooperating pair can converse as if they were face to face. To view a demonstration of the process, see http://www.growingstars.com.

The Tutoring Poll (Exercise 2.01) in this chapter detects how students perceive the importance of tutoring to overcome failure; ways of motivating them to admit a need for help; convenient times for tutoring sessions; anticipated response from friends and relatives to admission of a need for tutoring; reasons why individuals may recognize their need for support; preferred tutoring conditions, methods to handle difficult course content; subjects in which tutoring is needed most; ways teachers respond to requests for tutoring; schools making known availability of tutoring and progress of students who get tutoring, and willingness to be a tutor.

SCHOOLING IN THE FUTURE

In a global marketplace, all countries find it necessary to look ahead and try to figure out how to gain an advantage. Schools are recognized as one environment to nurture innovative thought and invention. There is a common desire to support creative thinking, using imagination to invent, revise or elaborate ideas. Cultures differ in how they are trying to support creative thinking. In the United States, this challenge involves significant changes in the role expectations of teachers and students.

Creative and Critical Thinking

Students can read about problems of the past but are unable to do anything about them. They cannot stop the assassinations of Presidents Abraham Lincoln or John Kennedy nor can they buy paintings of Adolph Hitler so he would become an artist instead of a dictator. However, it is possible to influence the future by cooperative planning (Craft, 2005). The physical and social technology is available to influence certain events that have yet to happen (Fagenberg, Mowery, & Nelson, 2005). First, there is a need to conceptualize alternative futures before deciding on priorities that public consensus leads us to pursue. For individuals and for societies, effective planning requires the application of creative thinking (Sternberg & O'Hara, 2002). Figure 2.4C (Future) shows the kinds of changes in education, learning, and thinking that are emphasized in a future-oriented society.

Torrance (1994, 1995, 2000a) defined *creative thinking* as the process of sensing problems or gaps in information, forming ideas or hypotheses, testing and modifying these hypotheses and communicating the results. Creativity presents a contribution of original ideas, a different point of view, or a new way of looking at problems. Creativity calls for making a successful step into the unknown, getting away from the common track, breaking out of the mold, being open to new experience and allowing one thing to lead to another, recombining ideas or seeing new relationships. Concepts like curiosity, imagination, discovery, innovation, and invention are prominent in discussions of creativity. Schools should include creative thinking skills along with critical thinking in the curriculum because both assets are essential and have to be nurtured simultaneously. Research has been devoted to both constructs but greater attention is needed on ways to merge them (Heilman, 2005).

People who possess creative abilities are more able than others to accommodate novelty, avoid boredom, resolve conflicts, manage broad consumer choices, accept complexity, tolerate ambiguity, participate in independent judgments, use leisure time constructively, and adapt to new knowledge (Elmer & Torem, 2004). Still, convincing the public to assign high priority to creative thinking remains difficult. There is little resistance when children enter school because most of them prefer to learn in creative ways. They reveal curiosity by asking questions, show a willingness to hypothesize by guessing, and freely use imagination. Later, by age 11 or 12, creativity has begun to show signs of decline for most students. For a long time this problem was ignored since it was assumed to be universal. However, cross-cultural studies have found that creativity can continue to increase as long as imagination is viewed as an asset to support successful adjustment (Beghetto, 2005; Torrance, 1995, 2000a).

Adjustment to Change

A commitment to creative and critical thinking can have the effect of enabling institutions and individuals to be more capable of coping with change. One condition for adaptation is assimilation of novel ideas. This asset is explored by Josep Burcet (2004). His premise is that each time mankind has experienced a substantial increase in communication, major cultural change has been the consequence. When applied to communications technology, Burcet's *communication leap hypothesis* suggests that, over the next several decades, people around the world will be presented with a need to absorb a huge amount of novel information in a shorter time frame than ever before. Many individuals and cultures might be unable to assimilate a rapid intake of novel data, especially when the new information contradicts the social framework they rely on for mental health, personal identity, and cultural cohesion (Hofstede, 2001; Whittle, 2005). To consider how Burcet's hypothesis could impact cultures, examine his Web site at http://www.burcet.net/b/cultural_change.htm.

Commitment to creative thinking can sustain the curiosity needed to foster learning throughout the lifespan. As technology makes it possible to attain a broader range of goals, society will have to decide which goals are to be pursued and the order of their importance. To shape the future in a democratic society, dialogue across generations must be common and people should respond to the needs of other age groups. Support for these goals is difficult to attain because interaction between generations is diminishing. For example, education programs are seldom available to help older adults stay in touch with the times, and there is no precedent for viewing adolescents as an essential source of learning to support adult adaptation to change (Santo, 2005).

Burcet's (2004) communication leap hypothesis appears implicated because younger age groups are more inclined to embrace novelty. This means that youth may have to be assigned some responsibility for helping older people who control societal resources to recognize and appreciate the potential benefits of accepting changes that could promote cultural evolution. Creative approaches for the education of all age groups are needed to cope with significant nontraditional challenges (Barth, 2006; Florida, 2005).

Integration of Technology

Adjustment to novel ideas is necessary to cope with rapid change. The Olympia school district in suburban Seattle, Washington, set a goal to integrate technology with the curriculum at all grade levels. Organizers agreed that one reason schools are slow in absorbing innovation is because student views have been ignored. For the first time in history, students understand more than their teachers about the tools on which future learning depends (Storey & Graeme, 2005). Students are disappointed by lack of opportunity to further develop their expertise in technology in school. Many claim a disconnect between life online after school hours and methods of learning used in classrooms. Teachers concede that their lack of technology skills and pressures for high stakes testing combine to prevent greater use of resources that could reduce boredom (Barth, 2006).

The strategy that Olympia, Washington schools applied was *reverse mentoring*, a concept which requires turning around the relationship in which an older person mentors a younger one. Reverse mentoring was popularized by the General Electric Corporation. When Jack Welch, the Chief Executive Officer, realized that he and other senior executives were out of touch with technology, he paired 500 of his leaders with younger employees whose task was to help older co-workers learn to navigate the Internet and use email. The experiment was successful, introduced a continuous sharing of expertise within the company, and credited for higher productivity. Many other businesses have adopted reverse mentoring (Frank, Zhao, & Borman, 2004; Greengard, 2002).

For the Olympia school district, reverse mentoring meant that each student was paired with a partner- teacher at the same school. These student-teacher teams plan a curriculum project together to be enhanced by some application of technology. Teachers provide knowledge about the topic, recognition of class needs, and lesson planning to guide the effort. The student contributes a technology element that can make the lesson more appealing and effective. The mutual creation becomes part of the curriculum in the partner-teacher's classroom. The student advantage is getting to practice and develop technology skills for practical projects while gaining collaboration experience needed for the workplace. The partner-teacher has access to technical support that matches current classroom needs and benefits from skills shared by a younger mentor.

Exciting technologies emerge at such a rapid rate that teachers cannot keep up with them (Gecke, 2006). Reverse mentoring permits the teachers to benefit from how fast students learn the latest technical skills and how willing they are to be helpful as mentors. Traditional models of professional development have been based on providing technology skills to teachers with the hope that it can improve student learning. Experience by Olympia schools suggests that more can be gained when the procedure is reversed. Allowing adolescents to practice technology and instructional skills can enhance teaching and thereby impact student learning.

The characteristics of a reciprocal learning relationship warrant reflection because they offer clues about how teacher-student interaction should proceed in the future. Both parties are involved in setting goals for mutual pursuit. Their product requires both parties to use complimentary strengths so they are interdependent. The teacher does not control the student but rather conveys freedom and trust that is essential for teamwork. The student and teacher alternate leadership. This shared dominance is a radical departure from the custom where the teacher is always the leader (Hample, 2005).

Students can assume shared leadership when they are given training to help them collaborate with adults as peers, show patience, and conduct the respectful dialogue expected in a workplace (Rader, 2005). So, when a teacher has a computer glitch that a student is able to solve, interaction does not include derogatory comments like "That is a silly way to do it." A more respectful comment would be "There is probably a better way for us to do it," followed by demonstrating the correct path, and monitoring the procedure as repeated by the teacher. Students have to understand that conversations with a teacher-partner must be confidential. Further, it is unacceptable to insult an adult partner during conversations with friends (Gross, 2004).

Dennis Harper, Olympia school district technology coordinator leading the project, maintains that linking student technology strengths with teacher academic strength can actualize creative methods proposed long before most students possessed distinctive skills. Vygotsky and Piaget are educational theorists featured in chapter 4 who proposed scaffolding and coaching concepts, beginning with what someone already knows and helping build on it. A basketball coach is not expected to demonstrate how to rise above the rim to dunk a shot to be viewed by players as the team leader. The track coach does not have to run a one hundred yard dash quickly to show athletes who are faster than him how it should be done. Similarly, teachers do not have to be able to make a Web page to effectively use Web pages. Students can make Web pages. Instead of supposing that teachers must always be more competent than students, a partnership paradigm is appropriate. In a partnership, the expertise of both parties is joined for mutual benefit (Barker & Erickson, 2005).

Over 1,200 schools have adopted the Olympia model of integrating technology with curriculum (Armstrong, 2001). This kind of on-the-job technology training where teachers participate in reciprocal learning with tech savvy students has proven to be an effective method for promoting change. Future classrooms should be more interactive, collaborative, and related to real life application. These outcomes are more likely when teachers recognize the possibilities of a problem-solving approach, allow students to move ahead at varying paces, alternate a leadership role with students, and relinquish control in favor of self-directed learning (Gross, 2004). The most enthusiastic and persuasive voices favoring reverse mentoring are middle school and high school students whose English, Mathematics, Reading, and History projects are described on the Generation YES (Youth and Educators Succeeding) Web site at http://www.genyes.com/programs/genyes/sample_projects/CD.

SUMMARY

Stages of Cultural Change

In a past-oriented society, change occurs so slowly that children are able to view their future by observing the lives of parents and grandparents. Therefore, the focus for most learning is historical and adults represent the nearly exclusive source of education. In contrast, change is relatively rapid in a present-oriented society. As a result, a large proportion of the population prefer learning from their same age group or persons who have experience with circumstances that resemble their own. In future-oriented societies that are driven by technology, adolescents are often exposed to situations never before encountered by people of their age.

Cultural Diversity and Cohesion

In every culture there is a need to listen to the voices of adolescents rather than have adults speak for them. This practice is necessary so that schools can improve based on views of students and cultures can change by taking generational differences into account. The effectiveness of educational innovation depends in part on related changes in families and communities. Adults need to abandon the notion that because youth are obligated to attend school, their generation should carry the full burden of adjusting to social change. Rather, it is necessary to think about education in a larger context, a new way that permits all age segments to undergo some aspects of change together. Adults must become as critical of their own development in order to prepare them for lifelong learning.

Cultural Preservation and Adaptation

Adolescents and adults complain that they tend to over schedule themselves and face expectations from others to complete tasks faster than is reasonable. There is a general aspiration for more effective planning and time management so personal and cultural priorities do not suffer. There can be benefit in reflecting on how individuals, cultures and education systems are stuck in the past, present, and future. Instead of passing on every aspect of the culture, it is relevant to determine which elements should be retained, modified, and abandoned. This task is vital for cultural viability so that members can adjust to changing times. Listening to adolescents is one key to success because the views of persons not old enough to vote must still be factored in when communities consider making decisions regarding change.

Schooling in the Past, Present, and Future

In a past-oriented society, schooling focuses on analytic thinking and attempts to perpetuate a focus of previous generations while also trying to avoid their mistakes. The primary sources of education are parents and other relatives. Critical thinking is emphasized in present-oriented societies along with decision making to cope with over-choice. There is also concern about giving everyone opportunities to learn compared with prior practices of denying rights to ethnic minorities and persons with disabilities. Learning from peers has greater prominence in a present-oriented society because most people prefer to be advised by others with similar experiences. In future-oriented societies like the United States, adolescents encounter situations never faced by previous generations. Accordingly, adolescents and adults of varying ages must engage in reciprocal learning. Determining effective ways to enable intergenerational learning represents a significant challenge.

The teacher role is gradually changing from a solo performer to a facilitator that links students with an array of resources including the Internet, television, cooperative learning groups, parental guidance, personal digital assistants, and direct instruction in class. This larger responsibility increases the complexity, demands, and satisfactions of teaching. These changes in instruction enable corresponding shifts in the student role. Active involvement is replacing a passive function for students who traditionally were obliged to remain quiet, work alone, and avoid interaction with others in class. Students need opportunities to practice teamwork skills that employers need in an interdependent work environment. Besides increasing the sources that students can access for learning, teachers are expected to broaden the scope of thinking, to enjoin benefits of analytical processes with critical decision-making and creative inquiry.

It is customary to suppose that adolescents need guidance from adults but grownups have little to learn from teenagers. A more promising orientation is that the impact of technology calls for a new teaching paradigm that reflects the current scene. Otherwise, further decline in communication and learning among the generations is inevitable. At every stage in life we are either too old or too young to know some things by direct experience. Adults must learn what growing up in the current environment is like or they cannot provide advice to match the situations young people face. Grownups only know what being a teenager was like in the past. However, lack of contemporary experience can be overcome by uninterrupted listening to youngsters. Teachers and parents who make it known that they value reciprocal learning will experience respect from young people. This unprecedented kind of interaction may be the most challenging aspect of providing guidance to adolescents.

CLASSROOM APPLICATIONS

1. Adolescent identity status remains less than adult status because of their need to complete extended education. Yet, for the first time, many students know more than their teachers about the digital tools on which future learning depends. Teachers can support identity for youth by acknowledging their expertise in technology skills and providing tasks to further develop these assets.

2. Adolescents are uncertain and anxious about the occupation they should pursue, curriculum to prepare for work, and relationship concerns. Teachers who are easy to talk with and willing to listen qualify themselves as confidants who can offer guidance by giving feedback about logic, raise questions for consideration, and suggest resources where more information is available.

3. Teens experience some conditions that are unique for their age group. Therefore, they are the most credible reporters about life at their stage of development. A source of satisfaction for many teachers is daily access to the best informants about adolescence and the opportunity for personal growth by exposure to the idealistic outlook many youth have about the world.

4. The constructive potential of peer influence to increase learning and to reinforce patterns of civil behavior is underestimated. Arranging group work can be an effective way to establish favor-

able norms for interaction with peers, promote maturity, practice team skills, and confirm that certain problems are better dealt with by collective effort.

5. Teachers can contribute to student adjustment by encouraging support groups at school. Meeting on a regular basis with peers who live with similar challenges like family separation, divorce, and other crises confirms for students that they are not alone in their predicament, sympathetic peers will listen, and everyone can share their solutions.

6. Faculty sponsored polls offer students suitable voting experience in the institution expected to teach them the merits of democratic government. Finding out how students see the learning environment can reveal ways to overcome obstacles, offer clues about how to improve instruction, and illustrates that showing respect means considering the views of others.

7. In a future-oriented culture, reciprocal learning should characterize the interaction between youth and adults. This approach can ensure that each generation is aware of the ideas and feelings of other cohorts so they become able to respond to needs. Teachers motivate this dialogue with assignments that call on relatives to share their views with students.

8. When adolescence is extended, students are often denied a chance to make decisions on their own. Opportunities to practice decision-making at school are essential to gain competence in selecting attainable goals, apply time management skills, use suitable criteria and critical thinking to assess progress, and set a course for self-direction.

9. The kind of education students receive at school has an enduring influence in shaping their attitudes about others, determining how they solve problems, and establishing ways of looking at events. These outcomes urge teachers to rely on a paradigm that matches the current environment and recognizes how educators and students can support mutual adjustment.

10. Creative abilities enable students to accept complexity, accommodate novelty, choose from many options, avoid boredom, manage conflict, and perceive possibilities that motivate their efforts. These valuable attributes are nurtured by teachers who encourage questions in class, make assignments that require divergent thinking, and model a sense of wonder.

11. Reverse mentoring is a new way of learning by which students provide instruction for teachers. This process of alternating leadership allows the student to contribute to a lesson using technology and

gain skills that are needed for collaborating with an adult. The teacher benefits from integration of technology with curriculum and skills shared by the student mentor.

12. The population of older adults without minor age children is growing. This large block of voters can improve or degrade the quality of schooling that students receive depending upon how well informed they are about what goes on in classrooms. Teachers should welcome older volunteers and find additional ways to acquaint elders with student progress and needs.

13. Interdependence theory provides a framework for understanding the ways in which a broad array of sources can impact students and schools. Teachers enhance learning when they value insights from the out-of-school adults that adolescents turn to for advice and prepare interview tasks that solicit their input on dealing with adversity finding satisfaction, and defining success.

FOR REFLECTION

Sometimes we have second thoughts about experiences. These afterthoughts are based on reflection that enables better processing of information. Reflect on some issues about cultural change and education.

1. Helping adolescents attain identity is an important contribution to development. How do you intend to support this possibility by the way things are done in your classroom?

2. What approaches could schools experiment with that will allow adolescents to impact thinking of grownups who might otherwise undervalue accomplishments of the schools?

3. Schools are expected to support creative thinking so this form of achievement should be assessed to detect progress. Give your reasoning to support or oppose this viewpoint.

4. How does the concept of reverse mentoring accord with your own expectations for the teacher role in the classroom and personal aspirations for professional development?

5. What are your greatest concerns about being able to serve disabled students in the classroom while also giving other students the help that they need to achieve success?

6. Identify some (a) obstacles that prevent reciprocal learning between adolescents and adults, and (b) recommend novel ways that could be used to overcome these difficulties?

7. How do you feel about seeking advice from sources that are outside your peer group, from people older or younger than yourself?

8. There are policies to facilitate racial and ethnic integration of schools. What do you think could be done to also support greater age-integration of the American society?

9. What strategies have you found to be most effective when faced with over-choice?

10. Identify some approaches you intend to apply that will lead students to recognize you as someone they can turn to for listening and advice?

11. How do you balance your attention, energy, and time to concerns about the past, present and future?

12. Some people feel a sense of obligation to preserve their subculture. Others believe that they would like to see changes in their subculture. Still others indicate they know little about their subculture and don't care to preserve tradition. Explain your position.

KEY TERMS

Analytic Thinking

Cohort

Communication Leap Hypothesis

Creative Thinking

Critical Thinking

Culture

Faculty Theory

Future Shock

Initiation rites

Over-Choice

Paradigm

Phrenological map

Reverse Mentoring

Schema

Support Groups

Transfer of Training

VISIT THESE WEB SITES

Link to these sites at http://www.infoagepub.com/strom-adolescents

Afterschool Alliance http://www.afterschoolalliance.org

Amish People http://www.800padutch.com/amish.shtml

Josep Burcet's Communication Leap Hypothesis
http://www.burcet.net/b/cultural_change.htm

Creativity Timeline http://www.gocreate.com/history/index.htm

Federal Interagency Forum on Child and Family Statistics
http://www.childstats.gov

Thomas B. Fordham Institute, Report on High-
Achieving Students in the Era of No Child Left Behind
http://www.edexcellence.net/detail/news.cfm?news_id=732&id

Growing Stars Online Tutoring Center
http://www.growingstars.com

Kaiser Family Foundation and Children Now
http://www.talkingwithkids.org

Martin Luther King, Jr., Research and Education Institute,
King Papers Project
http://mlk-kpp01.stanford.edu

Native American History of Gambling
http://www.santaynezchumash.org/gaming_history.html

Phrenological Chart
http://www.cerebromente.org.br/n01/frenolog/frenmap.htm

Teachertube, Learning to Change Changing to Learn
http://teachertube.com

World Future Society http://www.wfs.org

Youth and Educators Succeeding
http://www.genyes.com/programs/genyes/sample_projects/CD

EXERCISES AND ROLES

Exercise 2.01: Tutoring Poll

Role: Voter

The purpose of this poll is to find out how students at your school feel about tutoring. A common goal for tutoring is to help students gain skills that are needed to do well in a course or pass a test.

Directions: For each item, select the answer(s) that indicate how you feel. In some cases, you may select more than one answer. If an answer you want to give is not listed, write it down on the line marked "other." Your responses are anonymous and may be combined with those of other students at your school in a report to students, faculty, and parents.

1. Most students I know who need tutoring

   (a) recognize their need and will ask for help
   (b) deny they have a problem with the subject
   (c) feel embarrassed and refuse to ask for help
   (d) blame their difficulties on poor teachers
   (e) other

2. More students would seek tutoring if

   (a) it was more convenient and available
   (b) teachers would offer them this option
   (c) they cared about academic success
   (d) parents were aware that they needed it
   (e) other

3. Seeking help from a tutor

   (a) shows that I recognize a need for help
   (b) would embarrass me in front of friends
   (c) reflects my desire to learn and succeed
   (d) helps meet requirements for graduation
   (e) other

4. When students fail a class or a test required to graduate, they should

   (a) automatically be assigned a tutor
   (b) take monthly practice tests

    (c)   go to summer school
    (d)   access a computer program for help
    (e)   other

5.   The most convenient time for me to attend tutoring sessions is

    (a)   right after school
    (b)   during the evening
    (c)   on weekends
    (d)   at lunchtime
    (e)   before school
    (f)   other

6.   If I told my friends that I was going to get tutoring

    (a)   they would make fun of me
    (b)   they would try to talk me out of it
    (c)   they would suggest I drop the course
    (d)   they would encourage my efforts
    (e)   other

7.   If I told my parents that I was going to get tutoring

    (a)   they would suggest I drop the class
    (b)   they would encourage my efforts
    (c)   they would allow me to make the decision
    (d)   they would question if I really need help
    (e)   other

8.   The reasons I would seek a tutor are

    (a)   poor listening habits in class
    (b)   excessive absences from class
    (c)   difficulty focusing because of disruptions
    (d)   my teacher doesn't explain material well
    (e)   trouble reading or remembering materials
    (f)   not passing a section of the state test
    (e)   other

9.   If I were to seek help, I would prefer

    (a)   a small group setting
    (b)   one on one with a tutor

(c) computer program or online support
(d) video lessons to watch and repeat
(e) other

10. If a subject is difficult to understand, I

(a) ask the teacher questions
(b) meet with my counselor
(c) ask classmates or friends for help
(d) seek no help even though I may fail
(e) other

11. When I request tutoring, my teacher(s)

(a) arrange for help without delay
(b) put me off and ignore my request
(c) suggest checking with a counselor
(d) tell me that I should try harder
(e) other

12. I prefer a tutor to be

(a) my teacher whose class I am struggling in
(b) another teacher in the same subject area
(c) someone from a tutoring company
(d) classmates who know the subject
(e) other

13. My school should let students know about tutoring

(a) at orientation and in the handbook
(b) on the school Web site
(c) on daily announcements
(d) other

14. The subject(s) in which I am most likely to seek tutoring are

(a) Mathematics
(b) English
(c) Science
(d) Social Studies
(e) other

15. Students should receive school reports showing

    (a) group progress of students who receive tutoring
    (b) gains that tutored students make in specific subjects
    (c) number of dropouts and whether they had tutoring
    (d) comments by students about their tutoring experience
    (e) other

16. I am willing to volunteer as a tutor

    (a) in the subjects that I understand well
    (b) to help students from families who don't speak English
    (c) to help students with learning disabilities
    (d) for classmates in my cooperative group
    (e) other

Select your grade level, gender, ethnicity, and age.
My grade level is 5 6 7 8 9 10 11 12
My gender is female male
My ethnicity is Asian Black Hispanic Native American White Other
My age is 10 11 12 13 14 15 16 17 18 19

Exercise 2.02: Reciprocal Learning With Adolescents

Role: Improviser
At every age we are either too old or too young to know some things directly based on our personal experience. This is why teachers and parents must learn vicariously what growing up is like in the current environment so the advice they offer matches the circumstances faced by adolescents. Reciprocal learning can help adults compensate for their lack of contemporary youth experience. This kind of interaction is perhaps the most challenging aspect of providing guidance for teenagers. Identify some of the attitudes and behaviors that appear to be essential for supporting this nontraditional form of learning.

Exercise 2.03: Changes in Families and Institutions

Role: Discussant

1. In what ways are your parents stuck in the past? present? future?
2. In what ways are adolescents stuck in the past? present? future?

3. In what ways are you personally stuck in the past? present? future?
4. In what ways are secondary schools stuck in the past? present? future?
5. What are some cultures that seem stuck in the past? present? future?

Exercise 2.04: Cultural Tradition and Change

Role: Cultural Reporter

People of the same race and cultural origin vary in how they raise their children. However, some normative experiences differentiate societies. Consider the American experience in responding to these assertions.

1. We benefit from these traditions and should try to preserve them.
2. We no longer benefit from these traditions and should drop them.
3. We should create these new traditions to pass them on as our legacy.
4. We should consider adopting these traditions from other cultures.

Exercise 2.05: International Students and Diversity

Role: Cultural Reporter

Many high schools and colleges enroll international students in exchange programs. These classmates from overseas could help to appreciate other cultures if teachers offer opportunities allowing them to make their experiences known. One way to begin is by inviting the visiting students to serve on a panel presented with questions on growing up and schooling in their country. They should choose the questions they prefer to answer.

1. What differences are there between schools in your nation and the United States?
2. How do methods of instruction in classes here differ from your country?
3. What stress do you experience more in our schools than you do at home?

4. What aspects of U.S. schooling are most appealing and disappointing?

5. What school practices in your country should the United States adopt?

6. What is the relationship between teachers and parents in your nation?

7. In what ways do U.S. expectations of students differ from your land?

8. What aspects of American education would you adopt for your nation?

9. How is discipline for misbehavior handled by teachers in your country?

10. What arrangements are made for helping students with disabilities?

11. In what ways is peer pressure greater or less than in the United States?

12. What things do students like to do when their studies can be put aside?

13. What is a Web site that can acquaint outsiders with life in your nation?

Exercise 2.06: The Communication Leap Hypothesis

Role: Evaluator

Speculate about possible implications of Burcet's Communication Leap Hypothesis in the next decade.

Exercise 2.07: Differences Within Cultural Groups

Role: Cultural Reporter

Americans often identify themselves according to family origin. As a result, some call themselves African Americans, Hispanic Americans, Asian Americans, Italian Americans or other identities. Certain individuals are well informed about their cultural background while others have little knowledge. Before you get started on this exercise, re-examine Figure 2.2, An Example of Generational Differences of Experiences Within Black Groups or Figure 2.3, An Example of Generational Differences Of

Experiences Within Mexican Groups. The task is to identify generation differences and shared experience that appear specific to your subcultural (ethnic) group. Interview an older relative or a friend who understands your cultural heritage and can provide relevant observations. Organize your findings into a diagram like 2.2 and 2.3. Share your diagram with teammates and elaborate the findings.

Exercise 2.08: Parents in Perspective

Role: Challenger

There is always speculation when the present and past are compared. However, surveys of adults consistently conclude that parents today seem to be less successful than their own mothers and fathers were in raising them. Look at our society from another perspective. Describe ways contemporary parents seem more successful than previous generations of parents. Provide examples to support each of your assertions.

Exercise 2.09: Listening to Adolescents

Role: Evaluator

Most adults recognize that the self-esteem of youth is reinforced when others listen to their ideas, feelings, interpretations, and concerns. However, some adults responsible for the education of teenagers seldom listen to them. A typical excuse is that busy schedules prevent this desired but difficult to arrange situation.

Develop a list of ways schools might provide greater opportunity for adolescents to be listened to by the faculty. Provide justification for each item on your list.

Exercise 2.10: Observation and Recall

Role: Evaluator

Identify some common experiences of adolescents today that were not part of your growing up years.

CHAPTER 3

GOALS, IDENTITY, AND MOTIVATION

Dumbledore is Headmaster of Hogwarts School. In *Harry Potter and the Chamber of Secrets* (Rowling, 1999, p. 333), Dumbledore urges the adolescent wizard to always remember, "It is our choices, Harry, that show what we truly are, far more than our abilities." Learning to make choices is one of the most important outcomes of getting an education. The goals that students choose guide and motivate self-direction. When teachers are familiar with goals of individuals in their classes, it is easier to understand students and give feedback on progress toward their aspirations. For these reasons, it is necessary to find out the goals and motives students rely on to govern their behavior and make plans for the future (Blumenfeld, Marx, & Harris, 2006).

This chapter examines goals of adolescents based on developmental tasks and formation of identity, demonstrated by a willingness to explore possibilities. Deciding the kind of person to become and participating in activities at school that offer satisfaction are examined. Factors are identified that foster self-directed learning, help process failure and success, promote decision-making and enable amendment of goals. Determining how to interpret progress by using collaborative assessment, novel grading procedures, student portfolio evaluation, and guidelines for processing criticism are reported. Career orientation is described to help teenagers clarify their goals for job preparation.

Adolescents in the Internet Age, pp. 87–133
Copyright © 2009 by Information Age Publishing

ADOLESCENT IDENTITY AND GOALS

The amount of identity confusion adolescents experience depends in part on whether teachers recognize goals associated with this stage of development. There are tasks teenagers commonly strive to achieve as they pursue identity. In addition, some youth define themselves by their choice of personality goals. Schools have two cultures that can offer the satisfaction of getting ready for employment and the pleasure of participation in extracurricular activities.

Contemporary Developmental Tasks

There are certain goals that all adolescents should pursue to become healthy adults. These developmental tasks, originally identified by Robert Havighurst (1972) at the University of Chicago, were described in chapter 1. Many aspects of life have changed since Havighurst proposed his list. Updating the developmental tasks was the purpose of a Harvard University project which examined 300 studies about raising teenagers (Simpson, 2001). The 10 tasks that contemporary adolescents should consider as they make their transition to adulthood are identified in Table 3.1. See the Web site on Raising Teens: A Synthesis of Research and Foundation for Action at http://www.hsph.harvard.edu/chc/parenting.

Goal Exploration and Commitment

During adolescence a new perspective of self and others emerges because of physical and mental changes. In addition to looking more like adults, teenagers become capable of conceiving ideal environments or relationships and contrast them with their situation. For some students the result is discontent while others are motivated to promote constructive change. *Idealism* enables youth to picture how the world and its conflicting elements could be reconciled.

The inclination at this stage of development is to combine impressions that an individual has acquired about self in various roles as a daughter or son, student, friend, athlete, and member of peer groups. This task is fulfilled by the newfound integrative abilities that begin to surface in adolescence. When someone is able to bring these images together, recognize their continuity, and derive assurance, s/he can look to the future with confidence. Such persons have a sense of identity because they know who they are, where they come from, and where they are going. The

Table 3.1. The 10 Tasks of Adolescence

1.	Adjust to sexually maturing bodies and feelings	Teens are faced with adjusting to bodies that as much as double in size and that acquire sexual characteristics, as well as learning to manage the accompanying biological changes and sexual feelings and to engage in healthy sexual behaviors. This task also includes establishing a sexual identity and developing the skills for romantic relationships.
2.	Develop and apply abstract thinking skills	Teens typically undergo profound changes in their way of thinking during adolescence, allowing them more effectively to understand and coordinate abstract ideas, to think about possibilities, to try out hypotheses, to think ahead, to think about thinking, and to construct philosophies.
3.	Develop and apply a more complex level of perspective taking	Teens typically acquire a powerful new ability to understand human relationships, in which, having learned to "put themselves in another person's shoes," they learn to take into account both their perspective and another person's at the same time, and to use this new ability in resolving problems and conflicts in relationships.
4.	Develop and apply new coping skills in areas such as decision making, problem solving, and conflict resolution.	Related to all these dramatic shifts, teens are involved in acquiring new abilities to think about and plan for the future, to engage in more sophisticated strategies for decision making, problem solving, and conflict resolution, and to moderate their risk taking to serve goals rather than jeopardize them.
5.	Identify meaningful moral standards, values, and belief systems.	Building on these changes and resulting skills, teens typically develop a more complex understanding of moral behavior and underlying principles of justice and care, questioning beliefs from childhood and adopting more personally meaningful values, religious views, and belief systems to guide their decisions and behavior.
6.	Understand and express more complex emotional experiences.	Also related to these changes are shifts for teens toward an ability to identify and communicate more complex emotions, to understand the emotions of others in more sophisticated ways, and to think about emotions in abstract ways.
7.	Form friendships that are mutually close and supportive.	Although youngsters typically have friends throughout childhood, teens generally develop peer relationships that play much more powerful roles in providing support and connection in their lives. They tend to shift from friendships based largely on the sharing of interests and activities to those based on the sharing of ideas and feelings, with the development of mutual trust and understanding.

Table continues on next page.

Table 3.1.   Continued

8. Establish key aspects of identity.	Identify formation is in a sense a lifelong process, but crucial aspects of identity are typically forged at adolescence, including developing an identity that reflects a sense of individuality as well as connection to valued people and groups. Another part of this task is developing a positive identity around gender, physical attributes, sexuality, and ethnicity and, if appropriate, having been adopted, as well as sensitivity to the diversity of groups that make up American society.
9. Meet the demands of increasingly mature roles and responsibilities.	Teens gradually take on the roles that will be expected of them in adulthood, learning to acquire the skills and manage the multiple demands that will allow them to move into the labor market, as well as to meet expectations regarding commitment to family, community, and citizenship.
10. Renegotiate relationships with adults in parenting roles.	Although the task of adolescence has sometimes been described as "separating from parents and other caregivers," it is more widely seen now as adults and teens working together to negotiate a change in the relationships that accommodates a balance of autonomy and ongoing connection, with the emphasis on each depending in part on the family's ethnic background.

Source: From A. Rae Simpson (2001). The ten tasks of adolescence, in *Raising Teens: A Synthesis of Research and a Foundation for Action.* Boston: Center for Health Communication, Harvard School of Public Health. Reprinted with permission.

common quest for identity is better understood by reviewing observations provided by the best known theorist in this context.

Erik Erikson (1902–1994) was an artist when he was hired by Anna Freud, daughter of Sigmund Freud, to make paintings of children she was treating in her clinical practice. Later, Erikson was encouraged to study at the Vienna Psychoanalytic Institute. He never earned a college degree but became a faculty member at Harvard after migrating to the United States. His insights on developmental stages throughout life have been a prominent influence on psychology and education. A biography and discussion of Erikson's theory is available at http:/webspace.ship.edu/cgboer/perscontents.html

Erikson (1968, 1980) proposed that life consists of eight critical periods, each presenting a separate set of conflicts arising from unique polarities presented at that particular stage. The main task of adolescence is to establish identity instead of getting lost in role confusion. Erikson never conducted research to test his assumptions but his interpreters have devised structured interviews to classify teenagers according to identity status (Marcia, 1989, 1999; Marcia & Carpendale, 2004). Table 3.2

portrays these four categories related to the individual's combination of exploration and commitment: (1) Normal identity confusion, extreme identity confusion, or negative identity; (2) foreclosure identity, (3) moratorium identity, and (4) achievement identity.

(1) *Normal identity confusion* is the status of adolescents reluctant to engage in exploration and commitment. These persons seldom express curiosity or excitement about possible careers or religious and political beliefs to guide their behavior. They do not search for models or mentors they could emulate. Their meager awareness of options is sustained by an unwillingness to try out new roles or support benevolent causes. This malaise sometimes reflects concerns about being overwhelmed by too many choices (B. Schwartz, 2004). Normal identity confusion can also be a residual outcome of poor adjustment in stages preceding adolescence (Marcia, 1999). Students categorized by normal identity confusion, more than peers in other categories, reveal signs of apathy, anxiety, minimal self-esteem, and diminished sense of self-control (Baumeister, Campbell, Krueger, & Vohs, 2005). Normal identity confusion is usually temporary as most adolescents find their niche and sense of direction.

A small percentage of adolescents remain fixed in their opposition to exploration of a constructive role. Erikson (1980) suggested this decision often reflects *extreme identity confusion,* leading to *negative identity.* Individuals with a negative identity are alienated and they resist conforming to social customs or norms of behavior. In turn, peers reject them and, as outcasts, they formulate their own unhealthy rules. Social interventions are needed for students with negative identity. This group has been responsible for a disproportionate amount of school violence reflected by tragedies such as Columbine High school and Virginia Tech University (Tomsho & Golden, 2007).

(2) *Foreclosure identity* status describes individuals who make commitments without exploration as the basis for determining their goals. Adolescence is the time of maximum uncertainty in life and a broader range of choices complicate decision-making. One way to avoid uncertainty and anxiety is to choose without exploration. This response is characterized by teenagers who rely completely on advice of trusted persons when making decisions and commitments about career, lifestyle, and beliefs. This dependent behavior may provide comfort in the short term but experimentation yields more healthy identity formation (Locke & Latham, 2002).

Some teenage couples commit to going steady without exploring additional relationships by dating others. At the outset this premature decision to commit may be satisfying since it offers predictable companionship and eliminates worry about adjusting to new or unfamiliar situations. However, one party may later regret their action and decide they

Table 3.2.   Formation of Adolescent Identity Status Based on Individual Level of Exploration And Commitment

NORMAL IDENTITY CONFUSION	The student is reluctant to explore new roles or commit to decisions. John expresses little interest in possible occupational roles, religious beliefs to guide conduct, views of political figures about national problems, behavior patterns of sports heroes to resemble, or groups to join that practice to become competent.
Low exploration Low commitment	Outcome: Identity confusion is usually a temporary condition because most adolescents move on to determine their niche and acquire a sense of direction.
EXTREME IDENTITY CONFUSION {NEGATIVE IDENTITY}	The student is anti social and feels alienated from classmates and the school. Peter does not share interests or concerns with classmates so he is left out of group conversation and receives no approval or encouragement from them. His experience includes perceived and perhaps actual rejection. He lacks an sense of engagement at school so Peter does not feel the rules there such as dress code and smoking policy are applicable to him.
Low exploration Low commitment	Outcome: A small percentage of adolescents remain fixed in their opposition to exploring constructive roles. Negative identity produces alienation and resistance to conforming to accepted norms. As a result, peers reject them and, as outcasts, they formulate their own unhealthy rules.
FORECLOSURE IDENTITY Low exploration High commitment	The student makes commitments without exploration as a basis for decisions. Andrea views the broad range of curriculum choices at school to be overwhelming. The uncertainty leaves her feeling anxious about what to do. Her mother has some path in mind that she believes is just right so Andrea readily adopts it without doing any exploration of her own.
	Outcome: This dependent response may provide comfort during the short term but experimentation is more likely to yield healthy identity formation. Students in foreclosure status tend to score higher on conformity and obedience to authority.
MORATORIUM IDENTITY High exploration Low commitment	The student tries varied face-to-face and online roles and makes tentative choices. Michele has dated three boys in her junior year. Her intention is to explore how each behaves but not commit to being with one of them. She knows that being indecisive is reasonable and further exploration will help discover the attributes to prize most in a partner.
	Outcome: Continued exploration, accompanied by tentative decisions and the amendment of inappropriate choices is a sensible path to healthy adjustment.

Table continues on next page.

| ACHIEVEMENT IDENTITY

High exploration
High commitment | The student has moratorium experience and makes commitments based on exploration and goals. Jennifer was uncertain whether to enter business or engineering. She chose to take courses in both sectors before making a decision. She performed well in each but found the business track more appealing. So, her commitment to becoming a financial analyst is based on exploration followed by goal setting.

Outcome: These teenagers show greater competence in their ability to collaborate, demonstrate greater problem solving skills, and exhibit more favorable mental health indicators. |
|---|---|

want to explore relationships with others at a time when such behavior is no longer appropriate. Students in the foreclosure status tend to score higher than peers on conformity and obedience to authority (Elliot & Dweck, 2005).

(3) *Moratorium identity* allows adolescents to try out varied roles in face-to-face situations, experiment with multiple identities or "alias" on the Internet, and play different characters in video games (Rosen, 2007). They get to make tentative choices and amend them, explore ideologies and adapt beliefs to fit their circumstance. In effect, they experiment without locking themselves into roles that they later conclude are unsuitable. Teachers motivate role exploration when assigning multiple tasks for teamwork. Instead of feeling responsible to continue the pursuit of every goal they consider, students can defer commitments, realizing that being indecisive is reasonable and more exploration is needed before final decisions are appropriate. Erikson (1980) indicated that moratorium identity is limited to societies where individual choice is encouraged.

(4) *Achievement identity* defines the status of adolescents who have gone through the moratorium stage, enabling them to make decisions that motivate, guide, and govern behavior. They are self-directed because their commitments are based on personally driven exploration followed by goal setting. These teenagers show greater competence in ability to collaborate, demonstrate greater problem solving skills, and exhibit more favorable signs of mental health (Swanson, Spencer, & Peterson, 1998).

Friends are often a powerful influence during identity formation. One function of friends is to provide reassurance when someone doubts their worth or value of their opinions. Although a small proportion of youth underestimate themselves to such a degree that they adopt a negative identity, adolescence is the peak time in life when individuals are most inclined to question their views of the world. For this reason, they typically rely on friends to react to merits of their ideas. When asked to identify what they prize most in friends, 15- to 17-year-olds report they must be trustworthy, willing to keep revelations private (Kozminsky &

Kozminsky, 2003). The emphasis on being able to talk with friends as confidants continues into the late teens and then declines by the early twenties. This suggests that, by that time, most people have worked out their identity exploration and less often feel the need to discuss personal identity. Those who seek confidants during their 20s may be having difficulty resolving the next developmental task of early adulthood, called intimacy versus isolation (Frankenberger, 2000).

Erikson (1980) observed that the process of identity formation was likely to be extended in technological societies so that a prolonged period of adolescence would become a norm. Since then there has been an increase in range of possible occupations, greater need to attend school for a longer time, and higher age for getting married. Together these factors offer more opportunities for exploration as well as increased uncertainty and anxiety (Cote, 2000; Love, 2005). The status of identity achievement was once thought to be attained by age 18 but studies suggest this status describes only one-third of students graduating from high school (Marcia & Carpendale, 2004). For college students whose curriculum urges them to remain in an explorative mode about careers, political views, religious beliefs, and lifestyle choices, identity achievement status may be delayed until the mid-20s when they earn a degree and begin full-time work. These unprecedented conditions for identify formation explain in part why the duration of adolescence has been redefined to include persons from age 10 to 20 or 25.

Personality Goals and Achievement

Parents and teachers know that goal setting is an important skill that requires practice and wonder how opportunities in this sphere can be provided without jeopardizing student success. One way to begin is by encouraging children to select personality goals they can currently pursue before their consideration of occupation goals (Feist & Feist, 2006; Rader, 2005). This sequence of personality goals prior to career goals invites children to focus first on the kind of individual they want to become, the way they want to act, and the influence they hope to have on others. These aspects of maturing can be observed well before there is evidence about the type of job a student may become qualified to perform. When personality goals and the values they reflect are fostered by adults that provide feedback about progress, everyone can recognize the importance of this achievement domain.

Major problems of getting along with others such as abuse, divorce, crime, racism, and being fired from a job are caused more often by poor emotional health and immaturity than by lack of academic competence.

Reading, writing, and mathematics are essential skills; they are also the easiest lessons for everyone to learn. In addition, the education adolescents need has to equip them to cope with unpredictable adversity and demonstrate resilience based on hardiness. Bonanno (2004) defines *personality hardiness* as (1) interrelated attitudes of commitment rather than alienation, (2) a sense of control rather than feelings of powerlessness, and (3) a sense of challenge rather than threat. Maddi (2002) concludes that hardy attitudes define the courage and motivation needed to face stressors accurately rather than deny or exaggerate them. Personality hardiness is the context in which teachers and parents have their greatest opportunity to act as models for adolescents (Kamphaus & Frick, 2006).

Some goals adolescents might consider are portrayed in Table 3.3. Progress toward attaining these adolescent goals can be observed by teachers and parents who should confirm evidence of growth and identify the need for further development.

The collective personality goals show that relatives should not excuse themselves from a teaching role with claims that curriculum has changed so much that they are unable to help or lack the formal education needed to assist with academic work. The interpersonal skills on the list of personality goals will contribute to success no matter what occupation a student may follow (Larson, Wilson, Brown, Furstenberg, & Verna, 2002).

Personality goals individually chosen are a more appropriate long-term focus for self-evaluation than academic subjects. This focus allows feedback from adults who care about students. Personality is the key to identity, the way that we perceive ourselves and are seen by others. Personality and identity are linked because both are lifelong concerns whereas having a job is not. Uniting family and school support for personality development conveys the message that emotional and social growth require careful attention along with intellectual achievement (Feist & Feist, 2006).

When adults identify the qualities they want to be remembered for by their family and friends, they usually mention non-intellectual qualities that endear people to one another. These attributes can become more common when they are first chosen as goals. The example relatives set is important. Adults can acknowledge their personal shortcomings to younger relatives, describe plans to overcome them, and request feedback to evaluate progress and success. Thus, in addition to helping teens set short-term goals and long-term goals, wise adults review their own goals and make them known to loved ones. Everyone should continually strive to improve their personality for as long as they live. Persons who do not learn to judge themselves typically spend their lives only judging others. The Lions Quest program is offered in 30 countries to 250,000 youth with

Table 3.3.   Personality Goals and Achievement for Consideration by Adolescents

Goals for Individual Consideration	Achievement Perceived by Parents, Teachers	Achievement Perceived by Self
• Getting along with classmates		
• Treat people around me fairly		
• Show a willingness to help others		
• Look at the bright side of things		
• Make time for what is important		
• Develop a healthy sense of humor		
• Make feelings known to relatives		
• Learn to become a better listener		
• Settle arguments in a peaceful way		
• Ask questions if I don't understand		
• Avoid unkind statements about others		
• Keep trying as things get difficult		
• Ask for help when it is needed		
• Be patient in dealing with others		
• Be a person who others can rely on		
• Keep mind and body healthy		
• Reflect on behavior to improve self		
• Seek and accept criticism of others		
• Have self-control and self-discipline		
• Be a person that is self-directed		

the purpose of helping them identify their assets, set goals, and gain life skills. The Lions Quest Web site is at http://www.lions-quest.org/.

Think about the relevance of some of the goals in Table 3.3 above for the classroom and out of school.

- Getting along with classmates. A 14-year-old granddaughter of an 82-year-old African American told her, "Grandma Flora, I want to be just like you when I grow up." Flora replied, "Why? I have so little in the way of material things and did not make much of myself." Her granddaughter said, "Grandma, you have more friends than anyone I know." What a nice compliment.
- Treat people around me fairly—Society is struggling to get this right; it is an important lesson to learn and a difficult one to teach.

- Show a willingness to help others—this is what growing up and maturity are all about, moving away from being self-centered in favor of showing concern for the welfare of others.
- Look at the bright side of things—not perceiving every problem as a crisis that is unfair but looking at possibilities in other people, situations, and ourselves. Few things are worse for adolescents than to be around cynical adults who cause them to lose hope for the future.
- Make time for what is important—Setting priorities in life is a vital lesson that usually comes with growing older, discovering what really matters most. This lesson could be learned much earlier in life. Many parents do not devote enough time to being with their family and children suffer because of it. A Web site that provides a Time Management Guide to help students think about use of time is at http://www.time-management-guide.com/personal-goal-setting.html click goal setting guidelines and tips.
- Develop a healthy sense of humor. As people mature, they often discover that laughing at themselves is a way to support mental health.
- Settle arguments in a peaceful way—many youth are not learning this lesson and parents should not expect teachers at school to be the only source of instruction.
- Avoid making unkind statements about others—teenagers often report that they learn values from relatives indirectly by the way they respond to characters on television, and how they react to stories about neighbors or people in the news.
- Be patient in dealing with others—impatience is becoming more common and generally undermines relationships.
- Be a person others can rely on—this is one of the greatest accomplishments a person can achieve.

The final goal on the list is to be self-directed, capable of making decisions independently and performing tasks without outside control. Try to become aware of the listed personality goals that have high priority for students at their present age, and determine if they want to place additional goals on their list. Then, parents and teachers should encourage students to pursue their personality goals. Recognizing student gains in personality development are largely ignored by adults and providing guidance for those whose behavior signals significant problems deserves greater consideration in education (Morse, Anderson, & Christenson, 2004).

Instrumental and Expressive Cultures

Some goals adolescents adopt are selected for them by their schools. Education presents students with two cultures, one instrumental and the other expressive. The *instrumental culture* consists of academic requirements that everyone must develop competence in so they are able to graduate. Instrumental goals involve the content subjects of mathematics, science, and English. These aspects of curriculum are mandatory because they contribute to the skills, knowledge, and values typically stated as purposes for schooling. Students engage in the instrumental culture so that they can attain satisfactions to occur some time in the future—to get a diploma, be admitted to college, and find a job (Jennings & Likis, 2005).

The *expressive culture* consists of activities that students choose to participate in for the pleasure of involvement (Mahoney, Larson, & Eccles, 2005). Art, drama, music, and athletics define the expressive curriculum. Although participation in the expressive culture can include knowledge and skills, this outcome is generally not regarded as important as in the instrumental culture where everyone must pass state examinations (Anderson, Lucas, & Ginns, 2003; Furrer & Skinner, 2003). It is possible for a student to enjoy singing in the choir, working with clay in an art class, helping present a theatrical performance, or playing volleyball without gaining much knowledge. The criterion for student success in the expressive culture depends less on how well the individual performs in favor of how much the student enjoys being involved (National Research Council, 2004).

The instrumental culture sometimes has an expressive impact, such as when a student enjoys doing science experiments, reading novels or doing algebra problems for their own sake. Similarly, there can be an instrumental undertone to expressive activities so some students gain considerable skill and knowledge in art, music and drama. However, students usually distinguish between the expressive and instrumental cultures (Gewertz, 2006). Because most students are able to find satisfaction in the expressive culture, competition is deliberately minimized there, making it the most viable context in which to teach values such as appreciation for learning, commitment to personal development, and valuing participation (Assor, Kaplan, & Roth, 2002). Parents can more easily become involved in the expressive culture.

The motivation to remain in most situations usually depends on having some degree of satisfaction. People will endure disappointments when satisfaction is also part of their overall experience. This means that some experiences in school must be satisfying in order to motivate students to continue attending rather than drop out. Various combinations of satisfaction with instrumental and expressive cultures can sustain involvement or stimulate withdrawal. Table 3.4 shows that a high level of satisfaction in both cultures defines academic achievers who also feel good about extracurricular activities. A high instrumental and low expressive combination portrays someone who may gain satisfaction from the results of academic tests but does not care about extracurricular activities. A low instrumental and high expressive combination identifies those who have mediocre test scores but feel satisfaction from the extracurricular activities. Such a person has difficulty in mathematics or English but shines on the basketball court or football field. In this circumstance, the single incentive to stay in school is the pleasure and favorable self-impression gained from being involved with athletics, band or drama (Indiana University, 2004; Mahoney, Cairns, & Farmer, 2003).

Some schools have a No pass, No play policy that informs students they must perform to a standard in the instrumental culture or be barred from involvement with the expressive culture. This policy most often implicates athletes who, when cut from their team, may choose to quit attending school (Endresen & Olweus, 2005). In a similar way, students motivated to stay in school because of satisfactions from being in the band, drama or art are disappointed when budget cuts reduce the courses in expressive curriculum.

Some students are unable to find satisfaction in the expressive or instrumental culture. They dislike the required courses and refuse to take advantage of their expressive opportunities. Because they see school as a place of disappointment, they want to quit as early as permissible. Feelings of alienation motivate them to withdraw and hope they can find satisfaction in another environment. Schools have to discover ways to

Table 3.4. Level of Student Satisfaction With the Instrumental and Expressive Cultures at School

Culture and Satisfaction	Example of Student Reported Experience
High Expressive High Instrumental	Renaldo enjoys the math courses he has taken and wants to become an engineer. He also likes playing trumpet in the school marching band.
Low Expressive High Instrumental	Melinda likes the curriculum and has a part time job. Her busy schedule means that there is no time left to participate in extracurricular activities.
High Expressive Low Instrumental	Jason is 6 feet, 8 inches tall, lives for basketball, and is the top scorer for the conference. He struggles with required subjects but is grateful to get tutoring.
Low Expressive Low Instrumental	Avery does not like school and feels that his classmates look down on him. His friends left before graduating and he thinks this would be the best choice for him too.

appeal to such students so that they can find satisfaction within the institution (Rumberger & Palardy, 2005).

Creative use of the expressive culture can make school a place of satisfaction for more students and improve outcomes in the instrumental culture. This was demonstrated at a junior high school in Harlem, New York. Most participants were Black or Puerto Rican. The higher half of the 1,400 students was chosen for the Higher Horizons Project (Morrisey & Werner-Wilson, 2005). These students had average intelligence but typically scored 2 years below grade level in reading and mathematics. The principal told them, "We realize most of you do not like mathematics or reading, but these skills are important for your future. However, instead of increasing the time that you spend on these subjects by cutting back on other ones such as art, music, and physical education, we plan to take the opposite approach." So, motivating influences from the expressive culture were introduced to increase satisfaction and motivation to learn (Joussemet, Koestner, Lekes, & Houlfort, 2004). Students were taken to sports events, concerts, and movies. They went to parks, museums, and sightseeing trips while also continuing exposure to instrumental subjects.

Follow-up studies found that project members who went to senior high school graduated in substantially greater numbers than those from the same junior high in pre-project years. Then too, 168 graduates went on to higher education, compared with 47 in three classes preceding the experiment. It seems that being involved with expressive activities offered sufficient satisfaction to remain in school instead of leaving. The motivation effects included better performance in the instrumental culture (Morrisey & Werner-Wilson, 2005). This is why middle and high schools devote so much attention to encouraging student involvement with extracurricular activities and after school programming. For certain students, a lack of engagement in the expressive culture renders them less able to cope with daily pressures and makes them more vulnerable to stress and drug taking (Christie, Jolivette, & Nelson, 2005).

The school board of Pittsburgh, Pennsylvania determined that students who drop out are most likely to do so between Grade 8 and Grade 9. To prevent this tragedy, incoming ninth graders were provided a much different orientation from the usual half day of getting acquainted with their curriculum options, rules of the school, and tour of campus facilities. The main goal for a week long orientation was to target the hearts as well as minds of the incoming students, to establish a "Ninth Grade Nation" that moves through school together while feeling support and confidence. The expectation was that being a member of the Ninth Grade Nation would help adolescents feel cared about, connected to classmates and teachers, and convinced that courses they take will lead them to a place in the workforce (Gewertz, 2007). Some of the ways the expressive and instrumental activities were merged to change the school culture include:

- All students engage in hip hop acrobatics with their willing but more awkward teachers.
- Team scavenger hunts are arranged with clues on where to find things located in school.
- Taking an aerial rope course with teachers at a rural site where they travel suspended above gorges.
- Discussions about why everyone may need tutoring and the reasons each student is being assigned a mentor.
- Conversations on why the Ninth Grade Nation is assigned civic projects to improve their community.
- Discussing "The Last Chance Texaco," a novel they all read about teenagers coping with stress.
- Sessions with mental health experts about handling stress and building the competencies of resilience.
- Meetings with upper-class students to hear them describe expressive activities that they like at school.

Follow up with the students showed that some who were apprehensive about going on to high school had changed their mind, believed that getting a diploma was important for them, and liked how the teachers showed them that they care. One student reflected a common conclusion: "I thought I would be a number in this school but then I came here, and found that teachers are ready to try to learn about you. So I feel good about this school." The district has adopted a 5-year plan to increase experiences of the Ninth Grade Nation to include all ten of its high schools (Gewertz, 2007).

Unlike methods for dropout prevention or remedial education that focus on overcoming academic deficits, extracurricular activities appear to support adjustment to school demands by promoting individual interests and satisfaction. Benefits are enhanced when the after-school activities are based on activities students identify as enjoyable instead of activities that adults prefer to supervise like competitive sports (Smith, Roderick, & Degener, 2005).

MOTIVATION OF SELF-DIRECTED LEARNING

Setting goals, changing plans, and leaving some aspirations behind are part of growing up. Nevertheless, many students are denied these opportunities when adults insist on deciding plans for them. Grownups rationalize the takeover of adolescent decisions by contending that poor choices can have disappointing consequences. So, "I am doing this for your good." A more effective way to reduce chances for harm is by preparing students to make some decisions on their own. Teenagers encouraged to set goals feel more in control of their lives, establish a sense of personal direction, exhibit greater motivation to succeed, and are less vulnerable to being misled by others (Elliot & Dweck, 2005). For these reasons, teachers need to be aware of factors that support decision making such as self-reliance, trust, and opportunities for planning. Sometimes students adopt unreasonable goals so amending them is vital to ensure adjustment. The way individual students interpret failure and success should be understood by educators because these self-impressions influence motivation, renewed effort, and expectation.

Achievement Motivation Elements

Most parents want their children motivated to perform well in school because education is essential for the future. *Achievement motivation* is defined by the extent to which students strive for success. Persons with a high need for achievement share characteristics such as self-confidence, high estimate of what they can accomplish, and the uncanny ability to accurately judge personal limitations. These attributes were identified by the seminal studies of David McClelland (1917–1999), psychologist at Harvard. McClelland (1976) developed a game that simulated a manufacturing enterprise to test young adults. Using toy parts, participants were obliged to follow simple directions in assembling objects like rockets and airplanes. Before each five-minute assembly period began, individuals decided how many toy parts to purchase. Income was based on the number of units completed minus cost of materials. Because the goal was to maximize profit, it was important to estimate accurately how many units one could complete in the prescribed time limits.

Persons with a low need for achievement raised their estimates of how many units they could assemble and showed greater effort if offered $50 to surpass original production goals. Their behaviors were based on *extrinsic motivation*, a willingness to work harder in response to an incentive given by others. However, monetary rewards did not influence individuals with high achievement motivation as they estimated the work they could produce. They reflected *intrinsic motivation,* the ability to persist with tasks based upon personal desire rather than in response to external rewards. They reviewed past experiences as a basis for improving the accuracy of their estimates (McClelland, 1976; Reeve, 2006).

A related study by McClelland (1987) was conducted to find out whether an early assessment of achievement motivation could accurately predict future success. Situational tests were taken by 10,000 college students in 18 countries. One assessment involved competing in a toy slot-car race. For example, a driver in the left lane is eager to get ahead, but since his speed is too great, the car spins at a curve and crashes. This driver lost the race because the risks he chose were too great. Another competitor also wants to win but behaves differently. This person drives fast enough to be taking some risk, yet not so rapidly as to make an accident likely. Students with high achievement motivation consistently behaved as moderate risk takers and shunned games of chance or situations where they had no control over the outcome. McClelland's contributions to motivation theory is available at http://www.accel-team.com/human_relations/hrels_06_mcclelland.html.

Achievement motivation research offers insights about students. To support achievement motivation, the relation between taking risks and making choices should be understood. When students know that they can freely state their ideas in class, ask naive questions, expose opinions, and try new ways of thinking because the cost associated with these behaviors is minimal, they are more inclined to do so (Covington & Mueller, 2001). On the other hand, if the price of choosing to explore new ideas or unfamiliar subjects is high, when trying something different is seen as too risky in terms of influencing grade point average, students tend to continue studying only subjects in which they already are skilled. By avoiding unfamiliar curriculum, students deny themselves opportunities for development (Alderman, 2004; McInerney & Van Etten, 2005).

Origins of Achievement Motivation

Fifteen years after McClelland (1992) tested college students, he conducted a follow-up study. Findings revealed that most of the successful persons in business and industry, defined as having attained a leadership position in management, were the same men and women who years earlier scored high on achievement motivation measures. This result confirmed that motivation to achieve is a characteristic that remains stable from late adolescence until middle age. But these findings did not reveal origins of this asset. If educators knew how achievement motivation is formed and could identify forces that facilitate its development, they would be more supportive.

Can secondary teachers influence achievement motivation, or is this characteristic formed in elementary school? The answer to this question is evident from the results of McClelland's comprehensive studies to trace the origins of achievement motivation. He recruited young children to participate in the Ring Toss game. The object of this game is to toss rings onto a small post. The game pieces are made of soft vinyl. Points are scored based on distance a player stands away from the target. Each child was permitted to decide how close or far away from the post to stand before tossing the rings. Those with low achievement motivation typically stood so far away that failure was likely or moved so close to the post that success had little meaning. On the other hand, children with a strong need for achievement usually selected a middle distance where a certain amount of risk was involved so success had meaning, but where they were not so distant as to make likely the possibility of failure. The study concluded that being a moderate risk taker in approaching tasks is characteristic among high achievers from every age group (McClelland, 1992).

To find out whether factors in the parent-child relationship were implicated, McClelland (1992) introduced another game. This time participants were preschoolers blindfolded and obliged to build a high pile of blocks. As an additional obstacle, the children were restricted to using only one hand. They could get advice from their parent but the parent was not allowed to touch the blocks. If a child's pile fell down, the game was lost. When asked to guess how high a pile their child would build, parents of children scoring low on this task and other achievement motivation indicators gave low estimates. These parents often revealed dominance and shifted from advising to taking over and directing their child's activity. In contrast, the parents of high achievement motivation children behaved differently. They gave high estimates of what their children would accomplish, offered encouragement during the task, and left decision making to the child. These parents favored early self-reliance.

Other studies of high achievers have concluded that their parents favored early training in decision making and self-reliance (Wigfield & Eccles, 2002). A Gallup (2006) survey focused on 240 highly successful Americans working in business, politics, sports, entertainment, the arts, and sciences. The adults, in their thirties and forties, were asked about childhood. Nearly 300 of their parents were interviewed too. It was found that parents of the successful insisted that daughters and sons learn early to plan for themselves, served as advisors without dominating decisions, enjoyed frequent and extended conversations with them, and did not take credit for the accomplishments of their children. Many businesses engage employees in achievement motivation training to improve productivity. An example is provided by the Consortium for Research on Emotional Intelligence in Organizations—http://www.eiconsortium.org/.

Attribution of Success and Failure

The beliefs students have about causation of their success and failure are referred to as attributions. Bernard Weiner (1986, 1992, 2005, 2006) at University of California in Los Angeles proposed an *attribution theory* that explains the four most commonly perceived causes of academic success and failure. Table 3.5 shows that these causes, including task

Table 3.5. Student Attributions Regarding Causes of Their Academic Success and Failure

CAUSES OF SUCCESS OR FAILURE	STABILITY OF CAUSE *Stable or Variable*	LOCUS OF CONTROL *Internal or External*	ON-TRACK ATTRIBUTIONS	OFF-TRACK ATTRIBUTIONS
Task Difficulty	Stable cause	External locus of control	Teacher wrote easy test or was easy grader.	I did well on the test so I must be really smart.
Effort	Variable cause	Internal locus of control	Effort in studying affects test scores positively. Some need to study more than others but we all can succeed.	My friends don't have to study much to do well. If I have to study then I don't have ability in this area.
Luck	Variable cause	External locus of control	Mrs. Sampson is known for being the hardest grader in all algebra sections.	I was the only boy in class and felt that the teacher favored girls.
Ability*	Stable cause	Internal locus of control	I'm able enough so that time and effort leads to success in almost all cases.	I did poorly on test so it's all about ability that I don't have.

Note: Ability is a stable cause of achievement. However, student self-perception of ability can be greatly influenced by teacher expectations and behavior. When teachers with low expectations give high grades to most of the students, low performers believe their ability is greater than is true. Because the shortcomings of these students are never made known to them, they may not recognize their need to devote more effort to schoolwork. In contrast, high performing students in the same classes may doubt their distinction because everyone else gets high marks as well. Consequently, they may set less ambitious goals for themselves than are appropriate. Teachers also influence perception of ability by how they respond to student failure. For example, some students initially perform poorly with mathematics tasks. If a teacher prematurely decides that a student is incapable, no encouragement will be provided to stimulate greater effort. On the other hand, when a teacher is patient in presenting the steps of a mathematics process, chances to benefit from repetition may bring comprehension and motivate the continued practice needed for mastery.

difficulty, effort, luck, and ability, are classified in two dimensions—stability of cause and locus of control. The attributions of ability and task difficulty are stable whereas luck and effort are subject to change. This means that when someone is asked to repeat a task, their self-perception of ability and difficulty of the task are likely to stay the same. In contrast, perceptions of luck and effort can change from one time to another depending upon the situation. The other dimension, called locus of control, refers to whether or not achievements are seen as being subject to internal control (ability and effort) or seen as caused by external forces (task difficulty and luck).

Consider some ways students assign causes to their performance and how such explanations influence behavior and achievement. Marcy and John are in freshman English. Both received high scores on the first examination. Marcy attributes her success to having above average ability while John believes his performance was a product of good luck. Marcy's success is likely to have the affect of increasing self-confidence because she attributed getting a high score to her skill and preparation. In John's case however, the high score will be less meaningful because he takes no credit for his achievement.

Similarly, in failure situations, attributions influence expectations for future performance. Michelle, in the same English class as Marcy and John, failed the first test. She attributes her low score to not giving enough effort to preparing for the test. Michelle believes that if she devotes more time to studying, results of the next test will be better. Nancy also got a failing grade. Because she attributes the failure to lack of ability, Nancy has less hope for a better score next time even if she makes an effort to study.

Research has consistently found that most success-oriented students believe they can manage any challenges presented by the curriculum. Consequently, their ability is rarely thought to be the cause of poor learning. These persons view success and failure as mainly related to the quality of personal efforts. In effect, they attribute their success to sufficient ability augmented by concerted effort and, when they fail, interpret it in terms of inadequate preparation (Lattimore, 2005; Weiner, 2000, 2005). These explanations are helpful to enhance confidence since success confirms a capacity to perform well while failure is a sign indicating the need to try harder. Success-oriented persons do not feel threatened by exposure to failure because such experiences are not viewed as a reflection of their ability. Instead, they realize that non-defensive analysis of their failures can provide clues to avoid repeating them. This explanation also helps to understand why failure situations can be used to motivate students with a prior record of success.

Failure-avoidant students whose main goal is to avoid failure rely on different attributions than success-seeking peers. They suppose that failure is caused by lack of ability so they attribute their success to external factors such as exposure to easy tasks on a test or having a run of good luck. What happens is that they blame themselves for failure but take no credit when they perform well. This orientation does not provide the constructive motivation that is needed for self-improvement in any sector of living. Such students believe that they have little control over their destiny so they seek to minimize anticipated pain by trying to avoid failure (Weiner, 2005).

If success is an essential ingredient for durable self-esteem, then why do some students refrain from taking credit for their own success? Some observers suggest that success implies some responsibility to keep performing at a high level (Weiner, 2006). Those who have difficulty in meeting such expectations may believe that success is not of their own making. For this reason, they sometimes appear to sabotage personal effort when they find themselves in danger of reaching educational goals. If the failure orientation is extreme, learned helplessness can occur. *Learned helplessness* refers to individuals whose repeated failure causes them to conclude that outcomes of most events seem beyond their control, causing them to give up easily on many tasks (Dweck & Repucci, 1973). Therefore, those with an external locus of control see little relation between making an effort and goal attainment. Accordingly, they require considerable teacher attention to modify their attributions so they can pursue academic goals with confident expectations for success.

The literature on attribution suggests it is incorrect to suppose that low achievers, in general, lack motivation (Weiner, 2005). Instead, they may be more motivated to avoid failure than to perform well. Low achieving students or those displaying learned helplessness should be invited to discuss beliefs about the causes of their success and failure. In addition, classroom conditions should be established that help students to realize that sustained effort will usually result in success. Adjusting assignments into smaller, more easily attainable increments can increase likelihood of success (Seligman, 2006).

Amendment of Goals

Learning to amend goals is often overlooked as an essential aspect of decision-making. Steven, age 14, informed his parents that the occupation he wanted to pursue was to become a commercial airline pilot. The family had conversations identifying the appealing features of this occupation including satisfactions of flight, promising economic future, chances to visit new places, and responsibility for ensuring that passengers reach their destinations safely. Then Steve found a newspaper advertisement about flying lessons. The price was $500 for 20 lessons that included solo flights and landing experience needed to get the basic licensure to operate a small aircraft. The parents agreed that taking lessons would enable Steve to understand what is expected of aviators and figure out if this line of work would be satisfying for him.

Because Steve was not old enough to have a license for driving the car, his dad brought him to the airport for each lesson. After finishing the second lesson, Steve returned to the lounge where his father was reading. Steve's coloring seemed a bit off but he said nothing. The same pale and sickly appearance was evident after the third and fourth lessons. Then, on Thursday, the day before lesson five, Steve said,

> My lessons are not turning out as I supposed. Flying a plane is easier than I thought but each time we go up, I get sick to my stomach. First, I thought it was caused by something I ate before the lesson but it happens on a regular basis.

Further conversation revealed that Steve wanted to end his lessons. But, he said, "I know you spent a lot of money to give me this chance so I will keep going if you want me too." The father said,

> No, the tentative goal you had to become a pilot is no longer appealing. The money was well spent because the result showed that flying is not the right occupation for you. Finding that out is good because otherwise you might have continued to suppose the life of a pilot had greater promise than is the case. Many adults dislike the career choice they made and wish it were possible to change. Fortunately, you can amend the goal to be a pilot and consider other careers.

In every aspect of life goals should modify when they cannot be attained or become less appealing when knowledge of other possibilities emerge. Suggestions for preparing students to pursue self-direction are given by North Central Regional Educational Laboratory available at http://www.ncrel.org/sdrs/areas/issues/students/learning/lr200.htm.

There is a need to better understand the processes that support goal amendment. This issue is becoming more important because of exposure to over-choice. Wise amendment of goals supports adjustment to previously unrecognized requirements, underestimated difficulties, and opportunities that may have been overlooked in other sectors of the workplace. These questions can help adolescents reflect on whether to amend goals.

1. Have I written my goals so they are specific and could be conveyed to a confidante? It is difficult for relatives or friends to provide feedback about ambiguous goals.

2. Have I set goals in all significant areas of life including mental, social, emotional, physical, spiritual, career and family? When goals are too narrow, growth is limited in a corresponding way.

3. How long will it take to achieve each goal I have on my list? Unless a reasonable time limit is assigned, it is hard to know when to amend particular aspirations.

4. What are my reasons for pursuing these goals? Writing down pros and cons for each goal encourages reflective thinking. Sometimes goals cannot be attained and failure should be acknowledged. Then, it becomes necessary to amend goals and commit to achieving the revised purpose.

The National Center on Secondary Education, in collaboration with the University of Minnesota, maintains a Web site that offers students a research-based transition curriculum on goal setting that focuses on life after high school, available at http://www.youthhood.org/.

TEACHER AND PARENT GUIDANCE

Student self-impressions about capacity to learn are influenced by teacher expectations. Being able to perceive potential in students is a first step in contributing to their development. Sometimes students set poor goals that, unless challenged, can produce disappointment or harm. Reflective conversations that present advantages of goal amendment and choices offer greater benefit than trying to recover from experiencing adverse consequences. Adolescents worry about their occupational future and want to choose work goals wisely. Career education programs that include parents improve deliberations.

Influence of Teacher Expectations

Educators may wonder whether their expectations influence student performance. Robert Merton, professor of Sociology at Columbia University coined the term *self-fulfilling prophecy* whereby a person predicts an event and expectation of that event changes the prophet's behavior in order that the forecast will more likely occur. Merton (1948) maintained that once anticipation is set, even if inaccurate, people tend to behave in ways consistent with the expectations that are conveyed to them. The result is that, often, as if by magic, the expectation becomes reality.

The self-fulfilling prophecy was illustrated long ago in Greek mythology with the legend of Pygmalion and Galatea (Lind, 1957). Pygmalion was a lonely sculptor who had given up hopes of marriage. Then, while carving an ivory figure to resemble what he saw as an ideal woman, Pygmalion became attracted to the clay figure Galatea, and started to behave as though it was a real person. When he went to the festival of Venus, Pygmalion prayed, "If the gods can give what they may wish, grant me a wife like her." Upon return from the festival, Pygmalion found that his prayer was answered. Galatea was transformed to a living being who joined him as his lifelong partner.

How does the self-fulfilling prophecy apply to teaching? Kenneth Clark (1963), a Black psychologist and civil rights leader, maintained that low expectations of inner-city teachers often undermines the achievement of minority students. Many observers agreed with Clark but none could substantiate his claim. Then, Lenore Jacobson, a principal working with low-income families in San Francisco, read a presentation in the *American Scientist* by Robert Rosenthal (1963) of Harvard University. Rosenthal described his studies of experimenter effects on animal behavior. Specifically, he misled students to believe that the randomly chosen rats they would be training were genetically superior or inferior. Depending on what students were told, they treated rats differently. Those who supposed their rats were bright handled them gently, talked to them often, watched them a lot, encouraged them, and portrayed them as pleasant and likable. The students set high expectations for performance to solve maze puzzles.

Another group of students were led to believe the rats they cared for had little chance of success. They tended to handle rats roughly, seldom spoke to them, offered no encouragement, referred to them as unpleasant, and held low expectations for maze performance. After the experiment, it was discovered that the rats provided a more supportive environment and subjected to high expectations performed better than the rats with similar capabilities to learn but perceived by caretakers as dull and treated in less nurturing ways. In Rosenthal's (1963) conclusion, he wondered whether teachers who expect students to be slow might contribute to a self-fulfilling prophecy.

Jacobson was intrigued and wrote to Rosenthal proposing, "If you ever graduate to working with children, let me know if I can help." Soon the principal and researcher agreed to collaborate. Jacobson pointed out that it would be naïve to suppose teachers could be told that some students had unrecognized potential. Instead, a test that teachers were unfamiliar with should be administered to students. The faculty was informed that Rosenthal had developed a new instrument, the Harvard Test of Inflected Acquisition. The test, given to all students, would identify those "about to blossom" and show surprising growth over the next eight months. In fact, Rosenthal did not have such a test. Instead, the students took a nonverbal intelligence test that teachers did not recognize. Then 20% of the students from each class were chosen at random and identified for teachers as the "about to blossom" group (Rosenthal & Jacobson, 1968).

At the end of the school year, students were reexamined using the same intelligence test. Considering the school as a whole, the students from whom teachers had been led to expect greater intellectual gains improved achievement scores to a markedly higher degree than the control group of similar age, sex, and ability, but not labeled as "about to blossom." In Rosenthal's experiment there was no intervention, no special projects, no unique challenges for identified students. The only distinction was the creation of a favorable shift in outlook of teachers—a change in their expectations—that Rosenthal called the *Pygmalion effect*. When teacher expectations rose, students made better use of their mental capacities (Rosenthal & Jacobson, 1968).

Teachers can look for possibilities in each student or believe that some are capable of only low achievement. It is erroneous to suppose that students from minority homes or non-English speaking families are incapable. Yet, setting low expectations appears common because many teachers give high marks to students who demonstrate low performance. This contradiction between high grades and low test scores motivated Congress in 2001 to enact the No Child Left Behind Act (2002). All teachers should become familiar with the No Child Left Behind Act Web site at http://www.ed.gov/teachers/nclbguide/index2.html. Deceptive reporting practices mislead students about their prospects that implicate goal setting. In a national Learning Services poll, conducted by Knowledge Networks, 54% of 1,000 teachers and 43% of 800 parents agreed that low teacher expectations is a great problem (Tompson, 2006). In a related study, 135,000 adolescents at 295 middle schools in fifteen states were surveyed. There was agreement by students that their teachers did not have high expectations for them (Carpenter, Flowers, & Mertens, 2004). Most adolescents tend to adopt the expectations of teachers as an outlook to guide behavior and justify pursuit of goals. Educators can have substantial influence, including the possibility to instill a sense of optimism and willingness to persevere when work becomes difficult (Golden, Kist, & Trehan, 2005; Rosenthal, 2002).

Family Access to Student Records

Achievement test scores reflect how well academic goals have been attained. Whether these scores are helpful depends in part on who has access to them. Before 1974, parents were not allowed to see the school records of their children. Then Congress passed the Family Educational Rights and Privacy Act, which guaranteed parents the right to find out about abilities, performance and problems of their children. Every school must provide annual notification to parents regarding their right to inspect and review the records (United States Department of Education, 2008). Data includes scores from norm-referenced tests, criterion-referenced tests, and anecdotal statements of incidents at school, comments by teachers, and peer observation ratings of students. When parents suspect that records are inaccurate or violate privacy, there are informal and legal methods to request changes (Salend & Duhaney, 2005).

The home-school relationship has changed in several ways because of family access to records. First, by providing objective data about student achievement, schools acknowledge that families are a significant source of guidance. Second, informed parents are more able to share accountability with schools in helping students plan their future. Third, access to data enables parents to more adequately define their function. The most important outcome is that parents can be informed partners. To learn about the Family Educational Rights and Privacy Act, see http://www.ed.gov/policy/gen/guid/fpco/ferpa/index.html.

Exploration of Career Options

A growing number of adolescents admit to anxiety and stress about their career choice, how long to wait before examining options, and lack of guidance other than encouragement to just pursue higher education (Cizek & Burg, 2006). Most students identify parents as the most important persons helping them decide occupational goals (Hargrove, Creagh, & Burgess, 2002). For this reason, parents should be invited to attend career orientation with students. This recommendation is reinforced by Otto (2001) who examined perceptions of adolescents on parent influence for career choice. A class of 350 high school juniors was asked to identify persons they spoke with regarding career plans. Mothers were named by 81% of the students, followed by peers (80%), and fathers (62%). Mothers, as the most preferred source for guidance, were reported by both genders and across all of the ethnic groups. Even though a larger proportion of fathers were employed than mothers, students felt that their mothers were better acquainted with their interests and abilities.

Adolescents may look to mothers for advice on career options but mothers are keenly aware they lack knowledge in this context. A study of 700 White, Black, and Hispanic mothers identified self-perceptions of parent assets and limitations (Strom, Strom, Strom, Shen, & Beckert, 2004). The mothers ranked, "I need more information to help my adolescent explore careers" as their second greatest need among 60 items. In some cases students and parents are better able to consider options by attending a magnet school that offers an occupational emphasis such as South Texas High School for Health Professions where graduation rates are much higher (Buxton, 2005; South Texas High School for Health Professions, 2005). Career exploration has to become more widely available to fulfill the mission of secondary schools (Michelozzi, Surrell, & Cobez, 2004; Millar & Shevlin, 2003).

A resource for families to determine how the goals of individual adolescents relate to occupational opportunities is the Virtual Counseling Center of Arizona State University at http://vcc.asu.edu. Senior high students have free administration of the Personal Globe Inventory (PGI) to assess their vocational interests with immediate feedback on occupations that fit best with personal preferences. The Inventory of Children's Activities (ICA) presents the same topics as the PGI but targets middle school students and allows them to build a portfolio. An automated advisor imports results from the career interest inventory and connects the student and family to relevant information describing careers including streaming video, job forecasts, salaries, and necessary training to enter particular fields (in English and Spanish).

Students should also become acquainted with career opportunities that call for vocational training. This can be accomplished through presentations at school with skilled trade workers who can provide insights about specific jobs, required skills, satisfactions, and disadvantages in the workplace (Chao, 2006). Interaction with workers allows students to express personal goals and obtain feedback on whether their perceptions of jobs match reality as experienced by persons in that field (Johnson, Duffett, & Ott, 2005).

Teachers can expect questions regarding careers and exploration of options. A helpful recommendation is the Web site of the United States Department of Labor (2008)—http://www.bls.gov (click The Occupational Outlook Handbook for specific lines of work)—where information on many careers is presented in an easily understood format. The presentation for career alternatives includes nature of the job, work conditions, future outlook, and required training. The following questions are recommended for students to ask themselves as they think about whether certain career goals should be chosen or amended. Some of the factors to consider are also suggested.

1. How long will it take to reach this goal? Time and money are important factors.
2. Would I enjoy the tasks associated with this career? Awareness is crucial.
3. What are my reasons for wanting this job? Personal motivation should be clear.
4. Do my goals include intellectual, social, and emotional growth? Balance is a key.
5. Is this goal being pursued for myself or for other people? Follow your own dream.
6. What do trusted adults see as benefit and drawbacks of my career goals? Find out.
7. Does this career provide opportunities for advancement? Explore promotion issues.
8. Will this job offer the income needed for my desired lifestyle? Calculate the match.
9. What resources will I need to achieve this goal? Find out what help is available.
10. Is this a realistic and attainable career goal? Seek feedback about your capabilities.
11. Am I informed about requirements to reach this career goal? Know the steps necessary.
12. What are the differences between my original career goal and the amended goal? Clarify.
13. Am I aware of the stresses and demands related to this career? Think about adjustment.
14. How can achieving this goal affect my happiness? Discuss it with those in the field.

Voices of Adolescents

The main purpose of school is to prepare students for a place in the world of work. This goal is more difficult to reach when there are not enough opportunities during middle school and high school for students to explore possible careers. Many adolescents feel uncertain and anxious much of the time about their occupational future. By getting involved with exploration of careers, adolescents can begin to think about the options that might be best for them, become more motivated to study, and decide to remain in school to graduate. The poll for this chapter is about career exploration, a prominent concern of teenagers and their parents that schools should address in more effective ways.

INTERPRETATION OF PROGRESS TOWARD GOALS

A traditional school goal has been to track progress by assigning grades. Most students are motivated to earn good grades. They believe that the marks teachers give them accurately reflect their progress. However, in the past decade, a serious problem has arisen with marks. Scores on objective tests often indicate lower performance than is portrayed by grades, exposing students to a risk of being misled about their progress (Huhn, 2005; Strom & Strom, 2007). In response, the reliance on standardized testing has increased as a safeguard when grades are at odds with test scores. Some teachers explain their reasons for giving students of all performance levels high grades is to motivate self-esteem, prevent intimidation from parents, avoid student grievance, and maintain their mental health (Allen, 2005).

Grade inflation is evident when students get higher grades than they earn (V. Johnson, 2003). School records identifying most students as outstanding make it hard for employers and higher education institutions to identify the best performers, those who are average, and the poor. Teachers should make sure exceptional students get a grade that distinguishes them from the rest. New procedures for scoring and assigning marks are being tried along with methods to assist students in learning how to process feedback about their performance. Portfolios permit student to monitor their progress, detect obstacles, and recognize when goals have been achieved.

Blind Collaborative Grading

There is growing concern that grades have lost their meaning as reliable indicators of student progress. This assumption is corroborated by the high grade point averages of most students. Graduation ceremonies identify a large proportion of students as deserving academic honors. The task of interpreting grades is further complicated for parents, employers, and admissions staff at higher learning institutions when grades contradict test scores on competitive measures. The costs related to deceptive grading motivated the Congress to pass the No Child Left Behind Act of 2002. This law mandates frequent standardized testing as a uniform method to detect failure and trigger assistance. The expectation is that a focus on prevention will result in students getting help they need in a timely manner (Margolis & McCabe, 2006; Simpson, LaCava, & Graner, 2004). A comedy film that illustrates problems resulting from grade inflation and shows how this practice damages young people's motivation for achievement is called *Art School Confidential* (Zwitgott, 2006) starring John Malkovich and Max Minghella.

The contention that grading should be abandoned as evidence of growth is unreasonable. Additional options deserve consideration. For example, English teachers offering sections of a course can collectively judge all students instead of evaluate only those for whom they provide instruction. Think about some implications. First, this method obligates faculty to minimize ambiguity for what is required by agreeing on basic core content for a course and giving similar weights to a program wide assessment or test. Methods for scorer agreement should also include use of the same performance rubric or test for measurement.

For collective grading, assignments should have similar instructions and scoring criteria. Second, when faculty evaluate students who they do not teach, the process forces unison in consistently applying criteria such as in a performance rubric to fairly judge achievement. A willingness to have some common assignments is more likely when teachers feel they are not alone but can stand together in establishing and defending expectations and collective judgment. In this way, teachers become less vulnerable to external pressure for requests to change grades and do not compromise expectations (R. Strom & P. Strom, 2007).

The historic model of evaluation applied by Oxford and Cambridge Universities requires that instructors (called Dons) grade students whose identity is unknown to them. Each paper contains only a numeral matched with the responding student after grading is completed. Blind collaborative grading strongly discourages an otherwise common tendency to introduce bias and grade inflation. Bias, often motivated by interaction with students on a regular schedule, can evolve to dislike, sympathy, or favoritism that could enter an effect on individual assessment. Blind collaborative grading conveys the message that faculty are committed to objectivity in deciding about achievement. By requiring some course-wide assignments and tests judged by a blind-collaboration strategy, faculty can offer students more objective feedback about performance and identify deficits to overcome.

Innovative Reporting Practices

School districts are experimenting with new ways to help families interpret information about student achievement. Some have discontinued use of report cards with grades that are determined only by teachers. The rationale is that teacher grades are not uniformly based on a common set of criteria for judgment. The confusing outcome is that students given the grade of A at one school or from a particular teacher may receive the grade of C for the same level of performance at another school or teacher who maintains higher standards. To ensure that grade reports reflect the state single standard for grade level test scores as required by the No Child Left Behind Act of 2001, letter grades of A, B, C, D, and F determined by teachers have been replaced in some school systems by numerical reports of 1, 2, and 3 based on outcomes of standardized tests.

- Getting a 1 for a subject (English, History, Algebra) is interpreted as one or more years below grade level as assessed by the state test.
- Receiving a 2 for a particular subject is interpreted as performing less than 1 year below grade level as measured by the state test.
- A report of 3 is interpreted as being at grade level or above grade level for the particular subject as measured by the state test.

There are objections to this kind of reporting method but advocates maintain that their goal is to ensure that parents are informed of how well daughters and sons are doing in meeting the standards that are required by the state (R. Strom & Strom, 2007).

Portfolios and Self-Evaluation

Portfolios, a term adopted from the carrying case of paintings or drawings that artists present as proof of their talents, are collections of student work. One of the best opportunities for goal setting is developing a portfolio. During the past decade portfolios in middle school and high school have gained considerable support and become a familiar component of assessment. Portfolios require a student to state goals, monitor progress, and reflect on performance with feedback from teachers and sometimes peers. This process helps students to become more self-directed and less dependent upon others for always telling them how well they are doing. There is also benefit in students assuming the obligation for improvement of performance instead of placing the blame elsewhere. When failure is experienced, a student is expected to figure out how it happened and identify strategies to return to the right path. The usual outcome of portfolio assessment is a more responsible, self reliant student who can demonstrate the critical thinking and self-evaluation that is needed for success in school, work, and at home (Kish, Sheehan, Cole, Struyk, & Kinder, 1997; Theobald, 2006).

Some teachers believe that students lack the maturity needed to engage self-evaluation. Others suppose that students are unwilling to adopt the required attitudes of honesty and authenticity. Both arguments against portfolios could be used as reasons for helping students overcome such deficiencies through guided practice (Sunstein, 2000). Most educators favor allowing students to formulate some personal goals, monitor progress, and process feedback from others who critically examine their portfolio. The related dialogue with teachers, peers, and parents acquaints them with aspirations, sponsors reflection, and increases accuracy of self-appraisal (Sadler & Good, 2006). In addition, empathy often emerges because of the necessity to reconcile multiple perspectives about performance. There is no substitute for direct practice in this process needed by everyone to sustain growth during adolescence and adulthood (Pedersen & Williams, 2004).

There are some limitations of portfolio assessment. Some poorly oriented teachers mistakenly see it as an exercise for showcasing the best and worst work of a student. Instead, the purpose of a portfolio should be to set appropriate goals and evaluate progress by examining the quality of work as it changes over time in specific realms of learning. In this way teachers have a focus for their conversations that is uniquely relevant to each student. The emphasis on high stakes testing for graduation forces teachers to focus exclusively on that assessment. An important step forward is expected as more schools augment subject matter testing with portfolios to track student progress toward personal goals without comparison to classmates (Stefanakis, 2002; Stiggins & Chappius, 2005).

Portfolios are most prominent in schools where faculties have been thoroughly oriented to the potential of this form of evaluation. Four basic assumptions are associated with the design of a portfolio: (1) The process is important; (2) assembling the portfolio should reflect personal growth; (3) reflection and collaboration should be encouraged; and, (4) self-evaluation must be emphasized (Sunstein, 2000).

Schools often decide all learning objectives and put them in the course syllabus. As a result, success excludes the attainment of student goals that may differ from the uniform expectations that apply to everyone. Certainly, students are obligated to meet curriculum goals and minimal competency standards for academic skills. Nevertheless, when their learning is restricted to what others expect, students are denied practice in looking within themselves and reflecting on how they should grow as individuals. The schedule at school should include arranged time for students to participate in goal setting, reflect on the future, and examine personal progress (Sadler & Good, 2006).

There is increasing use of *electronic portfolios* consisting of resumes that reflect activities students participate in and evidence of accomplishments

(Montgomery & Wiley, 2008). Most of these portfolios are stored on Web sites, though copies can be burned on CD-ROM or other media. There is anticipation that transitioning from paper and binder versions of portfolios to digital presentation will facilitate organization of data and assist students with job searching as they make their availability known to a broader audience of potential employers on the Internet. Students need to examine where they are going and how much progress has been made. Minnesota has an electronic portfolio system that any high school or college student in the state is allowed to use.

Guidelines for Use of Criticism

Student willingness to accept criticism from teachers, parents, and peers is necessary for successful living with groups and working with teammates (Morrisey & Werner-Wilson, 2005). However, few adolescents are taught how to process criticism and engage in civil critiques of work by peers. Consequently, defensiveness is common and progress is limited because individuals rely on themselves alone to detect their needs for further growth (Drucker, 2005). Teachers have opportunities to provide timely feedback on assignments that reflect lower levels of thinking, tasks inadequately prepared, submissions for which directions were not followed, and incomplete work that should be revised. This kind of formative feedback can motivate improved effort without influencing the course grade.

Giving criticism is difficult but helpful when teachers use these guidelines:

1. Clarify for a student the reasons why you are offering them criticism.
2. Place your emphasis on a clear description of what can be improved.
3. Focus on particulars of an assignment rather than abstract behavior.
4. Invite discussion of possible consequences instead of giving advice.
5. Keep judgments tentative, indicating that this feedback is formative.
6. Present criticism in a way that allows the student to make decisions.
7. Focus criticism on behaviors that a student is capable of changing.
8. Include the recognition of positive outlook in your critical feedback.

9. Avoid providing an overload of concerns for the student to process.
10. Engage in perspective taking by inviting the student to respond.
11. Encourage reflection and state your willingness to provide help.

For students to benefit from criticism, they need to process observations of others. The following guidelines can be discussed in class and posted as a reminder for students to rely on:

1. Recognize the potential value of receiving constructive criticism.
2. Engage in perspective taking from the viewpoint of an observer.
3. Acknowledge criticism that focuses on behaviors you can change.
4. Listen carefully so that you fully understand the focus of concern.
5. Ask questions to clarify any aspect of the criticism not understood.
6. Welcome criticism to improve behavior instead of being defensive.
7. Seek constructive changes to the behavior that is being criticized.
8. Recognize that behavior change is a function of your own choice.
9. Arrange time to reflect on the criticism without any distractions.

SUMMARY

Adolescent Identity and Goals

The developmental tasks reflect goals that all adolescents need to achieve with support of their families and schools. Students benefit from exploring goals as they form their individual identity and should be urged to consider personality goals as a realm of achievement. Every student should be able to find satisfaction in school so they can commit to remaining in classes until graduation. Involvement with the expressive and instrumental culture can enhance the feeling of connection with classmates and the institution.

Motivation of Self-Directed Learning

High achievement motivation is characterized by students that are self-reliant, moderate risk takers, and able to accurately identify personal limitations. Teenagers benefit most from educators who trust them to make decisions about goals, project selection, homework tasks, and dialogue with them about goal amendment. Opportunities to practice planning skills in a low-risk setting enable students to identify a future of their own choosing, become more responsible individuals, and experience autonomy. Teachers should determine what individual students believe about causes of their success and failure, helping everyone recognize that continued effort will almost always result in achievement.

Teacher and Parent Guidance

Students from minority backgrounds, non-English speaking homes, immigrant newcomers, and everyone else should be told during the class introduction that the teacher perceives them all as capable of succeeding. The view that everyone who works hard and is willing to persevere when tasks become difficult can do much to support the school goal of academic achievement. When teenagers choose goals that can disadvantage them, reflective conversations with teachers is a better strategy than expecting disappointing consequences to provide learning. Parents need to examine school records of their children and join them in exploration of career options.

Interpretation of Progress Toward Goals

Adolescents count on teachers to inform them about progress. Grade inflation prevents individuals from knowing their actual level of performance. To minimize such hazards, the No Child Left Behind Act mandates external testing. Novel methods for scoring assessments and reporting progress are being explored along with ways to help students process constructive criticism. Teenagers practice self-evaluation as they engage in portfolio assessment by setting goals, monitoring gains, and detecting shortcomings. This process also reveals a need for goal revision. To change plans, students must recognize goals that are unattainable or too narrow.

CLASSROOM APPLICATIONS

1. Students whose teachers encourage them to set goals feel a greater sense of control, establish personal direction, show greater motivation to succeed, and become less vulnerable to manipulation by others. These benefits should motivate more educators to go beyond the usual effort of preparing students to meet the institutional goals expressed as graduation requirements. An added

challenge is to provide tasks enabling adolescents to identify, pursue, and evaluate the appropriateness of their goals.

2. When students are confident that their teacher will not penalize them for stating their ideas, asking what they believe are naive questions, exposing personal opinions for reaction, and exploring new paradigms for thinking, they are more inclined to take risks that lead to learning. Teachers govern the costs related to student inquiry and self-expression. Consequently, it is important to make known that interactive dialogue and reciprocal learning are expectations for student and teacher behavior.

3. Portfolio assessment can be an effective way to support goal setting. This method calls for individuals to reflect on their performance and to monitor progress toward goals. In turn, students become more self-directed and less dependent on others to always tell them how they are doing. When failure occurs, the student is expected to figure out how it happened and identify improvement strategies. The usual outcome is a responsible student who can apply critical thinking and self-evaluation skills.

4. Teachers should look for potential in each of their students instead of assume that the background of some individuals justifies low expectations for them. Most adolescents are inclined to adopt expectations conveyed by their teachers as a suitable guide for working toward goals. This means that educators have substantial power, including the possibility to communicate optimism, hope, willingness to persevere with tasks, and a commitment to resilience for coping with adversity.

5. Students should be urged to pursue personality development that is a vital aspect of identity in adulthood. Appearances may be difficult to alter but the kind of person someone aspires to become is a matter of choice that begins early in life and should be recognized as a realm of achievement. Teachers and parents need to realize that the pursuit of personality goals is the context where they have the greatest opportunity to act as models.

6. Adolescents need skills for setting a course of direction to follow and motivate persistence. The development of these attributes is jeopardized when students are over-scheduled by teachers or relatives, have too many choices made for them by adults, and are denied tasks to explore self-direction. Teachers should devise and give more tasks that motivate students to pursue separate paths and enable them to share with classmates the learning outcomes of their independent efforts.

7. Teacher trust is necessary to nurture aspects of student development. Trusting students means encouraging them to identify goals, soliciting their input about evaluation of group learning, supporting practice in self-evaluation, completing electronic polls to express opinions about the education process, assessing performance of the faculty, and working with peers on collaborative projects. Trust is a reciprocal process defining a healthy teacher-student relationship and can enlarge the scope of mutual learning.

8. Students should be urged to join extracurricular activities. Involvement with the expressive culture has been found to result in greater satisfaction at school, higher grades, lower dropout rates, and healthy adjustment to offset disappointment in other sectors of student life. These benefits are reinforced by evidence that participation in the expressive culture can support coping with daily pressures, make students less susceptible to undue stress, and more likely to choose appropriate methods of relief.

9. Students are faced with a larger array of choices than prior generations so there is a need for guided experience in school with processes to rely on for facilitating amendment of goals. Learning to revise personal aspirations is an often overlooked aspect of decision making that can enable a person to figure out when change in direction seems warranted and arrange time to reflect on alternatives. Teachers should avoid recommending persistence when a student actually needs to identify more appropriate goals.

10. Testing is the way schools detect deficiencies. In addition, adolescents need guidance to adopt and apply healthy criteria for the self-evaluation that should occur throughout life and motivate initiative for development. Persons who learn to become self-critical and monitor their school efforts can be expected to continue growth following graduation. Teachers must prepare students for a society where adults less often feel responsible to observe and report to parents the behavior of their children.

11. It is erroneous to suppose that low-achieving students lack motivation. Instead, they may be more motivated to avoid failure than to perform well. Teachers should arrange private conversations with individuals to find out the causes they attribute to their success and failure. Students should be informed that access to tutoring and sustained effort can lead to success. Helping students to acquire accurate perceptions of their ability is an obligation of teachers.

FOR REFLECTION

1. Which developmental tasks of adolescence require support from teachers?
2. What are the possible roles peers could play in the formation of identity?
3. How have your personality goals changed since you were an adolescent?
4. In what ways could instruction allow for greater student decision making?
5. What advantages and limits do you foresee in blind collaborative grading?
6. React to the use of grade level test scores as a basis for reporting to parents.
7. Which of your goals have you amended because they were unreasonable?
8. What lessons did you learn from negative consequences of poor choices?
9. Support or oppose the idea that all students can meet standards of No Child Left Behind.
10. How would you structure an innovative career program for adolescents?
11. What aspects of giving and receiving criticism are most difficult for you?

KEY TERMS

Achievement Identity
Achievement Motivation
Attribution Theory
Electronic Portfolios
Expressive Culture
Extreme Identity Confusion
Extrinsic Motivation
Family Educational Rights and Privacy Act
Foreclosure Identity
Grade Inflation

Idealism
Instrumental Culture
Intrinsic Motivation
Learned Helplessness
Moratorium Identity
Negative Identity
Normal Confusion Identity
Personality Hardiness
Pygmalion Effect
Self-fulfilling Prophecy

VISIT THESE WEB SITES

Link to these sites at http://www.infoagepub.com/strom-adolescents

Consortium for Research on Emotional Intelligence in Organizations
http://www.eiconsortium.org

Erik Erikson Theory, George Boeree
http://webspace.ship.edu/cgboer/perscontents.html

Family Educational Rights and Privacy Act
http://www.ed.gov/policy/gen/guid/fpco/ferpa/index.html

Lions Quest, Resources for Educators http://www.lions-quest.org/

David McClelland, Employee Motivation
http://www.accel-team.com/human_relations/
hrels_06_mcclelland.html

National Center on Secondary Education
http://www.youthhood.org

No Child Left Behind Act, A Toolkit for Teachers
http://www.ed.gov/teachers/nclbguide/index2.html

North Central Regional Educational Laboratory
http://www.ncrel.org/sdrs/areas/issues/students/learning/lr200.htm

Raising Teens: A Synthesis of Research and Foundation for Action
http://www.hsph.harvard.edu/chc/parenting

Time Management Guide
http://www.time-management-guide.com/personal-goal-setting.html

United States Department of Labor, Occupational Outlook Handbook
http://www.bls.gov

Virtual Counseling Center, Arizona State University
http://vcc.asu.edu

EXERCISES AND ROLES

Exercise 3.01: Career Exploration Poll

Role: Voter
The purpose of this poll is to find out how students feel about career exploration experiences and determine ways schools and families can support this aspect of education. Teenagers are the future work force so they naturally think about kinds of jobs that would be most appealing and appropriate for them.

Directions: Select the answer(s) that describes how you feel. In some cases, you may select more than one answer. If an answer you want to give is not listed, write it on the line marked 'other.' Your responses are anonymous and may be combined with those of other students at your school in a report to students, faculty, and parents.

1. Which factors will you consider in choosing your career?

    (a) amount of job stress
    (b) salary and benefits
    (c) reasonable hours
    (d) work satisfaction
    (e) other

2. How influential will relatives be in helping you choose a career?

    (a) very influential
    (b) some influence
    (c) slight influence
    (d) not an influence
    (e) other

3. Which of these sources do you talk to about possible careers?

    (a) family
    (b) friends
    (c) teachers

(d)   mentors
(e)   other

4. When you dream about a career, what kinds of things do you imagine yourself doing?

    (a)   helping others
    (b)   being a manager
    (c)   becoming wealthy
    (d)   being my own boss
    (e)   other

5. What steps have you taken to explore a possible career?

    (a)   talked to people in a job I like
    (b)   conversations with my relatives
    (c)   Web search of job requirements
    (d)   have not taken any steps so far
    (e)   other

6. How much education is required to enter the career that you want?

    (a)   a high school diploma
    (b)   vocational/trade school
    (c)   4-year college degree
    (d)   I don't know
    (e)   other

7. What advice have relatives or friends given you about career choice?

    (a)   choose a high paying job
    (b)   get a job with low stress
    (c)   find a job that is satisfying
    (d)   follow someone's footsteps
    (e)   other

8. How often do you think about your future career?

    (a)   often
    (b)   sometimes
    (c)   seldom
    (d)   never

9.   What career exploration help would you like from your school?

   (a)   guidance about Web investigation of careers
   (b)   orientation nights at school with speakers from different jobs
   (c)   scheduled observations of people on the job
   (d)   chances to interview workers online/ phone
   (e)   other

10.   What experiences have influenced your career choice so far?

   (a)   characters on television, Internet, movies
   (b)   talking to people who work in the field
   (c)   advice from faculty at my school
   (d)   advice from parent and other relatives
   (e)   other

11.   How stressful is it for you to choose a career?

   (a)   a lot of stress
   (b)   some stress
   (c)   a little stress
   (d)   no stress

12.   How certain are you about a particular career?

   (a)   I have definitely decided what job I want.
   (b)   I am considering several career options.
   (c)   I have no idea what career would be best.
   (d)   I am not ready to explore possible careers.

13.   What obstacles do you anticipate with your career choice?

   (a)   The job I want does not have a high salary.
   (b)   The job I want calls for being gone a lot.
   (c)   The job I want requires higher education.
   (d)   The job I want means relocating my home.
   (e)   other

14.   When I think about a possible career exploration program at school

   (a)   I would like to have my parents participate with me

    (b)   I would like to attend these meetings with classmates
    (c)   I would like to come to these meetings by myself
    (d)   I do not have any interest in being a participant.
    (e)   other

15.   How do you suppose the career you choose will change over time?

    (a)   There will be a need for continuous education.
    (b)   Job requirements will stay much the same.
    (c)   Demand for this work will increase salaries.
    (d)   Status of people in this field is bound to grow.
    (e)   other

Select your grade level, gender, ethnicity, and age.

My grade level is 5 6 7 8 9 10 11 12
My gender is female male
My ethnicity is Asian Black Hispanic Native American White Other
My age is 10 11 12 13 14 15 16 17 18 19

Exercise 3.02: Collaborative Grading

Role: Evaluator

The board of education has approved this new policy. "Teachers will evaluate progress but no longer decide grades. Course grades will be determined by teams of teachers that judge final tests and projects without knowing names of students." Describe advantages and disadvantages of this policy for (1) teachers and (2) students.

Exercise 3.03: Recollections of Career Choices

Role: Storyteller Role

How would you have answered these questions during your years as a teenager?

1.   When you dream of a career, what do you imagine yourself doing?
2.   What experiences have influenced your choice of an occupation?
3.   What steps have you taken to explore the career of your interest?
4.   How do you intend to prepare for the career path you will follow?
5.   What career pressures have you felt from your friends or relatives?

6. What career satisfactions and disappointments do you anticipate?
7. How much education is required to enter the career you prefer?
8. What are some careers that you considered but decided against?
9. How is the career you want to pursue likely to change over time?
10. How confident are you about reaching your occupational goal?
11. What are the greatest challenges you see in your chosen career?
12. What factors appeal to you most about your occupational choice?

Exercise 3.04: Goalsetting and Self-Evaluation

Role: Evaluator

Share Your Impressions With Teammates

1. What are some long-term goals adolescents should be encouraged to set?
2. What things do you think adolescents should plan for more than is usual?
3. What are some goals of students or relatives you make an effort to support?
4. In what ways has your family influenced methods you rely on to set goals?
5. What are some main goals that you are attempting to achieve at this time?
6. How do you feel about expecting students to acquire self-evaluation skills?
7. What can schools do to increase student chances to practice self-evaluation?
8. What memorable goals did you choose but later found it necessary to amend?
9. What are the greatest obstacles you encounter in setting personal goals?
10. What are some goals others have for you that turned out to be troublesome?
11. How can educators help the public emphasize long-term goals for students?

Exercise 3.05: Short and Long Term Goals

Role: Challenger

Short-term goals in school are defended on the premise that this provides early detection of student errors and feedback about state tests so mistakes can be corrected. In contrast, some observers see unfavorable effects when short-term goals receive exclusive attention without comparable consideration for students' long-term goals. Interview teachers and share their observations.

1. How do you view the relative balance of short-term and long-term goals emphasized in secondary schools?
2. How does the prevailing balance of short and long term goals affect the way that you provide instruction?
3. How do you assess the progress of your students toward achieving short-term versus long-term goals?

Exercise 3.06: Establishing Realistic Goals

Role: Generational Reporter

Recognizing personal limitations is an important aspect of setting goals. Some people commit themselves to the pursuit of more goals than they are able to fulfill. Perhaps they do not recognize that the decision to overload themselves can undermine their performance in a variety of situations. Even when others advise them to scale back, they may sustain the belief that overly ambitious plans can be attained if they are willing to remain persistent.

1. Why do you suppose many teenagers take on more goals than are reasonable?
2. How do adolescents cope when they decide to adopt some overload of goals?
3. What are some of the consequences of this behavior that you have observed?
4. How can teachers and parents help teenagers overcome this familiar problem?

Exercise 3.07: Teacher Goals

Role: Evaluator

All teachers have personal goals in addition to attainment of ones required of them by the school district. Interview a teacher with 10 or more years of experience and another who has taught less than 3 years. Ask them both to answer the following questions and provide an explanation for each one. If this exercise is chosen for an entire team, some members can focus on less experienced teachers while others interview those with more experience.

1. Which of your teaching goals do you think are being fulfilled?
2. Which of your teaching goals have you been obliged to amend?
3. Which goals for teaching have you found it necessary to abandon?

Exercise 3.08: Over-Choice

Role: Improviser

In some ways people have greater freedom today than in the past. However, over-choice has also become a familiar problem. Students need experience with setting goals, planning, and amending some of their choices. Describe an innovative activity to allow practice in these skills when there are so many issues competing for a place in the curriculum.

Exercise 3.09: Grading and Motivation Case

Role: Evaluator

Erik got a low A (90%) in his History class taught by Ms. Middleton. He discussed his grade and work submitted in an online chat room with friends who took the same course from another instructor, Mr. DeNiro. He also visited the site, "Rate your H.S. Teacher" and confirmed what he had been told via online chats. From these sources Erik concluded that had he been in Mr. DeNiro's class he would have received the lower grade of B. Based on Erik's case, reflect on these questions and provide your responses.

1. What might Erik's attributions have been for his A performance in History if he had known how other students who did the same quality work in another section of the course were graded? How are his attributions likely to change based on comparing the A

grade he received with the low B issued to his friends in Mr. DeNiro's section?

2. How might this variance in grading across different sections of the same course affect each instructor?

3. What are some reasons for why Erik got an A instead of a low B as others did who did the same quality work?

4. How could changes be made so that Erik's type of case becomes less common and is replaced by a higher level of consistent assessment and grading across sections of the same course?

Exercise 3.10: Trusting Students

Role: Evaluator

Trust is vital to build relationships and work in collaborative settings. Most teenagers want their teachers to trust them. Every teacher can make known that earning their trust requires students to demonstrate certain behaviors on a consistent basis. Add to this list some contingent behaviors that would motivate you to trust students.

1. Be on time and well prepared for classes.
2. Show a consistent sense of responsibility.
3. Complete the homework that is assigned.

PART II

COGNITIVE EXPECTATIONS

CHAPTER 4

MENTAL ABILITIES
AND ACHIEVEMENT

The public might suppose that educators and psychologists would have agreed long ago about the meaning of such an important concept as intelligence. Although varied definitions have been proposed, none has been given universal acceptance. Even though no intelligence test measures the full range of known mental functions, the scores students get on such tests greatly influence how others perceive them. The way learners are classified by intellectual abilities influence decisions about placement in special education or gifted and talented programs. Test results also impact expectations for accountability.

The goals for this chapter are to examine intelligence from several perspectives—as a quantitative concept, as qualitative levels of thinking, as consideration of actual and potential development, and as recognition of multiple intelligences. Consideration is given to environmental factors that teachers can arrange to facilitate learning, allow mistakes followed by corrective feedback, and address the overlooked instructional needs of exceptional students. Functions of the mind are compared with functions of computers to consider how learning occurs according to information processing theory. Recommendations for ways to improve comprehension are described along with memory and concept acquisition practices. Insights from neuroscience on brain development are discussed with implications for educators.

Adolescents in the Internet Age, pp. 137–181

PERSPECTIVES OF INTELLIGENCE

Setting standards for students requires careful consideration of intellectual abilities. The quantitative view of intelligence relies on measurement tools to produce scores indicating whether a student is above average, average or below average in capacity to learn. The qualitative view on intelligence identifies kinds of thinking that students can participate in at different stages of mental development. A more socially oriented approach to thinking about intelligence combines what students are able to achieve when given help and what they can accomplish alone as a broader index of potential. There is also a view that multiple intelligences emerge as sub abilities during adolescence.

Quantitative Assessment of Intelligence

Education authorities in Paris, France were puzzled about how to identify students that lacked sufficient mental ability to benefit from classroom instruction. Alfred Binet (1857–1911) was invited to develop some method that could detect students with mental deficiencies. The screening inventory Binet (1905) produced became the first intelligence test (Privateer, 2006). He established that a good test item is solved more readily as children get older. Therefore, Binet arranged items according to the age at which approximately 50% of students were able to perform them correctly, allowing the most able to differentiate themselves. The methodology Binet applied to selecting test items was adopted and continues to be standard practice (Sternberg, Jarvin, & Grigorenko, 2009). Binet explained his assumptions, rationale, and procedures for testing in *New Methods for Diagnosis of the Intellectual Level of Subnormals*, available at http://psychclassics.yorku.ca/Binet/binet1.htm.

Lewis Terman (1916) at Stanford University devised a measure he named the Stanford-Binet Test of Intelligence, to credit the French originator. The fifth edition of Stanford-Binet (Roid, 2003) is usually administered by school psychologists to evaluate student ability. Biographies of Binet, Terman, and other contributors to intelligence testing and theoretical development of mental capacity can be found at http://www.indiana.edu/~intell.

An *intelligence quotient, IQ,* is how the scores from an intelligence test are expressed. Originally, the IQ was assessed by dividing the mental age of a student (determined from responses on the test) by chronological age, multiplied by 100. Current measures like the Weschler Intelligence Scale for Children (WISC), allow examiners to interpret IQ using a score table that corresponds with the student chronological age (Thorndike, 2005). The common way to identify mental status is *standard deviation,* a measure of variability that shows how student scores are spread out. There are eight standard deviations in a normal distribution of scores, regardless of whether the focus is on height of seventh grade boys, weight of ninth grade girls, or scores of freshman on an intelligence test. Figure 4.1 illustrates that in a normal population portrayed by the bell shaped curve, approximately two-thirds (68.27%) of all cases fall between one standard deviation above the average score and one standard deviation below the average score. The range between plus or minus three standard deviations includes 99.7% of all students. In effect, one standard deviation is large, two is very large, and a difference of three standard deviations is huge (Herrnstein & Murray, 1996).

IQs depicted on the lower axis in Figure 4.1 reveals that a student who is two standard deviations below the mean has an IQ of 68. Two standard deviations below the mean have been used as the upper limit criterion to classify students as mildly retarded. Students in the *mildly retarded* range of 50–68 IQ represent 11% of all the students in special education. At the other end, students scoring two standard deviations above the mean, having an IQ of 132 or higher, are commonly chosen to join *gifted and talented* academic acceleration programs (Taylor, 2005).

Qualitative Differences in Thinking

Jean Piaget (1896–1980), a psychologist in Geneva, Switzerland, explored how children think and the ways they interpret the world. At the

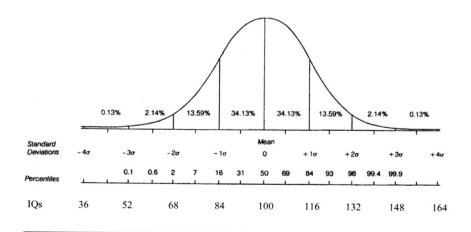

Figure 4.1. Standard deviation and the normal curve.

beginning of his career in the 1920s, Piaget worked on test development. His duties required tasks dealing with standardized measures until three observations led him to pursue a new direction for the assessment of mental abilities. First, instead of calculating correct answers, the method usually applied in analyzing responses, Piaget inspected incorrect responses to detect limitations that students of the same age had in common. He concluded that the way older children think is qualitatively different from younger children. This decision led Piaget (1954, 1963, 1969) to abandon the concept of quantitative intelligence.

A second observation led Piaget to a new technique for studying intelligence. A strategy was needed to give interviewers more freedom than methods required in standardized testing. Recalling his reading of Freudian psychology, Piaget tried an approach that would enable the interviewer to allow child answers to guide the flow of questioning. However, the abnormal children he worked with had verbal deficits so it was not helpful. Another novel feature was applied. Besides having students give answers as best they could, Piaget also invited them to manipulate objects that credited their actions as evidence of thinking instead of demonstrating knowledge only by use of words. Years later other researchers determined that verbal ability is greater among students from higher socioeconomic backgrounds (Eysenck & Keane, 2005).

A third way Piaget (1970) departed from other observers of child development was his recognition that, because the mind is an integrated unit, the best way to help students is to offer curriculum that they can comprehend at their current level of thinking. He referred to schemas in describing how children make sense of experiences. *Schemas* are temporary cognitive structures that determine how information is processed and situations are organized. As new experiences occur, schemas must either enlarge or change to allow adjustment in a complex environment.

According to Piaget (1970), people rely on two processes for their adaptation. First, *assimilation* calls for integration of new conceptual, perceptual or motor information into existing schemas. For example, Don is visiting the French Impressionist Exhibition at the Metropolitan Museum of Art. He has previously seen some pictures by Monet and Van Gogh in magazines. During his museum observation, Don's "impressionist schema" must expand to include the work of Toulose-Lautrec, Cezanne, Gaugain, Manet, Sisily, and Matisse, all artists of the late nineteenth century who explored the analysis of color and light. Assimilation enlarges the size of a schema, as in Don's case, but does not result in schema change. Instead, a second process that people rely on for adaptation is *accommodation*, which requires modification or replacement of schema so novel conditions can be accepted. When Don left the impressionist gallery, he took the elevator to another floor in the museum featuring modern art. Within this context Don was obliged to accept a different set of criteria in order to appreciate work by artists whose representations are more often symbolic than literal. The schema Don applied to enjoy Impressionism did not allow for an appreciation of modern art so the creation of new schema was necessary. An imbalance between what is familiar and novel creates tension until new schema categories have been formed.

When students sense *disequilibrium*, their motivation is to search for equilibration either through greater assimilation or by accommodation of looking at unfamiliar concepts and events in new ways. *Equilibration* occurs when a suitable balance is struck between the amount of assimilation and the amount of accommodation. If someone were to engage in assimilation only, s/he would possess a few very large schemas, perceive most situations as similar, and be unable to detect differences between things. Conversely, someone who engages in accommodation only would have many extremely small schema, perceive most situations as different from one another, and show an inability to recognize similarities.

Constructivism is the term often applied to theories such as Piaget's that describe how students actively develop their own meaning for events based upon personal experience (Fosnot, 2005). Piaget recognized that the thinking of children and many adolescents does not proceed in the same manner as among adults. He maintained that the thinking process evolves by stages roughly associated with chronological age. The elements of Piaget's stages of thinking in relation to elementary and secondary school students are referred to as concrete operations (ages 6–11) and formal operations (ages 11–adulthood) shown in Table 4.1.

The adolescent brain is no longer growing physically in size but changes as more complex thinking begins to differentiate students (Ward, 2006). The logic of some individuals remains restricted to involvement with concrete materials, situations, and contexts. Unless they have direct experience with a particular situation, or if the material is intangible, *concrete operations* thinkers are often unsuccessful with abstract problem solving. Other students who had attained a higher stage of mental development were called *formal operations* thinkers by Piaget (1970). These individuals are able to solve problems working without props, deal with hypothetical situations, and can manipulate abstractions. Evidence of formal operations appears between the ages of 11 and 15 for a majority of students, somewhat later for other students (in their 20s), and never occurs for some people (Medina, 2008).

Table 4.1 shows that *propositional thinking* is one element of formal operations. Formal thinkers are able to apply reasoning in solving problems verbally or propositionally without the presence of objects. They are no longer restricted to concrete thinking, working only with what they can see and feel. Students learn to use symbols, as in algebra. Their reasoning

Table 4.1.   Piaget's Stages of Concrete amd Formal Operations

Concrete Operations	
6 to 11 years old	Achievements and limitations
Reversibility	Carries thought forward and backward
Logic	Solves problems on tangible things or involving familiar situations
Decentration	Attends to several aspects of a problem at once
Classification	Uses multiple factors to organize or categorize; class inclusion
Seriation	Arranges things in order by sequence or according to some quantitative aspect
Formal Operations	
Ages 11 to 20 years old	Achievements
Propositional thought	Manipulates abstract symbols; addresses propositions, even those contrary to fact, and understands metaphor
Metacognition	Thinks about and analyzes the reasoning process of others and oneself
Experimental reasoning	Relies on tests to reach solutions on separation of variables and their relationships (proportional, inverse, etc.)
Understands historical time	Contemplates the future and past
Idealistic egocentrism	Identifies ways to improve life

permits them to transcend current situations and think about future possibilities. Even propositions that may be contrary to fact can be examined as if they were true. Formal operation thinkers can consider propositions like "Let's suppose that snow is black." In contrast, concrete stage thinkers cannot accept any premise that contradicts their own experience so they would dismiss this proposition by pointing out that "Snow is white, snow is not black." The ability to consider opposing views increases reliance on scientific methods, decreases self-centeredness, and improves relationships (Piaget, 1970; Rescoria & Rosenthal, 2004).

Metacognition is another element of formal operations thinking. Adolescents appreciate their new ability to engage in *metacognition*, a process of critically examining the logic of others or self. The benefits of metacognition are evident when someone seeks a professional counselor, relative or friend to help them monitor their thinking about specific concerns. There is an obvious risk if adolescents restrict themselves to guidance from peers simply because they share similar experiences. Classmates may be unable to participate in metathinking, critically examine the logic of a friend or fear the loss of friendship if they appear to be critical. Teachers usually lack many experiences of students but their ability to monitor logic and provide feedback is applicable for most situations (Berkowitz & Cicchelli, 2004).

When adolescents first acquire their capacity for metacognition, they practice this skill by arguing about almost everything. They are motivated to detect the weakness of logic that adults use at home or school. This response can be seen by the challenge of seventh and eighth graders to any school policies they consider unfair. It is great fun to catch teachers or parents in faulty propositions. Some parents are disappointed with transformation of their children from passively accepting ideas to challenging how authorities see things (McGue, Elkins, Walden, & Iacono, 2005). A more accurate interpretation is that the adolescent has arrived at the stage of formal operations and deserves encouragement for independent thinking.

A third element of formal operations, shown in Table 4.1, is *experimental reasoning.* This asset enables a student to go beyond personal observation as the basis for reaching conclusions. New information can be deduced from a generalized set of data when subjecting it to testing. In Biology, Chemistry and Physics students form hypotheses, test variables, and discover probable consequences. Unlike classmates at the concrete thinking level whose reasoning is limited to direct experience or what they call "reality," formal operations thinkers can consider potentiality, conditions that do not yet exist but might occur in the future (Kamphaus & Frick, 2006).

A fourth aspect of formal operations is *understanding of historical time,* depicted in Table 4.1. This strength is seldom in place during the elementary grades when most students rank social studies as their least preferred subject (Privateer, 2006). However, things begin to change as some students move to formal operations thinking and are able to comprehend historical time. For them the distant past assumes meaning, possible futures are contemplated, life in other cultures seems intriguing, and history is regarded as interesting rather than boring (Tally & Goldenberg, 2005).

Table 4.1 also shows that *idealistic egocentrism* is common during adolescence. Because formal operations thinkers can look ahead and identify possibilities, they often feel frustrated when comparing the world as it could be with the existing conditions that often appear inequitable. The idealistic perspective can get students in trouble with adults that do not share their ability to function at the formal operations level and are therefore limited to seeing only things in the present. Such persons label idealistic teenagers exhibiting formal operations as dreamers and often recommend that they become realistic (Alexander, 2005).

Adolescents who reach formal operations thinking usually direct their newfound ability for criticism and judgment on themselves. They may set standards and aspirations beyond their ability. Therefore, they feel unsuccessful at the same time friends and relatives describe them as performing well. Excessive self-criticism is nourished by the egocentric assumption of teenagers that everyone is observing their faults. The *imaginary audience,* a phenomenon that supposes our limitations are the object of attention is illustrated by a high school cheerleader who detects a pimple on her chin before going onto the football field to perform. Moments later, while doing cheer routines in front of the fans, she thinks all of them are looking at her pimple (Apter, 2006). Teachers should be aware that adolescents are more defensive in processing external evaluation than older age groups (Wormeli, 2006). The capacity for introspection and idealism that emerge in adolescence are essential assets that can be supported by training in how to process criticism, a topic described in chapter 3 on students goals and motivation.

An important reminder is that a student might function at the formal operations level in some classes but not in others. For example, Tom's spatial intelligence allows him to perform as a formal operations thinker in three-dimensional drawing for the advanced art class. However, Tom struggles and cannot function at formal operations in his mathematics course (Gardner, 2004). The Jean Piaget Society is available at http://www.piaget.org/links.html.

Piaget discovered that most adolescents (perhaps 2/3) and significant proportion of adults (half or more) do not use formal operational thought. He also found that individuals who are able to apply formal thinking vary in their scope of application. While some can use formal thinking across different school subjects, others appear limited to formal thought in a single area such as mathematics, science or three-dimensional art. Piaget's views about the proportion of students at the formal operational level of thinking were based on European studies. These estimates have been challenged in relation to cultures where school is perceived as less important and reflected by a lower proportion of boys and girls who perform at the formal thinking level. Such population deviations have led some observers to conclude that Piaget underestimated the effort, energy, and knowledge needed to engage in formal thought (Kuhn, 2005).

Because concrete thinking is sufficient for most daily tasks and formal thinking is more challenging, some people might avoid involvement even when they are capable. For example, secondary mathematics teachers describe their common dilemma of whether to allow students to use simple tools like calculators during tests. Students prefer these tools and claim that using them is what would be expected in situations outside the classroom. Nevertheless, some teachers forbid the tools, believing that it detracts from the more powerful thought processes that must be exercised when students have to do their calculations by hand. In another context, what is the objection to allowing rural African tribesmen who do not understand how cell phones work and relying on them to check the market prices for deciding when to bring crops to the city for sale? People throughout the world use Internet, iPods, MP3 players, and cell phones that provide functions that they do not comprehend but gratefully apply. Interdependence allows greater numbers of people to benefit from the insights produced by formal thinkers.

The proportion of students who participate in formal thinking might increase if schools incorporate more streaming video, DVDs that repeat steps in problem solving, graphic organizers, visuals to match verbal lessons, and Internet applications as contexts for skill practice. Examples later in this text include ways to enhance the appeal for guiding hypothetical deductive thinking with tasks formulated by the National Health Museum on its Web site at http://www.accessexcellence.org (click activities exchange & mystery spot) when students are given hints about the person(s) spreading a disease and learn by tracing steps in problem solving. In addition to acquainting students with new tools to support formal thinking, educators should assume the task of developing contemporary assessments implicating technology instead of criticizing the tasks that were created by Piaget long ago.

Social Constructivist Theory

Russian psychologist Lev Vygotsky (1896–1934) was a contemporary of Jean Piaget. Both men agreed that the key to durable learning is for students to build their own knowledge instead of gain it vicariously by listening to teachers or memorizing. Piaget's identification of thinking stages led him to recommend that teachers arrange opportunities for exploration that allows for personal knowledge building. Vygotsky (1978) did not propose new cognitive stages but emphasized collaboration as a condition that teachers can encourage to ensure greater learning. Vygotsky saw merit in having all students do some work with more competent peers.

Vygotsky (1978) joined Piaget in rejecting standardized testing as an exclusive procedure to determine intelligence. He believed that educators should go beyond detection of mental age to also link processes of development with learning abilities. To merge development and learning, he maintained that two separate levels of development must be assessed.

The "actual development level" identifies mental capacities, shown by customary intelligence tests, indicating what the individual can do alone without help. However, this awareness should not be the end of assessment. Vygotsky challenged the assumption that the tasks students are able to do by themselves represent the full scope of their abilities. What if, as a result of dialogue with a teacher or tutoring from a more competent classmate, students given questions or shown examples of how to solve problems become able to do so without help or nearly finish tasks on their own? Vygotsky's "potential development level" defines achievements that students can reach with help from others. He maintained that this broader view represented a more suitable index of mental development than only what individuals can accomplish alone (Vygotsky, 1994).

The importance of distinguishing between actual development and potential development is clarified with an example (Vygotsky, 1998). Two students are administered an IQ test. Both of the chronologically aged 10-year-olds obtain scores as being mentally 8 years old. This means they could independently solve problems consistent with the normative degree of difficulty that is dealt with by students 2 years younger than themselves. Generally, since both students had the same IQ, it is assumed that their prospects for learning are similar and it would frustrate them to be exposed to problems higher than their mental age of 8 years. However, in this case, a teacher demonstrates how to solve more difficult problems, invites the students to replicate her examples, arranges for repeated observation of specific steps in the process, asks them to finish the task, encourages reflection on personal logic, and offers guidance as needed. In the end, one student is able, with assistance, to solve problems considered appropriate for 9-year-olds while the other student can do tasks up to the level of 12-year-olds (Vygotsky, 1998).

Because performance of the two students varied to a high degree when given guidance, the expectations for learning as individuals should differ. The *zone of proximal development* is the distance between the actual level of a student's development as assessed by independent problem solving and the level of potential development as found by problem solving with guidance from an adult or in collaboration with more capable peers (Vygotsky, 1994). The zone of proximal development concept shows that learning can lead development. That is, the natural development process lags behind and this sequence results in zones of proximal development that call attention to the importance of tutoring, cooperative learning, dialogue with relatives, and interaction with other out-of-school mentors. Lev Vygotsky Archives explain his wide-ranging work at http://www.marxists.org/archive/vygotsky/index.htm.

A key process linked with the zone of proximal development is known as *scaffolding*, techniques used to adjust guidance to match levels of performance (Reiser, 2004). At the outset, a teacher may use direct instruction to introduce concepts. As the learner becomes more able, a gradual shift occurs so the teacher role centers more on monitoring progress, giving feedback, offering encouragement, and providing minimal correction. Middle school and high school teachers find the zone of proximal development and scaffolding concepts support better instruction. For example, the formal operations content of math and science is cumulative so it presents difficulty for many students. Vygotsky's insights encourage peer teaching and cooperative learning in secondary school because of the greater ability of some students who could tutor others (Cukras, 2006). When students admit that they are completely lost, they communicate a feeling of being outside their zone. When this occurs in a cooperative group, teammates should help a student ask questions so s/he can reconnect again. Otherwise, time will be lost for the learner and the motivation to put forth an effort may decline.

Vygotsky (1994) believed the social context of schooling is essential for special education students. He felt that it is inappropriate to rely on the actual level of development, as shown by test results, as the upper limit for expectations of students with disabilities. Because mentally retarded students perform poorly on abstract thinking measures, educators are inclined to give up on arranging activities for them that require any abstraction in favor of tasks that reflect Piaget's concrete stage of thinking. However, when instruction is limited to concrete experiences, retarded students are prevented from overcoming some limitations.

Vygotsky (1978) also contended that the most influential learning for students with disabilities is the social consequences of rejection by normal classmates who would not behave that way in a more humane society. Forty years after Vygotsky died, the high cost of social exclusion was acknowledged by the Education for All Handicapped Act (1975) as justification for abandoning the long-standing practice of isolating special education students (Kozulin, Gindis, Ageyev, Miller, Pea, Brown, & Heath, 2003). The replacement practice, originally called "mainstreaming," and more recently "inclusion," is considered the best way to encourage acceptance of differences by the normal population while also helping students with disabilities to acquire the social skills they need for adjustment in adult life (Giangreco, 2007).

Emergence of Cyber Constructivism

One premise of constructivism, originated by Piaget and Vygotsky, is that students learn best when allowed to build their own knowledge rather than receive it as ideas told to them by their teachers. Students invent personal theories by assimilating new information into existing schema or modify their understanding by accommodation of novel data. In this section an emerging theory of cyber constructivism is reviewed which is gaining global attention. The power peer influence can have on learning was elaborated by Vygotsky, but no one knows how much students could learn from peers in situations where they lack access to adult supervision. A contemporary theory called minimally invasive education (MIE), offers opportunities for students to learn cooperatively in resource-scarce environments. This context has been the focus of Sugata Mitra, an educational technology professor at New Castle University in England. Before Mitra joined academia in 2006, he was the director of research and development for India's largest software company located in New Delhi. During social gatherings, affluent parents often told him that their children could do computer tasks that the adults saw as complicated and impressive (Mitra, 2003).

Mitra (2005) wondered whether the parent reports were exaggerated, reflecting personal lack of experience with computers. If educated adults underestimate how well their children can perform with little or no training, perhaps disadvantaged youth can attain the same competence. Since children do not ask for or get much instruction on computing, maybe allowing more unsupervised use is a key to accelerating the acquisition of basic skills. To find out, Mitra put a Pentium computer with a fast Internet connection and touch pad within a kiosk located on the wall separating his company from a wasteland that poor people living in an adjacent slum used as an alley. The computer was always left on so any passerby would have a chance to tinker with it. All activity was monitored by a remote computer and video camera mounted in a nearby tree (Mitra 2006).

Most adults glanced at the kiosk without pausing to investigate. In contrast, 80 children from ages 6 to 16 and not enrolled in school, expressed curiosity. Within days, many of them had acquired basic computer literacy skills. Mitra defined basic literacy as the ability to carry out window operation functions like using a mouse, point, drag, drop, copy, and browse the Internet. After 3 months the low-income children had learned to load and save files, play games, run programs, listen to music, set up and access e-mail, chat on the Internet, do troubleshooting, download and play streaming video and games. Disney and Microsoft Paint were the favorite sites because everyone enjoyed drawing but no one had money for the supplies (Mitra, 2006).

When a second kiosk was placed in an illiterate rural village where no one had ever seen a computer, children helped one another gain basic skills. These "Hole in the Wall" projects have expanded to more than 100 sites in impoverished areas that have no schools or teachers. Half of the one billion people in India are illiterate (35% males and 65% females) and one third of the adults earn less than a dollar a day. Only 5 million Indians are connected to the Internet. The cost of setting up a kiosk and maintaining it for a year is about $10,000. On average, 100 children use a kiosk. Mitra's (2003) dream has been to install 100,000 kiosks. He speculates that the outcome would be 10 million more computer literate children who will change India forever by moving themselves toward prosperity.

The theoretical paradigms that merge to support MIE are unstructured collaboration and shared exploration as children use trial and error in opening the door to cyberspace. Because this approach to learning depends on discovery and sharing, working in groups is essential. Children teach one other and regulate the process. The ability to become computer literate in a short time seems independent of formal education, socioeconomic background, gender, ability to read or intelligence. The MIE concept has been adopted by other nations that also have a scarcity of teachers, schools, and hardware. Ninety hole in the wall kiosks have been established in Egypt and there are 10 operating in Cambodia (Mitra, 2006).

Learners tend to divide themselves into "knows" and "know nots." However, there is a recognition that someone who knows will part with his or her knowledge in return for friendship and exchange. The more mature participants, usually older females, commonly insist on proceeding in a civil manner. As a result, everyone enjoys the satisfaction of social experience and chance to learn more rapidly because they imitate one other, spur each other on, and pool their insights. When a group no longer produces breakthroughs, minimal intervention is welcomed from an online teacher who introduces a new skill for youth to use in generating more discoveries on their own Studies have shown that adults in the affected communities believe this method can spread literacy (85%), provide opportunity to learn about computers (80%), improve social cohesion (79%), develop confidence and pride (85%), and improve mental performance (79%) (Mitra, 2005).

These outcomes underscore the potential benefits of exposure to the Internet, the capability of students to accelerate their organization of knowledge by uniting efforts, and need for teachers to present tasks that support opportunities for student practice in collaborative constructivism. The creation of curriculum content is no longer as important as the provision of infrastructure and access to a world of information. Minimally invasive education is a self-structured system that assumes students can construct knowledge on their own. In this paradigm a teacher stands aside and intervenes only when assistance is needed. The custom has been to expect teachers to "make learning happen." Now teachers will be expected to "let learning happen." The distinction between these two expectations is illustrated by reactions of Indian adults. Unlike children, they just started at the kiosk and asked, "What is this for? Why is there no one to teach us something? How will we ever use such a device?" Mitra (2006) explains that, until now, people were taught to want teachers, and believe they cannot learn without them. Once upon a time, in yesterday's world, that was true. To view a video streaming presentation by Mitra as he explains his work, visit http://www.pbs.org/frontlineworld/stories/india/thestory.html. An additional report on how children teach themselves technology skills with the Hole-in-the-Wall experiments can be found at http://www.hole-in-the-wall.com.

Multiple Intelligence Theories

A long-standing controversy over the definition of intelligence has resulted in theories that reveal this aspect of human potential may be far more complex than originally supposed. However, the consequent impression that intelligence is fixed and therefore cannot be altered has been challenged by scholars who argue that IQ tests do not cover the full scope of intelligence. Raymond Cattell (1905–1998) at the University of Illinois thought that the theory of general intelligence (g) formulated by Charles Spearman (1863–1945) overlooked a key distinction between reasoning ability and acquired knowledge. Cattell argued that Spearman (1904) failed to recognize that these two broad factors have different trajectories over the life span. His insights led Cattell (1987) to devise the theory of fluid-crystallized intelligence that identifies particular realms of mental functioning in which cognitive stability and decline are associated with age.

Fluid intelligence is defined as the mechanics of how information is processed including memory capacity, speed of response, problem solving, and spatial ability. Fluid abilities account for a capacity to think and act quickly, solve novel problems, and encode short-term memories. These assets are the source of intelligence that individuals rely on when they do not already know what to do. There is abundant evidence that fluid abilities which are the focus of study in school show improvement during adolescence and then decline. In later life, most of the age-related loss that occurs in mental functioning implicates fluid intelligence as measured by instruments such as the Wechsler Intelligence scale. Memory capacity and problem solving also diminish and are accompanied by a consistent slowing of the capacity to process information as people get older.

Crystallized intelligence is defined as cultural and pragmatic knowledge, enhanced judgment, and experience which are gained through language, interaction, acculturation, and observing the strategies applied by others.

Tests of knowledge, general information, vocabulary, and a wide variety of acquired skills reflect crystallized intelligence. Cattell (1987) observed that, when people become adults, they move away from the kind of achievements featured in the classroom toward more personally relevant and advanced domains of expertise that he suggested should be recognized as intelligences. One of Cattell's students, John Horn (1928–2006) at the University of Southern California, determined that the weight of evidence is against a general factor (g) being responsible for all intelligent behavior (Horn, 1965). Horn extended Cattell's theory and showed how the two different sets of abilities, fluid and crystallized intelligence, have dissimilar trajectories from childhood through the end of life (Horn & Cattell, 1967; McArdle, 2007). For example, in comparison with 25 year olds, persons beyond age 70 show virtually no decline in verbal ability. One estimate is that the average graduate from college possesses half the size vocabulary that s/he will have at the time of retirement (Schaie & Uhlenberg, 2007).

In the emerging longevity society, the education recommended for older adults focuses on tasks that allow them to build on their crystallized intelligence. Similarly, many adolescents believe that their schooling could be enriched by more exposure to experiences they consider relevant for their preparation to enter the workforce. This condition could be met by arranging opportunities to explore careers, finding out directing what the employment sector requires of employees. Such initiative could take the form of work-study, volunteering, and interviewing people at work. School and work can become more integrated by reliance on a better balance of student tasks that emphasize crystallized intelligence along with fluid intelligence so these complimentary strengths can be attained at the same time.

Another theory of multiple intelligence was proposed by Louis Thurstone (1887–1955), President of the American Psychological Association and Professor at the University of North Carolina. Thurstone (1938) observed that before age 11 or 12, mental ability is of a general nature, identified as the *g* factor by Charles Spearman (1904). Later, during early adolescence, specific sub-abilities begin to emerge. The correlations between these capacities become smaller with the passage of years. This means that the building blocks which comprise total intelligence become more distinct and independent from each other (Eysenck & Keane, 2005). According to Thurstone (1938), there are seven distinct mental abilities or intelligences: (1) verbal comprehension, (2) word fluency, (3) use of numbers, (4) spatial visualization, (5) associative memory, (6) perceptual speed, and (7) reasoning skills.

A half-century after Thurstone's observations, the sub-abilities view of intelligence was further elaborated by Howard Gardner (1983, 1996,

2003) from Harvard University. Gardner described *multiple intelligences* (eight of them), and suggested that all students have strength in at least one of these multiple intelligences. Verbal-linguistic and logical-mathematical intelligences are typically valued most in the classroom. Visual-spatial, musical-rhythmic, and bodily-kinesthetic intelligences are associated with the arts. Naturalistic and interpersonal-social intelligences are called personal intelligences.

1. Verbal-linguistic abilities involve speaking, reading and writing skills.
2. Logical-mathematical abilities enable deductive and inductive reasoning.
3. Visual-spatial abilities allow a person to create representations and think in pictures.
4. Musical-rhythmic capacity presents sensitivity to pitch and rhythms of sounds.
5. Bodily-kinesthetic abilities implicate motor skills and graceful movement.
6. Naturalistic abilities allow one to observe patterns in nature and understand human-made systems.
7. Interpersonal-social capacity makes it possible to understand others and work effectively with them.
8. Intrapersonal-introspective abilities allow one to be deeply aware of personal feelings and goals.

In a presentation to the American Educational Research Association, Gardner (2003) reviewed his theory and described how he felt his work had progressed over two decades. To examine Gardner's assumptions, unanticipated obstacles, and the way his ideas have been implemented, visit http://www.infed.org/thinkers/gardner.htm.

The multiple intelligence orientation assumes that all students are not equally endowed with the same capacities for competence in every domain, even when two students record the same IQ score (Gardner, 2003). This distinction is reinforced by sub ability measures like the Differential Aptitude Test. When teachers and parents recognize that a student may be an average performer in mathematics but perform well in language arts, there could be less emphasis on discouragement about the lower marks in mathematics. All students should be helped to gain minimal competencies in the basic subjects. Beyond that, more emphasis could be placed on the pursuit of individual strengths than continually trying to move all students "up to the average" in their weak cognitive areas by placing them in remedial classes (Shearer, 2004). The concentration on areas of student weakness can and often does undermine confidence. Erosion of student self-esteem is a hazard because one of the major developmental tasks of adolescence is the formation of identity.

Teachers are grateful for the transformation in thinking about intelligence. The shift away from a preoccupation with traits such as IQ has fostered an emphasis on a "competencies" view of human ability. Traits are fixed and relatively stable through life and, even though people have enduring tendencies, they are capable of enormous learning and flexibility. Multiple intelligences are increasingly recognized as suitable contexts for training competencies. In effect, educators are becoming more open to determining the potential of individual students rather than judging them based only on their present performance.

Beginning with the seminal research of David McClelland (1987) (described in chapter 3), measurement tools have been devised to assess people in humane and rational ways, instruments that can detect "competencies," the actual and potential ability to behave in specific ways. When desired behaviors such as leadership are reduced to particular elements that define this domain, it is possible to measure and train for the relevant competencies. Instead of trying to identify "born leaders," leadership skills like those that are contained in the Teamwork Skills Inventory (described in chapter 7) become a focus for education. The competencies approach is recognized as appropriate for various aspects of achievement such as stress management, motivation, relationships, parenting, and creativity. The competencies perspective is welcome because it is positive and humane whereas the trait perspective can be wasteful and demeaning.

Voices of Adolescents

In *The Fellowship of the Rings*, the wizard Gandalf declares that everyone has to face the same daunting challenge in life. He points out "All we have to decide is what to do with the time that is given us" (Tolkien, 2003, p. 50). Time management is recognized as a goal that must be achieved to ensure quality of life. People who schedule time so their priorities receive sufficient attention typically feel more in control of their lives, experience greater satisfaction, and have a more productive work record. Parents who schedule too much activity inadvertently prevent themselves from being able to spend enough time with daughters and sons. Many adolescents are as busy as their parents, juggling schedules packed with after school programs, music lessons, and sports. The problem that begins early is reflected by a cartoon in which two young girls are standing at a bus stop, each clutching their personal planner. One girls says,

Okay, I will move ballet back an hour, reschedule my gymnastics session and cancel piano—while you shift your violin lessons to Thursday and skip soccer practice—that gives us from 3:15 to 3:45 on Wednesday the 16th to just hang out together.

It is essential that adolescents acquire the sense of balance that time management skills provide so they are able to avoid taking on too many activities, break promises to others, and ignore the people and activities that matter most to them. The poll for this chapter explores student experience with time management. How do they feel about the start time of first hour classes, spending the same amount of time studying subjects that vary in level of difficulty, and the schedule maintained by the school library and computer center? What do students think about the timing of their tests being scheduled close together, innovative options for attendance, access to educators outside class, and having discretionary time to do whatever they choose? How often do students feel hurried by teachers or family members and over extended with responsibilities? When faculties act as favorable models of time management and consider needs of students, they convey valuable life lessons.

FUNCTIONS OF THE MIND

Information processing theory seeks to explain how learning occurs and identify certain variables that promote and inhibit the acquisition of knowledge. The computer is viewed as the model, a frame of reference that describes how analogous components of the mind and machine function. Significant factors are considered including selective attention, establishing relevance, arranging review, offering feedback, and coordination of assessment schedules. Possibilities for more visual materials to enhance understanding of verbal lessons implicate all teachers. Greater consideration of visual memory also respects the preference of students for increased exposure to media learning.

Information Processing Theory

Information processing theory describes mental functioning, often referring to computers as an analogy to demonstrate how the corresponding elements of both operating systems function (Geary, 2005). Explanations commonly focus on three ways in which computer and their biological counterpart, the brain, appear to act in similar ways.

1. The sensory register (SR) provides input from the environment through our eyes, ears, and sense of touch. Similarly, a computer gets its information from some external source by input devices such as a CD and DVD loader, built-in camera or microphone.

2. Humans possess a short-term memory (STM) referred to as the working memory. Computers contain a random access memory (RAM) which resembles short-term memory of humans in having very limited capacity.

3. Like the long-term memory (LTM) of humans, computers have a hard disk where large amounts of information can be kept and stored for a lengthy period of time.

These similarities seem to suggest that computers and human beings process data in much the same way but this is only partially so. Human memory is transitory while the computer can accommodate information as rapidly as it is received. If someone chooses to increase the speed at which their computer "thinks," they can purchase a more rapid processor. This is not an option for speeding up the brain. The short-term memory of humans can contain only five to nine chunks of information composed of single words, numbers, or a combination. In contrast, it is possible to add RAM to a computer and increase the size of its working memory. Unless the hard disk of a machine crashes, computers never forget anything and have no trouble retrieving information as humans do (Daley & Wood, 2006).

Humans and computers appear reliant on similar processing elements. However, the use of these elements is quite different. Humans are able to multi-task, to think of multiple thoughts at the same time and perform a variety of activities all at once. Humans can also be sensitive to nonverbal visual cues like a smile, frown or tears while computers lack this capacity. Humans can be intuitive, emotional, creative, and inventive whereas computers are limited to following their programmed instruction (Cowan, Naveh-Benjamin, Kilb, & Sautts, 2006).

On the other hand, each component of a computer and aspect of the mind have particular functions that must be carried out efficiently so the system as a whole can operate at a high level of performance. When any of the processing components malfunction, effectiveness of the entire system is threatened by causing a significant loss in productivity and readiness to carry out expectations (Radvansky, 2005; Uttal, 2005). Teachers should be aware of how humans process, store, and retrieve information because the mission of schools is to equip students with skills, knowledge, and understanding required for success in the workplace, home, and community.

Figure 4.2 shows that learning is a progression of knowledge transformations beginning with input (stimuli) from the environment and concluding with output (student response) or information storage in the long-term memory. A beginning task for students is to filter incoming stimuli from what is seen, heard or felt within the sensory register. The amount of information students are exposed to at any one time can be enormous (Driscoll, 2004). This underscores the importance of *selective attention* to ensure that concentration is focused on just one aspect of incoming stimuli. Being able to attend to the most relevant data while ignoring stimuli that are less pertinent can be difficult in a media environment where there are lots of distractions (Gordon, 2006; Lozito & Mulligan, 2006).

Multitasking presents difficulties for selective attention. To illustrate, a student is having a cell phone conversation while paying for a magazine at the store and reading the horizontal line for CNN news on the television screen located above the cashier. Students continually participate in multi-tasking while on the computer. Some individuals poorly manage the complexity of dealing with simultaneous tasks, others overestimate the number of things they can do well at the same time, and still others admit to being distracted during Internet searches when attempting to follow links but lose their concentration. The prevalence of these and other obstacles means that finding ways to anchor attention and concentration of students are major instructional concerns. Selective attention is the perceptual process that implies having a specific goal, content to attend to while excluding unrelated stimuli (Posner, 2004).

Information for selective attention temporarily shifts from the sensory-register to short-term memory, called working memory (Baddeley, 1997, 1999). Unlike the expandable memory (RAM) of a computer, human *short-term memory* capacity is extremely limited and can retain information including just 5 to 9 ideas digits for about 30 seconds (Miller, 1956). This limitation is shown when you try to remember a number to call that you have just read in a phone book and will no longer need (Orey, McClendon, & Branch, 2006). The familiar rehearsal process and interference effects are shown in a streaming video on the Web site of Michael Orey at University of Georgia http://projects.coe.uga.edu/epltt/index.php?title=information_processing.

Sensory impressions are not stored in their original form. Before data is retained, it must be transformed. *Encoding* is the step by which data is recast into codes, symbols or representations for manipulation of meaning. Encoding, recoding, and decoding are accomplished by continuous transactions between the long-term and short-term memory (Parker, Wilding, & Bussey, 2002). Long-term memory knows the categories and organizational structures that must be applied for placement of knowl-

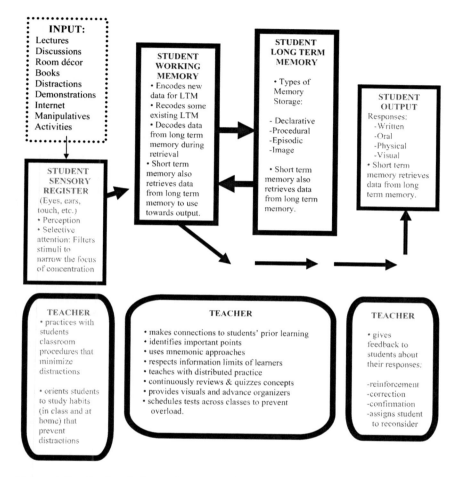

Figure 4.2. Student information processing and teacher actions.

edge. Accordingly, the short-term memory gets directions from the long-term memory about how new information should be converted into symbolic form to create meaning and ensure retrieval. Learning occurs when encoded information is transferred from short-term to long-term memory, the site of permanent storage analogous to the computer disk and hard drive. This secure placement means information is relatively accessible, usually on demand. *Long-term memory* performs two vital functions-- it directs the information processing system and stores coded material based on past experience and previous knowledge (Thorn & Page, 2008).

Opinions vary about the length of time information can be retained in long-term memory. Being able to recall information and having the ability to recover it within a reasonable period is often regarded as depending more on the retrieval strategies than on forgetting or deterioration of stored memories (Kandel, 2006). The information stored in long-term memory is everything that we know and know how to do. There are several types of memory. *Declarative memory* stores information we can declare such as the date and place of our birth and other facts, concepts, rules, principles or paradigms. People generally communicate using these common frames of reference. *Procedural memory* consists of the actions that we know how to perform such as driving a car or operating a computer. The domains of declarative memory and procedural memory account for most of the instruction and curriculum students are expected to learn in school (Pickering, 2005). *Episodic memory* is another domain that contains personal experiences that have happened over a lifetime. These memories can include events that occurred a long time ago such as when we got our first bicycle, met our spouse, and where we were during the national tragedy of 9/11/01 (Mayr, Awh, Keele, & Posner, 2005).

The series of knowledge transformations between initial sensory impressions and learning culminate in generation of a response, some physical movement, speech or thought. The resulting performance like being able to write or state a correct answer can be observed. Responses are confirmed or allowed to lapse, depending on the feedback received. Information processing ends with confirmation that a particular lesson is learned. Teacher feedback has a vital reinforcement effect that enables student knowledge to become more retrievable.

Critics of information processing maintain that what advocates see as strengths of this theoretical design, reducing the process of thinking into component parts, is actually its greatest shortcoming. This criticism suggests that a reductionism approach underestimates complexity of the human mind. In addition, the assumption that human cognition and operation of computers correspond in how all data is processed ignores the powerful impact of vision and emotions as major determinants of our behavior (Balcetis & Dunning, 2006). Granting these limitations, information processing theory presents clues to teachers about how learning occurs and what can be done to arrange more effective instruction.

Teaching for Comprehension

Teachers facilitate learning by applying methods that support information processing (see Figure 4.2, Student Information Processing and Teacher Actions). Knowing how to promote student attention is a priority (Driscoll, 2004). Selective attention can be protected when external distractions are minimized by orienting students to rules about leaving the classroom, tardiness, sharpening pencils, transition between and following lessons, turning in work, and arranging to retrieve directions for assignments missed because of an absence. When these procedures are understood, students can perform tasks without reducing concentration of peers, interrupting instruction, undermining collaboration, or denying reflective thinking of their classmates. Even distractions such as intercom announcements from the administration and minor discipline issues should be dealt with in ways that prevent sacrifice of attention from learning (Alexander, 2005).

Another obstacle to selective attention is poor study habits. Many students multi-task while studying by participating in other activities such as cooking, listening to music, watching television, chatting with friends, and surfing the Internet. These behaviors become dysfunctional when they interfere with the concentration needed to complete schoolwork. For example, some individuals benefit from listening to music because it provides a rhythm for their study. However, concentration is limited using these stimuli. Students should be challenged by teachers to monitor their progress in reading, writing, and studying under varied conditions to identify the situations that support or detract from comprehension. Some students can study with noise while others are easily set off course or require a longer time and produce less when they multitask. For persons easily distracted by noise, earplugs can help as can finding a quiet place to study where conversations or outside sounds are not bothersome (Alexander, 2005).

Elaboration is the process of adding support data to the understanding of students. This occurs when teachers make a continuous effort to clarify relationship between prior learning and how current lessons add to the knowledge that is essential for retention. These efforts increase the likelihood that students make connections across concepts and can transfer new information to their long-term memory (Gagné & Medsker, 1996). The significance of creating connections to prior knowledge so that students could perceive lessons as practical and important was described long ago by David Ausubel (1968), a psychology professor from the University of Illinois. Ausubel observed, "If I had to reduce all of educational psychology to just one principle, I would say the most important factor influencing learning is what the learner already knows. Find this out and then teach him accordingly." The organization and strength of already existing cognitive structures are the most prominent factors that govern meaningfulness of new material and efficiency of acquisition and rote. When adults are asked to identify teachers that helped them most, they usually select individuals who created connections between prior understanding and the new lesson being taught. In this way new information can be encoded effectively when related to familiar concepts.

Mnemonic devices are strategies teachers provide to assist with data retrieval from memory storage (Hwang & Levin, 2002). For example, the order of eight planets in our solar system, starting closest to the sun, are easier to remember when related to the sequence of words in this sentence "Man very early made jars serve useful needs." In translation, this means the order of the eight planets are Mercury, Venus, Earth, Mars, Jupiter, Saturn, Uranus, and Neptune.

The processing load of learners is respected when teachers rely on appropriate instruction practices and methods of assessment. Observers express concern about information overload for students who do not get enough support for organizing and processing large amounts of material. This problem becomes more complicated when teachers regard direct instruction as the only way to cover a large amount of material required in a course. This choice ignores the possibility to put some material on a Web site or podcast so that students can listen or watch as their homework. The monotony of direct instruction students identify as a cause of boredom can also be reduced by including one or more activities of at least five to ten minutes in length per class session that support active learning. The use of cooperative learning structures that encourage review and rehearsal of information can improve comprehension (Love, 2005; Roseth, Johnson, & Johnson, 2008).

Respect for information processing limits also implicates the methods of assessment used by teachers. *Distributed practice* allows students time to comfortably revisit ideas over several days or weeks in order to establish understanding. During this interval, the teacher reviews prior lessons, arranges team study, gives short quizzes, and provides feedback. Distributed practice is recommended because research has determined that it results in greater retention. Nevertheless, the dominant approach is *massed practice*, where students cram information from several classes into a one or two night review before final examinations. When the tests are finished, much of the information is quickly forgotten. The appeal of distributed practice is that material is reviewed at home the same day as presented in class on a continuous basis until the time of final examination so cramming becomes unnecessary. When material is revisited in reasonable amounts, students can rehearse several times as they review concepts and get feedback from a teacher. This strategy enables everyone to perform better on big tests because the course content has been taught and systematically reviewed in advance. Test study guides, provided a week or more ahead of time, help inform students of material to concentrate on when the course content is broad (Alexander, 2005; Sweller, 2003).

The use of massed practice is observed often when one or two large high stakes tests are given in a semester forcing an information overload that overwhelms slow learners and perhaps average students. In contrast, distributed practice favors scheduling three or four moderate sized tests augmented by brief quizzes. A similar problem occurs across courses. Final tests in all subjects are scheduled in the same week at many schools. A more reasonable strategy, based on research, is to coordinate test scheduling so no student has more than one examination over several days and can be better prepared (Brown, Anfara, & Roney, 2004). A common reason that high school students give for cheating is that too many tests and final projects are due at the same time.

Unless teachers use distributed practice, students experience an overload of material without deep processing, feel a keen sense of undue stress and memory interference across courses. These factors can contribute to a higher incidence of cheating. Effective school wide instructional practices based on empirical findings about information processing should be implemented. The faculty can facilitate better study habits by applying distributed practice and develop a coordinated testing schedule.

Memory for Visual Information

In addition to declarative, procedural, and episodic memory, there is also an *image memory* for visual materials. Studies have found that memory for pictures is far greater than memory for words. Shepard (1967, 1990) presented 600 pictures to students. When they were tested immediately following their observation, students correctly identified 98% of the pictures. A week later they were still able to accurately identify over 85% of the pictures. Similar results have been obtained in studies on recognition of visual information involving photographs and faces (Adams & Hamm, 2006; Standing, Conezio, & Haber, 1970). Comparison of text and oral presentations versus pictorial presentations have determined that visuals are always more effective. When information is given orally, people recall about 10% when tested three days after exposure. The recall rate rises to 65% if a picture or visual element is added (Medina, 2008).

So great is the advantage of visual memory that it has been designated as the pictorial superiority effect (Brockmole, 2008). This distinction had less relevance before the Internet introduced a broad range of visual resources. Given the enormous selection available from United Streaming, YouTube, and other Web sites, educators should incorporate visuals to optimize learning. The shift should include a place for three dimensional conversation tools such as Google's Lively that provides cartoon like avatars for chat rooms. Users can choose from handsome or

Disney-like characters, create their own rooms with up to 20 occupants, and post a blog or social network profile as easily as a YouTube video. Similar, 3D chat rooms like Vivaty run on Facebook and other sites.

This superiority of pictures for memory tasks is considered in the dual coding theory of information processing. This theory proposes that human long-term memory contains two distinct and interdependent codes, one verbal and the other visual based (Clark & Paivio, 1991; Kobayashi, 1986; Paivio, 1971, 1990, 1991, 2006; Sadoski & Paivio, 2001). The assumption is that the two codes produce additive effects so if data is coded visually as well as verbally, the probability of retrieval doubles. Another assumption is that the ways pictures and words activate the two codes are different. Pictures are more likely to be stored visually as well as verbally (Farah, 2000). For example, someone might recall the title of a particular book and be able to remember the color or image of the cover. Words alone are less likely to be stored visually. When it comes to memory, two codes seem better than one (Feinberg & Keenan, 2005).

Teachers can increase the probability that information will be dual encoded for long-term memory with a consequent improvement of retention, retrieval and transfer. Dual coding is more likely when lessons are partially presented by using imagery, graphics, visual networking of information, and spatial mapping (Orey, McClendon, & Branch, 2006). Graphic organizers such as webbing, concept mapping matrix, flow charts, and Venn diagrams help to illustrate, describe, compare, classify, and sequence concepts. Some benefits of graphic organizers and other visual procedures that support information processing can be examined at http://graphic.org/goindex.html.

Then too, students should more often be referred to observation of streaming videos. A teacher's Web site can include advance organizers outlining daily lessons in words or notes and use visual symbols and charts that draw connections between concepts (Adams & Hamm, 2006; Rock, 2004).

INSIGHTS FROM NEUROSCIENCE

Cognition refers to the range of mental processes such as thinking, perceiving, imagining, speaking, acting, planning, and remembering. *Cognitive neuroscience* explains particular mental processes in relation to brain-based mechanisms. The research technology tools often applied include magnetic resonance imaging (MRI), computerized tomography (CT), and positron emission tomography (PET). Discoveries of when brain growth spurts occur, timing required for maturity of the brain, explanations for how adolescents differ from grownups in judgment and emotional control present insights for educators. Adolescents usually go to bed later than their parents and prefer to get up later than is expected of them. This biological pattern can produce family conflict and require student effort to remain awake for early morning classes. The powerful impact that sleep deprivation has on readiness to learn, information processing, organization of thinking, consolidation of memory, and grades implicate student achievement and cooperative efforts by schools and families (Medina, 2008).

Brain Functioning in Adolescence

MRI experiments have led neuroscientists to conclude that the brain does not become mature during adolescence. This contradicts a previous assumption that the billions of neurons which constitute brain hardware are fully connected by puberty (Ward, 2006). Instead, studies have revealed that neural connections required for optimal information processing might not be fully installed until 20 to 25 years of age (Calvin, 2004; Uttal, 2005). Further, regions of the brain mature at different rates. Two regions that seem relatively delayed in development involve use of judgment and control of emotions (Tancredi, 2005). This uneven rate of growth could partially explain the inclination of adolescents to more often take unreasonable risks than adults, seek novelty and sensation, and to exhibit sudden shifts in mood from being joyful one moment to feelings of depression minutes later.

The *limbic system,* deep within the brain, is the source of strong feelings and instinctive emotional reactions (Damasio, 2003; LeDoux, 2002). These affective responses are mediated and restricted by the prefrontal cortex located behind the forehead. The executive functions that are performed by the *prefrontal cortex* include deciding how to handle ambiguous information, weighing evidence, and closing down or prolonging expression of instinctive emotions generated by the limbic system (Firlik, 2007). This arrangement works well for most adults but not for adolescents who have a less mature brain. For example, at Harvard University, Deborah Yurgelun-Todd (2005) showed 18 adults and 16 adolescents photographs of human faces, all expressing fear. Every adult was able to identify the emotion portrayed in each picture. In contrast, 11 of 16 teenagers made errors, sometimes interpreting fear as discomfort or anger.

To determine regions of the brain that were active when interpreting the photographs, magnetic resonance imaging provided a picture of mental activity every three seconds. When adults observed the portrait of frightened persons, their limbic system and prefrontal cortex lobes lit up showing both as active. In a similar way the limbic system lit up for teenagers but their prefrontal cortex remained dark. The adolescents relied more on the primitive emotional center of their brain and less on the more rational frontal lobes than did the adults. To benefit from an interview with Deborah Yurgelun-Todd titled "Inside the Teenage Brain," see   http://www.pbs.org/wgbh/pages/frontline/shows/teenbrain/interviews todd.html.

Yurgelun-Todd's findings have been corroborated by Jay Giedd (2004, 2008) at the National Institute for Mental Health. The longitudinal project he began in 1989 includes 2,000 subjects who visit NIHM at 2-year intervals for brain imaging, neuropsychological and behavioral assessment and collection of DNA. Of these subjects, about 400 who are aged 3 to 27 years, have remained free of psychopathology and serve as models for typical brain development. Giedd relies on an MRI that shows brain structure instead of brain activity for charting normal brain growth from childhood through adolescence. Over 1,000 subjects from ages 3 to 18 have been required to remain still for 10 minutes while their brain image was computerized. The initial hypothesis was that, after puberty, the adolescent brain would resemble the adult brain. Instead, it was discovered that, at age 9 or 10, a growth spurt occurs in the prefrontal cortex with a formation of new *synapses*, points of connection between neurons. Extra neural connections die off around age 12 so that the brain can nourish only useful neurons. The process of eliminating connections, known as *pruning*, has a different time table for separate brain regions and contributes to greater efficiency of cognitive processing. This important shift is the subject of "Adolescent Brains are Works in Progress" at http://www.pbs.org/wgbh/ pages/frontline/shows/teenbrain/work/adolescent.html.

Before the prefrontal cortex is fully developed, adolescents lack the cognitive power that is needed to render good judgment in many situations. It is suspected that excess synapses could prevent them from keeping track of multiple thoughts and obstruct a ready access to the essential memories and emotions that enable most adults to reach better decisions. Good judgment must be learned but it cannot be acquired until the necessary brain hardware is in place. An unfinished prefrontal cortex might also account for why it is often difficult for adolescents to organize multiple tasks and decide the order in which to do things when obliga- tions include checking e-mail, cleaning the bedroom, and reading an assignment for tomorrow's class (Medina, 2008; Goldberg, 2001).

Neurologists at the University of Chicago discovered that the cortex of children contains twice the number of synaptic connections as for adults (Kandel, 2006). Extra connections in the child brain would require more energy reflected by higher metabolic rates. Data suggest that, the pruning process in early adolescence results in a functional stabilization of the brain and lower demands for energy. An additional factor for consideration has emerged from measurement of sleep patterns for all age groups. These studies at the State University of New York show that children from 2 to 10 years old recorded twice as much deep sleep as did adults. However, deep sleep declined by 50% between ages 11 and 14. It would seem that the more metabolically active child requires greater amounts of deep sleep. Conversely, if the adolescent brain has fewer synaptic connections, less sleep would seem necessary. The dynamic of this shift and some implications for schooling is a focus of sleep and cognition research (Goldberg, 2001).

Family and School Support for Sleep

Growth spurts and fashion crazes are not the only signs that signal onset of adolescence. Changing sleep patterns are markers as well. Everyone's need for sleep is governed by a circadian timing system in the brain. This system regulates the production of melatonin, a sleep-inducing chemical responsible for setting the biological clock that lets us know the natural time for going to bed and getting up (Fogel, Nader, Cote, & Smith, 2007). Prior to adolescence, the circadian clock directs elementary students to fall asleep about 8 or 9 at night. However, the clock changes at puberty, delaying the time when adolescents start to feel sleepy by around 2 hours and urging them to sleep longer in the morning (Hobson, 2005). At Brown University, physiologist Mary Carskadon (1990, 2002, 2005) has explored how lack of sleep affects mental and physical skills. For a long time the speculation was that older students need less sleep than elementary school students. However, Carskadon discovered that adolescents require as much sleep as they did in childhood. From puberty until the early 20s, nine or more hours of sleep a night is regarded as optimal. The reason hypothesized is that hormones critical for growth and sexual maturation are released mostly during sleep (Carskadon, 2005). An interview with Mary Carskadon ("Insight the Teenage Brain") is recommended for teachers, administrators, nurses, teenagers and parents at http://www.pbs.org/wgbh/pages/frontline/shows/teenbrain/interviews/carskadon.html.

An important implication of these findings is that the average teenager's brain is not ready to wake up until 8 or 9 in the morning, well after most schools begin the day (Carskadon, Acebo, & Jenni, 2004; Wolfson & Carskadon, 2005). Unlike young children and adults, adolescents show elevated levels of melatonin in the morning. In effect, their brain informs them that it is still night despite an opposite announcement from the alarm clock or parents. Teachers report that, during the first hour class at school, many students doze off and seem unable to pay attention or concentrate (Wahlstrom, 2002). Those that are sleep-deprived try to compensate by micro sleep in the daytime. However, micro sleep is not a restorative process. On a broader scale, the risk of sleep-related car accidents is compounded because people cannot accurately judge the likelihood that they will fall asleep and suppose this is a slow process. In fact, sleep-deprived people often fall asleep for brief episodes lasting several seconds, during which they are perceptually blind (Saper, Scammell, & Lu, 2005).

When 3,000 Rhode Island adolescents kept a diary of their sleep patterns, the majority reported less than 7 hours sleep a night. Two-thirds reported that bedtime was 11 P.M. or later on school nights, even though they had to get up at 6:30 A.M. Students who struggle and doze during the day become energetic and are stimulated in the evening, often staying up past midnight (Wolfson & Carskadon, 2005). Many teenagers depend on caffeinated beverages to compensate for lack of sleep and remain attentive.

Adolescents begin their day before the biological clock goes off so they are denied access to the sleep stage that contributes most to memory and learning. During sleep the brain enters a stage involving rapid eye movement (REM) during which eyes can be seen to move back and forth under the lids. A common hypothesis is that during REM the brain resets chemicals in the emotional centers and clears short-term memory banks where current events are temporarily stored. Persons deprived of REM sleep have difficulty getting along with others and more often report depression. Experiments to induce REM deprivation have shown that, after lacking REM sleep for 2 days, people are disorientated and cannot function well (Hobson, 2005). Without sufficient REM activity, memory and judgment are impaired and reaction time for performance is poor (Fogel, Nader, Cote, & Smith, 2007). Studies reveal that teenagers who get less sleep than classmates who have ample rest earn lower grades and are more likely to have discipline problems (Wolfson & Carskadon, 2005).

The National Sleep Foundation (2006a) surveyed 1,600 households where respondents included one parent and one adolescent between 11 to 17 years of age. The findings suggest that many teenagers are practicing behaviors that disadvantage them at school and in their social life.

- Only 20% of the adolescents reported getting nine hours of sleep each night.
- Feeling too tired or sleepy to do any kind of exercise was expressed by 28%.
- Falling asleep in the classroom at least once a week involved 28% of students.
- Arriving late or missing school because they overslept was a problem for 14%.

- Many teenagers (31%) believe they may have a sleep problem but have told no one.

- Only 7% of the parents believe that their adolescent might be sleep deprived.

- Most parents and teens think teens have to stay up late to study and be successful.

- Students with A and B grades get more sleep than students receiving poorer grades.

A practical response to student sleep deprivation could be rescheduling the school day by starting and ending classes later. Field-testing of this solution was the focus of a five-year study of 7,000 high school students in Minneapolis where school start times of 7:30 were moved back to 8:40 (Wahlstrom, 2002). Results showed that, compared with students in schools where the usual schedule was retained, students with later start times reported more sleep on school nights, being less sleepy in the day, getting higher grades, and feeling depressed less often. School records and faculty identified improvements in attendance, daytime alertness, less irritability, higher tolerance for frustration, and less reliance on caffeine and nicotine stimulants. Similar outcomes have been found in Arlington, Virginia, and Wilton, Connecticut. More than 100 school districts have adopted later school start times and 17 states are considering this option (Carskadon, 2005; National Sleep Foundation, 2006b). The National Sleep Foundation Web site provides Videos about sleep and lifestyle http://www.sleepfoundation.org.

Sleep and Memory Consolidation

Some researchers theorize that sleep plays a crucial role in the organization of learning that occurs during the day. This process called *memory consolidation* refers to memory traces that are processed during sleep with earlier learning replayed and rehearsed while memory circuits become more firmly established. This is the conclusion of Robert Stickgold (1998, 2005), a neuroscientist at Harvard University. He taught adolescent participants a visual discrimination task before testing them. Several hours later the subjects were tested again. No improvement was made when retesting took place the same day as training. However, when allowed to sleep at least six hours after training and before retesting, most subjects showed progress on the visual discrimination task. Occurrence of sleep, not passage of time, made the difference. Sleep deprivation for even one night was found to permanently offset consolidation of memory. People kept awake for 30 hours following training showed no progress on a task, even after allowed two nights of restorative rest. The extent of improvement directly related to amount of slow wave and REM sleep during a total night cycle. The amount of sleep during these two phases accounted for 80% of the differences in task improvement among participants. The strong positive correlation between amount of sleep and a behavioral measure of learning was unexpected (Stickgold & Hobson, 2000; Stickgold, 2005).

What happens that is so important during the first night of sleep after learning? Steffin Gais at University of Lubeck in Germany tried to detect the processes responsible for sleep-related improvement. He compared the effects of late night sleep, occurring from 3 to 5 A.M., which is dominated by REM activity, and full night sleep, dominated by slow-wave patterns. Discrimination skills of participants significantly improved following a full night's sleep but did not improve after late night sleep alone. Whereas a full night of sleep appeared necessary for optimal improvement, slow wave sleep appears more valuable than has been supposed. Late night sleep only, dominated by REM activity, was insufficient for memory improvement (Gais, Plihal, Wagner, & Born, 2000). Stickgold and Luskin (2001) had adolescents participate in Terris, a computer game, for 7 hours over 3 days. When awakened each night soon after falling asleep, 75% of teenagers reported experiencing visual images of Terris, suggesting that their brain was continuing to address problems posed by the game. Stickgold (2005) explains that this is what "sleeping on a problem" is about.

Pierre Marquet (2000) found that areas of the brain activated while people learned a serial reaction time task were also significantly more active later in REM sleep than was the case among non-trained subjects. This means that the customary information processing portrayal of memory functioning as short and long-term storage should expand to include learning from experience, reorganizing the day's thinking during sleep, and building new constructs. When sleep is seen as a creative learning process that enables extrapolation and processing of events in new ways, perhaps better sleep arrangements will be adopted by adolescents and adults (Coltheart, 2004; Stickgold, 2005).

The assumption that successful people can get by with a few hours of sleep and that this activity is mostly a waste of time are misconceptions that reduce productivity and threaten health. Schools currently inform adolescents about the benefits of exercise, nutrition, and the need to avoid drugs. This strategy should include messages about the relationship between sleep and cognitive functioning.

SUMMARY

Perspectives of Intelligence

Intelligence testing, devised by Alfred Binet, is generally the method used for making decisions about special education or accelerated learning. Determining readiness for learning also implicates the cognitive development level governing kinds of thinking students should be expected to perform. Jean Piaget's qualitative view of intelligence has influenced curriculum so school tasks correspond with student stage of thinking.

Lev Vygotsky's zone of proximal development challenges setting academic expectations based solely on intelligence testing. Instead, his equation for learning includes recognition of how social interaction affects achievement. He maintained that what students can achieve on their own and what they can accomplish with help from others should be combined in estimating capacity for learning. During adolescence intelligence is transformed from a general ability to specialized sub abilities. Howard Gardner identifies eight intelligences and urges greater support for all of them.

Functions of the Mind

Information processing theory describes learning by using an analogy of how computer components operate in relation to corresponding functions of the human mind. Stimuli from the environment are provided via the sensory register of eyes, ears, and touch. When data arrives in the short-term memory, called the working memory, they can be held for about half a minute. In response to transactions between the long-term memory and working memory, information is transformed by symbolic encoding that provides interpretation, gives meaning, and categorizes data for transfer to storage in long term memory.

Student decisions about information to accept, transform, and store can be facilitated by instruction. Students benefit from teachers who help maintain selective attention with effective classroom management. Making connections between how new concepts are related to previous knowledge also supports comprehension. Reviews, giving timely feedback, and allowing rehearsal by quizzes are helpful techniques. Coordination of testing schedules to allow preparation time could prevent cramming and plagiarism.

The images memory is far greater than is memory for words. Dual information processing theory suggests that memory coded visually and verbally increases retrieval. Teachers can respect student preference for merging visuals and audio by incorporation of note taking support that uses graphic organizers, concept maps, and flow charts to assist in organizing and linking ideas, providing comparisons, and recognizing steps in a process being learned.

Because electronically stored data can be accessed more efficiently than human memory storage, some observers believe it is time to de-emphasize the prominence of memory as an aspect of learning. On the contrary, reliance on memory remains essential because of our continued need to recall: (1) key terms and concepts that enable mutual understanding, communication, planning, and cooperation; (2) correct sequence of the steps needed to carry out established processes. For example, to create a word file, it is necessary to use word software, choose a blank file, save the file by giving it a title that can be found on the desktop or include it in a folder of documents; (3) ideas that can be brought together for the purpose of enlarging perspective; and (4) combining data into novel configurations to figure out better ways of doing things.

Insights From Neuroscience

When children become adolescents, at the time of puberty, their brain is still not mature. Neural circuitry remains incomplete until age 20 to 25. There is also variance in maturity rates of separate regions in the brain, with the greatest lag involving judgment and control of emotions. This relative delay impacts decision making and may explain the greater inclination of teenagers than other groups to take unreasonable risks and demonstrate sudden polar mood shifts. The unfinished prefrontal cortex where decision making takes place may account for why teens are perplexed when faced with organizing a sequence of tasks to do first, later, and last.

Generally, adolescents sleep 7 hours or less a night. However, they need 9 hours from age 10 until the early 20s. As a result, significant sleep deficits are common. Many students are not fully awake when their classes begin. During first hour many students are less attentive or ready to concentrate. Teenagers who get less sleep than classmates getting ample rest tend to earn lower grades and are more likely to have discipline problems. Schools with later start times report that students get more sleep, are less sleepy during the day, get higher grades and less often feel depressed. The emerging knowledge linking sleep and learning should be carefully considered by schools and families.

CLASSROOM APPLICATIONS

1. Instructional planning should balance direct instruction and active learning. This strategy can prevent boredom, stimulate motivation, allow teamwork, and encourage higher order thinking.

2. Teachers can support retention with distributed practice allowing time to comfortably learn material in reasonable amounts, review daily lessons as homework, and revisit key terms in class. Distributed testing practice permits students to rehearse small amounts of learning and prepare for big tests.

3. Faculties should acknowledge the need to replace massed practice with distributed practice for final examinations. Teachers can develop a coordinated test schedule that gives students time to prepare for each examination reflecting what has been learned in a course.

4. Middle school and high school curriculum involve formal operations. However, given the variance in qualitative thinking, lessons should include formats allowing concrete thinkers to gain understanding and skills expected of the entire class.

5. Students think more abstractly and at higher levels of the Taxonomy of Educational Objectives when projects present disequilibrium. For example, they benefit from tasks that challenge them to accommodate new ways of thinking by temporarily abandoning existing notions to solve problems using another paradigm.

6. Students can learn from assignments in their upper zone of proximal development that require getting help from peers. These activities confirm teamwork as a way to solve problems that individuals may not be able to carry out alone.

7. Students should be encouraged to do their best and recognize that, for most persons, performance varies across courses that feature different intelligences. They may perform better in some subjects. Recognition of assets helps in decision making about careers.

8. Long term memory for visual images often surpasses retention for verbal material. Therefore, presentation of lessons can be more effective if teachers incorporate visual images like graphic organizers, concept maps, Venn diagrams flow charts and symbols that make it easier to remember curriculum content.

9. Help students maintain selective attention by routines that minimize disruption and interference. If teachers apply principles of classroom management, students are able to concentrate and complete assignments expected of them.

10. Information processing is enhanced by frequent review of concepts, taking quizzes with feedback, and linking lessons with prior knowledge. Teacher planning is a key in scheduling time so students participate in these aspects of information processing.

11. The extent to which students can influence learning for one another is unknown. However, evidence from resource-scarce environments using minimally invasive education (MIE) suggests that educators underestimate the potential of peer support and should consider new ways to take advantage of this powerful force for learning.

FOR REFLECTION

1. What guidelines can be drawn from Piaget's cognitive development theory and Gardner's multiple intelligences theory to support student thinking about careers?

2. What are some things teachers can do to help students more efficiently process information and become more able to retrieve relevant memories?

3. Identify and describe a theory of learning that makes the most sense to you and appears most useful based on the grade and subject you intend to teach.

4. How could teachers of first hour classes adjust their methods to deal with difficulties that occur because many adolescents are not fully awake?

5. What neuroscience findings do you think schools should communicate to secondary students and parents for family discussions?

6. What changes do you recommend in how gifted and talented students are educated that will better prepare them for leadership roles as adults?

7. What are some aspects of Lev Vygotsky's views about learning and its support in the classroom that you find appealing and other aspects you find problematic?

8. How has the concept of intelligence and its assessment evolved and what have been the main effects on how schools provide instruction for adolescent learners?

KEY TERMS

Accommodation
Actual Development Level
Assimilation
Cognition
Cognitive Neuroscience
Concrete Operations
Constructivism
Crystallized Intelligence
Declarative Memory
Disequilibrium
Distributed Practice
Dual Coding Theory
Elaboration
Encoding
Episodic Memory
Equilibration
Experimental Reasoning
Fluid Intelligence
Formal Operations
Gifted and Talented
Historical Time
Idealistic Egocentrism
Image Memory
Imaginary Audience
Information Processing Theory
Intelligence Quotient (IQ)
Limbic System
Long-term Memory
Massed Practice
Memory Consolidation
Metacognition
Mildly Retarded
Minimally Invasive Education
Mnemonic Devices
Multiple Intelligences

Normal Distribution Curve
Potential Development Level
Prefrontal Cortex
Procedural Memory
Propositional Thinking
Pruning
Scaffolding
Schemas
Selective Attention
Short-term Memory
Standard Deviation
Synapses
Zone of Proximal Development

VISIT THESE WEB SITES

Link to these sites at http://www.infoagepub.com/strom-adolescents

Alfred Binet Method of Testing
http://psychclassics.yorku.ca/Binet/binet1.htm

Alfred Binet and Lewis Terman, Human Intelligence,
Biographical Profiles http://www.indiana.edu/~intell

Mary Carskadon, Teen Brain and Sleep
http://www.pbs.org/wgbh/pages/frontline/shows/teenbrain/interviews/
carskadon.html

Howard Gardner, Multiple Intelligences and Education
http://www.infed.org/thinkers/gardner.htm

Graphic Organizers   http://graphic.org/goindex.html

Hole-in-the-Wall, Sugata Mitra http://www.hole-in-the-wall.com

Sugata Mitra, The Story—Hole-in-the-Wall
http://www.pbs.org/frontlineworld/stories/india/thestory.html

National Health Museum http://www.accessexcellence.org

National Sleep Foundation http://www.sleepfoundation.org

Michael Orey, Information processing
http://projects.coe.uga.edu/epltt/
index.php?title=information_processing

Jean Piaget Society http://www.piaget.org/links.html

Public Broadcasting System, Adolescent Brains are Works in Progress
http://www.pbs.org/wgbh/pages/frontline/shows/teenbrain/work/
adolescent.html

Lev Vygotsky Archive
http://www.marxists.org/archive/vygotsky/index.htm

Deborah Yugelun-Todd, Inside the Teen Brain
http://www.pbs.org/wgbh/pages/frontline/shows/teenbrain/interviews/
todd.html

EXERCISES AND ROLES

Exercise 4.01: Time Management Poll

Role: Voter

The purpose of this poll is to find out the time management experiences of students at your school. Time management can influence conditions of learning in favorable and unfavorable ways.

Directions: For each item, select the answers(s) that show how you feel. In some cases, you may select more than one answer. If an answer you want to give is not listed, write it on the line marked 'other.' Your responses are anonymous and may be combined with those of other students at your school in a report to students, faculty, and parents.

1. I could learn better if my school classes began at

   (a) 7 A.M.
   (b) 8 A.M.
   (c) 9 A.M.
   (d) 10 A.M.
   (e) other

2. I would benefit from a different schedule that allowed

   (a) more time in mathematics than other subjects
   (b) more time in English than other subjects
   (c) more time in Science than other subjects
   (d) more time in History than other subjects
   (e) other

3. All teachers work the same amount of time; it would be better if some teachers

  (a) came to school earlier or stayed later
  (b) were available after classes were over
  (c) were available during some evenings
  (d) were available on certain weekends
  (e) other

4. I would prefer the computer lab and library to be open

  (a) when classes are done
  (b) during the evening
  (c) over the weekend
  (d) during the summer
  (e) other

5. I would prefer that tests were scheduled:

  (a) not more than one in the same day
  (b) they can be spaced over a full week
  (c) I can take them ahead of time, if ready
  (d) I can delay taking them, if unprepared
  (e) other

6. I would like extracurricular activities (sports, band, drama) scheduled

  (a) after school instead of early morning
  (b) every other day instead of every day
  (c) only school days instead of weekends
  (d) whenever the coach or teacher want it
  (e) other

7. I would like the flexibility of scheduling some classes

  (a) over the Internet
  (b) in the evenings
  (c) during the summer
  (d) Saturday or Sunday
  (e) other

8. I would prefer to take

    (a) 2 or 3 intensive courses for half a semester
    (b) 4 or 5 courses during the regular semester
    (c) courses that last for the whole school year
    (d) required courses only so I graduate sooner
    (e) other

9. After school, I spend my time

    (a) participating in sports
    (b) with clubs: drama, art, student council, creative writing
    (c) at the job where I work
    (d) doing homework
    (e) other

10. If you have a job, how many hours a week do you work?

    (a) less than 10 hours
    (b) 10–20 hours a week
    (c) more than 20 hours
    (d) I do not have a job
    (e) other

11. Having time to myself is

    (a) not important for the lifestyle I prefer
    (b) not possible because my schedule is too busy
    (c) important so I am able to engage in reflection
    (d) important because I use it to reduce my stress
    (e) other

12. When absent from school, I would like the opportunity to

    (a) retrieve my homework on the Internet
    (b) submit assignments to teachers by e-mail
    (c) have access to video lessons I can repeat
    (d) other

13. I sometimes feel over-scheduled because

    (a) I am participating in too many activities
    (b) my parents want me to do too many activities

    (c)   my friends want me to do too many activities
    (d)   I do not feel like I am usually over-scheduled
    (e)   other

14.   My daily schedule is rushed

    (a)   always
    (b)   often
    (c)   seldom
    (d)   never
    (e)   other

15.   When my schedule seems hard to manage

    (a)   I feel helpless
    (b)   I feel confident enough to ask for more time
    (c)   I do everything expected but not as well as I could
    (d)   I ignore what I have to do
    (e)   other

Select your grade level, gender, ethnicity, and age.

My grade level is 5 6 7 8 9 10 11 12
My gender is female male
My ethnicity is Asian Black Hispanic Native American White Other
My age is 10 11 12 13 14 15 16 17 18 19

Exercise 4.02: Finding Academic Help

Role: Discussant

Describe your reactions for each of the scenario options along with an additional one you devise. Anne is a sophomore who is barely passing the state-required course in geometry. She feels bad about her marginal performance but is trying hard. Anne should—

(a) ask her parents to pay for the services of a mathematics tutor
(b) visit the geometry teacher and ask for individual assistance
(c) find a study partner from class who can help with homework
(d) join an extracurricular activity to get her mind off geometry
(e) other

Exercise 4.03: Scheduling Assignments

Role: Discussant

Four of Don's teachers make assignments on Monday that are all due on Friday. Not enough time is available to complete the combined homework. Don would appreciate your advice about what he should do.

(a) Accept the fact that unreasonable work expectations are just a part of life.
(b) Talk with one or more teachers and seek permission for a later deadline.
(c) Put the greatest effort into those classes where a better grade is needed.
(d) Ask someone from counseling or the principal's office to become involved.
(e) other

Exercise 4.04: Building Skill Versus Building Knowledge

Role: Evaluator

A century ago, manual labor was the way most people made a living. In contrast, the proportion of workers doing manual labor now is only 20%. The remainder employees are called knowledge workers. Even though workers need skills, acquiring knowledge is different. This is because skills change more slowly. If Michelangelo were to return now and take up his trade again as a stone mason, he would recognize most of the tools and quickly learn to use them. Skilled workers have always been apprentices who commonly learn what they need to know by late adolescence. This is not the case for the workers in an information society. Teachers and other professionals have difficulty keeping up with changes. List some things you can do to keep up to date as a teacher.

Exercise 4.05: Selective Attention

Role: Improviser

Students are exposed to a range of stimuli that can distract attention and prevent concentration on learning. Devise a list of things students, teachers, and administrators can do to minimize interference with instruction and reflection in class. This list can be posted in strategic places where everyone can read it and assume their share of accountability for implementation.

Exercise 4.06: Families and Report Cards

Role: Evaluator

Consider a familiar situation that illustrates how assets and shortcomings emerge during middle school and the range of possible interpretations. Robert is reading the report card his son John in seventh grade has brought home. The card indicates Language Arts = A; Social Studies = A; Music = B; Science = C; and Mathematics = C.

Which responses would you recommend to Robert during a discussion with John?

(a) I'm glad that you got passing grades in all the subjects; keep up the good work.
(b) You used to get all A's in elementary school, so what's changed since last year?
(c) I do not expect you to get the same grades in every subject that you are studying.
(d) It looks like the social sciences represent your center of strengths and interests.
(e) Some subjects are just more difficult than others depending upon the individual.
(f) It appears that you should start to work harder in science and mathematics class.
(g) I want you to understand that I'm disappointed by the inconsistency of grades.

Exercise 4.07: Gifted and Talented Programs

Role: Summarizer

Interview someone from a local school to find out (1) the processes used to select students for the gifted and talented programs and (2) nature of experiences provided in these programs. Ask teammates for help to prepare additional interview questions you will use and invite the school contact to identify other issues s/he thinks should be understood by prospective teachers.

Exercise 4.08: Scope of School Assessment

Role: Generational Reporter

State tests typically cover reading, writing, and mathematics skills. Interview adolescents to find out whether they believe changes are necessary in the scope of skills that are tested. What other skills do teenagers believe are basic for them and therefore should be required for graduation?

Exercise 4.09: Time To Get Up For School

Role: Challenger

The school schedule has remained the same for many years. However, studies of adolescent sleep have led some districts to alter schedules to start school later in the morning. Support or oppose the new practice and give reasons to justify your view.

Exercise 4.10: Slow Learner Program

Role: Improviser

The school board has decided something more must be done to help an estimated 14% of students who classify as slow learners, based on their IQs in the 70–85 range. These students usually fail some courses and leave school before graduation. The school board urges faculty to generate recommendations without regard to the cost. List your suggestions and reasons for each of them.

CHAPTER 5

THE INTERNET AND
MEDIA LITERACY

Most adolescents prefer an out-of-school environment dominated by the Internet, television, cell phones, computers, iPods, and the entertainment industry (Buckingham & Willett, 2006). Students view these influences as prominent sources for their identity, values, goals, and lifestyle. The schools are also undergoing a transformation to support greater involvement with tools of technology that can enhance the appeal and outcomes of student learning (Collins, 2006; Hastings & Tracey, 2005).

The goals for this chapter are to describe the relevance of technology and media for adolescents and show how the Internet is changing expectations of students, teachers, and schools. Strategies are recommended to help teenagers acquire the skills that are needed for conducting research online. A rationale is provided for inclusion of media literacy skills and the application of visual intelligence to improve the schooling experience. Examples reveal how student-teacher relationships can become more satisfying and beneficial when reciprocal learning includes the integration of technology. Enabling adolescents to attain identity status before they have full-time employment and financial independence are discussed. Virtual schools are examined along with concerns about the digital divide and solutions to remedy inequity of online learning.

Adolescents in the Internet Age, pp. 183–234

SCHOOLS AND THE INTERNET

When veterans returned from World War II in 1945, there was a substantial increase in the number of childbirths. These 76 million "baby boomers," born between 1946–1964, grew up when television was introduced as the most significant invention to support information technology. At the time parents acknowledged that their own upbringing had been limited to radio and newspapers as the ways they found out about current events (Mettles, 2005). Present technology promises to bring even more profound changes in communication. The 88 million Americans born since 1980 are referred to as the "Net Generation." Most of them know more about using tools of technology than their parents (Rosen, 2007).

Adults have historically been regarded as the authorities on most things of value. For this reason, the role of teachers and parents has always emphasized guidance for youth but without a corresponding obligation for adults to learn from adolescents. However, most parents and teachers admit that teenagers possess greater technology skills than themselves (Eastin, 2005; Friedman, 2005). This authority inversion is modifying the image of teenagers who interact with digital tools from early childhood. Because adolescents learn about use of computers by playing with them, they consider involvement with technology to be fun. Consequently, the assimilation or integration of new learning as part of the environment that they have always known comes naturally. In contrast, most adults perceive computers as tools, not as toys. As a result, the same lessons that students consider easy can be regarded as difficult by adults whose learning requires accommodation, replacing their long-standing thinking habits with new ways of looking at things. This circumstance presents ideal conditions for reciprocal learning to promote intergenerational harmony (Lancaster & Stillman, 2005; Sharez-Orozco, 2005).

Educating adolescents today requires a different set of strategies than were used for guiding instruction during the past. This change is occurring because of access to new tools that allow students to question, challenge, and disagree, thereby increasing their potential to act as critical thinkers. Watching television is typically a passive activity, but involvement on the Internet requires reading, evaluating presentations, making decisions about what is true, composing ideas, responding to messages, searching for information, interacting with friends, and collaborating with peers (Peter, Valkenburg, & Schouten, 2005).

The necessity to acquire Internet skills is reflected by changes in employer expectations. There have always been *knowledge workers,* people whose careers involved thinking more than working with their hands.

However, these employees become the majority in a knowledge-based economy. Nearly 60% of Americans are classified as knowledge workers with forecasts indicating that 80% of all new jobs created over the next decade will be in this sector (Drucker, 2005). Therefore, adolescents must be equipped with skills that employers need to be productive and profitable in a competitive global marketplace (Toffler & Toffler, 2006).

Adolescent experience with the Internet and other digital resources gives them a means to reach out and extract information they find interesting. Consequently, in a classroom, there are many things students may know more about than their teachers, simply because a few clicks of the mouse can enable adolescents to do research that was once tedious and depended on making many trips to a library. Teachers are gradually becoming facilitators who offer their student hints, directions, and advice for discovering ideas instead of trying to convey all the ideas and perspectives students should learn. The coming decade promises to be an exciting and difficult time as this transition takes place in schools (Spiro, 2006). As a teacher, you will have many opportunities to make an important contribution to this revolution.

Technology and Instruction

In the past teacher preparation was commonly based on models to provide direct instruction, augmented by field-based experiences. In this paradigm, teachers are considered experts who broadcast what students need to learn and the role of students is to pay attention, take notes, and memorize salient information for testing. Educational psychologists have devised theories about variables that can facilitate student motivation, comprehension, and retention (Schunk, 2007). Courses about methods of teaching often emphasize lesson planning, preparing presentations for students that feature power point or demonstrations, structuring tasks to practice skills in class, assigning homework, and reading from the textbook. All these tasks reflect the one-way type of communication that has been associated with learning in traditional environments (Clyde & Delohery, 2005).

The first wave of computer-assisted instruction during the 1980s continued the customary model, differing only in that programs replaced teachers as the primary source of authority. This minor shift meant that teachers were expected to expose students to curriculum developed by software specialists claiming to know the proper sequence for progression of content and skills in subjects like mathematics and science. Educators acknowledged that having access to instruction at convenient times and getting feedback quickly is beneficial. However, because the software excluded teachers from having an influential role, they felt undervalued and fearful that computers might replace them (Clyde & Delohery, 2005). Educators who had been trained to perceive themselves as the center of attention, the main performers in the learning enterprise, felt upstaged and resented being assigned a less important function. The predictable outcome was that, for over a decade, computer use was limited to drill, testing, and recordkeeping (Seidensticker, 2006).

Fortunately, public access to the World Wide Web became available in the 1990s. This stimulated a range of creative applications to unite media tools with the unique skills possessed by teachers. Because the Net Generation is able to locate and to process information differently than students of prior generations, their learning should expand to make a place for the enormous interactive potential offered by computers (Goldsmith & Wu, 2006).

Internet Learning Paradigm

Looking at things from a nontraditional view can sometimes provide the outlook needed to bring about favorable change. This was the observation of Thomas Kuhn (1962) in his classic presentation, *The Structure of Scientific Revolutions*. Kuhn's book was written while he was a graduate student in theoretical physics at Harvard. He introduced the term *paradigm* as a collection of beliefs that scholars share about how to understand and solve problems. Kuhn maintained that, contrary to public opinion, most scientists are neither objective nor independent thinkers. Instead, they are conservatives whose acceptance of theories they have been taught guides their behavior and can cause them to ignore findings that contradict the prevailing paradigm. Creative scientists like Isaac Newton and Albert Einstein who proposed new paradigms were initially subjected to ridicule and had their ideas rejected by colleagues.

Fast forward to the present. The dramatic rise in prominence of technology means customary paradigms used to guide instruction, motivation, assessment, and learning should be scrutinized for revision or possibly left behind. Joel Barker, an expert on institutional change, was the first author to apply Kuhn's scientific concept of a paradigm shift for education and business. A paradigm shift is a radical change in basic assumptions or approach to something that identifies conditions necessary to remain viable. Barker maintains that paying attention to trends which signal the need for paradigm shifting is necessary so students can be prepared to adapt when the traditional rules to achieve success undergo change. In *Five Regions of the Future: Preparing your Business for Tomorrow's Technology Revolution*, Barker presents a geography of technology used for mapping the future (Barker & Erickson, 2005). In a similar way that towns are located when we try to find them on a physical map, educators need to have a conceptual map that enables them to determine from the blizzard of new products and processes the ones to examine carefully, subject to trial, and adopt as new practices to improve schooling.

Theodore Sizer (2004), former Dean of Education at Harvard University, has identified reforms to apply in secondary schools. Raising expectations of students is at the top of Sizer's agenda. His recommendation is:

> High schools must respect adolescents more and patronize them less. The best way to communicate respect is to set high expectations for teenagers and insist on a level of accountability that is more adult in its demand than childlike. We should expect them to learn more while being taught less. Personal engagement with learning is crucial; therefore, unlike the past, adults can no longer "give students an education."

This conclusion urges questions such as—How much do schools rely on computers for instruction when this is the tool students will need for learning as adults? How can students be taught research skills so they can assume greater responsibility for their own learning on the Internet?

When adolescents talk about the Internet, they frequently state the wish that teachers would provide more opportunities for interactive learning (P. Strom, Strom, & Wing, 2008). A Teacher Tube presentation clarifies why educators should pay attention to this student concern. See http:/ /teachertube.com and enter search words pay attention then click pay attention final cut. The current generation of students is a digital generation, not a paper and pencil generation. Why keep pressing them into a pedagogical format that may have worked for adults but does not apply to adolescents. Of course, no one knows the best path for schools to achieve the broader mission that is being expected of them. However, the instruction strategies described here seem compatible with the cyber preference of adolescents, fit the instructional environment needed to support a tech-savvy society, and qualify as essential elements in the formation of an Internet learning paradigm.

1. *Expand linear learning to include non-sequential learning.* The custom has been to depend on linear-type tools as the single method of progression to acquire understanding. *Linear learning,* as applied to reading, means always beginning at the front page of a book, journal or magazine, and continuing until the last page is finished. Movies, programs on television and videotapes are typically linear presentations. However, Internet learning is often nonsequential and interactive, allowing students to surf and to choose links that connect to Web sites, blogs, or social network groups for persons with similar interests. These sites sometimes contain graphics, audio, and video elements along with the text. Students can also

learn by chatting with classmates, composing electronic messages, and downloading materials (Debevec, Shih, & Kashyap, 2006). This broader view of learning can accommodate differences among students in level of knowledge, pace of development, and benefit of visual enrichment. The Information R/evolution Web site explores changes in the way that information is found, stored, created, catalogued and shared and urges consideration of skills students need to be successful. Check it out at http://www.youtube.com/watch?v=-4CV05HyAbM&NR=1.

2. *Establish discovery as the expectation for self-directed learning.* This orientation encourages student discovery of knowledge to enhance direct instruction provided by teachers. So long as educators were the primary source of information, it was appropriate for their training to focus mostly on ways to communicate the content of lessons. Students still expect teachers to plan instruction, design and organize tasks, make themselves available to listen and offer guidance. However, students also prefer to learn by doing, finding out some things on their own instead of always being told and getting their knowledge secondhand (Buckingham & Willett, 2006). The pervasive interest in discovery means that learning based on personal experience brings greater meaning and can transfer more readily to real life situations than can ideas conveyed by teachers (Okojie & Olinzock, 2006).

3. *Student-centered learning should include responsibility to share knowledge.* This shift is needed because digital media offers unprecedented possibilities for working in teams (Hargis, 2005). Instead of students perceiving team discussions as a forum to express personal opinion, the larger expectation should be that everyone would share ideas and relevant resources they have found on the Internet or in the library. It is unreasonable to sustain the custom of students reading only from the textbook or materials assigned by the teacher (Gecke, 2006). The potential benefit of the Internet depends on greater expectations for students to locate reading on their own. Further, our studies show that expecting students to bring reading materials they have located to class for peers to examine and refer to reading materials during discussions will require a reorientation to what is necessary when working in cooperative groups (Strom & Strom, 2009). This transition toward increased student responsibility does not diminish the influence of teachers. On the contrary, teaching becomes more complex since it involves helping to structure student experiences that promote discovery, highlight competence, and encourage self-evaluation.

Even though there are computers in every school, teachers have mixed feelings regarding the contribution computers make to student achievement. Typically, educators are reluctant to discuss this issue because they do not want to be seen as standing in the way of progress. However, teachers agree that providing laptops and opportunity for Internet activity does not necessarily yield improved performance on skill tests required by most states (City, 2008). This conclusion reflects a dilemma over the contradictory pursuits of short-term goals to detect student knowledge versus long-term goals to acquire critical thinking and research skills (Popham, 2007).

There is no doubt that students need computer experience to secure their occupational future. However, many states still hold students accountable only for academic concepts that exclude computer competence. Scores on these state tests can be improved more readily by teaching to the assessment content than by using search and discovery assignments on the Internet. School boards are being lobbied to go beyond the short-term goal orientation to include long-term goals by adopting more comprehensive expectations for student learning, instruction, and assessment (Boudett & Steele, 2007). The National Education Technology Standards 2007, NETS, defines technology activities that students should be able to perform to learn effectively and live productively in a rapidly changing digital world. Each standard is related to acquisition of attitudes and skills that fit the following six categories:

1. Creativity and innovation.
2. Communication and collaboration.
3. Research and information fluency
4. Critical thinking, problem solving and decision making.
5. Digital citizenship, and
6. Technology operations and concepts.

Student profiles are presented that describe technology literate students at various grade levels (prekindergarten—Grade 12) and ages (4–18). The competency profiles recommended by NETS as expectations for students is available at the International Society for Technology in Education (2007) Web site—http://www.iste.org/ search: Profiles for Technology Literate Students. States vary from no expectations to high expectations for technology literacy but there is general agreement that in the near future the assessment of computer literacy will be common.

4. *Support student individuality with search and synthesis activities*. The goal of learning how to find things out has joined the customary classroom emphasis on memorizing information (Richardson & Newby, 2006). One aspect of this broader purpose is to provide opportunities for students to gain and practice the ability to synthesize. Teammates can be given the task of locating the same Web site, reading the material, and writing a paragraph summary. Everyone then critiques all the presentations to identify how the descriptions differ, note aspects that some students

captured better, and detect relevant elements that no one mentioned. Writing includes the skill of being able to synthesize the views of others and to express personal interpretation.

Being able to make connections and build upon the ideas of others is an important skill. Combining the intelligence of individuals by networking can often solve problems in a more efficient and less time consuming way than working alone. Instead of equating memorization with achievement, greater attention should be given to honing the abilities of locating data, merging together, and synthesizing information as a basis for reaching more informed conclusions. Students who can find information, organize it, and present results in a coherent way offer credible evidence of problem solving ability (Medina, 2008).

5. *Encourage the development of durable intrinsic motivation.* Learning in response to curiosity rather than in response to direction given by someone else defines *intrinsic motivation* (Elliot, 2008). The time available for learning in a longevity society is far greater than the past. Previous generations saw life as divided in two stages. During the growing up stage, students attended school, learned the skills needed to get a job, and then spent their adult years at work. In contrast, knowledge increases more rapidly now. The acceleration of new information motivates businesses to invest a greater amount of money in continuing education for employees than is spent by all American institutions of higher education combined (Davila, Epstein, & Shelton, 2006). The duration of relevance that education programs can offer is also diminishing. As a result, students have to gain intrinsic motivation so they are eager to keep on learning after graduation (Rodgers & Withrow-Thorton, 2005).

6. *Promote critical thinking by participation in a "fact-check" system.* Teachers can tell students that, for specified lessons, one or more aspects of a presentation will be incorrect. The perpetual homework task is to rely on the Internet at home as a tool to "fact-check" the lessons. Students will relearn and reinforce in memory facts from daily lessons that are accurate through Internet exploration while also detecting elements containing errors. Student reports in class can be made the following day to identify what was revealed through the process of fact checking. Because adolescents enjoy finding flaws in the thinking of teachers, parents, and other adults, this task motivates careful monitoring and is perceived as a reasonable process to challenge authority when inaccurate information is disseminated. Students may have to check several sources in order to find details of a lesson that are false. A sense of accomplishment follows when students locate "misleading" information. They may discover additional data contradicting what teachers say and create discussion reflecting the premise that truth is sometimes unrecognized and errors may seem to be correct.

Rotating student assignments so two or three share the "fact checker" role daily ensures that all lessons are covered and feedback provided for the previous day. That such practice is needed is underscored by national findings that only 16% of adults report going online to find or check facts on a daily basis (Cole, 2008). This nontraditional principle encourages self-guided learning in cyber space and helps students gain insight about teaching. Students come to realize that teaching is not as easy as it seems because educators must be well prepared and ready to back up assertions with facts. Parents and siblings should be enlisted as helpers, thereby encouraging more family interaction.

The need to help students become more critical of what they read on the Internet is illustrated by studies of Donald Leu, Professor in literacy and technology at University of Connecticut, and his colleagues. The team asked 50 seventh graders who had high scores on reading tests to evaluate the reliability of a cleverly designed Web site about the fictitious "endangered Pacific Northwest Octopus." Although this site is a hoax, 49 of the 50 students concluded that it was scientifically valid. Even after researchers told them that the site was bogus, half of the students remained convinced that the site was truthful (Coiro, Knobel, Lankshear, & Leu, 2008).

Access to an enormous amount of data on the Internet reduces our need to rely as much on human memory for storage of ideas. This shift signals a need for corresponding changes in the way education is provided so more emphasis is placed on information retrieval skills and data management. For example, the following skills are essential to become a self-directed learner:

- Data finding differs from reading what a teacher assigns to also locating what to read.
- Data analysis involves seeing connections and being able to combine related materials.
- Data synthesis calls for briefly reporting what has been learned using your own words.
- Data verification is confirming accuracy of material that can be less reliable than the information retrieved from articles or books that undergo review before being published.

The Inversion of Authority

Many adolescents are able to use technology more effectively than teachers and parents. The resulting *authority inversion* means that both generations recognize teenagers as possessing greater competence in this context. Researchers at Carnegie Mellon University conducted a study to explore dynamics of this new intergenerational relationship (Kraut, Brynin, & Kiesler, 2006). The participants were 170 people from 73 middle class homes in Pittsburgh. All the families included an adolescent and were given a free computer with access to the Internet. None of the households were previously connected to the Internet so they shared the experience of being newcomers to the Web. During the family orientation, researchers explained that the computers would be remotely monitored to find out how often they were used, length of time spent online, and sites visited but not the content. At several month intervals the parents and teenagers had to complete surveys that described self-defined computer skills, the amount of time spent together, and how often they helped one another overcome computer difficulties.

Monitoring detected that, on average, the amount of time teenagers spent online was six times greater than their parents. Adolescents got 10 times as much electronic mail as parents and explored the Internet to a far greater extent. Another type of data involved videotapes made during home visits to observe how each family used the computer. The observers did not give help when participants were seen to encounter technical problems. These difficulties seemed rampant in 89% of families where the usual adult reaction reflected an epidemic of helplessness. Adults offered a broad range of excuses for their inability to solve computer problems. On the other hand, teenagers seldom complained when difficulties arose and readily completed their tasks (Kraut, Brynin, & Kiesler, 2006).

Everyone was invited to phone the Home Net line anytime to get assistance. However, the adults were more inclined to turn to a daughter or son for help. When adolescents were not home, the grownups usually decided to defer a task rather than identify their needs to support sources at Home Net. Those who phoned the help desk most often were the teenagers, the same individuals who performed best. It appears that the most skilled persons realize what they do not yet know and show greater confidence in challenging themselves to attempt ever-more-difficult operations. In most families knowledge trickled upward as teenagers acted as consultants to their parents (Kraut, Brynin, & Kiesler, 2006).

One way to reduce the risks that are associated with this familiar situation is to encourage adolescents to adopt the attributes that characterize good teachers. Possession of a skill does not mean that someone can effectively convey and support development of that skill in other people. Patience and encouragement are important factors contributing to effective teaching. Impatience can erode motivation of students and cause them to doubt their capacity to learn (Elliot, 2008). The Home Net findings showed that adults may be more inclined than adolescents are to give up when faced with an unfamiliar learning situation. For this reason, adolescents who are expected to teach adult relatives should be aware of the emotional support needed to remain willing to keep trying following failure (Pinquart & Silbereisen, 2004).

Adolescents as Teachers

During middle school, most students surpass older relatives in computer skills for work on the Internet. Therefore, it is appropriate to make students aware of how to carry out their responsibilities for reciprocal learning. Teachers can suggest these guidelines as reminders to students about their potential as teachers of adults at home and in school.

1. Adults prefer teachers who show patience by not rushing lessons. When learners feel hurried, the usual outcome is reduction in comprehension. When there is enough time to practice new skills, satisfaction and success are the common result.

2. While explaining sequential steps, demonstrate by using slow movements and actions. Always narrate your behavior like sports commentators do when they inform fans about how a play was executed. This strategy allows the adult to observe and comprehend how a series of movements is the proper way to carry out a task.

3. Repeat examples several times to provide increased opportunity for observation. Most learners of all ages prefer to watch a competent person do a task before trying to imitate the behavior. The difficulty for some teachers who know a process well is to think of it as simple and therefore rush their explanation and demonstration. Take it slow.

4. Monitor behavior of the adult learner and give positive feedback when parts of a task are done correctly by saying 'You did it -- that's the correct way.' When an incorrect action is taken, encourage the adult to try again while you watch carefully to detect sources of the error and then explain how to correct it.

5. Set up situations in which the adult is required to go through a particular process several times. Continue to watch carefully and offer supervision until the person can repeatedly complete the task without making errors.

6. Have the adult describe the steps and give reasoning for certain actions. S/he should be able to go beyond just memorizing steps to show understanding as well by giving an accurate and reasonable explanation.

7. Encourage the continued effort necessary to become computer literate and remain up-to-date. Bear in mind that some adults

tend to give up when they fail with a technology task so receiving emotional support may be more important for them than yourself.

8. Recognize that a common problem arises when adolescent teachers perform a task for adults without insisting that the grownup go through the processes so they can learn to do it for themselves. The common approach of teenagers to quickly do a task for adults is intended to save time but in the long run actually leads to unnecessary dependence.

9. Invite questions to find out what the person finds confusing or wants to know more about. Good teachers always rely on questions as a way to identify needs of learners.

10. Guidelines for teaching should also be applied by adolescents in hierarchical cultures where adults are less appreciative of reciprocal learning. Adults in these environments should be advised by schools to demonstrate humility and commitment to learning that represents a good example for young people.

ADOLESCENTS AS RESEARCHERS

The long-term goals most educators express are that their students will become self-directed learners who pursue improvement by exploring new ways of thinking and adjusting to change. These goals are more likely to be achieved when schools equip teenagers with research skills that enable them to find out what they need to know and motivated to learn throughout life.

New and Old Media

The "old" media, defined by television, radio, telephones, magazines, and books compete with the "new" media that is represented by computers, cell phones, electronic mail, chat rooms, CDs/DVDs, iPods, handhelds, and video games for the time and attention of youth (Spiro, 2006; Thomas, 2007). Roberts, Foehr, and Rideout (2005) conducted a national study of 2,000 students, 8 to 18 years of age, to find out the amount of non-school time spent with media daily. Figure 5.1 that television is the dominant media for youth. Students spend nearly 4 hours (3:51) a day with television, videos, DVDs, and prerecorded shows. The observer role is changing too as teenagers time-shift their viewing to watch when they wish by relying on digital video recorders. In addition, many go online in conjunction with television programs they watch. Two-thirds of students (68%) have a television in their bedroom. This sub-group spends 1½ hours more a day watching television than peers without a television in their bedroom. About half (53%) report their families have no rules about television viewing; 46% say there are rules but only 20% indicate that parents enforce these rules.

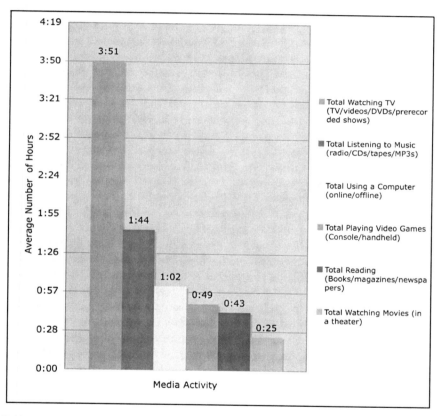

Source: *Generation M: Media in the Lives of 8–18 Year-Olds–Report (#7251),* by D. Roberts, V. Foehr, & V. Rideout, The Henry J. Kaiser Family Foundation, March 2005. Retrieved from Kaiser Family Foundation, Menlo Park, CA, April 19, 2008, http://www.kff.org This information was reprinted with permission from the Henry J. Kaiser Family Foundation. The Kaiser Family Foundation is a non-profit private operating foundation, based in Menlo Park, California, dedicated to producing and communicating the best possible information, research and analysis on health issues.

Figure 5.1. Time spent with media: Average amount of time 8- to 18-year-olds spend per day.

After television, the next highest media exposure involves listening to music on the radio, to CDs, tapes, or MP3 players (1 hour and 44 minutes a day). The most popular genre is rap/hip-hop and alternative rock. Interactive media is also a prominent activity. The appeal of computers continues to increase more rapidly than any other media form with adolescents devoting slightly over 1 hour a day (1:02) to being on a computer, excluding schoolwork. Most (86%) students have a computer at home and 74% have an Internet connection. Video games account for 49 minutes a day. Half of respondents (49%) had a video game player in their bedroom. Reading books, magazines, or newspapers for something other than schoolwork accounts for 43 minutes a day. Going to the movies at a theater averaged 25 minutes a day. The total average exposure for 8 to 18-year-olds to various media content is about 8½ hours a day. However, because some students use more than one medium at a time (reading and listening to music for example), their total exposure is actually packed into 6½ hours a day (Roberts, Foehr, & Rideout, 2005).

Table 5.1 shows the percentage of media budget time that is apportioned to television, videos, movies, print, audio, computers and video games in relation to student age, gender, race, education of parent, and household income. Younger students (ages 8 to 10) devote more time to television (39%) and videos (16%) than older ages. In contrast, older students (15 to 18 years) are more involved with reading (19%), listening to music (30%) and being on the computer (15%). Girls spend greater time listening to music (25%) than the boys (19%) while boys (13%) devote more time to video games than girls (5%). Blacks (40%) watch television more than Whites (33%) and spend less time reading (8%) than Whites (11%) or Hispanics (11%). Less formal education of parents implicates more television and less reading while household income has a negligible effect on amount of media exposure (Roberts, Foehr, & Rideout, 2005).

Educators should understand the enormous appeal of media for youth. In particular, students' feelings regarding the Internet and how this tool affects learning deserves attention (Greenfield & Yan, 2006). The Center for the Digital Future at University of Southern California conducts annual surveys to track the impact of online technology. Jeffrey Cole (2008), Director of the Center, reports that Internet users consider it to be the most important source of information, surpassing all other forms of media including television, radio, newspapers, and books. Cole indicates that amount of time users spend on the Internet is increasing each year to the current average of over 15 hours a week. Greater involvement with the Internet is reinforced by the Pew Internet and American Life Project survey of 1,100 students, ages 12–17 (Lenhart & Madden, 2007). Most (87%) reported going online after school each day and regard the Internet as a virtual textbook and reference library to quickly locate data, find

**Table 5.1. Percentage of Time for
Overall Media Budgets for 8- to 18-Year-Olds**

	TV	Video/ Movies	Print	Audio	Computer	Video Games
Total sample (*n* = 2,000) percentage of time	35%	13%	11%	22%	11%	9%
Age						
8 to 10 Years	39	16	12	14	7	12
11 to 14 Years	38	12	10	20	11	9
15 to 18 Years	28	11	19	30	15	6
Gender						
Boys	35	13	10	19	11	13
Girls	35	13	11	25	12	5
Race						
White	33	12	11	23	12	9
Black	40	15	8	18	8	10
Hispanic	39	13	11	19	9	8
Parent education						
High school or less	38	13	8	23	10	9
Some college	33	12	12	26	11	7
College graduate	33	13	12	21	13	9
Income						
Under $35,000	35	14	9	23	10	8
$35,000–$50,000	34	13	12	22	10	9
Over $50,000	37	11	10	20	14	9

Source: Generation M: Media in the Lives of 8-18 Year-Olds – Report (#7251), by D. Roberts, V. Foehr, & V. Rideout, The Henry J. Kaiser Family Foundation, March 2005. Retrieved from Kaiser Family Foundation, Menlo Park, CA, April 19, 2008, http://www.kff.org This information was reprinted with permission from the Henry J. Kaiser Family Foundation. The Kaiser Family Foundation is a non-profit private operating foundation, based in Menlo Park, California, dedicated to producing and communicating the best possible information, research and analysis on health issues.

materials for writing papers, exchange notes with classmates on assignments and sometimes access tutorial help. Adolescents (86%) and their parents (83%) agree that the Internet helps with schoolwork. Consider a project designed to inspire teachers to use technology for helping students develop higer level thinking skills at http://youtube.com search A Vision of K–12 Students Today.

Even though all public schools have Internet access, only one-third of teenagers in the Pew survey reported having significant Internet involvement during the school day (Lenhart & Madden, 2007). The reasons were not pursued and few investigations have focused on student obstacles to Internet learning. One notable exception is the work of Levin and Arafeh (2002) who found that the most common problems adolescents encounter are: (1) lack of Internet-based homework, and (2) poor and uninspiring quality of Internet assignments. A related observation is that teachers do not know how to devise Internet search tasks; instead, they over rely on end of chapter activities in textbooks which seldom implicate the use of other resources (Davila, Epstein, & Shelton, 2006).

Students wonder why teachers do not consider the Internet as a valuable tool for their education. They resent being denied opportunities to further develop and to practice important skills related to this fundamental resource (Gross, 2004). Most students (40%) report that they taught themselves to use the Internet or were helped by parents (30%), friends (23%), or siblings (10%). Only 5% credited school in teaching them about technology (Solomon & Schrum, 2007). School policies that restrict use of computers to certain courses, times, and locations should be reconsidered in favor of access in all classrooms on a continuous basis. Educators should become responsive to the reality that adolescents are Internet-savvy and their expertise causes them to have high expectations of the schools that are preparing them for a digital society (Messmer, 2006). The Public Broadcasting System created a documentary on "Growing Up Online" that shows how adolescence is being transforming by the Internet in every sector including relationships, self-expression, schooling, and conflict. View this program at http://www.pbs.org/wgbh/pages/frontline/kidsonline/.

Voices of Adolescents

Some aspects of the adolescent experience teachers need to know about cannot be found in books on development. This void exists for situations of recent origin where studies have yet to inform classroom practice (Carr, 2006). Knowing the responses of students to these poll questions can bring insights about ways to improve the institutions they attend.

1. Why are adolescents motivated to spend a lot of time on the Internet?
2. What benefits do teenagers feel they gain from being on the Internet?
3. What Internet research skills are necessary but are not being taught?
4. What problems do teens face in their efforts to learn on the Internet?
5. How could teachers help overcome the obstacles to Internet research?
6. What value do adolescents see in homework that requires Web search?
7. How often do teachers give homework that requires use of the Internet?
8. How does learning via Internet compare to other forms of instruction?
9. What role should parents have in supporting Internet research skills?
10. What Internet training should teachers have to become more helpful?
11. How do students feel about benefits and limits of virtual schooling?
12. In what ways should your school Web site change to be more useful?

Teachers need to understand development of adolescents in the particular school and community where they interact with students. One or more teams in your class can administer the Learning on the Internet Poll at the end of this chapter (see Exercise 5.01). Sharing results shows how adolescents you work with feel about this aspect of school.

Criteria for Internet Research

Students need to acquire research skills so they can pursue self-directed learning on the Internet. The motivation to acquire these skills is pervasive. Most adolescents report that they go online soon after returning home from school (D. Johnson, 2005–2006). Some homework tasks could facilitate greater student understanding of topics while allowing opportunities for search practice. The following six criteria, formulated by the authors, are used by middle school and high school teachers in all subject matters to help students become researchers:

1. Trace the cyber search path
2. Evaluate significance of the problem
3. Provide a synthesis statement
4. Determine application value
5. Assess credibility of sources
6. Recognize contexts where personal growth is needed

(1) *Trace the cyber search path.* Students select from a list of topics that the teacher presents as relevant to a curriculum theme. Everyone is expected to keep a record of where they go on their cyberspace journey. Teachers use these results as a type of road map to track student direction, retrace their steps, and then make recommendations for better routes to reach a desired destination. Some additional data that can be required include whether a search was based on key words or images, the choice of search engines, and succession of links that are followed. When team members are assigned the same topic, benefit comes from sharing the paths independently taken and gaining insights from experience of peers (Hargis, 2005).

(2) *Evaluate significance of the problem.* Students should be expected to confirm the importance of topics they select to explore, describing credible reasons for why the particular issue matters. The perceived significance of a concept influences student initial motivation as well as task persistence. Student response also reveals the extent to which a person is able to bring concepts together and enlarge the scope of inquiry. Sometimes students fail to recognize relevant connections. There are also times when students miss conceptual connections because teacher assignments are ambiguous (Gross, 2004; McKenney, 2005).

(3) *Provide a synthesis statement.* One important sign of comprehension is being able to process information accurately by restating a concept, idea or circumstance in one's own words. Knowing how to summarize is essential when others depend on us to report what we have read or heard that is not part of their own experience. Students who are able to summarize are also less inclined to plagiarize. For each Web search, students should identify URLs and provide a printout reflecting site content by posting on the classroom wall for teammates to examine. The materials should also include a summary of results that are stated in the student's unique way. The summary should combine data found and student interpretation including evidence of what has been learned. This is a constructivist process by which students create personal meaning from a lesson. Frequent practice with the role of summarizer promotes freedom of speech by encouraging students to state things in their own way. Teachers can assist

in editing summaries to make sure they effectively convey the outcome (Keller, 2005; R. Strom & Strom, 2007).

(4) *Determine the application value.* Students should describe how the information they locate could be applied in particular situations. Being able to recognize implications from data is a necessary skill for researchers because it results in better methods to replace existing practices. This ability should become more common, particularly among students who assume that locating data is sufficient evidence of learning without establishing whether they can make connections between the data and applicable situations (S. Lee, 2006).

(5) *Assess the credibility of sources.* Student should take steps to carefully examine and describe the sources of data they have relied on as the basis for their report. Determining that a site provides worthwhile information is basic. The background and qualifications of individuals cited should be identified along with the date of a posting, mission, and purposes of the Web site (Miller, Adsit, & Miller, 2005).

(6) *Recognize contexts where personal growth is needed.* New tools, procedures, and increasing knowledge are reasons to sustain learning (Solomon & Schrum, 2007). One way for teachers to assess their technology competence is to periodically carry out self-evaluations that reveals capability with computer use, instructional software, information literacy, Internet basics, electronic mailing lists, virus protection, World Wide Web search tools, real time and push technologies, obtaining, decompressing, and using files, Web page construction, online ethics, and current issues that implicate Internet use in K–12 schools. Teachers should monitor their readiness for Internet learning and helping students to perform well. You can assess your skill set by responding to a quiz prepared for the federal government by Doug Johnson (2002), Self-Evaluation Rubrics for Teacher Computer Use, available at http://www.ed.gov/pubs/EdTechGuide/appc-7.html.

Teenagers often use a cryptic vocabulary that adults may not use or understand. There is also a technical vocabulary that computer users of any age should try to comprehend. Matisse Enzer's Glossary of Internet Terms is a helpful resource to increase comprehension of writing and conversations related to computer literacy. See Matisse Enzer's Web site at http://matisse.net/files/glossary.html.

FUTURE OF LEARNING AND THE INTERNET

Teacher success depends on helping adolescents acquire skills to locate information from a vast array of sources in cyber space. When students have guidelines to rely on, they can pursue independent inquiry and work well with others in teams. These opportunities should be provided during middle school and high school with everyone exposed to some of their instruction online. The discipline and motivation required in this context can enable more students to become self-directed learners and carry the orientation to adulthood. Schools should ensure that all students have access to tools that support participation and adjustment in a technological environment.

Internet Assignment Guidelines

The Internet offers many resources to enlarge the scope of student learning. However, secondary schools seldom offer orientation for use of materials. The following guidelines can help teachers support adolescents as they go on the Internet for assignments or team projects.

(1) *Evaluate site reliability.* Before Web sources are used, check the site background. Keep in mind that the Internet consists of credible and dubious sources. It might be necessary to verify information by accessing an alternate source that is known to be accurate. Because students are accustomed to fast communication, teachers should insist that they take time required to analyze quality of the information retrieved, despite a desire for rapid response and reluctance to reflect on sources. Reflective thinking is an essential aspect of research. The amount of time required to corroborate data is justified because it prevents being misled (Watkins, 2006). For guidance on evaluation of Web sites by using criteria related to evidence, logic, methodology, balance, purpose, and authority, check out the McMaster University Web site in Canada http://socserv2.mcmaster.ca/Inquiry/neteval.htm.

The Internet Public Library (IPL) Web site for teens offers guidelines for school research projects http://www.ipl.org/div/teen/aplus/internet.htm. These questions are ones investigators should pose and try to answer before they give a report. What was the purpose for creating this Web site? What opinion does the page represent? When was the information on this page put up? Is this information current? Who are the parties that established the Web site? Do the authors have credentials that invite my confidence? How well documented is the work?

(2) *Demonstrate ethical behavior.* Authentic use of Internet materials must increase in order to support the integrity of academic performance. *Plagiarism* is unethical conduct demonstrated by copying what someone else has written or taking ideas of another person and portraying them as though they were one's own thoughts. Avoid involvement with the temptation of cut and paste plagiarism. Instead, rely on your own words to summarize articles and always provide a citation that includes author

name(s), presentation title, Web source and pages, journal volume, number, date, city, and publisher. Students should check with the teacher for directions on citing Web pages, e-mail, and research documents to accord with the format style required in a course (O'Bannon & Judge, 2005).

(3) *Determine a topic and write questions about elements you want to discover.* Having key points on an outline of the search focus can help stay on track and remain focused. Write a list of key words and short phrases to narrow the focus for a search engine. Write enough keywords and phrase options in case some searches come to a dead end. Start with a narrow frame and broaden the criteria as needed. The inclusion of links on every Web site and massive search engines can be overwhelming (an example of over-choice) if parameters are not established at the outset of a search (Vail, 2005; Watkins, 2006).

(4) *Locate search engines that provide a convenient supply of useful links related to your specific research topic.* Some useful Web sites include:

The Internet Public Library http://www.ipl.org
The WWW Virtual Library http://www.vlib.org
Search Engine Resources http://www.refdesk.com/newsrch.html

(5) *Maintain a balance of sources.* The convenience of the Internet motivates some students to overlook other relevant sources. In preparing for an assignment, balance Internet sources with additional references such as journals, books and interviews. Some things that are not found for free on the Web involve index and abstract services basic for a scholarly review. Estimates are that 90% of the content for library reference and circulating collections are not on the Web. This means researchers must spend some time in the library as well as on the Web (Valenza, 2006).

(6) *Keep a record of Web sites visited and used.* Maintain a list of helpful URL addresses as favorites so that they can readily be found again later if needed.

(7) *Avoid paid services.* Make known the consequences of having assignments done over the Internet through paid services. Teachers and parents should ensure that, in most cases, students do not use such services (Vonderwell & Zachariah, 2005).

(8) *Avoid and report unsuitable sites.* When a student comes across an unsuitable or questionable site, inform the teacher or school librarian. Fulfilling this responsibility reflects good citizenship and can help improve the Internet experience for other students (Wheeler, 2005).

(9) *Make use of parental controls.* There is a need to set parent controls on adult sites in an age appropriate way, whether a computer is at home or in school (Wang, Bianchi, & Raley, 2005).

(10) *Log out*. Students using the Internet for information transfer should understand the implications of a "secure server" space. After entering a user name and password to log on to the Web site, don't forget to log out before leaving. To go without logging out keeps information available to the other person that could be detrimental if the information contained sensitive material.

Virtual Secondary Schools

Looking ahead is an aspect of planning that calls for consideration of trends. A Sloan Consortium survey of 2,500 American colleges and universities found that, in 2007, nearly 4 million students were taking courses online, reflecting an enrollment growth rate of 10% a year over four years (Allen & Seaman, 2007). There is anticipation that the appeal of the Internet for adolescents will motivate a greater proportion of them to participate in online learning when they go to college (Revenaugh, 2005–2006).

Important changes are already taking place in secondary schools. *Virtual schools*, institutions that present online instruction, can provide offerings that go beyond what is available in the community. This is often a need for rural areas, inner city schools with difficulty retaining qualified teachers in key subjects, and neighborhoods where the schools are overcrowded. Distance learning provides families an option for school choice, enrichment of curriculum, and greater opportunity to become reliant on self-directedness. Communicating with each student and personalizing instruction are indicators of why online learning is becoming popular. The teacher can work one on one with class members, answer their questions and use time differently than in a classroom, as students proceed at their own pace. Certain students may need more time as they struggle with specific lessons while others may want to move on more quickly while continuing to receive feedback and intervention when necessary. Typically students report appreciation for a schedule allowing them to progress at their own rate. For some individuals it can mean completing high school in less than 4 years (Watson & Ryan, 2007).

Online learning requires commitment from state governments. For example, Governor Robert Riley of Alabama tied online learning to state technology infrastructure. Over three years Riley invested $30 million to upgrade state high speed network, put twenty-first century tools in every high school, trained teachers to teach online, and invested in conversion to digital content. The goal was to make courses accessible to every student in the state by online learning. Alabama makes available to all its youth chances to take Chinese, French, German and Latin; advanced placement (AP) calculus, AP English literature and composition. AP macroeconomics, and marine science courses are some of many other classes for choice. According to Governor Riley, "Using technology to provide these opportunities not only increases the rigor of instruction but acclimates students to the use of technology and prepares them for a 21st century workplace" (Patrick, 2008).

International Association for K–12 Online Learning tracks and provides participation reports for online learning in each of the states—http://www.inacol.org. Currently, 42 states have online learning programs where over one million students enrolled in physical schools take one or two courses outside the regular classroom. Florida operates the largest program with 90,000 annual course completions by 50,000 students. Generally, state completion rates for courses are in the 65–85% range. In 2007, Michigan became the first state to require that the high school graduating class of 2010 must participate in at least one online course as a prerequisite for graduation. The premise is that such experience will enable students to recognize that they will be able to obtain some of the future education they need in this context. Presently 30% of all work force training is done through e-learning (Patrick, 2008).

The University of Texas (2008) provides an opportunity for students to earn a high school diploma online, regardless of whether the participants reside in Texas. The diverse student body includes full-time workers, youngsters schooled at home, people in remote locations, older than traditional age, individuals wanting to accelerate, and many who prefer independence in their choices. All courses are aligned with state adopted texts and Texas Assessment of Knowledge and Skills Tests that every student has to pass for graduation. Self-pacing allows nine months for completion of a course. Examinations are taken at one of the state test centers or from a bonded proctor out of state. The comprehensive high school curriculum consisting of 48 courses and syllabi are available at http://www.utexas.edu/cee/dec/uths/.

There are similarities and variation in the way states provide virtual learning. Most of the programs are designed to meet state standards for graduation and commonly emphasize student acquisition of twenty-first century skills. Notable examples are the initiatives provided by Idaho Digital Learning Academy at http://Idla.blackboard.com, Florida Virtual School at http://www.flvs.net, and Michigan Virtual School at http://www.mivhs.org.

The North Central Regional Laboratory completed a meta-analysis drawn from 14 studies that, in combination, involved 7,500 students. Test performance of distance education students was compared with performance of control group students who did not have distance education (Cavanaugh, Gillan, Kromrey, Hess, & Blomeyer, 2004). Most (75%) of the students were in Grades 6–12 with the remainder enrolled in K–5. These studies were published between 1999–2004. Ten of the interventions were full year programs in which students participated 5 days a week. Subject matters included mathematics, science, reading, and writing. Results showed that, in all 14 studies, distance-learning students performed on matched examinations as well as students in classroom-based programs. Other investigators have reported similar results (Gecke, 2006). According to the North American Council for Online Learning, data evaluating online programs against face-to-face education are still lacking along with suitable criteria to assess how students perceive the teacher role and their own in a cyber learning environment (Watson & Ryan, 2007).

The problems associated with virtual schooling should be more widely understood. Online courses require that students have intrinsic motivation or there can be no progress. Greater numbers of students have to become more responsible for their learning (Revenaugh, 2005–2006). Even though a virtual classroom offers a front row seat, teachers must schedule time for one-to-one attention, usually without reduction in normal workload. Then too, preparing online courses are considered by teachers as more demanding. The reflection expressed by one teacher shows how regular and virtual classes differ, "I never realized how many student questions I never answered until I taught online." It seems that some blending will occur so that secondary students are exposed to learning online and learning in the classroom (Yarbrough & Gilman, 2006). The widespread growth of interest in virtual schooling suggests that teachers need to recognize the potential of distance learning and the emerging responsibility of students within this context (Egan & Akdere, 2005; Mupinga, 2005). The Southern Regional Education Board (SREB) describes online teaching principles and school learning initiatives by state—available at http://www.sreb.org.

Families and the Digital Divide

The *digital divide* refers to the gap between individuals and communities with greater or lesser access to technology resources and training (Monroe, 2004). Efforts to bridge the gap are necessary because:

1. Everyone needs access to information technology so they can be involved with the expanding communication environment;
2. Many employers are requiring technology skills as a requirement for hiring;
3. Students prefer the use of technology tools; and
4. Digital media can engage students who lose interest in traditional schooling.

There is growing recognition that, from now on, child and adolescent development will depend upon having opportunities for extensive practice with the technology tools needed for future learning. Government and the business sector have supported this goal by donating hardware so that there is free Internet access in every public school and 95% of public libraries (Rosen, 2007).

Most families have access to the Internet, but many do not. This circumstance should motivate educators to make use of their resources in more creative ways. For example, the Internet is available 24 hours a day in public schools. This means that opening elementary schools Saturdays, Sundays and some evenings could reduce the digital divide where this opportunity is needed. For example, one of the opportunities designed and provided by the authors is a free online community service course in which parents and their preschool children interact while encountering fun Web sites they can click on that we have chosen for them. The parents are provided guidelines for teaching appropriate attitudes and skills for online activity that are readily adopted because preschoolers are in the developmental stage of identification. Fathers and men of the community can provide school security as adolescent and adult volunteers orient and act as help agents for the parents. Considerable harm is being done by ignoring the need of disadvantaged parents to participate in learning with their children on the Internet all through the duration of their schooling (Ceci & Papierno, 2005). The digital divide is bound to increase if we continue on this path. There is a corresponding need to dispel the myths associated with online learning. For example, online learning should be mainly to provide acceleration for gifted and talented students, disabled students should be discouraged from participation, and parents should not be considered as teaching resources. The truth about access and equity in online classes and virtual schools must become understood to overcome these myths (Rose & Bloymeyer, 2007; Woessmann & Peterson, 2007).

The Children's Partnership conducted a study to identify how the Internet and other digital tools influence the opportunities for youth (Lazarus, Wainer, & Lipper, 2005). Data was gathered using the Digital Opportunity Measuring Stick consisting of 40 quantitative indicators related to educational achievement, health, economic opportunity, and community participation. Measuring stick findings are described at http://www.childrenspartnership.org/ (click Digital Opportunities Program).

Consider a National Science Foundation longitudinal study designed to assess effects of Internet use by students in urban low-income families. The 140 participants were 13 years old. Most were Black and 75% lived in single parent families. On average, they scored at the 30th percentile for standardized reading tests. All the families were given a computer and free Internet service. The Michigan State University team, led by Linda Jackson, monitored Internet usage, administered periodic surveys, and made home visits (Jackson, Von Eye, Biocca, Barbatsis, Zhao, & Fitzgerald, 2006). The results indicated that teenagers who used the Internet more had higher reading scores at the end of 6 months, 1 year, and 16 months later as well as higher grade point averages than peers who used the Internet less. The heavily text-based nature of Web pages is causing students to read more and resulting in higher achievement scores. Jackson speculates that there may be yet undiscovered differences between reading online and reading offline that make online experience more appealing to adolescents. Learning on the Internet may trigger greater motivation because it provides a fun environment.

There are also reasons to suppose that online reading could enhance some literacy skills that are fostered less with customary book reading. Studies of Donald Leu (2005) at the University of Connecticut and his colleagues found no substantial association between online reading comprehension performance and performance on state reading tests. Leu hypothesizes that the reason is because online reading depends on a different set of skills than those applied in reading books. Online reading relies on information-location skills of using search engines, being able to synthesize data, and participate in critical evaluation. Traditional studies focus only on outcomes of standardized reading tests that do not take into account the specific online reading comprehension skills students need before they can learn much on the Internet.

The Massachusetts Institute of Technology Media Laboratory sought to revolutionize how children are educated in remote and poor environments throughout the world. Nicholas Negroponte (2007), founder of the Lab, established the One Laptop Per Child Organization to produce a laptop so inexpensive, less than $200, that every child could have one. This unique laptop is powered by a wind up crank when no external power source is available and encased in rubber for durability to survive significant mistreatment. The designers wanted to construct a machine that would be a substitute, at one stroke, for desktop computers or traditional laptops, texts, libraries, maps, and movies often missing in the lives of low-income children. Negroponte reviews his journey at http://www.ted.com [click Speakers].

At the prototype unveiling, United Nations Secretary-General Kofi Annan identified this project as part of an international attempt to build an inclusive information society. Marketing has been limited to education ministries from developing countries. Several hundred thousand machines were purchased by Peru and Uruguay. Children in Rwanda and Mongolia, will also be recipients, based on a "give one, get one" U.S. based promotion where donors purchased two computers and either kept one or gave both to the country they choose to assist. Machines are donated to the students so they can keep them. Negroponte (2007) believes it is important for students to own the machines. When the laptops are brought home at night, students do homework and cooperate with peers making up their local network. There can also be a profound influence on the learning of other family members. Some of the implementation problems for One Laptop were not anticipated. For example, the concept is rooted in constructivism, a belief that children learn best by discovering knowledge on their own. However, educators in India and other countries continue to believe that the best way to learn is by listening as teachers provide lessons. The orientation of teachers to the constructivist view is now a major focus of the project (Hamm & Smith, 2008).

Besides connecting students to the Internet and assisting them with use of technology, the digital divide also implicates the kind of content desired by those at risk of being left behind. For example, Internet use is uniformly low among White (32%), Hispanic (31%) and Black (25%) people who did not graduate from high school (van Dijk, 2005). What kinds of information do low income families, those living in rural areas, persons with limited schooling or members of minority groups want provided by the Internet? Some topics they hope become more available include (1) help with employment and education, (2) information understood by limited English language users, and (3) culturally relevant material (House, 2006).

1. The Internet provides employment leads for persons who want to improve their work status but existing Web sites rarely advertise entry-level jobs. Then too, information on housing is widely available but not for those who can only afford low rent. Finding out about local service agencies and prospects for childcare, after school activities, and church programs are considered valuable.

2. Nearly 90% of all documents on the Internet are in English but this is not the primary language for 32 million Americans. Many affected by literary barriers would welcome a chance to increase their English competence by interactive sites that could help them gain grammar, vocabulary, and reading comprehension. Having information about responsibility to pay taxes and to vote are also important ways of enabling newcomers to become responsible citizens.

3. Some minorities want the Internet to help them explore cultural heritage in art, music, food, history, literature, and sports. Health information related to particular needs of racial and ethnic groups are desired. Greater consideration of these concerns could increase the appeal of the Internet for those who presently feel they are left out (Carreon, Drake, & Barton, 2005).

VISUAL INTELLIGENCE AND MEDIA LITERACY

Howard Gardner (1983, 2003), Professor of education at Harvard, proposed a multiple intelligences theory that involved eight separate ability domains discussed in chapter 4, Mental Abilities and Achievement. One of these domains is visual intelligence, composed of visual-spatial abilities that allow individuals to create views of the world and think in pictures (Baum, Viens, & Slatin, 2005). For a long time this vital asset was overlooked by schools, except in relation to a small minority of students identified as gifted in the visual arts (McCann, 2003). Over the past decade, however, it has become obvious that we live in an increasingly image-driven society. Media influence on communication, awareness, and decision-making through visual representations portrayed by computers, CD ROMs, digital cameras, PDAs, cell phones, and television is enormous (Grill-Spector & Kanwisher, 2005). The observation that "a picture is worth a thousand words" was intuitively recognized by prior generations. In contrast, scholars now suggest that lessons including use of digital images are likely to be retained by students to a greater degree than those gained only by reading or listening (Williams & Newton, 2006).

There is general agreement that much of what students learn outside school attributes to visual images presented by television, the Internet, and video gaming devices. The universal appeal of visual images is motivating educators to consider ways of integrating visual intelligence as part of the learning process (Rubin, 2006). George Lucas, creator of *Star Wars* and other classic films, recommends that schools teach communication in all its forms instead of continue the narrow focus on written and spoken words. According to Lucas,

> We all need to understand the importance of graphics, music, and cinema, which can be just as powerful and in some ways more deeply intertwined with young people's culture. When people talk to me about the digital divide, I think of it not being so much about who has access to technology as who knows how to create and express themselves in the new language of the screen. If students are not taught the language of sounds and images, shouldn't they be considered as illiterate as if they had left college without being able to read or write? (Lucas, 2008)

Elaboration of this issue is provided by a video interview with George Lucas on his Web site at http://www.edutopia.org search George Lucas teaching communication.

Preparation for an Image Driven Society

Education has been dominated by efforts to enhance two types of intelligence: (1) *Verbal-linguistic intelligence* consists of abilities that support student speaking, reading, and writing; and (2) *Logical-mathematical intelligence* consists of abilities that students rely on for deductive and inductive reasoning. This dual emphasis means that the basic skills everyone is expected to learn involve reading, writing and numeracy. These skills continue to be important but should be joined by visual thinking abilities, especially related to the media. When Howard Gardner (2003) reviewed his multiple intelligences theory after 20 years, he said,

> When I began the study of developmental and cognitive psychology, I was struck by the absence of mention of the arts. An early professional goal for me was to find a place for the arts in academic psychology. I am still trying.

The fact that being artistically incompetent is acceptable in our society reinforces the view that visual intelligence training is undervalued (R. Smith, 2005). In New York City, the Museum of Modern Art (MOMA) staff, in cooperation with adolescents, operates a Web site to foster greater awareness of visual intelligence. The teenagers, acting as reporters, interview prominent artists to find out how their ideas develop, ways they solve problems, and difficulties they face in trying to communicate their ideas in a visual format. These streaming video presentations focus on visual thinking abilities that are seldom discussed in schools. See http://redstudio.moma.org/about/.

Reforms in education to enhance visual intelligence would allow students to retain the benefits from customary forms of learning while also becoming capable of assimilating ever-increasing exposure to visual lessons provided by the media. Today's adolescents may be more visually than verbally literate. Boards of education across the nation are being lobbied to expand the outdated definition of basic skills to include media literacy and make it a requirement for high school graduation (Smith, Moriarty, Barbatsis, & Kenney, 2005). *Media literacy* is defined as the ability to communicate competently in all the media forms, print and electronic, as well as to access, understand, analyze and evaluate images, words, and sounds that comprise mass media culture. Media literacy could empower more people to behave as critical thinkers and become creative producers capable of using image, language, and sound. Support for this broader portrayal of literacy is explained in Martin Scorsese: "Teaching of Visual Literacy" available at http://www.edutopia.org/ search Martin Scorsese.

The Center for Media Literacy in Los Angeles maintains that convergence of media and technology in a global culture is changing the way people learn about the world and challenging the foundations of education. Being able to read the printed word is no longer a sufficient source of information. Everyone should also acquire the abilities needed to critically interpret images in a multimedia culture and express themselves in multiple media forms (Thoman & Jolls, 2005). An inquiry-based theory for learning about the media is proposed in conjunction with methods that can merge analytical (deconstruction) skills with creative communication (construction/ production) skills. The Center for Media Literacy Web site is available at—http://www.medialit.org.

Part of visual intelligence involves understanding symbols (Liungman, 2005). People rely on symbols when they use computers, cell phones, the Internet and PDAs. Visual symbols can facilitate communication in culturally diverse societies where multiple languages may separate people. As global interaction increases, there will be a need to invent ways of communicating ideas that rely on images as well as narrative. The capacity of adolescents to exhibit visual thinking skills for building symbols is evident when given the following assignment that you can try in class.

PREMISE OF ASSIGNMENT: Some restaurants display signs informing customers that smoking is not allowed. Symbols are shown at Hollywood events and at walkathons to remind us that certain diseases have yet to be overcome and, by uniting our support, we can attain the goal. Neighborhoods erect signs telling us that residents will alert the police whenever they observe suspicious behavior.

In contrast, some policies are less attended to because there are no symbols as reminders. For example, an important and relatively new custom is reliance on a designated driver to protect drinkers from driving. However, a symbol to remind and encourage drinkers about relying upon a designated driver is not seen. Perhaps such a sign that combined visual and text could be displayed in bars and worn by designated drivers.

In schools there are sometimes statements on the board urging "no putdowns" to remind students that civil behavior is expected of everyone. However, symbols or signs are usually lacking as gentle reminders regarding individuals about their obligation to avoid cheating, support gender equity, accept disabled peers, shun bullying, and make known those who take advantage of others.

TASK: Design a new symbol, image, or sign to promote some aspect of desired behavior at school. Figure 5.2 is a visual and text reminder that everyone on a cooperative team is expected to enhance productivity. Providing students this example can help to stimulate their thinking about the assignment.

Marc Prensky (2005–2006, 2008) has proposed a novel paradigm for adults as they look at adolescents and themselves. His premise is that technology has led students to process information differently than previous generations. Adolescents are identified as *digital natives* because they speak a digital language required for interaction with computers, the Internet, and video games. Even though students have dramatically changed in how they process information, many of the schools they attend continue using practices out of sync with ways of learning preferred by the digital native population. This institutional lag attributes in

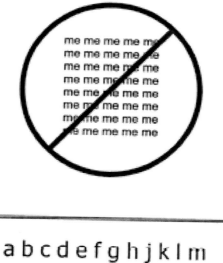

Figure 5.2. An example of symbolic and verbal thinking.

part to the *digital immigrants,* teachers and parents who were born or grew up before common access to technology.

Some digital immigrants seem reluctant to replace methods of instruction used in their own education. Teachers who choose to speak only in the language of the pre-digital age admit they have a difficult time trying to guide students who prefer immersion with the new language. The good news is that more teachers, digital immigrants and digital natives, are discovering how electronic resources can contribute to active learning and ways to blend these strategies with customary methods that support existing performance goals. Prensky's (2005–2006) observations of how digital natives and digital immigrants approach learning differently can be examined at http://www.marcprensky.com/writing/default.asp.

Differences in Visual and Verbal Intelligence

Consider the differences between visual intelligence and verbal intelligence. Mankind relied on pictures long before written words appeared as ways of communication and expression (Janson, 1986). *Verbal intelligence* can be expressive (active) or receptive (passive) but *visual intelligence* does not have a passive mode for thinking or for learning. It appears that visual intelligence occupies a more prominent function than verbal ability in the process of invention, originality, and discovery. That is, words come later than images in the creative process and may sometimes be inadequate for communication (Barry, 1997).

Every language has many words that people rely on to describe their ideas, feelings, and events. Relatively speaking however, there are fewer corresponding visual prompts or markers that are easily understood. The image of a flashing light bulb often is presented as an example to illustrate the insight experience prominent in creative thinking, the moment of sudden revelation that makes clear the solution for a problem. It is noteworthy that great thinkers whose insight experience has influenced history in science, art, mathematics and other fields identify visual thinking or visual images as at the center of their discoveries. The language of insight is sometimes reported as visual—I see it now. The English word "idea" derives from the Greek word Idein, which means, "to see." There are many words that link vision with thinking such as insight, foresight, hindsight, and oversight (Williams & Newton, 2006).

Roger Penrose, a famous mathematician, observes that visual thinking dominates thinking processes of gifted mathematicians. He explains that his own mathematical thought is done visually using nonverbal concepts, although the thoughts are quite often accompanied by inane and almost useless verbal commentary such as "that thing goes with this one and this thing relates to that" (Penrose, 2002). His conclusions are corroborated by the recollections of other well-known scientists. For example, Albert Einstein maintained that written or spoken words did not seem to play an important role in his thinking processes. Instead, physical entities serving as elements of thought were regarded as signs in more or less clear visual images Einstein was able to voluntarily reproduce and combine. He acknowledged that conventional words or other forms of expression had to be reached through struggle only in the second stage of creative thinking, after connection of ideas was sufficiently established and could be reproduced at will.

In a similar way, Frances Galton (1874) explained,

> It is a serious drawback to me in writing, and still more in explaining myself, that I do not think as easily in words as otherwise. It often happens that after being hard at work and having arrived at results that seem perfectly clear and satisfactory, when I try to express them in language I feel that I must begin by putting myself on quite another intellectual plane. I have to translate my thoughts into a language that does not run evenly with them. (p. 14)

These anecdotal self-reports, revealing that visual thinking and advanced mathematical functioning are linked, have also been confirmed by research studies (Geake, 2000, 2002).

Visual intelligence and media literacy training should become more prominent in the classroom as educators and the public recognize the limitations of analogies that inappropriately equate the brain with computers (Hubel & Wiesel, 2004). This comparison is based on capacity of computers for speed of information processing and access to data storage. However, what is now known about the brain places it far ahead of computers in terms of higher-order thinking. Specifically, it appears to be in the context of visual functioning, as contrasted to verbal functioning, that the brain is elevated to a higher status (Ward, 2006). This distinction was recognized some time ago by McKim (1980) who argued that computers are unable to see, dream or create. They are language-bound. Thinkers who cannot escape the structure of language often rely on only that small portion of their brain that resembles a computer.

Digital Images and Curriculum Enrichment

Merging digital images with direct instruction is a prominent approach to learning in secondary schools. Discovery Education (2009), the nation's largest digital video-on-demand service for schools, provides an illustration of how greater exposure to images can support instruction. More than half of American schools that together enroll 30 million students use this service. The appeal for teachers is to choose from a library of 80,000 video content clips as brief as two minutes, 8,700 full-length video titles, 20,000 photographs, and a gallery of 1,500 art images.

Discovery Education (2009) videos are categorized by grade and keyed to state department standards for subjects like mathematics, biology, and American history. The digital materials selected are stored on the local server by subscribing schools. Teachers can upload videos to seamlessly fit in a PowerPoint presentation or similar format in a classroom. New videos are added throughout the school year with 400 automatically downloaded to local servers for teacher consideration. There are closed caption titles for visual impaired learners, hearing impaired, and students acquiring English as a second language. Workshops online from the Teacher Center suggest ways for faculty to collaborate in designing interdisciplinary lessons. The Discovery Education Web site is at http://www.discoveryeducation.com/.

Independent proprietary evaluations were conducted for Discovery Education (2009). The results showed that greater exposure to visuals could increase student learning. For example, 2,500 middle school students in Los Angeles were administered a pretest to assess understanding of California mathematics standards. The same measure was administered as a posttest after the semester ended to determine progress. During the intervention, teachers randomly assigned to experimental groups were provided twenty standards-based core-concept video clips to enhance lessons. Teachers in control groups were not provided the visuals. Findings showed a statistically significant improvement of 3 to 5% greater for the experimental groups exposed to visuals than for students in control groups denied exposure. Teachers and administrators observed that inclusion of videos in lessons motivated greater student interest, more attention, recognition of relevance, and increased ability to see daily application. Similar results are reported for eighth grade students in Virginia where an experimental group of teachers exposed students to 30 content-relevant video clips as a supplement for lessons but control group teachers were not provided videos. Pretest and posttest comparisons found that the average improvement by students from the experimental group exceeded their peers in the control group by 13% (United Streaming, 2006).

There is a need for educational research to explore the relationship between use of digital video and the attention span of students (Clyde & Delohery, 2005). Think about your own experience with movies, video games, and Internet searching. For example, people watching movies seldom stop before the end of a film and even less often claim they had a hard time paying attention. Why is this the case for films that are often 2 or more hours in length? One line of speculation is that films enable the spectators to stay involved because they see pictures and hear soundtrack at the same time. In contrast, without some stream of images and related sound track, the lectures that teachers provide commonly produce student claims of distraction, loss of attention, and boredom (Daniels & Arapostathis, 2005).

Educators lack suitable measures of attention span but make estimates by observing how long students appear able to concentrate on verbal presentations. The typical conclusion is that students have short attention spans for this aspect of schoolwork. Therefore, teachers are often advised to restrict the duration of direct instruction. Sometimes attention deficits are attributed to television, supposedly creating a dependency for merging pictures with sound, and which may be interrupted by frequent advertisements (Poftak, 2005).

Multimedia presentations can be implemented by combining video clips and PowerPoint, exemplifying concepts through use of photos, diagrams, props, or artifacts, and Internet sites. In addition to increased visual imagery, it can be helpful to break up lectures with one or more group activities, each lasting for at least 10 minutes. This interaction minimizes monotony and, more importantly, encourages the students to actively process and reflect on material that has just been covered (Miller & Borowicz, 2006). Adolescents are more attentive in stimulating environments; in a non-stimulating environment, short attention spans are predictable (Debevec, Shih, & Kashyap, 2006). A promising explanation for teachers is to accept a challenge of providing support for the development of visual intelligence in school and plan instruction so presentations are augmented with digital video and student engagement.

Media Interpretation and Critical Thinking

When television was introduced in the 1950s, people saw it as an extension of human senses, a means for allowing viewers to immediately travel to far away places and vicariously observe events. The assumption was that spectators would be able to make rational decisions about the credibility of content they observed on the small screen. After all, television resembled photography by providing a window on reality while disseminating information at the same time. Subsequently, technology has produced vast changes that complicate the processing of visual intelligence (McCotter, Gosselin, Sowden, & Schyns, 2005).

A common experience is that images stream past viewers so fast that they are unable to rely on reflection as a basis for responding to the media-created reality. Even local news stories move quickly to emotionally involve the viewers while bypassing their critical thinking. When the video satellite systems present pictures from other countries in real time accompanied with a brief explanation, viewers must base their reactions primarily on the selected images and verbal excerpts provided them. This prospect of spectators observing events without training for critical interpretation and reflection caused Marshall McLuhan (1911-1980) to predict that, in a technological environment, the media becomes the message. McLuhan's (1964) contention was that everyone experiences more than they will ever understand but it is their experience more than understanding which has the greater impact on behavior (McLuhan & Flore, 2005). This is especially so in relation to media where people are unaware of the effect it has on them.

A notable model from television that established a media-created reality emerged in the 1990s with *ER*, a program originating in the emergency room of a hospital. Michael Crichton, designer of the show, reported that his formula for success was to speed up the pace with each episode including multiple stories and many speaking parts. This innovative format appealed to millions of observers who found the rapid action more exciting than their customary experience with in-depth treatment. This format is distinguished by a "long-take" in which vantage points of viewers are moved incessantly, scene changes take place quickly without interruption and visual continuity is retained by using a single camera outlook that drives through corridors and rooms in a roller-coaster fashion. Some of the characters lend credibility to the action by using medical terms. There are impressive sound bites that substitute for dialogue. Indeed, the hurried chain of events moves so rapidly that it is difficult for the characters to convey complex information. The same presentation format was later adopted by other programs.

Nonstop action that imitates truth without cognitively examining what is happening can disadvantage spectators because they are denied the active role necessary to weigh, balance, and make decisions about what has been seen. Continual exposure to programs in which there is no time or recognized need to participate in reflective thinking tends to discourage young viewers from acquiring listening habits and responding skills that are needed for problem solving and collaboration. When reflective activities are missing in the classroom, many adolescents announce their conclusion that school is a boring place (Carr, 2006).

Critical thinking is the habit of mind that resists being deceived by appearances. Everyone should be aware of the emotional power of visual images and the potential they have to exert subconscious influence, how programs as well as advertisements mimic logic while bypassing involvement with critical thought, consequences of abandoning reflection as the basis for making decisions, and implications of individual inattentiveness. Each of these concerns related to visual intelligence warrant consideration owing to a direct influence on media information processing, learning, and behavior (Gordon, 2004; Smith, Moriarity, Barbatsis, & Kenney, 2005).

SUMMARY

Schools and the Internet

The media often shapes the thinking, identity, goals, and values of adolescents. When schools support a wise use of technology tools, the scope of learning and comprehension of lessons usually improve and there is a corresponding decline in boredom. The chance to practice Internet skills motivates curiosity as illustrated by students more often presenting and answering their own questions, challenging ideas, and participating in critical thinking. These conditions also depend on adult willingness to recognize that students understand some things better than teachers because of their greater immersion with the Internet. Accordingly, teachers' reciprocal learning with students should become a goal they strive to achieve in the classroom.

The education of secondary educators should go beyond direct instruction type lessons as though they represent the complete curriculum. Instead, different principles to guide learning are needed that require students to discover some things on their own, read material without being assigned to do so, and share the findings of their self-directed search with peers and teachers. These changes can transform the role expectations of students and teachers to promote lifelong learning and adjustment to continued change.

Adolescents as Researchers

Some important conditions that support research are student motivation to seek answers for questions, access to suitable tools, and time to participate in searching. Adolescent surveys show that these conditions already exist. Many students have their own computer, spend time online each day, and regard the Internet as their informal curriculum. There is also awareness about the obstacles to becoming researchers. Students report that Internet-based homework is infrequent and of poor quality. These factors can cause boredom and disappointment with schools. Teachers should be urged to create more active learning assignments. Polls should be used to make known the experience of students.

Establishing a beginning set of criteria to guide student Internet research can help define the cooperative obligation of teachers and young investigators. Tracing the research path, evaluating significance of a problem, providing a synthesis statement, determining application value, assessing credibility of sources, and recognizing personal growth needs are steps students should follow with teacher monitoring and feedback at each stage. Young researchers are more effective when they know how to locate proper sources, follow ethical procedures, and maximize the benefit of using technology tools.

Future of Learning and the Internet

The rapid increase of online learning courses for secondary school students continues to exceed predictions. There is evidence that adolescent distance learners perform as well as peers who get instruction in the customary manner. More students can benefit from online experience of acquiring self-discipline needed for success. Similarly, more teachers should be aware of the advantages and how to minimize limitations of this new forum. Everyone needs technology in the new communications environment. Entrepreneurial efforts continue to overcome the digital divide by working to make computers accessible eventually at home for all students. There are also initiatives to develop Internet content to better serve the needs of low-income families.

Dramatic change describes the electronic potential for students over the next decade. For example, time management will become more possible when television programs students prefer to see can be scheduled at their convenience. Families and schools need to remain surveillant to protect youth from hazards on the Internet, particularly sex predators, purveyors of pornography, cyberbullies, and purchasing prescription drugs. Web sites about the prevention of exposure to indecent material and reporting criminal behavior along with sting operations by the government to identify and prosecute offenders can do much to improve student safety in cyber space.

Visual Intelligence and Media Literacy

Media has an enormous influence on communication and decision-making. Even though computers, cell phones, digital cameras, and PDAs fascinate adolescents, most schools offer inadequate orientation to how these tools should be used to advance learning. Some schools prohibit such devices for administrative reasons. Visual intelligence should be added to the customary emphasis on verbal-linguistic and logical-mathematical abilities so that students can better assimilate the visual lessons surrounding them. Media literacy has been proposed as a requirement for high school graduation, vital skills to support likelihood of student success.

Well-known contributors to progress describe their discoveries as initially presented to them in visual image form before they could be translated into words. Sound bite strategies for news shows that report events from around the world in 80 seconds are frequently utilized with nonstop images of visuals that deny observers enough time for reflection. In this way, cognitive evaluation of media for a balanced interpretation in reaching decisions is seriously compromised. Adolescents get much of their learning from the media so they need training in order to become spectators able to apply critical thinking abilities rather than be misled by appearances.

CLASSROOM APPLICATIONS

1. An important aspect of research is dissemination, sharing findings with others. When students conduct Internet searches, they can post their self-stated summaries alongside printouts on the classroom wall. This procedure does not require time for oral reporting in class. Instead, students can be expected to review the collective work and benefit from a pooling of findings discovered through cooperative learning. Readers can write brief phrases identifying their learning about key concepts and questions rather than making evaluative statements. This type of peer feedback can confirm and challenge how to communicate ideas in team settings.

2. Teachers should inform students that they are expected to read beyond their textbook. The Internet allows individuals to make decisions when they participate in self-directed learning. This experience should replace the notion that students read only what a teacher assigns. Instead, the more appropriate emphasis is to take initiative and explore without being told and then share findings and insights with peers.

3. Students need opportunities for search and synthesis activity. Acquiring the skills to find information, becoming adept at communicating in one's own words what has been learned, and being able to recognize connections between data and application is replacing memorization as an indicator of achievement. Students who can locate information, combine data, and present the results in a coherent manner offer evidence of their comprehension and organization.

4. There are things students know more about than teachers do because it is more convenient than ever to carry out research on the Internet. This shift means that direct instruction is no longer the gateway to most learning. Instead, the role of teachers is transitioning to become facilitators as they provide clues, monitor direction, give feedback, and offer advice. These functions permit students to become active learners and make teaching a more exciting task.

5. When teachers acknowledge that technology skills students possess may exceed their own, a more equitable relationship can emerge based on shared leadership and reciprocal learning. This choice enables students to contribute to curriculum through infusion of technology, grow by further practice with technology, and learn to work cooperatively with adults. Teachers can benefit by learning from student mentors who share their technology skills.

6. A new paradigm to support Internet learning requires going beyond the linear approach to include a branching format, establishing discovery as an expectation for self-directed learning, focusing on student-centered work that requires sharing accountability, and encouraging intrinsic motivation that can drive continued growth throughout life.

7. Students prefer the Internet as the source for much of their learning. Teachers can take advantage of this widespread motivation by devising homework assignments and projects that involve application of research skills, practice of online collaboration with teammates, improve attitudes and understandings regarding media literacy, and encourage exploration of personal goals related to higher education and possible work careers.

8. Inventors are building low cost hardware that can help diminish the digital divide. Schools have an important role too. One task is making sure all parents understand the importance of having a computer in the home, preparing assignments that call for family involvement on the Web, provide free classes for parents, and maintain a multiple language school Web site that addresses academic and social needs.

9. Virtual schooling enrollment is increasing in every state and can offer greater opportunity for students to take courses from qualified teachers who, in many cases, are not be available at their institution. Current data indicate virtual students learn as much as peers instructed in classrooms. The challenges for teachers are to prepare and post materials for online instruction, provide timely

assistive feedback by e-mail, post-grades, and convey high expectations for students.

10. Most students want to learn by doing, find out some things on their own instead of gaining knowledge secondhand by being told. This self-directed approach is necessary for a teacher's accommodation of individual differences in interest and ability. The discovery method is also necessary to establish intrinsic motivation to trigger growth after formal schooling is over.

11. Much of what students learn relates to what they see and read on the Internet and television. This preference of sources for learning deserves consideration by schools. By including lessons involving visual thinking and visual media in presentations, students can be prepared to function more effectively in an image-driven society that requires greater reliance on visual intelligence.

12. Media literacy curriculum should be adopted by school districts so that students continue their benefits from traditional subjects while also becoming capable of assimilating a growing exposure to visual lessons. Administrators should assume a leadership role in advocating for this addition to instructional content.

13. The national goal to make creative thinking more prominent depends in part on the public acceptance of visual intelligence as a basic skill suitable for the curriculum. In a media driven society of dominant visual images, students should be provided lessons to support visual communication.

FOR REFLECTION

1. Based on your teaching subject, what Web sites would you recommend adolescents visit to enhance understanding about content of the class?

2. What are some ways to ensure that your students share with classmates what they have learned independently from the Internet?

3. What are your impressions about the potential of adolescents to become researchers who apply technology tools for exploration on the Internet?

4. What aspects of providing online courses for secondary students do you find appealing and what others are bothersome for you?

5. What Internet-related topics would you favor including in a community–based course offered for parents of students attending your school?

6.   Explain your reasoning for support or opposition to the notion that media literacy should be added to the curriculum as a requirement for graduation from high school.

7.   Describe how some of your learning at school could have been enriched by the inclusion of media literacy practices as an aspect of the curriculum.

8.   Identify some obstacles that you foresee in providing support for visual intelligence at school and ways each of these difficulties can be overcome.

9.   Why do you suppose adolescents so often identify the Internet as the source of learning that offers the greatest appeal for them?

10.   How will you help students to transition from nearly exclusive external direction about what to read to taking initiative for self-directed reading?

11.   What topics should be included in a workshop for adolescents on how to reverse mentor relatives so that they can benefit more from the Internet?

12.   What are your observations of how multitasking by students supports and obstructs their learning at home and in school as they complete assignments from teachers?

KEY TERMS

Authority inversion
Baby Boomers
Digital divide
Digital immigrants
Digital natives
Intrinsic motivation
Knowledge workers
Linear learning
Logical-mathematical intelligence
Media literacy
Net Generation
Paradigm
Plagiarism
Verbal-linguistic intelligence
Visual intelligence
Virtual schools

VISIT THESE WEB SITES

Link to these sites at http://www.infoagepub.com/strom-adolescents

Children's Partnership, Digital Opportunities Program
http://www.childrenspartnership.org

Discovery Education, Classroom Resources
http://www.discoveryeducation.com

Edutopia, George Lucas Teaching Communication
http://www.edutopia.org

Edutopia, Martin Scorsese: Teaching Visual Literacy
http://www.edutopia.org/martin-scorsese-teaching-visual-literacy

Florida Virtual School http://www.flvs.net

Growing up Online
http://www.pbs.org/wgbh/pages/frontline/kidsonline/

Idaho Digital Learning Academy
http://Idla.blackboard.com

International Association for K-12 Online Learning
http://www.inacol.org

International Society for Technology in Education, Profiles for Technology Literate Students
http://www.iste.org

Internet Public Library for Teens, Research and Writing Info Search
http://www.ipl.org/div/teen/aplus/internet.htm

Internet Public Library, Subject Collections
http://www.ipl.org

Matisse Enzer, Glossary of Internet Terms
http://matisse.net/files/glossary.html

Media Literacy Center http://www.medialit.org

Michigan Virtual School at http://www.mivhs.org

Museum of Modern Art, New York City
http://redstudio.moma.org/about/

Nicholas Negroponte,
The Vision Behind One Laptop per Child
http://www.ted.com

Marc Prensky http://www.marcprensky.com/writing/default.asp

Search Engine Resources http://www.refdesk.com/newsrch.html

Self-Evaluation Rubrics for Advanced Teacher Computer Use
http://www.ed.gov/pubs/EdTechGuide/appc-7.html

Southern Regional Educational Board http://www.sreb.org/

Teacher Tube, Pay Attention Final Final Cut
http://www.teachertube.com

University of Texas High School
http://www.utexas.edu/cee/dec/uths/

Web site Evaluation
http://socserv2.mcmaster.ca/Inquiry/neteval.htm

WWW Virtual Library http://vlib.org

YouTube, A Vision of K–12 Students Today
http://www.youtube.com

YouTube, Information R/evolution
http://www.youtube.com/watch?v=-4CV05HyAbM&NR=1

EXERCISES AND ROLES

Exercise 5.01: Learning on the Internet Poll

Role: Voter
   The purpose of this poll is to find out how students at your school feel about learning from the Internet. Directions: For each item, select the answers(s) that indicate how you feel. In some cases, you may select more than one answer. If an answer you want to give is not listed, write it on the line marked "other." Your responses are anonymous and may be combined with peers at your school in a report to students, faculty, and parents.

   1.   Homework assignments on the Internet

        (a)   Encourage me to learn things independently
        (b)   Provide me more information about a topic
        (c)   Improve my understanding of search skills
        (d)   Require sharing with other students in class
        (e)   other

2. The ways parents can support Internet learning are

    (a) monitoring the Web sites visited by their teenager
    (b) discussing information found on the Internet
    (c) assisting students in carrying out their research
    (d) make sure student has computer access at home
    (e) other

3. The Web sites I find beneficial contain

    (a) streaming video or audio material
    (b) quizzes with corrective feedback
    (c) visuals that help organize content
    (d) written summaries of the content
    (e) other

4. My teachers could use training on how to

    (a) develop more assignments involving the Internet
    (b) organize students in teams to do Internet searches
    (c) advise parents to support learning on the Internet
    (d) help students understand Internet ethics
    (e) other

5. Virtual schools, where students may work from home,

    (a) could help responsible students make greater progress
    (b) should replace the traditional schedule of school
    (c) would motivate students to be more self-directed
    (d) would be ineffective for lazy students
    (e) other

6. The main reasons that I use the Internet are to

    (a) find things for school work
    (b) play games
    (c) chat with friends
    (d) send e-mail messages
    (e) download music
    (f) shop online
    (g) other

7. My school Web site could be improved by

   (a) listing all events with times and places
   (b) posting homework and course grades
   (c) posting tutoring schedules for help
   (d) recognizing students for good behavior
   (e) I do not have a school Web site
   (f) I have never visited my school Web site
   (g) other

8. I learn best through

   (a) discussions with my classmates
   (b) books and other print sources
   (c) reading on the Internet
   (d) direct instruction from teacher
   (e) videotapes and television
   (f) other

9. I wish my school offered instruction on

   (a) how to evaluate Web site credibility
   (b) methods to improve my search skills
   (c) how to block inappropriate sites/materials
   (d) ways to deal with cyberbullying
   (e) other

10. In the interest of Internet safety, I choose to

   (a) not reveal personal information
   (b) ask my parents before downloading any software
   (c) keep a log of all the Web sites that I have visited
   (d) let my parents know when I find dangerous materials
   (e) access the Internet only with the consent of an adult
   (f) other

11. My homework requires that I use the Internet

   (a) daily
   (b) twice a week
   (c) weekly
   (d) never
   (e) other

12.   When doing homework on the Internet

    (a)   I find it difficult to decide which sites to access
    (b)   I plagiarize/cut and paste instead of using my words
    (c)   I get sidetracked while conducting a search
    (d)   I have a hard time identifying key words for my search
    (e)   other

13.   Internet learning is beneficial because it

    (a)   helps teachers learn from their students
    (b)   it enables students to discover information
    (c)   it encourages a more global outlook about things
    (d)   it allows students to progress at their own pace
    (e)   it enables students to share information
    (f)   other

14.   The amount of time I spend daily on the Internet is

    (a)   none
    (b)   less than 1 hour
    (c)   1–2 hours
    (d)   2–3 hours
    (f)   other

15.   My school can support Internet learning by

    (a)   making the computer lab available evenings and weekends
    (b)   offering classes for parents about learning on the Internet
    (c)   making online courses available for the students to take
    (d)   providing more assignments that require use of the Internet
    (f)   other

16.   My greatest obstacles to Internet learning are

    (a)   teachers don't make assignments involving the Internet
    (b)   school computers are in labs only, not in the classrooms
    (c)   too many filtering restrictions that limit ability to search
    (d)   lack of access to the use of a computer in my own home
    (f)   other

Select your grade level, gender, ethnicity, and age.

My grade level is 5 6 7 8 9 10 11 12
My gender is female male
My ethnicity is Asian Black Hispanic Native American White Other
My age is 10 11 12 13 14 15 16 17 18 19

Exercise 5.02: Internet for School-Home Communication

Role: Improviser

When cable television was introduced, vendors were obligated to provide free airtime for communities to use regarding public service projects and public school programming. These disappointing presentations consisted mostly of meal menus and meetings of the school board. Technological resources should be used in more creative ways to support students and involve parents. Use your creativity to identify helpful information parents should be able to access on the Web site maintained by their child's school.

Exercise 5.03: Electronic Mail

Role: Summarizer

Electronic mail is part of the school environment. Identify some advantages and disadvantages that e-mail presents for secondary teachers. Then recommend three guidelines you believe could help faculty with electronic mail challenges.

Exercise 5.04: School Attendance and Distance Learning

Role: Voter

An increasing number of adults prefer online learning because it offers scheduling convenience. However, little is known about the choices that would be favored by adolescents. To increase insight, administer this poll to high school students. Use a handout or an overhead projector so students see their choices as a teammate reads them aloud. Tally a show of hands for each of the options and find out reasons for preferences.

Directions to Adolescents

We are approaching a time when it may no longer be necessary for students to attend classes 5 days a week. Distance learning technology is widely used and increasing in higher education. While any decision on changing the school schedule is likely to create controversy, it is important to find out how middle school and high school students feel about choices that may be possible for them as individuals. When I read aloud each choice, please raise your hand if you favor that option for yourself. You can raise your hand for more than one choice. I will ask for reasons why each choice is selected or opposed. One team member will take notes about your comments. Let's begin.

OPTION 1. I would like to attend classes 3 days a week and stay home 2 days a week where I would do my reading and assignments on the computer by distance learning. If you like this option, raise your hand (count the hands). What are your reasons for choosing or opposing this choice? (Write comments.)

OPTION 2. I would like to attend classes 1 day a week and stay home 4 days a week where I would do reading and assignments on the computer by distance learning. If you like this option, raise your hand (count the hands). What are your reasons for favoring or opposing this choice? (Write comments.)

OPTION 3. I would like to keep things the way they are and go to school 5 days a week. If you like this option, raise your hand (count the hands). What are your reasons for favoring or opposing this choice? (Write comments.)

OPTION 4. I would like to take one course for college credit by distance learning during each semester of my junior and senior year in high school. These courses would be taken in addition to meeting requirements for graduation. If you like this option, raise your hand (count the hands). What are your reasons for favoring or opposing this choice? (Write comments.)

Exercise 5.05: Technology in the School

Role: Generational Reporter

There is increasing reliance on technology to support learning in the classroom. Concern is also growing about misuse of technology tools that students own and bring to school. Privacy and fair use issues are implicated. Teachers wonder what can be done to prevent and minimize inappropriate practices by students. Ask adolescents to describe some misuses of technology they have observed at school and recommend suitable methods for prevention.

Exercise 5.06: Distance Learning

Role: Evaluator

Public support for distance learning at the middle school and high school levels is growing. This is a chance to look ahead and generate possibilities. Describe (a) ways this paradigm shift could improve schooling; (b) present obstacles that must be overcome; (c) identify opportunities for faculty collaboration; and (d) suggest novel methods that could enrich the online experience.

Exercise 5.07: Learning About Adolescents From the Movies

Role: Improviser

George Lucas, creator of *Star Wars*, recommends that educators should take media more seriously as a source of insight about the lives of students. Perhaps we can learn something from the movies about experience of adolescents, challenges they encounter, abilities they possess, and ways to be of help to them.

Identify two films that you believe offer understanding about teenagers. For each film provide the (1) title, year, actors, length and other relevant data; (2) describe the storyline in a paragraph; and (3) explain why you think that teachers and parents can gain from watching the film. *Videohound*, *DVD and Video Guide*, and *Halliwell's Film Guide* are among many annotative resources regarding film.

Exercise 5.08: Distance Learners

Role: Improviser

List and describe some strategies that can enable distance learners to contribute to education of their online teammates.

Exercise 5.09: Creating Internet Homework Assignments

Role: Improviser

Teachers should encourage family collaboration and dialogue for some homework assignments. Use of the Internet for homework in middle or high school could be based on these guidelines:

1. Enable parents to understand social network sites by adolescents who provide a tour showing how shared interest information is organized and provides chances for interaction (e.g., Facebook, MySpace).

2. Adolescent and parent choose a controversial topic on a list given by the teacher. Both generations read about the issue from Web sources they independently locate. Following a discussion, they submit to the teacher their shared reactions along with issues of disagreement.

3. Student and parent choose from teacher topics that reflect greater knowledge by the adults (finances, adolescence in the 80s) including discussion agenda, augmented by questions that arise spontaneously and can be checked on the Internet.

4. Parent and adolescent work together, side by side for a specified period (30 minutes) to search for understanding about a teacher assigned topic. The pair identifies their progression of keywords and search processes, sites visited, and insights gained by each party. This dialogue stimulus could be helpful practice encouraging other conversations.

5. Describe an additional guideline that teachers could consider as they try to enable parents and children to learn together.

Exercise 5.10. Multirole Exercise—Cell Phones

Roles: Storyteller, Improviser, Challenger, Generational Reporter

Many issues arise with cell phones. Positive uses and obnoxious purposes both are commonly observed. Each team member should choose at least one of the four roles below and perform the exercise (task) associated with it.

Role: Storyteller

TASK: Tell a story about a time when you found a cell phone to be of considerable help. Then share another story about a time when a cell phone was problematic for some reason. Provide details.

Role: Improviser

TASK: Brainstorm a list of the general possible benefits and disadvantages of cell phones. This can be done by the entire team during a session, or, done outside of class by one improviser. The list can be shared later with the team.

Role: Challenger

TASK: Choose a position to defend which argues for or against the access to cell phones in college classrooms. You may qualify under what conditions the access should be allowed or disallowed as long as rationale is provided and explained to teammates.

Role: Generational Reporter

TASK: Interview teenagers and their parents. Ask them the following questions:

1. What are some advantages about the use of cell phones as commonly seen by people your age?
2. What are some important concerns about the use of cell phones as commonly seen by people your age?

CHAPTER 6

CREATIVE THINKING AND PROBLEM SOLVING

Myth has been a common source of information about creative people throughout recorded history. Explanations of the inventive mind, original thinking, and novel ideas have often been pejorative. According to ancient people, creative individuals were possessed, driven to innovation and unconventional behavior by some unseen power that selected this manner of revelation. That creative behavior could be an outcome of learning was seldom considered. Instead, inspiration was attributed to the gods. And, because evil and good were supposed to be in constant dispute, individuals who manifested signs of creativity were often suspect. Original thinking might be a deception by the forces of evil, particularly in cases when the creative persons challenged prevailing beliefs and customs of their time (Bourke, 2006).

In the twentieth century, unfavorable impressions about creative individuals continued but their behavior was then linked to a supposed relationship between inventive thinking and mental break down. Creative persons were no longer perceived as pawns of an unseen force. Instead, they were viewed as personally responsible for their deviation from the norms of society. Creativity was acknowledged to be an internal function but unrelated to education. Mental illness afflicted few geniuses but eminent examples were used to make exceptions appear as though they were the rule. There was no recognition that willingness of creative people to

Adolescents in the Internet Age, pp. 235–283

press their nature to its limit is the supreme test of sanity. Instead, individuals who failed in such efforts were singled out as proof that giftedness comes at too high a cost to make it a desirable condition for most of the population (Ludwig, 1995; Saunders & Macnaughton, 2005).

The goals for this chapter are to describe how the stigma that was once attached to imagination has been replaced by cautious support for education to encourage creative behavior. The empirical distinction between creativity and intelligence is presented with an overview of creative abilities, priority for mental operations of thinking, and progressive steps that define the creative process. Discussion considers how teachers perceive creative students, often as difficult to work with because they provide offbeat answers, refer to concepts that appear irrelevant to conventional thinkers, display humor and sarcasm, and often engage in daydreaming. Emphasis is placed on ways to improve classroom conditions so creative thinking becomes more common, and creative students are respected by peers and teachers. Student reports of boredom are explored along with ways it affects learning and implicates revision in school practices.

CHARACTERISTICS OF CREATIVITY

The need to support creative behavior in schools became widely recognized following Joy Guilford's (1950) presidential address to the American Psychological Association. He argued that the customary views of mental growth were focused too narrowly on *convergent thinking* with an emphasis on knowing the single correct answer for a problem and giving a speedy response. These aspects of achievement are important but should not dominate conceptualization of mental functioning at the expense of other dimensions of thought essential for creativity. Guilford specifically referred to *divergent thinking,* the ability to branch out and generate alternative answers for problems where there might be more than one solution, and having an ability to perceive many possibilities in situations.

A few years later, in 1957, Russia launched Sputnik I, the first artificial satellite. There was a feeling of national embarrassment because the United States had lost the first round in the space race. Navy Admiral Hyman Rickover (1959), a nuclear scientist, placed the blame on public schools, citing the "inability of our institutions to find a place for the creative expert and their persistence in believing that novel projects can be carried out using routine methods" (p. 16). Soon there was public agreement about the need to encourage creative thinking and improve science curriculum so the nation could catch up (Torrance, 2000a). Within weeks Congress passed the National Defense Education Act (1958) providing funds for research on ways to nurture creativity in the classroom. Paul

Torrance (1965) defined *creative thinking* as the process of sensing difficulties, problems, gaps in information, missing elements, making guesses, or formulating hypotheses about these deficiencies, testing guesses, possibly revising and retesting them, and finally in communicating the results.

The resulting studies of creativity focused mostly on establishing a common basis for collaborative efforts (Cropley, 2003). However, first it was necessary to determine whether creative potential is measured by intelligence tests or if creativity is a separate domain of mental functioning requiring alternative tools for measurement. There was also speculation about the cognitive processes creative people rely on to produce their work. Identifying progressive steps in the creative process would be useful in orientation of students. Teacher willingness to nurture creative abilities had to be assessed and educational objectives modified so that expectations of students would reflect the newly adopted goals of society (Bonner, 2005).

Creativity and Intelligence

Michael Wallach, Professor of psychology and neuroscience at Duke University, and Nathan Kogan, of Educational Testing Service, are recognized for their seminal study that changed how educators think about creativity. Their purpose was to determine whether creativity, defined as the ability to produce many associations among ideas and many that are unique, is independent of individual differences in the domain of general intelligence (Wallach & Kogan, 1965). The researchers also wanted to determine whether creativity, like Spearman's (1904) g concept of intelligence, includes a large degree of generality across different types of verbal and visual tasks (Jensen, 1998). The 151 participants were fifth graders (10- and 11-year-olds) that attended a suburban public school. The students (70 girls and 81 boys) completed creativity instruments that called for the production of idea associations. These tests resembled an earlier battery of measures that had been devised by Guilford (1950) but conditions of speed and evaluation were de-emphasized. Instead, a game-like setting without time limits was allowed. For each instrument (all were oral), the number of unique associations and total number of ideas served as correlational variables (Wallach & Kogan, 1965).

On the instances task, students were expected to produce instances for a class concept specified in verbal terms. For example, "Name all the round things you can think of." The number of unique responses for an item was defined as the number of associates given by only one child to the item in question. Thus, while "lifesavers" was a unique response for things that are round, "buttons" was not unique. The alternate uses task required students to generate possible uses for verbally specified objects.

To illustrate, "tell me all the things you can do with a shoe." A unique response was "trap a mouse" but it was not unique to "throw it at a noisy dog." A third task was to think of similarities between two given objects. For the question "Tell me the ways in which milk and meat are alike," a conventional response was, "They come from animals" whereas a unique response was, "They are government inspected."

In addition to these verbal tasks, there were two procedures that involved abstract patterns and line-visual stimulus materials for which students produced meanings or interpretations (see Figure 6.1) (Wallach & Kogan, 1965). Students were also administered 10 indicators of general intelligence, including verbal and performance subtests of the Wechsler Intelligence Scale for children (WISC); verbal and quantitative aptitude tests drawn from the School and College Ability Tests (SCAT); and the Sequential Tests of Educational Progress (STEP), a measure of achievement in various subjects (Spies, Plake, & Murphy, 2005).

The measures of creativity and intelligence were first determined to be valid and reliable and then the dimensionality of these indicators was examined to find the degree to which they were related, referred to as *correlation*. Generally, a correlation of .40 or higher between two measures is considered substantial. The measures of creativity were highly intercorrelated (average .40); similar internal consistency was found for the general intelligence tests (average .50). However, the degree of relationship between creativity and intelligence was low as evidenced by a correlation of .10. This lack of association led to the conclusion that individual differences in the ability to generate many cognitive units and many that are unique is a cohesive realm and independent from what is referred to as general intelligence. Within an assessment context free of evaluative threat and time constraint, being able to produce unique ideas comes from a different source than intelligence as it has been historically perceived. Consequently, it can be asserted that the ability of students to demonstrate creativity, as defined in the Wallach and Kogan (1965) study, has little to do with whether or not they reveal behaviors that produce high scores on tests of general intelligence. This result is even more significant when remembering that all the measures of creativity in this investigation were oral, calling for verbal facility, and verbal facility plays a major role in the assessment of general intelligence.

Wallach and Kogan's (1965) findings suggested that it might be possible to educate to a greater degree many students who have been unsuccessful in traditional classroom environments. Operationally, the term "intelligence" has included the abilities needed for reading and mathematics, subjects that are not conspicuously demanding of creative behavior. It should be mentioned, however, while the creativity and intelligence domains seem to be separate, a person might rate high in both sectors.

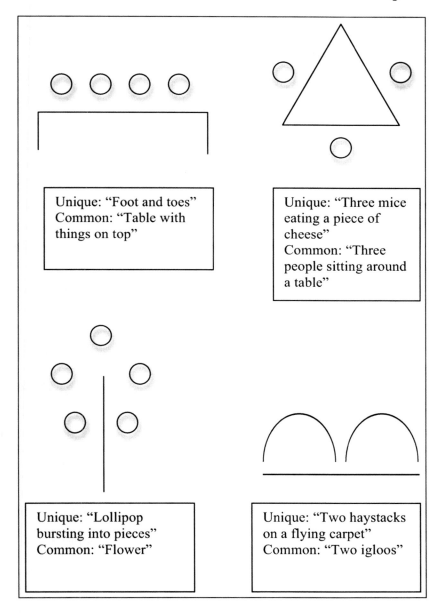

Figure 6.1. Children's Responses to Abstract Drawings.

One estimate is that, in a group of students that are either highly creative or highly intelligent, 30% qualify in both categories (Torrance, 2000b). Finally, the statistical independence of these two domains has been documented at a point in the lifespan (ages 10 and 11), well below the age at which maximum differentiation of types of cognitive performance would be expected. This means that even greater independence could be revealed at later ages. These considerations strongly suggest that a concerted effort is warranted to educate students for creative behavior (Heilman, 2005). For an alternate explanation of creative thinking, see Robert Harris' Web site at Virtual Salt—http://www.virtualsalt.com/crebook1.htm.

Creative Thinking Abilities

Writing a story, painting a picture, and doing science experiments can be creative activities, but their success depends upon different subabilities. However, are there some common abilities implicated in every kind of creative activity? Guilford (1977) maintained that the creative abilities he identified as: (1) sensitivity, (2) fluency, (3) flexibility, (4) originality, and (5) elaboration are aspects of divergent thinking (i.e., creative problem solving). Unlike most thinking in school that requires convergence upon a single correct answer, divergent thinking is generating a number of alternative solutions for particular problems. Sensitivity and redefinition are additional traits of creative production.

(1) *Sensitivity.* Showing sensitivity to a problem is necessary to trigger the creative process. Two witnesses of the same event can differ considerably in the degree to which they are sensitive to the scene. For example, the training of chemists and teachers make them both sensitive to different aspects of experience. The chemist working alone in a lab can perhaps be relatively insensitive to interpersonal relationships and remain successful but this is not the case for a teacher. Similarly, the educator supporting students may have little sensitivity to temperature as is necessary for chemists. The solving of problems in any field begins with appropriate sensitivities (Bonner, 2005).

Sensitivity in creative persons accounts for keen awareness of a problem and is associated with a desire to favorably change situations. This tendency has been observed among creative individuals across generational groups. Rossman (1964) distinguished patent inventors from less inventive peers by noting that, whereas non-inventors tend to complain about environmental defects, inventors were motivated to find ways of improving the conditions. Similarly, Torrance (2000a, 2000b) determined that less creative children had little difficulty cataloging defects in toys and pictures but they lacked constructive responses. For example, when shown a plastic toy dog and requested to think of ways in which it might be changed to be more fun, most of the non-inventive students suggested that the dog should move but offered no way of accomplishing movement. In contrast, inventive children who also felt that the plastic dog should become mobile proposed alternatives like attaching a string to pull it, adding wheels, giving the dog a motor or battery, constructing a mechanism for winding it up, or placing a magnet in its nose.

(2) *Fluency.* The relationship between creative process and the field of application in which it is manifested is best described by fluency factors. *Fluency,* the proliferation and ease with which ideas are generated and expressed, is further divided into ideational and associational for purposes of assessment (Bonner, 2005). *Ideational fluency* is the ability to produce a large number of ideas within a specified time limit when free expression is encouraged and quality is not evaluated. Although number of ideas produced might appear to be relatively unimportant as a criterion for creativity, persons who have more ideas more frequently generate better ones too. Thomas Edison and Alfred North Whitehead asserted that quantity and quality of ideas are related. Support for this contention also comes from studies which show that, in group activities, the greater the variation of ideas presented, the more likely a final decision will be reasonable (Russo, 2004).

One way to assess ideational fluency is by asking students to enumerate as many ideas as they can about some assigned topic in five or ten minutes. This could also be an assignment for students if given a practical prompt or directive, such as "Devise several ways to improve how time could be better spent at school." Another task requires students to list in a specified time period all the things they can think of that are circular. The total number of responses constitutes the ideational fluency score. Applying this idea in the classroom, for practice or as an assignment, teachers can assign students to think of various new titles for a story or news report they have read, or generate a list of endings for an incomplete story.

Associational fluency includes extensive awareness of relationships and ease in producing words or ideas from a restricted context of meaning. For example, a student might be asked to generate synonyms for a particular word. For the word gifted, some responses could include intelligence, smart, talented, sharp, and outstanding. Teachers of all grades support associational fluency by tasks that involve a Thesaurus offering students opportunities to recognize word relationships, words of similar and opposite meaning, to detect irrelevant words, and select words with precise meanings. Fluency factors might have little importance for creative production in a physics laboratory but they are crucial for areas such as creative writing. Ideational fluency provides writers with something to write about and associational fluency offers word finding ability and helps writers arrange words into organized form.

(3) *Flexibility.* This quality is frequently mentioned as an attribute that everyone needs to acquire in a rapidly changing society (Craft, 2005). *Flexibility* is the capacity to shift readily from one particular pattern of thought to another. Individuals demonstrate this ability when thinking is not bound by history, tradition, or familiar social restraints. Whereas ideational fluency centers on the number of ideas that are produced, spontaneous flexibility concerns number of categories into which ideas are channeled (Cheng & Cheung, 2005). There is little doubt that some people get into ruts and cannot change tracks, devise new approaches, or see alternatives. Torrance (1995) studied the extent of such rigidity by asking students to think of unusual, clever, or interesting uses for tin cans. The percentages of persons in each of the sample groups who were unable to break away from the idea that cans must be seen as containers were: schizophrenics 87%; graduate students 40%; and middle school children 15%.

(4) *Originality.* While almost everyone mentions originality as an important aspect of creative thinking, there is disagreement over what this term means. One suggestion is that to be original is to do something that is without precedent, the first of its kind. This definition is unworkable when we measure originality because it is impossible to verify that no one throughout time has ever thought of a particular idea before. A related difficulty arises if two inventors or researchers independently arrive at the same solution to a problem. It would be incorrect to identify as creative only the person officially credited with the discovery. Further, there is little merit in attaching value to some behavior simply because it is novel. Dreams and hallucinations are frequently unique yet usually lack relevance and worth.

For purposes of measurement, Guilford (1977) hypothesized that originality is a quality possessed by everyone to some extent and therefore is best characterized as a continuum. Instead of defining as original only ideas or things that are new or without precedent, Guilford relied on the following three alternative criteria for originality: uncommonness of response, remoteness of association, and cleverness. *Originality* is an ability to produce ideas that are statistically infrequent for the population of which the person is a member. On an Unusual Uses test, the subjects were asked to enumerate six additional functions for each of several items having a familiar use. The criterion of originality was tested by presenting subjects with 25 pairs of words. The relationship between members of each pair was not immediately obvious, and subjects were asked to suggest a third word to link each pair. Finally, cleverness was assessed by a panel of judges responding to titles that individuals submitted for several stories they had been assigned to read. These three approaches to the assessment of original response seem sensible. If novel ideas are by definition impossible to judge by conventional standards, then pejorative labels such as "silly," or "odd" have no place among the criteria. More of us should become reluctant to prejudge new ideas without careful examination and reflection (Cropley, 2003).

(5) *Elaboration* refers to the ability for working out implications of an idea or filling in details of a structure. Original thinkers sometimes achieve less than might be possible because they lack elaborative ability. Others who may follow them could receive credit for explaining the same issues as translators. Elaboration involves following through on ideas. It has been recognized for a long time that as much genius is displayed in explaining a design and bringing out the hidden significance of a work of art as in creating it (Ghiselin, 1987; Mill, 2000). Finally, *redefinition* is the ability to transform an existing object into one of a different function, design or use. This ability implies a freedom from fixedness and the skill to reinterpret what is already known.

The Creative Process

The support of student creativity as a priority in the classroom and finding ways to develop this capacity are becoming common goals. Those who conduct research in this context admit that the creative thinking process is only partially understood. Yet, there is agreement that several specific phases precede invention. These respective stages are (1) Preparation, (2) Incubation, (3) Illumination, and (4) Verification (Ghiselin, 1987; Torrance, 1995). Characteristics of the four stages of the creative process are illustrated in Figures 6.2 (Preparation), Figure 6.3 (Incubation), Figure 6.4 (Illumination), and Figure 6.5 (Verification).

(1) *Preparation*. Some people are surprised to find out that preparation is essential for creative thinking. Instead, they tend to suppose "inspiration" just comes to certain people and not to others. This assumption makes it easier to avoid the struggle in which those who create are participants. *Preparation* (see Figure 6.2) begins after creative persons experience vague insights and set out to examine some particular problem or realm of difficulty by literally flooding themselves with the diverse impressions held by others. Many obstacles that undermine production characterize the preparation phase. First, the literature about a problem may be so extensive that the task seems overwhelming. This appears to be the case when many search engines can be applied to locate an enormous database for consideration. At this point the person might decide to withdraw from further exploration and go on to some other concern that is less complicated (Starko, 2001).

A second related danger is that side issues can capture a person's attention and divert interest from the original purpose. This is a familiar

Figure 6.2.   Stage 1 of the creative process—Preparation. Search data, brainstorm with a partner, try to see the main pieces of problem, and begin to question assumptions. Illustration by Paris Strom.

shortcoming among people whose indiscriminate curiosity often causes them to leave their line of direction (Starko, 2001). They may be pursuing a particular area of inquiry but along the way Web sites they explore present links that lead them away from their intent. Remaining focused is essential and can be difficult when conducting searches on the Internet or in a library (Cropley, 2003).

Third, the impatience that causes students to grapple with an issue can destroy their chances for success if they prematurely reach conclusions about the data (de Bono, 1999; Getzels & Jackson, 1962; Lewandowski, 2005). This is a widespread hazard in situations where rapid production is an expectation. Whenever teachers set deadlines that are too early, they inadvertently encourage superficial consideration of data. The emphasis on doing everything in a hurry is not conducive to creative thinking. It is necessary to recognize that a fundamental aspect of the preparation phase is immersion in the ideas and insights already expressed by others. Awareness of these impressions produces the material on which synthesizing ability will operate. Abandoning a problem or project is easier at this stage than later because little work has been invested and the degree of emotional involvement is minimal (de Bono, 2007).

Many adolescents see themselves as lacking creative potential because novel ideas have not come to them without preparation. Reading about the lives of eminent individuals including their failures, successes, and courage can correct this perception (John-Steiner, 2000). Courage is required to move alone toward uncertainties, counter to one's classmates, to do battle with one's own prejudices. It takes persistence to begin a task again and again. Persistence brings both success and failure. More than most of us, the creative person experiences failure because s/he does not run from complex tasks. Many of us do not fail because we are so easily discouraged and quit; at the same time we can never fully succeed. Persistence enables a person to sustain a question, a problem, or task, and work it through to completion. The history of creative persons who have contributed the most to society is an account filled with persistence and courage (Bandura, 2004; Delisie, 2005; Desetta, 2005).

Preparation is a difficult period for all creative persons. Those who underestimate the value of preparation typically end their search process too soon. Potentially creative students frequently give up because they suppose inventive thinking is either simple or beyond their reach. The fact is that quite often what seems to be a creative achievement is really a matter of being able to sort abundant information and organize it well (Barron, Montuori, & Barron, 1997).

(2) *Incubation*. The second stage of the creative process centers on incubation (see Figure 6.3). During incubation there is an irrational, intuitive encounter with the materials that have been gathered in the search process. At this stage people experience unrest as they try to produce an ordering structure, a recombination of information that will merit their expression into some unique as well as practical form. They may be preoccupied to the point that they fail to attend to routine tasks expected of them by others. As they try to allow the intuitive idea to take conscious form, creative persons are dissatisfied with themselves and often difficult to be around. Sometimes conflicts ensue with relatives or friends who consider the inattention to them as a deliberate insult (Guilford, 1979).

During the incubation stage, self-doubt can pose a great hazard. Confidence is essential when unconscious activity bring up new possibilities for combination one after another. It is imperative that the conscious mind

Figure 6.3.   Stage 2 of the creative process—Incubation. In-depth pondering, sketch or test ideas, get frustrated, recognize paradigm paralysis, look for one's niche. Illustration by Paris Strom.

refrain from disapproving these ideas as they emerge, defer judgment until a wide range of unconscious products become available. Feeling obligated to withhold judgment until the associative flow ends is a difficult and demanding task that requires a high tolerance for ambiguity and frustration. Mental health is usually delicate during the incubation phase, which can vary from a few minutes to months (Torrance, 2000b).

Students are often discouraged by their pace of production. Teachers and parents add to the frustration when they construe lack of speed as lack of ability, being slow as an indication of failure. It should be known that the time needed for production depends on the individual. The example of Mozart and Beethoven represent a contrast in musical production. Mozart thought out quartets and symphonies in his head while traveling or exercising. Then, upon returning home, he would write out the innovative melody in its entirety. On the other hand, Beethoven often wrote his work note by note, fragments at a time that he recorded in a little booklet for years. Often his initial ideas were so clumsy as to make one wonder how, at the end, such beauty could emerge. Ernest Hemmingway (1964) admitted, "I didn't know I would ever write anything as long as a novel. It often took me a full morning of work to write a paragraph" (p. 154). The same man later wrote a classic novel in 6 weeks.

During incubation, anything disruptive to the focus of concentration is likely to be rejected. There are some individuals for whom incubation can take place on and over a long period of time. However, for others the attempt to produce ideas leads to excessive measures for sustaining touch with the unconscious in an environment that may be noisy and distracting. Not everyone seems psychologically capable of spending the same amount of time in the tension-producing phase of incubation. Yet, creative persons usually prefer to work in long blocks of time so they can become fully engaged. This is without question the stage when classmates, relatives, and teachers should be aware of the seeming self-punishment that a person appears to experience. Giving up at this stage is done at great expense since creative persons typically consider not achieving the next stage, called Illumination, as total failure (Hargrove, 1998). Albert Einstein observed, "The intuitive mind is a sacred gift and the rational mind is a faithful servant. We have created a society that honors the servant and has forgotten the gift" (Ghiselin, 1952, p. 43).

(3) *Illumination*. If the incubation stage presents for most creative persons what Van Gogh called a "prison" in which they are confined by conversation and debate with themselves, then the illumination phase may be analogous to release from jail with a full pardon. Illumination (see Figure 6.4) is the inspirational moment that the artist Paul Cezanne described as being a liberation, the mysterious becoming external, the time when everything falls into place. It is the exhilarating triumph creative persons like so much to relive, the time that is beyond words. Charles Darwin, whose search for the theory of evolution came to an end on a dusty lane, recalled the very spot on the road while traveling in his carriage that, to his joy and surprise, the solution occurred to him (Darwin & Wilson, 2005). Creative scientists, inventors, artists, and writers all look back in nostalgia at this brief but cherished moment and often speak of it as mystical. With illumination, the burden of tension is lifted and creative persons regain touch with those around them (Bennis & Biederman, 1997).

Certain creative persons, especially those who have long awaited illumination, often make an effort to retain their joy by sharing it. Usually

Figure 6.4.   Stage 3 of the creative process—Illumination. "Ah-ha"—finding one's niche, loving the idea, taking the leap, and assembling the main pieces that fit well. Illustration by Paris Strom.

their accounts of how an idea occurred are less than exciting to others who regard the rapid shift from total preoccupation with the work and seeming depression to happiness and conscious delight as an additional sign of mental illness. They may wonder at the extremes in the creative person's behavior and especially at the sudden elation expressed over something they may not comprehend and thus regard as unimportant. Further, in returning to a normal state of consciousness, some individuals cannot figure out why some people have become distant toward them during the interlude (Ludwig, 1995).

For some persons, the creative process ends with the illumination stage because they have achieved the tentative answer and shed their tensions. At this point, they may move ahead to confront another problem. Persons of this inclination seldom attain recognition or contribute as much as possible because they do not go on to make the form of their invention coherent to others who could enable its broader application or modify it to fit a wider range of prevailing situations (Jacobs & Klaczynski, 2005).

(4) *Verification*. The stage of verification occurs after an idea or plan has emerged from unconscious activity and must then be consciously evaluated (see Figure 6.5). Some creative persons find the need for verification difficult or impossible to accept because emotional certainty about the worth of their idea or product precludes any criticism or adaptation. Nevertheless, the pleasure of illumination must give way to rational judgment as the determinant of final production. If a writer is to communicate, the inspired work must become organized and edited. There must be a coherent flow so that readers can share the message. Similarly, the successful

Figure 6.5.   Stage 4 of the creative process—Verification. Testing final idea to see/ correct faults- "final editing," assessment by outsiders, experience closure and recognize success via individual or social judgment criteria. Illustration by Paris Strom.

experiment that elates a scientist must be clearly described (Storey & Graeme, 2005).

Unlike the brief illumination phase, verification is typically lengthy, arduous, and at times disappointing to a person whose patience declines because of eagerness to begin another project. The hazard that awaits many writers, scientists, and creators in technology and art is the temptation to avoid follow through. This temptation has often prevented good work from becoming public knowledge. There are well known writers such as Samuel Coleridge and Percy Shelley who left fragments of unfinished work because they could not revise it, feeling that inspiration could not be improved on and that any alteration would destroy the illumination. Hart Crane was an exacting author, and a look at his manuscripts reveals that revisions involved as much doubt as decision. In contrast, Gertrude Stein intensely disliked the drudgery of revision and the obligation to make certain of her writing projects intelligible (Barron, Montuori, & Barron, 1997; Ghiselin, 1987). Being willing to seek and constructively interpret criticism from reviewers is essential at this stage. Sadly, most people have not been taught in school or at home to benefit from the criticism of others and this presents an enormous obstacle to creativity. It means that growth is restricted because they rely on themselves alone for criticism. Notwithstanding the attachment of some writers to their work, insight during the revision process can improve organization, structure, and narrative flow (King, 2000).

Students of the creative thinking process are disappointed that the phase-sequence explanation focuses only on only events that happen after an individual has originally sensed a particular problem, become aware of some gap in knowledge, or experienced a vague insight into some area of difficulty. It is as though someone who is interested in knowing about the elaborate design of a novel began to read midway through the book. We do not know how much of the creative process precedes what have been described as its phases. Maybe our explanation of the process starts not at the beginning but closer to the end. In addition, educators have much more to discover about ways to support creativity when students work in teams. Some groups appear to have a unique chemistry with members able to trigger insights from one another and rely on their collective imagination to generate better solutions than they could produce alone (Sternberg, 2003).

Psychology of Thinking

Paul Torrance (1965), an early leader in the measurement of creative thinking, speculated on what schools should be like in the future. He predicted the mission of teachers would enlarge to satisfy employers that seek graduates capable of making discoveries, finding solutions to recurrent problems, and retaining the lifestyle balance needed to preserve mental health. To ensure this possibility, education objectives that center on learning should expand to include thinking as well. Torrance (1995, 2000a) observed that professors offer courses called the psychology of learning but not the psychology of thinking. This means teachers are shown how to construct tests that reveal only what students have learned but almost never to find out what they can do with what has been learned.

Teachers are expected to state their objectives in the language of learning, particularly in terms of students being familiar with facts, conforming to behavior norms, and learning correct attitudes. Teachers rarely state their objectives in the language of thinking such as creative, critical, constructive, independent, logical, and analytical. Teacher methods of instruction, the tasks that they assign students, and relationships with adolescents are mostly intended to produce evidence of convergent learning. Seldom do these efforts focus on stimulating learners to leap the barrier from learning to thinking. Furthermore, most educational research is restricted to examining the learning process and seldom considers thinking process (Carr, 2006).

To assess the slowness of change in adopting educational objectives that reflect thinking, Torrance (2000b) invited secondary social studies educators throughout Minnesota to submit a unit they teach that included their three most important objectives. These objectives were then classified by mental operations students would have to engage in to attain each of them. The five mental operations of cognition, memory, convergent behavior, divergent thinking, and evaluation were originally identified by Guilford (1950, 1986) in his structure of intellect. *Cognition* objectives called on students to recognize, be familiar with, aware of, know about or appreciate. For *memory* the teacher objectives included remembering, knowing thoroughly, and acquiring knowledge. *Convergent thinking* objectives were ones that require conforming to behavior norms, adopting the proper attitude, and finding the single correct solution. *Divergent thinking* consisted of tasks calling for independent thinking, constructive thinking, creative thinking, original work, questioning, inquiring, and similar activities. *Evaluation* included critical thinking, assessing, evaluating, judging, making decisions, comparing, and contrasting (Guilford, 1971, 1986; Guilford & Hoepfner, 1971).

Torrance's (2000b) results suggested that an overwhelming majority of the social studies objectives fall into the cognitive category (66%). Most of the remaining objectives involved convergent behavior (20%). When memory (5%) was added, very little attention was left for divergent thinking (2%) or evaluation (7%). Bearing in mind that intelligence tests focus mainly on cognition and memory, there is a clear need to replace tradition and implicate measures that accord with contemporary challenges adolescents must be prepared for in the workplace. Fortunately, a growing number of teachers are engaging students in discovery learning, giving them opportunities to become self-directed, and participate in self and peer evaluation (Florida, 2004, 2008).

CONDITIONS FOR PROBLEM SOLVING

Since the year 2000, many countries have elevated the priority that schools assign to creative thinking. A National Commission on Educational Reform in Japan concluded that educators at all levels were not nurturing the creative behavior the nation needs to remain competitive (Baker & LeTendre, 2005). Similarly, the Republic of China Ministry of Education (2001) has begun to plan reforms to educate more broadly and to reward creativity. Recommendations to transform schools are encouraged by business leaders in the United States and Europe (Sharez-Orozco, 2005; R. Strom & Strom, 2002a, 2007). Derek Pink (2008) observes that a paradigm shift is emerging, moving educators from the Information Age of the 1990s that rewarded linear, logical, analytical talents measured by SATs and deploying CPAs. We have arrived at a new era called "the Conceptual Age" in which the economy more often requires inventive and empathic abilities. The skills of computing, calculating, diagnostics, and basic legal work are losing value in the United States. They retain their importance but any activity that can be reduced to rules and instructions is likely to become a software program such as TurboTax, replacing tax accountants or end up migrating to China or India.

This shift to the goals for creative thinking can be achieved when the rules that guide educational policy and teaching practice are modified (Runco, 2006). Specifically, teachers should be reminded to avoid the usual response of their predecessors who actively discouraged creative behavior. Student accountability should include divergent thinking as evidence of personal development. Student polling that detects obstacles to creative thinking could help teachers find ways to improve the classroom experience. Novelty has been found to stimulate greater learning and should become more common.

Assign High Priority to Creative Thinking

Thomas Friedman (2005), in *The World is Flat*, observes that place is no longer as great an influence on creative production. Technology has leveled the global playing field, making the world flat so that "anyone can innovate without having to emigrate." An opposite view is expressed by Richard Florida (2008) in *Who's Your City: How the Creative Economy is Making Where You Live the Most Important Decision of Your Life.* He has identified lists of cities on each continent where creative persons move because their talents are accepted, collaborators for projects can be found, and people enjoy working together on interdependent productions. According to Florida (2004), innovation is best encouraged with the geographic concentration of creative people because they can be counted on to permit ideas to flow freely, more often suggest ways to improve products, and their projects are put in practice sooner when creators, implementers, and financial supporters are in continuous contact. A small number of communities generate most of the innovative ideas and products used throughout the world. Dialogue occurs easily and constantly in these settings because of the revolution in communication and transportation.

Most people are not highly creative although everyone needs to acquire problem-solving abilities for adjustment to the ever-changing. environment. Therefore, students from every town and city should find that others accept their divergent thinking without having to move to places where favorable reactions are known to be more common. One context where the necessary transformation should begin involves teacher training. The attitudes of teachers are a powerful force in determining the kind of behavior expected of students. Some observers wonder how teachers and schools will respond to the emerging priority societies across the world are assigning to creative behavior. Some clues can be drawn from the "Ideal Student Checklist" consisting of 62 characteristics discriminating between persons of high and low creative ability. Torrance (2002) provided this list, based on input from experts in creative learning, to 1,000 teachers in the United States, India, Germany, Greece, and the Philippines. Educators checked the characteristics that described the kind of person that they would like their students to become and crossed out the characteristics they believed should be discouraged or punished.

Low correlations were found between the behaviors teachers favored and the behaviors that are usually exhibited by creative thinkers (Torrance, 2002). Educators from all five countries were inclined to undermine creative thinking by encouraging only behaviors like obedience, memorizing material or what the teacher says during lectures, and accepting the judgment of authorities. Students who presented questions, enjoyed speculating, became preoccupied with tasks, acted like visionaries, and showed a willingness to take risks found that these behaviors were discouraged by most teachers. This helps to explain the assertion of Pablo

Picasso that "Every child is an artist. The problem is how to remain an artist once we grow up."

It seems natural that teachers would emphasize the cognitive skills that reflect their competence. However, when expected to facilitate development of mental abilities that differ from their own strengths, some teachers may do so reluctantly, ineffectively, or not at all (Stover, 2005). Consequently, before most students become willing to risk involvement with creative thinking, changes are necessary in teacher training. The need is to prepare educators who comprehend the importance of cognitive abilities that they may lack themselves, and understand ways to nurture the long-term development of imagination. For insight about creative thinking techniques, see Robert Harris (2002) Web site at Virtual Salt—http://www.virtualsalt.com/crebook2.htm.

Much of instruction today relates to preparing students to pass state-required tests. Competence in this realm is important but evaluation of mental abilities should also include creative behavior (Bowkett, 2005). We do not know how much of cognitive potential goes undetected by the exclusive reliance on current measures of intelligence. However, the evidence suggests that it is considerable. Guilford (1977) was the first scholar to identify this problem based on his study of scientists that were nominated by colleagues as making outstanding contributions to their field. The nominees were presented with a list of 28 mental functions and asked to rank order them based on perceived contribution to success in their field. All but one traditional intelligence test factors ranked below 20th; that is, 19 of 20 characteristics considered by scientists as being most important on the job involved attributes that are not measured by traditional tests. Subsequent studies have determined that considering only persons with IQs of 130 or more (the traditional definition) as gifted overlooks 70% of the most creative students. The Torrance (2002) Tests of Creative Thinking are the most widely used instruments and should be familiar to teachers.

Teachers are not alone in discouraging creative thinking. A stimulating Web site tracks significant events that have contributed to the advancement of creative problem solving throughout history along with events that have acted to suppress creative behavior (Lloyd, 2007). The reader selects any period in history for examination, by century, from B.C. to the present time. One benefit of reviewing any aspect of the presentation is a renewed awareness that each generation is indebted to its predecessors for their willingness to persist in discovering new ways to improve the quality of life. See the creativity timeline at http://www.Gocreate.com.

Student Leadership and Problem Solving

Many problems are more complex now than in the past and require a merger of efforts by individuals with varied talents. A fundamental task is to make sure that creative persons are not excluded from becoming leaders. A generation ago, Paul Torrance (1978) discovered this obstacle while he was working with students who were identified as highly creative. Torrance founded the Future Problem Solving Program that aims to develop critical, creative and futuristic thinking skills. The participants work in groups of four and focus on problem solving for real world issues such as transportation, education, health and the economy. More than 300,000 students in Grades 4–12 participate in the annual competition—http://www.coe.uga.edu/torrance/ (click Programs, Georgia Future Problem Solving Program). Several studies by Torrance (1995) revealed that many talented students admitted their performance in team projects was poor even though they were able to excel with tasks working alone. They engaged in practice sessions using collaborative skills to experience success for the bowl competition. In the end, 98% rated "Learning from peers" as the most exciting aspect of the program, a much higher proportion than cited "Learning from teachers." In his *Manifesto for Children*, Torrance (2002) reinforced this lesson by encouraging students to recognize the value of interdependence (see Figure 6.6).

Manifesto For Children*

By E. Paul Torrance

- Don't be afraid to fall in love with something and pursue it with intensity.
- Know. Understand. Take pride in. Practice. Develop. Exploit and enjoy your great strengths.
- Learn to free yourself from the expectations of others and the games they impose on you.
- Free yourself to play your own game.
- Find a great teacher or mentor who will help you.
- Don't waste your energy trying to be well-rounded.
- Do what you love and can do well.
- Learn the skills of interdependence and gladly share your infinite creativity.

Source: *From *The Manifesto: A Guide to Developing a Creative Career,* by E. Paul Torrance. Charlotte, NC: Information Age Publishing, 2002. Reprinted with permission of The Torrance Center for Creative Studies, The University of Georgia.

Figure 6.6.   Manifesto for Children.

The need for enabling the gifted and talented to become involved as leaders while still in school is underscored by an investigation of 1,600 students from the upper 2% of their 10th grade in Los Angeles (Barron, Montuori, & Barron, 1997). They expressed self-esteem, felt in control of their lives, viewed school as an acceptable place, and shared a typical schedule in amount of time spent on academic and extracurricular activities. Yet, 64% of them felt unpopular or very unpopular with their peers. There is no reason to suppose that being valued by classmates is a condition that gifted students should forfeit. In a democratic society, popularity plays a major role in selection of leaders. Talented students can experience esteem of peers when their role includes obligations to help others. When adolescents participate in cooperative learning teams, the ability possessed by gifted students is not seen as a threat. Instead, it is viewed as a powerful resource to rely on. Cooperative learning situations requiring problem solving present gifted students with opportunities to practice team skills and improve their chances for being recognized as leaders (John-Steiner, 2000).

Self-Directedness and Divergent Thinking

Adolescents like to interact with classmates. For this reason, working together in teams is a way to reduce boredom in class. However, the contribution group conversations make to learning depends on the tasks assigned and arrangements to ensure there is individual accountability (Benson, Scales, Hamilton, & Sesma, 2006). Most courses rely on a textbook that all students are expected to read. This practice has meant that students encounter only materials that are assigned by a teacher. A better strategy is to make all students aware at the beginning of the course the each individual will be responsible to find some of their own sources on topics that their cooperative groups pursue without being told to do so by the teacher. Students who bring Internet materials, books, and articles to share contribute to mental stimulation of teammates (Brown, 2006).

Group discussions are more stimulating when students identify external sources that support or oppose their own views. Too often conversations focus on opinions of individual students without sufficient attention to the larger information base needed to sustain productive interaction (Fosnot, 2005). Those who are able to connect what they have read in newspapers, journals, books, the Internet and what is observed on television to topics considered in class discussion increase their credibility, expand the scope of dialogue with teammates, and reduce the likelihood of boredom for everyone (Apter, 2006; Buckingham & Willett, 2006).

Novel and Stimulating Learning Activities

Human beings continually seek stimulation. When someone or some thing looks different, appears out of the ordinary, or triggers a sense of fright, it attracts attention. Indeed, people lacking stimulation often try to combat feelings of boredom by turning to action-oriented films, horror movies, thrill rides, video games that simulate risky situations, euphoric drugs, pornography, talk shows about bizarre topics, reality programs with unpredictable, fast moving or violent presentations (Morrissey & Werner-Wilson, 2005). Most students expect stimulation in their classroom too. When they experience boredom instead, some attempt to create excitement by interfering with the learning of their classmates, writing on walls of restrooms, exchanging notes with friends, ditching class to go to a mall—anything to break monotony of boredom. The disturbing feelings associated with monotony and generalized attraction to novelty characterizes the human condition, a search for new ways of seeing things. Comparative studies have determined that adolescents have greater interest in novelty than do children or adults (Kelly, Schochet, & Landry, 2004). Adolescents are attracted by experiences that involve risk taking and thrill seeking that stimulate the dopamine system in the brain (Goldberg, 2002).

Students report that school lessons taught with visual images are more readily retained (Burns, 2005). This is why computers, Web site streaming video like YouTube, videotapes, slides, overheads, lecture outlines, and graphic organizers are viewed as stimulating (Orey, McClendon, & Branch, 2006). Additional ways to introduce novelty are telling stories, doing something unexpected to energize students, and pausing in a presentation to invite examples of how specific concepts could be applied. Such strategies can stimulate students to make vital connections between lessons and out-of-school experiences (Okojie & Olinzock, 2006). Another example of novel learning environments is a chairless classroom designed by the Mayo Clinic that includes wireless technology, podcasting, and standing desks allowing students to move around and exercise (Levine, 2006). This approach, intended to reduce obesity, is described in chapter 10 on health and lifestyle.

Instructables, Step-By-Step Collaboration, is a Web site that gives directions about build-it projects at http://www.instructables.com/group/howtoons/. These "tools of mass construction" can inspire teenagers to think about hopeful futures while allowing them practical skills and nurturing imaginative abilities to solve problems that involve the community as well as themselves. The Web site also contains action videos along with relevant links (Griffith & Bonsen, 2006).

SCHEDULING AND RESOURCES

Time is a resource everyone should use wisely. Time management skills are encouraged for people of all ages. Many students report that they are kept perpetually busy because of schedules teachers and parents impose on them. A more suitable strategy is to allow discretionary time so adolescents explore constructive ways to act when they are responsible for their own timetable. Similarly, creativity can be retained if there are opportunities to examine new concepts in class without fear of formal evaluation or excessive criticism. The benefits of solitude, deliberation, and reflection are appreciated by students whose teachers arrange these experiences and explain how they can make a difference in success. Creativity flourishes in classes where teachers expect students to ask questions as preparation for becoming self-directed adult learners and acknowledge inquiry as evidence of achievement.

Constructive Use of Unscheduled Time

Creative behavior is more likely when scheduling and resources are considered. Adults are agreed that time management is an important asset that must become more common. However, students that lack discretionary time are unlikely to acquire these skills (National Institute for Out-of-School Time, 2005). One approach for encouraging students to use unscheduled time in constructive ways is illustrated by the case of 12-year-old Jeffrey.

Jeffrey is a sixth grader who always finishes the worksheets ahead of classmates and gets all the assignments correct. After finishing work early, Jeffrey usually sat still and watched peers at work. He felt bored waiting for them. After he thought about how to deal with this problem of filling extra time, Jeffrey decided that he would bring a book to read. He considered his choices carefully, realizing that a comic book would be inappropriate. He selected "Creatures of the Amazon," a book with many pictures and descriptions of exotic animals and their habitats. The next day when his mathematics worksheets were done, Jeffrey took the book from his backpack and started looking at the pictures. Soon the teacher stopped beside him and suggested that he put the book away, reminding Jeffrey that he did not have permission to read, particularly a book brought from home. She pointed out that "free" reading was reserved for a designated period at the end of the day. When Jeff explained that he was just filling time by reading until the others did their assignment, the teacher told him to "put the book away or go sit in the office until lunch time." Jeff continued suggesting that he was bored when he finished working in less time than classmates did. He could not understand why he could not look at a book instead of sitting and doing nothing. At that point, Jeff was given a referral slip for "arguing with the teacher" and directed to go to the office until the lunch bell rang about 45 minutes later.

That evening Jeff told his mother about the incident. The following morning she phoned the teacher. Jeff's teacher said that he had been sent to the office for arguing and she could not permit a student to bring material from home to read whenever he wants to because this would mean she would have to permit others to bring books as well, and she does not have time to monitor what the children are reading. Jeffrey's mother, herself a high school teacher, was saddened and puzzled by this practice which seemed designed to prevent too much reading at school.

Jeffrey had tried to transform what he saw as a boring situation into one that could be interesting. He took the initiative of carrying out a quiet task that would not disturb classmates nor cause them to feel rushed while they did their work. Teachers should encourage students like Jeffrey to utilize their unscheduled time in constructive ways. Parents have an important role too. By urging students to plan and set goals, children can become future-oriented and thereby avoid getting locked into concentrating only on current events. People limited to present-oriented thinking become excessively dependent on external sources for stimulation.

Chances to Practice Creative Abilities

Imagination is a powerful remedy for boredom because it provides an internal source of stimulation when the external world of movies, videos, music heroes, sports celebrities, the Internet, teachers, friends, and family become boring. Creative people rarely complain of boredom during discretionary time because they have an internal capacity to stimulate themselves. This asset can promote self-directed learning. Since boredom often means "not knowing what to do next," creativity is implicated. Persons unable to think of what to do with themselves seem destined to become dependent on others for their sense of direction.

Everyone possesses creative abilities to some degree. Most of what young children learn before going to school involves guessing, questioning, searching, manipulating, and playing. These activities are consistent with definitions of the creative process. Given the natural creativity of students, the main concern should be to preserve and to enrich this dimension of potential (Girod, Pardales, Cavanaugh, & Wadsworth, 2005; Wu, 2005). David Straker's (2008) goal for his Web site, Creating Minds, is to offer useful principles, tools, articles, and quotes to help build creative abilities—http://creatingminds.org.

When students encounter simulated events, it is easier to evaluate problem-solving choices and generate options than having to assume the risks of real life situations (Stuhlman, Hamre, & Pianta, 2002). Scenarios encourage reflection on how to respond to particular events, explain reasoning for choices, and monitor the logic of teammates. Using scenarios helps broaden the range of solutions that students can see and discourages hasty conclusions. For example, the National Health Museum presents animated medical mysteries that appeal to secondary students in bioscience and health courses. Solving each mystery requires careful reading, keeping organized notes, and applying logic. All the scenarios offer clues with an option to solve a mystery any time or continue to obtain more clues. A glossary of medical terms is available for reference along with the teacher guide. Finding solutions usually takes about an hour so scenarios can be homework for individuals or teams to report their decision making. See http://www.accessexcellence.org/ (click activities exchange).

Parents and teachers who over-schedule adolescents to enrich their experience and prevent trouble can undermine creativity because this practice denies opportunities for the solitude that is needed to reflect and produce new ideas (Mahoney, Larson, & Eccles, 2005). Adults should become aware of two observations about creative behavior based on a decade of research at Brandeis University (McCabe, 1985). First, the best motivator for creativity is freedom. Something happens when the interests of students are accommodated, allowing them to decide their goals and how to achieve these purposes (Chen, Kasof, Himsel, Dmitrieva, Dong, & Xue, 2005). Self-control increases the possibility that students will explore unlikely paths, take risks, and in the end produce something unique and useful. Second, frequent evaluation and criticism smother creativity. This conclusion differs from the common assumption that students need to have continuous feedback.

When creative behavior is the goal, people do better if productivity is reviewed less often (Margolis & McCabe, 2006). Adults that have been found to be most inhibited and least capable of expressing themselves in imaginative ways are those working in high-pressure occupations where they are subjected to weekly or monthly evaluations (Beghetto, 2005). The importance of encouraging imaginative thinking is illustrated by what the authors think might have been the response of a high school teacher to William Shakespeare's beginning efforts for becoming a creative writer (see Figure 6.7).

Solitude, Reflection, and Deliberation

Boredom has become a more prevalent experience because of the significant increase in external stimulation. Technology enables people to

William Shakespeare
English I
April 24, 1578

Tomorrow is one word
To-morrow, and to-morrow, and to-morrow, — *Redundant*

Creeps in this petty pace from <u>day</u> to <u>day</u>, — *Redundant*
Childish
         ↗ time is a <u>one</u> syllable word
To the <u>last syllable</u> of recorded time;

And all our yesterdays have lighted <u>fools</u> *insulting to the reader*

The way to dusty death. <u>Out</u>, <u>out</u>, brief candle!
                          → Redundant <u>again</u>!

Life's but a walking shadow, a poor <u>player</u> *→ insulting again - watch this*

That struts and frets his hour upon the stage *→ How can the reader identify with a shadow? Be realistic!*
There are two sexes ↗
You'll learn that in sophomore year.
And then is heard no more; it is a tale

Told by an <u>idiot</u>, full of sound and fury,
Insulting again

Signifying nothing.
A tale should always signify something.

The average life span is more than one hour.

Everyone doesn't want to be an actor, Will.

Bill, I am disappointed! Frankly, you seem to underestimate the craftsmanship that goes into becoming a writer. Rework the assignment in a more realistic fashion and submit it to me before tomorrow's class.
                              Mr. Johnson

Figure 6.7.   An example of divergent thinking.

watch rental movies, cable and satellite television, respond to interactive programs, play electronic games, and join chat groups on the Internet. Listening to music as well as recorded lessons and books on tape are common activities that occur at the same time people run, ride a bike or drive a car. Despite these additions to external stimulation, some teachers remain puzzled over why student interest in learning for its own sake has less appeal than it did in previous generations. Such an observation overlooks stimulation of media to capture the attention of a young economic market (Thomas, 2007). CNN, MTV, Fox and Nickelodeon rely on stimulation strategies that educators could apply. On the other hand, students need to become aware that some essential learning might be monotonous, call for perseverance, and a willingness to confront failure. In the end, concentration and hard work remain vital keys for success (Strong, Silver, Perini, & Tuculescu, 2003).

In a rush-oriented society, there is a need to recognize that some goals cannot be attained quickly. Instead, students must learn at home and in school to tolerate ambiguity (Elmer & Torem, 2004). Persons who are strictly present-oriented often emphasize only short-term goals shown by insistence on immediate feedback. However, for more complex learning, there is a need to invest significant amounts of time and effort before applying evaluation is appropriate. In this context, all students should have time alone, apart from peers, to reflect, evaluate, and dream (Holverstott, 2005). Autobiographical studies of highly creative adults have shown that, as children, they spent more time alone and with adults than with peers. They also learned from an early age to enjoy the company of their own imagination. Now, however, many students spend more time with peers during the day and in after-school programs. The fact is that creative thinking is facilitated when students have time to spend alone (Easton & Allensworth, 2005).

Teachers can present an exercise and set a timer for 5 minutes while students reflect. This experience can enable some individuals to appreciate the value of deliberation. Periods of reprieve should be built in to the schedule. Anyone engaged in the creative process recognizes that, on completion of a project that has required extensive preparation and emotional energy, there is a temporary need to have more moderate expectations and time to partially withdraw to recover. Teachers who fail to honor this natural and necessary response pattern are unreasonable and are not fulfilling the important obligation to support mental health of their students (Menzies, 2005).

Family and School Support for Curiosity

People express individuality by the questions they ask. When teachers encourage inquiry, students become self-directed learners (Falk & Blumenreich, 2005). This is not a problem when boys and girls are young. Indeed, many preschoolers ask their parents a hundred questions a day reflecting the enormous influence that curiosity has on the motivation to learn in early childhood. Unfortunately, by the time children arrive in middle school, few of them still ask questions of teachers and parents. What is it that happens between early childhood and adolescence that curtails the drive to discover new knowledge, causes students to give up exploring how the world works, and eliminates a fascination with mysteries of the unknown? There are no satisfactory explanations for why these losses are so pervasive. However, it seems clear that when people cease to be curious, they also give up their opportunity to be a self-directed learner. The right to be a self-directed learner is one of the greatest freedoms in a democratic society (Lee & Olszewski-Kubilius, 2005).

The most visible sign that students lack mental stimulation is their failure to raise questions. Parents seldom recognize when this decline begins and few help their children recognize that generating questions is a necessary part of getting a good education. One way for teachers to determine whether the concepts they convey are understood is for students to comfortably express confusion and seek guidance for aspects of lessons they do not comprehend. Parents should introduce this practice by inviting questions during the times the family watches television. Teachers spend more time asking questions than other activities. However, they should not be the only persons that express curiosity through questioning (Torrance, 1994, 2000a). Problem-solving depends on asking suitable questions and the application of rational procedures to reach answers. An effective way to help students retain the curiosity they need is to enlarge the basis for receiving credit. By this strategy students can be credited for curiosity in raising questions as well as answering questions from the teacher. Adults should try as many ways as possible to support inquiry (Bonner, 2005). Motivation to ask questions can come from Jay Walker's Library of Human Imagination available at http://www.ted.com (click Speakers).

Mothers and fathers have an obligation to be examples for children showing that they find reading on a regular basis to be stimulating. High achieving students usually come from homes where, regardless of income, parents are observed to gain satisfaction and avert boredom through reading. Unfortunately, there are many homes in which children never see their parents spend time reading for pleasure (Segrin & Flora, 2005).

Extensive reading and curiosity often are the basis for another aspect of creativity called problem-finding, identified by Jacob Getzels, a University of Chicago psychologist (Getzels & Jackson, 1962). Whereas most approaches to creative thinking refer to advantages for problem solving, what really differentiates a creative thought from a less original one is that it deals with some issue that no one has seen as a problem before. In effect, *problem finding*—formulation of a previously unperceived problem rather than its solution—is the hallmark of creativity. Problem finders are rare and usually years ahead of their time (Vangundy, 2004). Courage is necessary to stand alone and essential to sustain a vision they may not be recognized for in their lifetime but could set the course for progress in the future.

RESPONSIBILITIES OF STUDENTS

The future of innovation will feature teams of creative individuals more than efforts by individuals that characterized the past. Prospects for productivity depend on how creative students are treated by teammates. When everyone supports inventive thought, creative persons come to value interdependence and appreciate working with others instead of withdrawing to solve problems on their own. Being talented typically results in rejection when classmates regard such persons as curve raisers who lower the status of everyone else. In contrast, creative students whose teachers assign them the task of helping others find that peers come to see them as a resource and recognize them for their leadership.

A difficult task for teachers and students is giving and receiving criticism. Honest and accurate criticism can support team improvement and is more likely to be considered by persons able to process recommendations without defensiveness. Teams are more effective when all members show competence in providing constructive suggestions. This process can begin with brainstorming practice in which students are urged to express creative perceptions before subjecting them to judgment.

A growing number of adolescents representing all ability levels are expressing boredom with experience at school. One interpretation identifies them as less diligent than previous generations of students. A more accurate outlook emerges from their reports on lack of stimulation in the classroom. Teachers and students together can find ways to reduce the boredom often attributed to lessons that appear irrelevant, presentations that do not stimulate interest, and lack of opportunity for students to have an active role in learning. Many teachers wonder if students who bring laptops to their class are using them for taking notes or for surfing the Web during direct instruction. A 4-minute look at the perceptions of students about relevance of classroom instruction is available at http://www.youtube.com search "A Vision of Students Today."

Mutual Support for Creativity

Cooperative teams should more often be a source of motivation for creativity. However, divergent thought is often suppressed during work groups (de Bono, 1998, 2007). This negative reaction causes creative students to dislike being placed in teams and motivates them to state the preference for solving problems on their own (John-Steiner, 2000). Nevertheless, teamwork and creative thinking are an essential combination for success in the emerging economy (Maciariello, 2005). Consequently, all students must learn to explore views and suggestions they may not like at first, apply logic to challenge the thinking of peers and team methods, avoid making hasty decisions, build on ideas expressed by others, and discover new ways of looking at things.

The merger of cooperative learning and creative thinking calls for different types of assignments (Chen & Gardner, 2005). When teachers provide enough roles so that each team member can make a unique contribution, collaboration is more productive. There is a corresponding decline in boredom, and, by rotation of the roles, each student performs functions that allow sufficient observation by peers to fairly evaluate them. In combination, these factors define the collaboration integration theory (CIT) described in chapter 1. This approach facilitates the behaviors characteristic of creative thinkers.

Peer Criticism and Brainstorming

Societies and subcultures should more often engage in being self-critical because this is an essential condition to trigger readiness for change. Thomas Friedman (2005), in *The World is Flat*, describes processes and implications associated with globalization. He speculates that countries must begin to look at themselves with greater scrutiny by using introspection. He asserts the need for a strategy analogous to Alcoholics Anonymous by which all members are obliged to examine themselves as they really are and make their condition known by standing up to publicly announce "My name is John Jones and I am an alcoholic." In a corresponding way, countries that are Anonymous Club members might admit "My name is France and I don't work hard enough," or "My name is North Korea and I need more healthy goals." The point is that every nation needs to transcend the customary self-impression that centers mostly on pride to also include becoming self-critical, followed by a decision to make progress, to evolve. Unfortunately, schools do little to equip students with the constructive tools they need to become critical of the small society that defines their own classrooms. Peer criticism is an often overlooked but potentially valuable source of perception for improvement (Gardner, 2004; Sadler & Good, 2006).

A helpful way to pool resources is for students to improve written work produced by another cooperative team in class. Creative thinking, finding ways to make something better, and learning how to offer suggestions can result in a better product. This strategy can help students become more constructive in how they express their criticism and more willing to consider criticism of colleagues without resorting to defensiveness (Grzegorek, Slaney, Franze, & Rice, 2004; Rachlin, 2004). Students can be asked to speculate, state hunches about the outcomes of a project before the details of an experiment are fully reported to them. Ask students to tell what they anticipate is going to happen next in a sequence of events that are only partially known to them. A panel can be invited to discuss their opinions and reasoning about controversial issues. Creative tasks can stimulate inventive thinking by offering novelty and reducing monotony (de Bono, 1999, 2007).

Brainstorming is a technique for eliciting, without evaluation, many solutions to situations implicating local, state, nation, and global problems. Students at every grade level can benefit from this approach because it encourages creative thinking. Four rules guide brainstorming (de Bono, 2007):

1. Record each suggested alternative without criticism. Defer judgment until many alternatives have been proposed.

2. Encourage freewheeling discussion. The more remote, unusual, and wild the ideas, the better.

3. Generate a large list of ideas, including both obvious ones and uncommon or clever alternatives.

4. Combine alternatives, and use these combinations to stimulate the generation of new ideas.

A time limit should always be specified for brainstorming. When the time is up, usually after 10 to 15 minutes, the participants shift their thinking pattern to use of logic and reasoning (forms of judgment) to decide which of the alternatives proposed requires further consideration. This sequence of perception first and judgment afterwards is crucial. Options must be generated before they can be evaluated. In short, during creative problem solving the irrational is engaged first and then the rational (de Bono, 2007).

Brainstorming is difficult for persons who are quick to judge and lack appreciation for divergent thinking. Even creative students may find it hard to apply all the procedural rules at first. Consequently, it is a good idea to have classmates begin by working in pairs, practicing only the first rule until it is mastered. In turn, each of the remaining rules can be added. Before long, larger groups can be formed and all rules applied at once. The Web site for Infinite Innovations Limited describes the presession preparations, materials and organization needed to conduct a successful brainstorming session—visit http://www.brainstorming.co.uk.

Computer-assisted brainstorming (CAB) has been in existence since the 1980s. Because the computer takes the initiative by asking questions, the mental blocks that people sometimes experience are eliminated and less time is required. The computer can produce more ideas within a shorter period and takes notes about the process which frees the user from this mundane task. Asynchronous brainstorming is fundamentally different from the usual synchronous venue because participants do not have to be physically present. In turn, this allows for global think tank processes that have become common in many sectors of international problem solving (Hakkarainen, Palonen, Paavola, & Lehtinen, 2004). "Computer-Assisted Brainstorming and the Global Think Tank" (Trost, 2004) is provided by the Creative Center of the Universe at their Web site http://gocreate.com/Articles/agtt.htm.

Overcoming Boredom Together

A powerful and little understood obstacle to productivity is that state of mind referred to as boredom. *Boredom* produces feelings of irritability because of an exposure to something that seems uninteresting or having nothing to do. Many adults describe themselves as bored with daily affairs. When people say, "Thank goodness it's Friday," what do they mean? Do they mean that their job gives such pleasure that the sheer ecstasy of it cannot be sustained more than 5 days at a time? Perhaps they mean that the obligations at work fail to meet their need for a sense of purpose and cause them to look forward to more interesting activities during weekends and vacations? Maybe they mean that it would be nice to quit working. Winning the lottery and having enough money to quit a job are a common dream. Another way of looking at the prevailing impression is that it confirms that alienation from work is widespread (O'Toole, & Lawler, 2006). And, as boredom increases for adults, more adolescents are also having difficulty finding stimulation in the classroom.

The gravity of boredom for educators is reflected by the observations of a visitor regarding what she saw at Owen Middle School. In one classroom most of the students appeared motivated to learn, paid attention, expressed curiosity, generated imaginative ideas, persisted with difficult tasks, demonstrated self-direction, and enjoyed being involved with reflective thinking. Things were not the same in the classroom across the hall. Here most students appeared to lack interest in the curriculum, continually distracted one another, avoided asking questions, provided low level responses, gave up quickly in the face of difficulties, looked to others for direction instead of making an effort to figure things out, and disliked assignments requiring deliberation. Instead of attributing such differences to learning as a function of income, culture, learning disabilities, or parent indifference, educators should explore without defensiveness how they may influence the phenomenon of boredom.

Historically, high achieving students have expressed boredom about having to wait while teachers helped slower students catch up. Today, average and below average students assert that they are bored, some as early as the primary grades (Joussemet, Koestner, Lekes, & Houlfort, 2004). Complaints offered by a growing proportion of secondary school students are perceived as ominous signs of discontent with the existing system of education (Kelly, Schochet, & Landry, 2004). Boredom is a topic teachers seldom discuss with students but warrants attention to minimize its negative effect on the pursuit of knowledge. Studies have determined that boredom restricts attention, interferes with concentration, and is often cited as one of the main reasons for dropping out of school (Bridgeland, Dilulio, & Morison, 2006). Many adolescents perceive school as a disappointment. They feel that school is boring, lessons are uninteresting, assignments have little practical application, and there is a lack of community and sense of belonging in class (Rosen, 2007; Thomas, 2007).

In a national longitudinal study of 526 high school students, efforts were made to find out how they spent time at school. They experienced a greater sense of engagement when teachers allowed options for tasks, when they had some feeling of control, and were allowed to work together in teams than when their role was to only listen or discuss with their teacher (Shernoff, Csikszentmihalyi, Schneider, & Shernoff, 2003). Similarly, in a survey of 800 middle school adolescents, it was found that teachers can enhance three types of autonomy which are recognized and highly valued by students: (1) ensuring that tasks are perceived as being relevant for them, (2) allowing criticism of the classroom environment without suffering a penalty, and (3) providing choices that can contribute to autonomy (Assor, Kaplan, & Roth, 2002). Collaboration between teachers and students seems to be the best way to increase mental stimulation. To support this goal, Eisenhower National Clearinghouse for teaching Science and Mathematics offers Internet resources that teenagers find appealing and can help to enrich their learning at http://www.goenc.org.

Families and Home Schooling

Boredom is one of the reasons given by parents for the choice to home school children (Romanowski, 2006). This movement began during the 1980s when Christian conservative parents who doubted the quality of learning in public schools wanted to limit the exposure of their children to drugs and other negative peer influences they felt characterized many schools. The families who decided to educate their elementary grade children at home initially suffered criticism from the community and were subjected to court challenges from school boards claiming their children were being deprived because the parents did not have state certification required of teachers. However, after repeated confirmation that home-schooled students perform as well or better than their peers on standardized tests, the focus of objection changed. The revised contention was that the relative isolation of home schooling meant that students were missing out on the social development provided by schools. The courts did not agree. Generally, they ruled that public schools neither plan nor provide experiences in social development and do not evaluate this aspect of development by testing, grading or reporting to the parents. Consequently, since 1993, home schooling has been a legal activity in all 50 states (Romanowski, 2006). States differ in what they require of families that choose home schooling. In New York parents are expected to file a home-instruction plan and submit quarterly progress reports along with annual results of student performance on the state standardized tests. A summary of legal options for home schooling in every state is available from the Home School Legal Defense Association—http://www.hslda.org/laws/default.asp.

The National Center for Educational Statistics (Bielick, 2008) estimates that over 1.5 million children from ages 5 to 17 were educated at home in 2007. The three reasons selected by parents of more than two-thirds of students were (1) concerns about the school environment, (2) to provide moral or religious instruction, and (3) dissatisfaction with the academic instruction available at other schools. These students are as diverse as peers attending classrooms, representing all religions and races. Until recently, most parents concluded that they could only educate their children at home through the elementary grades. Recent distance learning opportunities have motivated an increase in number of homeschooled secondary students (Patrick, 2008). For example, Keystone is a national distance learning high school that collaborates with parents and enrolls 20,000 students. Visit the Web Site at http://keystonehighschool.com/ and go to online learning, interactive lessons. and online course demo.

The financial sacrifice associated with home schooling presents a major challenge. The choice to home school requires giving up one parent's income to stay home and act as the teacher. Only a minority of American families are able or willing to make this economic adjustment and investment of their time. Many home schooling parents report that the Internet has made teaching easier and reduced boredom for children (Bauer & Wise, 2004).

VOICES OF ADOLESCENTS

Many businesses rely on marketing research techniques to determine preferences of teenage consumers as well as identify things adolescents do not like. This strategy is illustrated by the IRV Research International Web site at http://www.teenresearch.com. In a similar way, there is benefit when secondary schools solicit adolescent perceptions about the obstacles to creative behavior they encounter in school (Black, 2005; D. Mitra, 2004). Mutual efforts by teachers and students can then be made to reduce the extent of boredom.

The Boredom Poll in this chapter makes known the amount of school time students feel bored, reasons for their boredom, the way they tend to respond when bored, and the typical consequences (see Exercise 6.01). The poll also solicits student recommendations about things that teachers could do to be more stimulating, views of boredom involving homework, identification of the subjects perceived as the most boring, and classroom activities that should be used less or replaced. There is opportunity to speculate about how teachers would respond if students told them they were bored, and the obligations students feel they should assume in situations where they must deal with lack of external stimulation.

SUMMARY

Characteristics of Creativity

Creativity and intelligence have been found to represent separate domains of mental ability. Accordingly, it seems that schools may be able to better educate many students who have been unsuccessful in mastering traditional curriculum. Fluency, flexibility, originality, and elaboration are aspects of divergent thinking that enable students to discover multiple ways for solving problems when there is no single correct or convergent answer. Inventive thinkers from diverse careers report similar steps in the creative process they rely on that includes preparation, incubation, illumination and verification. The mental operations called divergent thinking and evaluation tend to be overlooked by educators in favor of cognition, convergent thinking, and memory despite claims to the contrary. When student involvement with the full range of mental operations is in balance, thinking and learning become dual purposes for instruction and achievement in the classroom.

Conditions for Problem Solving

Creativity is considered the key to productivity and can determine winners and losers in the global competition for business. This is why the public endorsement of education for creative behavior is rising and must be accompanied by willingness of teachers to sanction and encourage some mental abilities that differ from their own strengths. Teachers who allow students to choose tasks and obligate them to share with peers what they have learned on the Internet and from other sources contribute to the development of divergent thinking. Leadership for creative students is enhanced when they are given a helper role to assist peers. Presenting lessons in novel ways stimulates the interest of students since they are intrigued by unfinished stories that call for involvement and the unpredictability of departing from the usual way things are done in class. Students enjoy Web site exploration, watching video clips or slides, reviewing and editing graphic organizers to fit their view of a lesson and other procedures that unite verbal and visual memory.

Scheduling and Resources

There are more choices for ways to spend time than were available in the past. Adults commonly try to maximize opportunities by scheduling too many things for teens to do. A more appropriate strategy is to ensure they have discretion about some of the events in their schedule. Teenagers should be aware that, while they enjoy interaction with friends, they also need private time for reflection about concerns of importance for them and to consider decisions that require deliberation rather than being made under the influence of peers. Spending time alone allows students to avoid becoming overly dependent on peers, enables them to stand alone if needed, and represents a condition valued by highly creative persons. Asking questions can be discouraged or encouraged by peers depending on how they view the learning process. Teachers should explain that creativity and asking questions are linked, individuality is expressed by the questions we ask, and peers should encourage inquiry because it supports creativity.

Responsibilities of Students

Creativity has historically been associated with efforts of individuals. Currently greater emphasis is being placed on productivity in teams because this strategy allows persons from different fields to combine expertise in solving complicated problems. Satisfying experience with teamwork helps students appreciate interdependence and motivates mutual support for creativity. Learning how to process criticism as individuals and in teams is a largely unmet need in most classes. Practice in giving and receiving constructive criticism should be arranged so students become less defensive. If the growing expression of boredom is viewed as a wake-up call, it can encourage greater focus on preservation of imagination and capacity for internal stimulation. Teachers should go beyond the customary forms of instruction to include work on the Internet, the method of learning most preferred by teenagers. By alternating student tasks, it is possible to increase novelty, diminish monotony and curb boredom. Creativity is most prominent when curiosity is the norm, there are opportunities to practice reflective thinking, and access to imagination becomes a common asset.

CLASSROOM APPLICATIONS

1. Developing assignments that call on individuals and teams to generate alternative solutions for complex problems allows practice with divergent thinking. This mental operation, typically ignored in homework and project tasks, should become more prominent so that students can acquire the outlook and skills needed to deal with the often complicated situations encountered in the current environment.

2. Awareness that intelligence and creativity represent different domains of mental ability should caution teachers against reaching unfair conclusions about the performance students are capable of based solely on their scores from intelligence tests. Such measures cannot identify the students who are highly creative nor indicate which ones excel in creativity and intelligence. Schools intending to support creativity should use suitable tests to detect performance and track progress.

3. Acquaint your students with the progressive steps of the creative process and discuss how this process can serve as a guide for the way projects and tasks are scheduled, worked on, reviewed, and completed for the course. As students become aware of how your planning efforts and arrangements for the class schedule supports their engagement with the process, they should also recognize aspects of accountability to be expected of themselves.

4. Students who ask a lot of questions, enjoy speculating, tend to become preoccupied with tasks, act like visionaries, and show a willingness to take risks are often creative. Teachers should encourage

them to sustain these behaviors, a departure from the custom of discouraging them. In the effort to stimulate creative talents, teachers need to approve and support some mental abilities that may be more prominent in students than themselves.

5. Tell students that you expect them to enrich the curriculum through searching the Internet or journals for ideas and materials that could augment content of the course. Their insights, drawn from self-selected out-of-school sources of learning, should be shared with teammates or the whole class as arranged by the teacher. Teenagers who are accountable for sharing learning with others soon appreciate the concept of interdependence, usually adopt a broader view of the student role, are recognized by peers for their leadership in helping them, and benefit from teammates who enrich their experience by assuming the same teaching function.

6. Express your creativity by combining visual and verbal methods in original ways to communicate concepts. Students report that they are stimulated by the freedom that comes with being able to seek their own information on the Web. The enormous appeal of novelty and its favorable influence on motivation can be experienced by sometimes departing from the routine to have students participate in an unexpected activity or pause in a lesson to find out how students believe the lesson can be applied. Such strategies help to sustain interest and can often link academic lessons with real life.

7. Students have greater opportunity to learn time management skills when they do not have excessive homework that prevents using after school time for pursuit of other activities. When class projects involve due dates, it is appropriate to have planning discussions with students to decide on when certain aspects of their obligation should be completed. This monitoring ensures that procrastination is recognized as unacceptable. There is also merit in discussing the importance of balancing work with play to support optimal mental health, a guideline that should be respected by the faculty.

8. Students should adopt curiosity as an aspect of lifestyle so they will remain learners after completing school. This is difficult because peers, starting in early adolescence, discourage inquiry and make individuals feel conspicuous. Given the power of peer influence, teachers should try to use it to their advantage. During orientation of cooperative learning groups, specify that they are expected to encourage teammates to ask questions because making known what is not understood is necessary for learning, and the active role students want to have requires this kind of behavior.

9. Creative students must feel comfortable when they participate in groups or they tend to withdraw. One way to improve their status is encouraging them to help teammates with difficult tasks or concepts where there is lack of comprehension. When classmates begin to view the talented student as an asset to their team, the individual is usually recognized for leadership, valued for willingness to act as a source of assistance, and becomes aware that communal achievement can make individual success more satisfying.

10. Every teacher should experiment with ways to help students give and take peer criticism. Unless teams are able to process critical feedback in a non-defensive manner, they are likely to forfeit the benefits of insights that could be provided by external observers. Practice with giving constructive suggestions in response to peer work and offering recommendations that can be readily implemented are skills that students need so they can contribute more to the success of their own groups and others they are invited to critique.

FOR REFLECTION

1. What aspects of the creative process do you think students should get to practice more and better appreciate?
2. What do you see as advantages and disadvantages of including divergent thinking items on teacher-made tests?
3. In what ways do you perceive yourself to be like and unlike persons who are identified as highly creative?
4. How do you intend to reconcile pressures to provide frequent homework with student needs for discretionary time?
5. What teaching tips will you share with creative students so they can help classmates and be more favorably seen by them?
6. What are some questions you could present to introduce a discussion with the class about giving and taking criticism?
7. In your estimate, what changes are needed in the training of prospective teachers so they can effectively support creative behavior of students?
8. What novel methods of instruction have you found most appealing and hope to replicate for your students?
9. What are some situations in classrooms that have turned you off because they produce boredom?
10. How do you feel about schools administering creativity measures along with high stakes testing?

11. How do you suppose highly creative students are viewed by most of their teachers?

12. What can teachers do to help some students shift from being overly critical to becoming more capable of recognizing many possibilities in situations?

KEY TERMS

Associational fluency

Boredom

Brainstorming

Cognition

Convergent Thinking

Creativity

Divergent Thinking

Elaboration

Evaluation

Flexibility

Fluency

Ideal student checklist

Ideational fluency

Illumination

Incubation

Memory

Originality

Preparation

Problem Finding

Redefinition

Sensitivity

Verification

VISIT THESE WEB SITES

Link to these sites at http://www.infoagepub.com/strom-adolescents

Creating Minds, Build Creative Abilities Resources
http://creatingminds.org

Creative Center of the Universe,
Computer-Assisted Brainstorming and the Global Think Tank
http://www.gocreate.com

Eisenhower National Clearinghouse,
Teaching Science and Math Internet Resources
http://www.goenc.org

Robert Harris, Introduction to Creative Thinking
http://www.virtualsalt.com/crebook1.htm

Robert Harris, Creative Thinking Techniques
http://www.virtualsalt.com/crebook2.htm

Infinite Innovations Limited,
Brainstorming Preparation and Organization
http://www.brainstorming.co.uk

Instructables Step-By-Step Collaboration
http://www.instructables.com/group/howtoons/

Keystone National High School,
Curriculum, Online learning,
Interactive lessons, and Online course demo
http://www.keystonehighschool.com/

National Health Museum, Activities exchange
http://www.accessexcellence.org/

Torrance Center for Creativity and Talent Development
http://www.coe.uga.edu/torrance/

TRU, Research International http://www.teenresearch.com
Jay Walker's Library of Human Imagination, Speakers
http://www.ted.com

YouTube, A Vision of Students Today
http://www.youtube.com

EXERCISES AND ROLES

Exercise 6.01: Boredom Poll

Role: Voter

   The purpose of this poll is to find out the causes and effects of boredom experienced by students at your school. Directions: Select the answer(s) that describes how you feel. In some cases, you may select more than one answer. If an answer you want to give is not listed, write it on the line marked "other." Your responses are anonymous and may be combined with those of other students at your school in a report to students, faculty, and parents.

1. I feel bored at school

    (a) all of the time
    (b) most of the time
    (c) some of the time
    (d) rarely
    (e) never

2. The reason(s) I get bored at school is because:

    (a) some courses do not interest me
    (b) the course content is too difficult
    (c) the course content is too simple
    (d) my teachers are not interesting
    (e) other

3. When I get bored in class, I

    (a) talk with other students
    (b) spend time daydreaming
    (c) draw or write notes
    (d) text message my friends
    (e) other

4. The result of boredom for me is usually

    (a) getting in trouble with a teacher
    (b) falling behind in my schoolwork
    (c) receiving lower scores or grades
    (d) a poor attitude toward the school

5. Teachers could make school more interesting if they:

    (a) let me plan some of my own projects
    (b) used more visuals to increase interest
    (c) assigned homework that is practical
    (d) spent less time lecturing to the class
    (e) other

6.   Homework is boring for me because

   (a)   I don't understand some of the work
   (b)   it is too easy and I don't need to do it
   (c)   assignments don't apply to real life
   (d)   it is repetitive, always the same thing
   (e)   other

7.   The subject(s) I find most boring are:

   (a)   Mathematics
   (b)   Science
   (c)   English
   (d)   Social Studies
   (e)   other

8.   The most boring kind of school work is

   (a)   reading the textbook
   (b)   doing the worksheets
   (c)   end of chapter exercises
   (d)   oral reports by students
   (e)   other

9.   If I told a teacher that I was bored, s/he would

   (a)   ask for my suggestions
   (b)   ignore what I have to say
   (c)   tell my parents about it
   (d)   blame boredom on me
   (e)   other

10.   The way I can overcome boredom at school is

   (a)   ask questions about the lessons
   (b)   tell my teacher that I feel bored
   (c)   realize long-term benefits of study
   (d)   participate more in discussions
   (e)   other

11. I am bored outside of school

    (a) less than in school
    (b) more than in school
    (c) about the same as school
    (d) rarely
    (e) other

12. My best friend is bored at school

    (a) all of the time
    (b) most of the time
    (c) some of the time
    (d) rarely
    (e) never

Select your grade level, gender, ethnicity, and age.

My grade level is: 5 6 7 8 9 10 11 12
My gender is: female male
My ethnicity is: Asian Black Hispanic Native American White other
My age is 10 11 12 13 14 15 16 17 18 19

Exercise 6.02: Dreams, The Story of Myself

Role: Storyteller

Everyone has dreams that they wish would come true. Sometimes these dreams provide a sense of direction, guide behavior, inspire perseverance, and keep people from becoming pessimistic. It is possible to acquire insight about another person's motivation by hearing about their dreams. Tell some personal stories in response to this agenda.

1. What are some dreams you have held onto for a long time?
2. What are some dreams that you have changed or given up?
3. Who listens to you when you try to describe your dreams?
4. What dreams do you have for other members of the family?
5. What happens when people quit dreaming about the future?
6. What dreams do you have that probably will not be achieved?
7. How important is it to be around people with similar dreams?
8. How do your dreams compare with dreams others have for you?
9. Which of your dreams are other people unwilling to support?
10. Which of your dreams have already started to come true?

Exercise 6.03: Boredom and Stimulation

Role: Summarizer

1. Why do you suppose people claim boredom more now than in the past?
2. What kinds of situations or events do you usually consider to be boring?
3. What things distinguish boring teachers from those who motivate you?
4. How does boredom affect the relationships you have with other people?
5. What are some methods you rely on to reduce possibilities of boredom?
6. How does boredom influence your involvement in watching television?
7. What are some of your own characteristics that others might find boring?
8. What things would you change about schools in order to reduce boredom?
9. Who do you interact with on a regular basis that is stimulating? boring?
10. How are you trying to help other family members minimize boredom?

Exercise 6.04: Manifesto for Children

Role: Evaluator

Figure 6.6, Paul Torrance's Manifesto For Children, is a document that reflects the outcome of long-term research with students. Identify the elements of the Manifesto that seem most difficult for you and share this self-evaluation with teammates.

Exercise 6.05: School Days

Role: Generational Reporter

Parents commonly want more conversations with their adolescents but feel they sometimes lack an agenda. Ask an adolescent to use this guide for a dialogue with parents and write answers of both parties so you can share in class.

Directions: The nature of schooling changes for every generation. Nevertheless, life in the classroom involves experiences that every age group finds easy to remember. Take turns answering each of the questions.

1. What are some things about school that have pleased you the most?
2. What kinds of changes do you think are needed to improve schooling?
3. How are the students who misbehave at school punished by the faculty?
4. What kinds of peer pressure do you have to deal with daily at school?
5. What benefits have you gained from being in extracurricular activities?
6. How do friends make a difference in the way that you feel about school?
7. How can relatives be more helpful with your homework assignments?
8. What can be done to lower the rate of students who drop out of school?
9. What sorts of things have happened at school that bothered you most?
10. What kinds of help do you need that are not provided by the school?
11. How do you feel about computer aspects of learning at the school?

Exercise 6.06: Boredom Reduction

Role: Improviser

Teachers of all grades are concerned about the growing number of students who express boredom with their school experience. Prepare three side-by-side lists. In the first column, list some school practices you think may contribute to boredom. In the middle column, list school replacement practices that could result in some reduction of the boredom experience. In the right column, list some behavior changes students need to make to diminish the frequency of their boredom.

Exercise 6.07: Multiple Models

Role: Evaluator

Life in an age-segregated society is sometimes portrayed as undermining adolescent development because teenagers are exposed to more pressures from peers. On the other hand, it is recognized that peers can be a valuable source of learning. Instead of supposing that adolescents would be better off looking to adults as their only models, it seems wise to recognize that peers can be powerful and beneficial models too. Think about the realms where adult models and peer models can provide benefits in adolescence.

1. What lessons can teachers and parents model better than classmates?
2. What lessons can peers teach one another more effectively than adults?
3. How are peer and teacher instructional methods similar and different?

Exercise 6.08: Evidence of Learning

Role: Improviser

The practice has been for teachers to lecture, assign readings, and give examinations based on information in a textbook. Besides the boredom associated with this approach, understanding gained from other potential sources of learning such as the Internet and television are not recognized. Suggest some creative ways teachers can evaluate and credit students for some relevant learning that takes place outside the classroom.

Exercise 6.09: The Creative Process

1. Identify steps in the creative process that are most difficult for you and suggest possible solutions.
2. How should learning in the classroom change in order to better support conditions for creativity.

EXERCISE 6.10: How Do You Do?

Role: Storyteller

In 1904, a few months before 25-year-old Albert Einstein (1879–1955) published his theory of relativity, he met 23-year-old artist Pablo Picasso (1881–1973), who would also later receive worldwide recognition. When the two men came together at Lapin Agile, a cafe in Paris, France, they attempted to educate each other about the world. The pair expressed conflicting views about values and the meaning of life. Their back and forth exchange of values in art and science is the theme of Steve Martin's provocative play called *Picasso at the Lapin Agile* (1996). Your task is to generate a list of famous persons you would like to observe as pairs having conversations about how they perceive the world. First, everyone on the team should take 4 to 5 minutes to think alone. When your list is developed, share it along with your reasoning.

PART III

SOCIAL EXPECTATIONS

CHAPTER 7

SOCIAL MATURITY AND TEAMWORK

The importance of getting along with others is confirmed every day. *Social intelligence* is the ability to recognize differences in moods, temperament, motivations, and intentions of the persons we meet and act wisely on these distinctions in order to fit in different social situations (Goleman, 2006). Most parents strive to nurture social intelligence because they recognize that this attribute can greatly influence chances of their daughter or son being able to form close and durable friendships, cooperate with classmates, and co-workers, build a satisfying marriage, and care about others who are less fortunate. The ways to achieve these broad goals are not entirely known but some promising alternatives deserve teacher consideration.

This chapter describes how adolescents influence socialization of classmates and peers outside of school. Emphasis is placed on the importance of friendships as a basis for building long-term durable relationships. Dating practices are considered along with methods to support healthy interaction. Explanations are given for ways learning in cooperative groups differs from traditional instruction, how students acquire social skills through participation in teams, use of appropriate criteria for assessment of peer and self performance, and importance of providing individuals and groups feedback on teamwork skills and deficits. The social challenges associated with integrating regular students and students with disabilities as they work together in cooperative groups are examined.

PEERS AND SOCIAL DEVELOPMENT

Teachers and parents are recognized for the guidance they provide students. However, the positive ways in which adolescents contribute to their social development are less understood and appreciated. Teenagers are motivated to learn from age mates in almost all dimensions of life (A. Thomas, 2007; Weber & Dixon, 2007). Teachers are aware that peer influence is one of their greatest assets as well as the most difficult resource for them to manage. Peers are a powerful force that can either support or inhibit socialization (Prinstein & Dodge, 2008). A *peer group* consists of students in the same age group or grade at school. Recognizing the social contexts in which peers influence behavior enables teachers to arrange better conditions of learning.

Voices of Adolescents

School classrooms and after-school programs support student interaction. These settings should be seen as natural environments for the development of social skills. For example, when the dialogue in a classroom is mostly between teacher and students, there are chances to observe how individual boys and girls handle conversations where expected to explain their ideas or offer some rationale for disagreement. The customary classroom in which teachers monitor most interaction are being replaced by active learning that requires scheduling more time for students to work in teams. Teachers are unable to observe the dynamic that occurs simultaneously in multiple teams. Consequently, they are bound to lack awareness about how some students get along, help others, and are willing to learn from teammates (Gillies, 2007).

Teachers are aware that students must be equipped with teamwork skills. Still, there is uncertainty over what goes on during group work and how the quality of classmate interaction can be optimized. For example, what do you suppose the answers to these questions would be in courses or other settings where you are engaged with field experience, labs or service learning?

1. Do students seek and value impressions of all teammates or are conversations based on social dominance?

2. Do teammates treat one another in ways that contribute to self-esteem and motivate achievement?

3. Is each person expected to perform a fair share of the collective workload as well as demonstrate initiative?

4. How do students feel about the involvement of classmates with disabilities as members of their team?

5. Do members provide feedback on logic of peers and acknowledge insights they acquire from one another?

6. How do students feel about the amount of class time that is set aside for working together in team activities?

7. How do students feel about group assessment of the cooperative skills and performance of teammates?

8. What do students think about teacher methods used to credit individuals for their group contribution?

The answers to these peer support inquiries are important since they provide indicators reflecting group work success of students in your classes. Because adolescents interact with each other often in the absence of teacher observations, they are the most credible sources of perception about these issues, so their voices should be heard (Girod, Pardales, Cavanaugh, & Wadsworth, 2005). One method for assessing student views is for them to complete polls. A polling approach encourages honesty because it can be anonymous. You can conduct the Peer Support Poll (Exercise 7.01) at the end of this chapter. The results will reveal how this aspect of education is viewed and detect how it might be improved.

Lessons From Peers

The potential of teenagers to influence socialization is revealed by lessons most students learn mainly from peers. The relevance of these lessons is that they support or interfere with personal adjustment across a wide range of situations.

(1) Peers provide the first substantial experiences with equality. Everyone likes companionship and enjoys attention others give them. The peer group is in the best position to satisfy these needs. When members act in an approved manner such as dressing according to the norm, their group rewards them with attention, acceptance, and emotional support (Bowker, 2004; Prinstein & Dodge, 2008).

(2) The peer group presents a separate set of standards for how to act than what is expected by adults at home and in school. Peer standards are more attainable and offer a rationale for behavior in opposition to

directives from adults. The greater resources that adults have make it difficult to declare complete autonomy from them. Nevertheless, classmates show a consistent willingness to listen to friends report on common dilemmas, and they encourage one another to express differences in the presence of grownups (Hamm & Faircloth, 2005).

(3) The positive influence of peers is commonly overlooked and undervalued by adults (Harris, 1998, 2006). Peers provide lots of experiences that support social and emotional development. To illustrate, adolescents need someone of their age as a reasonable basis for self-comparison, opportunities to express themselves without fear of punishment, and the opportunity to share leadership. They encourage others to strive for independence and convey a sense of belonging to another important group besides the family or the class (Kroger, 2005).

(4) Peers learn about friendship mainly from one another, how to get along with people of the same status (Chadsey & Han, 2005). Becoming part of a group requires gaining skills motivated by peers. These skills include cooperation, sharing, striving for independence, expressing discontent and anger, and making up. All of these lessons are more easily acquired from peers than parents. Students find out what friends will tolerate and identify conduct they will not condone. Most youth are able to gain a sense of belonging in peer groups and to feel accepted. Students discover that they must learn from one another how to peacefully resolve arguments even though, like adults, aggressive and dysfunctional approaches are sometimes prominent (Chu, 2005; Crothers, Field, & Kolbert, 2005).

Belonging and Rejection

Helping students perceive themselves as successful is a way to support healthy personality development (Feist & Feist, 2006). Youth can also grow by learning to look at others in positive ways. Before age 10, students less often engage in social rejection. Most activities of young children tend to be noncompetitive so self-concepts are not threatened. Students who perform better than classmates in elementary school seldom announce superiority and those who are below average do not sense inferiority because norms of performance have yet to be established. During childhood, the status of parents represents the primary source of child self esteem. Children accept as their own the value they perceive their parents to have attained (Tropp & Pettigrew, 2005).

Things change dramatically when students enter middle school or junior high. They can no longer depend on what their parents have accomplished as the basis for self-pride. Another shift is that, instead of meeting the expectations of just one teacher, they are now obliged to satisfy the demands of multiple teachers, each of whom provide instruction in different subjects. From this time on, students have to earn their own social standing. In classes they begin to encounter more competition and failure along with critical and unfriendly remarks from their classmates. Peers are quick to seize on weakness, expressed either by insults or even more hurtful statements. As a result, middle school students generally exhibit a sharpening sense of self and overall decline on measures of self-esteem. Middle schools should provide experiences that enable students to see themselves favorably without having to find fault with others (Ponterotto, Utsey, & Pedersen, 2006).

As peers replace parents in supplying norms, roles, and models with whom to identify, adolescents look more to classmates for acceptance, information, and emotional support. It is so important to belong that students seldom challenge peer group methods. Instead, most are eager to conform. Group members feel less anxious when they behave the same as others without quite knowing why. This tendency to adopt values and attitudes without understanding the reasons for them can sometimes lead to acceptance of behaviors students would otherwise recognize as being wrong (Way, Gingold, Rotenberg, & Kuriakose, 2005).

For a group to have special significance, becoming a member must be somewhat exclusive. Beginning about age 10, students form *cliques* in which those from similar backgrounds and standards hang out and usually refuse to accept classmates who differ from themselves (Desetta, 2005). Although this can be a reasonable way for people to find and develop friendships, there can also be negative outcomes. Sometimes rejection escalates to verbal expression of intolerance and prejudice. Social prejudice is more common among 10–year-olds than high school seniors (Adams, Biernal, Branscombe, Crandall, & Wrightsman, 2008; Hamm & Faircloth, 2005).

Although it is gratifying to realize that negative social prejudice (i.e., rejection) is likely to decline as level of education rises, research has consistently shown that the consequences of peer rejection in early adolescence can last for a lifetime (Thompson, 2006). Persons who become a target of racial, religious, ethnic, and other prejudices have to divert some energy from healthy development to self-protection (Inzlicht, McKay, & Aronson, 2006). Acceptance, rejection, and self-concept are inseparable. To suggest that minority students who suffer prejudice ought to disregard the low estimate the dominant group has of them is to presume they can avoid being affected by peers. On the contrary, how others feel about us influences the way we are treated by them and, to some extent, how we view ourselves (Baumeister, Campbell, Krueger, & Vohs, 2005).

Peer Pressure Protectors

One cost of a strong sense of belonging to a group is conformity. This is alright when a group expects the person to adopt healthy patterns of behavior. When this is not the case, individuals must be capable of withstanding pressure from peers because caving in to their demands could compromise health, integrity, and personal goals. Teachers and others working with adolescents are valuable sources of guidance in preparing students to overcome pressures to adopt dysfunctional behavior in order to avoid rejection. Every adolescent needs access to peer pressure protectors. Teachers can be influential in establishing constructive peer norms and enabling students to withstand negative pressure (Baumeister, 2005).

1. Families rely on educators to take initiatives because school is the place where peers are together most often. Encouraging involvement with extracurricular activities and after school programs is one way to support healthy interaction with others who have similar interests and goals that might not be known in the classroom. The benefit for students is more likely attained when teachers are willing to act as advisors for after-school activities and clubs.

2. Teachers can set peer influence on a healthy course by arranging cooperative learning teams in which peers support one another to think critically and creatively.

3. By showing acceptance of imagination, teachers can modify peer judgment. For example, John is a creative sixth grader. In the past when he proposed original ideas, his classmates laughed and the teachers felt it was their role to protect John by insisting the laughter end. However, this year the teacher listens to John's ideas and, when peers begin to jeer, she says, "Let's pursue John's idea." She writes the idea on the board and challenges the students to explore beyond a surface reaction. We want to consider whether John's idea has value and what some implications could be for us. In this manner the teacher obligated the class to consider John's thinking instead of dismissing it without reflection. During the ensuing conversation students came to the following conclusions: (a) Sometimes good ideas are not recognized when they are first expressed. (b) Judging a concept before understanding it is a form of ideational prejudice. (c) John's ideas are really good. These conclusions contribute more to John and the class than trying to protect him from those choosing to laugh when they do not understand.

4. Teachers encourage self-reliance and individuality by rewarding questions in the face of peer pressure to prevent questions, beginning during middle school and junior high. The common unwillingness to be viewed by peers as curious inhibits growth and suggests the false impression that students can be self-directed without pursuing questions. Instead, if we want students to continue learning after they finish school, asking questions must be part of the attitude and skill set they develop. Support for questioning does more to improve teaching than any other student response.

5. One reason for urging students to ask questions is so that they will challenge the thinking of their peer group instead of supposing that all norms make sense and deserve support.

6. Students should have opportunities to discuss the nature of clique groups, how they affect others, and what can be done to prevent inappropriate rejection. If someone is behaving in unacceptable ways toward others, then peer rejection is the natural response.

7. If teachers help adolescents establish friendships, students are less vulnerable to rejection from cliques. Two can stand apart easier than one. While all students need opportunities to make friends at school, some classes appear more conducive to friendships. These relationships are more apt to flourish when teachers make assignments where students work as pairs or triads instead of only in large groups or alone.

8. Most students are achievement oriented and adopt actions that produce recognition. Extra credit is sometimes given for competition. Caring about others is observable and could be seen by students as a form of accomplishment that deserves consideration in status and leadership (e.g., giving blood, tutoring, volunteering in a hospital or a nursing home, peer counseling). Similarly, when teachers see how newcomers are treated without directing students to welcome them, recognition can be given to students whose initiative enabled newcomers to feel that they belong.

9. Teachers can counter peer dependence by making themselves available for conversation outside class. This allows students somewhere else to turn with problems than to one another. To fulfill this role, teachers must be regarded as approachable and trustworthy. Students feel that some teachers are too hard to talk to, leaving them without a potentially valuable source of assistance.

Parents also have an important role in providing peer pressure protectors for their children.

1. The best way to minimize the influence of peer pressure is to encourage individuality. Parents do this by avoiding comparisons of achievement or shortcomings among their children. When one child is used as a standard of behavior for a sibling, the result can be sustained rivalry and jealousy instead of lifelong reciprocal support and pride.

2. Encourage teenagers to value solitude as a time to reflect, self-evaluate, and look at things anew. Solitude allows the individuality and creativity adolescents need so that being around age mates for long periods does not lead to peer dependence.

3. Parents need to make themselves available to listen, especially about difficulties of maintaining friendships. This task requires high priority, takes time, and is inconvenient. Do it anyway. From grade 5 onwards problems involving classmates and friends are likely to be continuous and, depending on how parents respond, they may be asked for advice often or not at all. Help children learn how to get along without threatening withdrawal in order to force concession by others. Share your mistakes—this requires self-disclosure.

4. Allow privacy. Let adolescents confide in you when they will, without insisting that you be told everything that is happening in their lives. Trust is essential for building intimate relationships and parents play the most prominent role in helping adolescents acquire this attribute.

5. Recognize that the status of a daughter or son no longer depends exclusively on their place in the pecking order at school. For example, students with low social status can satisfy their need for acceptance and belonging and enjoy interaction after school when they go online to communicate with cyber friends. The opportunity to build friendships in a broader context has expanded with the Internet and there may be more interaction with peers online than face- to-face communication at school. Parents can encourage adolescent conversations with cyber friends who attend other schools and live in other communities (Peter, Valkenburg, & Schouten, 2005).

FRIENDSHIP AND DATING

When boys and girls become adolescents, between ages 10 and 13, a corresponding change occurs in the worries that preoccupy their parents. Mothers and fathers start to worry less about strangers and more about friends, particularly boyfriends and girlfriends. Adolescents commonly place friendship and dating on the top of their list of concerns as well (Chadsey & Han, 2005). *Friendships* are relationships based on mutual feelings of trust and affection (Brown & Klute, 2005). Being able to form friendships is essential for socialization. *Dating*, to go out with someone as a social partner, allows adolescents to practice building friendships and to explore romantic connections. The majority of students from 12 to 18 years of age report that they have experienced a romantic relationship. By age 16, many adolescents interact more often with romantic partners than with their parents, siblings, or friends (Bouchey & Furman, 2005). *Cyber dating*, exploring romantic relationships online, is increasing among teenagers (Gallagher, 2006). Wiredsafety, the largest online safety and help group, provides important tips for older teenagers about cyber dating—http://www.wiredsafety.org/internet101/aromance.html.

Some students fail to learn to build healthy friendships because parents disregard the learning sequence of attitudes and knowledge needed to attain this goal. The orientation parents provide on dating should include an emphasis on equality, mutual respect, and consideration of the dating partner's goals. Instead, the fears of parents about sexual involvement and pregnancy often motivates them to ignore lessons on friendship building in favor of warnings about premature sex and discussions about condoms. Concerns of parents are reinforced by health reports that, every year, three million teenagers are diagnosed with a sexually transmitted disease (STD) and a million adolescent girls become pregnant (Gurvey, Adler, & Ellen, 2005; O'Donnell, Stueve, Simmons, Dash, Agronick, & JeanBaptiste, 2006). Parents are also frustrated by scenes of intimacy on television, especially situations where couples become sexually involved quickly after meeting for the first time. The fear is that teenagers will conclude this speeded up level of involvement is acceptable and incorporate it as part of their expectations for dating (Rosen, 2007).

Sexual Harassment of Students

One problem adolescents face inside and outside school is *sexual harassment*, unwanted sex-related advances toward someone. Touching a person improperly or making suggestive remarks are examples of harassment. Students who are disabled, gay, or lesbian appear to suffer the most from suggestive and pejorative remarks (Ladd, 2005). Girls sometimes encounter comments or improper touching by boys who excuse themselves with claims that "I was just kidding," or "She is my friend so it's ok." Pamela Haag (2001) interviewed 2,000 girls, ages 11–17, regarding what they considered the most important issues in their lives, how they would like conditions at school to change, things they believe girls their age should know, and how they had been hurt by others. The only age segment that did not identify sexual harassment was the 11-year-olds. By age 12, girls commonly faced requests from boys to have sexual intercourse. Haag found that the majority of girls felt they lack opportunities in school for friendly conversation with boys. Other studies have shown that boys also share the view about needing more time to talk socially with girls (Meyer, 2008).

Most schools have sexual harassment policies but few provide curriculum to address the issues. Lessons can be helpful to curb this problem. In addition, communities should increase the after school, no-cost places where students can hang out, talk, play games, dance, have guided discussions on healthy relations and daily concerns. Most after-school programs are too goal-oriented, too competitive, and too gender-segregated (Meyer, 2008; National Institute for Out-of-School Time, 2005). Teenagers benefit from opportunities to practice being around and learning to feel comfortable talking with persons of the other gender. There is a need for more diverse after-school activities on campus and in community centers than the prevailing domination of sports teams. Adequate time spent together in enjoyable wholesome activities and discussions about respect can establish a foundation for what can become genuine, caring friendships and dating.

Dating Abuse Among Teenagers

Dating abuse is "when someone resorts to a pattern of violent behavior by means of verbal, physical or sexual intimidation to gain power and control of a partner." Some adolescent boys suppose that it is cool to call girlfriends bad names or mistreat them in the presence of guys they wish to impress. These put-downs make further mistreatment of the girls easier to justify (Foshee, Bauman, Linder, Rice, & Wilcher, 2007). It seems that many adolescent boys receive conflicting and harmful messages about what constitutes "being a man" (Cosby & Poussaint, 2007; Jouriles, McDonald, Garrido, Rosenfeld, & Brown, 2005). These boys need better advice on how to treat girls (Marquart, Nannini, Edwards, Stanley, & Wayman, 2007). The Family Violence Prevention Fund (2006) offers a set of helpful guidelines called "Coaching Boys Into Men—What You Can Do" to prevent violence against girls and young women—http://endabuse.org/cbim/. Parents and teachers need to become informed and more accountable for their responsibility to teach gender respect to boys and girls from an early age (Kindlon, 2006; Sax, 2005).

Literature confirms that intimate bullies represent a growing health and social problem for adolescents. About 85% of rapes are committed by dating partners or by acquaintances. National data indicate that Hispanic girls are more likely than girls from other groups to report being victims of dating violence (Fields, 2008). The Annie Casey Foundation provides state-by-state indicators of well being for children and adolescents including teen pregnancy rates, available at—http://www.kidscount.org/datacenter/databook.jsp

The United States House of Representatives has recognized that parents and educators are poorly informed about adolescent dating violence (Congressional Record, 2005). Part of the House Resolution 483 to support greater awareness included these facts.

1. One in three female high school students report physical abuse by a dating partner.

2. Forty percent of high school students have been victims of dating violence at least once.

3. Violent relationships in adolescence can have serious consequences for victims, who are at higher risk for substance abuse, eating disorders, risky sexual behavior, suicide, and adult re-victimization.

4. Severity of violence among intimate partners increases if the pattern was established in adolescence.

5. Eighty one percent of parents surveyed believed teen dating violence is not a problem or admitted that they did not know it is a problem.

Dating Rights and Responsibilities

Some of the education adolescents need about dating should take place in the classroom where they can have guided discussions with other students. There is a need to understand that roles like driving a car, going to school, playing on an athletic team, and dating all come with rights and responsibilities. Figure 7.1 and Figure 7.2 provide middle school and high school students guidelines for dating behavior. Schools can post these guidelines as a reminder of how to act and encourage students to self-direct the following questions: Do I violate the rights of my dating partner? Am I fulfilling my responsibilities to the person I date? Am I respecting my rights and the rights of the person I date? As part of someone's cell phone message or e-mail "signature," teens could include one or more guidelines, abbreviated or an acronym, which could serve as conscience reminders. After all, these media provide for the arena in which many adolescent relationships occur. Perhaps the guidelines, if they are "forwarded" across these technologies, could become a healthy norm.

Most teenagers have lots of questions about dating and want to do whatever they can to prevent exposure to mistreatment. For example, "I thought my boyfriend must really love me when he started to call me a lot on my cell phone. Now he wants to know where I am all the time. Is this normal?" Most counselors would suggest that the partner is becoming possessive and trying to control behavior. *Possessiveness* is when someone treats another person like one of their belongings. The possessive person does not want the partner to share time or to give attention to anyone else. This is similar to jealousy but more extreme. A controlling attitude is evident when a person rules a relationship and insists on making all decisions. The dominated person's view is ignored. Often a controlling person tells the partner how to dress, who to talk to, where to go and what they cannot do. Frequent calling on the cell phone is a way to maintain control, keeping tabs on her activities and whereabouts. Sometimes a boyfriend monitors his girlfriend's chat room or e-mail activities. If this is the predicament a girl finds herself in, she should speak with a teacher, parent, or other trusted adult to seek guidance (Apter, 2001).

Dating Rights

I have the right:

1. To be treated with respect always.
2. To my own body, thoughts, opinions, and property.
3. To choose and keep my friends.
4. To change my mind—at any time.
5. To not be abused—physically, emotionally, or sexually
6. To leave a relationship.
7. To say no.
8. To be treated as an equal.
9. To disagree.
10. To live without fear and confusion from my boyfriend's or girlfriend's anger.

Source: Copyright © 2008 State of Washington, Washington State Medical Association and National Crime Prevention Council, retrieved November 1, 2008, from http://www.atg.wa.gov/page.aspx?id=1968. Reprinted with permission.

Figure 7.1.   Dating rights.

Dating Responsibilities

I have the responsibility:

1. To not threaten to harm myself or another.
2. To urge my girlfriend or boyfriend to pursue her/his dreams.
3. To support my girlfriend or boyfriend emotionally.
4. To communicate, not manipulate.
5. To not humiliate or demean my girlfriend or boyfriend
6. To refuse to abuse—physically, emotionally or sexually.
7. To take care of myself.
8. To allow a boyfriend or girlfriend to maintain individuality.
9. To respect myself and my girlfriend or boyfriend.
10. To be honest with each other.

Source: Copyright © 2008 State of Washington, Washington State Medical Association and National Crime Prevention Council, retrieved November 1, 2008, from http://www.atg.wa.gov/page.aspx?id=1968. Reprinted with permission.

Figure 7.2. Dating responsibilities.

Some other dating concerns frequently expressed by teenagers include:

1. What forms of abuse occur in dating relationships? What are some early warnings that my partner might mistreat me? I tried several times to end my relationship, but my partner rationalizes that we should stay together based on our investment of time together so far.
2. What should I do? I have a friend who I think is enduring an abusive relationship and would like to provide help but I don't know just what to do.
3. Are there things I can do to increase my chances for dating success? I am not in a relationship but want to have a healthy friendship when I find the right partner.
4. Am I "cheating" on someone if I date others from time to time just to get to know what other people are like? As long as I am not physically intimate with anyone else, other than my special other, is it cheating by just seeing a movie or doing dinner with another person?
5. If we are going together, is it just like a marriage, or do I have the right to talk to and to see others?

Responses to similar questions from adolescents are provided by the Washington State Office of the Attorney General (2006). This Web site provides an awareness curriculum titled "Teen Dating Violence" intended for eighth graders http://www.atg.wa.gov/violence/curriculum.shtml. The 50-minute lesson includes a helpful handout on dating rights and responsibilities, brochure on expectations for dating, a video clip featuring adolescent problems with partners, and a discussion guide for teachers. After students observe the video, they can meet in small mixed gender groups to reflect on a set of related questions. This focus for dialogue is most relevant to their life stage. As things stand now, teenagers speak mostly to friends of the same age and gender about dating but seldom hear the thinking and opinions of opposite gender peers. Schools should give high priority to arranging these conversations (Rathus, Nevid, & Fichner-Rathus, 2005).

Family Dialogue on Relationships

The purpose of *dating* should be to get to know someone while having fun at the same time. No one has to convey false impressions or commitments beyond "getting to know you." Nevertheless, concerns that daughters and sons may rush into sexual relationships distract many parents from their responsibility to provide a healthy orientation to dating (Bogle, 2008; Bozick, 2006). *Empathy* is the ability to identify with and understand another person's feelings or difficulties. Some ways of showing empathy in dating include listening to hurt feelings and considering the other person's goals and aspirations. Building trust and respect are vital ingredients for emotional ties that are durable and mutually satisfying (Crouter & Booth, 2006).

Some parents defer lessons on dating until adolescents reach the same age as when the adults were first allowed to date. In contrast, studies of 17,000 American girls have confirmed that puberty and menstruation arrive earlier than in the past (Fingerson, 2006). The age of first intercourse occurs earlier too (Fields, 2008). Family dialogue on these issues should begin in grade four because some girls enter puberty as young as age 8. Studies of 2,000 Black, White, and Mexican American parents of adolescents and adolescents (ages 10–14) were conducted to rate parental guidance. Both generations agreed that parents are not involved to the extent they should be in discussing dating (R. Strom, Strom, Strom, Shen, & Beckert, 2004). Teachers are sometimes asked by parents to recommend sources on adolescent friendship and sexuality to focus conversations at home. A helpful Web site to recommend draws on the expertise of a medical board who respond to questions of teenagers and parents about dating, emotions, sex, and other problems—see Teen Growth http://www.teengrowth.com.

TECHNOLOGY AND SOCIAL INTERACTION

Most of the literature on peer relationships and composition of youth groups reflects a bygone era when face-to-face interactions were the exclusive focus of concern. Adolescents saw each other mostly at the mall or the movies, driving around with friends, or hanging out in someone's home. In the present environment, friendships are more reliant on cell phones, chat rooms, buddy lists, instant messaging, e-mail, PDAs, and blogs. How will these technology forums for communication alter the way adolescents build and preserve their friendships? What skills are required to develop virtual friendships with peers from other places and cultures? What guidance should parents provide about online friendships and cyber dating? How can friendships on the Internet be linked to school goals about socialization, communication, and appreciation of cultural diversity? During the next decade, these questions about peer relationships will be the focus of studies.

What we know is that technology is a common tool that facilitates social interaction. Two ways in which this influence is particularly visible are for adolescents to create multiple identities on the Internet and frequent use of blogs to express themselves. Although technology offers new ways for teenagers to communicate, it also presents new hazards. By interacting in cyber space without caution, personal data can be accessed by predators and others who would inflict harm (Willard, 2007).

The Internet and Multiple Selves

The ability of adolescents to create multiple identities on the Internet adds a new consideration for their social development. While the online identities of many will be the same as their real life identities, others will choose to present themselves in other ways. An interesting focus to explore social interaction on the Internet involves the concept of multiple selves devised by Carl Rogers (1961). Rogers, a leader in counseling psychology, maintained that each person represents three selves—the ideal self, the real self, and the perceived self. The *ideal self* is the person we would like to be; the *real self* is the self as observed by others; and the *perceived self* is the way that we perceive ourselves to be. Jamie's aspiration, his ideal self, is to become popular with others in his class at school. In contrast, the way that peers see Jamie, his real self, is as reluctant to join them in the common challenge against most aspects of adult authority. According to Jamie, his perceived self, he is a person whose shyness is misinterpreted as a lack of courage or lack of assertion. Rogers (1961) maintained that the purpose for counseling therapy is to help clients find ways to their ideal selves while increasing the accuracy of their perceptions of where they currently are and how much of their ideal self has been realized (see Figure 7.3).

Rogers would have been intrigued by how his concept of multiple selves could be applied to people using the Internet. Adolescents who join chat rooms can have multiple aliases allowing them to masquerade, try out new roles, and discover what it is like to act differently than their typical daily behavior (Liau, Khoo, & Peng, 2005; Subrahmanyam,

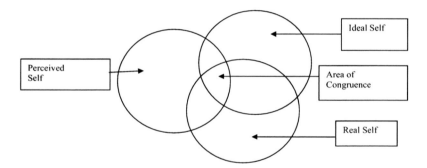

a. Small area of congruence suggests poor psychological health and the advisability of therapy to bring the selves closer together.

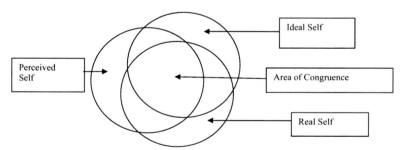

b. Large area of congruence suggests psychological health and little anxiety, and hence efficient life functioning about where they currently are and how much of their ideal self has been realized.

Figure 7.3.   Congruence of ideal, real, and perceived selves as an index of psychological health.

Greenfield, & Tynes, 2004). A teenager like Jamie who is shy might wish to be assertive on the Internet before incorporating assertive behavior during face-to-face conversations. There are students who prefer to present themselves online as less dominant than they are in person. Both genders claim to have learned courtship skills online such as finding out as much as possible about another person's interests and preferences because of opportunities that do not occur in other situations. The chance to practice unfamiliar but desired roles is appealing (Kelsey & Kelsey, 2007).

Teachers should remind students about their accountability for social interaction online. Adolescents need to know that anything they do on the Internet could be traced and, therefore, while anonymity may be felt, it cannot be ensured. A priority goal should be to reconcile the different impressions one chooses to make on others via the Internet with interaction reflecting honesty along with guarded privacy to avoid sharing sensitive information anyone can see. In this way, misrepresentation does not occur and online selves are integrated with off line conditions (Horak, 2007).

Blogs and Social Networks

A growing number of teenagers document personal experience by recording the events that capture their attention as well as expressing feelings and interpretations. However, unlike the guarded privacy cherished by diary writers in previous generations, many authors now prefer to post their journals in the public domain. This recording of events usually appear on a weblog, commonly called a blog. A *blog* is an online journal frequently updated with news, opinions, pictures/ audio/ video files intended for the public and open to responses from password protected visitors or, on some sites, anybody in cyber space (Gardner & Birley, 2008). An *online community* is defined as a group that shares thoughts or ideas, or works together on projects by using electronic communication only. Online communities represent a broad range of interests that are social, hobby-oriented, political, spiritual or professional. Teenagers consider Myspace, Facebook, YouTube, Hi5, Xanga, Live Journal, Bebo or Nexopia (Canadian equivalent of Myspace) appealing because they present opportunities to meet new friends, dialogue with others having similar interests, and encourage postings on topics of interest.

By using a blog anyone can comment on matters that they feel are being ignored or distorted by the media and express rants that are unlikely to be published by public news outlets. Blogs have a special appeal to teenagers because this forum allows them to control how they present themselves online without interruption or correction from adults. In this way, blogs facilitate a measure of independence (Horak, 2007). Looking from another vantage, social network blogs such as www.facebook.com and www.myspace.com can serve other constructive functions adults may overlook. For example, having someone pay attention to your opinions and provide feedback could contribute to growth. Teenagers can benefit from reciprocal sharing with bloggers from other ethnic groups or nations. This context permits them to practice their developing logic in debates that are seldom possible with the adults in their lives. By reading the postings of peers, adolescents also receive confirmation that they are not alone in the way they interpret contemporary situations and events. These benefits increase when teachers make assignments that connect student motivation with existing resources (Buckingham & Willett, 2006). The Web site for the Internet Public Library offers a selected list of blogs about a range of topics, including how to create your own blog. Subjects include law, books, food, travel, medicine, history, politics, business, and other topic—http:// www.ipl.org/div/blogs.

Most online teenagers (75%) report using instant messaging, with nearly half (48%) counting on this method for communication daily. The greatest leap in activity takes place between Grade 6 and Grade 7 when the proportion of users jumps from 60% to 82%. Girls are more likely than boys to rely on instant messaging and they begin involvement at earlier ages. For example, 79% of sixth grade girls use the Internet compared to 44% of boys (Lenhart & Madden, 2007).

The National School Boards Association conducted a survey to find out how much time students devote to social networking. The conclusion was that those in the 9–17 age range spent nearly as much time socializing on the Web as watching television (Karlin, 2007). An example of a beneficial social network is Youth Noise, sponsoring blogs catering to 13-18-year-olds from all 50 states and 176 countries. The site supports maximum volume and encourages the racket that a group of teenagers can generate when they wish to make their voices heard. This is a place on the Web where students can discuss the things they dislike and work together attempting to reach solutions. Specifically, the goals for Youth Noise blogs are to (a) inspire adolescents to explore concerns that affect their age group throughout the world, (b) connect with other teens, realizing that two or more voices can be louder and therefore are better heard than one, and (c) empower adolescents to engage in communal efforts that support the development of maturity while improving lives of others. The adults who supervise Youth Noise communicate information from 300 nonprofit partners in order to motivate the middle school and high school students to become noisemakers who post their impressions. Students are also expected to access links where they are encouraged to read articles that offer background data about issues. These sources enables youth to debate more persuasively by accessing informed judgment as a basis for their personal opinions. Some global topics for noise board reaction are stories about current relief efforts where people have been affected by natural disasters; exploitation of children in the workplace throughout the world; and concerns on health and what youth can do to improve their environment and other conditions. Students also get to use the youth noise interactive tools that were devised to inform them about opportunities to participate in volunteer activity, either online or in their community. Youth noise can be found at http://www.youthnoise.com/blog.php.

Studies evaluating the influence of blogs on adolescence have yet to be published. However, these potential benefits can be anticipated.

1. When peers explain their dissimilar perspective without interruption reciprocal learning can occur.
2. There may be a sense of assurance in confirming that personal views are shared.
3. The chance to practice emerging logic in friendly dialogues and debates could be welcome, especially by teenagers whose conversations with adults provides too little opportunity to express opinions.
4. Communicating with peers from other backgrounds could result in an appreciation for cultural diversity that is not represented in class (Columbo & Columbo, 2007).

Rules for bloggers are beginning to emerge as a standard that teenagers can use to guide behavior. The rules for What Not To Do when participating on Youth Noise blogs warrant discussion by students.

1. Share personal/private information
2. Harass or threaten another Noisemaker
3. Cyberstalk, spam, or send unwanted messages to or from anyone related to Youth Noise
4. Bash another member's race, heritage, culture, gender, sexual orientation, religion, and so forth.
5. Post, transmit, promote, distribute or facilitate the distribution of any obscene, sexually explicit, vulgar, pornographic, libelous, ethnically offensive or untrue content.
6. Solicit sexually explicit photographs or text from anyone.

7. Post or transmit photographic violently graphic images or representing youth below age 18.

8. Disrupt flow of blogs or other folks' spaces with vulgar language, abusiveness, repetitive posts, and off-topic content.

9. Impersonate another Noisemaker, Youth Noise staff member or anyone else.

10. Attempt to get or steal a password, other account information, or other private information from another Noisemaker, harvest e-mail addresses or other information.

11. Post copyrighted material or material prepared or created by others without direct permission and authorizations.

12. Post advertising and solicitations for goods and services.

13. Include URLs for outside sites that violate any of the rules stated here.

14. Post anything that Youth Noise decides (in its sole discretion) is inappropriate for the Youth Noise Web site.

Jeffrey Cole (2008) directs the Digital Future Project at the University of Southern California. This group surveys 2,000 households each year to explore how online technology affects the lives of Internet users. Findings show that social networks are increasing dramatically and a majority of users report feeling as strongly about their online communities as they do about their real-world communities. In fact, 75% report that they use the Internet to participate in communities related to social causes. Nearly 90% of online community members are participating in social causes that are new to them since their involvement with online communities began. This growth of online communities is opening a range of opportunities for social connection, involvement and communication that could not have been anticipated a few years ago.

In addition to the advantages of social networks, certain disadvantages also warrant consideration. A majority of the parents (63%) responding to the annual Digital Future Project survey in 2008 feel uncomfortable about the participation of their adolescent daughter or son in online communities; only 15% of these parents stated that they feel comfortable with this aspect of behavior (Cole, 2008). Many of the parents worry that they are being replaced by adolescent peers who have become a main sources of teen guidance.

In *The Case Against Adolescence*, Robert Epstein (2007) argues against blaming brain development as the principal cause for foolish risks taken by many adolescents. He suggests that instead of tracing poor judgment to the delayed rate of growth in the frontal cortex, more attention should be placed upon the 24/7 immersion in a peer culture that is facilitated by cell phones and the Internet. Many teenagers are in contact with their friends 70 hours a week but lack any meaningful contact with the important adults in their lives. Some spend brief periods with their parents but often this is time watching television, eating, or checking in by phone. Epstein contends that adolescents have been infantilized by our culture which has caused their isolation from adults and motivated them to communicate almost exclusively with age mates.

A potentially powerful solution to increase the amount of time that teenagers spend with relatives is allowing them to join the adult world in as many ways as possible. However, this shift requires a different way of looking at youth, recognizing their capabilities and nurturing their talents. More contact with adults online and in person along with a gradual increase in responsibility is necessary to replace what is in many instances becoming a strictly peer-driven communication environment. A trajectory for more mutually beneficial relations between adults and adolescents requires sustained interaction rather than allowing Internet social sites for peers to substitute for dialogue within families. To illustrate, when 116 grandmothers were asked how often they communicated online with their 116 adolescent granddaughters, the response of "Never" was given by 95% of the respondents (R. Strom, Lee, Strom, Nakagawa, & Beckert, 2008). Teachers can play a role by devising online homework to involve parents and grandparents, a creative challenge that should be addressed.

Prevention of Exploitation

A predictable hazard arises when students divulge personal information or photos online by e-mail or blogs. Most of what has been written about experimentation with multiple identities on the Internet has concerned dangers that can occur when people exploit others. For example, pedophiles visit chat rooms and social blog sites to find and lure children to meet them (Macgill, 2007). Another group of users is intent on describing or selling sexual experiences, and sharing pornographic images that can be downloaded. The National Center for Missing and Exploited Children (2008) reports 1,200 incidents annually of online enticement of adolescents by adults. See http://www.ncmec.org/ and a related video depicting kidnapping called "Runaway Train" by Soul Asylum at http://www.youtube.com/watch?v=psP1bKKEtHg.

The Federal Bureau of Investigation maintains a task force to monitors the Internet for criminal behavior and protects the vulnerable, particularly minors. The FBI reports that computer sex offenders are mostly White, professional, upper middle-class males. The predators' multiple identities appear to resemble the personality polarities first described in the *Strange*

Case of Dr. Jekyll and Mr. Hyde written by Robert Louis Stevenson (1886). In this classic tale, Dr. Jekyll, is the main character that people believe they know well and affirm to be a model citizen. However, he is periodically transformed into the monster Mr. Hyde, whose evil deeds are seldom observed. In a similar way, when online predators are publicly identified, neighbors often express surprise stating they never observed that side of the person's dual nature. If the Internet was not available to these men to comfortably express themselves online, they would probably be more reclusive. Many predators have been arrested as a result of Internet electronic surveillance conducted by the FBI. The U.S. Department of Justice offers information regarding predators online, *A Parent's Guide to Internet Safety*—http://www.fbi.gov/publications/pguide/pguidee.htm. Another Web site parents can turn to for a comprehensive overview of the problem and ways to protect their children from potential dangers is called Enough is Enough, available at http://www.enough.org.

To protect students, some school districts prohibit them from using their school e-mail address to register for blogs that focus on meeting others or provide cyber dating. The most popular source is http://www.myspace.com a clearinghouse where members can find others by their location, age and interests. Participants are supposed to be at least 14 years old but younger students often misrepresent themselves. Some schools offer seminars for parents regarding ways for them to protect youngsters online. They emphasize that it is not a matter of whether to trust daughters and sons but to show concern for safety. A Web site by teenagers directed to adolescents that provides articles such as cyberdating, birth control, love and relationships is from Rutgers University at http://sexetc.rutgers.edu/index.php Wiredsafety at http://www.wiredsafety.org—addresses questions regarding blog problems and suggest methods for teenagers and their parents to deal with them.

Prevention of student exposure to sex offenders should become a priority for schools as well as parents. A national resource that all educators should be familiar with is Family Watchdog—http://www.familywatchdog.us/. This Web site provides a map of the city and state that you type in. The map legend shows school locations and addresses where identified convicted sex offenders live and work. In each case, there is a description of the conviction, picture of offender for ease of recognition, and indication of how close the person lives to the school or home address given in the inquiry. Bear in mind that it is a misdemeanor to harass anyone listed on the offense registry. The purpose of this national service is to make faculty and students aware of sex offenders in their community so children can be warned to avoid talking or interacting with them.

Significant changes are transforming the context for socialization in adolescence. There is increasing reliance on technology tools for communicating online with friends and strangers. Blogs facilitate these mostly out of school conversations where teenagers are exposed to opinions of others, elaborate their own opinions and feelings, report on satisfactions and disappointments, disagree on how to resolve concerns, and identify community needs that are of concern to youth (Gardner & Birley, 2008). Preventing predators from harming teens that feel invulnerable remains a challenge for schools and parents. Although there are many complaints about the lack of etiquette in use of technology, there is little dispute that cell phones and the Internet have increased the number of persons listening to adolescents. On the other hand, periodic cell calls from teens to check in should not be seen by adults as a substitute for the face to face conversations needed to discuss things that matter (Weber & Dixon, 2007).

COOPERATIVE LEARNING CLASSROOMS

One way for teachers to directly support an essential aspect of social development, acquisition of teamwork skills, is by arranging conditions for cooperative learning. *Cooperative learning* is an approach to instruction that engages students in groups as a method for them to study course content. This orientation is rapidly becoming one of the most significant elements of digital literacy by allowing students to enlarge their scope of inquiry beyond what has been possible while merging their efforts through connecting with others from distant locations (Gillies, 2007). Students work on one or more tasks in pursuit of mutually understood goals. Besides learning the intended content, they get to practice team skills that are needed in the workplace. There is an expectation that each team member will contribute something to build a group product or to construct knowledge that could not otherwise be attained without extra individual effort.

Social Interdependence Theory

The theoretical origins of cooperative learning began with the inquiries of Morton Deutsch at Columbia University (Pippert, 2007). He informed student in one class that their grade for the course would depend on the quality of their discussions. Each student would get the same grade as teammates to reflect how well they performed as a group. This *social interdependence* arrangement meant that everyone would have to depend upon one another. Other students with similar backgrounds as the first group in another class were informed that their grades would be based on individual contributions as compared with performance of classmates. This was the competitive situation. Deutsch (1949a, 1949b) discovered that students assigned to the interdependent cooperative situation produced better products and were more satisfied with their course experience than peers in the competitive arrangement. The cooperative groups generated more and higher quality ideas during their discussions than the competitive groups. They communicated more effectively by considering the comments of teammates, liked one another better, and tried to motivate colleagues. In contrast, the competitive group students usually tried to dominate or to overshadow peers. Results favored the interdependent cooperative situation.

Building on Deutsch's findings, Muzafer Sherif (1958) discovered that cohesiveness of groups increases when cooperation is required. He randomly placed 22 fifth-grade boys in two groups called the Rattlers and Eagles for competitive games of baseball, football, and tug of war at a summer camp. Initially the groups were good sports but soon grew hostile, accused others of cheating, resorted to put-downs, and refused to interact. To attempt to solve the conflict, the groups were put into situations necessitating cooperation. For example, Sherif deliberately broke the water line that supplied the camp. He then informed all the boys that there was a problem with the water supply. The Rattlers and Eagles searched for the problem and, after a lengthy collaboration period, found and fixed it. When the boys had to unite, their hostility was temporarily set aside. After arranging other cooperative activities, friendships emerged between the Eagles and Rattlers. Sherif (1966) replicated the experiment several times with similar results confirming the importance of interdependence.

Cooperative learning can produce numerous benefits when conducted effectively. Some of the observed social-emotional outcomes include more frequent engagement in helping and tutoring, more careful listening to the views of others, encouraging and recognizing contributions of teammates, avoidance of put-downs or placing blame on others, greater willingness to accept compromise as a way to deal with differences of opinion, enhanced sense of belonging, increased perspective taking, greater willingness to try new and difficult tasks, and increased expression of optimism and hope regarding group success. Cooperative learning research has found that academic performance improves. Students show greater problem solving abilities, more favorable attitudes toward school, increased appreciation of cultural and racial diversity, better understanding about principles of democracy, closer relationships among classmates, and lower incidence of discipline problems (Forest & Balcetis, 2008).

Cooperative Models of Instruction

Since Deutsch, (1949a, 1949b) carried out his experiments 60 years ago, cooperative learning has been the focus of many studies to determine how social relationships influence student behavior and achievement. The collective results were summarized in a meta-analysis of 148 studies that compared the relative effectiveness of cooperative, competitive, and individualistic goal structures. These studies included 17,000 students, ages 12–15, from 11 countries. As predicted by social interdependence theory, students in classrooms with cooperative learning goals where teams worked together were more accurate on test outcomes, earned higher problem solving scores on reasoning and critical thinking tasks compared to classes where the goal focus was on competitive or individualistic learning. In the cooperative settings students felt a greater sense of support from and connection with peers. The implications are that when teachers structure classrooms in a cooperative way, the goals of academic achievement and social development can be promoted simultaneously while student goals for interaction are also met (Roseth, Johnson, & Johnson, 2008).

Five common elements of cooperative learning were defined by Johnson and Johnson (2003) as follows.

Element 1. Positive interdependence among teammates. Teachers can support social interdependence by structuring goals that can only be attained when students function as a team. These shared and mutually understood goals require that each team member use whatever resources are necessary to fulfill particular tasks assigned by the group. The interdependence emphasis is on "we" instead of "me." Those who are more able or more assertive are not allowed to dominate the group. Teammates are responsible for their own learning and helping peers by tutoring and encouragement. Everyone sinks or swims together because the team product depends on collective performance, not individual performance. Ways to facilitate this outcome are to design a task that is complex enough to warrant the efforts of a few people, to include activities that allow for diverse ideas from the perspective of different people, or to have limited access to task resources (information) or roles.

Element 2. Face-to-face promotive interaction. Discussion and group consensus can ensure that everyone understands how each task assigned or chosen contributes to the team purpose rather than representing independent efforts of individuals that are combined at the end. Peers are encouraged to ask questions and to express confusion or doubt. Lessons are reviewed together to improve comprehension for all the members. Put-downs are unacceptable ways of responding to frustration with team performance.

Element 3. Individual and group accountability. Monitoring progress is essential for productivity. Each member must be responsible for quality work and to help others. The assets of individuals should be used without limiting them to tasks they perform well. Some students ignore their obligation, assuming that conscientious peers will do their work for them to avoid team failure. An important aspect of accountability is that slackers are not to be excused nor given credit when they do not perform their fair share of the workload. A single performance standard is relied on with each individual receiving peer feedback.

Element 4. Team and interpersonal skills. This can be accomplished with each student having a different role or task that supports group goals. In addition, this element helps students be accountable to demonstrate team skills, to help peers learn and to do their fair share of work. Teachers should identify and define the teamwork skills that everyone in class are expected to practice and attain. Discussions and reading should ensure there is common understanding of why the designated skills are relevant to the occupational future of everyone. Besides prescribing team skills, teachers must make assignments that encourage and facilitate their learning. Group procedure departs from a single leader tradition in favor of shared leadership so all teammates get to try this role.

Element 5. Group processing of performance. Teachers agree this element of cooperative learning is the most difficult for them to manage. The reason is because teacher judgment about quality of team products is only one aspect of appropriate assessment. There is a need to also acquire the observation of peers regarding how each member performed their teamwork skills. Including the views of students to credit individuals for team contributions and detect needs for further growth requires teacher trust that providing practice in peer and self-assessment can be accurate, fair and helpful.

There are many strategies to implement cooperative learning. Some prominent methods include Jigsaw, Think Pair-Share, Pairs Check, and Think Quest.

Jigsaw, by Elliot Aaronson (1978) is a cooperative learning strategy requiring each team member to be responsible for one piece of a required group task. Like a jigsaw puzzle where each piece is needed in order to construct the complete picture, the part that each student is assigned in a jigsaw task must be fulfilled for completion and understanding of a team product. Because the role that each student performs is essential, each student is essential. This dynamic offers everyone a sense of individualization and awareness that they are contributing to their team. For example, Margaret Mead's innovative work described in chapter 1 led to wide support for the study of environment as a factor that influences learning. In a biographical jigsaw assignment John would research Mead's growing up years and her schooling. Laura would describe Mead's work in the South Seas and her findings. Lenny will examine the obstacles Mead encountered throughout her career; and Dianne will identify Mead's legacy, the contributions for which she is remembered. Some jigsaws may be organized so that before Laura teaches peers what she has learned, she first meets with another 'expert group' from the class to discuss and crosscheck understanding before going back to the base 'home' team to teach them. The directions for using Jigsaw and other possibilities for this structure are found at Jigsaw Classroom—http://www.jigsaw.org.

Think-Pair-Share is a cooperative learning structure designed to foster reflection as an active engagement during the course of direct instruction (Kagan, 2008). In this approach students process material using interaction with peers to supplement teacher comments. A teacher, after presenting some material, then transitions into the Think Pair Share mode with a question or directive calling for analysis, evaluation, or synthesis that students consider and write their response (Think). Several minutes later the students turn to partners allowing them to share responses and to get immediate feedback on their ideas (Pair). In the third stage, responses are shared in teams or with the class (Share). For example, a teacher is presenting on the principles and possibilities of handheld-Internet connected technology. After discussing a few main ideas for about 15 minutes, she stops and gives the class the following directive to solve in a Think-Pair-Share mode.

> For the next 10 minutes, generate a list of possible things that you could do with such devices. Try to be creative and remember our brainstorming rules. Think about it for 3 minutes alone first and write your own list of ideas. Then share with a partner your ideas and expand the combined list. After 10 minutes I will choose some dyads to share their ideas with the class. This method offers everyone a chance to reflect and vocalize ideas at a given moment, unlike a traditional class where only a teacher is active or one student at a time gives answers.

Pairs Check is a structure used to ensure that the steps of a process are learned. For example, students are learning the technical steps needed to insert video and photographs into PowerPoint presentations they will be expected to offer several times during the semester. John reads the directions he has on these steps to Briella and coaches her. He watches and corrects Briella as needed. Then they switch with Briella acting as the checker/coach and John becoming the learner. Later, the pair confers with another dyad on the sequence of steps they followed. If there is agreement, the task is finished. If help is still necessary, they can try to provide it for each other. But, if there is disagreement without resolve, then all four students raise their hands as it signifies to the teacher the collective need for assistance. The good part of this method is that it makes students accountable for providing considerable help whenever possible, rather than an over-reliance on the teacher (Kagan, 2008).

ThinkQuest is a cooperative learning structure that goes beyond the classroom and uses the Internet to enable students from different countries to unite their efforts. This approach can also expand the composition of teams to include teachers as well as students for the benefit of both groups. ThinkQuest is an international competition for student and teacher teams whose goal is to produce a creative Web site that enhances global learning about concerns shared across cultures. Each Web site features an adolescent contribution of technology tools. The teacher role is to help plan goals and suggest how they can be attained while also advancing personal development by technology mentoring from their student partners. Online teams must overcome barriers of distance, language, and culture. Over 5,000 Web sites have been completed on topics such as the Internet, social science and culture, health and safety, mythology and religion are hosted in the free ThinkQuest Library sponsored by the Oracle Education Foundation (2006) Visit http://www.thinkquest.org.

Additional cooperative learning structures for teacher consideration are explained and illustrated on the University of Texas Division of Instructional Innovation and Assessment (Millis, 2005) Web site at—http://www.utexas.edu/academic/diia/research/projects/hewlett/cooperative.php.

Social Skills and Team Assessment

Major corporations like Bank of America, Disney, Ford, General Motors, Hewlett-Packard, Intel, Microsoft, and Motorola use group methods to evaluate the teamwork performance of individuals. The most common approach, referred to as 360° feedback, comes from an analogy to a compass. The circular compass is a navigational tool with 360 points of reference used to determine direction and monitor whether we are on or off course. The 360° feedback consists of perceptions about someone's work performance as provided from multiple points of reference. There may be differences in how we perceive ourselves and the way in which others perceive us. A comparison of multiple impressions can detect aspects of poor performance and also identify achievement (Evans & Wolf, 2005).

Employees like using multiple sources of observation because coworkers see them often, know how well they perform, and are able to identify their limitations. Team assessment is supported by management too because it has been proven to have a favorable effect on productivity (Klaus, 2008; D. Smith, 2008). Because group evaluation is widely used in the workplace, adolescents should gain teamwork and self-assessment skills employers will expect.

How do the marketplace models match accountability for teamwork in the classroom? There are three considerations that link conditions in the workplace with conditions in school.

(1) *The focus should be on how each individual contributes to other group members.* Teachers generally believe that this condition is appropriate for judging their own performance in the classroom. Educators try to help everyone in class but, in the final analysis, each student is responsible for her or his own personal growth and development. When the same condition is applied in judging how someone contributes to learning of peers in cooperative groups, it means that students are responsible for their own conduct but cannot be held accountable for actions of teammates. Instead, the motivation to support one another is expected to grow as individuals recognize they will be judged by teamwork skills they demonstrate as observed by peers (Van Vugt, De Cremer, & Janssen, 2007).

(2) *Teachers should share responsibility with students for evaluation of group learning.* Most teachers are subject matter experts so they are the best qualified to judge work products submitted by student teams. However, teachers are not the best judges of what happens in groups because they are seldom present to witness student interaction and, even when they are around, cannot tell how initiatives of some individuals affect others in a group. Consequently, when teachers alone judge the dynamics of groups, they risk overlooking some benefits and obstacles experienced by students. Adolescents are in the best position to identify persons who influence them and describe the nature of help given (Gillies, 2007).

(3) *Self-evaluation reports should be compared with the observations reported by peers.* Students are administered national tests, state tests, and teacher-made tests. Feedback on these measures can be beneficial. In addition, students need suitable criteria to consider as they participate in the task of self-evaluation. Otherwise, they may not make the adjustments needed in an environment characterized by over-choice and a job market where collaboration skills are essential (Klaus, 2008). Cooperative learning provides ideal conditions to compare self-evaluation with teammate observations. In this way students practice an ability to judge themselves. Everyone needs guided practice in self-evaluation to become self-critical, a vital ingredient for effective performance in teamwork. Self-evaluation helps students know when to think well of themselves and when to change their behavior based on perceptions of others. In adolescence students become capable of using *introspection,* the detailed mental self-examination of feelings, thoughts, and motives.

Cooperative learning highlights and supports one among the multiple intelligences that have been described by Howard Gardner (1983, 1997) in chapter 4. *Interpersonal intelligence* consists of abilities that make it possible to understand others and work effectively with them. Interpersonal intelligence is essential for cooperative learning and teamwork. How can teachers assess interpersonal intelligence? One way is to present hypothetical situations and then rate student predictions of how they would expect to behave. This procedure is sometimes inaccurate because projections of imagined behavior could vary greatly from how the person might actually respond in a real situation. Another way to assess interpersonal intelligence is to hold students accountable for behavior that can be verified by classmates. Multiple observers with sufficient interactive experience are able to corroborate or refute self-impressions that individuals report on their performance as team members. By aggregating perceptions of teammates, greater reliability is attained (Chen & Gardner, 2005).

Trusting students is also necessary to assess interpersonal intelligence. Trust determines whether students are allowed and encouraged to engage in peer and self-evaluation. In this arrangement, teachers continue to judge quality of work produced by teams and to test results of individuals while students gain experience with the kind of peer and self-evaluation they can expect to encounter in the workplace (D. Smith, 2008). A model of interpersonal intelligence can enable students to identify and record observations of teamwork skills shown by peers and themselves (P. Strom & Strom, 2002). These impressions, reported on the *Teamwork Skills Inventory* (P. Strom & Strom, 2009), inform teachers about the interaction among teammates from a student view (see Table 7.1). Specifically, the Inventory can

- Identify teamwork skills that are demonstrated by individuals,
- Provide individual profiles of anonymous feedback from peers,
- Compare peer observation of performance with self-impression,
- Detect individual and group learning deficits to guide instruction,
- Credit conscientious learners for their initiative and contributions,
- Discover slackers that fail to carry out their fair share of the work,
- Yield an easily understood record of team skills for use in portfolios.

Importance of Inclusion Practices

During adolescence it is common for students to form cliques with classmates who share their interests. This practice can inadvertently lead to exclusion of classmates, most often those with disabilities. The treatment of students with disabilities has varied through history. During

Table 7.1.   Team Skills Adolescents Need to Learn for the Work Place

Attends to Teamwork

1   Demonstrates reliability by keeping a record of good attendance

2   Shows dependability by arriving on time for group participation

3   Focuses attention on the team task so there is no waste of time

4   Fulfills rotation roles such as summarizer, discussant and improviser

5   Can be counted on to do a fair share of the team assigned work

Seeks and Shares Information

6   Admits uncertainty when in doubt about what should be done

7   Asks questions that help to understand and complete class lessons

8   Teaches peers by explaining or reviewing concepts and assignments

9   Brings relevant reading materials for teammates to examine in class

10   Refers to reading materials as a basis for enhancing the discussions

Communicates With Teammates

11   Can be counted on to disclose feelings, opinions, and experiences

12   Speaks clearly and uses vocabulary that can be easily understood

13   Limits the length of comments so other people have a chance to talk

14   Listens to everyone in the group and considers their points of view

15   Encourages teammates and recognizes contributions of individuals

Thinks Critically and Creatively

16   Explores viewpoints and suggestions that may not be liked at first

17   Uses logic to challenge the thinking and work methods of the team

18   Practices reflective thinking and avoids making hasty conclusions

19   Combines and builds upon the ideas that are expressed by others

20   Discovers different ways of looking at things and solving problems

Gets Along in the Team

21   Responds well whenever peers disagree or express their criticism

22   Avoids blaming and judging teammates for difficulties or mistakes

23   Accepts compromise when it is the best way to overcome conflicts

24   Keeps trying even when the task or situation becomes demanding

25   Expresses optimism about the team being able to achieve success

Source: "List of 25 Team Skills" from *Teamwork Skills Inventory* by Paris Strom & Robert Strom. Copyright 2009. Reprinted with permission of Scholastic Testing Service, Inc., Bensenville, IL 60106 USA.

certain periods they were viewed as enemies disliked, imprisoned, and even killed. In modern times, the common response has typically been to segregate them (Osgood, 2007). Fortunately, great improvements have occurred over the past generation with the realization that persons with disabilities are neither helpless nor hopeless but require assistance to develop their talents (Burns, 2007). This perspective has been reinforced by government regulations for employment, access to buildings, and educational opportunities as well as influence of the positive psychology movement applied to the preparation of professionals. The expectation that disabled students can become productive contributing members of society is now shared by teachers, parents, employers, and the disabled. Transforming their potential into achievement is facilitated when regular teachers and special educators are partners, support is provided, appropriate standards of conduct are applied, and instructional strategies enable students with disabilities to integrate with their non-disabled peers (Salend, 2005).

The stimulus for reform was a revelation in the 1970s that more than one million students were excluded from public schools and denied education services (Osgood, 2007). *Mainstreaming* refers to the schooling of special education students in regular classes, a practice that began when Congress passed the Educatioin of All Handicapped Children Act in 1975 (Osborne & Russo, 2007). The tradition of setting a duration period for school related laws was waived. Instead, this reform is intended to govern the nation's education policies permanently. Over the past generation the law has been changed several times to reflect needed alterations. The latest revision, called the Individuals with Disabilities Improvement Act of 2004 (IDEA), requires the *inclusion* of special education students in all aspects of school life including extracurricular activities (Thomas & Loxley, 2007). There are 13 categories of disabilities including autism, specific learning disabilities, speech and language impairments, emotional disturbance, traumatic brain injury, visual impairment, hearing impairment, deafness, mental retardation, deaf-blindness, multiple disabilities, orthopedic impairment, and other health impairments.

Six million students are in special education and 70% of them attend regular classrooms. The conditions for serving this 10 to 12% segment of the entire student population are:

- Free public education for disabled persons between ages 3 and 21.
- Access to education in a regular classroom is guaranteed unless a person's handicap is such that services cannot be properly offered there.
- School placement and other education decisions are made only after consultation with a child's parents. Continuation in a program

requires a reevaluation once every 3 years based on testing at no cost to the parents.

- Parents can examine and challenge all records bearing on identification of their child as disabled and the kind of educational setting for placement. The expense of this independent educational evaluation is borne by the school.

- Previous federal legislation aimed at elimination of architectural barriers to the physically handicapped is applied to funding school construction and modification (Osborne & Russo, 2007).

Most people will eventually face disabilities in their family or on the job. It can be predicted that a certain proportion of regular students will suffer impairments or disabilities, whether through accidents, illness, age, or changes in social conditions. Further, some non-disabled students will grow up to be parents of disabled sons or daughters or employers of impaired workers (Villa & Thousand, 2005). These reasons underscore why learning to accept differences has become an important aspect of the school curriculum. The University of Kansas offers examples of lesson modifications to meet special education student needs in all subjects, ways for teachers to answer questions that regular students have about why special needs classmates are given less rigorous tasks or allowed longer time limits, and links to creative methods to support the disabled in extracurricular activities—http://www.powerof2.org./ Students and teachers report greater appreciation for the disabled when some challenges they experience and obstacles that must be overcome are presented through films. In this context, a valuable resource is the Films Involving Disabilities Web site in the United Kingdom. These visuals include 2,500 feature films related to disabilities, such as blindness, AIDS., deafness, retardation, and cancer—http://www.disabilityfilms.co.uk.

Enabling inclusion practices to succeed requires being aware of and avoiding certain mistakes of the past (Bon, Faircloth, & Chapple, 2005). The following guidelines can support inclusion practices: (1) recognize the high cost associated with social segregation; (2) develop cooperation between regular teachers and special educators; and (3) arrange cooperative learning to support interaction and avoid social isolation.

(1) *Recognize the high cost associated with social segregation*. The landmark legislation during the mid 1970s provided economic support to make free and appropriate schooling available for students with disabilities. Part of the directive for schools was to place disabled students in regular classrooms. Before that time many teachers excluded the disabled from their classes by rationalizing that if a student cannot do the work required, the rest of the class cannot be abandoned just to assist one person. A special education environment seemed justified because it allowed for a lower

pupil-teacher ratio and access to more help. This was seen as a humane and reasonable decision; but, the consequence was elimination of an equally critical ratio of regular students to disabled students (Lasky & Karge, 2006). When disabled students are separated from their non-disabled peers for the sake of greater teacher attention, the regular population cannot learn how to accept differences. Studies consistently have shown that segregation leads to an unfair assessment by outsiders. This means that, if disabled students are isolated in school, they will remain isolated as adults. This social cost overrides the cognitive benefits of smaller, segregated classes (Burns, 2007; Mannix, 2008).

(2) *Develop cooperation between the regular teachers and special educators.* The initial legislation of Congress presented a strategy viewed as more suitable than social segregation. That method of *mainstreaming* placed special education students in regular classrooms most of the school day to support their social integration augmented by extra help given elsewhere by special education teachers. Merging the influences of regular teachers and special educators was seen as sensible. However, getting faculty members to collaborate was underestimated. Disputes arose over competition for student schedules. Regular teachers complained that classes were out of control because special education students would come and go through the day to attend sessions with special educators. These interruptions created a need to repeat lessons for absentees when they returned after instruction had already been given to the rest of the class (Burns, 2007).

Regular teachers were not alone in being reluctant to cooperate. Special educators also had misgivings about the benefits of mainstreaming. In their opinion, some regular teachers were not sufficiently committed to the education of students that deviated from the norm. Instead, it was supposed that such children could benefit more by spending their entire day with caring and trained special educators. This rationale led to new categories of disability and programs that grew to include almost 20% of students in some states. Robert Sternberg, Professor at Yale and President of the American Psychological Association, referred to the growth rate of special education as an epidemic (Spear-Swerling & Sternberg, 1998). A related concern that has continued is the disproportion of minority students placed in special education (Thurlow & Wiley, 2006). Blacks represent 12% of the school population but 41% of all students in special education and only 3% of the gifted and talented (Klinger, 2006).

Accommodations are distinctive expectations for instruction and assessment of students with disabilities. Accommodations requested of regular teachers by special educators range from extra time to complete tests, less homework, and longer deadlines for assignments. The methods, benefits and problems associated with accommodations remain controversial among regular classroom teachers (Osgood, 2007).

(3) *Rely on cooperative learning to facilitate interaction of regular students and students* with disabilities. The law focuses on inclusion to ensure special education students participate in nonacademic affairs at school such as lunch time interaction, assemblies, and extra curricular clubs or organizations (Osborne & Russo, 2007). Extending social involvement is intended to further support the development of age-appropriate social skills. It is not enough that regular students learn to accept peers with disabilities. Persons with disabilities should also gain social skills that enable them to become more acceptable to others.

Research has identified cooperative learning as an effective method to implement inclusion (Gillies, 2007). More than other approaches, this strategy ensures that students with disabilities have chances to interact with non-disabled students. Further, meta-analyses have found that cooperative learning favorably impacts classroom management when special education students are present (Roseth, Johnson, & Johnson, 2008). Teachers report that special education students in cooperative groups have greater self-esteem, feel less frustrated, and learn to listen. Peer encouragement enables them to overcome obstacles they might not surmount when working alone (Newman, Lohman, & Newman, 2007; Osgood, 2007).

SUMMARY

Peers and Social Development

Peers have a powerful influence on socialization. They provide the first substantial experience with equality and present standards more attainable than those imposed by grownups. Teenagers consider peer group norms to be a proper criteria to apply for self-evaluation. They learn about friendship mostly from their peers and encourage cooperation, empathy, compromise, and pursuit of independence. These lessons are often learned more effectively from peers than adults. Adolescents discover what friends will tolerate and conduct they will not accept. Most middle and high school students join a clique in which they feel accepted. However, some students suffer racial, religious, and ethnic discrimination. Prejudice is more common in early adolescence and those who are targeted suffer more than is generally supposed. The way others feel about us motivates the way we are treated by them and consequently how we view ourselves. Middle schools should include experiences that help students see themselves favorably without having to find fault with someone else.

Friendship and Dating

Being able to build friendships is essential for getting along with others. Dating provides a context for the practice of friendship skills and exploration of romantic connections. In many homes the concern of parents about early sexual involvement leads them to overlook fundamental lessons that they should teach about healthy relationships. One outcome is that teenage dating violence is a greater health and social problem than estimated by most parents. Girls and boys express frustration that, even at school, they lack opportunities for friendly conversations with the other gender. Some education about dating should take place in the classroom during discussions. All students should understand dating rights and responsibilities and recognize where to turn if they are abused or know someone who is mistreated.

Technology and Social Interaction

Cell phones, chat rooms, e-mail, blogs, PDAs, buddy lists, Web sites and after-school programs expand the scope of social interaction available for adolescents. The ways these forums should link with school purposes for socialization have yet to be determined. Adolescents on the Internet often assume multiple aliases allowing them to masquerade and experiment with new roles. A shy teenager could be assertive online before acting the same way in face-to-face conversations. Both genders report that social opportunities in cyber space are appealing. However, because anything online can be traced, students should reflect on the potential consequences of misrepresentation. Similarly, danger can occur when adolescents reveal personal information that could be used by others who wish to exploit them. Prevention of student exposure to sex offenders should be a priority for surveillance by teachers as well as parents. Web site resources identify convicted sex offenders, show their pictures, and indicate how close they live to schools. Protecting students is a collective obligation of the adults in every community.

Cooperative Learning Classrooms

Teachers who arrange cooperative learning understand the student need for teamwork skills to meet the entry-level expectations of employers. This form of instruction promotes social connections among students of culturally different backgrounds, encourages constructive norms of behavior, and motivates optimism that most problems can be solved by collective action. Teams in a classroom become more like teams in the workplace when teachers share responsibility for assessment of group learning. This shift from tradition requires that students be trusted to gain experience in making judgments and reporting their perceptions honestly. Classroom observations in schools across a wide range of income and ethnic backgrounds show that, when student-engaged instruction is emphasized, there is greater academic achievement than when the emphasis is on teacher-directed instruction and students are relegated to a passive role. Teachers support inclusion more effectively when they remain aware of the high cost associated with social segregation, build relationships with special educators, rely on suitable criteria for student placement, and arrange cooperative learning that supports interaction and prevents social isolation. Inclusion depends on developing mutual respect between disabled and regular students and the dynamic of their combined effort to plan and solve problems together.

CLASSROOM APPLICATIONS

1. The distinguishing feature of cooperative learning is reciprocal instruction. Every team member is expected to contribute to peer learning. This approach is different from tutoring where only one party knows a subject or has a skill and tries to pass it on.

2. To establish conditions of interdependence, teachers should structure tasks that students can only attain through teamwork. Enough tasks should be prepared so that each team member can add to the scope of group learning.

3. Cooperative learning typically produces improved academic skills, greater ability to work with others, and enhanced maturity. In combination, these strengths help equip students to demonstrate the teamwork skills that most employers will expect of them.

4. The need for students to gain team skills requires scheduling time for cooperative learning. Student achievement levels are higher when they engage in active learning.

5. Cooperative teams can be highly productive when members are united in purpose, understand individual tasks and group expectations, and feel encouraged to do their absolute best in performing a particular role. Teachers should emphasize team skills adolescents need to learn for the work place.

6. Teachers should share responsibility with students for appraisal of teamwork skills. Acknowledging that peers are the most relevant

source of observation on interaction that takes place during group work demonstrates trust and respect for student judgment.

7. Cooperative learning presents ideal conditions that allow students to compare their self-evaluations with observations of peers who interact with them regularly in problem solving groups. The combined assessment of peers is a good indicator of performance.

8. Adolescents should examine their own behavior. In addition, they need guided practice with self-evaluation to become self-critical, a vital ingredient for being able to make changes in behavior.

9. One sign of good teaching is that students participate more in higher order thinking skills such as synthesis and evaluation than lower order thinking such as memorization of knowledge. Try to build tests that reflect higher order thinking.

10. Special education placements should be based on appropriate criteria and present classroom conditions that support attainment of cognitive and social goals stated in the Individualized Education Plan (IEP).

11. Teachers should encourage student participation in extracurricular activities. This social context builds connections with others having similar interests and contributes to the social capital that motivates united efforts to improve communities.

12. Friendship and dating are priority concerns for adolescents so they are relevant issues for teachers. The entire faculty should plan for guided discussions that enable students to discuss dating and learn their rights and responsibilities as partners.

13. Disabled students should acquire social skills, follow the same rules for behavior, and be held accountable for misconduct when it is unrelated to their disability.

14. Teachers should find out how team skills of disabled students are seen by non-disabled peers because they are in the best position to render an accurate judgment.

15. Cooperative learning structures like Jigsaw and Think-Pair-Share can be used to introduce students to the challenges and benefits of cooperative learning.

FOR REFLECTION

1. What do you regard as (a) most favorable and (b) least favorable contributions adolescents make to the socialization of peers in the classroom?

2. How can middle school and high school teachers help students adopt healthy and safe guidelines to rely on for (a) face-to-face dating and (b) cyber-dating practices?

3. What attitudes and skills do you recommend that students acquire to form and maintain (a) online and (b) face-to-face friendships?

4. What do you consider the (a) short-term and (b) long-term benefits students can gain from interdependence and reciprocal learning in cooperative teams?

5. What expectations for special education inclusion do you anticipate will be the most difficult to implement as you attempt to integrate students and support their progress?

6. What alternatives would you consider when non-disabled students want to know why a particular special education student gets "privileges" that other students are denied?

7. Traditional networking involved joining community groups to solve problem. What steps do you suggest for digital networking to solve problems in a technological setting?

8. What are your concerns about sharing responsibility with students for the assessment of group learning that takes place during cooperative teamwork?

9. Schools do not give grades for social development: (a) What would be some of the advantages that might occur if social development was added to student evaluation?

10. How can teachers help to make the dating rights and responsibilities principles more of a norm among adolescents?

KEY TERMS

Accommodations
Blog
Cliques
Cooperative Learning
Cyberdating
Dating
Dating Abuse
Education for All Handicapped Children Act
Empathy
Friendships
Ideal Self

Inclusion
Individuals with Disabilities Education Improvement Act, IDEA
Interpersonal Intelligence
Introspection
Jigsaw
Mainstreaming
Online community

VISIT THESE WEB SITES

Link to these sites at http://www.infoagepub.com/strom-adolescents

Blogs Listing, Internet Public Library
http://www.ipl.org/div/blogs/

Annie E. Casey Foundation, Kids Count Data Center
http://www.kidscount.org/datacenter/databook.jsp

Coaching Boys Into Men—
What You Can Do, Family Violence Prevention Fund
http://endabuse.org/cbim/

Cooperative Learning Structures, University of Texas,
Division of Instructional Innovation and Assessment
http://www.utexas.edu/academic/diia/research/projects/hewlett/
cooperative.php

Enough is Enough http://www.enough.org

Facebook Online Directory for Social Network
http://www.facebook.com

Family Watchdog http://www.familywatchdog.us

Films Involving Disabilities http://www.disabilityfilms.co.uk/

Jigsaw Classroom, Cooperative Learning Structure
http://www.jigsaw.org

Myspace, A Place for Friends http://www.myspace.com

National Center for Missing and Exploited Children
http://www.ncmec.org/

Runaway Train by Soul Asylum
http://www.youtube.com/watch?v=psP1bKKEtHg

Sex, Etc., Rutgers University, by Teens for Teens
http://sexetc.rutgers.edu/index.php

Teen Dating Violence, State of Washington Attorney General
http://www.atg.wa.gov/page.aspx?id=1968

Teen Growth, Help with Relationships
http://www.teengrowth.com

ThinkQuest, Oracle Education Foundation,
Global Competitive Teams
http://www.thinkquest.org

United States Department of Justice,
A Parent's Guide to Internet Safety
http://www.fbi.gov/publications/pguide/pguidee.htm

Wiredsafety, Tips for Blogs and Cyberdating
http://www.wiredsafety.org

Youth Noise, Blogs for Adolescents
http://www.youthnoise.com/blog.php

EXERCISES AND ROLES

Exercise 7.01: Peer Support Poll

Role: Voter

The purpose of this poll is to find out how students at your school feel about working together in cooperative teams.

Directions: For each item, select the answer(s) that show how you feel. In some cases, you may select more than one answer. If an answer you want to give is not listed, write it on the line marked 'other.' Your responses are anonymous and may be combined with those of other students at your school in a report to students, faculty, and parents.

1. Students on my team usually

    (a) make me feel like I belong
    (b) treat me like an outsider
    (c) tutor me when I need help
    (d) reject me for achievement
    (e) other

2.   The team activities that I prefer are

    (a)   planning how to do a project
    (b)   sharing ideas in conversations
    (c)   chat rooms/ discussion boards
    (d)   reporting on Internet sources
    (e)   other

3.   In teamwork situations, I usually

    (a)   do not have to work as hard
    (b)   take on too much of the load
    (c)   do my faire share of the task
    (d)   regret being a group member
    (e)   other

4.   In team discussions, someone usually

    (a)   takes over and dominates
    (b)   drifts away from the topic
    (c)   invites quiet people to talk
    (d)   argues without compromise
    (e)   other

5.   In my experience, teammates with disabilities

    (a)   do their fair share of the work
    (b)   express their ideas and feelings
    (c)   lack the social skills for teaming
    (d)   distract a group from their task
    (e)   other

6.   The teachers prepare us for team work by

    (a)   discussing possible ways to work together
    (b)   talking about obstacles that prevent success
    (c)   suggesting reflection before making decisions
    (d)   giving definitions of the expected team skills
    (e)   other

7.   I find that team members typically
    (a)   challenge the logic of one another
    (b)   allow everyone the chance to talk

    (c)   bring reading material for sharing
    (d)   recognize individual contributions
    (e)   other

8.   I would like feedback from my teammates to

    (a)   identify strengths shown in group work
    (b)   detect behaviors that I need to work on
    (c)   recognize improvement in team skills
    (d)   be known by the teacher of our class
    (e)   other

9.   My teammates usually help me

    (a)   stay focused on the assignment
    (b)   admit uncertainty when in doubt
    (c)   build on ideas expressed by others
    (d)   see ideas or problems in new ways
    (e)   other

10.   I need to learn more about how to

    (a)   accept feedback from teammates in a friendly way
    (b)   provide constructive feedback to my teammates
    (c)   compare how teammates see me with how I see myself
    (d)   provide honest feedback to classmates that I like
    (e)   other

11.   The insights that teammates share are

    (a)   very helpful
    (b)   somewhat helpful
    (c)   not very helpful
    (d)   no help at all

12.   Given the choice to have teammates with disabilities, I would

    (a)   always want to have them on my team
    (b)   sometimes want them to be on my team
    (c)   seldom want them to be on my team
    (d)   never want them to be on my team

13.   I prefer that evaluation of teamwork be based on

(a)   teacher observation of team behavior
(b)   teacher judgment of project submitted
(c)   peer and self-evaluation
(d)   student self-evaluation only
(e)   other

14.   My classes involve teamwork

(a)   too often
(b)   about right
(c)   not enough
(d)   never

15.   We evaluate teammate performance and self-performance

(a)   always
(b)   often
(c)   seldom
(d)   never

Select your grade level, gender, ethnicity, and age.

My grade level is 5 6 7 8 9 10 11 12
My gender is female male
My ethnicity is Asian Black Hispanic Native American White Other
My age is 10 11 12 13 14 15 16 17 18 19

Exercise 7.02: The Group Award

Role: Challenger

Each spring Hollywood celebrities compete to receive individual academy awards. Most people believe that it is a good idea to honor persons who demonstrate exceptional talent. Society has also begun to recognize that some achievements cannot occur unless people work together in teams. Perhaps team awards should become more common. Your assignment is to nominate a group from any sector of society that should be recognized for their achievement. The collective accomplishment should represent an example of the importance of cooperation. Present a justification for your nomination and invent a name for this award.

Exercise 7.03: Collaboration and Unlearning

Role: Evaluator

When new ways of doing things become necessary, the greatest challenge can be leaving old habits behind. Identify some behaviors students have usually acquired that they must unlearn to perform as effective members in cooperative learning groups.

Author afterthought: This exercise can help recognize challenges associated with what we call 'unlearning.' In our view, this phenomenon will pose unprecedented concerns for educators at all levels. *Unlearning* is a willful activity requiring people to change their minds, perhaps about ways of doing things that are strongly habituated. In some cases, unlearning can be more difficult than new learning and it is likely that some people will fail as they try to unlearn customary ways of responding. The matter is more complex than may be supposed. For example, all of us have friends whose concern that we may worry unduly cause them to recommend that the best solution is to just "forget it." However, we realize how difficult it is to follow such advice since forgetting is not a deliberate and conscious activity.

Exercise 7.04: Thinking About Dating

Role: Generational Reporter

Dating is an opportunity to practice friendship building skills and relating to a partner. Interview adolescent girls or boys using some of these questions as your partial agenda.

1. What are some qualities that you look for in a person to date?
2. What are some of your favorite things to do while on a date?
3. What expectations should dating partners have of each other?
4. What are some problems that you have experienced on dates?
5. How does peer pressure influence the things you do on a date?
6. In what ways has dating changed since your parents were teens?
7. What concerns your parents the most when you go on a date?
8. What are some important things that dating has taught you?
9. How do you feel about people your age only dating one person?
10. How would you handle unfair demands of a dating partner?

Exercise 7.05: Friendship

Role: Generational Reporter

Adults should be better informed about the friendships of teenagers. Interview adolescents to discover their perceptions about these aspects of friendship.

1. How do you choose friends differently now than in the past?
2. How does your school arrange chances to meet new people?
3. How could schools give sufficient time for student socializing?
4. What clique groups at school tend to exclude other students?
5. How do you resolve differences of opinion with your friends?
6. How do your parents feel about the friends you have chosen?
7. How does family opinion influence your choice of friends?
8. Where do you go most often to spend time with your friends?

Exercise 7.06: Reflection on Choice of Friends

Role: Improviser

Parents are fearful when they suspect that friends of their daughter or son could be an unhealthy influence. Such parents often turn to teachers or school counselors for guidance. Describe the advice you would offer and provide your reasoning.

Exercise 7.07: Conversations About Success

Role: Generational Reporter

Everyone wants to succeed. However, discussions seldom consider how to define success at different ages. Listening to adolescents makes it easier to understand what they expect of themselves and what they expect of those who teach them. Interview adolescents and share the outcomes in a discussion with teammates.

1. What qualities do you think are necessary to be successful at your age?
2. What qualities do successful people of all ages seem to have in common?

3. What are some activities in which you are usually able to obtain success?

4. Who are some successful people that you would like your life to resemble?

5. How do personal views of success compare with what teachers expect of you.

6. What do you consider to be your most important accomplishment so far?

7. How are the factors that you use to define success change as you get older?

Exercise 7.08: Teamwork and Self-Esteem

Role: Discussant

An important aspect of preparing students for the workplace is working in teams.

1. Identify ways teams contribute to self-esteem that are less likely if working alone.

2. Identify self-esteem issues more prominent in teamwork than independent activity.

Exercise 7.09: Inclusion of Students With Disabilities

Role: Discussant

1. What could regular students be taught about their role to ensure inclusion of disabled peers?

2. How should the progress of special education students in gaining social skills be assessed?

3. What can teachers do to determine how well regular students support disabled students?

4. How could the parents of regular students be more supportive of inclusion at school?

5. What are your concerns or questions regarding the nature of special education programs?

Exercise 7.10 Privacy for Adolescents

Role: Challenger

1. Identify some problematic contexts for teen privacy from the view of adults.
2. Identify problematic issues with privacy as seen from the view of adolescents.
3. Recommend privacy guidelines for consideration by adults and adolescents.

CHAPTER 8

RISKS FOR
ADOLESCENTS AND SCHOOLS

Risk is the possibility that something may go wrong, the chance that an injury, damage or loss could occur. Taking risks can also bring benefits that would not occur otherwise. Adolescents are more willing than adults to take risks. Poor judgment by teenagers is a major concern of parents and teachers. Parents often tell daughters and sons to "just be careful." This vague advice is intended to be a gentle reminder that taking unreasonable risks could produce disappointment. Everyone has to make decisions about risks that can jeopardize or contribute to their health, safety, and success. Learning to recognize risks worth taking and detecting ones to avoid is a lifelong challenge (Johnson & Malow-Iroff, 2008).

The goals of this chapter are to identify risks that adolescents face and ways to help make decisions that protect their health, adjustment, academic progress, and opportunity to pursue personal goals. A need to gauge and monitor risks is shown to apply to institutions as well as to individuals. Educators commonly identify out-of-school situations over which they lack control such as poverty and crime as the critical factors that place students at-risk for failure in the classroom (Zaff & Smerdon, 2008). In addition, some school practices and policies should be seen as presenting risks (Harpine, 2008). *Underperforming schools,* defined by the No Child Left Behind Act of 2002, are institutions that fail to make adequate annual progress towards measurable objectives. Teachers should be

Adolescents in the Internet Age, pp. 335–377
Copyright © 2009 by Information Age Publishing

familiar with elements of the No Child Left Behind Act explained on the Web site at http://www.ed.gov/teachers/nclbguide/index2.html.

Some dubious risks that schools take include (a) tests focused on low levels of thinking; (b) retention policies that contradict research outcomes; (c) teachers offering subjects in which they lack expertise; (d) instruction that excludes the Internet as a tool for learning; (e) standardized test scores are ignored when assigning student grades; and (f) low expectations for achievement. In contrast, success for students and schools depend on taking risks that can yield benefit. This chapter identifies sensible risks that should be taken by adolescents and their schools.

FACTORS IN RISK TAKING

Teachers are concerned about students that are at risk for dropping out of school, individuals who feel they are socially disconnected from their classmates, truants who choose to be somewhere else than the classroom, youth without sufficient emotional support from relatives, and persons misled by gangs that encourage unlawful behavior. When teachers are informed about the risks adolescents encounter in the community and at school, plans can be made to address the factors they can influence.

Families and Students At Risk

The literature about obstacles to academic achievement often identifies disproportionate risks experienced by minorities (Knitzer, 2008). American Indian (40%), Black (33%) and Hispanic (27%) students more often reside in low-income households than is the case for Asians (12%) and Whites (10%) (Fass & Cauthen, 2006). Growing up in a single parent family is normative among Black (65%) students and more common among Hispanics (34%) than it is for Whites (24%). See the Federal Interagency Forum on Child and Family Statistics (2008) Web site at http://www.childstats.gov. Minority students experience more health and safety risks because they lack medical care, have greater nutritional deficits, are more exposed to violence, early pregnancies, and hazards in the environment (Evans & Kim, 2007). The National Center for Children in Poverty at Columbia University was established to promote strategies to improve lives of low-income students and their families. See http://www.nccp.org/about.html.

Dropouts are former students who quit school without completing the requirements for a diploma. There is abundant evidence that reports of success in educating low-income students are often inflated. This assertion is corroborated by a study of dropout rates in the nation's 50 largest cities, conducted for the America's Promise Alliance and the Bill and Melinda Gates Foundation by Christopher Swanson (2008a, 2008b). Results indicated that about half (52%) of all students in the biggest cities complete high school, far below the estimated national graduation rate of 70%. The lowest level of success was reported by Detroit with a graduation rate of 25%, followed by Baltimore, Cleveland, and Indianapolis where less than 35% of students earn a diploma. Great disparity was also found when graduation rates for the cities were compared with rates for schools in the suburbs. Baltimore graduates 35% of its students while suburban Baltimore districts graduate over 80%. The graduation rate in Cleveland is 34% compared to 78% in the Cleveland suburbs.

The proportion of 16- to 24-year-olds that no longer go to school and lack a high school diploma is highest among minorities. Details related to conditions of education (such as family characteristics, student disabilities, languages, age, and race) are provided by the United States Department of Education, National Center for Education Statistics (2008), available at http://www.nces.ed.gov/programs/coe. According to the government, the school dropout rate among Hispanics is (30%), American Indian/Alaska Natives (15%), Blacks (14%), Whites (8%), and Asian/Pacific Islanders (4%) (Federal Interagency Forum on Child and Family Statistics, 2007). The figures become more troubling with the recognition that the minority group with the highest school failure rate, Hispanics, is also the most rapidly increasing subpopulation. The proportion of Hispanics is forecast to double by 2050 and become 24% of the national population (United States Bureau of the Census, 2004). The Pew Hispanic Center in Washington DC was established to provide public understanding about the Hispanic population and to chronicle Latino impact on the nation—see http://www.pewhispanic.org/index.jsp.

Demographics and Destiny

Demography is the study of human populations regarding characteristics like birth, death, and disease rates along with related indicators of well-being (Yaukey, Anderton, & Lundquist, 2007). Some educators express feelings of helplessness when they believe demographic conditions predict student destiny and conclude that not much can be done to reduce risk factors (Englund, Egeland, & Collins, 2008). Conventional thinking identifies race, ethnicity, income, and family structure as the explanation for why adolescents more often engage in health-related risks like smoking, drinking, early sexual intercourse and violent behavior (Thomas-Presswood & Presswood, 2008).

A less ominous forecast comes from the National Longitudinal Study of Adolescent Health that focused on 12,000 Black, White, and Hispanic students from Grades 7–12 (Blum, 2005; Blum & Mmari, 2006). Co-director of the project, Robert Blum, is a professor of reproductive health at Johns Hopkins University. He and his team found that demographic conditions accounted for only a small proportion (less than 10%) of individual differences in adolescent health risk behaviors. On the other hand, some factors that can be more easily modified such as school performance, how teens spend free time, behavior of friends, truancy, becoming involved in a romantic relationship, and interaction with relatives were identified as far more powerful predictors of health risk behaviors. These risks and protective features explained the behavior of teenagers to a greater extent than various demographic variables. Individual, peer, and family influences were responsible for 24% to 49% of the individual differences in smoking, depending on race and gender. Involvement with sex and drinking alcohol followed similar patterns. Blum (2005) warns that when we make predictions about adolescents based on the color of their skin, parent income or number of parents they live with, we will be right only a small percentage of the time.

Demographic data provide the context in which adolescents live and, while they impact conduct, cannot be accurately identified as the main cause of high-risk behavior. To increase educator optimism and hope about risk reduction, it is necessary to abandon excessive referral to race and income because these are weak predictors of adolescent behavior. A more promising approach is to acknowledge powerful influences over which schools have some control and that are more amenable to change (Bronfenbrenner & Morris, 2006). The Annie E. Casey Foundation provides indicators of adolescent well-being by state, available at http://www.aecf.rg/kidscount.

Families and Truancy

Truancy is being absent from school without permission or having a good reason. The National Center for School Engagement indicates that truancy is a powerful early warning sign that drop out is imminent (Martinez & Porter, 2008). When students have difficulty and continually skip classes, their learning problems are bound to accelerate (Wise, 2008). In Philadelphia 500 parents have been trained and serve as truant officers for the school system. They patrol shopping malls, neighborhood hangouts, and visit parents of truants and absentee students to make them aware of likely consequences of skipping school and sources of academic help for students. Philadelphia Mayor John Street (2007) states,

Truancy and curfew violations are among the strongest indicators for identifying children at risk for delinquency or violence. Parent Truant Officers are an important component of our increased efforts to ensure our children have a successful life. Parents and guardians are the first line of defense and the home is where the important message of attending school must originate, but everyone in the community must play a role in ensuring children are in school.

The Philadelphia anti-truancy program is described at http://ework.phila.gov/philagov/news/prelease.asp?id=296.

The Amherst Wilder Research Center in St. Paul, Minnesota reviewed school-based intervention programs, community-based initiatives, law enforcement and court-based approaches to identify effective procedures to reduce truancy (Gerrard, Burhans, & Fair, 2003). Projects conducted since 2000 using a control group and follow-up of attendance records were examined while projects that provided only descriptions about services without evidence of program effect were excluded. The most successful school-based interventions emphasized three factors.

1. Relationship building such as cooperative learning groups helps students feel a sense of belonging. Individualized teacher attention was also identified as a common element. The importance of peer support is corroborated by studies showing that social reasons are the most often given by truants for their decision to stay away from school (Martinez & Porter, 2008).

2. Keeping parents involved through family counseling ensures greater awareness of problems and support.

3. School policies about attendance and reasons for them should be conveyed to students and parents (Gandy & Schultz, 2007).

RISK ASSESSMENT PRACTICES

Adolescence is the stage in life when there is a greater willingness to take risks. Some dangerous risks include pregnancy, sexually transmitted diseases, drugs, online predators, lack of sleep, drinking alcohol, truancy, becoming a dropout, joining a gang, getting involved with criminal activity, bringing a weapon to school, cheating, lying to parents and teachers, procrastination on assignments, inadequate study for examinations, smoking cigarettes or chewing tobacco, lack of exercise, poor nutrition, failing to get help when needed, and running away from home (Johnson & Malow-Iroff, 2008). Additional risks include reckless driving, being the passenger of a driver that has been drinking, ghost riding when a driver leaves the car to do stunts while a vehicle is moving, car surfing where there is a driver and a stunt passenger lays, kneels or stands atop the car. A girl in a high school class taught by one of the authors was seriously injured in this manner (Harpine, 2008). The MTV program called *Scarred* features adolescents and young adults that participate in stunt behavior and the physical consequences that follow. Video clips of the crashes, wipeouts and accidents drawn from the Internet can be viewed at http:// mtv.com/ (enter Scarred). The physical costs associated with adolescent risks are described by the Centers for Disease Control and Prevention Youth Risk Behavior Surveillance System Web site at http://www.cdc.gov/ HealthyYouth/yrbs/index.htm.

Adolescents can make better decisions when they recognize the benefits of risk analysis involving adults whose perspective and feedback they trust. Educators can also reduce the risk of harm by becoming aware of findings about student retention. The way teachers make decisions about responding to failure improves by examining how medical professionals communicate risk data to patients.

Origins of Risk Analysis

Some observers believe that teachers should discourage all forms of risk taking including failure in the classroom. The opposite conclusion is drawn from research about how risks influence behavior. First, being able to accurately gauge risk is a skill that everyone needs to learn because it prevents foolish choices. Consider what can happen when people are unable to accurately assess whether particular risks are suitable or believe their courage is confirmed by becoming involved with situations shunned by others as being too risky.

During the Korean Conflict of the 1950s, military leaders began a new practice to protect soldiers at war. *Risk analysis* is the practice of monitoring ability of individuals to accurately gauge risks they face. Psychological teams were assigned to conduct risk analysis with air force squadrons (Torrance & Ziller, 1957). The purpose was to identify fighter pilots who should temporarily be withdrawn from the battle zone. Prior to this strategy, the only consideration for relief from a war environment had been completion of a specific number of combat missions. This policy was amended to include risk analysis for pilots who flew too low or too close to the enemy response system so that they would jeopardize lives of crew members, aircraft, and the mission. Because of severe stress associated with their task, some pilots took on the characteristics of high-risk takers. They were no more courageous than fellow airmen but appeared to lose the common fear necessary for carrying out successful bombing runs.

Therefore, whether or not they had flown the minimum number of flights to justify a furlough, pilots identified by risk analysis as needing relief were sent to Hickham Field in Honolulu for mandatory recuperation. The reason for removal from the battle scene was to help pilots recover their usual sense of caution, the normal degree of fear essential to effectively perform their dangerous task (Torrance, 2000b).

This risk analysis strategy implemented by psychological teams has been credited with saving many lives. It also revealed that individual capacity to accurately gauge risk is a fundamental survival skill that can sometimes cease to function, even among highly intelligent people (Vose, 2008). This aspect of adolescent behavior should be continually monitored by adults who are concerned about their well being. Certainly, classrooms rarely present dangers comparable to a battlefield. However, school can present significant risks. Students who decide to dropout are more likely to become casualties than survivors (Cosby & Poussaint, 2007).

Just as the American fighter pilots required external feedback to identify when their ability for risk assessment was impaired, teachers and parents should help adolescents with risk analysis. In particular, it is necessary to challenge the *personal fable* causing teenagers to believe that they are exempt from consequences of taking risks others choose to avoid. A broad spectrum of behavior implicated by the personal fable is evident from these comments of ninth graders, "I will not get a sexually transmitted disease because my boyfriend told me he has never done it with anyone else." "The television warnings are wrong; tobacco does not have to be a tumor causing, tooth staining, smelly puking habit because I am an occasional smoker, not a chain smoker."

Another example of unreasonable risk taking by adolescents involves driving. Teenagers typically surpass adults in physical ability to respond quickly. However, they are responsible for a disproportionate number of car accidents. The leading cause of death among 16- to 20-year-olds is car accidents. Poor judgment is the main reason for most fatalities (Medina, 2008). A related consequence is that insurance rates are higher for teenage drivers than adult drivers. And, rates for boys, who take greater risks behind the wheel than girls, remain more expensive until age 24 when risk taking moderates and similar rates obtain for both genders (Kelly, 2005).

Many teenagers are reluctant to ask adults for their advice before taking risks that could carry a high price. Discussions on gauging risk can be more helpful than trying to instill fear or assuring adolescents that they are trusted unconditionally. There is greater benefit when, in a low risk setting with adults who care about them, teenagers can calmly reflect on possible outcomes of actions that have not been taken yet than to consider the damage from poor decisions after the fact (Reyna & Farley, 2006). A teacher, relative or friend who has a reputation for willingness to listen is often allowed by adolescents to review problematic options and anticipated costs linked with each choice (Apter, 2006). These dialogues provide adults an opportunity to monitor the risk assessment ability of the adolescent and urge that choices always consider the effects on long-term plans. When students commit to long-term goals, it is easier to avoid foolish risks (Benson, Scales, Hamilton, & Sesma, 2006). In the event teens find themselves in a crisis, sources of help are available like The National Runaway Switchboard with their Web site at http://www.1800runaway.org.

When students recognize the rewards that can come from taking growth-oriented risks, they become more willing to take such risks. For example, setting goals is a risk that can provide a sense of purpose, guide behavior, and minimize boredom. Asking questions in class presents a risk of admitting ignorance but holds the promise of becoming more informed. Providing authentic feedback to teammates in cooperative learning groups is a risk that can enable awareness and preserve honesty. Giving advice is a risk revealing the scope and limits of one's perceptions. Becoming a volunteer is a risk that requires helping others whose needs could be ignored. Self-assertion is a risk that involves acquainting others with how we stand on matters of importance. Sharing differences of opinion poses the risk of conflict but can promote mutual learning. Taking elective courses about unfamiliar topics risks exposing novice frames of reference but offers new perspectives. Trusting friends and relatives is a risk that can be a basis for reciprocal support. And, risking spontaneity requires departure from a predictable routine but may offer worthwhile experiences that could not be planned (Crouhy, Galia, & Mark, 2005).

Retention and Promotion

Teachers participate in risk analysis whether they recognize it or not. *Retention*, holding a student back instead of allowing promotion, is a decision teachers make each semester. During the 1990s, rates of non-promotion rose dramatically as many school districts and state departments of education adopted strict standards linking student performance with standardized test results (Swanson & Chaplin, 2005). Most states use *high stakes testing* as a basis for decisions about retention (Nichols & Berliner, 2007). The Center for Education Policy predicts that, by 2012, 70% of students will attend schools that require high school exit examinations (Dillon, 2006). However, instead of just raising the bar for promotion, New York City, in 1995, became the first large system to revise its policies on retention. Officials cited evidence that the dropout rate for students held back was higher than for students promoted who recorded comparable reading scores, even though those retained got more special services (National Governors Association, 2005).

Chicago public schools reported similar findings with the school board concluding that (1) retention does not have a favorable effect on progress; (2) matched counterparts of retained students and promoted students show higher actual gains by those who are promoted; (3) students retained are significantly more likely to quit; (4) students held back have more misconduct problems than peers with similar test scores but not held back; and (5) the retained tend overwhelmingly to be minority, male, and low-income (Allensworth & Easton, 2007). Although retention is a poor strategy, promotion alone is an inadequate response because students are not held accountable for learning and left unprepared for expectations in the workforce. These findings led to a revocation of the basic skills testing practices in Chicago as a basis for retaining students. Instead, a reform law was enacted that established reduction of retention rates as a priority for the system. *Tutoring*, working with individuals to detect deficiencies and help them to perform at capacity, was implemented as the strategy for increasing student success.

A longitudinal study of grade retention provided evidence that refutes retention (Jimerson & Ferguson, 2007). State studies have also found that (1) retained students are more likely to drop out and have trouble with the law than peers recording similar test scores but not held back; (2) students who repeat courses or grade levels learn less the second time instead of becoming more competent; (3) repeaters suffer in terms of self-esteem and confidence; and (4) schools seldom make an effort to try new or more suitable ways to help students the second time through a course or grade (Edwards, Mumford, Shillingford, & Serra-Roldan, 2007).

It seems that most elementary and middle school teachers do not realize the emotional damage that follows retention. A University of Michigan team studied retention by following 16,000 students from kindergarten through eighth grade. Contrary to popular assumption that holding students back would have the effect of waking them up to adopt favorable motivation to study, investigators were unable to find any positive outcomes for retention. It was discovered that eighth graders retained were four times more likely to have lower grades and test scores as well as greater learning problems than their classmates. Based on the findings it was recommended that intense tutoring to keep failing children in step with classmates is less expensive and more effective (Lillard & DeCicca, 2001). This means that a lot of money has been spent on a practice that does not offer benefit and, in fact, produces harm (Anagnostopoulos, 2005; Frey, 2005). In 2002 President George Bush signed the No Child Left Behind Act aimed at increasing accountability of schools to ensure that all students are provided the support they need. To check on how well your state is responding to the challenge, consult Education Commission of the States and enter the key words promotion policies—http://www.ecs.org.

In view of the strong case against retention, it might be supposed that educators would seldom choose such a risky practice. However, surveys indicate that from half to two-thirds of elementary teachers regard retention as a sound educational practice (Jimerson, Pletcher, Graydon, Schnurr, Nickerson, & Kundert, 2006). The rationale of some teachers include comments like these: "My experience tells me that keeping a student back is necessary to preserve academic standards." "Holding students back puts everyone on notice that they must be responsible for work or suffer the consequences." "Retention is the best way to motivate slackers in the classroom to take their studies seriously." "One of the main outcomes of retention is a student who demonstrates better behavior and moves toward higher achievement."

Teachers in primary and middle grades lack feedback on the long-term effects of their retention decisions. Otherwise, they would understand the reasons why researchers agree that educators should respond to failure with intensive tutoring for as long as necessary (Wright & Cleary, 2006). The audience for this message is not only elementary teachers because, for some time, the highest rates of retention have been in Grade 9 (Swanson & Chaplin, 2005). Grade retention is one of the most powerful predictors of high school dropout (National Association of School Psychologists, 2003). The National Dropout Prevention Centers at Clemson University is a clearinghouse and describes model programs—http://www.dropoutprevention.org/.

The Medical Risk Model

Contrast the view of elementary teachers about risking retention with the process for making decisions in the medical profession. Jack is a friend of ours. He is energetic, on the go, and busy nearly all the time. However, after one of his many trips to provide workshops for teachers, he arrived at home exhausted. A few days went by and Jack continued to feel tired. So, he scheduled a checkup with his physician. After examining him, the doctor asked, "How long ago did you have the heart attack?" Jack was surprised and replied, "What heart attack?" He had never felt pain, passed out, or been unable to go to work. His impression was that he was just fatigued.

The doctor said, "We need to conduct further tests. I will arrange a catheter screen to learn more about your condition." The next day the test was completed. As the physician introduced the results to Jack he observed, "Now, that test wasn't so bad, was it?" Jack replied, "No, it was ok." Then the doctor reported, "However, there is some bad news. One of your arteries is completely blocked, and there is 85% blockage in the other."

Jack said, "What can be done?" The doctor explained,

We could try angioplasty where a balloon is inserted in an attempt to clear the walls. The risk in that case is usually 1 to 2%. In other words, 1 to 2% of patients die during the procedure. On the other hand, there is open-heart surgery. In that case the risk of not making it through the operation is 5%. It is up to you to decide which option is best.

Jack hesitated, "What do you recommend?" The doctor said, "I favor open-heart procedure."

"Wait a minute," Jack responded. "You told me the risk for open-heart surgery is 5%, and it is only 1 to 2% with angioplasty. Why would you suggest surgery if the risks are greater?" The doctor smiled,

Yes, the risk factors that I stated are correct. However, in your case, with complete blockage in one artery and nearly complete obstruction in the other, if something went wrong during angioplasty, I could not intervene and would have to watch you die. But, even though there is generally a higher risk in heart surgery, I will be better equipped to provide additional help if needed.

"So, what's your choice the doctor inquired?" Jack concluded, "I prefer the open-heart procedure." "Good choice," said the doctor.

Now that you made that decision, I can share some good news. You have a *Type A personality*, defined as an anxious, hardworking person with a strong drive to succeed That will be in your favor for recovery and reduce the odds. I believe that you will do just fine.

Consider what occurred in this conversation. The physician shared the data, made the risks clear, and then allowed Jack to make the decision. However, many teachers do not behave in this manner. Instead, they tell parents their adolescent is behind and should be held back a year without acknowledging the risks. What if the parents were to ask,

Can we send him to summer school, arrange tutoring, pursue other alternatives? We know little about the advantages and disadvantages of holding students back a year. Tell us what research indicates about the effects of retention so we can make a more informed decision.

In that case, a teacher familiar with the literature would reply,

Evidence suggests that retention makes a student four times more likely to dropout later, he is much more likely to experience poor self-esteem, reduced motivation to learn is a common result, and he is likely to have more difficulty getting along with classmate. On the other hand, my own experience suggests these risks are worth taking. I think that your son will benefit from repeating the class.

Recall that the physician informed Jack about the risk factors and then gave him the choice of which heart procedure to use. The doctor relied on data first, and then gave observations based on his personal experience. In contrast, when teachers do not know the research on retention or choose to ignore it, they fail to present parents with the facts they need to make an informed decision. Instead, many teachers are inclined to share their intuitive hunch that a retained student is likely to become more motivated, better behaved, and more productive. Sometimes the defense is that a student needs more maturity that will be provided by spending an additional year in the same grade (Dalton, 2008).

Educators should realize that professionals rely on research as a basis for making decisions rather than just personal observation that excludes awareness of the long-term consequences. The achievement scores of students in a sixth-grade class typically range from Grade 4 to Grade 10. That is, some students perform as low as fourth grade on tests while others have scores equivalent to high school sophomores. Teacher unwillingness to accept a broad range of mental differences among students is a prejudice that can have more devastating effects than racial, cultural, religious or gender intolerance. Schools should rely on tutoring to meet the wide range of mental abilities that are bound to exist in any classroom (Jimerson & Ferguson, 2007; Rimm, 2005).

RISK REDUCTION STRATEGIES

Schools can limit undesirable risks for students and help them build satisfying interactions outside school. Students need time management skills in order to avoid risks related to hurrying and over-scheduling. Teachers model these skills when they arrange schedules for instruction and homework that preserve mental health. Similarly, there is a need to protect teachers' time so they are seen by students as mentors instead of dysfunctional models helpless to cope with their overload. Teaching students to protect themselves from risky communication online is a practical and satisfying aspect of curriculum that relates to daily life.

Hurry and Over-Scheduling

Many people risk the predictable consequences of rushing others and themselves. This inclination can be observed in every sector of life, from getting ready for work in the morning to expecting a driver in front of us to move as soon as the traffic lights turn green. When teachers are pressured to have students reach their learning goals in less time than is needed, educators feel overwhelmed, and some respond by imposing unreasonable expectations on classes (Elkind, 2006). Efforts to rush instruction or abbreviate amount of time students have to practice new skills guarantees that some will fall behind and others will demonstrate mediocre performance (Honore, 2005).

Similarly, when students lack sufficient time to consider relevant information or think about ways to solve problems, they could reject reflective thinking in favor of hasty methods of processing information. Instead of deferring judgment until a possible range of alternatives in a situation is examined, persons accustomed to being hurried often draw premature conclusions based on partial information. This can be a high price to pay for trying to compress time for learning. Time and learning are linked. People learn what they spend their time doing and from whomever participates with them. These two factors affect how conditions of instruction should be arranged for students (Carroll, 1963).

Students who suffer most from being hurried are those who must also cope with learning, emotional, or behavior problems. To discover and establish ways of helping these students, the University of Minnesota developed a Check and Connect program. This project matches community volunteers with at-risk early adolescent students to monitor for early warning signs of failure and alienation from school. Clues that signal student withdrawal are tardiness, absenteeism, disciplinary conduct referrals, detentions, and suspensions. The volunteers function as mentors and advocates who help students stay connected with school by making sure that tutoring is given, making weekly contacts with the family, talking about the importance of staying in school until graduation, checking on progress in every course a student takes, identifying overdue assignments, examining grades, acting as a liaison with faculty, and giving feedback to the student and parents (Reschly & Christenson, 2006).

Check and Connect volunteers continue monitoring tasks over several years. A follow-up evaluation was conducted after 5 years to assess overall effects of this strategy to reduce unnecessary failure. Results revealed that 91% of participants who started in seventh grade were still in school by grade 10 as compared to 68% of a control group with similar characteristics but not assigned a monitor. Having a responsible adult who cares and provides continued support appears to be a necessary condition that every student should be able to count on (Lyst, Gabriel, O'Shaughnessy, Meyers, & Meyers, 2005). The Check and Connect model for promoting student engagement with school can be found at http://ici.umn.edu/checkandconnect/default.html.

Some parents over-schedule their children to prevent problems that might occur if adults are not home to provide supervision. Fight Crime: Invest in Kids—http://www.fightcrime.org—reports the time between 3–6 P.M. on school days are peak hours when teenagers commit crimes, innocent students become victims, 16- and 17-year-olds are involved in car accidents, teen sex happens, kids smoke, and drink or use drugs. After-school programs can be an effective way to reduce these risks, especially when they provide students with a menu of activities. However, if the only programs available include competitive expectations similar to the classroom, the consequence is that students have to demonstrate peak performance all day long. The usual results of over-scheduling are high stress, inadequate relaxation, and no arrangement for solitude and reflection (Mahoney, Larson, & Eccles, 2005).

Many parents do not recognize that they hurry their children. They may expect youngsters, from an early age, to remain home alone after school hours, cook their own dinner, and look after younger siblings. In most cases young caretakers still need to be nurtured themselves (Savage, 2007). In many families the time set aside for sharing and discussion is often fast-paced or multitasked and thus continually interrupted. This pattern prevents in depth conversations and signals a low priority for such sharing. The outcome is that sustained conversations are not held that would permit parents to model qualities they say are important across the lifespan such as patience, empathy, reflection, critical thinking, setting goals, and giving feedback to relatives about their behavior (Epstein, 2007).

A hectic pace in school presents undesirable risks (Greenberg, 2006). There are concerns about lost learning if lessons are rushed, impulsive thinking replaces reflective thinking when there is not enough time, and stress prevails if everyone feels obligated to do everything faster than before. Consider some ways that the expectations and pace of activities for students could moderate to promote mental health.

1.   The tendency to rush students is more common in 50-minute classes than in larger scheduled blocks like 90 minutes. Larger blocks allow for greater time on task, support sustained inquiry, allow for concentration, incubation, and persistence that is needed to pursue difficult tasks. Being interrupted by a bell soon after getting into a problem can be frustrating and restrict attention span.

2. Letting students practice essential skills in class can reduce homework. This means that student time after school is available for visiting friends or family, exercising, working, hobbies or self-directed learning. The sense of control and relief that comes from choosing activities helps maintain a sense of balance and autonomy.

3. Forcing students to move quickly from one class to another is intended to reduce hallway conflicts. Slowing down the movement by permitting 10 minutes between classes can permit students to talk to friends and reduce pent up energy accumulated in the previous class, relax and be ready to focus in the next course. Calm and relaxed students are likely to learn more than those who feel helpless because of being rushed.

4. Students should have opportunities to reflect about what they learn. Teachers can encourage this habit by requiring students to maintain a journal or submit daily summaries of reflections. During the final 10 minutes of a class students can write a paragraph describing what they have learned, ways they found it relevant, and questions about the topic. These reflections are submitted before leaving class.

5. Many schools in a hurry to raise test scores jeopardize student health by focusing only on sedentary activity. All students need physical exercise every day. Establishing this regimen while going to school can become a powerful habit that ensures such participation is a lifestyle maintained after graduation.

6. Teachers are expected to make decisions about what to include from a rapidly growing base of information, inventions, and history. This task causes some teachers to present instruction too fast, provide less depth, and continue without pause when student misunderstanding is evident. When faculty who teach the same subject together identify the skills and knowledge that deserve prominence, they can devote greater attention to fewer priorities, emphasize depth for comprehension, and allow time for student questions and discussion.

7. Tell students that when you ask questions, everyone is expected to take the time needed to reflect rather than quickly raise their hand. Using a timer that rings at the end of a designated period such as three minutes is helpful. This procedure acknowledges the importance a teacher assigns to contemplation and motivates students to reject risky impulsive response patterns in favor of participating in higher order thinking. In this process the thoughtful students get a chance to have their ideas heard instead of

perpetuating the myth that the first persons to raise their hands are high achievers.

Protecting Teacher Time

Consider the reciprocal when students cause teachers to feel rushed. This pressure often takes the form of expecting quick feedback about the quality of performance for every written task. Boards of education and principals generally support this practice because they do not consider the toll it can take on teachers who must take papers home at night for scoring so they can be returned the next day. Then too, students who need perpetual reassurance to persist in their studies dread uncertainty and can become overly dependent on teachers to confirm progress that can often be self-determined by comparison with an answer sheet (Whittle, 2005).

What seems to have happened in the past decade is that common reliance on immediate feedback that computers provide has become an expectation for teachers too. Yet, teachers should gather considerable data about student thinking before reaching any conclusions about their performance. Premature evaluation is prejudice. Projects and teamwork efforts that require greater time are de-emphasized because the outcomes cannot be assessed in a short period. Many high school teachers complain about being expected to spend too much time monitoring attainment of short-term goals (Rimm, 2005). A heavy class schedule does not take into account the need to prepare lessons, devise and respond to homework, and plan with colleagues.

In contrast, teachers in Japan spend half of every day providing instruction and the remainder half to reading papers, preparing lessons, meeting with individual students, and planning with colleagues. In Japan and Germany beginning teachers are assigned to mentors recognized for their skills (Baker & LeTendre, 2005). These mentors observe and consult with newcomers over their first 2 years in the classroom. This kind of help often occurs in American schools only during student teaching before someone has responsibility for their own classes. When a person becomes a member of the faculty, they are typically on their own and get few chances to exchange lesson plans or discuss teaching techniques with colleagues who have more experience (Barker & Erickson, 2005).

A much needed school reform is reallocation of the way teachers spend time so their work can be more productive and satisfying to themselves and students. For an online tour of some innovative classroom practices, examine the National Forum to Accelerate Middle-Grades Reform—http://www.mgforum.org.

Voices of Adolescents

Most sectors of life require being able to deal with some frustration. Depending on the ability to manage frustration, people experience disappointment, helplessness, and disinterest or they can become upset, angry and confrontational. The student role is bound to present frustrations, some of them easy to manage and others that may threaten motivation to learn. Certain frustrations are inevitable and students should be given guidance to process these in healthy ways. There may also be frustration with school practices that undermine motivation and learning.

Adolescents report that feelings of frustration increase when the pace of instruction is too fast or too slow, expectations for achievement are too high or too low, they are limited to a passive role, and final examinations for all courses are scheduled too close together. Teachers and administrators need to understand what can be done to make the school environment more satisfying and less frustrating to students. The poll for this chapter centers on student frustration with school experience (see Exercise 8.01). Examining the results of this poll can make known how adolescents you work with feel about frustration at school and possible solutions.

Cyber Risk Taking

Safety is the highest priority for every school. Teachers are expected to protect students while on campus and offer education that helps them avoid unreasonable risks online (Provenzo, 2005). The public expects progress to reduce the risk that adolescents might become victims of predators surfing social network sites. The Federal Bureau of Investigation has a Web site containing safety tips for parents and teachers to share with teenagers about predators, cyberbullies, spam scams, online shopping fraud, file sharing, and identity theft at Government On Guard Safety http://onguardonline.gov/index.html.

Teachers should collectively and often caution adolescents against taking these risks online:

1. Reveal detailed personal data such as address, phone number, full name or name of the school.
2. Agree to see someone met online without approval of parents. Restrict the relationship to chat.
3. Enter inappropriate topic related chat lines such as conversations that focus on pornography.

4. Be wary of any information appearing online because there are many sources that lack credibility.

5. Believe everything about how people represent themselves because their portrayal may be deceptive.

6. Beware of innocent terms like "teen" and sites that may lead to pornography pictures of adolescents.

7. Believing sales pitches that are presented. Realize that you are a target for advertising campaigns.

8. Beware of Web sites that include inappropriate language or picture groups of people in unfair ways.

9. Buying anything online without the supervision of parents. Make sure you use only secured sites.

10. Downloading e-mail from an unknown site. A computer virus could infect your operating system.

11. Be suspect of advertisements that offer free products, market surveys, and unsolicited messages.

INSTRUCTIONAL RISKS

Risks related to instruction can detract from student motivation to learn. This happens if the entire class is expected to proceed at the same pace. A better approach is to monitor progress of individuals by using assessments that detect needs for remediation and ensure that everyone meets minimal competencies. This strategy overcomes the customary risk in which some students are left behind. A related strategy is determining how students perceive their need for tutoring help and the potential to support success. Keeping families informed of student progress on minimal competency tests and describing their normative standing on achievement tests can prevent the risk of students being overwhelmed by uncertainty and being unable to share feelings with adults.

Fast and Slow Learners

A dangerous risk for educators is to suppose that the rate at which students gain knowledge reflects their capacity for learning. This assumption was first challenged by John Carroll (1963). He hypothesized that nearly all students can learn whatever schools expect of them but differ in amount of time and help they require to learn. When teachers think of ability as an indicator of learning rate rather than as an index of capacity to learn, they recognize their class is composed of fast and slow learners rather than good or poor students. Carroll speculated that if teachers allowed sufficient time and ensured that time is spent on task, instructional goals can more often be met. When all students are expected to achieve in the same amount of time, those who are slow will be unable to reach the goals expected by teachers.

Benjamin Bloom (1913–1999) was intrigued by the implications of Carroll's theoretical model of learning for schools. If ability is mainly a function of speed at which students learn, it should be possible to help more of them meet academic expectations by modifying the conditions of instruction. Bloom (1976) elaborated an approach called mastery learning (Block, 1971). In *mastery learning,* students must pass a test at a specified level for a unit of instruction before being allowed to move ahead to a more advanced lesson. Bloom observed that educators usually organize lessons to match the content of text chapters for a course. After reading and instruction, students are evaluated to determine the extent of learning. Given the cumulative aspects of much knowledge, students who test poorly on measures covering content for the first unit are likely to do worse on assessments for succeeding units. In this way students can fall behind peers and fail to acquire the skills and understanding needed for entry to the labor force. The current national resolve reflects a promise to ourselves that No Child will be Left Behind.

Efforts to ensure mastery learning begin by dividing course content into short instructional units of one or two weeks' duration. Bloom (1976) recommended reliance on continuous evaluation as a basis to guide instruction. *Formative assessment* is a diagnostic tool to track individual progress and serve as a basis for providing feedback by detecting learning needs students must spend more time on. A high level of performance is generally required (usually 75% of items correct) to meet the definition of mastery before students can go on to a more advanced lesson. Those who fail to demonstrate mastery are provided help following formative assessment. This help takes the form of tutoring, videotape lessons, discussions, computer practice, reading or worksheets (Dalton, 2008).

Formative assessment occurs again after help is given to determine if the student performance warrants going ahead to the next lesson. Those who quickly show an understanding of materials should not be held back or have to wait for their slower classmates. Instead, enrichment activities should enable faster students to expand their knowledge. *Summative evaluation* comes at the end of a course, covers all aspects of learning, and is the basis for judgment on overall student performance or final grade. When mastery programs succeed, nearly all students record high scores demonstrating that they have attained the required minimal understanding of content (Gall, Gall, & Borg, 2005).

Testing and Progress Reports

In the past tests were administered mainly to compare students with one another so that the most talented could be identified and admitted to college. However, now that attending college is common, the purpose of testing has shifted to monitoring individual competence. By continually tracking the progress for each student, educators can detect deficiencies early and provide remediation to meet minimal goals. The necessity for this approach has been encouraged since the 1990s when allegations arose that the high school diploma was losing credibility because many students were allowed to graduate without possessing basic skills in reading, writing, and mathematics. In response to such claims, states and school boards adopted more stringent policies. Since then, the emphasis has been on *minimal competency tests* that require all students to demonstrate that they have attained the basic skills before being permitted to graduate (Loveless, 2005).

What type of measurement is appropriate to assess minimal competence? A Norm-Referenced Test (NRT) compares individual performance with the performance of a specified group such as students in the same grade for a district, state or nation. For example, Tom's *test percentile rank* of 60 shows that he scored as well or better than 60% of the norm group who took the same test. However, this information does not give specifics about what Tom understands and has yet to learn in mathematics. NRT tests are not designed to detect particular strengths or weaknesses. They are designed to produce scores that reveal an individual's relative position in a particular group so education decisions based on performance differences can be made. To illustrate, the selection of a limited number of students for an accelerated mathematics program can proceed more fairly if it is recognized that Tom's score at the 60th percentile rank is much lower than Michelle's score placing her at the 96th percentile rank. To allow for such comparisons, there must be some reasonable spread of scores that would not happen if a test were so easy everyone performed well. For this reason, the items on a NRT that do not contribute to variance are subject to change. Consequently, items on concepts or skills considered basic will, over time, be eliminated from a norm-referenced achievement test. The ideal test item for maximizing variance on a NRT is one where only half (50%) of the respondents answer correctly. An item that is answered correctly by 80% or more of the students is often eliminated because it does not spread out the range of student scores (Ceci & Papierno, 2005).

A Criterion-Referenced Test (CRT) is the most appropriate way to assess student competence in basic skills. In a CRT the required performance level is decided ahead of time so it is not influenced by how well other students in the class or grade perform. Mastery at the 75% to 90% level is the typical minimal standard chosen. For example, if there are four items related to reading comprehension, a student must get three out of four items correct to attain 75% mastery. Whatever standard is set, it becomes the absolute criterion against which the performance of every student is compared. Because a criterion-referenced test is diagnostic, it is intentionally success-oriented. Most students are expected to pass, if not the first time around, then on a retest following corrective instruction. In this context, the student who does not reach the required standard for one or another basic skill is not seen as a failure. Instead, the student is identified as someone able to learn the necessary skill and pass the test but has yet to do so (Thorndike, 2005).

An important distinction between CRTs and NRTs is that the criteria for judging success on CRT are preestablished, decided before a test is administered to anyone. Ideally, everyone will pass the CRT, if not on their first try, then later after tutoring and before being allowed to graduate. In contrast, the criteria for success on NRT are not decided in advance. Instead, success of individuals depends on the performance of the group taking the test. The range of scores becomes a basis for identifying standing of individuals in relation to one another. Generally, the purpose of CRT, used for mandated high stakes tests by the states, is to assess minimal competence whereas NRT are for selecting students to enter advanced classes where competitive selection is necessary. For example, the number of places in an advanced course is limited so it may be decided that only students scoring in the top 10% are allowed to enter.

CRT is the dominant form of assessment used by states for compliance with the No Child Left Behind Act (Hursh, 2008). This type of evaluation has merit but shortcomings too. By definition, it is recommended only when the emphasis is on attaining limited instructional objectives and mastery is considered as a reasonable expectation for all students. Neither condition obtains once a student moves ahead to advanced learning. Then broad educational objectives are implicated, calling for integration of concepts and ideas from different subject matters. For such complex achievements, it is necessary to rely on NRTs. The relevant point is that educators do not choose between CRTs and NRTs as the best for all situations. Schools need both kinds of measures because they serve different but complementary purposes for evaluating development.

Parents want to be informed about the progress of their child. Table 8.1 illustrates a basic skills report received by parents of high school students. All of the reading and mathematics skills required for graduation are stated, the minimal expected performance is specified (75% mastery), and sections of the test already passed by the student are identified. Minimal competency tests that include a section on writing skills as well are administered annually beginning in Grade 9. Results are used to schedule tutoring. All of the required subjects must be passed before a diploma is issued (Hursh, 2008).

Besides the results of minimal competency testing, parents want to know how the achievement scores of their daughter or son compares with classmates at the same grade level. Such information, as provided by norm-referenced tests, is helpful for career planning. Percentile ranks used with NRT are the most informative way of reporting comparative achievement to parents, provided two characteristics are made clear to them; (1) the norm group is identified (city, state, national); (2) *percentile score* is defined as the percent of the norm group whose performance a student has equaled or surpassed. The range of percentile ranks reported are from 1% (lowest possible standing) to 99% (highest standing surpassing almost everyone).

Table 8.2 is a report to students and their parents about performance on a comprehensive test of skills. It provides several ways of looking at performance in comparison with other high school sophomores throughout the nation. Percentile ranks are given along with *test stanine*, dividing students in achievement groups with one as the lowest and nine as the highest. A below average, average or above average rating is also portrayed. To comply with the Family Rights and Privacy Act, passed by Congress in 1974 to allow parents access to all their child's school records, this report appears in Spanish and in English because the school serves both populations (Brier, 2007; United States Department of Education, 2008).

Observations of Dropouts

The Bill and Melinda Gates Foundation supported an investigation to find out from school dropouts how they saw their school experiences and what could have been done to prevent them from leaving (Bridgeland, Dilulio, & Morison, 2006). The observation sources were 467 ethnically and racially diverse males and females, ages 16 to 25 who had left public schools throughout the nation. To ensure that each participant could respond in their own words and elaborate their reasoning, individual interviews were held using the same set of agenda questions for all. The top five reasons given by dropouts as major factors for leaving school and proportion identifying each were:

1. The classes were not interesting to me (47%)
2. I missed too many days and could not catch up (43%)
3. I spent time with people who were not interested in school (42%)

Table 8.1. A Sample of Minimal Competency Criterion-Referenced Test Reports on Basic Skills

Student Number	*Student Name*	*Date*

READING SKILLS AREAS—The high school reading basic skills requirements are that each student demonstrates 75% proficiency in each skill area prior to graduation. X indicates proficiency.

Comprehension Skills:		**READING**
1. Identify stated main idea	PART 1	
2. Identify stated detail	PART 2	
3. Identify stated cause/ effect relationships	PART 3	
4. Identify inferred main idea	PART 4	
5. Identify inferred cause/ effect relationships	PART 5	
6. Identify inferred sequence	PART 6	
7. Identify inferred conclusions	PART 7	
8. Identify fact/opinion statements	PART 8	
9. Identify relevant/ irrelevant data	PART 9	
Study Skills:		
10. Follow written directions	PART 10	
11. Extract information from diagrammatic/ pictured materials	PART 11	
12. Use dictionary, index, table of contents	PART 12	
13. Identify prefixes, suffixes, roots	PART 13	
14. Use context clues	PART 14	
	Proficiency Met	

MATHEMATICS SKILLS AREAS—The high school mathematics basic skills requirements are that each student demonstrates 75% proficiency in each skills area prior to graduation. X indicates proficiency.

1. Adding whole numbers	PART 1	**MATHEMATICS**
2. Subtracting whole numbers	PART 2	

Figure continues on next page.

Table 8.1. Continued

Student Number	Student Name	Date
MATHEMATICS SKILLS AREAS—The high school mathematics basic skills requirements are that each student demonstrates 75% proficiency in each skills area prior to graduation. X indicates proficiency.		
3. Multiplying whole numbers	PART 3	
4. Dividing whole numbers	PART 4	
5. Adding fractions	PART 5	
6. Subtracting fractions	PART 6	
7. Multiplying fractions	PART 7	
8. Dividing fractions	PART 8	
9. Adding decimals	PART 9	
10. Subtracting decimals	PART 10	
11. Multiplying decimals	PART 11	
12. Dividing decimals	PART 12	
13. Finding percent of a number	PART 13	
14. Interpreting scales, graphs, charts	PART 14	
15. Equivalent expressions for measurements	PART 15	
	Proficiency Met	

4. I had too much freedom and not enough rules in my life (38%)
5. I was failing in some of my subjects (36%)

Most dropouts expressed regret about their decision, admitted they were responsible for their predicament, and wished they could have done things differently. When asked to identify conditions that may have improved their chances of remaining in school, the most prominent factors cited were (Bridgeland, Dilulio, & Morison, 2006):

1. Opportunities for real-world learning (internships, service learning, etc.) to make classroom more relevant (81%);
2. Better teachers who keep classes interesting (81%);
3. Smaller classes with more individual instruction (75%);

Table 8.2. A Sample of Norm-Referenced Test Reports on Basic Skills

School	Student No.					Student Name		Form		Date
Percentile	Below 5	5–10	11–22	23–40	41–59	60–77	78–89	90–95	96 & Above
Stanine	1	2	3	4	5	6	7	8	9
National Norms	Below Average Promedio Bajo			Average Promedio			Above Average Promedio Superior		
Reading Vocabulary Vocabulario de lectura									
Reading Comprehension Comprension de lectura									
Spelling Deletreo									
Language Mechanics Expresion escrita									
Language Expression Uso de la lengua									
Mathematics Computation Computaciones de matematicas									
Mathematics Concepts Conceptos de matematicas									
Mathematics Application Aplicacion de matematicas									
Reference Skills Uso de libros de consulta									
Science Ciencia									
Social Studies Civismo									

4. Better communication between parents and school, and get parents more involved (71%);

5. Parents make sure their kids go to school every day (71%);

6. Increase supervision at school to ensure students attend classes (70%).

One of the greatest risks schools take is to ignore the need to find out how students view conditions of learning (Strom & Strom, 2008). Sadly, many of the most disappointed students make their point of view know by withdrawing from education, dropping out of school. All faculties should consider ways to diminish frequent complaints about lack of real world learning, need for more interesting classes, and demonstration of relevance for the content. This is the approach used by the Chicago, Illinois, public school 2010 plan for 50 high schools in collaboration with the Gates Foundation providing support with a $21 million grant (Daley, 2006). See http://www.gatesfoundation.org.

The Chicago Public Schools (2005) have also devised a warning form for declared dropouts to make them aware of the gravity of their decision. When a student wants to quit and has reached age 16, s/he is required along with parents or guardian to read and sign a waiver of educational rights to complete the process of leaving school. The intention is for everyone in the family to realize the impact this decision will have on a student's future. The Consent to Withdraw From School Form was devised in cooperation with the school reform group. Statistics show that most prison inmates lack a high school diploma, dropouts are far more likely than high school graduates to be unemployed, in poor health, live in poverty, and get public assistance. Therefore, accurate information is being communicated to the family without sugar coating the harsh realities. The project director expressed hope that the form will be adopted by schools nationwide. Figure 8.1 presents this Consent to Withdraw From School Form.

A further contribution to the reduction of dropout rates involves findings attained by the University of Chicago Consortium on Chicago School Research (Allensworth & Easton, 2007). Investigators determined that information on high school students' freshman year course credits and failures can be used to predict at a high degree of accuracy whether they will receive a diploma and provide an early detector of drop out risk for parents, teachers, and schools. Students are on track if they earn at least five credits and no more than one semester "F" grade during their freshman year. On-track students are 3.5 times more likely to complete graduation requirements in 4 years than off-track students. There is evidence that on-track students are not just those with better scores on achievement tests. High school success requires that students have skills in addition to those that are evaluated by achievement tests (Allensworth & Easton, 2007).

Figure 8.1. Consent to Withdraw From School Form

CHICAGO PUBLIC SCHOOLS

CONSENT TO WITHDRAW FROM SCHOOL*

I _____ (*student name*) acknowledge that by dropping out of high school, I am voluntarily giving away my educational rights, privileges and opportunities. Under State law and CPS policy, enrolled students are entitled to a free, full-time public education until the age of 22 unless I graduate from high school, I am expelled for misconduct, or I withdraw from enrollment. By dropping out, I am withdrawing from enrollment.
By dropping out of school, I further acknowledge that:

1. *I will be less likely to find a good job.*
2. *I will be less likely to be able to buy many things*
3. *I will be more likely to get caught up in criminal activity.*
4. *I will be more likely to spend time in jail.*
5. *I will be more likely to be on welfare.*
6. *I will likely have fewer choices about where to live.*
7. *I will be less likely to be able to properly care for and educate my children.*

I _____ (*student name*) confirm that I am 17 years old or older. I have read and fully understand the consequences of my dropping out of high school. Yet, I choose to withdraw from school. I understand that even after I dropout, I have the right to return to school and be reenrolled. The school may challenge my reenrollment only on the grounds that, because of my age and lack of credits, I cannot graduate before turning 21. If they do challenge my reenrollment, I am entitled by State law and CPS policy to a due process appeal.

_____ **Student signature**

(*For students between 17 and 18 years old*) I _____ confirm that my child is between the ages of 17 and 18. I also have read and fully understand the consequences of my child dropping out of high school. Yet, I will allow my child to withdraw from school.

_____ **Parent/Guardian signature**

The above-named individuals have been fully informed of the consequences of dropping out of high school. I have also informed them of alternative and adult educational services that are available in the community, and provided them with the phone number for the Reenrollment Center in CPS Department of Dropout Prevention and Recovery.

_____ **Principal signature**

It's Not Too Late To Stay In School

_____

Source: *From Chicago Public Schools (2008), School Dropout Withdrawal Form, Retrieved November 1, 2008 from http://clear.cps.k12.il.us/AboutCPS/Departments/ Dropout%5FPrevention%5FRecovery/consent.html
Reprinted by permission.

Taxonomy of Educational Objectives

Performance objectives are another element of mastery learning. Bloom (1976) thought that it was possible to analyze any learning sequence into specific objectives and teach them in a way that would allow most students to attain course goals. The *Taxonomy of Educational Objectives* provides a rationale for sequencing instructional activities to ensure that higher order thinking becomes prominent (Bloom, Englehart, Furst, Hill, & Krathwohl, 1956). The assumptions for sequencing are that attainment of goals higher in the taxonomic hierarchy rest upon mastery of goals lower in the hierarchy. This taxonomy can be relied on as a conceptual outline to order and to reorder learning tasks. By using this schema teachers can ensure that instruction and learning are not restricted to just the lowest levels of performance in the cognitive domain.

The six levels of instructional objectives in the taxonomy that should be acquired by students are:

1. *Knowledge* is the lowest level of learning outcomes, defined as an ability to remember facts, names, dates, principles, or other data.

2. *Comprehension* goes beyond the recollection of knowledge in being able to translate meaning by explaining concepts, interpreting data, and predicting consequences.

3. *Application* refers to solving new and unfamiliar problems by recognizing implications of specific rules, methods, concepts, principles, laws or theories provided by comprehension.

4. *Analysis* involves recognizing relationships, organizational principles, and implications. These outcomes transcend comprehension and application because they require understanding of both the content and structural forms of knowledge.

5. *Synthesis* is the ability to reconstruct data by creating a new whole such as a unique communication (theme or speech), plan (research proposal), or set of relationships (scheme for classifying information).

6. *Evaluation* requires an ability to assess the value of material (novel, statement, report) by using internal criteria (organization) or external criteria (relevance to a purpose). These outcomes are highest in the taxonomy because they contain elements of all other categories plus conscious value judgments based on clearly defined criteria. Using the evaluations of students to monitor self and peer progress gives opportunities to engage in higher levels of thinking. There is justification to let students practice evaluation skills that

will be required of them in the interdependent workplace and in personal relationships throughout life.

To summarize, the taxonomy involves cognitive processes ranging from strict memorization of knowledge to more complex mental operations involving synthesis and evaluation. Higher levels of cognition require students to apply what they learn, discriminate, generalize, and form judgments based on evidence and reasoning. Studies that span two generations have consistently shown that, at every grade level including college, teachers are inclined to overemphasize knowledge (level 1) and comprehension (level 2) while giving insufficient attention to the higher cognitive levels of application (level 3), analysis (level 4), synthesis (level 5), and evaluation (level 6) in questions for class discussions and tests (Krathwohl, 2002; Kuhn, 2005). A Web site describing the Taxonomy of Learning and Benjamin Bloom's work is at http://oaks.nvg.org/taxonomy-bloom.html.

Teachers who develop test items that cover all cognitive levels of the *Taxonomy of Educational Objectives* can enable students to demonstrate what they have learned. Some questions that could be considered in reference to topics described in this text are shown in Table 8.3.

The *Taxonomy of Educational Objectives* is undergoing a resurgence of attention much greater than when it initially appeared a half century ago (Krathwohl, 2002). This is because quick obsolescence of information requires teaching and evaluation practices that must go beyond remembering knowledge to include a greater emphasis on interpretation of knowledge, application of knowledge, analysis of knowledge, synthesis of knowledge, and the evaluation of knowledge. The group of scholars who originally worked with Bloom held meetings on a regular basis over a 5-year period, from 1995–2000, to discuss how they could bring the taxonomy up to date so it would match contemporary conditions in schools. This collaborative effort is titled *Taxonomy for Learning, Teaching and Assessing: A Revision of Bloom's Taxonomy of Educational Objectives* (Anderson, Krathwohl, Airasian, & Cruickshank, 2000).

The main features of Bloom's (1976) concept of mastery learning are: (a) sequencing learning tasks so they encompass simple to complex cognitive processes; (b) providing students clear statements that specify the expected levels of performance; (c) use of formative assessment to identify the particular learning needs of individuals; (d) teacher application of suitable methods of remediation and enrichment for those who need correction as well as those attaining mastery; and (e) construction of test items and class questions that allow students to make known what they learn at each level of the hierarchy of cognitive skills.

Table 8.3.   An Interpretation of Performance Outcomes for Taxonomy of Educational Objectives

Performance Outcomes	Behavioral Evidence	Test Item Example
KNOWLEDGE of facts, terms, procedures, basic concepts, principles and theories	Defines, describes, identifies, labels, lists, matches, names, outlines, selects, reproduces	Who was the scholar who began the formal study of adolescence?
COMPREHENDS and translates material; interprets graphs; uses procedures correctly	States, explains, illustrates, distinguishes, summarizes, paraphrases, infers, predicts	How does adolescence now differ from the experience of previous generations?
APPLICATION of concepts and principles to practical problems faced in unfamiliar situations	Computes, modifies, discovers, demonstrates, produces, solves, relates, justifies, operates	How should pda's and pagers be used by teachers to improve parent awareness about behavior of students?
ANALYSIS recognizes unstated assumptions, logical fallacies, distinguish fact and inference	Differentiates, breaks down parts, diagrams, discriminates, separates	What factors contribute to a lack of education classes for parents of adolescents?
SYNTHESIS by a well organized speech/paper, formulate a new method for classifying ideas	Categories, combines, revises, compiles, designs, generates, reconstructs, plans, organizes	Prepare a paper about polling as a method to improve the school learning environment.
EVALUATION of judging how well the data supports conclusions, judging value of art or music or writing with external criteria	Appraises, compares, contrasts, criticizes, explains, discriminates, justifies, interprets, summarizes, describes, concludes, justifies	How effective is education in helping students learn to assess teamwork skills of teammates?

SUMMARY

Factors in Risk Taking

Some students are referred to as being at risk for failure in school because of demographic factors such as household income or minority status. Yet, these factors typically have less influence on student success than do opportunities provided by schools and teachers. The way adolescents perform in class, spend time after school, choice of friends to hang out with, and interaction with classmates are more powerful predictors of health-related risks like drinking, smoking, sexual activity, and violence than are demographic factors educators are less able to influence. Truants commonly identify lack of satisfying relationships with classmates as a prime reason for their absenteeism. Feeling connected to school is a more common experience when teachers arrange learning conditions that support a sense of belonging, friendship, and peer support.

Risk Assessment Practices

The adolescent experience includes an extensive array of risks that can threaten or enrich development. Deciding in advance how much risk is acceptable in situations clarifies the true range of choices available and eases decision making. Interpretation of risks and responding in constructive ways requires a capacity to accurately gauge and consider possible costs associated with situations. This ability is commonly overridden by the personal fable causing teenagers to suppose they are invulnerable and will not suffer harmful consequences that might affect others who take the same risks. Teenagers need to count on their teachers, parents, and friends for monitoring and giving feedback on their ability to gauge risk. Educators should be aware of educational research on retention outcomes or they place students at greater risk for quitting school. Encouraging adolescents to identify and pursue growth-related risks is an important contribution of teachers and parents. As students experience rewards of growth-oriented risks, they become more willing to take such risks.

Risk Reduction Strategies

A serious risk is the increasing pressure to rush learning, to forego reflective thinking because it takes time, and examine options in a superficial way before making decisions. The observable outcomes are that some students feel helpless, others seek pharmaceutical solutions to cope with the stress, many fall behind, and still others perform less well than their capacity. Teachers can control the pace of lessons and should recognize that time and learning are linked. Practicing desired skills is the best way to ensure they are learned and adopted by students for future reliance in problem solving. Related risk of compromising the effectiveness of teachers can be overcome by more reasonable work schedules that include time to prepare homework and in class tasks, assess learning, meet with students, and collaborate with colleagues. In addition to protecting students at school, teachers have a role in helping adolescents to protect themselves outside school when oriented to guidelines for safe practices on the Internet.

Instructional Risks

Almost all students are capable of acquiring the skills and understanding schools require but there is variance in the pace at which individuals learn. The strategy to ensure that everyone masters basics, no matter how long it takes, involves minimal competency testing to identify achievement and detect remediation needs responded to by tutoring. Formative assessment is repeated until goals are reached, thereby eliminating a risk that some students will be left behind. Parents are kept informed about student progress toward minimal competency standards and comparative achievement by norm-referenced reports. Effective teachers arrange tasks that allow students to participate in higher order thinking levels identified on the *Taxonomy of Educational Objectives*.

People of every age who stop taking potentially beneficial risks become narrow and less capable of coping with change. They demonstrate more rigid behavior and less flexibility in thinking. It is ironic that the pattern they choose to prevent danger leads to one of the most ominous risks, the abandonment of learning. The reason why this choice is dangerous is because individuals who cease to change can no longer adapt and so their development ends. A better response to the prevalence of over-choice and lack of time everyone must deal with is learning to accurately gauge risks and invite trusted relatives and friends to monitor this delicate ability that is essential for survival and improvement. When such conditions exist, taking risks can do much to support the quality of life in adolescence and the years of adulthood.

CLASSROOM APPLICATIONS

1. Educators should avoid interpreting demographic variables as destiny because they are actually weak predictors of risk behavior in adolescence. A more optimistic outlook comes from focusing on powerful influences at school that teachers can control such as detecting skill deficiencies, tutoring, emphasizing higher order thinking, implementing research-based retention policies, and being properly prepared for the courses they offer students.

2. Building relationships with students, providing individualized attention, encouraging peer support, and making sure parents are informed about signs of trouble are elements of intervention that reduce truancy. Truants typically identify lack of social connections with classmates at school as a major reason for staying away. This admission underscores a need to arrange cooperative learning

teams that facilitate social connections and enable a feeling of belonging.

3. Students are more likely to adopt reflective thinking than hasty judgment for dealing with complex problems when teachers arrange enough time to process information, deliberate, and reach thoughtful conclusions. Sensible scheduling for completion of tasks in class and homework assignments can help students understand importance of time management as a way to prevent unnecessary stress.

4. Teachers become isolated professionals when their entire day consists of meeting classes and direct instruction. An important lesson from teacher schedules in other nations is that time must be allowed for preparing instruction and assignments, marking papers for feedback, meeting with individuals who require assistance, collaborating with colleagues to plan, detect student problems as well as monitor effects of united intervention, and communicate with parents.

5. Teachers should consider the consistent results from large scale studies of retention that show holding students back is a less effective way to overcome low achievement than is detection of skill deficits followed by intensive tutoring. Professionals rely on research findings to help guide decision-making rather than believe that personal experience trumps empirical results to determine the best courses of action for solving problems.

6. The quick obsolescence of information requires that instruction and assessment practices change to go beyond memorization of knowledge. The emphasis should include the entire *Taxonomy of Educational Objectives*. Instead of limiting learning to the lowest levels of the cognitive domain, teachers should also focus on the more complex mental operations related to comprehension, application, analysis, synthesis, and evaluation.

7. The basic skills taught in school should reflect what people of a particular era need to know. Acquiring Internet research skills for finding information and media literacy skills for digital communication and interpretation should be recognized as basics along with traditional curriculum in reading, writing and arithmetic.

8. Teachers should vary in the ways they provide course materials each semester. Otherwise, the risk of sameness of delivery can be loss in the level of teacher excitement and consequent lack of student interest or possible boredom. Taking risks means applying constructivist approaches, exploring Internet resources, and arranging cooperative learning.

9. Communicate to students your concerns for them and their work. One short term related risk is confrontation with frustrated or insincere adolescents who respond to suggestions with defensiveness. Nevertheless, in the long term the greater risk is student perception that you do not care about them.

FOR REFLECTION

1. Hispanics are the fastest growing subpopulation. How can schools and parents cooperate to reduce the higher than average risk of dropout for these adolescents?
2. Truancy is an early warning that there is a risk of alienation from school. How could student influence become a greater force to limit this problem?
3. What can teachers do to be chosen more often by students to advise them regarding their ability to gauge risks?
4. Retaining a student in the same grade for a second try is recommended by some educators while others view this as an unreasonable risk. What factors will you consider in this situation?
5. How could the medical risk model be applied to choices for students and their parents regarding retention?
6. What kinds of things can teachers and schools do that will establish an environment where students are not hurried, rushed or overscheduled?
7. How could school curriculum address the adolescent need for safety on the Internet?
8. In what ways can the Taxonomy of Educational Objectives support your goals and methods of providing quality education for adolescents?
9. How much training do you think teachers should have in the subject they intend to teach so that students are not at risk for poor instruction?
10. What are the advantages and disadvantages of using minimal competency testing in secondary schools?

KEY TERMS

Criterion Referenced Test (CRT)
Demography

Dropouts

Family Rights and Privacy Act

Formative Assessment

High Stakes Testing

Mastery Learning

Minimal Competency Test

Norm Referenced Tests (NRT)

Percentile Score

Personal Fable

Retention

Risk

Risk Analysis

Summative Evaluation

Taxonomy of Educational Objectives

Test Percentile rank

Test Stanine

Truancy

Tutoring

Type A Personality

Underperforming Schools

VISIT THESE WEBSITES

Link to these sites at http://www.infoagepub.com/strom-adolescents

Annie E. Casey Foundation http://www.aecf.org/kidscount

Centers for Disease Control and Prevention,
Youth Risk Behavior Surveillance System
http://www.cdc.gov/HealthyYouth/yrbs/index.htm

Check and Connect, Student Engagement Intervention
http://ici.umn.edu/checkandconnect/default.html

Conditions of Education 2008, National Center for
Education Statistics http://www.nces.ed.gov/programs/coe

Education Commission of the States http://www.ecs.org

Federal Interagency Forum on Child and Family Statistics
http://www.childstats.gov

Fight Crime: Invest in Kids http://www.fightcrime.org

Gates Foundation http://www.gatesfoundation.org

Government On Guard Safety http://onguardonline.gov/index.html

MTV "Scarred" Program on Risks and Consequences
http://mtv.com/

National Center for Children in Poverty, Columbia University
http://www.nccp.org/about.html

National Center for School Engagement
http://www.schoolengagement.org

National Dropout Prevention Centers, Clemson University
http://www.dropoutprevention.org/

National Forum to Accelerate Middle-Grades Reform
http://www.mgforum.org

No Child Left Behind, A Toolkit for Teachers
http://www.ed.gov/teachers/nclbguide/index2.html

Pew Hispanic Center http://www.pewhispanic.org

Philadelphia School District, Attendance and Truancy
http://ework.phila.gov/philagov/news/prelease.asp?id=296

Taxonomy of Educational Objectives, Benjamin Bloom
http://oaks.nvg.org/taxonomy-bloom.html

Teens in Crisis, National Runaway Switchboard
http://www.1800runaway.org

EXERCISES AND ROLES

Exercise 8.01: School Frustration Poll

Role: Voter

The purpose of this poll is to learn about the frustration that students experience at your school.

Directions: For each item, select the answer(s) that apply to you. In some cases, you may select more than one answer. If an answer you want to give is not listed, write it on the line marked 'other.' Your responses are anonymous and may be combined with those of other students at your school in a report to students, faculty, and parents.

1. Some school situations that frustrate me are

    (a) students who misbehave in class
    (b) course content presented too fast
    (c) course content presented too slow
    (d) too much work due the same day
    (e) other

2. My usual reaction when frustrated at school is

    (a) seek out my friends to talk about it
    (b) try to withdraw from the situation
    (c) become upset and express my anger
    (d) try to demonstrate greater patience
    (e) other

3. I get frustrated trying to earn a good grade because

    (a) teacher requirements for grading are not clear
    (b) tests do not reflect what was studied in class
    (c) teammates do not get to evaluate my efforts
    (d) the teacher and I do not get along very well
    (e) other

4. The school could reduce my feelings of frustration by

    (a) having students work more together in teams
    (b) allowing participation in more active learning
    (c) having the classes begin later in the morning
    (d) slow things down so that we are not hurried
    (e) other

5. Sometimes I cause my own frustration by

    (a) taking on too much work without enough time
    (b) not scheduling time for fun and to be alone
    (c) waiting to do homework until the last minute
    (d) not speaking up when given too much work
    (e) other

6. Some qualities that I need to develop are

    (a) demonstrating patience
    (b) better set of study habits
    (c) setting reasonable goals
    (d) managing time wisely
    (e) other

7. Homework is frustrating for me when

    (a) the teacher does not give clear directions
    (b) assignments take up too much of my time
    (c) teachers don't provide feedback on tasks
    (d) I do my work but other students copy
    (e) other

8. When I get frustrated at school, I generally get over it

    (a) in a few minutes
    (b) in a few hours
    (c) in a few days
    (d) after a long time
    (e) other

9. When I am frustrated with an assignment

    (a) I can discuss it with the teacher
    (b) I do not complain but just do it
    (c) I do not finish or submit the work
    (d) I am inclined to copy from others
    (e) other

10. My main outlet for expressing frustration is

    (a) writing in a journal or a blog
    (b) doing some kind of exercise
    (c) talking to friends or relatives
    (d) cool down by listening to music
    (e) other

11. The grades I get at school frustrate me when

    (a) personality factors seem to influence teacher marks
    (b) low achievers get the same grades as high achievers
    (c) no grades are given for work that students do in teams
    (d) they do not reflect the scores I get on the state tests
    (e) other

12. Testing at school is frustrating when

    (a) no class time is given to review concepts on the tests
    (b) final exams in all subjects are scheduled the same week
    (c) there is no feedback on concepts that are not understood
    (d) content we are expected to learn does not seem practical
    (e) other

13. I would be less frustrated if the school

    (a) scheduled tests a few days apart so I could prepare for each
    (b) gave more short quizzes about key concepts in the courses
    (c) changed schedules so classes could start later in the morning
    (d) allowed exploration of new subjects without getting a grade
    (e) other

14. I feel frustrated in courses where the teacher

    (a) is unable to maintain discipline in the class
    (b) only lectures instead of also allowing active learning
    (c) does not permit working together in teams
    (d) ignores the Internet as a source of learning
    (e) other

15. The frustration that classmates present for me are

    (a) difficulties in making friends
    (b) interfering with class learning
    (c) being pressured to misbehave
    (d) concerns about being bullied
    (e) other

16.   In general, my frustration level at school is

    (a)   high
    (b)   moderate
    (c)   low
    (d)   none

Select your grade level, gender, ethnicity, and age

My grade level is 5 6 7 8 9 10 11 12
My gender is female male
My ethnicity is Asian Black Hispanic Native American White other
My age is 10 11 12 13 14 15 16 17 18 19

Exercise 8.02: Risktaking in the Classroom

Role: Challenger
What risks do you intend to take in the classroom that might promote greater learning for your students?

Exercise 8.03: Grading and Risk

Role: Discussant
Identify some risks that arise when teachers give higher grades than warranted by student progress or achievement.

Exercise 8.04: Recent Risks

Role: Discussant
Some risks have been around for a long time whereas others are of recent origin or have become more prominent than in the past. Brainstorm a list of risks for adolescents that have originated or increased during the past decade.

Exercise 8.05: Risktaking and Culture

Role: Cultural Reporter
The literature on education often refers to populations considered at risk for failure in the classroom. Low income is usually identified as a

risk. It is less common to consider how cultural factors are implicated because the custom has been to think of culture only in terms of pride. Critical comments from outsiders regarding a culture are considered politically incorrect and attributed to prejudice or lack sensitivity. These conditions make it unlikely for people to apply the objectivity that is required to become constructively critical of their own subgroup and recognize when departures from tradition are appropriate. Interview someone well informed about your subculture or ethnicity to identify (a) trends taking place in the subculture s/he does not approve of, (b) changes s/he supports and hopes will become more common, and (c) customs or trends seen as confusing about people from other backgrounds.

Exercise 8.06: Parents and Risktaking

Role: Generational Reporter

1. What are some risks you took as a teenager but would not consider now?
2. What are some risks that people should continue to take throughout life?
3. What do people of your age consider the most risky behavior for them?
4. What are some risks that you encourage your adolescent children to take?
5. What risks do your adolescent sons or daughters take that concern you?
6. What risks would you like to take if there were no adverse consequences?
7. What risks did you avoid in the past that you now wish had been taken?
8. What do you consider to be the greatest risk that you have ever taken?
9. What risks are you more inclined to take than most people of your age?

Exercise 8.07: Tests and Risktaking

Role: Challenger

It has been customary for students to take academic tests without the benefit of written resources. This seems contrary to the advice typically given on how to solve everyday problems by using as many resources as possible. When students are found to have notes written on their hands or access information in other ways that could improve the quality of their performance, this behavior is commonly identified as cheating, evidence of dishonesty and sign of poor character.

1. Provide some reasons why traditional conditions for testing should change.
2. Suggest replacement policies and practices related to testing and assessment.

Exercise 8.08: Sharing Failures

Role: Storyteller

Most people tell friends or relatives stories about things that happen to them each day. Yet, some parents seldom share lessons of personal failure, plans that did not work or unrealistic goals that were abandoned. Instead, many adults suppose that, to be seen as a model, memories they share with teenagers should highlight achievements with occasional mention of trivial mistakes in order to portray themselves as having shortcomings. However, it is the willingness of adults to risk disclosure of failures that causes adolescents to consider them able to comprehend their struggles. For this reason, talking to adolescents about our failures can be a good idea. Because most people fail daily, we have a broad range of situations from which to choose in telling our stories. Take turns answering any of the following questions you feel comfortable sharing.

1. What are some of your plans that turned out to be unsuccessful?
2. What failures bother you less than they bother other relatives?
3. How do you respond to relatives when they encounter a failure?
4. What failures did you later look back upon with some pleasure?
5. How do family members react when they learn you have failed?

Exercise 8.09: Guidance About Failure

Role: Storyteller

Some adults are wary of revealing their failures to adolescents. They maintain that, "If I tell my daughter or son about my failures, s/he is likely to bring them up in a future argument." That may be true, but it is a risk everyone takes when they make their failures known to others. On the other hand, if your goal is to be viewed as a person who rarely makes any mistakes, then teenagers will conclude that you cannot comprehend their problems. Grownups who teenagers most often turn to for advice are persons who admit their own shortcomings. People who care about us should become aware of our failures or they are denied an opportunity to help in coping with them. For this task the risks associated with self-disclosure are reduced because the audience for stories are teammates. Take turns answering these questions in a story narrative.

1. In what activities will you risk failure to learn something new?
2. Which situations are ones where you are the most likely to fail?
3. Of all your failures, what was the most difficult one to accept?
4. Who usually helps identify your failures and ways to recover?
5. Which friendship failures would you now handle differently?

Exercise 8.10: National School System

Role: Challenger

List some risks that might occur if the United States adopted a national school system. Then, in a second list identify some risks that might occur if the United States chooses not to adopt a national school system.

CHAPTER 9

VALUES AND ETHICAL CHARACTER

In the story of *Alice in Wonderland* (Carroll, 1865/2004), she comes to a crossroad and seeks advice from a Cheshire cat. "What road should I take?" The Cat replies, "That all depends on where you want to go." Alice admits, "I don't know where I want to go." The thoughtful cat says, "Well, then, any road will do." Adolescents have more roads to choose from than previous generations. Selecting values that contribute to personal growth supports responsibility, happiness, and maturity. When students develop coherent values and plan goals, they are less likely to be misled by those who seek to take advantage of vulnerability, confusion, and indecision.

Growing up and becoming mature requires the adoption of healthy values. *Values* are accepted principles used to guide behavior of an individual or group. Adolescents get their values from parents, other relatives, friends, classmates, teachers, clergy, musicians, sports figures, movie and television performers, Internet respondents, politicians, and reality program participants. When these sources offer conflicting advice, it can be difficult to decide which messages to believe. The goals for this chapter are to identify dishonest practices in schools, recommend procedures to minimize deceptive patterns of behavior, and consider ways to support constructive expression and tolerance of differences. The methods schools have used to teach character development are described, theories

Adolescents in the Internet Age, pp. 379–423
Copyright © 2009 by Information Age Publishing
All rights of reproduction in any form reserved.

of moral development are reviewed, and the impact of values on success and delinquent behavior are explored.

CHEATING IN SCHOOL

Many parents believe that growing up today presents more complicated challenges. Teenagers need to acquire certain attributes in order to cope with predictable difficulties (Seligman, 2007). A national sample of 1,600 parents with students attending middle school or high school was surveyed to determine the relative importance of teaching 11 values related to character development (Farkas, Johnson, Duffett, Wilson, & Vine, 2002). The value parents ranked highest, chosen by 91% of them as absolutely essential to teach their children, was "to be honest and truthful." One procedure to evaluate how well parents perform, in their own estimate, is to compare the proportion that identify a goal as essential with the proportion reporting that they have succeeded in teaching the specific value to their children. The survey results indicated a gap of 36 percentage points between the 91% of parents who saw honesty and truthfulness as fundamental lessons and the 55% reporting that their instruction had been successful. These findings confirm that, even for aspects of role performance parents consider indispensable, significant differences exist between their education intentions and what they have been able to accomplish.

Prevalence of Dishonesty

Teachers and students are also appropriate sources to judge whether lessons related to being honest have been learned. *Honesty* represents the combined qualities of being fair, just, truthful and morally upright. The Josephson Institute of Ethics in Los Angeles conducts annual surveys that monitor the ethics of 30,000 adolescents attending 100 randomly selected high schools nationwide, both public and private. All students are given the survey during a class and their anonymity is assured. Using the past year as their reference, 64% of students admitted cheating on a test. Cheating on homework is also widespread; 82% reported that they had copied another student's work at least once in the past year. Lying was prevalent too with 83% indicating they lied to a parent about something important and 40% lied to a teacher two or more times about issues of importance. To underscore the view that lying, cheating and stealing go together, 30% of the students admitted they had stolen something from a store in the past year. Despite these disappointing indicators of moral development, the students maintained high self-esteem with 93% expressing satisfaction with their personal ethics and character. Indeed, 77% stated, "When it comes to doing what is right, I am better than most people I know." Although these survey results reflect a trend toward deterioration of ethics among youth, it would seem that the main question for consideration is not whether things are getting worse but whether they are bad enough to mobilize concern and action by families, schools, and the community. Michael Josephson (2008), Director of the Institute suggests, "What we need to learn from these results is that our moral infrastructure is unsound and in serious need of repair."

Cheating is behavior intended to deceive or mislead others for personal advantage. During the past it was usual to suppose that cheaters had marginal abilities, leading them to resort to dishonesty, lying or forms of deceit, as the only way to keep pace with more competent classmates. However, when 3,000 students that were selected for recognition in Who's Who Among American High School Students were asked to report on their experiences, 80% acknowledged they cheat on tests (Lathrop & Foss, 2005). This high proportion of academic achievers engaging in deception reflects a 10% rise since honor students were first presented the same question 20 years ago. Among adolescent leaders that admitted cheating on tests and assignments, 95% said they were never caught and therefore did not have feelings of guilt or shame and viewed themselves as morally responsible.

Plagiarism involves copying what somebody else has written or taking somebody else's idea and trying to pass it off as original. The Center for Academic Integrity at Clemson University collaborates with 250 colleges to find ways of restoring ethical behavior in higher education. *Integrity* characterizes persons that possess high moral principles or professional standards and consistently act in accord with them. The consortium devises principles that define conditions of integrity to expect of students and strategies to help faculty influence students to adopt honesty as an aspect of lifestyle. The Center for Academic Integrity Web site is at http://www.academicintegrity.org.

Cheating is an international concern. A survey of 900 college students in China found that 83% of students had cheated. Frustration over cheating practices by late adolescents motivated Peking University, the most prestigious school in the nation, to begin expelling students caught plagiarizing (Dan, 2005). The government of China has been debating a National Examination Law with proposed tough penalties for cheating including jail sentences up to 7 years (Dongdong, 2005). Cheating among middle school, high school and college students is reported to be widespread across the globe in Australia, England, India, Japan, Korea, Spain, and Scotland (Callahan, 2004).

Cheating can influence admission to higher education, favoring dishonest students while disadvantaging those that show integrity. The Graduate Management Admissions Test (GMAT) taken by aspiring corporate executives from 100 countries is considered a vital criterion for decisions regarding applicants to business schools. Officials indicate that the GMAT will not be altered since it requires people to respond to an individually tailored series of questions designed to gauge mathematics and verbal ability levels. However, the fraudulent practice of "proxy" test taking in which imposters take a test for someone else is being targeted. Everyone is required to undergo a "palm vein" scan when they check in for test taking and each time they reenter the exam room. The scan takes an infrared picture to reveal a unique pattern of veins in a person's hand. Vein patterns are 300 times more complex than fingerprints; even identical twins have different vein patterns. Results of the palm scanner along with a digital photograph and signature become a permanent part of the record for each test taker at 400 centers worldwide (Hendricks, 2008).

Motivation for Cheating

Why do students from all age groups and levels of achievement cheat? One line of speculation is that academic dishonesty is merely a reflection of the broader erosion of ethics that support self-centeredness over concerns for fairness and equality. Another view is that fear and anxiety about high stakes testing causes dishonesty, especially among students who have difficulty acquiring minimal competency skills required for graduation (Callahan, 2004). Other observers contend that teachers are partially responsible because they ignore evidence of character failure and choose not to hold students accountable. Then too, educators agree that more and more parents appear obsessed with wanting their children to perform better than classmates, regardless of what it takes to get desired results (Anderman & Murdock, 2006).

Every school district should establish policies and procedures on cheating so faculty are able to respond to incidents they observe or have reported to them without experiencing fear of being subject to duress by students or their parents. While 80% of students responding to the Who's Who Among American High School Students survey admitted cheating on tests, a separate survey administered to their parents found 63% expressing confidence that their child would never cheat. Perhaps these parents suppose that teaching the distinction between right and wrong is enough instead of also linking this understanding with responsibility to behave in honest and truthful ways at school (Lathrop & Foss, 2005).

A familiar outcome is that educators feel vulnerable to parent threats of lawsuits if the honesty of their child is questioned without proof. Many teachers worry that they may erroneously accuse a student and have to suffer dreadful consequences. Indeed, 70% of educators agree their concern about parent reaction discourages them from identifying and punishing cheaters (Whitley & Keith-Spiegel, 2002). An unintended outcome is student awareness that misconduct seldom produces punishment and therefore poses a low risk for them (Carter, 2005).

Technology and Test Monitoring

Teachers are advised to be vigilant when they monitor students taking tests. A perennial form of dishonesty involves referral to messages that cheaters write on their body, clothing or belongings kept nearby. A common practice has been to remind test takers not to glance at papers of others during a test. The emergence of technological devices has spawned new and more sophisticated approaches to deceptive conduct. Students with handhelds or cell phones can "beam" or call data silently from across the classroom or, with a cell phone, from anywhere off campus. During a test such tools are frequently hidden under the table or in baggy pockets. Both devices can be equipped with text messaging, instant messaging, email, and a camera or video recorder that makes capture or transmission of answers a relatively simple task. Cell phones could have a hands-free function allowing the user to listen to sound files (i.e., prerecorded class notes). Applying the same method of sound files, others use music playing devices like iPods. The listening piece connected to a cell phone or some music-playing device can be concealed beneath long hair of a student, covering their ears from the teacher's view. An interview about modern cheating methods is available from *ABC News* at http://abcnews.go.com/search?searchtext=modern%20cheating%20methods&type. Additional contemporary reports about cheating can be found at http://www.youtube.org enter cheating.

Some teachers allow personal data assistants and graphing calculators during tests because these tools offer helpful functions for solving problems. Nevertheless, educators must be aware that, whenever a device displays data on the screen (liquid crystal display), it might also have a minimized screen containing cheat data that can be accessed for a few seconds and then entirely hidden (minimized) from a teacher's view with the press of a key. In a similar way, screen protectors include decorative patterned holograms intended to allow only the user to observe the screen and prevent viewing by onlookers from other angles. If a teacher permits use of calculators or PDAs, certain rules should be understood. Technology contributes to learning and assessment but devices must be applied in a responsible and ethical way. Barbara Davis (2002) at the University of California in Berkeley provides helpful tips about prevention of cheating, scoring and returning test results, handling fraudulent excuses to postpone an examination, turning in a late assignment, missing class, and clarifying expectations for course performance at http://teaching.berkeley.edu/bgd/prevent.html.

When a course has multiple sections, tests are typically scheduled on different days and times. This practice allows students to buy questions from someone that has already completed the examination. In such cases, buyer and seller are both cheating. A more daring risk involves paying a person to take a test for someone else (Anderman & Murdock, 2006). The identity of all students in an examination should be verified and the test for all sections of a course should be scheduled on the same day and at the same time. In addition, teachers should modify course tests of their own making each semester in order to lessen impact and likelihood of cheating by students able to access the previous answer keys. Administration of multiple versions of a test helps because items appearing in different sequence prove frustrating to anyone who tries to borrow answers by peering over the shoulder of another individual thought to know the material better than them. Changing the seating location of students is beneficial during testing because students are less likely to copy from classmates whose record of achievement is unknown. When a teacher leaves the room or permits students to during an examination, the chances for cheating increase. No student should be out of a teacher's sight while taking a test.

Giving periodic open book examinations and allowing students to bring notes can increase their familiarity with the content of a course, improve the review process, and reduce the incidence of cheating. While some considerations that have been described may seem unduly cautious, collectively these steps do much to prevent dishonesty and support the integrity of a test environment. Students take honesty more seriously when they see that their teacher makes an effort to ensure fair conditions for assessment.

While forms of student cheating increase in complexity, a related but unexpected threat has also become more common. During a period of high stakes testing, faculty and administrator salaries and career paths are tied to the academic performance of students. Some teachers and principals have been fired for giving students the answers to tests, prompting change in responses of students while being tested, changing answers after tests are completed and before they are submitted to a school district for processing, and giving students more time than the directions allow to finish tests (Axtman, 2005).

The extent to which educators will go to fabricate student achievement is shown by a case in Long Island, New York. A student taking the Regents' annual high stakes test was caught with blue writing on his hand that matched all of the correct responses. The source of answers was traced to the student's father, an assistant principal who was responsible for state examinations in a nearby district (Lambert, 2005). Public outrage over this illegal activity is prompting new initiatives as well as policies to protect the evaluation process. In Ohio teachers must sign a code of conduct and receive a warning that inappropriate monitoring of examinations could lead to revocation of their certification licensure. Kentucky administers six different versions of their state tests to frustrate the practice of teaching students answers that might be easier known by faculty where there is only a single version of the measure (Callahan, 2004).

Delaware, North Carolina, South Carolina and Texas are among the growing number of states contracting with Caveon, the nation's premiere test security company that monitors annual assessments for the No Child Left Behind Act. This company has developed data forensics, a process that searches for unusual test response patterns like getting difficult questions correct while missing easy questions, an abnormally high pass rate for a classroom or school, tests where incorrect answers have been erased and replaced with correct ones. The service includes protection of instruments from fraudulent practices, erecting barriers to prevent unauthorized access to copyright materials, and applying sophisticated statistical and Web patrolling tools that track cheaters, and hold them accountable by providing evidence to school administrators. The Caveon Web site— http://www.caveon.com—includes articles related to cheating methods, research and statistics.

INTERNET ETHICS

Congress passed the Children's Internet Protection Act (2000) requiring public schools and libraries to install filters that minimize exposure to objectionable materials like pornography. Another feature of cyber legislation, the body of law that pertains to computer information systems and networks, involves safeguard guarantees for the copyright material of authors and artists whose music or ideas are made available on the Internet. The national rush to make sure that every age groups can be online has overlooked the training everyone should have to support ethical behavior on the Internet. There is a growing population of young computer pirates that bootleg music and misrepresent themselves as authors of materials submitted to their teachers without identifying original sources. Dishonesty is not unique to students but seems widespread among adults in the workplace and presents similar challenges involving integrity, trust, and giving credit where credit is due (Evans & Wolf, 2005).

There are Web sites like http://www.schoolsucks.com/ that warehouses term papers students can access without cost. The papers can be downloaded for presentation instead of having to write a document containing personal views based on student reading and citation of proper citations. Another site—http://academictermpapers.com—offers research papers at a per page cost for the preparation of custom papers to fit the unique needs of a client.

When students lack training regarding the ethical commitment necessary for searching the Internet, they may suppose it is alright to present the words and views of someone else as if they represent their own thinking. Plagiarism on the Internet is a monumental problem that educators in middle school, high school, and college are struggling to confront (Axtman, 2005). Cyber law proposals that define offenses and penalties have begun to emerge as agenda that, in the future, could be determined in the courts instead of by teachers and administrators. Ronald Standler (2000), a copyright attorney, has an informative Web essay about plagiarism in colleges that illustrates the wide range of issues involved along with results of court cases at http://www.rbs2.com/plag.htm.

Parents share responsibility for helping daughters and sons realize that looking up a topic on the Web is only a first step in research, similar to visiting a library. Copying from books, journals or sources on the Internet and portraying these products as one's own invention is dishonest and defined as cheating (Moore & Robillard, 2008). Because of a growing access to the Internet, deceptive practices by students have been reported as moving downward to earlier grades. The Center for Academic Integrity surveyed middle schools throughout the nation and found that 73% of seventh graders and 66% of the sixth graders admitted to regularly borrowing materials without giving credit to their sources (McCabe & Pavela, 2004). Cut and paste plagiarism is increasing with students acting as though whatever they find on the Internet can be submitted as their own work. Bruce Leland (2002), Professor at Western Illinois University, provides suggestions for teachers on how to deal with plagiarism and what to tell students about ethical expectations. See http://www.wiu.edu/users/mfbhl/wiu/plagiarism.htm.

Prevention of Plagiarism

Teachers want students to practice search skills on the Internet but are finding it difficult to cope with plagiarism. To encourage originality and prevent students from taking credit for the writing of other people,

schools are contracting with a service that quickly detects work that is pla-
giarized. iParadigms—http://www.turnitin.com—the world's first Internet-
based plagiarism service, detects when more than eight copied words are
used in a paper, identifies the original source, and provides evidence
when confronting students and parents. This prevention resource is used
by public schools and universities. On a typical day, 30,000 papers are
submitted to the service for checking, and more than 30% of these documents include cheating. The annual cost of this software license can be
substantial (Moore & Robillard, 2008).

Adolescents are rarely asked to evaluate the practical worth of assignments given by teachers. Another way to better understand student reaction is from conversations in which they describe aspects of their
experience. For example, Jamal is a sophomore from Montgomery, Alabama. He believes that it is misleading to focus only on inappropriate
motives of students. Jamal suggests,

> Maybe a bigger problem is that teachers require students to memorize
> material instead of teaching them to think. You can cheat if all you are
> going to be tested on are facts but it is harder to cheat when you are asked to
> attack or defend a position and actually write an essay.

Jamal's outlook may not reflect consensus. Nevertheless, his view that
teachers could minimize cheating by devising more challenging tasks that
are less vulnerable to cheating is gaining support. Assignments that
motivate students to learn by doing, encourage reciprocal learning in
cooperative groups, support self-directedness, and foster original thinking are essential shifts in teaching that will allow students to become
actively involved in construction of their own knowledge. Traditionally,
teachers have devoted their preparation time mostly to instruction they
present to a class and little time developing assignments allowing students to learn on their own.

Individual and team projects are another realm of academic cheating.
Teachers can reduce the likelihood of deception by considering the following recommendations.

1. The purpose of every project should be clear, identify anticipated
   benefits, and invite dialogue about methods, resources, and types
   of products acceptable for submission.
2. Relevance for students should be established. The connection
   between curriculum and real life is confirmed when students can
   get credit for interaction with informants of other generations or
   cultures whose experience goes beyond the perspective offered by
   the teacher or text.

3. Encourage students to express their feelings and describe the processes they use to reach their conclusions. These presentations are more interesting to write and more satisfying to read.

4. Emphasize higher order thinking and creative behavior. Instead of reporting only knowledge, student participation should involve practice with higher-level abilities identified in the Taxonomy of Educational Objectives.

5. Go beyond the customary scope of problem solving. Students are often presented questions the teacher already knows answers for or could readily find. Yet, generating alternative solutions and then making choices is often the key to overcoming personal challenges in life.

6. Encourage varied types of information gathering. Submissions might include a hard copy of the located Web data accompanied by the same information summarized and interpreted in a student's own words, results drawn from polls or interviews, and descriptions of steps in an experiment.

7. Identify the criteria to be used for evaluating the quality of performance. When students know in advance the criteria that will be applied in judging work, they can focus instead of being anxious and reporting at the end "I wasn't sure if this is what you wanted."

8. Allow students to reflect, revise, and improve a project product they submit. Having access to suggestions of classmates who read their work and being expected to revise products supports perseverance, and motivates learning to accept constructive criticism.

9. Consider the use of oral critique. This procedure allows students to make their views known verbally, permits classmates to practice offering helpful criticism, enables teachers to call for clarification when points are unclear, and eliminates the use of technology tools for deception.

Student Integrity and Maturity

Legalistic syllabi and tough policies alone are insufficient to prevent cheating. Instruction is also needed. Students are able to understand that honesty is an important indicator of developing maturity. Indeed, maturity cannot materialize without a sense of obligation to treat other people fairly (Sternberg & Subotnik, 2006). Adolescents benefit from periodic discussions about the need for integrity across all sectors of life. They should also be informed about some seldom considered damaging effects of cheating, those gaps in knowledge and skills that can adversely affect later success when the foundation of knowledge necessary to understand processes in higher-level courses has not been acquired.

Academic dishonesty has another significant disadvantage. The moral compass that students need to guide conduct in class and outside of school can be thrown off course. This message is portrayed in *The Emperors Club* (Hoffman, 2003), a film starring Kevin Cline. As a teacher and assistant principal at St. Benedict's High School for Boys, he motivates the students to choose a moral purpose for their lives in addition to choosing occupational goals. The story illustrates how great teachers can have a profound influence on students and how cheating during the teen-age years can become a life-long habit. The interactive Web site for this film includes an interesting quiz on how to define morality at http://www.theemperorsclub.com.

Educators cannot provide all the guidance students need to choose honesty as a lifestyle. Some parents tell youth that cheating is a fact of life in the world of work and this has forced them to cheat to succeed (Berns, 2005). When parents condone dishonesty or deception as being norma-tive and defensible, it becomes more difficult for educators to counter the message that the prevalence of cheating makes it an acceptable practice (Carter, 2005). Schools could provide workshops for parents that focus on the range of cheating issues adolescents face and offer agenda questions for family discussions on honesty, integrity, and trust. In this way, mothers and fathers are enlisted to sustain their efforts to nurture these attributes in children. Successful performance rooted in honesty enables students to take pride in work that is their own and make known when tutoring is needed (McCabe & Pavela, 2004). Ultimately, student success depends on the positive values they adopt and level of maturity they attain. These aspects of healthy development warrant greater attention in a society that aspires to provide world leadership (Wallace, 2008).

Voices of Adolescents

Fairness and equality are core values that families and schools expect to pass on to youth. However, neither value is conveyed in situations where students are placed at a disadvantage because others cheat. When dishon-esty is common, high achievers cannot distinguish themselves, gaps in learning remain hidden, tutoring needs go undetected, reports of group progress are inaccurate, and schools lack indicators of change that must be made known to trigger institutional improvement. Scandals in the workplace and in government have shown how unethical practices by leaders can erode the public trust, reduce productivity, and motivate cynicism.

Adolescence is the stage of development when most individuals establish their sense of moral direction, define the meaning of commendable behavior and misconduct, and determine relationships they approve of and ways of treating others they reject. For these reasons, adolescents benefit from guidance that leads them to choose integrity to shape their behavior rather than rely on cheating to get ahead (Adams & Hamm, 2006).

After administering the cheating poll for this chapter, you will become aware of how students where you work feel about dishonesty in education. Faculty can reinforce honesty, fairness, and equality better if they know the student experience. Specifically, there is a need to learn the prevalence of dishonesty, reasons why cheating occurs, and forms of deception that cheaters rely on in using technology tools. The poll also identifies circumstances that would cause students to act in dishonest ways, how they react when someone they know is involved with deceptive practices, and punishment they regard as appropriate. Students are also asked to speculate on how their parents and friends would respond to them if they were caught cheating at school. The reasons to avoid cheating are also explored with ways to combat deception in testing and misuse of the Internet.

EXPRESSION AND TOLERANCE OF DIFFERENCES

A fundamental value that is cherished by Americans is allowing everyone to express their thoughts freely and to show tolerance for views that differ from our own. When student disagree in elementary school, teachers and relatives often find it necessary to intervene. However, more responsibility for resolving conflict is expected of adolescents because of the belief that citizens in democracies must be able to accept conflicting opinions, beliefs, and lifestyles. When adolescents learn to manage disagreements, they are better equipped to get along with their families, co-workers, and other members of a diverse community (Twenge, 2006).

Normative Family Conflicts

Family conflicts increase during early adolescence. Children who previously were agreeable now seem to have issues that trigger daily debates. These arguments often relate to procrastination in doing household chores, cleaning an untidy bedroom, monopolizing the bathroom, scheduling transportation, spending beyond a budget, and agreeing about time for curfew. Students in middle school and high school regard these topics as suitable agenda for their struggle to gain independence. The resulting hassles bring pressure on parents to communicate with their children in more equitable ways (Combrinck-Graham, 2006).

Contemporary families also face new challenges. For example, students have to attend school longer than ever before so they cannot leave home at an early an age to be on their own. Many remain in the home of their parents a decade or more after the onset of adolescence. This arrangement means children and parents can anticipate family disagreements for a more extended length of time than has been the norm throughout history (Fogel, Garvey, Hsu, & West-Stromming, 2006). This issue is further explored in chapter 12.

Parents of early adolescents, particularly in Grades 7 and 8, are so involved with current squabbles that they prefer not to think about a forecast of long-term disputes. Surveys of parents identify teenagers as the most difficult age group to guide, providing less satisfaction, greater feelings of inadequacy, and more stress than raising younger children (Apter, 2006). While emotional tension and arguments are normal during adolescence and can facilitate the transition to adulthood, awareness does little to ease the anxiety of parents who sometimes feel that their teenager has a mission to engage them in perpetual arguments (Johnson & Malow-Iroff, 2008).

Models of Disagreement

Parents can be motivated to pursue modeling opportunities when they realize that disagreements can produce benefits. Adolescents are acquiring the ability to examine logic so they monitor the reasoning of others. They practice this newfound ability mostly by debating with parents and educators in conversations. This continual challenge of their ideas can be an exhausting experience for mothers, fathers, and teachers. Those who do not recognize these daily debates as opportunities for sharing feelings and reciprocal learning often attribute the turmoil to the undesirable influence of peers (Harris, 1998). A more accurate appraisal is that youth are motivated to instigate arguments so adults can show them how differences can be dealt with in a civil way (Blumberg, Hare, & Costin, 2006).

More parents should become aware of their unique potential to provide instruction at this stage of development (Tersman, 2006). One father said, "The experiences I had were different from what Larry is going through but my logic still applies to most situations." Giving feedback about their logic is a useful form of advisement even though such lessons may be met by resentment. Above all, parents should strive to demonstrate patience and perseverance rather than anger and frustration that may be expressed by their adolescent. Self-control and self-restraint are needed to resolve complex problems. There is growing awareness that these characteristics may be in decline for all age groups (Baumeister & Tice, 1995).

Early adolescence is an opportune time for parents to model self-conflict, show how they examine and judge themselves. Most parents of teens are 35 to 45 years of age and engaged in self-evaluation. They are attempting to revise goals they chose as young adults to accord with what they want to achieve during middle age. At the same time, their children are becoming able to examine themselves in a critical way. Self-examination requires measuring oneself against criteria that immature classmates are less likely to generate than adults. This process supports dealing with conflict because reflection triggers behavior changes that may be key to resolving disputes (Velleman, 2005).

The internal processes that adults use for self-evaluation can be shown to teenagers by talking out loud in front of them. For example, a series of self-dialogues by a teacher can proceed in this way, "Some things I said to a colleague when we had an argument at work yesterday were unfair. Maybe I should apologize." A day later students hear their teacher report, "I apologized to my colleague and he did the same so we've patched up the relationship. I feel better not staying angry and taking the initiative to say I was sorry." In situations like this, youth get to observe how an adult enacts self-evaluation and takes constructive action (Drucker, 2005).

Generational Differences at Work

Working in teams at school can be easier in some ways for middle school and high school students because teammates are from the same cohort. They were born at around the same time, exposed to many of the same key events, rely on a similar set of references, and tend to embrace similar values. These conditions seem to support the observation that people resemble their times more than they resemble their parents. Certainly, every person has unique experiences but also shares a place in history with others representing their generation (Lancaster & Stillman, 2005). In the twenty-first century there have been some significant changes in demographics of the workforce, resulting in a much broader range of age and value diversity than ever before. Depending on how these differences are perceived, they can either support harmony or promote conflict among employees and thereby affect productivity (Mannix & Neale, 2005; Moses & Chang, 2006).

Americans have increasingly segregated themselves on the basis of age over the past generation. One consequence has been a steady decline in the amount of interaction between older and younger people (Fogel, Garvey, Hsu, & West-Stromming, 2006). Growing up now also differs from the past in that children and adolescents spend far more time with peers. As a result, over half of high school students begin employment with insufficient experience in understanding how to get along with people from other age groups (O'Toole & Lawler, 2006). The initial job is often the first encounter where adolescents have consistent and sustained communication with older adults (M. Johnson, 2006; Lancaster & Stillman, 2005). In addition, each generation has distinctive views and attitudes that define their work ethic, criteria for job promotion, commitment to the company, seniority practices, employee benefits, and ways of talking, thinking, and solving problems (Toffler & Toffler, 2006). The common shift away from organizational stratification has meant younger and older workers are less separated in space and status. In combination, these circumstances present nontraditional difficulties that challenge the well being of everyone (O'Toole & Lawler, 2006). While cultural diversity issues receive a lot of attention in the work place, generational differences are often problematic and deserve attention (Lancaster & Stillman, 2005). Getting along with co-workers of all age groups is essential for productivity. Employees get fired more often because of relationship problems than lack of job skills (Dunning, Heath, & Suls, 2004).

Studies that chronicle workplace interaction show that when younger employees interact with age mates over coffee, the following complaints can be heard in relation to older co-workers. "When he asked me to work overtime, I told him—no way man, I have a life and want to be out of here at 5 o'clock." "My reaction to the supervisor's reminder about showing loyalty to the company was that if you're looking for loyalty, buy a dog." "The manager gets upset because I call him by his first name." "The old guy sends handwritten notes that I am expected to respond to because he doesn't like to use e-mail." "When I suggested that we could do something in a more efficient way, he said we tried that a few years ago and it didn't' work." At the opposite end of the spectrum, older co-workers sometimes describe younger colleagues in these ways. "She disrupts the office by bringing her infant daughter when a babysitter is not available." "He does not demonstrate any loyalty to the company but expects a promotion after being here a few months." "He comes late to meetings and blames it on the traffic." "He claims to want to be a professional yet refuses to wear suitable clothes and instead dresses like a construction worker" (Drucker, 2005; Zemke, Raines, & Filipczak, 2000).

Conflicting norms of behavior can limit productivity and morale. Therefore, high priority is given to making sure that everyone demonstrates the respect and collaboration needed for success (Dunning, Heath, & Suls, 2004). Employers agree that training for interdependence should occur in high school as preparation for entry to the world of work. The qualifications employers look for in recruiting young people include a record of punctuality and attendance, gets along with others, shows willingness to work hard, and demonstrates courtesy. These factors often overshadow school grades (Handel, 2005). High schools are being urged to provide community service activities that give students opportunities to interact with people older than themselves and gain insights while sharing their own ideas and skills as well (Senge Scharmer, Jaworski, & Flowers, 2005). This experience with *intergenerational perspective taking*, becoming aware of and respecting how other age groups see things, is vital for a work setting that is responsive to everyone's needs and offers mutual satisfaction (Goleman, 2006; Mannix & Neale, 2005).

CHARACTER BUILDING

Morality is defined as the conduct society considers to be right and appropriate. Besides preparing students for work, schools are seen as the one place where everyone should be exposed to an orientation on the consensus values and moral standards of society (Nucci, 2008). Therefore, when social problems increase, the public expects schools to act as their agent for corrective intervention. Commentators and journalists urge schools to reduce drug taking, pregnancy, misbehavior in classes, and juvenile crime. Schools are supposed to build character, urge students to obey the laws, and motivate concern for those less fortunate (Russell, 2007; Sternberg, Roediger, & Halpern, 2006). A review of moral education reveals the benefits of varied approaches.

Religion and Citizenship

Early in the nation's history, religious training was the main purpose for schooling. The curriculum and teachers were expected to foster *character development*, qualities of mind and feeling that make a person responsible and contribute to a good reputation (Kirtley, 1919). Disagreement regarding the definitions of morality, standards accepted as proper, became common with the immigration of varied ethnic groups. From 1830–1920, called the "melting-pot" era, *McGuffey Readers* were the texts for 80% of all students attending Grades 1–8 in the public schools (McGuffey, 1989). Over 120 million copies of Reverend William McGuffey's (1800–1873) character building readers were sold, placing them in an exclusive category with *Webster's Dictionary* and *The Bible* (Pulliam & Van Patten, 2006).

The anthologies that McGuffey edited were drawn from literary sources such as *The Bible*, Milton, Longfellow, Shakespeare, Dante, and Dickens. These presentations gave competent readers exemplary values to reflect on but the texts were too difficult for beginners. McGuffey made an effort to match his desired curriculum with child literacy. He met with students of various ages to identify their interests, level of comprehension, and ability to read. Based on these conversations, the book of moral lessons was formulated. This effort to respect limitations of students was the origin of grade level lessons and resulted in McGuffey becoming known as the nation's moral school master. *McGuffey Readers* explored a broad range of moral concerns like love, greed, faith, temptation, conflict, drinking, swearing, wise use of time, and procrastination (Pulliam & Van Patten, 2006). Building character with exemplars from literature remains a popular approach to character development (Carr, 2005).

The goal of an informed public became essential after the Revolutionary War. For a democracy to succeed, people have to be enlightened as well as moral. This broader goal allowed for the addition of new subjects in the curriculum. Another influence involved the battle to free education from sectarian influence, to bring about a separation of church and state. Different faiths competing for prominence had to relinquish claims and consent to secular curriculum before community taxation to support schools could become law (Carter, 2005).

Educational research also influenced a decline of moral instruction at school. By the 1930s, most boards of education knew about studies by Hugh Hartshorne and Mark May (1928) from the University of Iowa. Their research determined that the study of morality, ethics, and religion in the classroom did not prevent lying, stealing, and cheating. Direct teaching of morality fell to its lowest point during the 1950s. Released time became the common replacement method, permitting students with parent permission to leave school for part of one afternoon a week to get moral instruction from their pastor, priest, or rabbi (Power, Nuzzi, Narvaez, Lapsley & Hunt, 2007).

In response to national student unrest in the 1970s, another values approach became prominent (Simon, 1978). The premise was that teaching predetermined right and wrong behaviors to students was no longer appropriate. No teacher has the "right" set of values to convey that will fit other people's children. Instead, the approach called *values clarification* focused on the valuing process rather than on a particular set of values. Students exposed to values clarification could learn to examine their feelings and beliefs so decision making would be conscious, deliberate, and consistent. The rationale for values clarification was supportive of the emerging self-esteem movement that emphasized the importance of individual choice (Raths, Harmin, & Simon, 1966).

Values clarification techniques were widely adopted. Teachers were directed to stop lecturing and discontinue rewards and punishments as methods of imposing adult values. Instead, students had worksheets presenting possible ways of thinking or behaving in response to problems of personal choice. For example, eighth graders were asked: Which freedom would you give up if it became necessary to leave one behind? (a) economic freedom, (b) religious freedom, (c) political freedom (d) freedom of speech, or (e) freedom of privacy? The pros and cons with consequences for each alternative would be weighed based on discussion. The teacher was morally neutral while listening, reflecting, and trying to elicit responses from everyone and ensuring that no one's views were belittled. The guiding assumption was that if students were allowed to make decisions and learn how to evaluate the outcomes of their choices, they would be able to determine their own set of values (Merry, 2005; Nucci, 2008).

Moral Development Theories

Moral Reasoning Theory

Lawrence Kohlberg (1927–1987), psychologist at Harvard, proposed a theory of moral reasoning that includes three levels on which judgments are reached. Kohlberg's (1973, 1975) levels are further divided into six separate stages (see Table 9.1). The preconventional, lowest level of moral reasoning, is reflected by making decisions based upon personal needs and perceptions. Stage 1a reflects the thinking of young children that obey rules only to avoid punishment. During Stage 2b the decision to follow rules is related to a desire to please authorities that have the capacity to provide reward and contribute to self-interest. When students become adolescents, most of them transition to the conventional level of moral reasoning in which the expectations of law and society are given primary consideration (Jacobs & Klaczynski, 2005). Stage 3a gives highest priority to emotional ties with relatives and friends as factors to consider in deciding any course of action. At stage 4b, a law and order emphasis is based on the intent to preserve rights for people of all backgrounds that comprise the nation. Postconventional thinkers decide their moral choices by reliance on underlying principles that are used to guide construction of laws. Stage 5a reasoning emphasizes validity of laws regardless of whether the authorities are present to enforce them and need for safeguards to provide balance between group and individual rights. Stage 6a moral reasoning identifies actions that protect and honor the welfare of all mankind rather than limiting justice to the community or national domain (Kohlberg, 1984).

Table 9.1. Kohlberg's* Theoretical Stages of Moral Development

Age	Stage	Moral Reasoning
		Preconventional Level
		Judgments are related to personal needs and perceptions
4–10	1a	Moral behavior based on fear of physical consequences; avoid punishment by not breaking the understood rules.
	2b	Moral decisions based on pleasing those in power; being obedient to serve self-interest such as receiving rewards.
		Conventional Level
10–20		Judgments consider the expectations of society and law
	3a	Moral judgment based on preserving relations with relatives and friends, avoiding disapproval; Being good is defined by what others expect requiring trust, loyalty, and gratitude;
	4b	Societal expectations and rules are followed because they ensure stability; a law and order orientation defines what is right for everyone to coexist in the larger community.
		Postconventional Level
20+		Judgments are based on principles that go beyond laws
	5a	Moral principles underlying laws are viewed as valid even when authorities are not present to enforce them; focus on balancing protection of individual rights with needs of the majority population.
	6b	Recognition of universal principles of justice, reciprocity, equality of human rights and a respect for human dignity that should be applied by peoples throughout the world.

Source: *Based on Kohlberg (1963, 1971, 1975).

Kohlberg (1973, 1975) maintained that moral reasoning stages are progressive with each reflecting a higher and more mature level of judgment. However, he indicated that individuals advance at various rates and development can become arrested at any stage. There was no claim that cognitive moral reasoning and moral behavior were correlated. A person might reason at one stage but act at a lower stage.

To test his assumptions, Kohlberg (1987) conducted longitudinal research that began with 84 White males, aged 10, 13, and 16. They were administered assessments at regular intervals for 30 years. The method that Kohlberg relied on to evaluate moral reasoning was to present individuals with hypothetical dilemmas. Then he assigned scores based on how a person's responses matched criteria for his hierarchical stages

398 P. S. STROM and R. D. STROM

(Gilliand, 2008). Nine dilemmas were followed by interviews to detect the course of action someone considered right or wrong along with a justification to explain their choices. For example, in one dilemma a woman is dying of cancer. The only possibility to survive is to take a drug that has been proven effective. However, the pharmacist refuses to sell her the prescription below cost. Heinz, the woman's husband, tries to raise money but is able to get only half the amount needed to purchase the drug. Pleading with the pharmacist to show compassion produces no effect. Thus, the dilemma—should Heinz break into the pharmacy to steal the drug to save his wife or stand by and do nothing to prevent her death? (Kohlberg, 1987). Some common real life dilemmas that adolescents face are presented in Table 9.2.

Kohlberg agreed with the advocates of values clarification that moral development is restricted when adults impose values (Merry, 2005). He wanted to radically change the student and teacher roles to create equality in school. He believed that only when all parties have equal status does it become possible to avoid coercion, obedience, and inauthentic behavior. By collaboration with everyone acting as equals, a "Just Community" could be formed and education could be improved (Russell, 2007).

Table 9.2.   Real Life Dilemmas For Adolescents

These dilemmas represent moral decisions that adolescents may face. What additional dilemmas can you identify that should be included on the list?

1. Should I tell the teacher if I know that someone in our class is cheating?
2. Should I try to stop bully behavior I observe or just remain a bystander?
3. Should I go along with friends who want me to do things that are wrong?
4. Should I challenge name-calling and racist statements or overlook them?
5. Should I cheat in school or do the right thing no matter what the cost?
6. Should I send anonymous threat messages to someone that I do not like?
7. Should I turn in the money or valuables that someone left and I found?
8. Should I apologize to someone for things I said or did that were wrong?
9. Should I pass on rumors about someone that can be hurtful to them?
10. Should I skip classes to hang out at the mall with some of my friends?
11. Should I procrastinate in studying for a test scheduled soon at school?
12. Should I tease my classmates because they are tall, short, fat, or thin?
13. Should I listen to hurtful comments about others or challenge them?
14. Should I let friends copy my work so they won't have to do their own?
15. Should I betray the trust of a friend if s/he appears to be in danger?

As an experiment, Kohlberg (1984) set up an alternative school in Cambridge, Massachusetts. This high school included 30 students, 6 teachers, and many volunteers. Participants accepted the possibility that adolescents could transform society if they first had opportunities to influence their education environment. The assumption was that discussion, listening to and respecting the views of others, role-playing, and due process would support the transition to a democratic process. Incidents of theft, drug taking, cheating, and absence from class provided the focus for moral decision making. To judge misconduct, town hall meetings were convened. The process of democratic confrontation made it difficult to reach agreement. Gradually however, more reasoning and less self-interest became a norm. After 5 years, in 1979, the Just Community project ended and the Cluster School closed (Hunt, 2005).

Kohlberg's (1987) experiment with school reform led him to alter his theory of moral reasoning. The amended version excluded stage 6b because no one qualified for this high level of maturity. A meta-analysis of 40 studies provided support for Kohlberg's assumptions about moral reasoning (Snarey, 1985). The most ambitious program at Brookline High School in Massachusetts involved 2,000 students, teachers, administrators, and staff that worked with Kohlberg to combine participatory democracy and moral education (Powers, Higgins, & Kohlberg, 1991). Variations of the Just Community concept have respected the opinions of students and recognized that adolescents should have input to guide institutional change (Block, 2008). Contemporary research suggests that adolescents are less rational than Kohlberg supposed (Reyna & Farley, 2006; Stanovich, 2006).

Ethics of Caring Theory

Carol Gilligan (1936–) was Kohlberg's research assistant until she became disenchanted with the criteria that he used to evaluate moral development (Kohlberg & Gilligan, 1971). Specifically, Gilligan thought that Kohlberg (1) ignored gender differences in the perspective most males and females rely on when processing moral decisions; (2) demonstrated traditional male bias in underestimating the ethical strengths of women; and (3) relied on impractical tasks to judge how ethical choices are made in real life (Gilligan, Ward, & Taylor, 1988).

First, Gilligan contended that gender orientation influences perspective taking in moral choices. Kohlberg's criteria relates to abstract and impersonal justice, rights, and responsibilities. Males typically rely on these criteria in judging themselves as guilty if they do something wrong. In contrast, females tend to use caring as a basis for judging themselves, making moral choices contingent on whether personal actions will produce harm or help others. While Gilligan attributed these perspective differences to gender identity, she acknowledged that these were tendencies with some individuals deviating from their gender norm (Gilligan, 1982).

Gender identity is rooted in early experiences with the person that provides the most nurture, usually a mother. Girls discover that they are like their mothers so growing up is usually defined as taking care of and protecting others. This responsibility requires giving up some freedom of self-expression to attend to the well being of others. Gilligan and Brown (1993) portrayed how 100 White adolescent girls that they interviewed described this internal process. Typically, the girls felt compelled to listen to other voices, including older relatives and friends when making moral decisions implicating loyalty, self-sacrifice, and peacemaking. Looking beyond oneself to broaden moral perspective is supported by neuroscience showing that the frontal cortex, the region of the brain that is responsible for judgment, is perhaps not fully mature until age 25 (Kandel, 2006).

On the other hand, young boys realize that they will never be like their mother and formation of masculine identity depends less on caring relationships than achieving autonomy and competing for status. Concern over the differential in power between themselves and adults motivate boys to assign inequality, individual rights, and justice the highest priority (Sternberg & Jordan, 2005). Because identity is a powerful force in shaping perspective, the gender link is pronounced at the time self-consciousness is maximized in the teen years. The adult outcome is a population of men inclined to see themselves as separate from others so they favor impersonal justice that is unaffected by feelings (Power, Nuzzi, Lapsley, & Hunt, 2007).

Gilligan's second realm of disappointment was that psychology has historically misunderstood women, their motivations and strengths (Capeheart & Milovanovic, 2007). In her view, this customary error was reflected in Kohlberg's moral development theory by underestimating the maturity of females based on their common scoring at stage 3a of his hierarchy. Stage 3a morality is defined by interpersonal relationships, being willing to help and please others with whom one is connected. Gilligan saw this interdependent outlook as a wonderful strength of most women and objected to having it placed one step below stage 4b of the impersonal rules that more often govern male decisions. Kohlberg's (1984, 1987) impression of stage 3a was that this represented ethical relativism, a flip-flop orientation of trying to please everyone. He regarded stage 3a as appropriate for mothers staying home to care for children but saw this view as inappropriate for employed women. In his opinion, employed females must acknowledge the inadequacy of a caring perspective in the workplace and instead strive toward higher stages of morality in which relationships are subordinated to rules (stage 4b) and individual justice (stage 5a) (Kohlberg, 1975).

Gilligan's contention that the interdependent perspective motivating most females warrants greater respect is reinforced by events that emerged since her arguments were framed. *Interdependence* means reliance on mutual assistance, support, and cooperation. This concept has become a prominent goal of societies trying to compete in the global market, students preparing for jobs that require team skills, and families that must consider views of multiple generations to preserve harmony. Perspective taking, listening to how other people feel and the way they see things before deciding actions to be taken are behaviors currently recognized as criteria for leadership and teaching (Butler & Green, 2008; O'Toole & Lawler, 2006). For example, one innovative high school used cooperative learning across the curriculum. After 303 students worked in teams for a semester, they evaluated contributions others had made to group learning and their own development. Both sexes (152 boys, 153 girls) gave the girls higher scores on 23 of 25 social skills needed to perform well in interdependent situations (P. Strom & Strom, 2009).

Gilligan's interviews with adolescent girls shaped her Ethics of Caring Theory presented in Table 9.3 (Gilligan & Brown, 1993). *Ethics* is the study of moral standards and how they affect conduct. According to Gilligan, the central moral concern women face involves internal conflict between their own needs and needs of others. Her theory includes three progressive stages which define changes in the way women perceive self rather than changes in their cognitive ability for moral reasoning. In the preconventional stage, self is the exclusive concern so survival is the focus. Then, a transition occurs that motivates advancement, allowing girls to shift from selfishness outlook to accepting the obligations that enable welfare of others. In the conventional stage, goodness is equated with self-sacrifice. Another transition broadens the concerns for a woman, from goodness to acknowledging that she is an individual with personal needs. In the postconventional stage, the specific needs of self are identified so that a woman becomes able to consider consequences that her behavior may have on others and on herself (Gilligan & Roader-Roth, 2005).

The third concern Gilligan expressed about moral development theory involved use of improbable dilemmas as a basis for judging ethical reasoning. She believed that Kohlberg also overlooked the fact that women generally dislike reacting to hypothetical situations as shown by their inclination to ask questions about a situation, character, and their relationships to discover a solution that would not include any harm. Gilligan preferred real life dilemmas. An example is the moral struggle that some women must contend with when they consider having an abortion. Following the Supreme Court legalization of abortion, in 1973, Gilligan

Table 9.3.   Gilligan's* Stages for an Ethics of Caring

Stage	Goal
Preconventional	Individual survival
	Example: Taking advantage of classmates by cheating to achieve the desired status.
Transition: Advance From Selfishness to Responsibility for Others	
Conventional	Self-sacrifice is good
	Example: Helping classmates with skill deficits by tutoring them instead of devoting time only to personal interests
Transition: Advance From Goodness to the Truth that I am also a Person With Needs	
Postconventional	Nonviolence principle: Do not hurt others or harm oneself
	Example: Telling a hurtful lie can harm another person's reputation while eroding self capacity to show concern for others

Source: An adaptation of *In a Different Voice: Psychological Theory and Women's Development* (1982) by Carol Gilligan. Cambridge, MA: Harvard University Press. Goals and examples developed by Robert Strom and Paris Strom.

interviewed 24 women in the first trimester of their pregnancy that were considering an abortion.

Most of the women were interviewed again a year later. Their discussions about possible courses of action reflected the ethic of care much more than an ethic of justice. They often referred to selfishness and responsibility as a consideration in self debates. Women expressing a preconventional view were egocentric, considering only factors that would help them survive. Women at the conventional stage defined their worth in terms of willingness to accept self-sacrifice, to look out for the welfare of others. Postconventional thinking was reached by only a few of the women who accepted responsibility for their choice while realizing the harm that was bound to occur regardless of what decision was made (Gilligan, Ward, & Taylor, 1988). Although some adolescents have to consider an abortion, teenage girls in general do not confront this dilemma.

Like most theorists, Gilligan has been subject to criticism. Christina Sommers (2001), author of *The War Against Boys*, maintains that Gilligan never followed the standard protocol for doing qualitative research, relied on small, single sex samples, reported findings without subjecting them to peer review, and continues to deny anyone access to the data from which her conclusions are drawn. Nevertheless, Gilligan's theory has led to a broader outlook about moral reasoning in which the ethics of caring should be joined with the ethics of justice (Cohen & Wellman, 2008).

Curriculum and Community Service

By the late 1990s a dramatic rise had been recorded in drug taking and pregnancy for adolescents. Departments of education in most states decided they should no longer remain neutral about the subject of values (Smagorinsky & Taxel, 2005). There was agreement that new curricula should be devised to support personal and social values of people in a democracy, regardless of their religion, income or race (Beachum & McCray, 2005). Thomas Lickona (2004), Professor of developmental psychology at the State University of New York, provides these reasons for efforts to reinstate the goal of character education in public schools:

1. Add meaning to education. Character learning is needed because moral questions are among the dominant issues that are experienced by individuals and nations. There is no value-free education because schools are bound to teach students values every day by design or by default.

2. Sustain and strengthen our culture. Communicating values to students remains one of the most important functions of society. Democracies have a special need for ethical education because this form of government depends upon leadership drawn from the public.

3. Model civility. There is consensus regarding core values of decency, including the need for everyone to embrace honesty, responsibility, self-discipline, compassion, altruism, and perseverance.

4. Build true character. A person of character is trustworthy, treats others with respect, maintains self-control, is fair and just, shows kindness, pursues excellence, and is an all-around desirable citizen.

The most prominent contemporary strategy to foster character development assumes that students must be exposed to emotionally maturing experiences. Being informed about problems through reading or discussion alone does not enable adolescents to become responsive to others who require assistance. As the length of compulsory schooling lengthens, society must ensure that the need to experience responsibility is also met. When students participate in social obligations along with academic assignments, they will more likely show concern for others, continue to mature, and eventually grow up (Holloway, 2006; Putnam & Feldstein, 2003).

This conclusion is reinforced by a study involving 8,000 students and 10,000 of their parents to find out the fears of youth and how accurately mothers and fathers assess such feelings (Benson & Lerner, 2005). It was determined that, by fifth grade, students are much more affected by television news regarding war and natural catastrophes than was supposed by parents. Students are expected to be aware of troubles that occur throughout the world yet schools have been slow to develop constructive ways for boys and girls to respond to such knowledge in a helpful way. Unlike adults, adolescents do not pay taxes, contribute to charitable causes, or view problems from a historical perspective. Instead, they are expected to attend classes, remain informed about contemporary problems, and wait until their generation is in charge. However, when their response to the needs of others is limited to just discussions rather than doing anything constructive, many students experience guilt, frustration, and helplessness. Over time, the inability to act on caring emotions can lead to cynicism. Cynical people doubt the motives, goodness, or sincerity of others, and suppose that there must be a selfish motive for helping someone else (Rizzo & Brown, 2006).

Adults must find ways to keep the caring capacity alive by allowing adolescents to help in solving civic problems in humane and effective ways. *Community service* is a way to attain this goal because it provides responsibility, lets students enact their feelings of compassion, focuses on the local setting as a context for serving others, and invites parent approval (Berkowitz & Bier, 2005). In a survey by the Carnegie Foundation for the Advancement of Teaching, many adolescents expressed feelings of being isolated from the larger world (Jackson & Davis, 2000). This may seem strange given the ready access teenagers have to media enabling them to instantly monitor events anywhere in the world. Instead, what students meant was they disagree with the practice of having 12 years in formal education during which social problems are continually observed, read about, and discussed but never confronted. Instead, there should be expectations to spend time in constructive responsive ways such as tutoring children needing academic help, assisting frail elderly, cleaning up the school environment, or public places (Hebert, Sallee, & Stock, 2008). Emotional detachment can happen at the same time students are supposed to decide who they are and the kind of person they wish to become. The Carnegie Foundation survey led to a recommendation that community service, helping others without remuneration, should be a requirement for high school graduation.

A national cohort of 25,000 eighth graders were followed over a period of 12 years to assess the connection of their secondary school experiences to early adulthood civic participation. The focus was on experiences that can be shaped by education policy such as arranging for opportunities in community service, extracurricular activities, and acquisition of civic knowledge. The main finding is that community service in high school is a strong predictors of adult voting and volunteering. There was also evidence that urging student involvement in extracurricular activities is a good choice by policymakers interested in grooming adolescents for citizenship (Hart, Donnelly, Youniss, & Atkins, 2007).

Adolescents are often described as idealists. An *idealist* is someone who aspires to high standards and principles. Idealism should not be an exclusive adolescent perspective that adults outgrow. Because there can be no maturity without ideals, the duration of idealism should extend from adolescence until death. Societies can control more aspects of the future than ever before so long-range planning is recognized as a necessity. This means that being idealistic and being practical should no longer be seen as incompatible. Unless youth are allowed to connect ideals with behavior, and thereby enact their caring aspirations while still attending school, ideals might be left behind. And, the cost is considerable because to lack ideals as an adult is to lack moral direction. Adolescents prefer to retain their ideals, commit themselves to great causes and be responsive to community needs. Families, churches, and schools should support this desire (Hebert, Sallee, & Stocks, 2008; Laursen, 2005; Reeb, 2006). The Corporation for National and Community Service involves all ages to strengthen communities—http://www.nationalservice.org.

Values as a Predictor of Success

The media often presents stories about people whose poverty places them at risk for failure. Less common are reports regarding persons that succeed despite their low-income origins. This group includes immigrants from Southeast Asian whose record shows that values can often be a more accurate predictor of academic achievement for children and financial success for adults than socioeconomic status. For 5 years, a University of Michigan team conducted multiple interviews with 7,000 immigrants to the United States from Viet Nam, Cambodia, and Laos (Caplan, Choy, & Whitemore, 1996). The purpose was to find out how adaptation to a new homeland was influenced by prior cultural concepts regarding ways to approach difficult challenges of life.

A list of 26 cultural values were presented to the immigrants whose task was to rate each value, using a five scale ranging from "this value is very important for me" to "this value is not important for me." Three of the values were chosen by 98% of people as very important to them. These core values consisted of education and achievement, a cohesive family and hard work. Another group of values were identified as normative, based upon 90% of respondents identifying them as "important" or "very important." These eight normative values were: family loyalty, freedom, morality and ethics, carry out obligations, restraint and discipline, respect for elders, perpetuate ancestral lineage, and cooperative and harmonious family.

It was found that certain values could predict economic achievement and academic success. Those who gave high ratings to "the past is as important as the present," "seeks new experiences," and "security and comfort" came from households where the average annual income was 125% of the poverty level and the children had an average grade point of B+ in school. In contrast, parents who regarded these values as "not very important" earned incomes that were 70% of poverty and their children had grade point averages of B− in school. These outcomes suggest that the newcomers most likely to succeed are those with the strongest respect for their past and its application to challenges of life in the present, are willing to try new ways to deal with unfamiliar demands, and give priority to physical well being and freedom from danger.

Two values were inversely related to achievement. Nearly 95% of parents and children ranked "material possessions" and "fun and excitement" at the bottom of their list. In contrast, people that identified these values as being "very important" had much lower family incomes and their children recorded lower grade point averages in school. These values of "material possessions" and "fun and excitement" were observed by immigrants to be "very important" to their nonimmigrant neighbors. Because most of the participants lived in poor neighborhoods at the time of their arrival in the United States and were no better off financially than others in their neighborhood, this contrast likely reinforced common impressions of what it takes to get ahead.

The relationship of values to achievement reveals that certain aspects of the culture that immigrants brought with them served as valuable mechanisms for adjustment to making a living and learning in school. Boys and girls are not born with a sense of their heritage; they acquire it because of conscious and focused effort by their parents. The close agreement between value ratings reported by the parents and their children (correlation of .83) confirms parents achieved the goal of transmitting their culture. When questioned about the greatest obstacles to becoming successful in the new environment, 65% of parents and 98% of children reported lack of English proficiency.

This study of immigrants reveals a need to become more accurate about defining the problem of nonachievement in schools, reconsider the role of family influence and cultural pluralism in education, and recognize the potential parents have to support child learning. The outstanding academic performance of students who attended the same classrooms that are often identified as inadequate to support the education of nonimmigrants suggests that the capacity of schools to provide instruction remains viable. Even though few of the students were living with single-parents or in blended families, many had undergone traumatic separation from relatives and were limited in previous exposure to English. Except for mathematics, their curriculum in Indochina focused mainly on nonwestern languages and subject matter. Despite such limitations, students attained high performance in the classroom. These findings confirm that schools can educate students from low income and culturally diverse backgrounds.

It seems justified to speculate that the family and its value priorities represents a more profound influence than instructional reforms introduced by the schools. The rationale for this hypothesis is that, because the immigrants attended schools in Los Angeles, Chicago, Seattle, Houston, and Boston, they experienced diverse teaching methods and access to resources and yet performed uniformly well. These outcomes clearly attribute to noncognitive factors of their family and cultural background. Predictions of achievement that rely only on intelligence and aptitude scores would not have been as accurate as the values were in this investigation (Caplan, Choy, & Whitemore, 1996). More assessments of this kind in which cultural values and family interaction have a central role should be used to improve learning and success for students.

Asians generally have different assumptions about education than Americans. When students, parents, and teachers from Asia are asked to identify the most important factor contributing to academic success, they always mention "hard work" whereas Americans often believe intelligence is the key to success. As a result, Asians push their children and children push themselves because they believe that effort makes a great difference. Asians assume that almost everyone can achieve success with the required subjects. Their justification for holding such high expectations is the level of success that is attained by most Asian students (Baker & LeTendre, 2005).

In contrast, Americans are inclined to suppose that some fugitive proportion of students cannot perform well because they lack intelligence or are constrained by some special challenge. Consequently, their academic deficits cannot be overcome just by increasing personal effort. Generally such students are thought to suffer from one of an ever-expanding list of vaguely defined learning disabilities (Spear-Swerling & Sternberg, 1998).

Another common explanation for failure already described is that most students cannot succeed because they come from low-income families. These assumptions have been used to support compensatory programs such as Head Start and programs of special education for many years. In contrast, the lesson from the immigrant study is that poor people are not all the same and those who adhere to particular values are not likely to remain poor for long. Immigrants and other minorities become successful because of the values that govern their behavior even when they have meager financial means. Recall the closer correlation of values with the grades of students than the association between grades and family income. The same conclusion held true of success for adults. Immigrants who valued their past (the source of their values) as much as the present earned higher incomes than peers who chose to depreciate and abandon their past. Values are nonintellectual factors that have a significant impact on success throughout life.

Values and Delinquent Behavior

Values can favorably influence other aspects of well-being than academic achievement and income. The largest investigation to assess causes of crime and delinquency took place in Chicago (Sampson, 2008). Chicago was selected as the target site because this city closely matches racial, ethnic, economic, and social characteristics of the nation as a whole. After Chicago was divided into 350 neighborhoods, interviews were conducted with 9,000 residents. It was determined that, in neighborhoods with a strong sense of community values, crime rates were much lower. The report concluded that, by far, the largest predictor of violent crime was level of *collective efficacy*, a term reflecting common values, trust, and cohesion among people in the neighborhood

The Project on Human Development in Chicago Neighborhoods found that the most important characteristic of collective efficacy is a willingness by residents to intervene in the lives of all children from their neighborhood. This means that adults take action to stop juvenile misbehavior as soon as it appears even in the mildest of forms such as skipping school, writing graffiti, and disorderly conduct demonstrated by gangs. Corrective responses by adults emanate from a shared vision that intervention is necessary and requires everyone to show social trust, a sense of engagement, and ownership of public space. The findings are considered significant since they challenge the prevailing theory that crime can be mainly attributed to poverty, unemployment, single parenting, and racial discrimination. Certainly such factors make it difficult to maintain cohesion. However, some neighborhoods in Chicago that are largely black and poor have low rates of crime. Therefore, other explanations are needed to account for the causes of delinquent behavior and violent crime. Values of families and communities seem to be key factors (Sampson, 2008).

SUMMARY

Cheating in School

High rates of cheating, even among honor students, reveals moral development is not keeping pace with other areas of mental development. In response, initiatives are underway to motivate ethical behavior and define conditions of integrity that should apply to govern student conduct. Explanations for why so many students engage in academic misconduct include erosion of ethics throughout society, reaction to high stakes testing, pressures from parents to excel, and a desire to get ahead regardless of the cost. Schools should poll students to detect prevalence of cheating, reactions to deceptive behavior, personal definitions of cheating and involvement, and ways to reduce misconduct that makes progress reports on individual and group achievement inaccurate. Technology to detect cheating, devising multiple versions of tests, teacher surveillance, and provision of alternative forms of assessment deserve consideration. Faculties should devise ways to police themselves because some individuals give students answers to raise scores. The emergence of companies that monitor test security and detect fraud is a necessary form of protection.

Internet Ethics

Everyone needs training to understand their ethical behavior obligations on the Internet. There are Web sites that offer students, for free or a price, term papers that can be submitted in school so they do not have to write their own. Consequently, plagiarism presents teachers with situations of uncertainty over whether they are grading students on their work or efforts of someone else. Educators are reluctant to express their doubts about the dishonesty of any student without absolute proof because they are fearful of retribution from parents and the administration. To assist the teachers, schools pay for services that can detect plagiarism. Another way to reduce cheating is for teachers to devise more challenging assignments in which students defend or oppose particular views and offer opportunities for reciprocal learning as generational reporters or cultural reporters gathering input from relatives or other sources. Use of legalistic syllabi that clearly state school policy and tough punishment for students participating in deceptive practices can influence thinking and motivate responsible behavior. Instruction is necessary as well. Students are able to recognize that becoming mature cannot be achieved unless they demonstrate fairness and equality toward others. They should become acquainted with cyber laws, why these are needed, and situations that could place decision making on punishment for school offenses in the courts instead of the schools. There is also a need to educate parents with agenda for family discussions about the importance of honesty, trust, and integrity.

Expression and Tolerance of Differences

A fundamental value of democracies is allowing everyone to make their opinion known without fear of rejection. Teaching this value becomes important in adolescence when conflicts with adults accelerate and students initiate a struggle to be independent. The emerging ability to monitor logic motivates adolescents to engage adults in frequent quarrels. These confrontations can have value because they provide a chance to practice debating skills needed for constructive conflict. Parents should realize that arguments give them opportunities to demonstrate problem solving and show tolerance for opposing views. There is also merit in modeling self-conflict, allowing daughters and sons to witness how adults examine and judge themselves. A capacity to introspect emerges in adolescence so youth benefit from the adoption of healthy criteria for self-evaluation. They also benefit from recognizing that this form of assessment is often the key to conflict resolution because reflection can produce changes in personal behavior.

Character Building

Values instruction in schools has reflected societal transformation. When public education was established, religious training was the main emphasis. Student readings were chosen to reinforce moral principles. Later, legislation to separate church and state caused schools to shift to teaching the values of being responsible citizens. A succession of education reforms has taken place since 1950. One approach was to schedule weekly school time for faith-based learning provided by family chosen religious leaders. Another practice involved values clarification in which students considered scenarios, discussed options, and stated reasons for their personal choices. In the past decade, districts have offered a range of character education courses including ethics and comparative religion. The most popular strategy to support responsibility and social maturity is a requirement for community service.

CLASSROOM APPLICATIONS

1. Extensive schooling does not ensure that students will choose honesty and ethical behavior as a lifestyle. These aspects of development depend more on exposure to tasks that are emotionally maturing than academic study alone. Giving students opportunities to respond directly to social problems by community service generates concern for welfare of others, keeps the caring capacity alive, and provides the satisfaction of meeting needs.

2. Character development is motivated by observation of commendable behavior. This is why the public expects teachers to behave as models of honesty and integrity, maintain ethical standards, and, when problems arise, offer nonacademic lessons that contribute to growing up. Teachers have the awesome responsibility to consistently demonstrate maturity for impressionable observers.

3. Class discussions often stimulate arguments among students eager to express strongly held opinions. Such conditions are ideal for teachers to encourage and monitor respectful listening, allow speakers to state their ideas without interruption, provide the interpretation of what someone has said to confirm that it corresponds with the message a speaker intended to convey, and invite comments about what is learned from others that have explained their different points of view.

4. Teachers, students, parents, administrators, and librarians should make a concerted effort to reform the school culture from one where cheating is ignored or tolerated to an environment where creative initiatives are taken that emphasize the values of honesty, fairness, and equality. Faculties can develop agenda for dialogue about moral issues in school and family discussion that can support progress in becoming responsible adults.

5. Educators can reduce the odds that students will portray the work of others as being their own by preparing assignments that require higher order thinking in response to issues studied during class. Students can be asked to oppose or support propositions and ideas, requiring them to engage in evaluation. Challenge them to demonstrate an ability to synthesize by preparing a list of questions that can be answered based on the lessons in class and a related list

of questions they are unable to answer. Scenarios and cases can be presented for which students select and justify the best answer or generate alternative solutions with their explanation. Brainstorming practice is a good way to start because the process requires suspending judgment.

6. The tendency to interpret every disagreement as a competition where the only goal is to defend one's point of view is a narrow outlook and can prevent the reflective processing of another person's perspective. Teachers should encourage students to recognize that taking the time to weigh opinions that differ from our own is essential to appreciate diversity, cause us to change our minds, and adopt new paradigms to guide behavior.

7. Teachers have a responsibility to identify outstanding academic performance so hardworking students remain committed to studies and have confirmation that their achievements are valued. This motivational aspect of teaching can have greater impact when corresponding efforts are devoted to discouraging as well as detecting cheating. In this way, undeserving students are less likely to get academic distinction under false pretenses.

8. Students disagree with the school tradition of reading about, observing and discussing social problems but never actually confronting them. They want teachers to blend studies with community service tasks that enable them to grow by spending time tutoring children with deficiencies, visiting the frail and isolated, and taking responsibility to improve the community. Emotional detachment undermines personality development by allowing individuals to remain egocentric and not develop a concern for others.

9. Helping teenagers live with disagreement should include careful consideration and adoption of specific conflict goals, the desire to strive toward their attainment, and a willingness to consider feedback about personal progress from parents and teachers who observe them on a regular basis. Giving attention to this domain of development is more often seen as important when teachers reveal the conflict goals that they are still trying to reach as educated adults.

10. Educators should always be willing to apologize to their students, colleagues or anyone that they may offend. When teachers do not acknowledge their mistakes, students may refer to such behavior as a justification for their own similar actions. Reaching out to make amends, asking for forgiveness, and seeking reconciliation to

restore harmonious relationships is a sign of humility, one of the important aspects of maturity.

11. School initiatives to support character development should provide students opportunities to discuss, consider, and apply suitable criteria for self -evaluation. Many students admit that they cheat on academic work yet still consider themselves satisfied with their ethic and character. This contradiction suggests that there is a need to revise the criteria students rely on to declare personal success. Although educators are reluctant to permit self-evaluation related to classroom performance, it is pertinent to promote such involvement to improve self-perception of ethical progress.

12. Teachers and administrators that break the rules for administering tests so that scores of their students improve are increasingly obliged to resign their position, lose certification, and have their identity revealed to the public. Educators cannot justify misconduct with claims of trying to help students perform well. With a rise in number of security breaches, some districts are employing independent test proctors or hiring organizations that monitor test fraud by erecting barriers to unauthorized access and applying Web patrolling tools that assess answer patterns that detect cheaters.

FOR REFLECTION

1. How is helping students acquire values easier and more difficult than in the past?

2. Parents rank honesty and truthfulness as the most important qualities they want to convey to children yet students commonly admit to cheating in school. Describe some possible solutions.

3. Describe some advantages of including in your student orientation a set of guidelines for conducting conflict when disagreements arise during the class.

4. What are some ways you could incorporate community service into assignments?

5. Explain your view on whether honesty could become a norm in secondary education.

6. How could the "Just Community" concept be adapted to fit your school?

7. Adolescents commonly admit to cheating on school work but express satisfaction with their ethical development. Speculate on why students do not recognize the contradiction.

8. Some reasons for cheating are " I didn't have time to do the work;" "This subject is not important to me;" Everyone else is cheating; " and "I must get good grades." Comment on each of these explanations.

9. Parents sometimes act as advocates for misbehaving students. What factors will you consider in dealing with parents that seek confrontation?

10. Schools have performed poorly in curbing plagiarism. How do you feel about law enforcement handling justice in such cases instead of schools?

11. Describe some types of assignments that you intend to give students that will minimize plagiarism.

12. What punishment seems appropriate for educators that cheat to raise test scores of their students?

13. Identify some topics that could be helpful in an ethics course designed for secondary school students.

KEY TERMS

Character development
Cheating
Collective Efficacy
Community Service
Cyber legislation
Cynics
Data Forensics
Dishonesty
Ethics
Honesty
Idealist
Integrity
Interdependence
Intergenerational Perspective Taking
Morality
Plagiarism
Released Time
Values
Values Clarification

VISIT THESE WEB SITES

Link to these sites at http://www.infoagepub.com/strom-adolescents

Academic Term Papers http://academictermpapers.com

Center for Academic Integrity http://www.academicintegrity.org

Corporation for National and Community Service
http://www.nationalservice.org

Film for Discussion: The Emperors Club http://
www.theemperorsclub.com

Turn It In, Plagiarism Prevention http://www.turnitin.com

Josephson Institute, Ethics of American Youth 2008 Survey
http://charactercounts.org/programs/reportcard/

Bruce Leland, Plagiarism and the Web
http://www.wiu.edu/users/mfbhl/wiu/plagiarism.htm

Modern Cheating Methods
http://abcnews.go.com/
search?searchtext=modern%20cheating%20methods&type

School Sucks, Warehouse of Term Papers
http://www.schoolsucks.com/

Ronald Standler, Plagiarism in Colleges in USA
http://www.rbs2.com/plag.htm

University of California at Berkeley,
Preventing Academic Dishonesty
http://teaching.berkeley.edu/bgd/prevent.html

Steven Wright Comedy
http://www.weather.net/zarg/ZarPages/stevenWright.html
and http://www.steven-wright.com

EXERCISES AND ROLES

Exercise 9.01: Cheating Poll

Role: Voter

The purpose of this poll is to find out how students at your school feel about cheating, plagiarism, and other forms of academic dishonesty.

Directions: Select the answer(s) that describes how you feel. In some cases, you may select more than one answer. If an answer you want to give is not listed, write it on the line marked 'other.' Your responses are anonymous and may be combined with those of other students at your school in a report to students, faculty, and parents.

1. How common do you suppose cheating is among your classmates?

    (a)   the majority of them do it
    (b)   my guess is half of the class
    (c)   less than half of the class
    (d)   hardly any of the students

2. How common do you suppose cheating is among adults you know?

    (a)   the majority of them do it
    (b)   my guess is half of them
    (c)   less than half of them
    (d)   hardly any of the adults

3. How often do you cheat or plagiarize on schoolwork?

    (a)   daily
    (b)   weekly
    (c)   monthly
    (d)   never

4. What method do you think teachers use to detect cheating at your school?

    (a)   software
    (b)   reporting by other students
    (c)   comparing assignments with other teachers
    (d)   I don't know
    (e)   other

5. Which of these behaviors do you think of as cheating?

    (a)   taking information from the Internet without citing the source
    (b)   copying the answers someone else has already completed
    (c)   allowing a friend to copy the work that I have finished

    (d)   having other people do my assignments for me
    (e)   other

6.   How should students who are caught cheating be treated?

    (a)   have a discussion with their teacher and parent
    (b)   they should receive a lower grade for the course
    (c)   place them on in-school or at-home suspension
    (d)   require them to take a class on ethical behavior
    (e)   other

7.   What circumstances might cause you to cheat at school?

    (a)   to get the kind of grades that I need
    (b)   to make up for not studying enough
    (c)   I would not cheat in any circumstance
    (d)   being overscheduled with things to do
    (e)   other

8.   If you knew a classmate was cheating, how would you react?

    (a)   report the incident to one of the teachers
    (b)   tell the student that it is wrong and to stop
    (c)   ignore the person and not take any action
    (d)   other

9.   The main reasons students give for cheating are

    (a)   I need good grades to get into college
    (b)   there is not enough time to do the work
    (c)   everyone else is cheating
    (d)   this course is not important to me
    (e)   other

10.   If my parents knew I had cheated with schoolwork, they would

    (a)   be disappointed and discuss the incident
    (b)   punish me
    (c)   defend my actions
    (d)   ignore the situation
    (e)   other

11. Sometimes I have lied to teachers in order to

    (a) postpone taking a test
    (b) turn an assignment in late
    (c) explain a reason for being absent
    (d) improve my grade in a course
    (e) I never lie to any teachers

12. The way(s) that I cheat in school are with

    (a) handheld device
    (b) cell phone
    (c) iPod/ MP3 player
    (d) hidden notes
    (e) term papers from the Web
    (f) I don't cheat

13. The reasons that keep me from cheating are

    (a) my moral beliefs about doing what is right
    (b) fear that the teacher might catch me
    (c) feeling competent to achieve on my own
    (d) awareness that I can learn what is required
    (e) other

14. My philosophy about cheating is that

    (a) it is ok to cheat if you do not get caught
    (b) cheating means having less work to do
    (c) everyone else does it so why not me too
    (d) cheaters do not succeed in the long run
    (e) other

15. Which of these methods could reduce cheating?

    (a) having open book tests and allow use of notes
    (b) taking oral tests so no other resources are used
    (c) giving unannounced tests that surprise students
    (d) other

16. The way I feel after getting a good grade or test score that I did not earn because of cheating is

    (a)   I feel ok because my goal is good grades
    (b)   I have feelings of guilt for a short time
    (c)   I don't give the matter a second thought
    (d)   I just hope the teacher will not find out
    (e)   I don't cheat so I feel good about my work

Select your grade level, gender, ethnicity, and age.

My grade level is 5 6 7 8 9 10 11 12
My gender is female male
My ethnicity is Asian Black Hispanic Native American White Other
My age is 10 11 12 13 14 15 16 17 18 19

Exercise 9.02: Adoption of Values

Role: Generational Reporter

Transmission of values has been viewed as a responsibility of adults to pass their lifestyle on to younger people. However, in a rapidly changing society, there may be some values that adolescents should pass on to adults. List some prevalent values among teenagers that you think more adults should consider learning. Justify each of your recommendations.

Exercise 9.03: Teach The Wright Things—Top 10 List

Role: Challenger and Evaluator

Your mission: As secondary teachers, you need practice in deciding what kinds of things are acceptable and unacceptable for sharing with adolescent students when giving examples of works in literature, poetry, songs lyrics, art images, body gestures, your own humor, school dress code, or body movements in dance, cheer, theater or sports. Here is a way to begin "on the same page." Explore two Web sites and read the comedy material of Steven Wright at: http://www.steven-wright.com/ and http://www.weather.net/zarg/ZarPages/stevenWright.html. Much of Wright's work is acceptable for adolescents. Teens enjoy his humor and consider him to be highly creative. However, there may be an occasional joke of his that you would hesitate to share with this age group, especially in school settings, because of possible unacceptability (age inappropriateness) for one reason or another. It is inevitable that you will have to do this for (on behalf of) your own students and their parents.

First, write down the five best jokes based on creativity (most clever and acceptable as well) you could share with teenagers. Second, record the five jokes you might not feel comfortable sharing with them. For each unacceptable joke, explain why it is unacceptable (sexual overtones, too violent, etc.). The explanation will allow teammates to understand your choices. Submit the assignment double-spaced with the jokes recorded verbatim. We will share and compare in class!

Exercise 9.04: Living With Conflict

Role: Discussant

1. Why do you suppose so many people are fearful of involvement with interpersonal conflict?
2. How did parents feel about conflicting in your presence when you were a child? A teenager? Now?
3. How do you feel about expressing differences with another adult in front of your students?
4. We seldom view conflict of adolescents in terms of benefit. Identify some conflicts they experience and suggest possible outcomes that implicate personality development.
5. Which goals of conflict learning are more possible to reach at home? at school?
6. In what ways do changes resulting from technology stimulate conflict? How might these types of conflict contribute to emotional growth?

Exercise 9.05: Heroes as Models

Role: Cultural Reporter

Heroes are often drawn from cultural history and mythology. They are a powerful source of motivation that adolescents look to imitate before they establish their personal course of direction. Talk with someone who is well informed about your culture to identify past and present figures that your ancestors and living relatives looked to as sources of inspiration. Identify some commendable attributes of each hero and share with teammates.

1. Who are the heroes from our culture in literature? Television? Real life?

2. What qualities make these heroes models that we should want to follow?

3. What things does our culture have in common with these heroes?

4. Why do you suppose heroes are such an important part of our lives?

5. In what ways have heroes influenced the way that you behave?

6. If you could meet one of your heroes, what questions would you ask?

7. How do other family members feel about the heroes that you admire?

8. How has your choice of heroes changed as you have grown older?

9. Who do your age peers seem to choose most often as their heroes?

10. What kind of behavior should society expect of heroes in private life?

Exercise 9.06: Goals for Living With Conflict

Role: Discussant

Students need to know how they can live with conflict. When this goal is stated in general terms, it seems vague or overwhelming. However, if the goal is divided in smaller tasks, a more comprehensive picture emerges to deal with disagreements. Show this list of conflict goals to adolescents and ask them to identify the ones they are trying to attain. Then, share goals on the list that you are currently striving to reach.

Conflict Goals

- Recognizing that people who love each other may experience conflicts

- Learning to share possessions as well as to take turns with other people

- Realizing that respect for personal property is a way to reduce conflict

- Helping others may involve conflict, by not watching and standing back

- Deciding to talk things over instead of trying to settle issues by fighting

- Being able to accept changes in people that we would wish to prevent
- Knowing that self-conflict is essential for moral behavior (conscience)
- Developing the ability to respect others by willingness to compromise
- Being able to accept defeat when it is the outcome of some competition
- Having the will power to stand alone when it seems necessary to do so
- Accepting that living with a certain amount of uncertainty is necessary
- Finding ways to disagree without suffering a loss in status or affection
- Being willing to apologize after making hurtful comments about anyone
- Realizing that there may be some differences that are irreconcilable
- Listening to others while they express contrary feelings or opinions
- Analyzing the conditions needed to result in mutual reconciliation
- Sharing dominance and demonstrating an ability to be cooperative
- Coping with complex situations that offer unfamiliarity and anxiety
- Learning to assert personal opinions without having feelings of guilt
- Perceiving differences as possible opportunities for reciprocal learning

Exercise 9.07: Values and Political Correctness

Role: Generational Reporter

Should Americans have the right to be protected from comments in opposition to their lifestyle or beliefs? The stated purpose of political correctness is to reduce the disappointment some would otherwise endure as victims of insensitive others. Another viewpoint is that political correctness prevents the expression of free speech and discussion about controversial issues. When columnists or talk show hosts are critical of ideologies, they can expect to be accused of intolerance, bigotry, or racism. In the past the United States was distinctive among nations because people were comfortable stating feelings that did not accord with those of the government. Interview an adolescent using these questions

1. What are your impressions about following political correctness?
2. How does political correctness affect any of the people you know?
3. What are your predictions about the future of political correctness?
4. How does political correctness differ from political censorship?

Exercise 9.08: Community Service as an Obligation

Role: Challenger

A group of parents believe that their adolescent daughters or sons should not have to participate in a community service program at school. Because the program is involuntary, parents see it as coercion. You are on a faculty panel that will meet with these parents. What perspective will you provide about the value of community service for secondary school students?

Exercise 9.09: Ethical Code of Conduct for Students

Role: Evaluator

Obtain a copy of the Student Code of Conduct from a secondary school.

Examine the document for the following conditions and share in class.

1. Aspects of ethical behavior for which students are accountable
2. Description of the reasoning for requiring particular expectations
3. Referral sources for students or families wanting code clarification
4. Your suggestions to improve the code and processes used with it

Exercise 9.10: A New Government Department

Role: Improviser

Looking at situations in new ways can sometimes produce more effective solutions. Suppose that Congress were to establish a new component called the Department of Immigrant Education.

List some (a) anticipated benefits and (b) anticipated disadvantages of this strategy.

PART IV

HEALTH EXPECTATIONS

CHAPTER 10

PHYSICAL HEALTH
AND LIFESTYLE

Parents are the decision makers that society expects to protect the welfare of young children. This situation changes somewhat in adolescence when boys and girls assume greater responsibility for choices that could influence their health. They benefit by adopting guidelines that support having a nutritious diet, regular exercise, and weight management. Refusing to take drugs or risk sexually transmitted diseases are added safeguards. The goals for this chapter are to describe patterns of normative growth, discuss nutrition, consider the dangers of early sexual activity, suggest ways to encourage decisions about smoking, drinking, drug taking, and identify reasons why adolescents should give high priority to personal care and well being (Federal Interagency Forum on Child and Family Statistics, 2008). The choice of lifestyle habits is key to development of a healthy body and mind.

GROWTH AND DEVELOPMENT

Adolescence is characterized by uneven physical growth in height and weight. These changes and variance cause youth to compare themselves with others of their gender. Such comparisons, combined with idealized physical expectations portrayed by the media, often motivate a

---

Adolescents in the Internet Age, pp. 427–470

427

preoccupation with personal appearance and body image. Boys and girls differ in their timing of puberty. This transition in sexual maturation presents parents and schools with the need to introduce accurate information about sexual development and appropriate expectations for behavior. Student learning is enhanced by good vision but sight problems often go undetected unless regular screening is arranged and teachers observe for difficulties. Hearing loss requires prevention and treatment so students are not disadvantaged in understanding instruction or interacting effectively with classmates.

Height and Weight

Many adolescents feel insecure because they are shorter or taller than friends or classmates. Schools should inform all students that the physical growth rate is not the same for everyone in their age group. Understanding that being normal does not mean being exactly alike is more helpful than to avoid discussions about physical differences which create anxiety (Darst & Pangrazi, 2008). Consider that a physical growth spurt typically begins about age 10 or 11 for girls and peaks by age 12. Most girls stop growing around age 15 or 16. In contrast, the growth spurt for boys begins at age 12 or 13, peaks at 14, and usually ends by age 19. Consequently, for a brief period in middle school, girls are taller than boys of their age. However, at the peak of their growth spurt, boys grow faster than girls, sometimes 3 to 4 inches a year. A sure sign of the growth spurt is that a youngster has outgrown shoes or clothes, again (Gilbert, 2006). During growth spurts limbs grow at different rates, leaving teens relatively uncoordinated and clumsy. Sometimes growth is so rapid that the connective tissues of tendons and ligaments tighten. For young athletes this means that they should stretch before involvement with playing sports or growth-related pain is felt in the knees and lower legs. Many athletes report discomfort in these areas until their bones stop growing (Ripkin & Woolf, 2006).

Growth processes are accelerating throughout the world. Adolescents in North American, Europe, and the other advanced nations are taller and heavier than previous generations. In the United States, on average, boys grow to become 1-inch taller and 10-pounds heavier than their fathers. Similarly, girls typically become 1-inch taller and 5-pounds heavier than their mothers. These generational differences might be even greater were it were not for the fact that puberty starts earlier and growth ends correspondingly early (Sun, Schubert, Liang, Roche, & Chumlea, 2005).

Height is not the only physical change that happens during adolescence. While growth spurts occur, both sexes evidence collection of fat on the buttocks and around the abdomen. Boys, however, mostly gain muscle and bone whereas girls add more fat, particularly in their hips and breasts. The result is that about 25% of the total body weight for girls is fat while fat accounts for only 15 to 20% of the total body weight for boys (Shannon, 2006).

Sexual Maturation

Puberty, the time when sexual reproduction first becomes possible, is the biological onset of adolescence. This sexual maturation process starts a couple years earlier for girls than for boys. The changes in girls may begin anytime between ages 8 to 13, while sexual changes in boys typically occur from ages 9 to 14 (Asby, 2005). Parents whose daughters or sons are entering puberty should have conversations that are informative, allow for questions of all kinds, and reduce anxiety. A source to suggest for families as they begin this dialogue is at http://www.4parents.gov/.

The male body prepares for a biological transformation by creating additional androgen hormones. These hormones, made primarily by the testicles, produce the physical changes of puberty. A familiar indicator of change is the presence of pubic hair at the base of the penis. There is also enlargement and darkening of the scrotum. These alterations occur well before physical growth reaches its peak. Although a penis can become erect from infancy, it is generally not until 2 years following the onset of puberty and 1 year after the penis begins to lengthen that it becomes capable of ejaculating semen. Beginning ejaculation is sometimes spontaneous in reaction to a sexual fantasy, a nocturnal emission, or the outcome of masturbation (Pfiefer & Middleman, 2006).

Another visible change in males is that hair begins to appear under the arms and on the face. As the voice box enlarges, the Adam's apple is more observable. There is a corresponding change as the voice shifts to a deeper tone with periodic cracking as the higher younger voice continues to be heard. During the sexual maturation period lasting four or five years, the testicles continue to enlarge while the penis grows longer and thicker. By the end of the process, the testicles, penis, and pubic hair are developed and facial hair appears that can form a beard or moustache (Madaras, 2007a).

Sexual changes in girls occur because of the increase in hormones produced by ovaries and adrenal glands. The initial visible change is either origin of breast development or the appearance of light pubic hair. Girls need to know that the two breasts do not typically grow at the same rate.

Even when breasts are fully developed, they are unlikely to be exactly the same size. When breast growth is underway for about a year, the overall physical growth reaches its peak. A year after this spurt, girls experience the *Menarche*, their first menstrual period. *Menstruation* is a monthly process of discharging blood and other matter from the womb that occurs between puberty and menopause in women who are not pregnant (Asby, 2005; Madaras, 2007b).

Menstruation signals a need for parents to discuss sexual behavior and contraception. The National Campaign to Prevent Teen and Unplanned Pregnancy (2006a, 2006b) reports that only 29% of girls and 34% of boys report having conversations with parents about condoms. Studies show that parents overwhelmingly support sex education in schools (Ito, Gizlice, Owen-O'Dowd, Foust, Leone, & Miller, 2006). Parents also have an obligation to talk with adolescents about tough issues (Kaiser, 2005a). Talking With Kids About Tough Issues is a national campaign providing resource agenda for parent/adolescent discussions, available at http://www.talkingwithkids.org./

There may be occasional increase in white or yellow vaginal discharge during the months preceding first menstruation. Girls should be aware that their menstrual periods might be irregular the first year with an average cycle consisting of a 3- to 7-day period that occurs every 24 to 34 days. The first few menstrual periods are not painful but over half of all later adolescent girls suffer mild abdominal cramps during the first day or two of their periods. About 10% experience such pain that they cannot follow a normal schedule of activities without reliance on medication (Kaplowitz, 2004; Madaras, 2007b).

Vision and Hearing

One in four students have sight problems. There is a broad range of visual disabilities, from the need to wear glasses in certain situations to a total loss of vision. Even blindness is not a unitary concept. There are the legally blind, medically blind, and occupationally blind, as well as the partially sighted and visually impaired. A person is considered blind when the better eye tests no better than 20/200 after correction, and visually handicapped when the better eye tests from 20/70 to 20/200 after correction (Hinz, 2006). The Sight and Hearing Association Web site at http://www.sightandhearing.org includes an online vision test with descriptions of detecting common eye problems.

Annual vision screening should be available at school and teachers need to become aware of signs of visual handicap. Specifically, educators should watch for squinting, tilting the head, rolling the eyes, inattention to visuals, avoiding work that requires reading or close vision detail, and lowering the head to gain closeness to paperwork. Nearsightedness, *myopia* as it is medically referred to, is a condition in which near objects are seen clearly but distant objects do not come into proper focus. It is estimated that about 30% of Americans are nearsighted (Kitchen, 2007). Farsightedness, *hyperopia*, is a condition where distant objects are seen clearly but close ones do not come into proper focus. Approximately one-quarter of the population is hyperopic, and incidence increases with age. At least half of all persons over age 65 have some degree of hyperopia. The American Optometric Association maintains a Web site with video illustrations of a broad range of vision conditions and their correction—see http://www.aoa.org/x4692.xml. Students with visual problems should have the best seat placement in a class to view the blackboard, overhead or activity center. Tasks requiring prolonged focus should be interrupted periodically. The visually impaired also need regular physical exercise (Stuart, Lieberman, & Hand, 2006).

Two million students are estimated to have significant hearing loss (Kochkin, 2005). A hearing handicap is not an either/or phenomenon but a matter of degree. Persons may adequately hear low-pitched voices but miss high-pitched voices. Some may hear in a room where there are no competing sounds like other voices, traffic, fans, and music or where echoes are minimized by room structure and acoustical tile ceilings. To maximize achievement and adjustment, annual hearing examinations should be available at school since less than 15% of physicians routinely screen for hearing loss during physical examinations. The Sight and Hearing Association provides an online hearing assessment, identifies common hearing problems and describes methods for overcoming them at http://www.sightandhearing.org.

During the past half century there has been a 150% increase in hearing problems among youth (Luterman, 2006). Estimates indicate that 15% of all adolescents have permanently lost some hearing, about the proportion expected of people that are 45 to 65 years old. Medical theorists refer to the rising epidemic of ear damage as "a disease of civilization" created by difference between the world that bodies are designed for and the environment we have developed. Nature designed human ears for detecting predators approaching or prey moving away but modern technology has produced a decibel level that exceeds what people can safely handle.

Over 5 million students ages 6 to 19 have some degree of hearing damage because of amplifier music (Luterman, 2006). Amplifiers have transformed the volume of music at concerts, movies, clubs, home and car stereos and personal listening devices that often jeopardize auditory health. Many teenagers like music as loud as it can be and seem indifferent to dangers of high decibel levels since debilitating results are not

evident for years. To help teenagers define how loud is too loud and recognize the ways they can protect themselves, suggest that students and
their parents go to http://www.abelard.org/hear/hear.php#how-loud. The
National Institute for Occupational Safety and Health Preservation also
promotes ways to protect hearing at http://www.cdc.gov/niosh/topics/
noise/.

Electronic sound enhancement systems have been applied for a generation in classes serving the hearing impaired. A few years ago, however,
evidence began to mount that a microphone and speaker system could
also enhance the learning of students without hearing impairments
(Luterman, 2006). Consequently, in an increasing number of schools
observers can detect small black devices that hang from the neck of students. These infrared microphones are designed to raise the volume and
clarity of a teacher's voice so as to overcome competing student whispers,
fluorescent light noises, air conditioners, and other distractions. Teachers
who use the electronic sound enhancement systems no longer suffer from
laryngitis and do not have to project their voices. Being able to hear well
makes it easier for everyone to learn. The system that includes roving
microphones like those used by television entertainers has an appeal for
students when they respond to teacher questions or make reports in class.
The cost of ceiling speakers, microphones, and related equipment is
about $1,800 per classroom but considered good value by schools adopt-
ing this innovation. The possibility of fire has always discouraged schools
from having fabric wall coverings or carpets that could absorb background noise. Some families also oppose carpets because they could
aggravate student allergies, and architects seldom emphasize sound in
designing classrooms (Matthews, 2008).

Body Image Concerns

An important aspect of maturation that calls for support from adults is
helping teenagers to accept a realistic image of their body (Durkin, Paxton,
& Wertheim, 2005). Nancy Redd (2007), a former Miss Virginia and
Harvard graduate, exposes many myths adolescents accept about their
bodies and describes some negative consequences they are bound to
experience. For adolescents whose physical maturity initiates earlier or
later than it does for classmates, the inclination is to be embarrassed.
Teasing by agemates that results in lower social status reinforces these
feelings. Body image concerns are further complicated by acne eruptions
that appear on the face, neck, and shoulders. *Acne* is a relatively harmless
condition beginning about puberty for about 75% of both sexes and usually
disappearing in several years. However, teenagers with acne suppose that

few conditions could be worse since blotches detract from their appearance (Swami & Furnham, 2007). In contrast, adolescents often explain that tattoos and body piercing reflect their independence and attract attention to having a distinctive appearance (Huxley & Grogan, 2005; Larzo & Poe, 2006). Take a quiz and learn about the conditions that motivate involvement with tattoos during adolescence at http://www.kidsgrowth.org/resources/articledetail.cfm?id=434. Counseling adolescents about tattoos is a topic that many teachers feel uninformed about and would like to better understand (Montgomery & Parks, 2007).

Exposure to unrealistic expectations for body models can begin for girls in childhood when they are given Barbie type dolls with exaggerated proportions instead of American girl dolls that resemble the shape, fashion, and childhood concerns of their owners. Idealized male bodies can present a similar preoccupation for boys (Stout & Frame, 2004). Teens face continuous challenges to their self esteem from television, the Internet and magazines that portray images of perfection which are closely linked with being thin. Only 15% of girls are happy with their body while more than half of them think they should lose weight (Schroeder & Wiatt, 2005). A reflective reminder is that most successful people do not have perfect body measurements. Of 6 billion residents on the planet, less than a few hundred are supermodels. Caring about someone should not depend on how tall or thin they are or on the shape of their face and body. Being capable of looking beyond physical appearances to see who people really are is an important sign of growing up and maturity.

Many teachers and parents underestimate the anxiety of teenagers related to appearance and body image. This concern is illustrated by *Real Women Have Curves* (Cardoso, 2002) a film starring America Ferrera. Ana, a bright Latina high school senior, is torn between her duty to the family and pursuing a promising future. Will she accept a college scholarship or keep working in the family's small bridal gown factory? Ana, in a poignant scene, inspires overweight girlfriends to strip down to their underwear, laugh about and, at least temporarily, accept their less than perfect bodies. A related need for awareness is that persons recognized for their beauty should not be judged as less intelligent as though a compensating principle exists. Stereotypes about beautiful girls are usually inaccurate and reflect jealousy that can result in mistreatment.

NUTRITION AND DIET

Americans of all ages are becoming more motivated to make good decisions about their nutrition and diet. Energy requirements and nutritional needs increase during adolescence. However, when teenagers feel rushed to meet unreasonable expectations of teachers, when they participate in after-school programs or engage in part- time employment, the busy schedule often means eating in a hasty fashion and failure to get enough calories or nutrients they really need. Over scheduling can cause teenagers to skip meals or to eat more often. Many adolescents eat away from home so they have to decide the diet that is suitable for them. Frequently the choice is a fast food restaurant or a vending machine with meals that compromise good health. Overeating and restricting food intake can result in eating disorders with serious consequences. The government provides guidelines for teenagers on what to eat and selection of portion sizes.

Nutrition Deficiencies

Sufficient iron is essential in adolescence because of an expanding volume of blood in the body and increase in muscle mass experienced by teenagers. During growth spurts extra iron is required because it is vital for muscle development and healthy red blood cells. A need for additional iron is especially acute for teenage girls because of the loss of iron that occurs during menstruation. When there is a lack of iron in the diet, the resulting *iron deficiency anemia* is reflected by a tendency to fatigue, feelings of lightheadedness, loss of appetite, and pale appearance. Teens should be advised to eat enough iron-containing foods such as meat, fish, poultry, eggs, peas, beans, potatoes, and rice (Katz & Smith, 2006).

Another nutrient required by bodies of teenagers but frequently overlooked is calcium. Strong bones and teeth depend on calcium. Lack of calcium in the diet increases risk for a bone-thinning disease called *osteoporosis*, a quite common problem for women from middle age onwards. Parents and teachers should encourage adolescents to more often choose calcium as an essential choice for their eating lifestyle. Only 14% of adolescent girls and 35% of boys meet the government calcium recommendations of 1,300 milligrams a day for persons aged 9–18. One glass of milk contains about 300 milligrams of calcium. Girls should be told, "Here's the deal. You are in the biggest most important growth spurt in your life and this is the critical time for you to learn to eat right and treat your body with the respect and nutrition it deserves" (Schroeder & Wiatt, 2005).

Certain nutrients and adequate calories are necessary for teenagers to meet their physical growth and activity needs. When these nutrients are lacking because teenagers choose to diet, they can prevent the attainment of their full height. Those concerned about their weight should adopt healthy eating habits and increase their daily exercise rather than just try to cut calories. When a serious weight problem is indicated, guidance from a dietician associated with the school can help (Casazza & Ciccazzo, 2006).

Family Dietary Guidelines

Students from 4,500 public high schools were surveyed regarding their food perceptions (Zullig, Ubbes, & Pyle, 2006). Over 40% reported not eating breakfast within the past week and a similar proportion were trying to lose weight. Excessive diet practices like fasting, taking diet pills or laxatives and vomiting to lose weight were reported by 25% of the students. The findings suggested that these adolescents are skipping breakfast as part of a patterned lifestyle of unhealthy weight management and that schools must make greater efforts to encourage healthy diets (Story, Kaphingst, & French, 2006).

An information system to help consumers translate recommendations for nutrition into action was devised by the United States Department of Agriculture (2008a, 2008b). These *Dietary Guidelines for Americans* describe a healthy diet, by age level with a focus on fruits, vegetables, whole grains, and low-fat milk and milk products. This diet includes lean meats, poultry, fish, beans, eggs, and nuts, and is low in saturated fats, trans fats, cholesterol, salt (sodium) and added sugars. The government Web site at http://www.mypyramid.gov offers suggestions for what individuals should eat based on information they provide about their age, sex, and daily level of physical activity. To help monitor personal diet and exercise progress, the Web site at http://www.mypyramidtracker.gov presents an assessment tool with feedback on diet quality, physical activity status, and nutrition messages. A feature is the Food Calorie Energy Balance that calculates an individuals' energy balance by subtracting energy expended on physical activity from the food calories/energy intake. This tool increases understanding of one's energy balance and supports the link between good nutrition and regular physical activity.

When Internet users identify foods they eat for a specific period such as a month, they are given an overall evaluation that compares their intake with the recommended consumption. In a similar way, physical activity status can be monitored. After indicating the amount of daily physical activity, an overall score is assigned based upon comparison of the person's record with recommendations by experts that reflect optimal lifestyle. The government report concludes that, unless current trends of poor dietary habits and sedentary behavior are reversed, adolescents may be the first generation that cannot look forward to a longer lifespan than their parents (United States Department of Agriculture, 2008b).

Another method the government is using to encourage self-monitoring is to help teenagers become aware of the *Go, Slow,* and *Whoa* foods. *Go* foods can be eaten almost anytime whereas *Slow* foods should be eaten a few times a week. *Whoa* foods should only be eaten on occasion as special treats. The Web site of the United States Department of Health and Human Services and the National Institutes of Health (2008) is available at http://www.nhlbi.nih.gov/health/public/heart/obesity/wecan/live-it/go-slow-whoa.htm. Choosing proper foods and limiting the amount is important. In recent years restaurant portions have grown so that the size of a single meal is actually more appropriate for two persons (Schroeder & Wiatt, 2005). To illustrate the problem, adolescents should click the Portion Distortion line and quiz located on the just described government site. This presentation describes how food portions have changed over the course of an adolescent's lifetime, offers a quiz on portion sizes along with feedback and gives a serving size card that can be downloaded and put on the refrigerator or in a wallet for reference.

Families and Eating Disorders

Many teenagers are preoccupied with how their body looks. If dieting becomes an obsession, it may be a sign of a potential eating disorder. Eight million Americans suffer from some eating disorder and 90% are young women. The incidence of disorders has doubled in the past decade and implicates ever-younger age groups (Costin, 2006). Forty percent of 9-year-old girls have dieted. Eating disorders have the highest mortality rate of any mental illness. *Anorexia nervosa* (self-imposed starving) and *bulimia* (overeating followed by vomiting and purging) are health hazards presenting as great a danger as the rising incidence of obesity. Ninety percent of the anorexic victims are females from 15 to 25 years of age (Chavez & Insel, 2007).

The cultural pressure that "thin is in" can motivate anorexia. A motivation to be thin, having body fat 15% or more below expected levels, can lead to extreme loss of weight and create complications like anemia, hormonal changes, and cardiovascular problems. One estimate is that 10% of anorexia cases end in death, half attributable to suicide. The National Association of Anorexia, Nervosa, and Associated Disorders (2007)—http://www.anad.org provides guidance for adolescents and their families. Most studies conclude that the cultural factor is less influential than personality disorder. An inability to cope with stress appears to be the dominant cause but the facade of fat provides a convenient excuse (Costin, 2006).

The half million victims suffering from bulimia, ingest large amounts of food (usually carbohydrates) in private and then purge themselves by using laxatives, enemas, diuretics, and self-induced vomiting. The word Bulimia comes from the Greek language and means "huge appetite." The term is actually a misnomer because bulimics do not eat up to 50,000 calories a day because of hunger. Instead, they rely on food for self-medication in a similar way as others may use drugs to cope with unmet personal needs. Most researchers believe that bulimia, like anorexia, masks personality problems of low self-esteem and inability to cope with stress. However, the personality traits associated with these two disorders are different (Wilson, Grilo, & Vitousek, 2007).

Anorexics shun food in order to cope with stress, tend to withdraw socially, maintain rigid self-control, deny that they have problems (despite the loss of up to 25% of their body weight), and feel like they are fat. In contrast, bulimics eat to cope with stress, are sociable, lose self-control, recognize that something is wrong, yet because of the purging are able to maintain near normal weight. Another negative effect of bulimia is tooth decay because of the chemicals related to vomit. The cure for anorexia and bulimia is not just a matter of controlling eating habits. Body image and self-confidence, anxieties, fears, and goals must be considerations. The complexities are illustrated by reports that 25% of anorexics will be helped, 25% not helped, and 50% will gain some control but remain vulnerable to a recurrence (Striegel-Moore & Bulik, 2007).

Families and Obesity

According to the Centers for Disease Control and Prevention (2008), children are defined as *overweight* if their BMI (body mass index) is in the 85th to 94th percentile and *obese* when they are in the 95th percentile or higher. The proportion of overweight among children aged 6 to 11 has tripled during the past generation, rising from 6% to 19%. During the same period, overweight among 12- to 19-year-olds more than tripled, increasing from 5% to 17%. The government estimates that 9 million students are fat enough to endanger their health and 5 million more are on the verge of joining the high risk group (Anderson, 2008; National Center for Health Statistics, 2006). Table 10.1 presents data for selected years over a generation, from 1976–2004. About 25% of Hispanic and Black adolescents are overweight as compared with 15% among Whites (Ogden, Carroll, Curtin, McDowell, Tabak, & Flegal, 2006; Ogden, Carroll, & Flegal, 2008).

Obesity is the greatest public health threat, accounting for more fatalities than AIDS, cancers, and accidents combined (Davies & Fitzgerald,

Table 10.1.   Prevalence of Overweight Among Children and Adolescents Ages 6–19 Years, for Selected Years 1976–2004

Age (Years)	1976–1980	1988–1994	1999–2000	2001–2002	2003–2004
6–11	6.5	11.3	15.1	16.3	18.8
12–19	5.0	10.5	14.8	16.7	17.4

Source: From National Center for Health Statistics (2006). *Prevalence of overweight among children and adolescents: United States 2003–2004.* Hyattsville, MD: U.S. Department of Health and Human Services.

2007). The problem begins during childhood with the number of fat cells becoming fixed by age 10. Parents should understand that obesity in childhood merits immediate concern. Studies have found that 7% of children with normal weight parents grow up to be obese whereas 80% of children that have two obese parents will become obese adults. There is an increase in gastric bypass surgery that drastically reduces the stomach capacity, causing people to feel full from meager amounts of food. The medical community is agreed that weight-loss programs generally do not work. A 1% success rate is the norm. Physical activity must be part of the strategy because exercise and weight management have to go together (Schumacher & Queen, 2007). The University of Minnesota Obesity Center offers periodic reports on research, available at—http://www1.umn.edu/mnoc.

What concerns health-care professionals is the cost in lives. Obese youth are three times more likely than peers of healthy weight to develop high blood pressure and twice as likely to suffer heart disease (Paxson, Donahue, Orleans, & Grisso, 2006). There is a saying that you are as old as your arteries, implying that the condition of your arteries is more important than chronological age in the evolution of heart disease and stroke. Geetha Raghuveer, a cardiologist at the University of Missouri in Kansas City led a team that examined 70 obese boys and girls whose average age was 13 (Laino, 2008). Ultrasound imaging was applied to measure the thickness of the inner walls of their carotid arteries in the neck that supply the brain with blood. The intention was to gauge their vascular age, referring to the age at which the level of arterial thickening would be normal. For these teenagers their vascular age generally was three decades older than their chronological age. That is, the thickness of their arteries was more typical of persons 45 years old. The lifestyle changes implicated in this study are reinforced by an American Academy of Pediatrics policy revision reflecting the fact that some children as young as 8 years of age need to be treated with statin drugs if they have certain cholesterol levels (Daniels, Greer, and the Committee on Nutrition, 2008).

Other dire predictions indicate that one of every two children will develop type 2 diabetes because of excess weight, raising the probability that they will die at a younger age than their parents. Diabetes is the sixth leading cause of death and major cause of kidney failure, blindness, and non-traumatic leg amputation. An obese adolescent can expect to live 12 to 14 years less than a peer of desirable weight. The cost of medical treatment for children with obesity is three times more than treating the average child. These statistics should lead to reflection, especially because it is easier to prevent obesity than treat it (Daniels, 2006).

Eric Hoffman (2008) directs the Research Center for Genetic Medicine at the Children's National Medical Center in Washington, DC. Hoffman observes that people today are not living as our genes intended because sitting down most of the time does not match the historical norm of human activity. From an evolutionary view the body is still programmed to hunt for food and survive famine. This means that if the body is not moving, as is the case for most of us much of the time, the brain thinks the body is starving and directs the quest to cannibalize protein-rich muscle to feed the brain and conserve fat stores. In effect, sedentary lifestyles are causing people to kill themselves, and this tragedy must be reversed by helping them adopt a healthy regimen counter to prevailing behavior patterns of all age groups. The main focus should be lifestyle choices rather than dieting. When a child watches a lot of television, the initial goal should be to reduce viewing. Similarly, if a student consumes several sugar based drinks a day, the strategy is to cut back. Taking time to eat instead of hurrying is helpful. One reason to eat slowly is because it takes 15 to 20 minutes for the stomach to signal the brain that it is full. Many overweight teenagers have acquired uncontrollable eating habits and cannot recognize when they are full. They have to relearn to listen to their internal hunger drive. Finally, when the body is sleep deprived, a common condition, there is more craving for fatty, high sugar foods. Arranging for sufficient sleep is fundamental to healthy living and involves personal choice.

Some implications from studies are (a) obesity can be indirectly attacked by giving more attention to issues of social adjustment; (b) obesity can be directly overcome by establishing required exercise and fitness programs for all students; and (c) obesity persists throughout adult life (Powell, Calvin, & Calvin, 2007). Professional athletes are among the most admired people with fans spending great amounts of time watching their favorite players perform. Adolescents should be persuaded to exchange some of the time they spend as spectators to play themselves. The resulting exercise and fitness will support long-term health. The American Obesity Association offers information on childhood obesity at http://www.obesity.org.

EXERCISE AND FITNESS

For most boys and girls adolescence is more sedentary than in the past and includes less physical activity. Students sit at desks in school or at a computer and in front of the television set at home without getting sufficient exercise. In addition to giving up the considerable health benefits that come from pursuit of fitness, adolescents are becoming obese in unprecedented numbers. This condition contributes to a range of life threatening diseases and presents a significant challenge for schools. Students are rarely consulted about the dress codes imposed on them at school. Given the preoccupation of teenagers about body image and appearance, it could be a good idea to consult with them regarding options for school uniforms and find out their reaction to details of the dress codes.

Benefits of Exercise

Choosing to exercise regularly is a beneficial lifestyle choice because it contributes to overall health. More specifically, it helps control weight by using excess calories that would otherwise be stored as fat. Exercise helps reduce the risk of chronic diseases like diabetes, high blood pressure and cholesterol, heart disease, osteoporosis, and some cancers. Other benefits of exercise include building strong muscles, bones, and joints, improving flexibility and balance, warding off depression, improving mood, sense of well being, and better sleep (Mitchell, Church, & Zucker, 2008). Physical activity may include structured activities like walking, running, biking, hiking, basketball, tennis, golf and other sports. It may also include daily tasks such as household chores, yard work, or walking the dog. Teens who adopt exercise as a part of their daily regimen are likely to continue the practice in adulthood that may lengthen life expectancy (Beets, Pitetti, & Cardinal, 2005; Darst & Pangrazi, 2008; Morrow, 2005). In a study of Harvard male graduates, those who burned 2,000 or more calories each week by walking, jogging, climbing stairs or playing sports lived an average of one to two years longer than those burning fewer than 500 calories a week by exercise. Teens might not only live longer by exercising regularly but live more years independently and with a better quality of life (Mayo Clinic, 2007).

Moderate to intense physical activity is recommended for at least 30 minutes on most, if not all, days of the week (Darst & Pangrazi, 2008). An expert panel reviewed the research about effects of physical activity on young people's health and well being. More than 850 articles and 1,120 abstracts were examined. The conclusion was that, overall, children who participate in moderate to vigorous physical activity one hour or more a day gain significant physiological, health, and psychological benefits (Siegel, 2006a, 2006b). Less than half of adolescents are physically active on a regular basis. Instead, many of them maintain a lazy lifestyle that includes sitting at a desk or computer during the school day and watching television or spending time on the Internet while they are home (Kahn, Huang, Gillman, Field, Austin, & Colditz, 2008).

Schools and Exercise

Less than half of the nation's schools require fitness training or physical education. Many schools no longer allow breaks, hoping that more time on task will promote better academic performance and reduce student conflict between class periods (Kerner, 2005). Two-thirds of adolescents do not participate in organized physical activities scheduled in after school hours (Mohr, Townsend, & Pritchard, 2006). Some observers perceive the No Child Left Behind Act as part of the problem because it forces educators to curtail studies outside the core curriculum in favor of teaching to standardized tests. In response to the sedentary norm, lack of exercise, poor diet, and need to develop life long health habits, Congress in 2006 passed a law to promote wellness in schools (Story, Kaphingst, & French, 2006). Vending machines providing high sugar and caffeine drinks were replaced by water, milk, and fruit juice. Lunchroom menus featuring fast foods were changed to include more nutritious options. Schools cannot overcome this problem alone but they have an important role. A relevant question is, "Why are schools training students to be basketball, baseball, and football players when after graduation, only 1% will continue?" (Ripkin & Woolf, 2006). The common focus should be on promoting the health of all students, reflected by walking, running, and other forms of exercise that boys and girls will likely continue and enjoy through life. All adolescents should wear a pedometer and arrange to walk at least 10,000 steps each day or approximately 5 miles.

The Mayo Clinic and the National Institute of Health designed a new kind of classroom environment that does not confine students to desks or sedentary activity. Instead, this classroom located in Rochester, Minnesota, features laptops, iPods, exercise machines, dance movement video games, personalized white boards instead of one large blackboard, vertical magnetic work spaces that double as projection screens, and standing desks. Students stand, sit, walk around, exercise, and solve problems together. All 60 early adolescents participating in the program have their movement monitored with specialized telemetry called Posture and

Activity Detectors (PADS) worn on the leg to measures time spent standing and walking. At the end of a school day, the equipment can be stored so the site is a community center at night (Levine, 2006).

Cross-cultural studies also underscore the relationship of exercise and health. There has been speculation about the extent to which developing type 2 diabetes is due to the genes we inherit and our environment (mainly diet and lifestyle). A National Institutes of Health project compared Pima Indians in Arizona with Pima living in the Sierra Madre mountainous of Mexico (Schulz, Bennett, Ravussin, Kidd, Kidd, Esparza, & Valencia, 2006). The Pima groups have a similar genetic heritage and, for comparative purposes, resemble identical twins that grow up apart. The Arizona Pima Indians have the highest rate of type 2 diabetes in the world; 34% of the men and 41% of the women are affected. However, prevalence of the disease for the Mexican Pima was previously unknown. When the researchers completed a physical examination of 224 Mexican Pima (77% of that population), it was found that only 8% of Pima men in Mexico and 9% of women had diabetes, a rate only slightly above the 7% for 193 other non-Pima Mexicans living in the same area. The pattern was the same for obesity rates.

What aspects of the environment protect Pima south of the border from obesity and diabetes? The diet of Mexican Pima actually contains more fat and less fiber than the Arizona Pima while similar numbers of calories are consumed. The main difference between the groups involves greater physical activity by the Pima in Mexico. Most of them make a living by physical labor and they grow their own food. They plow their fields with the help of oxen, then plant and harvest by hand. On the other hand, the Pima north of the border drive trucks or cars and farm with the aid of highly mechanized equipment. Most of them purchase their food from a grocery store. According to the researchers, the lower prevalence of type 2 diabetes and obesity in Pima Indians of Mexico than in the United States indicates that, even in populations genetically prone to these conditions, their development is influenced mostly by environmental circumstances, thereby suggesting that type 2 diabetes is largely preventable. This investigation offers compelling evidence that changes in lifestyle associated with westernization has a major role in increasing the global epidemic of type 2 diabetes (Schulz, Bennett, Ravussin, Kidd, Kidd, Esparza & Valencia, 2006).

Voices of Adolescents

In this chapter, we have drawn attention to the importance that adolescents attach to appearance and body image. Nevertheless, many secondary schools impose dress codes without considering the views of students. The usual rationale is this policy supports the sense of belonging everyone needs, promotes school pride, and prevents status differences based on ability of families to purchase expensive clothes. Some students who oppose dress codes state that "when we dress in our regular clothes, it expresses how we feel." Others welcome the code because it frees them from being captive to fads of fashion (Boutelle, 2008).

The poll for this chapter is about dress codes (Exercise 10.01). Specifically, you can learn how students at your school feel regarding whether the dress code is beneficial, if it enhances the sense of community, improves safety, and diminishes gangs. This poll reveals how students feel about wearing shirts that contain bad language, and whether hairstyle, jewelry, tattoos, or body piercing should be regulated. Students can express views about whether adults on the faculty and staff should have to follow a dress code and if students should be involved in choosing a uniform.

Compare your results with findings we have obtained from hundreds of adolescents. For example, the same proportion of boys (87%) and girls (87%) feel that it is unfair to be told what they must wear at school. When adults impose such policies, 90% of girls and 83% of boys feel that students should be consulted in choosing the uniform. A majority of boys (75%) and girls (66%) believe that teachers and staff should be expected to follow a dress code too. The inclusion of hairstyle as part of a dress code was agreed to as appropriate by only 3% of boys and 4% of the girls. Just 6% of boys and 8% of girls agree that jewelry, tattoos, and body piercing ought to be regulated. School officials are uninformed about this issue and have done little to educate students regarding the health risks of tattoos and piercing, particularly for minors (Huxley & Grogan, 2005).

SEXUAL BEHAVIOR AND KNOWLEDGE

Adolescent sexual activity usually proceeds from vicarious experiences with daydreaming to sharing questions or stories about sex with one friend of the same age and gender. Later, teenagers rely on a larger peer group that may support their sexual experimentation at the time a relationship begins with a partner of the opposite gender. Although sexual intercourse and oral sex is common during adolescence, many students are poorly informed about ways to avoid pregnancy as well as reduce the risk of exposure to sexually transmitted infections. The medical profession and most parents advocate making comprehensive sex education available as the common approach to prevention. Their reasoning is that this strategy provides information that can protect the health of teenagers who might become sexually active and gives a more informed message to students taking a virginity pledge to remain abstinent until marriage.

Sexual Activity and Diseases

Early adolescents, ages 10 to 13, usually identify one friend of their same sex as the closest relationship they have outside the family. At the same time teenagers are curious about anything sexual and want to learn about intercourse. Sexual feelings, especially among boys, are often expressed with dirty jokes or raunchy stories. When teenagers first become capable of sexual intercourse, they are years away from having the emotional maturity needed for an intimate relationship (Pfiefer & Middleman, 2006).

During middle adolescence, from age 14 to 16, a shift usually occurs from being with just one friend to spending more time with a group of peers. Most are interested in developing a relationship with someone of the opposite sex and the group often influences the kind of involvement. Dating and double dating begins and is soon followed by sexual experimentation. Peers can impose pressure to lose virginity, causing some youth to have sexual intercourse (Moore & Rosenthal, 2006). By later adolescence, ages 17 to 20, sexual identity is no longer a common main concern. However, even though they view themselves as emotionally ready for sexual intercourse, they are not prepared for parenthood and need to know ways to avoid pregnancy and exposure to sexually transmitted infections (Gilbert, 2006).

Sexual activity typically begins with reliance on *daydreaming*, a mental process that offers a desired content and safe outlet for imagination. Teenagers generally report having sexual fantasies, vicarious experiences useful in development of sexual identity because they allow the exploration of situations that would be socially unacceptable to act out. A second way emerging sexuality is expressed involves fantasy and *masturbation*, the stimulation of genitals for sexual pleasure. Some youth have misgivings or feelings of guilt about masturbating because it violates their religious beliefs or they have been exposed to myths alleging this habit could lead to blindness and insanity. Masturbation offers a way to release sexual tension, gain pleasure, repeat sexual fantasies, and lessen the likelihood of getting involved with dangerous sexual activity involving others. So long as an adolescent masturbates in private, this behavior is considered normal (Madaras, 2007a, 2007b).

Sexually active adolescents are those who have had intercourse at least one time. The Centers for Disease Control and Prevention (2006) surveys indicate that half of 17-year-olds report having engaged in sexual intercourse with slightly higher percentages indicated for Blacks and Hispanics than for Whites. The average age of first intercourse for girls in the United States is 17 and 16 for boys (see Table 10.2).

Reaction to first intercourse differs by gender. Generally, girls report that they felt scared, guilty, worried, curious or embarrassed while boys report feeling excited, satisfied, thrilled, happy, and mature. Two-thirds of teens report they first had sexual intercourse in their partner's family home (34%), their own family home (22%) or home of a friend (12%) (Kirby, 2007; National Campaign to Prevent Teen and Unplanned Pregnancy, 2003, 2006a, 2006b). This means that parents should be aware of activities when a boyfriend or girlfriend is visiting, not be shy about making their presence known around the house, and ensure that a responsible adult is present and paying attention when their teenager visits the home of a boyfriend or girlfriend. Studies reveal that the likelihood of first sexual experience increases with the number of hours that teenagers spend unsupervised (Albert, 2006).

There is a wide range of dating practices. Students may not date at all in middle school or in high school or they may have one romantic partner. The common pattern is to have two or three close emotional rela-

Table 10.2. Percentage of High School Students Who Engaged in Sexual Behaviors by Sex, Race/Ethnicity, and Grade

Category	*Ever Had Sexual Intercourse*		
	Female %	*Male* %	*Total* %
Race/Ethnicity			
White	43.7	42.2	43.0
Black	61.2	74.6	67.6
Hispanic	44.4	57.6	51.0
Grade			
9	29.3	39.3	34.3
10	44.0	41.5	42.8
11	52.1	50.6	51.4
12	62.4	63.8	63.1
Total	45.7	47.9	46.8

Source: From Centers for Disease Control and Prevention (2006 June 9). Youth Risk Behavior Surveillance—United States, 2005. *Morbidity and Mortality Weekly Report, 55* (SS05), Table 44, 1–108. Retrieved January 5, 2009, available at http://www.cdc.gov/mmwr//preview/mmwrhtml/ss5505a1.htm

tionships in succession. Typically, in the course of each relationship, neither partner dates others and, when their relationship includes sexual
intercourse, has no other partners (Sommers & Surmann, 2005). About
15% of sexually active students in high school report having four or more
partners, a choice that reflects lack of maturity and increases the chances
of getting a sexually transmitted disease (Centers for Disease Control Prevention, 2006).

Teenagers are at greater risk for sexually transmitted diseases than
older age groups partly because they are more likely to have a partner
who has been sexually active with others, engage in oral sex, and are least
likely to consistently use protection (Kaestle, Halpern, Miller, & Ford,
2005). In addition, the decision making ability and communication skills
of adolescents are being formed and lag behind their capacity for sexual
activity.

The rate of sexually transmitted infections (STIs) among adolescents is
growing at an unprecedented rate. Each year three million teenagers are
diagnosed with Gonorrhea, Chlamydia, or viral infections like Herpes
and human Papilloma virus, HPV (Houck et al., 2006; Moscicki, 2005).
Most of these diseases are treatable with medication but while antibiotics
can destroy bacteria, this is not so for AIDS virus. Medication can slow
progression of this disease but there is no cure. Diseases like herpes and
HPV (the leading cause of cervical cancer) may recur even if there has
been treatment. The longer STD treatment is delayed, the greater the risk
for complications (Alford, 2003; Valdiserri, 2004). Video interviews about
sexually transmitted diseases like Chlamydia (major cause of infertility),
cervical cancer, HPV vaccine, and HIV are available at NBC Digital
Health Network http://www.healthvideo.com—click menu for teen health.

Gay, lesbian. and bisexual teenagers are often reluctant to identify their
sexual preference because of doubts about accuracy of their feelings and
concerns about ridicule or rejection by peers and family (Goodenow,
Szalacha, & Westheimer, 2006). Sexually active teenage male homosexuals
are at much greater risk for acquiring Chlamydia, Hepatitis B, Gonorrhea, AIDS, and Syphilis. Persons at even higher risk are homosexuals
having multiple partners. Using a *condom*, close fitting rubber covering
the penis during intercourse, can reduce but not eliminate the risk of
becoming infected (Albert, 2006).

Contraception and Pregnancy

The good news is that rates of teen pregnancy and child-bearing have
declined by one-third since the early 1990s. However, evidence suggests a
more targeted approach for prevention is needed. More specifically, *one*

of *two* Latina teenagers (51%) get pregnant at least once before age 20; this *pregnancy rate* is nearly two times higher than the national average of 31%. Latinos now comprise 14% of the population. By 2025, one-quarter of all teens will be Latino. Whatever happens in this group will undoubtedly affect the nation as a whole (National Campaign to Prevent Teen and Unplanned Pregnancy, 2008).

When pregnancy happens, the reasons can sometimes be traced to student reliance on longstanding myths (Madaras, 2007b). One myth is that a girl cannot become pregnant the first time she is involved with intercourse. The fact is one encounter can result in pregnancy even when the girl was a virgin. A second myth is that pregnancy can be avoided if the penis is pulled out before ejaculation. However, fluid-carrying semen commonly leaks from a penis before and after ejaculation. A third myth suggests that girls cannot get pregnant during a menstrual period. Although the odds of pregnancy are less likely during these times, it is possible to become pregnant any time. A fourth myth supposes that pregnancy will not occur if the girl uses a douche. However, flushing the vagina with water or some other liquid does not prevent pregnancy.

Contraception is the prevention of pregnancy by methods like condoms or birth control pills. Sexually active teenagers that do not use contraception have a 90% chance of becoming pregnant within a year. The Centers for Disease Control and Prevention (2006) report that 60% of high school students reported using a condom during their last sex. Ironically, ninth graders (75%) applied condoms most and 12th graders (60%) least. Teenagers should know about types of birth control, limitations of each method, and where to access them. Birth control techniques include hormonal contraceptives and the barrier method using a condom (rubber) or diaphragm. Each kind of birth control has advantages and disadvantages. Condoms provide the most protection from infection. But, they may not be as helpful in prevention of pregnancy. For unmarried people the recommended practice is to use condoms with another method of birth control such as oral or patch contraceptives. The way to ensure full protection from pregnancy and sexually transmitted disease is abstinence.

The United States has the highest rate of teenage pregnancy among Western nations. One half of these pregnancies occur within six months of a girl becoming sexually active. Teenage mothers are more likely than older mothers to have a poor diet, receive welfare, lack prenatal care, and sustain anemia. They have twice the normal risk of delivering a low birth weight baby (less than 5 ½ pounds) that exposes infants to a higher probability for mental retardation and other developmental problems (Klein & Committee on Adolescence, 2005). The main reason adolescent girls quit school is because of pregnancy. Less than half of teen mothers graduate and fewer than 2% obtain a college degree. Eight of 10 fathers do not marry the teen mother of their child and rarely pay child support. The daughters of teen mothers are three times more likely to become teen mothers themselves than women who had a child at age 20 or older. Sons of teen mothers are twice as likely to spend time in prison than sons of mothers age 20 or older. Communities must strive to be more comprehensive in helping teen mothers complete high school, fulfill their parenting obligations, and prepare for a job. The National Campaign to Prevent Teen and Unplanned Pregnancy presents *Too Young*, an online video adolescents and their parents can benefit from, available at http:// www.thenationalcampaign.org.

Abortion is a form of intervention to end a pregnancy by removing an embryo or fetus from the womb. The Supreme Count, in 1973, ruled in the Roe versus Wade case that abortion was legal (Hull, Hoffer, & Hoffer, 2003). During the past decade, abortion rates have declined in every state. Approximately half of 700,000 teen pregnancies annually end in live births, 35% end by abortion, and 14% end in miscarriage (Centers for Disease Control, 2006). Teenagers generally do not believe that getting married is the best solution for an unplanned pregnancy. The fact is 60% of adolescents who marry just because of pregnancy divorce within 3 years. Unwed mothers are less likely to experience social disapproval now than in the past. Consequently, fewer than 5% of them surrender their babies for adoption.

Biologically, sexual activity and pregnancy is normal for teenagers. However, students must attend school for an extensive time so they usually get married later than the past. The lengthy interval between physical maturity and starting a family typically includes sexual activity (Centers for Disease Control and Prevention, 2006). This means that every student needs to have a sexual plan based on personal long-term goals and values. Most parents are willing to help adolescents plan for their education, and they should also assist them to have a decision-making plan about sexuality. The National Campaign to Prevent Teen and Unplanned Pregnancy presents an interactive quiz about pregnancy that has been prepared by teenagers and is available at http://www.thenationalcampaign.org.

Researchers and policy makers concerned about teenage pregnancy focus mostly on romantic relationships between adolescents and partners within the same age group. The assumption is that their newfound passion is the main cause of pregnancy. Less well known is the fact that minor-age girls (under 18) are often impregnated by much older men (Cocca, 2004). The evidence was first discovered over a decade ago when vital statistics for California revealed that men over age 25 fathered twice as many teenage births than did males under age 18; men over 20 years of age fathered five times more births to middle school girls than middle school males (Males & Chew, 1996). Data for 46,500 births to mothers aged 10–18 years living in California was examined to determine extent of adult male involvement in school-age childbearing. In 85% of these births, ages of fathers were available on birth certificates. In only 34% of all births, the fathers were a school-age peer of mothers; 66% of the fathers were post-school-age adults who were 4.3 years older than the mothers. Post-school-age adult fathers made up a majority of the school-age births, regardless of ethnicity (67.8% for Hispanic births, 62.9% for Whites, 58.8% for Blacks, and 63.6% for Asians). The younger the mother, the greater the age difference between herself and the baby's father.

To assess whether these figures were unique to California, the Population Reference Bureau carried out a national study. Finding indicated that two-thirds of births to teenage girls are fathered by men age 20 or older (De Vita, 1996). The National Longitudinal Study of Adolescent Health data on 2,000 teenage girls were analyzed to find out how the age gap between a female and older partner might influence the relationship (Halpern, Kaestle, & Hallford, 2007; Kaestle, Wiley, & Wiley, 2002). The age difference between partners was found to be an important predictor of whether they would engage in sexual intercourse. Adolescent females involved with an older partner have higher odds of intercourse with that partner than females do involving partners their own age. The magnitude of this association is most dramatic among younger females. For example, the odds of intercourse among 13-year-old females with a partner 6 years older are more than six times the odds among 13-year-old females with a same age partner. Females age 17 with partners 6 years older have twice the odds of intercourse when compared with those who have a same age partner.

Sex educators in schools should consider that they might be reaching only half of a couple at high risk for sexual activity. Additional efforts may be needed to reach adult male partners about their responsibilities and legal ramifications (Lettenberg & Saltzman, 2000; Marin, Coyle, Gomez, Carvajal, & Kirby, 2000). Then too, because adolescent females in education programs may not have the same power in a relationship as their older partners, they may need help to identify their own interests and assert personal decisions. Educating females about abstinence and safe sex practices may not be enough when the romantic partners are significantly older. Education materials on dating older males could be helpful, especially for younger adolescents who are unaware of laws about *statutory rape*, the offense of having sexual relations with someone that has not reached the legal age of consent (Cocca, 2004; Kogan, 2004). *Legal age of consent* is the minimum age defined by each state at which a person is old enough to participate in consensual sexual relations, usually 18 or 19 years of age.

Involvement With Oral Sex

There is anecdotal evidence that many adolescents are turning to behaviors that avoid pregnancy but leave them vulnerable to sexually transmitted diseases such as Herpes, Chlamydia, Gonorrhea, and perhaps HIV (Brewster & Tillman, 2008). Although empirical studies are scarce, extant data suggests that one-third to half of high school students have given or received *oral sex*, using the mouth and tongue to stimulate the genitals of a partner. Fewer females than males report having received oral sex. Researchers from the University of California Division of Adolescent Medicine in San Francisco assessed perceptions of 580 ninth graders about oral versus vaginal sex. More participants reported having had oral sex (40%) than vaginal sex (30%). They evaluated oral sex as less risky than vaginal sex and believed that oral sex is more acceptable for their age group in dating and non-dating situations (Halpern-Felsher, Cornell, Kropp, & Tschann, 2005). Some adolescents, especially those in abstinence programs, may regard oral sex as a method to preserve their virginity while still providing the intimacy of sensual pleasure. In such cases, they misinterpret public health messages about disease as relating only to vaginal sex. Sex education programs should include discussions on oral sex and risk-reducing strategies like barrier protection (Paul & Freshman, 2006).

Researchers at Yale University surveyed 200 10th graders to assess involvement with oral sex in relation to peer correlates for three reasons. First, it could be that adolescents participate in oral sex to avoid risks they perceive are related to vaginal and anal sex. In that case, social influences and benefits tied to this behavior can be considered in intervention efforts. Second, if oral sex presents health risks, the estimated proportion of teens that report involvement should become a community concern. Third, data is scarce on adolescent use of sexually transmitted infection protection during oral sex and number of oral sex partners. Therefore, it is difficult to know whether many teenagers participate with oral sex in a way that increases their risk (Prinstein, Meade, & Cohen, 2003).

The findings showed that students were significantly more likely to engage in oral sex than vaginal sex, whether they were boys (38%) or girls (42%). Sexually active teens reported a greater number of oral sex partners than sexual intercourse partners. Most reported never using protective devices while having oral sex. Of those having oral sex in the past year, 57% perceived that their best friend also engaged in oral sex. Among students who did not have oral sex, 83% reported that their best friend also did not have oral sex. No significant association was found between reports of involvement with sexual intercourse and the perceptions of their best friends' involvement with sexual intercourse (Prinstein, Meade, & Cohen, 2003).

Overall, the results suggest that oral sex may be more amenable to social influence and intervention than prevention of sexual intercourse. Not only were adolescents' involvement with oral sex related to perceptions of their best friends' oral sex habits but also number of oral sex partners was also associated with perceptions of number of friends' partners. No such pattern was found for sexual intercourse. This means less risky behaviors like oral sex may pose a greater threat to health because teens appear more strongly influenced and reinforced by perceptions of peers' behavior. Even though there are current efforts to improve protection during oral sex by providing flavored condoms, changes in social attitude and norms among students seem necessary before discernible risk reduction occurs in this form of sexual behavior (Prinstein, Meade, & Cohen, 2003).

Comprehensive Sex Education

Comprehensive sex education programs emphasize abstinence as the best way to prevent pregnancy, guidance to avoid sexually transmitted diseases, advice on family planning and contraception, and, when appropriate, prescriptions for contraceptives or referral to a birth control clinic and prenatal care (Martin, 2005). The American Academy of Pediatrics, American Medical Association, Society for Adolescent Medicine, and American College of Obstetricians and Gynecologists support comprehensive sex education because it provides information about abstinence as well as contraception and condoms (Klein & Committee on Adolescence, 2005). Most parents and students feel adolescents have a right to accurate and complete sexual health information as a part of their education (National Campaign to Prevent Teen and Unplanned Pregnancy, 2006b). This view reflects a belief that knowledge supports better decision making than lack of knowledge and can help teenagers protect themselves from sexually transmitted infections, know how to avoid unintended pregnancy, value abstinence, and make choices that enable fulfillment of personal ambitions while maintaining physical and mental health (Barlow, 2005).

Comprehensive sex education begins with personal goal setting, decision-making, and responsibility. There are discussion on topics such as masturbation, birth control, sexually transmitted diseases, premarital sex, abortion, and homosexuality. Research has found this strategy generally promotes favorable health. Specifically, some behavioral outcomes include delaying initiation of sex, reducing number of partners, curbing incidence of unprotected sex, and increasing use of condoms and contraception among sexually active participants. The long-term consequences are lower pregnancy rates and less sexually transmitted diseases (Santelli, Ott, Lyon, Rogers, Summers, & Schleifer, 2006).

Despite the demonstrated benefits of comprehensive sex education programs, none are eligible for federal funding because they do not meet the mandates prohibiting education that identifies any benefits of condoms or contraceptives. Government involvement with abstinence education began with passage of the Adolescent Family Life Act in 1981. This legislation which made grants available to community and faith-based groups was challenged as unconstitutional in violating separation of church and state. Lower courts agreed but the United States Supreme Court, by a five to four vote, upheld the law maintaining that the government had a right to promote abstinence (Young & Penhollow, 2006). Consequently, the single approach supported by the federal government since 1998 has been *abstinence-only-until-marriage curriculum*. In these classes, students learn about the failure rate of condoms, are discouraged from using them to prevent sexually transmitted diseases and pregnancy, and sign pledges of virginity (Hauser, 2004; Santelli, Ott, Lyon, Rogers, Summers, & Schleifer, 2006).

The Mathematica Policy Research Institute in Princeton, New Jersey conducted a multiyear evaluation of abstinence programs for the U.S. Department of Health and Human Services (Trenholm, Devaney, Forston, Quay, Wheller, & Clark, 2007). The purpose was to assess the impact of four programs on 1,200 students in rural and urban communities in Florida, Wisconsin, Mississippi, and Virginia. Six years after students began the program at age 11 or 12, they were compared with 800 similar peers who had not participated in abstinence classes. Results showed that the classes had no effect on sexual abstinence. Students enrolled in the program were just as likely as those not attending classes to have intercourse. Adolescents from both groups reported beginning intercourse at the same average age of 14 years, 9 months. About 25% of students in both groups reported having sex with three or more partners and 23% reported always using a condom.

Columbia University researchers report that virginity pledges increase the risk for sexually transmitted infections and pregnancy. It was found that 88% of pledge-takers' initiated sex before marriage even though some delayed sex. The rate of sexually transmitted diseases among pledge-takers and non-pledge takers were similar, even though the pledge-takers delayed sex. Pledge-takers were less likely to seek testing for sexually transmitted infections and less likely to use contraception when they had intercourse (Brückner & Bearman, 2005). A federally supported study by the University of Pennsylvania found that abstinence—based programs in middle school make students aware of potential adverse consequences of nonmarital sex but do not appear to improve their refusal skills or communication with parents on topics related to sex (Honawar, 2005). Similarly, University of Washington researchers studying 1,700 teenagers found that students who took comprehensive sex education had a lower risk of pregnancy than adolescents who received abstinence only or no sex education (Kohler, Manhart, & Lafferty, 2008).

The overall conclusion from research on sex education is that encouraging abstinence and contraception are compatible goals. Abstinence-only-until marriage curriculum teaches teens about abstinence but not birth control; this approach makes it more likely that once teenagers begin sexual activity, they will have unsafe sex and risk greater exposure to sexually-transmitted diseases. Discussions of contraception in comprehensive sex education programs does not increase amount of sexual activity, and abstinence programs that provide medically accurate information on contraceptives for those already sexually active can support better health (Kohler, Manhart, & Lafferty, 2008).

SUBSTANCE ABUSE

The scope of protection needed to foster adolescent health goes beyond the sexual domain and includes substance abuse. Public rejection of hard drugs like cocaine and heroin has been motivated by studies showing how lives are destroyed by dependence on illegal substances and from personal observation of the damage to individuals (National Center on Addiction and Substance Abuse, 2006). A generation ago many adults decided to quit smoking and pay more attention to physical fitness. Attitude shifts were reflected by preferences for beverages with less alcohol. In the past decade, use of inhalants and synthetic drugs like methamphetamines have become appealing to adolescents at great cost to health. While the proportion of teenage smokers is in decline, this behavior continues to be a hazard with potentially fatal consequence. The Partnership for Drug-Free America (2006) provides an overview of drug descriptions and their effects that can be helpful to teenagers, parents and educators— http://www.drugfree.org.

Marijuana and Cocaine

Monitoring the Future is an annual survey of 50,000 students in Grades 8, 10, and 12 established in 1975 at the University of Michigan in collaboration with the National Institute on Drug Abuse. The usage for each type of drug is reported on their Web site at http://www.monitoringthefuture.org. From the outset, marijuana has been the most prevalent illicit drug each year, typically smoked, or sometimes mixed with food. About 35% of 12th graders, 30% of 10th graders, and 15% of eighth graders report that they use marijuana and it is easily available. The appealing effects include feelings of relaxation, euphoria, elevated self-confidence, vivid visual and auditory experiences and altered perceptions of time and space. However, teenagers seldom realize that marijuana is a gateway drug leading to more dangerous substances like cocaine (Brown & Snyder, 2008). Similarly, parents who may have used marijuana as teenagers view it as harmless because they are unaware of how the drug has changed since the time of their youth. Because of technology with hydroponics, plant cloning, and sophisticated lighting systems, adolescents now smoke Marijuana that is 10 times more potent than a generation ago. Each year more teenagers enter treatment with a diagnosis of marijuana dependence than all other drugs combined (Johnston, O'Malley, Bachman, & Schulenberg, 2008).

Two-thirds of marijuana users are younger than age 18. They are less likely to smoke marijuana if their parents strongly disapprove. Only 3% of teenagers whose parents strongly disapprove report using marijuana compared to 29% of those whose parents do not disapprove. Marijuana can impair judgment, coordination, balance, and ability to pay attention, reaction time in driving accidents and increases rate of age-related hippocampus neuron loss, leading to persistent memory loss. The drug has adverse affects on the respiratory system and is associated with bronchitis, emphysema, and lung cancer. Users have a risk of head and neck cancers two to three times greater than nonusers (Nistler, Hodgson, Nobrega, Hodgson, Wheatley, & Solberg, 2006). A drug knowledge quiz that teachers can recommend to parents and students for acquainting them with the dangers is available at The National Youth Anti-Drug Media Campaign site—http://www.theantidrug.com/advice/parenting-drug-knowledge-quiz.asp?id=banner.

Methamphetamine

Methamphetamine (meth) is known by many names such as "speed" and "glass." Use of speed that began as a fad by motorcycle gangs during the 1970s has become a major concern. Law enforcement ranks meth as the number one drug they battle (Owen, 2007). To respond, Congress passed the Combat Methamphetamine Epidemic Act in 2006 (Kennedy, 2006). Teenagers should be aware of how meth could affect them. Dopamine is the brain's natural pleasure chemical. Meth, whether smoked or injected, has the effect of releasing a powerful stimulant causing the brain to release a surge of dopamine that creates a euphoric high lasting 6 to 24 hours. Meth can also cause a dramatic increase in heart rate, resulting in an irreversible narrowing of brain blood vessels, leading to a stroke and severe respiratory problems (Lee, 2006). The drug also influences the central nervous system, making it difficult to fall asleep. Users frequently become confused, have tremors, and suffer convulsions, anxiety, paranoia, and aggression. A loss of teeth and sores all over the body are common signs that a person is taking meth. Researchers have found that meth changes wiring of the brain by destroying the dopamine neuro-receptors. Changes in rewiring require a year or more to regrow the receptors; during that time, users often slip into deep depression that may cause relapse (Braswell, 2006).

The low cost of meth is especially appealing to adolescent girls and young mothers who may try the drug because someone told them it suppresses appetite, enables weight loss, provides energy and enhances concentration. In Montana, where the epidemic got underway, 85% of women inmates in state prisons have been placed there because of meth-related crimes. Users are entering prison in record numbers while their children often overwhelm the social services system. During the 1990s foster care in cities increased dramatically because of crack babies but meth originated as a rural phenomenon where batches are more easily cooked in barns without notice of neighbors (Owen, 2007). As a result, orphans began to appear in places where there are no social service net-works to support them when courts took them away from their parents (Lee, 2006).

Montana's effort to confront the meth epidemic has been supported by Thomas Siebel, a Silicon Valley billionaire raised on a ranch in Mon-tana. He began by donating $6 million to fund a prevention campaign that is like no other. In an attempt to learn from adolescents, focus groups were held with teenagers to assess their views about meth. Nearly half of the students expressed their belief, based on stories they had been told that meth can be more beneficial than dangerous and worth a try (Langton, 2007). Civic leaders decided to adopt a novel strategy by presenting striking visual images with stories by teen addicts telling how they became involved and their tragic results. Graphic pic-tures appear on the Internet, billboards, and television showing addicts and the ways in which their lives have been damaged. Radio spots discourage youth consideration of the drug. Streaming video and addict comments with articles are at the Montana Meth Project Web site http://www.montanameth.org and sister site directed to teenagers is available at http://www.notevenonce.com.

Unlike cocaine, a natural drug derived from plants that are grown throughout the world, meth is a synthetic drug requiring ephedrine or pseudo ephedrine, chemicals that are found in over-the-counter cold, cough, and allergy medicines. Additional chemicals are used to isolate the ephedrine, cook it into meth, and process it for consumption (National Center of Addition and Substance Abuse, 2006). There is agreement that two solutions seem feasible to combat the meth crisis and neither has been fully tried. First, during the mid-1980s the Drug Enforcement Agency (DEA) proposed control of retail sales of ephedrine in cold medicines by having customers register and limit how much they could buy. Pharmaceutical companies resisted so the government exempted cold medication from the regulatory process. A second solution proposed by the DEA was to regulate source of ingredients. Ephedrine and pseudo ephedrine are chemicals that can only be produced in a few huge legal laboratories worldwide, making them potentially easy to trace. However, Washington's focus on cocaine and heroin meant that meth was not given high priority. The government focus shifted in 1994 when a customs agent discovered a large shipment of ephedrine on a plane from India to Mexico. Over an 18-month period, a Mexican drug cartel purchased 170 tons of ephedrine from manufacturers in India and smuggled into the United States to become 2 million hits of meth (Braswell, 2006).

Cold medicines remained unregulated and the cartel began to scoop up pills by the tens of thousands. Currently there are nearly 2 million users in the United States, and 1 million in the rest of the world. When 3,400 drug enforcement agencies across the nation were surveyed in 2005, meth (40%) was identified as the number one drug problem followed by cocaine (35%) and marijuana (12%) (National Center of Addiction and Substance Abuse, 2006). Only nine factories in the world manufacture the bulk of the world's supply of ephedrine. Tightening control over the supply of these chemicals has been pursued off and on for fifteen years but loopholes remain. For communities the consequence is a crime wave because addicts need money to support their habit. The Combat Meth Epidemic Act of 2006 imposed restrictions of wholesale and retail pseudo-ephedrine sales, toughened penalties against traffickers, and are intended to stem the flow from foreign manufacturers (Lee, 2006b).

Inhalants

Inhalants are the most frequently reported class of illicit drugs used among adolescents aged 12 or 13 (3.4 and 4.8%, respectively) (U.S. Department of Health and Human Services, 2008). There are over a thousand *inhalants* that are abused, including gasoline, paint thinner, aerosol sprays, nail polish remover, and household cleaners. Sniffing inhalants offers an inexpensive alternative to consuming illicit drugs and are readily accessible. Teenagers can also huff by soaking rags in inhalants and then pressing the rags to their mouth. Another option is known as bagging—inhaling fumes from chemicals poured into a plastic bag. Inhalants produce a quick and powerful lift. Inhalant abuse can start as early as elementary school and continue through adolescence. About 17% of American teenagers report using inhalants at least once in their lifetime (Whitehouse Drug Policy, 2008). When children sniff, huff, or bag, they take in a host of toxic chemicals such as butane, propane, fluorocarbons, and nitrates. Chronic abusers are at risk for weight loss, muscle weakness, lack of coordination, and addiction. Other possible effects include damage to the brain, heart, kidneys, and liver.

Youth who abuse inhalants often act as if they are intoxicated with alcohol. Some manifestations are excitation followed by drowsiness, lightheadedness, dizziness, loss of inhibitions, irritability, insomnia, hallucinations, and disruptive behavior. Adults often overlook inhalant abuse because they are preoccupied by concerns regarding use of nicotine, and illegal drugs. The Consumer Product Safety Commission (2007) Web site available at http://www.cpsc.gov/CPSCPUB/PUBS/389.html offers a parent observation guide to detect these signs: unusual breath odor or chemical odor on clothes; slurred or disoriented speech; drunk, dazed or dizzy appearance; signs of paint on finger or face; spots or sores around the mouth; nausea or loss of appetite; anxiety, irritability and restlessness.

Alcohol

Alcohol use is widespread among teenagers. Forty percent of 8th graders and 73% of 12th graders have consumed alcohol. Over half (56%) of 12th graders and 20% of 8th graders report being drunk at least once. Fortunately, the overall rate of alcohol use by adolescents is in decline (Johnston, O'Malley, Bachman, & Schulenberg, 2008). The adverse effects that drinking has on schoolwork and behavior are documented (Crosnoe, 2006). Instead of viewing this behavior as a rite of passage, neurological evidence shows that alcohol damages brain development making teenagers more likely to become alcoholics than was once supposed. In a national study of 43,000 adults, 47% who started drinking before age 14 became alcohol dependent compared with 9% of those who waited to drink until they were at least 21 years old (Hingson, Herren, & Winter, 2006).

The recognition that half of alcohol-related deaths on the highways involved teenage drivers triggered the formation of a group called Mothers Against Drunk Driving (MADD) in 1980—http://www.madd.org. From the outset this organization planned a campaign to save lives that eventually led all 50 of the states to raise their age for purchasing and drinking alcohol to 21 years. Nevertheless, automobile accidents continue to be the leading cause of teenage death, accounting for 6,000 lives lost each year—a fatality rate four times higher than for drivers aged 25–69 (K. Kelly, 2005). Many injuries can be prevented by seatbelts. Still, even though driver education courses, school programs, and state laws urge drivers to buckle up, teens are less likely than other age groups to heed the warning (Elliott, Shope, Raghunathan, & Waller, 2006).

Tobacco

The Centers for Disease Control (2007) reports that 22% of high school students smoke cigarettes. Each day an estimated 1,500 persons younger than age 18 begin smoking on a regular basis. Tobacco usage is the most preventable cause of death, causing 450,000 fatalities a year, more than AIDS, alcohol, accidents, murders, suicides, and drug taking combined. On average, smokers die 13 to 14 years earlier than nonsmokers. Adolescents that smoke underestimate the health risks and overestimate their ability to quit once a habit has been established. The reality is that, among high school seniors who smoke several cigarettes each day, 70% will still be smoking 5 years later (Substance Abuse and Mental Health Services Administration, 2005). The younger students are when they begin to smoke, the greater their chances of becoming a heavy smoker as adults (Centers for Disease Control, 2005, 2006, 2009). Teenagers report that it is easy to get cigarettes (Jason, Pokorny, Muldowney, & Velez, 2005). Adolescents who smoke are more inclined than nonsmokers to experiment with other illegal substances that can produce harm. The Centers for Disease Control offer tips for youth to avoid smoking, see "I Quit! What to do when you are sick of smoking, chewing or dipping" at http://www.cdc.gov/tobacco/youth/index.htm. The Tobacco Control Program in British Columbia, Canada, is a resource for teachers, parents, and teenagers about the effects of tobacco use http://www.tobaccofacts.org.

For most adolescents, the health commitment that is needed to refuse tobacco and other drugs comes from supportive families, relatives who do not smoke but listen, make suggestions, encourage goal setting, and provide help. This orientation that makes a family more able to function effectively implicates education. According to the Centers for Disease Control (2007), the likelihood of adolescent exposure to smoking in their family differs substantially by the amount of formal education of the parents. Respectively, 8% of parents with a bachelor's degree smoke, compared with 20% who attended some college, 29% of those completing high school and 30% with less than a high school diploma. Parent education on the school Web site might produce a change in these figures.

Peer influence has a powerful affect on the decision to smoke. There is evidence that most adolescents see smoking as an unattractive habit and have developed norms that act as a deterrent to the use of tobacco. Table 10.3 Teen Opinions on Smoking, presents results of a national survey about reasons why smoking is unpopular among teens (Centers for Disease Control, 2005). Being exposed to secondhand smoke concerns teenagers who believe they have a right to breathe clean air. The facts supporting this point of view are that secondhand smoke: produces 6 times the pollution of a busy highway; causes 30 times as many lung cancer deaths as all the regulated pollutants combined; contributes to 300,000 lung infections like pneumonia and bronchitis in children; produces reddening, itching and watering eyes, wheezing, coughing, earaches, and asthma; fills the air with many of the same poisons found in toxic waste dumps; and distorts the smell and taste of food while making the person's clothes and hair stink.

All high schools and most middle schools offer anti-drug education. These programs acknowledge that peer influence has been found to have greater impact on substance abuse than all other factors (Johnston, O'Malley, Bachman, & Schulenberg, 2008). A longitudinal investigation with 2,000 adolescents related to five risk behaviors including alcohol, marijuana, smoking, tobacco chewing, and sexual debut. For each risk, friends were identified as the most influential source for adopting

Table 10.3.   Teen Opinions on Smoking

All Numbers are Percentages	*Agree*	*Disagree*	*No Opinion or Don't Know*
Seeing someone smoke turns me off	67	22	10
I'd rather date people who don't smoke	86	8	6
It's safe to smoke for only a year or two	7	92	1
Smoking can help you when you are bored	7	92	1
Smoking helps reduce stress	21	78	3
Smoking helps keep your weight down	18	80	2
Chewing tobacco and snuff cause cancer	95	2	3
I strongly dislike being around smokers	65	22	13

Source: Centers for Disease Control and Prevention (2005). *Teen opinions on smoking survey.* Atlanta, GA: Centers for Disease Control and Prevention. Retrieved January 21, 2009, from http://www.cdc.gov

unhealthy behavior and for enabling cessation (Maxwell, 2002). Once teenagers start consuming any drug, therapy can yield progress but if they return to interact with the same drug-taking friends after rehabilitation, chances are that the treatment effect will not last (Flanagan, Elek-Fisk, & Gallay, 2004). In such cases, advising someone to adopt refusal skills is seldom effective since the most powerful influence in their lives remains a negative force. Accordingly, some students need to have a new group of peers who will encourage them and monitor a healthier path (Martin, 2005).

Peer counseling programs are the most effective form of drug prevention for adolescents (National Center on Addiction and Drug Abuse, 2006). Using this strategy, the students who sign a contract pledging to stay tobacco, alcohol or drug-free get extensive training by the school counseling staff for roles allowing them to act as positive peer leaders. They learn ways to build self-esteem in classmates who lack friends, offer alternative support as well as constructive goals for those whose peer group is moving in the wrong direction, and help acquire and practice refusal skills. Peer leaders are examples to others in their classes, on sports teams, and in extracurricular clubs (Bachman, O'Malley, Schulenberg, Johnson, Freedman-Doan, & Messersmith, 2007).

SUMMARY

Growth and Development

One challenging aspect of adolescence involves the acceptance of a realistic body image. Daily observation of peer differences from oneself in height, weight and sexual maturation is a continual source of anxiety. For teens appearances matter because their status and identity are implicated. Changes associated with puberty for boys include growth of the scrotum and penis, capacity for ejaculation, appearance of body hair, bone and muscle gain, and deepening of the voice. For girls puberty starts with breast development and menstruation. There is a need to know in advance that the breasts may not develop at the same rate and menstrual periods may be irregular as well as accompanied by cramps with possible pain. Parents and schools should have discussions with middle school students regarding sexual intercourse and protection from sexually transmitted infections. Schools also contribute to health by conducting vision screening and hearing tests to identify disabilities that can reduce learning and detract from student quality of life.

Nutrition and Diet

Teenagers like being the decision makers about what they eat but frequently choose foods that are not good for them. Schools have inadvertently contributed to poor diet by profiting from vending machines that offer sugar based sodas and lunch menu options ignoring the nutritional needs of adolescents. Congress passed a law in 2006 intended to bring schools into compliance with guidelines that support healthy eating habits on campus. Many teenagers who want to conform to the idealized thin body image skip meals and experiment with dieting plans that cut calories but ignore needs for nutrients such as iron and calcium. Adolescents, especially girls, may suffer from anorexia nervosa (self-imposed starving) or bulimia (overeating and then vomiting and purging) that can jeopardize their pattern of growth and long term health.

Exercise and Fitness

Exercise is essential to promote health. However, most adolescents have a sedentary schedule at school that includes being seated most of the day and this habit continues upon returning home with chatting on the computer or watching television. Because schools are expected to prepare students for life, education should include daily-required involvement with exercise. Parents should become models of exercise while schools develop new ways to ensure that all students get physical activity. One aspect of lifestyle involves fashion, the way that a person dresses and takes care of their appearance. When schools solicit the views of students during formation of dress codes, teenagers are more likely to believe that their views count, value the rationale for policies, and conform to them.

Sexual Behavior and Knowledge

Many high school students and a growing number in middle school report that they have had sex. These sexually active adolescents are less likely than older persons to rely on condoms consistently, more likely to have a partner who has been active with others, and to participate in oral sex. Exposure to myths about prevention of pregnancy, underestimates of dangers related to oral sex, and female involvement with older partners combine to yield unexpected trouble. Half of all teenage pregnancies result in live births for girls who more often than in the past become single mothers. Comprehensive sex education in schools is widely encouraged as the way to ensure that teenagers understand the importance of abstinence, become aware of their responsibility toward sexual partners and know how to prevent pregnancy as well as avoid sexually transmitted infections.

Substance Abuse

Adolescents want to become independent but instead some of them lose their ability for self-control when they take drugs like Cocaine, Heroin, and Methamphetamine. One effective prevention strategy has been to blanket the media by providing teenagers a graphic portrayal of the meth epidemic including direct reports from addicts who describe the loss of their autonomy. Under-age drinking also presents health risks, especially when combined with driving. Car accidents are the leading cause of death among teenagers. Smoking is an addiction for many teenagers who find themselves unable to quit. The forecast that teenage smokers who continue as adults may shorten their life by a dozen years urges schools to create more effective methods to help students choose a tobacco-free lifestyle.

CLASSROOM APPLICATIONS

1. Middle school students need to know that it is normal for people in their age group to differ from one another in height and weight. Boys and girls who learn at school about growth patterns can better anticipate change and understand that peers face the same challenges.
2. Classes should discuss teasing, defined as "making fun of someone, either playfully or maliciously." Body size and sexual maturation are a focus for teasing. Unlike bully victims, teasing victims are urged to endure hurtful comments, be strong, look at these situations as a part of learning to cope and as opportunities to develop character and resilience.
3. Schools should acquaint adolescents about the increase of hearing loss among people of their age, explain the potential consequences that can be expected, and describe ways to protect themselves. Faculty, student and parent initiatives can motivate the community changes that are needed.
4. The school library should have a designated section where information about health concerns of teenagers can be found including

recommended Web sites. Knowing about the resources can be part of student orientation.

5. Understanding ways to promote and to preserve personal health is one of the most important aspects of learning that can be provided by schools. Districts should provide adolescents a systematic health curriculum that covers development, exercise, nutrition, drug awareness, and sexuality.

6. Oral sex among teenagers is a topic most parents and educators refuse to discuss with students and believe is the responsibility of physical education faculty or the school nurse. The result of evasion is that teenagers lack a credible source of guidance about this risky behavior. Schools should organize in-service training on this topic and invite parents to attend.

7. Provide a homework assignment for your students to examine messages from the Montana Web sites highlighting the methamphetamine epidemic. This assignment should also call on the students' parents to see these same messages followed by a family conversation reported on later in the class.

8. Efforts to dissuade adults from using tobacco have resulted in a decline in proportion of smokers. Related initiatives might have a similar influence on teenage smokers if schools were to go beyond just forbidding the presence of tobacco on campus and also utilized education as means of persuasion.

9. Assign teams to visit the federal nutrition and exercise Web sites in this chapter. One team can report on the Portion Distortion issue and quiz on portion sizes as well as the serving size card. Another group can discuss their trial of the pyramid tracker with feedback on diet quality, physical activity status, and nutrition. A third group can talk about the distinctions between Go, Slow, and Whoa foods in formulating a plan for nutrition.

10. Teachers usually regard themselves as examples of intellectual curiosity and sustained learning. Students can benefit when they adopt such behaviors. The scope of influence teachers have on adolescent lifestyle could enlarge if they were recognized as good models of exercise and nutrition habits.

FOR REFLECTION

1. What are some of the social implications for adolescents who mature earlier or later than their classmates?

2. How would you respond to reports from overweight students that others are teasing them in your classes?

3. How should schools acquaint students and parents with Web sites on health issues for family discussion?

4. How could faculty ease the problems pregnant girls face as they try to obtain their high school diploma?

5. Why do you suppose so many teenagers smoke when they are aware this habit causes health problems?

6. What curriculum changes should schools make so teens are better informed about nutrition and exercise?

7. How can schools help obese students with challenges without causing them to withdraw or sense alienation?

8. How can teachers across subjects integrate health issues into their curriculum so students see a broader relevance?

9. Why would you support or oppose a school district policy that forbids faculty from smoking while on campus?

10. In what ways could teachers mobilize student norms of behavior that encourage adoption of healthy lifestyle?

KEY TERMS

Abortion

Abstinence Only Until Marriage Curriculum

Acne

Anorexia nervosa

Bulimia

Comprehensive Sex Education Program

Condom

Contraception

Daydreaming

Hyperopia

Inhalant

Iron Deficiency Anemia

Legal age of consent

Masturbation

Menarche

Menstruation

Methamphetamine

Myopia
Obese
Oral sex
Osteoporosis
Overweight
Pregnancy Rate
Puberty
Statutory rape

VISIT THESE WEB SITES

Link to these sites at http://www.infoagepub.com/strom-adolescents

Adolescent Tattoo Quiz
http://www.kidsgrowth.org/resources/articledetail.cfm?id=434

American Obesity Association http://www.obesity.org

American Optometric Association http://www.aoa.org/x4692.xml

Centers for Disease Control, Youth Tobacco Prevention
http://www.cdc.gov/tobacco/youth/index.htm

Consumer Product Safety Commission,
A Guide to Preventing Inhalant Abuse
http://www.cpsc.gov/cpscpub/pubs/389gph.html

How loud is loud? http://www.abelard.org/hear/hear.php#how-loud

Minnesota Obesity Center http://www1.umn.edu/mnoc

Monitoring the Future, National Results on Adolescent Drug Use
http://www.monitoringthefuture.org

Montana Meth Project http://www.montanameth.org

Montana Not Even Once http://www.notevenonce.com

Mothers Against Drunk Driving http://www.madd.org

National Association of Anorexia,
Nervosa and Associated Disorders
http://www.anad.org

National Campaign to Prevent Teen and Unplanned Pregnancy
http://www.thenationalcampaign.org

National Youth Anti-Drug Media Campaign,
Drug Quiz for Parents and Teens

http://www.theantidrug.com/advice/parenting-drug-knowledge-quiz.asp?id=banner

NBC Digital Health Network, Teen Health
http://www.healthvideo.com

Partnership for Drug-Free America, Drug Guide
http://www.drugfree.org

Sight and Hearing Association, Online Assessments
http://www.sightandhearing.org

Talking with Kids about Tough Issues
http://www.talkingwithkids.org

Tobacco Control Program in Victoria, British Columbia, Canada
http://www.tobaccofacts.org

United States Department of Agriculture,
Assess Your Food Intake http://www.mypyramidtracker.gov

United States Department of Agriculture,
Steps to a Healthier You http://www.mypyramid.gov

United States Department of Health and
Human Services & National Institutes of Health
http://www.nhlbi.nih.gov/health/public/heart/obesity/wecan/live-it/go-slow-whoa.htm

United States Department of Health and Human Services,
For Parents http://www.4parents.gov/

EXERCISES AND ROLES

Exercise 10.01: School Dress Code Poll

Role: Voter

The purpose of this poll is to find out how students at your school feel about dress codes.

Directions: For each item, select the answer that shows how you feel. Your responses are anonymous and may be combined with those of other students at your school in a report to students, faculty, and parents.

1. I want my school to have a dress code.
   Agree   Disagree   No Opinion
2. School uniforms provide a sense of belonging.
   Agree   Disagree   No Opinion
3. Safety at school would improve if there is a dress code.
   Agree   Disagree   No Opinion
4. Having a gang-free campus is supported by a dress code.
   Agree   Disagree   No Opinion
5. Shirts with bad language on them should be prohibited.
   Agree   Disagree   No Opinion
6. Hairstyle of students should be part of a dress code.
   Agree   Disagree   No Opinion
7. Jewelry, tattoos, and body piercings should be regulated.
   Agree   Disagree   No Opinion
8. Teachers and staff should have to follow a dress code too.
   Agree   Disagree   No Opinion
9. Students are treated more fairly when they wear uniforms.
   Agree   Disagree   No Opinion
10. Students should be involved in choosing the dress codes.
    Agree   Disagree   No Opinion
11. It is unfair for students to be told what they have to wear.
    Agree   Disagree   No Opinion
12. A dress code should apply to all school functions.
    Agree   Disagree   No Opinion
13. Students are treated differently depending on what they wear.
    Agree   Disagree   No Opinion
14. Students are distracted when classmates dress inappropriately.
    Agree   Disagree   No Opinion

Select your grade level, gender, ethnicity, and age.

My grade level is 5 6 7 8 9 10 11 12
My gender is female male
My ethnicity is Asian Black Hispanic Native American White Other
My age is 10 11 12 13 14 15 16 17 18 19

Exercise 10.02: Appearance and Fashion Choice

Role: Summarizer

Some adolescent girls do not want to dress like Hollywood celebrities. A group of students at Mountain View High School in Mesa, Arizona, collected 1,500 signatures on a petition urging that department stores offer them a broader selection of fashion choices. These girls wanted more modest clothing options than having to buy only low-rise midriff-baring and spaghetti-strap wear that are popular. One 16-year-old said, "I don't want to feel like people are constantly looking at my body." Even boys signed the petition. The girls then met with Dillards Department Store, bringing photos along to show what they wanted to wear and be able to purchase. Shopping is difficult the girls said as they look for shorts that are longer and tops that are not too low cut and cover the shoulders and midriffs. Dillards welcomed the input and responded, as did Nordstroms when teenagers in California presented a similar petition to them. List some problematic types of student clothing and appearance that should be excluded by a school dress code. Be specific about why your exclusions are appropriate for a secondary school environment.

Exercise 10.03: Drug Tracking And Response

Role: Evaluator

1. You are teaching a first hour class and walking around the room to examine the work of students. You pass by a particular student who smells strongly like marijuana. How do you respond and why?

2. Interview an assistant principal at a secondary school to find out the policies that apply in cases when students are suspected of drug abuse. Ask about the procedures teachers are expected to follow in such cases. Identify what schools do on their own to handle such problems and ways in which other agencies like the police department become implicated. Report the findings to your teammates.

EXERCISE 10.04: Media Campaigns to Prevent Smoking

Role: Generational Reporter

The society is concerned about a growing number of boys and girls who develop the habit of smoking. In order to reduce the incidence of adolescent smoking, Phillip Morris and other tobacco companies have invested in public service advertising campaigns targeting this age group. Interview some teenagers to learn their impression of how successful this strategy is to reach them.

EXERCISE 10.05: MOBILIZING INFLUENCE ON OBESITY

Role: Challenger

Many adolescents are overweight and they risk long-term health problems. There is public ambivalence about how to respond to this rapidly growing danger. In the estimate of one group, it is demeaning to draw attention to people who are obese because it could damage self-esteem and represents cruelty. An opposite opinion is that failing to say anything condones a lack of self-regulation, and people should be reminded to adopt good eating habits and exercise in much the same way society has gone after adult smokers. Describe ways that you feel would be helpful in dealing with this issue.

Exercise 10.06: Exercise Homework for Students and Parents

Role: Challenger

The topic for a faculty meeting is whether once a week homework should exclude academic assignments in favor of expecting students and parents to participate together in a range of exercise options that can promote physical health. Some teachers believe this is a sensible reaction to reports by the Surgeon General and other medical authorities that a sedentary lifestyle undermines the health of adolescents and their relatives. Prepare a brief statement describing the reaction and rationale you will present when asked to comment in the meeting about the proposed "Home workout."

Exercise 10.07: Sex Education

Role: Improviser

Explain what you perceive to be the benefits and disadvantages of (a) abstinence only classes, and (b) comprehensive sex education classes.

Exercise 10.08: Health and Fitness

Role: Improviser

An epidemic is underway and must be stopped so that the lengthy lifespan expected for today's adolescents can be healthy. Obesity, type 2 diabetes, high blood pressure, ulcers, and additional danger signs have begun to emerge for teenagers because many maintain sedentary habits, lack exercise, and observe dysfunctional adult models for diet and fitness. Your high school faculty is going to make a presentation on "Adolescent Health" to parents of adolescents. Suggest (a) healthy activities parents and teenagers could participate in together (perhaps qualifying as homework), and (b) agenda questions to guide family conversations about this issue.

Exercise 10.09: Health Portfolio

Role: Improviser

Portfolios help students set goals, monitor progress, and showcase their academic achievement. Apply this concept to the development of a health portfolio that individual students would maintain in middle school and high school.

Describe the content to be included and suggested procedures for students to carry out their task.

Exercise 10.10: Breaking the Dress Code Policy

Role: Evaluator

Generate a scenario (i.e., case) where a student violates the dress code policy. Then recommend some procedures and precautions that teachers should take in confronting the adolescent and his family in resolving the situation.

CHAPTER 11

SELF CONTROL AND
SAFE SCHOOLS

Providing a safe environment is a national goal. There are efforts to prevent child abuse, violence against partners, coercion at work, and harassment by government or religious officials. Rejection of such offenses and public demands that misconduct result in punishment are signs of progress toward becoming a civil society. Bullying is the most frequent discipline problem for the schools, involving 30% of students as bullies or victims (Williams & Guerra, 2007). Victims of peer abuse describe their ordeal as including fear, humiliation, hopelessness, pain, depression, loneliness, social anxiety, inability to concentrate on studies and reluctance to come to school (Kowalski, Limber, & Agatston, 2008). Students who depart from norms are the most likely to be singled out for harassment. In a national school survey involving 6,200 middle and high school students, 86% of those who identified themselves as gay or lesbian reported verbal abuse in the past year and 44% stated they had been physically mistreated (Kosciw, Diaz, & Greytak, 2008). Other studies also indicate gay and lesbian youth are often exposed to homophobic hatred and violence (Mason, 2007). Another group exposed to greater abuse are the disabled, particularly students with social skill deficits whose lack of friends makes them more vulnerable (Carter & Spencer, 2006). Surveys also reveal that over half of the gifted and talented report being a target of bullies (Peterson & Ray, 2006).

Adolescents in the Internet Age, pp. 471–518

Many victims do not report their intimidation because they believe that relatives cannot help, adults do not understand, they would find themselves in trouble, and parents are too busy to assist them. There can be a reluctance to tell teachers because students believe privacy and confidentiality do not exist at school, faculty do not recognize limitations of safety policies, teachers cannot intervene in effective ways, and lack the time and willingness to listen. Those who have been victims are the most hesitant to tell teachers. One-third believe teachers cannot help anyway so it is better to deal with situations alone (Agatston, Kowalski, & Limber, 2007).

Teachers report that they are concerned about the growing number of students who seem unable to deal with frustration, react with outbursts of anger in the classroom, taunt or persecute others, and present discipline problems that interfere with the learning of everyone. The goals for this chapter are to explore several theories related to the promotion of self-control, identify kinds of intimidation some students experience, consider how individuals and institutions can respond to cyberbullies, examine characteristics of bullies, explain effects of bullying on the bystanders, outline abuse prevention programs, and show why parents must become more involved with their role in providing corrective guidance.

THEORIES OF CIVIL BEHAVIOR

Educators choose theories to rely on based on perceived relevance for particular problems. Sometimes however, the insights needed call for seeing an issue from more than one point of view. The juxtaposition of theories makes it possible to gain a broader perspective on factors implicated in self-control and school safety. Specifically, the main concern of some teachers is identifying methods of instruction that motivate conformity to classroom and school rules. A prominent concern of other teachers is how observation of good and bad behavior affects students and ways to restrict the amount of their exposure to unacceptable conduct. The third set of issues centers on arranging conditions that can encourage students to become caring individuals that will take action to prevent exploitation of others. In combination, these matters implicate behavioral conditioning theory, social cognitive theory and hierarchy of needs theory.

Behavior Conditioning Theory

When the study of psychology began, most human behavior was attributed to instincts. Scholars defined *instincts* as an inherited network of emotional drives that predispose individuals to avoid or approach particular stimuli (McDougall, 1916). John Watson (1874–1954) became the most formidable opponent of instinct theory. To assess innate emotions (instincts), he presented infants with objects that they were thought to instinctively fear. Instead, he discovered that babies did not show fear of black cats, reptiles, monkeys or white rats. If there are no avoidance instincts at birth, how is it that only a few years later children have so many fears? Watson concluded that fear is a learned behavior, the environment has the greatest impact on development, and planning wise interventions can mold people to pursue whatever pattern of behavior is intended by those who manage the environment (Watson & Rayner, 1920, 2000). Watson's often cited assertion was,

> There are inheritable differences in structure but we no longer believe in inherited capacities. Give me a dozen healthy infants and my specified world to bring them up in and I will guarantee to take any one at random and train him to become any type of specialist I select—doctor, lawyer, artist, merchant, chief, and, even beggarman or thief regardless of talents, penchants, tendencies, abilities, vocations and race of his ancestors. (Watson, 1930, p. 104)

Watson maintained that psychology would not become a credible science unless scholars could verify findings as researchers do in other fields. He suggested that the purpose of psychology should be the prediction and control of behavior. To attain this goal, the objective method needed would be to focus on recording observable events. Feelings, aspirations, and beliefs are subjective mental states that cannot be observed. Similarly, hypothetical internal factors such as the id and ego described by Sigmund Freud cannot be seen. Consequently, these unscientific considerations must be replaced with a behavior conditioning theory that emphasizes the external shaping of human behavior and records progress in modifying conduct (Watson, 1925, 1928).

B. F. Skinner (1904–1990), a psychologist at Harvard, built on the legacy of Watson and became the most well known behaviorist. His *operant conditioning* paradigm explains that behaviors are learned mainly because of the consequences (rewards or punishments) that follow them. Accordingly, the conditioner (experimenter, teacher, or parent) provides rewards such as a kernel of corn to a chicken, a piece of candy to a student or a word of approval to a friend for actions considered appropriate when they occur. The probability for a particular response is increased when that response is immediately followed by positive consequences called *reinforcements* (Skinner, 1965, 1976). Teachers use positive and negative reinforcements. Positive reinforcement involves a reward such as recognition while negative reinforcements allow learners to escape an unpleasant consequence such as extra homework on the condition they behave accordingly. Punishment is a last resort when conditioning behavior does not lead to the acceptance of class rules. There is considerable evidence that operant conditioning is an effective method for reduction of temper tantrums (anger management), helping smokers give up the cigarette habit, and being able to lose weight (Martin & Pear, 2006).

Skinner (1985) was convinced that since behaviors resulting in reward are learned, consequences are the key to governing the direction of development while cognitive activity is inconsequential. For this reason, operant conditioning ignores inappropriate or incorrect behaviors that are destined to die or become extinct because they are not rewarding or rewarded. Because rewards should only be applied for acceptable responses, Skinner (1971) predicted that computers would eventually provide more effective instruction than teachers who may be inconsistent and sometimes reward the wrong things.

Operant conditioning was explained to the public as the best method of instruction to deal with misbehavior and also the most suitable approach for constructing a safe society. In Skinner's (1948) novel, *Walden Two*, he tried to illustrate that, by carefully rewarding conformity it would be possible to eliminate selfishness, bullying, and criminal conduct. He explained,

> My preference for positive rather than punitive control is based on my observation that human behavior is wholly determined by environment. Some psychologists may try to explain behavior by what happens inside people's heads, so-called states of mind or feelings. However, we need to look outside of individuals rather than inside them for solutions. Teachers do not change minds; they only change the world in which their students live. (Skinner, 1980, p. 80)

The education context in which behaviorism remains most powerful is special education where teachers are expected to help students modify unacceptable conduct and conform to rules (Rachlin, 2004).

In *Beyond Freedom and Dignity*, Skinner (1971) argued that concepts such as freedom, choice, and autonomy should be abandoned. He argued that only a technology of behavior could save democracy from the problems of abuse that threaten safety. A more suitable emphasis would be to identify stimuli and reinforcing contingencies that would produce desirable behavior. Critics warned that the real danger was Skinner's belief that some person or select group would decide what is best and shape uniform expectations for everyone. Given that scenario, what would happen to future Picassos, Einsteins, and Gates? They would be so conditioned that none of them could depart from the conventional, expected, and rewarded behaviors (Kohn, 2006).

Social Cognitive Theory

The benefits of behaviorism to improve conduct merged with the mental processes referred to as cognition in the theory of Albert Bandura (1925–) at Stanford University. Bandura was a behaviorist who decided that external shaping does not fully explain the learning process. Instead, he believes that mental processes are involved and most learning is based on observation. Watching how another person, a model, acts can lead to behavior changes within the observer. The viewer's attempt to imitate or reproduce mannerisms and performance of what has been witnessed is referred to as *modeling*. Everyone learns some things by modeling. Another common outcome of observational learning is *vicarious conditioning*, paying attention to the positive or negative consequences that follow actions of a model, and then adjusting personal response accordingly (Bandura, 1977).

Observation of human behavior can be time consuming and difficult to analyze but it is necessary for accurate understanding. Careful viewing of adolescents while they participate in unstructured contexts can provide data about ways they imitate, experiment, and rely on models when adopting new forms of behavior. Bandura's (1977, 1989, 1997) social cognitive theory assumes that human learning begins with observation followed by partial or complete imitation. This significant departure from the view of other behaviorists meant that Bandura recognized cognitive processes determine how people interpret what they observe. Teachers support appropriate observational learning when they provide examples of steps and skills that students are expected to reproduce in a lesson, illustrate relevance of assignments by referring to situations students consider important, and giving feedback that identifies errors as well as ways to correct them. Mentoring programs also provide students with peer or adult models whose exemplary behavior warrants reproduction as a key to success (Milsom & Gallo, 2006).

Studies of aggression and abuse especially confirm the enormous power imitation has in formation of personality and underscores a need to understand how observation guides behavior. In a classic experiment to assess modeling in childhood, Bandura, Ross, and Ross (1963) arranged for a group of preschoolers to observe an adult while he punched and kicked an inflated plastic doll. When the adult model sat atop the doll, he described each of his physical actions, making such comments as "sock the doll in the nose" and "hit the doll in the stomach." While using a hammer he shouted "pow" as each leg of the doll was repeatedly banged. Later on, when the observing children were left alone with replicas of the doll and other toys, most of them imitated the sequence of destructive behavior that had been seen, usually duplicating in detail the punching and hitting episodes. Another group of children that observed a different adult model playing with Tinker Toys did not show any destructive behaviors when presented with the inflated doll. The researchers concluded that violent behavior and gradual development of insensitivity toward abusive behavior is learned by observation. Further, as youngsters watch television programs that include repeated episodes of violence, abuse, and other unacceptable conduct that do not result in punishment, they decide that acting the same way presents a low risk of punishment. Bandura's findings have been replicated (Baumeister, 2005).

The scope of observational learning and vicarious conditioning implicate the entire range of student experiences. When they are at home students may watch violence, abuse, pornography or other unhealthy behavior in video games, movies, the Internet, television and the neighborhood. Parents are uncertain about the extent of precautions they should take to restrict what a child is allowed to see. At school adolescents often observe cheating, teasing, bullying, and rejection, intimidation by threats, outbursts of anger, and physical conflict. Lessons regarding self-control and personal responsibility for the safety of others are being learned and reinforced daily in these situations (Agliata, Tantleff-Dunn, & Renk, 2007). Students must decide whether to show courage in directly opposing or reporting bullying they witness as bystanders or remain silent to protect themselves (Salmivalli, Kaukiainen, & Voeten, 2005). Vicarious conditioning is cited as student justification for cheating when they see that being caught or punished is rare and therefore involves minimal risk (Maxwell & Reichenbach, 2005).

Hierarchy of Needs Theory

Abraham Maslow (1908–1970) proposed a novel way to conceptualize human motivation. He was stimulated by discontent with theories of Sigmund Freud and other psychoanalysts whose counseling practice involved mostly troubled people who did not represent the norm. Consequently, the writing of clinical psychologists emphasized the dark side of human nature and often portrayed aberrant problems as common. Maslow (1968, 1973, 1994) suggested that a better focus for the study of mental health should center on self-actualizers, persons whose lives personify a desire to support the welfare of others. Examining the attributes of people like Franklin Roosevelt, Martin Luther King, Caesar Chavez, and Billy Graham could offer examples of how to achieve self-control and civil behavior.

Maslow (1987, 1998) hoped to identify the characteristics resulting in healthy ambitions and emotional maturity. His hierarchy of needs theory premise is that everyone is driven by an ever-expanding set of unsatisfied wants. As soon as the primary needs are satisfied, other needs become prominent, starting with basic biological necessities and proceeding through a series of levels that are each more intangible than preceding ones. When a specific need has been met, its urgency declines and the next higher need assumes priority. By this manner of progression, satisfaction of lower order needs become the basis for allowing greater concentration on fulfillment of higher order needs.

Maslow's hierarchy of needs includes five levels that generate motivation. Respectively, the demands are

1. physiological needs for food, water, air, shelter, rest, and exercise;
2. safety needs for freedom from fear of deprivation, threat, and danger;
3. belonging needs to be with others, socialize, feel accepted, and loved;
4. esteem needs to establish a personal reputation and enjoy self-respect; and
5. self-actualization needs to be fulfilled by using abilities to benefit others (Maslow, 1973, 1998).

The first four levels of the hierarchy—physiological, safety, belonging, and esteem—are identified as *deficit needs*. Until students have enough to eat, regard the environment as safe and secure, feel accepted by others, and are satisfied with themselves, teachers cannot effectively appeal to their higher level needs for growth that motivate learning and aspiration. This means that safety and psychological security are preconditions for teacher success in supporting education, health, and overall student development (Black, 2006). Maslow (1973) estimated that average Americans satisfied 85% of their physiological needs, 70% of safety needs, 50% of belonging needs, 40% of esteem needs, and 10% of self-actualization needs. He speculated that if this record could be improved, then regardless of individual differences in intellectual achievement, more people would grow toward the ideal of becoming self-actualized. Self-actualization means giving up the desire to be better than others in favor of striving to do the best one can. Self-actualizers can be counted on to take the actions needed to meet the deficiency needs of others.

CHARACTERISTICS OF BULLIES

Most adults recall school bullies that they tried to avoid and may still wonder what led them to mistreat classmates. Similarly, opinion varies regarding the normality of bully behavior, types of individuals that become involved, and kind of relationships they have with relatives and friends. There is also speculation about the influence bullies have on peers that watch while they torment victims. These considerations are best informed by a review of research findings.

Misconceptions About Bullies

When bullies stop bothering peers, schools become safer places. One way to begin is to abandon the misconception that bully behavior is normal, a stage some people go through but are likely to outgrow as they become adults. Research supports an opposite conclusion and suggests that ways must be found to modify the behavior of bullies while they are young. Psychologists at the University of Michigan conducted a longitudinal study of 500 students, following them from age 8 until age 30 (Huesmann, 2007). Assessments showed that bullies experienced far greater adjustment problems than classmates. About 25% of those who started fights in elementary school by pushing, hitting or stealing the belongings of others had a criminal record by age 30; the comparable record was less than 5% among non-bullies. Furthermore, waiting longer to intervene seems to make matters worse.

Bullies often become adults with unstable relationships. In comparison with the general population, male bullies more often abuse their wives, drive erratically on the highway, get fired from jobs, commit more felonies, and less often achieve vocational success. Females that bully classmates in childhood are more inclined to severely punish their own children. Male and female bullies have higher than average rates of alcoholism, more frequent personality disorders, and require greater use of mental health services than non-bullies (Larson, 2008).

Although bullies get lots of attention from teachers and administrators, responses seldom include instruction to improve behavior. Later on the same pattern of behavior that make bullies troublesome to classmates are portrayed on a larger scale in their employment histories where rejection is the typical response of co-workers. Parents of school-age bullies should be made aware that harassing others will eventually harm the perpetrators as well as victims (Dutton, 2007). Teachers should recognize that helping students develop their own internal guidance system is a more constructive response to violence than recruiting more guidance counselors. New Zealand educators have devised tips on establishing the Whole School Approach to reduce peer abuse. See http://www.police.govt.nz/service/yes/nobully/kia_kaha/whole.html.

Contrary to popular opinion, bullies are often intelligent, get good grades, and express self-confidence (Huesmann, 2007). These assets can lead teachers to underestimate the dangers that might occur if such children grow up without a sense of empathy and continue to mistreat others (Bianco, 2005; Denison, 2005). Policymakers encourage educators to take the problems of bullies as seriously as if they had another disability teachers feel more comfortable trying to remediate. When students experience difficulty reading, tutoring is given with the expectation that intervention will yield improvement. However, educators less often express hope when a student lacks self-restraint or concern for the feelings of others. In such cases, the potential for learning is ignored in favor of considering punishment options.

Social skill deficits and emotional immaturity are issues educators lack confidence in confronting once a student shows signs of failure. Many schools give up on these individuals. Yet, specialized classes are available for students that take illegal drugs because it is assumed they are capable of recovery if provided instruction. This same optimistic attitude should apply to curriculum for students whose emotional and social difficulties are exhibited by lack of self-restraint and empathy toward others (Ybarra, Diener-West, & Leaf, 2007).

Low self-esteem is often suggested as an explanation for motivation of bullies. Research does not support this opinion. In fact, there is a strong relationship between high self-esteem and violent behavior (Baumeister, 2005; Baumeister, Campbell, Krueger, & Vohs, 2003). Violence is often perpetrated by people with unrealistically high self-concepts, attacking others who challenge their self-impression. This troublesome group includes bullies, racists, gang members, persons associated with organized crime, rapists, and psychopaths. Challenging their self-esteem can be dangerous. Interventions that concentrate on self-control rather than self-esteem are more successful.

The favorable self-impression of bullies is usually based on a lack of awareness about what their peers think of them until they reach late adolescence. While they are growing up bullies typically hang out with one or two companions, often lackeys who feel constrained to help them carry out hostile wishes. Bullies mistakenly suppose that their own social situation is normal (Henkin, 2005). Owing to the social blind spot making makes them oblivious to how they are seen by peers, bullies characteristically lack empathy and ignore views of classmates they intimidate. Acquiring empathy is an essential purpose for education of bullies (Orpinas & Horne, 2006).

Female bullies need rehabilitation too (Chemelynski, 2006). Male bullies rely on physical aggression like shoving, hitting and kicking whereas females more often resort to relational aggression. To get even they spread rumors about someone so classmates will reject the victim. Female bullies strive for domination by threatening social exclusion, "You cannot come to my party unless you…" Threats are made to withdraw friendship in order to get one's own way, "I won't be your friend unless…" Often the silent treatment is applied to produce social isolation. These expressions of coercion are effective because they jeopardize what most girls value, their relationship with other girls. Social exclusion is especially powerful when girls make the transition to adolescence and are more susceptible to conflict (Goldstein & Brooks, 2005).

Family Relationships

Abuse of others is a behavior often learned at home where young bullies are victims of mistreatment. Family studies have found that parents of bullies interact with children much differently than families of nonviolent children. Parents of bullies do not use even a fraction of the praise, encouragement, or humor other parents use in communicating with sons and daughters. Put-downs, sarcasm, and criticism are responses that bullies experience at home (Dutton, 2007). The punishment of a young bully often depends more on mood of a parent than gravity of misconduct. If the parent is angry, harsh punishment is usual. If a parent is in good spirits, the child may get away with almost anything (Kowalski, Limber, & Agatston, 2008). This is a global issue in education. The Centre for Children and Families in the Justice System (Canada) provides advice for parents and teachers of bullies as well as victims at http://www.lfcc.on.ca/bully.htm.

Dysfunctional homes sponsor an outlook that life is essentially a battleground and threats are anticipated from any direction at almost any time (Hardy & Laszloffy, 2006). Even when bullies grow too strong for parents to physically abuse them, they continue to observe the mistreatment of younger siblings or a parent. The lesson is always the same—whoever has the greatest power is right. Based on erratic attacks from parents, bullies become wary and they misinterpret motives of people outside the family too. They often see hostility where there is none and this suspicion precipitates conflict with classmates (Larson, 2008). Schools must be given authority to educate dysfunctional families by giving instruction to parents of bullies as well as their children. This approach can help parents adopt constructive goals, better methods of communication, and suitable forms of discipline. In the long-term, counseling cannot compensate for failing to provide parents of bullies with the skills needed to give humane guidance at home (Larson & Lochman, 2005). The Family Violence

Prevention Fund provides information on domestic disputes with implications for parents, teachers, and communities—http://www.endabuse.org.

Influence on Peers

Students who are spared as targets of bullies can still be harmed by social lessons learned from them. Researchers at York University in Toronto, Canada found that bullies who do not get negative feedback about misconduct present classmates with a dysfunctional model that suggests there are no consequences for aggression (Mishna, Scarcello, & Pepler, 2005). This observation can motivate bystanders to behave in the same way themselves. Evidence about the influence of bullies comes from studies where peers have been observers in over 80% of bully episodes at school (Lodge & Frydenberg, 2005). The willingness to remain spectators and acquiesce encourages greater intimidation (Coloroso, 2004).

A more favorable outcome can be expected with training. In Finland, 1,200 students from 48 classrooms attended a year-long course in which appropriate behaviors were rehearsed as ways to respond to bullies. Results included a reduction in the school reported frequency of bullies and victims, student observed and experienced intimidation. A corresponding increase was reported in belief that action can bring an end to abuse (Salmivalli, Kaukiainen, & Voeten, 2005). These responses accord with the self-actualizer behavior Maslow described, evidence of maturity by showing concern for the safety of others.

In the United States, a study of 1,000 elementary students found that an experimental group who were provided guidance about ways to respond to bullies later reported enhanced bystander responsibility, greater perceived adult responsiveness, and less acceptance of bullying and aggression than peers in an untreated control group (Frey, Kirschstein, & Snell, 2005). Barbara Coloroso (2004, 2005) portrays the bully, bullied, and bystander as three characters in a tragic play and shows how their scripts can be rewritten, new roles created, and the plot changed to yield responsible behavior.

It is important to identify conditions that would motivate bystanders to intervene in behalf of those being mistreated. Few students challenge bullies but most who do take action have high social status. To increase peer intervention, it is necessary to make students aware of their individual responsibility to take action and demonstrate empathy for anyone being abused. In addition, students need effective intervention strategies and should be encouraged to show the courage necessary to offset a silent majority whose lack of caring can deprive victims of support while jeopardizing their own future as compassionate individuals (Beran & Shapiro, 2005). The benefits of breaking the code of silence and stepping forward to identify bullies is described by the United States Secret Service at http://www.ustreas.gov/usss/ntac_ssi.shtml (click Threat Assessment in Schools).

When bully behavior is seen as a group phenomenon, the participant role of observers is recognized and attention can be given to training them to facilitate social change by becoming willing to report incidents. Besides victims (who suffer humiliation, anxiety, and pain), bullies (who harm others and endanger their social and emotional development), the witnesses (who are in the process of forming lifelong responses to injustice) deserve consideration (Salmivalli, Kaukiainen, & Voeten, 2005). Bully behavior may begin with minimal harm but historical records show that it can escalate to devastating treatment of others (McGrath, 2006).

When parents and students discuss worries about school safety, the fear that someone will bring a weapon is mentioned more often than other concerns. This attributes to many killings by middle school and high school students in recent years and the recognition that, annually, more than 4,000 students are expelled for having a gun at school. Nevertheless, nearly half of students report that they would not tell teachers or administrators if they knew a classmate brought a weapon. The reason given is possible retaliation, a fear that the person would "Get them back." Clearly, student unwillingness to report peer abuse is a perilous norm. Following cases of violence, it has often been discovered that some students were previously aware of threats but did not take them seriously or decided not to tell faculty (Fein, Vossekuil, Pollack, Borum, Modzeleski, & Reddy, 2002).

There may be other explanations for the reluctance to confide in faculty about peer abuse. One speculation for why students do not reveal mistreatment or potential danger is that, from an early age, adults have discouraged them from "tattling" about everyday indignities suffered at the hands of hair-pulling siblings or playmates that take their possessions or tease them. Often they are urged to show independence by resolving such issues themselves without adult intervention (Coloroso, 2004, 2005). However, when they enter school, all students should be made aware of the important distinction between tattling and telling. The goal of *tattling* or snitching is to get someone in trouble while the purpose of *telling* on someone is a way to get the help they need. Figure 11.1 provides a way for students to inform a teacher about a bully incident.

Student who is being bullied _____	
Teacher _____	
Today's Date _____ Time _____	
Name of Bully _____	
Grade _____ Period _____	
Date and period that he/she bullied you _____	
Place where he/she bullied you _____	
Who else saw what happened _____	

Directions: Check how the person acted like a bully.

Threatened me or wanted me to have a fight_____

Called me names or made offensive gestures_____

Pushed, shoved, hit me or threw things_____

Took cuts in line ahead of other students_____

Copied my test or other school work_____

Stole my money or personal belongings_____

Damaged my work or personal belongings_____

Told others hurtful rumors or lies about me_____

Made fun of me in front of other kids_____

Mistreated my friend by threatening or hurting_____

Attention: Give this form to your teacher today before or after class! Do not tell classmates about your problem.

Today or tomorrow the teacher will talk to the bully privately.

Figure 11.1.   Example of a School Bully Report Form.

Formation of Gangs

The U.S. Department of Justice (2008) estimates there are 800,000 gang members in 30,000 gangs across the United States. Many parents, particularly in low-income areas, admit that gangs top their list of worries. The motivation of adolescents to join a gang puzzles many adults. Gangs are appealing because they offer group identity, friendship, protection, and excitement. Some reasons that students give for joining a gang are that they feel unimportant and powerless, seek respect, crave attention, lack involvement with school extra curricular activities, have poor communication and problem solving skills, live with a single parent, alcoholic or drug user (Covey, 2003). The peak period for recruitment to a gang is grades 9 and 10 when youth begin their search for identity. Differences in the drug related penalties for youth offenders than for adults has increased recruitment of teenagers as gang members. Teens are often expected to carry out drug sales and lessen the danger for older gang members who would be prosecuted as adults. Gangs promote vandalism, shootings, burglary, extortion, trafficking in drugs, rape, and assault (Franzese, Covey, & Menard, 2006). The Center for Study and Prevention of Violence at University of Colorado focuses on adolescents and offers advice for schools about juvenile gangs—http://www.colorado.edu/cspv See the Web site for U.S. Department of Justice regarding Gangs -http://www.cops.usdoj.gov/default.asp?item=1593.

Parents have the main role in preventing adolescents from joining a gang. Urging participation in extracurricular activities at school, community centers, or religious sites has been found to be an effective deterrent (Struyk, 2006; Umemoto, 2006). Such activities provide an alternative way to achieve common goals of belonging, recognition, and attaining satisfaction. Spending time with a daughter or son is essential so that sharing feelings continues because this communication is vital for guidance and safety. Some teenagers avoid bringing friends home. However, parents should try to get acquainted with their child's friends. As parents and community leaders establish programs like Block Watch and keep the neighbors informed about gang activity, there are more arrests and unlawful behavior declines (King, Walpole, & Lamon, 2007).

Many schools engage in violence prevention programs with the police (Larson, 2008). The lessons center on what a gang lifestyle is really like, increase knowledge about the causes and effects of violence, and recognition of how the company that one keeps can determine trouble or success. These courses present alternatives to gang membership, teach problem solving skills and methods for dealing with peer pressure, offer guidance on how to resolve conflict in nonviolent ways including walking away from a fight without feeling a loss of face, and active exploration of lawful career opportunities. Follow-up studies have shown that over 90% of students exposed to such curriculum express unwillingness to associate with a gang on a post-survey as compared to 50% on a pre-survey (Franzese, Covey, & Menard, 2006).

Trying to cope with abusive peers alone often prevents students from seeking adult help and has tragic consequences. Consider Yo Hirano, a Junior High School student in Japan who did not tell parents or teachers about constant bullying he endured (McNeill, 2001). Finally, unable to take it any longer, the 14-year-old committed suicide. Yo's parents sued the school for not helping him when the faculty knew about repeated peer abuse. This was the first time a Japanese school and bullies were ever prosecuted. Judge Ryoichi Ikeda said that, given the facts, he could not conclude anything other than the faculty was negligent. Therefore, the school as well as the parents of nine students who bullied Yo were held liable for financial damages.

VIRTUAL WORLD HARASSMENT

William Golding's (1954) classic novel, *Lord of the Flies*, begins with a group of boys who are being evacuated during a war when their plane is shot down. The tube in which the passengers are packed is released and falls onto an island, scattering boys over a wide area of jungle terrain. No one is seriously hurt. Following a search of the island, the boys conclude that there are no adults to tell them what to do, make decisions for them, or correct their misconduct. Adapting to this new environment requires the boys to develop their own rules for behavior and determine what should be expected of others. They soon discover that to control or intimidate companions is easier if they disguise themselves by painting their faces to ensure anonymity and convey fear when attacking enemies.

In a similar way, adolescents visiting the virtual island called the Internet are aware that adults are not watching, cannot know when misconduct occurs, and will not intervene when there is a need for corrective action. This means that if someone wants to harass or abuse others, s/he can hide behind pseudonyms and well-disguised IP addresses to facilitate the masquerade while victims are unable to figure out the source of threats to their mental health. Parents often are too busy with their own lives and careers to find out what their children do on the cyber island.

Students have always encountered bullies at school and in their neighborhood. However, adolescents now must also be concerned about unseen enemies that seek to harm them online. In some ways, cyberbullies are more destructive than customary foes because their action can often produce greater hurt and sorrow. Electronic intimidation also presents obstacles for the detection of bullies, reluctance of victims to report their mistreatment, access to counseling for individuals suffering from persecution, presentation of education programs to diminish cyberbullying, and formation of rehabilitation programs to assist bullies and their parents. Safety is supposed to be a priority for schools and the faculty should not flinch but instead decide to address these issues.

Uniqueness of Digital Abuse

The new threat from cyberspace is one for which educators and parents admit they are poorly prepared (P. Strom & R. Strom, 2005). Cyberbullying involves use of an electronic medium to threaten or harm others. E-mail, chat rooms, blogs, cell phones, instant messaging, pagers, texting, and online voting booths are tools employed to inflict humiliation, fear, and a sense of helplessness. Surveys show from 20% to 40% of middle and high school students have been victims of online bullies (David-Ferdon & Hertz, 2007). This form of harassment differs from customary bullying in several ways. Unlike cases that most adults recall where the threatening party is bigger and more powerful than the victim, cyberbullies can be physically weaker than those they attempt to frighten. The cyberbullies typically hide behind a mask of anonymity that the Internet allows by using fictitious screen names. Because abusers may lack face-to-face contact with the individuals persecuted, they may be unaware of the level of stress produced by their misconduct. Consequently, they are less likely to feel regret, sympathy, or compassion toward their victims.

The assumption of a relationship between physical bullying and cyberbullying appears to be unwarranted (Ybarra, Diener-West, & Leaf, 2007). In a national cross-sectional online survey of 1,600 students between ages 10 to 15, two-thirds of the students who reported being harassed online did not report that they were bullied at school. Nonetheless, youth who were harassed online were significantly more likely to also report two or more detentions or suspensions and skipping school in the previous year. Especially concerning, those who reported being targeted by Internet harassment were eight times more likely than all others to report carrying a weapon to school in the past 3 days.

Harmful messages intended to undermine the reputation of a victim can do more harm than face-to-face altercations. Instead of remaining a relatively private matter, known by a small group, text or photographs can be communicated to a large audience within a short time. Whereas bullies at school can be identified by victims, cyberbullies are often difficult to trace. This means that cyberbullies can avoid responsibility for misconduct, thereby reducing fear of getting caught and being punished (Wolak, Mitchell, & Finkelhor, 2007).

Cyberspace represents new territory for mistreatment, often leaving school administrators with doubts regarding the boundaries of their jurisdiction. School leaders may be unable to respond when unknown parties send hate messages from a location outside school like a home-based computer or mobile phone. Some students are reluctant to inform adults about the anxiety they experience at the hands of cyber enemies, fearing that parents may overreact by taking away their computer, Internet access, or cell phone. Many teenagers are unwilling to risk having their parents choose such extreme forms of protection. The reason is because, without technology tools, they would feel socially isolated and less able to stay in immediate contact with their friends (Rosen, 2007).

A common misconception of cyber abuse is that nothing can be done about it. *Cyber harassment* is a crime that, like other forms of unlawful behavior, is subject to prosecution (Willard, 2007). The University of Dayton School of Law offers resources to help understand legal issues related to cyberbullying. The Web site http://www.law.udayton.edu/cybercrimes describes cyberstalking and cyber intimidation, current news about cyber crime, and presents articles explaining legal processes and penalties associated with a wide range of cyber crimes.

Examples of Cyberbullying

Until recently, victims of bullying saw their homes as a place of safety, a sanctuary from peers who would abuse them. This is no longer the case. Most secondary students go online as soon after they return home from school. Some find themselves target of threats, rumors, and lies without knowing the identity of the persons creating fear and frustration or how to end the damage. The following examples of adolescent cyberbullying in several countries reveal the scope and complexity of arranging for safety in cyberspace.

Shinobu is a high school freshman from Osaka, Japan. When his gym period was over, Shinobu got dressed in what he believed was the privacy of the changing room. However, a classmate who sought to ridicule Shinobu for being overweight secretly used a cell phone to photograph him. Within seconds, the picture of the naked boy was sent wirelessly by instant messaging for many students to see. By the time Shinobu finished dressing and went to his next class, he had already become a laughing stock of the school (Paulson, 2003).

Sixteen-year-old Denise is a high school junior from Los Angeles, California. She had an argument with her boyfriend and broke up with him. The rejected boy was angry and he wanted to get even. The devious method he chose was to post Denise's contact numbers, including her e-mail address, cell phone number, and street address on several sex-oriented Web sites and blogs. Denise was hounded for months by instant messages, prank callers, and car horns of insensitive people who drove by her house to see whether they could catch a glimpse of her. In this case, identity of the cyberbully, her former boyfriend, was detected quickly. Nevertheless, his apprehension did not eliminate the sense of helplessness and embarrassment felt by Denise (Rachman, 2004).

Jealousy is frequently a motive in cyber abuse cases. Fourteen-year-old Amy lives in Montgomery, Alabama. She is enrolled in a home school curriculum and plans to earn the high school diploma by age 16 so that she can start college early. Darin, a neighbor who attends public school, is

Amy's friend. Darin's girlfriend began sending Amy e-mail messages threatening to cut herself if Amy did not stop talking to Darin. The guilt that someone might do herself bodily harm because of her led Amy to tell Darin about the e-mails. Darin confessed his girlfriend had cut herself once before. Amy wanted to do the right thing, but did not know who to contact. She told her mother, and the police were called to investigate.

Donna attends eighth grade at a parochial school located in Montreal, Canada. Donna and her mother went to Toronto for a week to visit her grandmother who was recuperating from cancer surgery. When Donna came back, a cyberbully circulated the rumor that Donna contacted SARS (Severe Acute Respiratory Syndrome) during her stay in Toronto. Donna's girlfriends were afraid and unwilling to be around her or talk on the phone. Without exception, classmates moved away when Donna came near them (Wendland, 2003).

Some cyber cases involve more than one bully and a single victim. Others could involve a group of bullies that persecute multiple parties. The latter occurs when students respond to online trash polling sites. These Web sites invite students to name individuals they feel qualify for unflattering characteristics, such as the most obese person at school, boys mostly likely to be gay, and girls who have slept with the most boys. The usual consequences for those who suffer from this shameful treatment are depression, hopelessness, and withdrawal (Assuras, 2004).

Teachers can also become targets of cyberbullies (Bubb, 2006). When students are disrespectful in class or challenge authority of the school to govern behavior on campus, they decide on discipline. The limits of this practice to prevent student harassment of faculty are shown by the experience of Joseph, a high school teacher in Phoenix, Arizona. He offered computer classes to juniors and seniors and consistently got high ratings for instruction. Joseph was known for preparing students well to get a good paying job right after graduation. He was disappointed and shocked when told of a Web site where he was the subject of messages on "What I hate about my teacher, Mr... " The site contained statements Joseph recognized as comments that he recalled saying to a student. Joseph explained, "I taught this young man how to apply a technological tool for constructive purposes, and he decided to use it against me."

Sophisticated cyberbullies sometimes target schools or other institutions by releasing worms to compromise integrity of computers or make them unavailable. The result is often disruption leading to a significant loss of time and money. The U.S. Department of Justice (2008) Web site http://www.cybercrime.gov lists the names of criminals and summary of computer intrusion cases, including juvenile or adult status of perpetrators, type of harm done, estimated dollar loss, target group, geography, and punishment. That list includes one hacker who directed worm-infected computers to launch a distributed denial of service attack against the main Web site of Microsoft, causing a shutdown of 4 hours for the public. The 14 years old hacker pleaded guilty of damage and trying to disable protected computers.

Teasing and Cyberbullying

Teasing is making fun of someone playfully by using claims such as "I was just kidding" or with malicious intent to create feelings of embarrassment and humiliation. Adolescents report that being teased is stressful. When students who suffer physical abuse at the hands of their peers report to teachers, they are typically urged to identify the responsible classmates. However, when students are teased, adults sometimes give a contradictory response. The dilemma begins with a false assumption by adults that classmates who tease others lack an intention to harm and would stop if the persons being made fun were to make known their disappointment. Accordingly, the victim may be urged to suck it up, view the incident as an aspect of life that everyone must cope with, and consider their ordeal an opportunity to build character and develop resilience. Studies of adolescent teasing have shown that two-thirds of cases involve name-calling, mostly focused on physical appearance or dress, followed by attention to deviance from group behavioral norms, deficits in academic subjects, and other imperfections (Agliata, Tantleff-Dunn, & Renk, 2007).

A strong correlation has been found between popularity and bullying among sixth grade students (Swearer, Espelage, & Napolitano, 2009). Those nominated by peers as doing the most teasing were also the students nominated as most popular and having the most friends at school. Given the reluctance of adults to condemn teasing in the same way physical bullying is rejected, it is not surprising that students adopt the same perspective. As a result, many of them trivialize such mistreatment when it is applied to harass others on the Internet. In effect, students are being led to believe that physically hurting someone is unacceptable but teasing is a relatively harmless prank and could even enhance someone's ability to handle adversity.

There is a need for greater public recognition of the high cost when students call one another undesirable names. The name callers are seldom identified as bullies even though their behavior undermines the mental health of others. When victims of teasing respond with violence against classmates, their motivation more often implicates teasing than being physically bullied. Reports from teenager murderers who said they could no longer bear being called nasty names usually identify ridicule as the main reason for taking such desperate actions (Watchler, 2005).

In 1999, at Columbine High School in Littleton, Colorado, two teenagers used guns and bombs for killing 12 students and a teacher while wounding 30 others before killing themselves. Following the massacre a suicide note from one shooter was found. In his explanation for why he and Dylan Klebold carried out their bloody rampage, Eric Harris warned against blaming the rock music they listened to like Marilyn Manson or trench coats worn by members of their social outcast group. Instead, he repeated the message communicated to students while killing was going on. According to Eric's note,

> Your children who have ridiculed me, who have chosen not to accept me, who have treated me like I am not worth their time are dead. I may have taken their lives and mine—but it was your doing. Teachers, parents, let this massacre be on your shoulders until the day you die. (Johnson & Brooke, 1999)

When Marilyn Manson was asked what he would say to students at Columbine and the community, he replied, "I wouldn't say a single word. I would listen to what they have to say and that's what no one did" (Moore, 2002).

School and family cooperation can support development of norms for students to treat others with civility. This goal should have high priority among initiatives to reduce school violence (Willard, 2007; Worthen, 2007). Consider some practical actions faculties can take to reduce incidence of face to face and online teasing situations.

1. Encourage healthy criteria for self-evaluation so student confidence does not come from demeaning others.
2. Have students periodically identify the positive attributes they have observed in each of their classmates.
3. Portray the growth of social maturity as an achievement to strive for and shown by acceptance of diversity
4. Help students see that teasing means being unable to accept the differences between ourselves and peers.
5. Bystanders should be expected to show courage in challenging mistreatment in any set of circumstances.
6. Cooperative learning teams could support feelings of belonging and develop a class sense of community
7. Provide gentle reminders around the classroom about no name calling, eye rolling, or laughing at peers.

8. Teach students how to process comments of teasers from all age groups that are presented in many situations.

9. Discuss why people want to fit in and how being made fun of has harmful effects regardless of intention.

10. Create a list of words that students agree are not to be used when they talk to each other on school grounds.

11. Help students identify the kind of person they wish to become and choose goals for personality development.

12. Ask each student about a time they teased someone, their reasons for doing it and the observed outcome.

13. Ask everyone to describe a situation in which they were teased and tell how they felt about the situation.

14. Help students acquire conflict resolution skills instead of resorting to pejorative remarks about classmates.

15. Invite parents to dialogue with their student who is a teaser or student being teased.

Solutions for Cyberbullying

What actions should be taken against cyberbullying? State departments of education have begun training principals to build awareness about options (Willard, 2007). Other personnel must also should assume responsibility for prevention. The information technology staff and business technology faculty could share the task of designing and delivering curriculum to acquaint students, teachers, and parents with etiquette on the Internet, methods of self-protection, and ways to react to persecution. A related initiative involves helping the community to recognize that adolescents interact with technology differently than adults. Most grown-ups regard computers as practical tools used to locate information and send electronic mail without the expense of postage stamps. In contrast, teenagers consider instant messaging and chat rooms an essential part of their social lives—a vital connection with peers. Chatting is the most prominent online activity among teenagers (Rosen, 2007).

These generational differences partially explain why few adults are able to give advice about dealing with cyberbullies. Their solutions are simplistic and result in minimal protection. For example, purchasing or setting online filters would appear to be suitable solutions because these preventive measures block reception of unwanted messages. However, by altering screen names, bullies can easily override these obstructions. Responding to bullies online to persuade them to stop the harassment may seem reasonable. Yet, student experience indicates this approach usually motivates a bully to apply even more severe methods of intimidation (Kowalski, Limber, & Agatston, 2008).

Teachers and parents can follow these practical guidelines to minimize cyberbullying:

1. Adults should develop close communications with adolescents and encourage them to relate problems such as episodes of digital harassment.

2. Students should be told not to share personal information, such as their e-mail password, with anyone except a parent.

3. Students, parents, educators, and law enforcement personnel should know where to go for information about online abuses, such as cyber intimidation, cyber dating, con artists, identity theft, predators, stalkers, criminal hackers, sexting, social networks, child pornography, and privacy problems—see WiredSafety, http://wiredsafety.org.

4. The U.S. Department of Justice (2008) http://www.cybercrime.gov offers guidelines on cyber ethics for students, parents, and teachers and identifies government contacts for reporting Internet crimes.

5. Adults should ensure that students realize people may not be who they say they are in a chat room. For example, someone could claim to be a 14-year-old female but in actuality be a 50-year-old male predator seeking to take advantage of a vulnerable adolescent.

6. Teenagers never should agree to meet someone they have chatted with online unless their parents go with them and the meeting is in a public place.

7. People should avoid sending impulse messages or staying online when angry. Wait until self-control and a sense of calm is restored so that the message is more sensibly written and excludes hostility. People usually regret sending a *flame* (angry) *message* that can motivate someone to become a cyberbully for revenge (Willard, 2006). Messages written in capital letters are usually interpreted as shouting.

8. When adolescents tell teachers or parents about Internet harassment, the cooperating adults should immediately inform the local FBI at U.S. Department of Justice—http://www.cybercrime.gov/reporting.htm#cc.

9. Victims should never respond to cyberbullies, but always should keep their messages as evidence, including the text and source of information detailing the originating address of the e-mail. Whether they are read or not, bully messages should never be

erased. The police, Internet service provider, or telephone company often can use the narratives for tracking purposes. Victims may notice words that are used by people they know. Most cyberbullies who post messages are not as anonymous as they suppose. If a legitimate threat exists, law enforcement can subpoena records of all Web users for a particular Web site. From there, users can be tracked to individual computers.

10. The mission of Channel One, a broadcast network watched by students in 400,000 classrooms daily is to keep them informed about current events and the role of media. Their Web site offers a video about cyberbullying and an interactive quiz that adolescents, parents, and teachers can take to check their knowledge regarding coping with bullies in cyberspace. Channel One's Web site is at http://www.channelone.com/news/cyberbullies/.

SCHOOL INITIATIVES

Teachers can influence student views about bullying. The feelings of resignation that little can be done or expecting adults to deal with every incident should be replaced by a collective resolve of students to assume their unique responsibility related to misconduct by their cohort. When students have a structured agenda allowing them to describe their impressions about abuse and ways to prevent it, constructive norms can emerge. In a similar way, faculties should avoid supposing that students who exhibit anger and lack self control are incapable of change so it is reasonable to give up on them. A more favorable outlook reflects an awareness that class discussions and anger management classes can promote more healthy responses to frustration.

Guided Student Discussions

Class discussions on bullying and safety can support the motivation students need for their role in ensuring safety. These conversations also improve adult perspective taking. Studies have shown that, compared with students, teachers and administrators underestimate the scope of bullying, consider the school as being more safe, and judge incidents to be less serious (Willard, 2007). A suitable agenda can invite student opinions that are seldom heard in classes. Teachers can reinforce accurate impressions by summarizing research findings. The following questions are recommended for use in your classes.

1. What does it mean to be a bully? (students share their definitions based on personal experience)

2. How does it feel to be the victim of a bully? (encourage awareness based on hearing feelings of others)

3. What can happen to someone who is bullied a lot? (effects of bullying on mental health)

4. Why do you suppose people bully others? (speculation and first hand accounts about bully motivation)

5. What do you think will happen to bullies when they grow up? (guesses about long-term consequences accompanied by teacher reports of research findings)

6. What problems can school bullies expect to face later in life? (difficulty forming intimate and durable relationships; rejection by co-workers and neighbors in the community)

7. How can bullies change to become someone that other people like? (identify possibilities for rehabilitation)

8. How do you suppose bullies are treated at home by their parents? (conjecture about the parent-child relationships compared to what is revealed by research literature on bullies)

9. What should someone do when they are picked on? (finding out the best ways to respond is of great interest to students)

10. How can students expect adults to protect them from bullies? (identify ways teachers and parents can be counted on to enforce the civil rights of everyone)

11. What factors should bullies consider when they reflect on their behavior? (provide healthy criteria all students should use for self-examination)

12. What are some myths about bullies? (speculation followed by review of research about bullies)

13. Why should students tell when they know of peer abuse (individual obligations in a civil society)

14. What are some names that you do not want to be called in the classroom or outside of school?

15. What results from the bully poll completed by our class (Exercise 11.01) do you want to discuss?

The United States Secret Service investigated Columbine and other school shootings. The findings revealed that most attackers had experienced long-term severe peer harassment and bullying. In fact, more than 70 percent of them reported being persecuted, threatened and, in certain cases, injured before they chose violence as their solution. "In some cases being bullied had a significant impact on the attacker and seemed to be a factor in deciding to attack the school." More than three-fourths of school shooters were found to have announced suicidal thoughts that were ignored by friends or family (Vossekuil, Fein, Reddy, Borum, & Modzeleski, 2002).

The expectation to use class time efficiently means that teachers are confronted with choices on balancing instruction and giving attention to concerns of students. Educators and parents wonder whether discussions about relationships are appropriate when the main purpose of curriculum is to prepare students for the world of work. This perspective seems shortsighted. In the past decade substantial evidence has revealed that students who are unable to get along with classmates have a higher rate of absenteeism, dropout, truancy, incarceration, suicide and murder. Devoting class time to talking about issues that bother students is justified.

Anger Management Curriculum

Students with self-control issues benefit from *anger management curriculum* that offers them:

1. opportunities to practice self-evaluation skills and receive anonymous feedback from peers;

2. empathy-building exercises to learn how others feel and training to respect such feelings;

3. examples of civil ways to cope with frustrations and conflicts that occur in daily relations;

4. activities that call for showing patience, self-restraint, and nonviolent expression of anger;

5. self-direction by setting goals along with reasonable criteria to evaluate personal progress;

6. awareness of how social and emotional growth impacts adjustment as well as satisfaction;

7. realization that good grades cannot make up for failed relations based on mistreatment; and

8. acceptance of responsibility for personal misconduct instead of placing blame on others.

Skeptics may doubt whether providing classes for bullies is the most effective way to rehabilitate them. Others opposed to anger management strategies may contend that making students take remedial social instruction is degrading and could lead to lawsuits. However, *rehabilitation* calls for efforts to improve behavior with corrective instruction. Helping adolescents overcome social skill deficiencies and emotional immaturity is likely to become a prominent expectation for schools as being more developmentally appropriate than just punishment (Larson, 2008).

John Lochman, psychologist at Duke University, devised a course for boys meeting forty-minute meetings twice a week (Larson & Lochman, 2005). The length of student attendance in class varied, from 6 weeks to 12 weeks, depending on teacher reports about student behavior. The focus was on gaining skills to accurately interpret friendly or neutral behaviors of peers that bullies tend to misread as hostile. A frequent task was to examine events from the perspective of classmates to comprehend their feelings and thoughts that were inaccurately interpreted by bullies, thereby causing them to lose their temper and coerce others. The need for intervention programs that can correct interpersonal misperceptions of bullies is reinforced by 2 decades of research with a cohort of 1,000 males and females in Dunedin, New Zealand. This longitudinal tracking project found that, among 10- to 12-year-old students, impulsivity is three times more powerful than is verbal IQ in predicting delinquent behavior (Lahey, Moffitt, & Caspi, 2003; Moffitt, Caspi, Rutter, & Silva, 2008).

The Lochman intervention with bullies also involved role playing to acquaint them with their need to monitor feelings and understand the trigger point at which their self-control is jeopardized (Larson & Lochman, 2005). Other activities call for reflective discussions about substituting more constructive methods for solving problems. For example, being bumped in the hallway as students try to move quickly between classes is a familiar student experience. This situation could be viewed as a challenge that calls for a fight to avoid the label of coward or writing the incident off as being an accident that only warrants reminding the other person to "Be more careful." Choosing a civil response demonstrates self-control, preserves self-esteem, and makes others aware of frustration caused by their careless behavior. Three years after graduating from anger management, the boys were compared with a matched group identified as aggressive but who did not participate in the program. Findings showed that those who completed the curriculum were less often identified by their teachers as a disruptive influence in class, had more healthy views about themselves, and were less likely to consume alcohol or illegal drugs. Moreover, the boys who participated longest, remaining for 12 weeks instead of the minimum 6 weeks, showed the least amount of aggressive conduct during their years of senior high school. Similar successful outcomes have been reported by other researchers (Carter, 2004).

Time Out is when students are upset and need to cool down, reduce their anger and regain composure. By setting aside a place for time out, schools confirm this is the first step toward coming to terms with negative feelings

(Rachlin, 2004). The common assumption is that while students are in Time Out they will confront themselves in a rational way and consider behavior change. A more supportive approach is to provide questions that students can use in Time Out to direct their self-evaluation. These questions should be discussed during student orientation and periodically assessed for benefit. The procedure can be applied at school or at home and modeled by adults to support social responsibility. Figure 11.2 offers a guide for students to rely on when they confront themselves in private.

When students return to class from Time Out, they may not be ready to make amends for their misbehavior. The important thing is that students have a chance to practice a constructive way of confronting themselves, and gain experience with a process that ensures safety of others and themselves. If a student decides to apologize, it should be based on genuine regret and the resolve to improve a relationship instead of fear regarding punishment for not declaring "I'm sorry" regardless of whether or not this is an honest expression of feelings (Nay, 2003).

Voices of Adolescents

Every school has a responsibility to assess students exposure to cyber-bullying and take steps necessary to create a safe environment. There is a

---

When You Are Sent to Time Out, Use These Questions to Talk to Yourself

1. What did you hope to accomplish?
THINK OF THE REASONS WHY YOU DID IT.

2. Why do you suppose your way didn't work?
THINK ABOUT WHY IT DIDN'T WORK.

3. What are some other ways you could handle the situation?
THINK OF NEW WAYS TO HANDLE THE PROBLEM.

4. What might be the consequence for each of your choices?
THINK ABOUT WHAT WILL HAPPEN NEXT.

5. What do you think are your best choices?
CHOOSE THE BEST WAY TO SOLVE YOUR PROBLEM.

Figure 11.2. Agenda for self-evaluation in Time Out.

need to find out the prevalent forms of mistreatment students endure, ways they respond to electronic threats to manipulate them, and their perceptions of teachers as resources to help them cope with cyberbullies. The extent to which students lie by misrepresenting themselves on line is unknown as is the reaction students would anticipate from their relatives and friends if they were told about being abused by bullies. There is a need for common polls to collect data so that results can be compared. You can find out the experience of students in your classes by administering the cyberbully poll (Exercise 11.01).

School-wide results should be reported to all the stakeholders including faculty, students, parents and the community. There is benefit in discussing findings in classes, identifying bully conduct as unacceptable, and affirming the right of everyone to be free from harassment. Another reason for student discussions led by teachers is to establish the norm needed to bring about zero tolerance among youngsters for violence at their school. A third reason for dialogues is that they acquaint bullies with how classmates feel about intimidating behavior (Bosacki, Marini, & Dane, 2006; Henkin, 2005).

Currently bullies seldom get to hear such conversations at school. This is because the public has erroneously supposed that bullies are fully aware of how their victims feel but do not care. Unfortunately, 65% of students in elementary school report that teachers never talk about the problems bullies present to peers. In middle school, 85% of students report this topic is never discussed in classes. Nearly 40% of grade school students and 60% in middle school complain that the frequency in which teachers try to stop bullying is "once in a while" or "almost never" (Salmivalli, Kaukiainen, & Voeten, 2005).

FAMILIES AND CORRECTIVE GUIDANCE

Parent support is necessary for helping students develop self-control. This possibility is undermined when teacher reports of student misconduct are ignored by parents who refuse to confront their sons and daughters or administer suitable punishment. Instead of assuming responsibility for corrective guidance, such parents take the side of their misbehaving student and become an adversary of the school. A more beneficial response describes the majority of parents who want to cooperate with teachers. This desirable response is more common when teachers report good behavior of students as well as misconduct. Parents seldom get favorable feedback on their efforts to raise a well behaved adolescent and they are glad to reinforce commendable behavior at home. Internet and television safety must become the focus of education for parents provided by the school. Guidance in this realm is needed so parents can properly monitor student Internet and television experience.

Families and School Discipline

There is an urgent need for more parents to effectively teach self-control (Rachlin, 2004). The challenge is reflected by a national survey of 725 secondary school teachers and 600 parents of students from Grades 5 through 12 (Public Agenda, 2004). The findings showed that 82% of teachers and 74% of parents ranked parent failure to teach self-control as the most influential factor contributing to student misbehavior. About 20% of the parents considered transferring their child to a private school where discipline is more stringent. A minority of students account for nearly all problems that interrupt classroom learning. Disruption of instruction is so pervasive that one-third of teachers know colleagues who left the profession for this reason and another third have thought about quitting themselves.

Nearly 80% of teachers in the Public Agenda Survey (2004) said misbehaving students have reminded them that they have rights and their parents could sue the school district. Over half (55%) the teachers felt that administrators and school boards who back down from assertive parents prevent consistent discipline. Almost all teachers (94%) felt that treating special education students the same as every other child unless misbehavior is related to a disability would be an effective solution. A primary reason for inclusion is to help special education students learn social skills that enable them to be more readily accepted by others. However, this does not appear to be what is happening. Instead, most teachers (76%) agree that when special education students are sent to the administration because they interrupt learning of others, they are treated too lightly, even when misbehavior has nothing to do with their disability. The solutions recommended were stronger enforcement of rules, establishing zero tolerance policies so students know that they will be expelled for serious violations, finding ways to hold parents more accountable, limiting law suits to serious situations like expulsion and removing a possibility of monetary awards for parents who sue over discipline. The Public Agenda (2004) report on "Teaching Interrupted: Do Discipline Policies in Today's Public Schools Foster the Common Good?" is at http://www.publicagenda.org (enter Teaching Interrupted).

State reports also provide troubling evidence that special education students account for a disproportionate share of violence and disciplinary problems in school. Texas, Minnesota, and Missouri reports show that special education students are suspended at twice the rate of regular students. In the large districts of Dade County, Florida, and Fairfax County, Virginia, they are suspended four times as often as other students. In Massachusetts, special education students are 17% of the total enrollment but responsible for over half of all incidents related to weapons, assaults or physical threats in 2006. In Pennsylvania, 683 special education students were removed to attend alternative settings because of weapons or drug violations in 2005, more than twice the total 5 years earlier. When the General Accounting Office of the federal government investigated these matters, it found 50 incidents of serious misconduct such as violent behavior or bringing weapons to school for every 1,000 special education students in middle school compared to 15 for every 1,000 general education students. These figures challenge the assertion that special education students integrated with regular students adopt more civil behavior (Tomsho & Golden, 2007).

Families and Student Misconduct

Some related observations come from high school teachers responding to two questions: (1) What changes would you like to see in the way students treat teachers; and (2) What changes would you like to see in the ways parents treat their child's teachers? Educators report there are a growing number of students whose lack of self-control is shown by unhealthy reactions in coping with day-to-day challenges. Signs of dysfunction include periodic outbursts of anger, swearing, threatening peers or teachers, and withdrawal from class activities (Greene & Ablon, 2006). These problems are compounded by similar responses from parents when informed about the unacceptable conduct of their student (Tyson, 2006).

Becoming emotionally upset and making threats happens far more often now than in the past according to teachers with lengthy classroom experience. When new teachers were asked to identify their biggest challenge, nearly 75% said, "Too many parents treat schools and teachers as adversaries" (Gibbs, 2005). The most troubling parent reaction is denial, a refusal to ever consider negative feedback about their child. Such men and women usually take the child's side instead of accepting their unique and necessary responsibility to correct misbehavior (Whitted & Dupper, 2005). A poor response by parents can lead misbehaving students to suppose that the family condones misconduct. What appears to happen is that with a gradual erosion of their authority at home, many parents adopt the erroneous perception that their function is to be an advocate for the children against outside authority figures such as teachers and principals. Parents spend less time than they would like with their children and want their moments together to be mutually satisfying. Therefore, instead of administering punishment when needed, they suspend discipline. They may suppose this behavior will endear them to a child but it prevents learning self control (Rachman, 2004; Worthen, 2007).

What happens when schools do not confront parents about their responsibility to correct a student who misbehaves in class or abuses peers? Perhaps a lesson can be learned from England where 34 local education authorities conducted a survey to find out why the number of families deciding to home school their children was increasing at such a rapid pace. The major factors identified by parents who had chosen this option included a broad range of motivations including more students in the class diagnosed as having special needs, parents wanting to spare their child the state school emphasis on incessant testing, readily available teaching materials and guidance on the Internet, and doubling of private school fees in recent years. However, the most prominent factor was bully behavior. A substantial proportion of the parents, 44%, cited bullying as the primary reason for withdrawing their child from public schools. The parents indicated that they do not believe schools respond to problem children, or hold their families accountable as should be the case. Therefore, when faced with bullying, some parents manage the situation themselves in a way they feel is best (Blackhurst, 2008). The extent to which American parents who transfer daughters and sons from public schools to homeschool, charter, private, or parochial institutions based on wanting to ensure safety and psychological well being of their children is unknown.

Good Behavior Reports to Families

Recording the commendable behaviors of students and reporting them to parents should become common practice. Most parents acknowledge the need to be aware of their child's good behavior as well as misconduct. Mothers and fathers realize that attaining their goal of character development depends on reinforcing favorable actions whenever they occur. In this connection, a study of 108 high school students, their parents and teachers demonstrates the benefit of feedback about positive behavior in the classroom (P. Strom & R. Strom, 2003). Faculty were trained to use a personal digital assistant (PDA) to record student notable favorable and unfavorable behaviors and notify parents by pager the same day about their need to give corrective guidance or reinforce good conduct. Most parents (98%) and students (83%) felt encouraged by pager messages from teachers on commendable behavior. Teachers (92%), parents (92%), and students (82%) expressed their belief that most adolescents will behave better if good conduct receives timely recognition. One mother stated a consensus view,

Before this project, I used to suppose that "no news is good news." Now I realize that no news is really just not knowing. It is a great boost to sometimes receive feedback indicating that our son is becoming mature.

Reporting favorable behavior to encourage and maintain good conduct matches findings that nurturing healthy relationships in school is a more effective way to reduce discipline problems than zero tolerance policies and punitive penalties. This view is confirmed by the National Longitudinal Study of Adolescent Health that found attachment to the school can be a protective factor against violence (Franke, 2000). The most significant predictor of well-being for adolescents was feelings of connectedness with the school. Other studies indicate that when students feel they are accepted by peers and vested in the institution, they are less likely to engage in risky behavior (Orpinas & Horne, 2006).

Most secondary schools keep records of student misconduct by using software purchased from companies like Rediker or STI or Sasci. Although these records are systematic and uniform for state purposes of data collection, they commonly exclude commendable behavior. School communication should reflect positive psychology in presenting individual progress toward social maturity observed by teachers. This frame of reference goes beyond comments about how well students follow rules because many aspects of development are not required by rules. One example is the School Code of Positive Events (SCOPE), a listing of 20 study skills and social skills teachers refer to when tracking the incidence of these behaviors for a class over a semester or reporting timeframe (P. Strom & R. Strom, 2003). See Table 11.1, School Code of Positive Events.

The relative frequency of each behavior is tallied and communicated to students and parents. Faculty discuss the outcomes as a way to gauge group progress and detect types of conduct deserving greater attention. This same method is used to monitor study skills and social skills for special education students except that they are tracked as individuals with each person having a separate column on the form shown in Table 11.1. This report is given to a coordinator of special education for the Individualized Education Plans (IEP) of students. Similarly, the conduct of individuals from groups at-risk can be monitored with this format (P. Strom & R. Strom, 2003).

SUMMARY

Theories of Civil Behavior

Behavioral conditioning theory provides methods of shaping student behavior to ensure greater conformity to rules, increased safety, and more

Table 11.1.   School Code of Positive Events—(SCOPE)

Semester _____Individual _____

STUDY SKILLS	Name	Name	Name	TOTAL
1. Asks questions during class				
2. Requests teacher help				
3. Learns during free time				
4. Shares readings with class				
5. Refers to text in discussions				
6. Summarizes in own words				
7. Keeps trying when difficult				
8. Organizes ideas well				
9. Practices self-regulation				
10. Finds Web resources on one's own initiative				
SOCIAL SKILLS				TOTAL
11. Works well with peers				
12. Opposes abuse of peers				
13. Shows empathy for others				
14. Compromises with others				
15. Reports school incident				
16. Asserts respect for rules				
17. Helps teacher with chore				
18. Encourages peer success				
19. Questions thinking of group				
20. Provides tutoring for peers				

civil treatment of others. Evidence shows that behavior modification is effective as a means of classroom management. However, there is ambivalence because while this method improves behavior, it may not foster cognitive processing about reasons for not engaging in misconduct. There is also concern that this strategy places restrictions on personal choice and could lead to external dictation of lifestyle. This fearful possibility is reinforced by pressures to enforce political correctness restricting the language that people use to express feelings and ideas.

Social cognitive theory contends that observation is the basis for most human learning. Watching others leads to imitation. Mentoring programs can offer positive models that give students a sense of direction. However, they also see many negative conduct models in movies, video games, on the Internet and television. Schools and parents are challenged to balance the freedom of media expression with a need to limit adolescent exposure by filters and monitoring online activity. The hierarchy of needs theory identifies a progression of needs that must be satisfied before persons can attain the status of being self-actualized. Self-actualizers can be counted on to stand up for others whose deficiency needs are not being met, and take action to bring about changes necessary for a civil society. Schools must provide safety before there can be an effective appeal to student curiosity for academic learning.

Characteristics of Bullies

Bullies are typically intelligent, get good grades, and show confidence. These attributes lead teachers to suppose that the misbehavior is temporary and will stop when these bullies get older. However, the more likely future is that they will continue to be abusive as adults. The best way to help students that lack self control is to require rehabilitation classes along with their parents. The dysfunctional attributes of bullies have an adverse effect on peers that witness their abuse of others without standing up for victims or reporting misconduct to teachers. Students need to understand their role in ensuring safety and the courage that will be required. Joining a gang can be appealing because it offers a sense of belonging, friendship, support, feelings of power, acceptance, and identity. These needs can also be met when educators provide conditions that cause students to regard school as a place where they feel welcome, safe, and enjoy relationships.

Virtual World Harassment

Cyberbullies rely on electronic tools to humiliate, threaten, taunt and terrorize others while they remain anonymous. Victims are reluctant to inform the school or parents about their abuse. Dissemination of embarrassing photographs, spreading lies and rumors, and sending messages that promise harm to individuals are common methods of harassment. Schools must convince students that, like adults, their role as human beings requires protecting others. Instead of perpetuating the false impression that nothing can be done, schools should establish prevention programs. Victims must become aware of their obligation to report incidents so that intimidation ends, perpetrators are identified, and a civil environment is in place. Those suffering from cyber persecution should be provided with counseling at school (Hall, 2006). Educators have to develop curriculum for all students that can guide civil behavior on line. Instead of punishment as the exclusive deterrent to cyberbullying, rehabilitation programs should be offered and require participation of parents. Similarly, parents of victims need support and guidance.

School Initiatives

Teachers can be influential in guiding class discussions on bullying. Dialogue can clarify how students define bully behavior, ways to respond when being picked on, and why informants are the key to having a safe environment. Feelings of those that have been bullied should be heard along with speculation about long term consequences for victims and bullies. Myths about bullies, possibilities for motivating them to change, and the potential of methods of rehabilitation deserve attention. A widely recognized need is for bullies to participate in anger management classes. This curriculum should focus on nonviolent ways to cope with frustration, acquiring patience, learning social skills for conflict resolution, and recognition that good grades cannot excuse failure to develop healthy relationships. Anti-bully programs should be in all schools. These programs are more effective when parents know their reinforcement role at home. The extent to which bullying occurs, forms it takes, and views about what can be done should be the focus of student polling.

Families and Corrective Guidance

There is evidence that many students are not acquiring self -control and suppose violence is an appropriate way to settle disagreements (Rachman, 2004). The failure of parents to teach civil behavior is seen as the most difficult obstacle to overcome in maintaining classroom discipline. Becoming emotionally upset and displaying outbursts of anger when faced with frustration is a pattern that is becoming more common (Henley, 2003). Student behavior often appears to imitate that of their parents whose reaction to teacher reported misconduct is denial. As a result, more schools have initiated a zero tolerance for abusive behavior. Schools cannot provide students with the corrective guidance and forms of punishments that must occur at home to set limits on self-control that can deter misconduct (Combrinck-Graham, 2006). Developing better communication with parents happens when teachers send reports about commendable behavior as well as misbehavior. This strategy acquaints parents with aspects of student development they care about, informs them that their guidance is succeeding, and allows them to reinforce good behavior. Safety issues related to the Internet and television mainly implicate parents because online activity occurs mostly at home. The school Web site should offer guidance and sources for information on use of filters, monitoring Internet activity, and ways to protect students from exploitation online.

CLASSROOM APPLICATIONS

1. Teachers convey two kinds of messages. One involves the subject matter for which they are responsible. The second message involves modeling how to treat others and readiness to protect those that are vulnerable and need help to ensure their safety. As students grow older, they may not remember the subject matter acquired from individual teachers but generally recall how the teacher responded to peer abuse, efforts to protect victims, and educate bullies.

2. Faculty as models should be augmented by recruitment of mature volunteers that provide assistance in the classroom. In addition, schools should link students with mentors (Burns; 2005; Carnell, 2005). The life lessons that such individuals are able to provide students about goal setting, understanding what is required for success in the work environment, respecting dignity of peers, and standing up for the rights of others can do much to facilitate development of civil behavior.

3. Monitoring student growth requires more than assignment of grades. Some students get good grades but fail to make satisfactory progress in self-control. Good academic performance does not excuse poor performance in the social sphere. Communicating this distinction is difficult because most parents assume that good academic grades and good behavior are synonymous. They also want to believe that their child has good conduct. When teachers provide evidence for concern and enlist parent support, the usual result is intervention and improved behavior.

4. Bullies often come from dysfunctional homes where parents lack attitudes and skills needed to exercise humane guidance. These adults need to adopt constructive goals, better communication methods, and more suitable forms of discipline. Therefore, efforts to assist bullies must include a component for parents. If parents refuse to help their child by participation in family education, the school should involve other agencies while suspending the student.

5. The school orientation of students should make it known that the preservation of freedom from threat and danger is not the responsibility of law enforcement or school faculties alone. Instead, the entire society is obligated to defend community safety. For students this means demonstrating concern for others by showing courage to inform teachers or parents about information related to abuse. When students choose not to reveal such information, they jeopardize the safety of others and undermine development of integrity.

6. Cyberbullying is a topic that parents are highly motivated to learn about and would welcome guidance on from the school Web site as well as meetings. Student victims are often reluctant to tell parents about their suffering because they suppose their access to electronic communication will be discontinued and they will be isolated from friends. Parents should become aware of this reasoning, have conversations with daughters and sons about online experiences with chat rooms and exposure to exploitation. Because most of the abuse students face occurs when they are on their computer at home, parents should be the first line of defense.

7. There is a serious instructional void in most schools relating to protection from cyber abuse. District boards of education should designate the technology staff at each school responsible for educating everyone on campus about electronic abuse and safety. Some essential topics should include Internet etiquette, methods of self protection, ways to respond to persecution, limitations for sharing personal information online, ways the school can help victims of abuse, rationale for cyber laws and punishments, and collaborative efforts by the faculty with law enforcement to detect and prosecute abuse on the Internet.

8. Teachers can be influential in guiding student discussions on self-control, abuse and safety. Such conversations can trigger the motivation that individuals and the class as a whole need to accept responsibility for creating safe environments. Conversations about changing unacceptable behaviors of bullies allow for consideration of intervention options and their relative success. In turn, students realize that abuser behavior can be modified. Talking about reliance on informants to help solve crimes such as murder, robbery, rape and assault enable students to recognize that the same obligation is needed to support safety within the school (Hutchins, 2004).

9. Every school needs to develop a parent education program that defines the separate and shared responsibilities that schools and families have in supporting student safety. A clarification of expectations and instruction tasks can enhance cooperative efforts,

reduce parent denial about student misbehavior, increase their willingness to provide corrective guidance, and allow mutual observation at home and school to assess the progress of interventions to change behavior.

10. Teacher reports to parents about student progress should include observation of good behavior. Although grades are not given for study skills and social skills, parents realize their important contribution to success as an adult. When teachers report good behaviors the same day students demonstrate them, parents are able to reinforce commendable conduct in a timely manner and renew their commitment to encouraging this aspect of adolescent development. Parents can be contacted by using the SCOPE code via e-mail or by cell phone with text messaging or online school reporting area.

11. Anger management classes have been found to have a more beneficial effect on the behavior of disruptive students than only administration of punitive measures such as suspension and expulsion. Each school faculty should petition their district board of education to make these classes available for students that are identified as lacking self-control. Participation of parents should be stipulated as a requirement of the intervention program.

12. The observation of violence, sex, risk taking, and verbal abuse on television programs and the Internet can adversely affect adolescent attitudes and behavior. Consequently, cyber space and video dangers are of great concern to families and the community. Faculties need to recognize that student safety, whether in class or off campus, is part of their mission. Providing the larger community with online resources that can help protect youth is a reasonable expectation for contemporary schools.

FOR REFLECTION

1. Describe the civil behavior theory that you find most appealing and elaborate your reasoning.

2. What are some advantages and disadvantages of giving grades for study skills and social skills?

3. Express your view about the likelihood that schools will be able to rehabilitate student bullies.

4. Identify some myths regarding adolescent bullies that have you previously thought to be true.

5. Explain the rationale you favor for persuading students to become informants about peer abuse.

6. Speculate about the long-term effects on adolescents who are cyberbully perpetrators or victims.

7. How can schools help students gain the courage needed to oppose bullies in all sectors of life?

8. What preparation do you recommend for teachers so they can report good behavior to parents?

9. Suggest some ways for communities to motivate greater parent accountability for civil behavior.

10. What proportion of the students at your school do you estimate are harassed and feel unsafe?

11. How effective do you suppose student suspension is as a means for reducing misbehavior?

12. What possibilities can you think of for recognizing positive behaviors of students in school?

KEY TERMS

Anger management curriculum
Behavioral Conditioning Theory
Channel One
Cyberbullying
Cyber harassment
Deficit needs
Flame message
Hierarchy of needs theory
Instincts
Modeling
Operant conditioning
Rehabilitation
Reinforcements
Self-actualization
School Code of Positive Events
Social Cognitive Theory
Tattling
Teasing
Time out
Vicarious conditioning

VISIT THESE WEB SITES

Link to these sites at http://www.infoagepub.com/strom-adolescents

Center for the Study and Prevention of Violence,
University of Colorado at Boulder, Juvenile Gangs
http://www.colorado.edu/cspv

Centre for Children and Families in the Justice System, Canada,
Bullying Information for Parents and Teachers
http://www.lfcc.on.ca/bully.htm

Channel One, Cyberbullies
http://www.channelone.com/news/cyberbullies/

Family Violence Prevention Fund, Preventing Family Violence
http://www.endabuse.org

New Zealand, Whole School Approach Programs for Peer Abuse http://
/www.police.govt.nz/service/yes/nobully/kia_kaha/whole.html

Public Agenda,
Teaching Interrupted: Do Discipline Policies in Today's
Public Schools Foster the Common Good?
http://www.publicagenda.org

United States Department of Justice, Gangs
http://www.cops.usdoj.gov/default.asp?item=1593

United States Department of Justice, Reporting Cyber Harassment
http://www.cybercrime.gov/reporting.htm#cc

United States Department of Justice, Cyberethics
http://www.cybercrime.gov

United States Secret Service, Safe School Initiatives,
Threat Assessment in Schools http://www.ustreas.gov/usss/
ntac_ssi.shtml

University of Dayton School of Law
http://www.law.udayton.edu/cybercrimes

Wired Safety http://wiredsafety.org

EXERCISES AND ROLES

Exercise 11.01: Cyberbully Poll

Role: Voter

The purpose of this poll is to find out about student experiences with cyberbullying. Cyberbullies use some type of electronic medium, such as cellular or vision/picture phones, e-mail, instant messaging, text messages, chat rooms, Web sites or online voting booths, to inflict humiliation, fear or helplessness to others.

Directions: For each item, select the answer(s) that show how you feel. In some cases, you may select more than one answer. If an answer you want to give is not listed, write it on the line marked 'other.' Your responses are anonymous and may be combined with those of other students at your school in a report to students, faculty, and parents.

1. Common cyberbullying at my school includes

    (a) cell phone calls or text messages
    (b) picture or video on cell phones
    (c) online instant messaging or live chat rooms
    (d) Web sites or message boards
    (e) other

2. Common cyberbullying messages at my school include

    (a) threatening to hurt someone
    (b) telling lies about a person
    (c) exposing secrets to an audience
    (d) sexual harassment
    (e) other

3. Common reasons for cyberbullying at my school are

    (a) boyfriend/girlfriend jealousy, rejection or breakups
    (b) winning/losing a school event, contest or competition
    (c) being picked on for not acting or looking like others
    (d) revenge for being mistreated by someone
    (e) other

4. My understanding of cyberbullying is based on

    (a) being a target of cyberbullying
    (b) friends talking about cyberbullying
    (c) teachers talking about cyberbullying
    (d) reports presented on television
    (e) other

5. If someone tried to cyberbully me, I would

    (a) tell a teacher or my parent
    (b) ignore it
    (c) tell the bully to stop
    (d) change my screen name or block the message
    (e) other

6. When teachers are told about cyberbullying, they say

    (a) tell the principal or your parent
    (b) ignore it
    (c) tell the bully to stop
    (d) change your screen name or block the message
    (e) other

7. When parents are told about cyberbullying, they say

    (a) tell the principal or your teacher
    (b) ignore it
    (c) tell the bully to stop
    (d) change your screen name or block the message
    (e) other

8. When friends are told about cyberbullying, they say
    (a) tell the principal or your parent
    (b) ignore it
    (c) tell the bully to stop
    (d) change your screen name or block the message
    (e) other

9. In the past year my teachers discussed cyberbullying

    (a) Never
    (b) 1–5 times

(c)   6–10 times
(d)   More than 10 times

10.   In the past year I have been a target of cyberbullies

   (a)   Never
   (b)   1–5 times
   (c)   6–10 times
   (d)   More than 10 times

11.   In the past year, one or more of my friends has been a target of cyberbullies

   (a)   Never
   (b)   1–5 times
   (c)   6–10 times
   (d)   More than 10 times

12.   In the past year, I have participated in cyberbullying

   (a)   Never
   (b)   1–5 times
   (c)   6–10 times
   (d)   More than 10 times

13.   In the past year, one or more of my friends has participated in cyberbullying

   (a)   Never
   (b)   1–5 times
   (c)   6–10 times
   (d)   More than 10 times

14.   In the past year I have presented myself online as someone else

   (a)   Never
   (b)   1–5 times
   (c)   6–10 times
   (d)   More than 10 times

15. In the past year I have told lies online

    (a) Never
    (b) 1–5 times
    (c) 6–10 times
    (d) More than 10 times

16. In the past year my parents discussed cyberbullying

    (a) Never
    (b) 1–5 times
    (c) 6–10 times
    (d) More than 10 times

17. In my opinion, cyberbullying is

    (a) worse than the face-to-face bullying
    (b) about the same as face-to-face bullying
    (c) less damaging than face-to-face bullying
    (d) just having fun and results in little harm

18. Overall, cyberbullying at my school is

    (a) not a problem at all
    (b) a minor problem
    (c) a common problem
    (d) a worse problem than any other

19. The school should provide information to students about cyberbullying.

    (a) yes
    (b) no

20. The school should provide information to parents about cyberbullying.

    (a) yes
    (b) no

21. The amount of time I spend daily on the Internet is:

(a) I don't use Internet
(b) Less than 1 hour
(c) 1–2 hours
(d) 3–4 hours
(e) 5 or more hours

22. The amount of time I spend on a cell phone daily is:

(a) I don't use a cell phone
(b) Less than 1 hour
(c) 1–2 hours
(d) 3–4 hours
(e) 5 or more hours

Select your grade level, gender, ethnicity, and age.

My grade level is 5 6 7 8 9 10 11 12
My gender is female male
My ethnicity is Asian Black Hispanic Native American White Other
My age is 10 11 12 13 14 15 16 17 18 19

Exercise 11.02: Learning Self Control

Role: Improviser

Self-control means being able to regulate conduct instead of resorting to impulsive behavior. Teaching self-control implicates management of negative emotions like anger and frustration, coping with stress, establishing personal direction, and substituting long term goals for pursuit of immediate gratification. Students who are guided by long-term goals are more able to wait and to look ahead with anticipation, factors that contribute to persistence instead of giving up. Identify attitudes and skills teachers can encourage to help adolescents move toward greater self-control.

Exercise 11.03: Hierarchy of Needs and Environment

Role: Evaluator

There have been many changes since Abraham Maslow proposed the hierarchy of needs theory. At that time he estimated the average American had 85% of physiological needs met, 70% of safety needs, 50% of belonging needs, 40% of ego needs, and 10% of self-actualization needs. Think about the contemporary scene and provide your estimate of the extent to which physiological, safety, social, ego, and self-actualization needs are met at the present time for teenagers at the school where you are working. Explain your reasoning.

Exercise 11.04: Reporting Peer Abuse

Roles: Summarizer

Adolescents are forming lifelong attitudes about social injustice. Education should help them learn that it is their responsibility as individuals to prevent abuse.

1. Why should students join teachers and parents to identify peers who abuse others?
2. Support or challenge the practice of telling teachers when friends are the abusers
3. What situations do you recall where failure to inform authorities led to tragedy?
4. What assurances should be given to someone willing to identify abusive peers?
5. What sequence of processes should take place when someone reports peer abuse?
6. What are some ways to establish a norm of telling rather than hiding peer abuse?

Exercise 11.05: Educating Parents of Bullies

Role: Challenger

Schools may not have the legal authority necessary to mandate intervention classes for parents of bullies as one method to support rehabilitation. It has been customary to suppose that parents should handle their own affairs without any intrusion from the public education system. Generate a list of reasons to justify why parents of bullies should participate in classes designed for them by the school district.

Exercise 11.06: Volunteers in the Classroom

Role: Improviser

Teachers sometimes complain that discipline problems are increased by having too many students and not enough help. The preferred solution is smaller classes. This solution is seldom attained because of budget constraints. Another way to handle the need for students to access help is by recruiting volunteers to for the classroom. Three million retirees volunteer in school, 90% of them at the elementary school level. They report that this activity enriches their lives. Because volunteers are eager to perform well, they need feedback that helps to increase their effectiveness. Develop a list of five favorable criteria to record observations of volunteer behaviors as perceived by students, teachers, and volunteers.

Exercise 11.07: Rules for Conduct

Role: Improviser

Devise a list of six rules for student behavior in your classroom and provide reasons for each rule. Remember that students respond better to rules that are stated in a positive manner and include justification for them so students recognize the need for them.

Exercise 11.08: A Bully I Won't Forget

Role: Storyteller

Most people can remember a bully who persecuted them or a classmate. Tell a story about a bully you knew. Provide details on events that happened, your feelings, options considered, responses tried, and eventual outcome.

Exercise 11.09: Reporting Good Behavior of Students to Parents

Role: Evaluator

Most parents feel that "No news is good news" when it comes to school communication about their adolescents. The prevailing custom has been for a school to inform parents only when the misbehavior or failure of a student warrants corrective instruction in the family. Parents also should know about commendable behavior of students that occurs at school. Speculate on some of the possible effects that could accompany reporting good behavior to parents.

Exercise 11.10: Bullies in History

Role: Generational Reporter

Have your team identify prominent bullies in history. These bullies might be individuals or nations. For each case, report the consequences of bullying and what was done to make it end. You can use this same exercise in class with students to find out their take on mistreatment throughout time.

CHAPTER 12

EMOTIONS AND RESILIENCE

Emotional success in a technological society requires being able to adapt to rapid change, manage stressful events, cope with frustrations, and keep worries in perspective. There are increasing signs that mental health must become a more prominent concern for the society and focus for education in families and schools. The goals for this chapter are to show how people vary in amount of stress that they can handle, describe how emotional intelligence contributes to well being, and illustrate the benefits of acquiring emotional balance. Patience, hope, and reflection are documented as important factors in becoming mature and resilient.

Parents face unfamiliar challenges that call for increased knowledge about the experience of adolescents today and a willingness to accept assistance from sources outside of the family. Specific ways for communities to provide developmental assets that promote healthy choices for youth and prevent dangers of drugs, violence, and failure are explored. Living at home while attending college is a financial necessity for many students and can be a more mutually beneficial experience when adolescents and their parents are informed in advance about ways they can overcome predictable difficulties together.

Adolescents in the Internet Age, pp. 519–566

INFLUENCE OF STRESS

Student conversations often include reports about their stress experiences. The concept of stress in relation to mental health was first identified by physician Hans Seyle, Director of the Institute for Experimental Medicine at University of Montreal. Selye (1956) defined *stress* as "the nonspecific response of the body to demands made on it." Stress can be physiological including excessive cold, heat, food, and water deprivation or stress can be related to psychological experiences such as anger, frustration, conflict, anxiety, and discomfort. There are two types of stress. *Eustress* involves good situations people adapt to like graduating from high school, making the transition to college, or getting a promotion. *Distress* results from disappointing events that require adaptation such as breaking up with a boy/girl friend, being abused by a bully, or getting a ticket for speeding (Greenberg, 2006).

The concept of emotional, physical, and mental stress may seem vague but must remain that way because conditions that produce feelings of strain are not the same for every person (Harris, 2006). A high school basketball player or student taking a biology test must be "up" for the event. However, if the felt burden is too great, performance could be significantly impaired. This means that it is not just the weight of an external stressor that enters an effect but how the particular situation is viewed that is crucial. This section examines causes of anxiety among adolescents, focus of worries, symptoms of depression, and results of treatment (Aldwin, 2007).

Resilience—The Hardiness Asset

Personality differences correlate with how well individuals are able to perform under pressure (Bonanno, 2004; Maddi, 2002). At one pole of vulnerability are persons who appear stress resistant in their capacity to manage a heavy amount of stress and carry on effectively. At the other extreme is the personality that folds when exposed to slight pressure. Stress resistant individuals appear to have these characteristics in common. They (1) recognize negative forces in their environment but choose not to engage them; (2) remain open to possibilities for change; (3) perceive challenging events as opportunities for growth; (4) feel the need to be involved because they believe their actions can make a difference; and (5) possess an *internal locus of control,* feel in charge of most things that happen in their lives. The contrasting orientation, an *external locus of control,* describes individuals who believe their destiny is mostly controlled by fate, luck, or other people (Goldstein & Brooks, 2005).

There is evidence that the way someone perceives a particular event or a situation can sometimes be more important than what actually exists. The people who readily adapt to new conditions and feel they are in control display a psychological hardiness reflected by a much higher level of tolerance for stress (Sternberg & Subotnik, 2006). This hardiness quality is the basis of *resilience*, being able to work toward good outcomes despite having to deal with threats to development (Elliott, Menard, Elliott, Rankin, Wilson, & Huizinga, 2006). Parents, teachers, and friends should encourage teenagers to acknowledge their setbacks and work to overcome them. This experience can become the basis for confidence that difficult challenges in the future can be seen as contexts for success. Being on a sports team that frequently loses requires accepting defeat gracefully and determining how to perform better the next time. Failing a school class should motivate a request for tutoring and then working hard to gain the necessary skill. When adults try to protect adolescents from having to deal with any adversity, they render them less able to cope with the unforeseen challenges everyone must face. Ann Masten (2000, 2001, 2007) at the University of Minnesota has conducted a longitudinal study of risk and resilience involving 205 low-income children since the late 1970s. The ways that they have overcome adversity to attain success are described on her Web site at http://www.extension.umn.edu/distribution/familydevelopment/components/7565_06.html.

Parents and teachers should consider the involvement of allies in supporting resilience. Mentors can be an important source of support in adolescence. The concept of mentoring originated with the Greek myth in which Mentor was entrusted to educate the son of Odysseus when he left to fight in the Trojan War. A *mentor* is a wise and trusted advisor, a tutor, coach, counselor, and faithful friend (Rhodes, 2005). Mentor influence can be strong even when the two parties never meet face-to-face but instead communicate via the Internet. The Computer Clubhouse is a joint venture of the Museum of Science in Boston and Massachusetts Institute of Technology Media Laboratory—http://www.computerclubhouse.org. This center, and 75 others like it around the world, provides teenagers from underserved communities a safe after-school learning environment where they can explore ideas, develop skills, and build confidence. Each student gets to choose a mentor after reviewing biographical sketches online which include visuals prepared by volunteers willing to dialogue with adolescents. The participating mentors have successful careers and are able to offer valuable advice on how to interpret failure situations, provide feedback on critical thinking, encourage interdependence, and monitor planning skills.

Anxiety and Uncertainty

Anxiety is the feeling of uncertainty that arises whenever something new or different is anticipated. Because social change was less rapid in previous generations, teenagers then could look toward a more predictable future. In contrast, today's students experience greater anxiety because of increased uncertainty about their choice of career, identity formation, and alternative lifestyle options. Feeling uncertain and sensing doubt can be beneficial when the result is stimulation of curiosity or creative thinking. However, when the amount of uncertainty is excessive, the consequent stress can produce emotional disturbance. Schools and families should help students avoid this dangerous outcome of anxiety (Aldwin, 2007). Focus Adolescent Services describes the forms of anxiety adolescents experience and some common disorders at their Web site http://www.focusas.com/Stress.html.

The preconditions for anxiety are the same as for being human. As far as we can tell, animals do not lie awake at night thinking about the difficulties that make them dread the next day. Animals do not worry about how to pay the rent or mortgage on the tree where they live, cover the costs of higher education for many offspring, or whether they will be infected by a sexually transmitted disease. In short, animals lack the capacity to imagine, that wonderful attribute which is unique to the human mind, but also leads some people to anticipate every conceivable danger. Mankind worries because of awareness that we have a future and that what might happen tomorrow is less certain than was the case in earlier times (Blonna, 2006).

Philosophers and psychologists have recognized the need to accept uncertainty as part of life. Epictetus, the Greek scholar, explained how our thoughts can influence feelings when he observed that "Men are disturbed not by things but by the views they take of them." Asians have also been exposed to the similar view of Buddha suggesting, "All that we are is the result of our thoughts." A prominent psychologist, Erich Fromm (1992), warned that the quest for certainty can block the search for meaning. Uncertainty is the very condition that impels man to unfold his powers.

The unprecedented level of uncertainty that adolescents encounter requires learning how to be flexible and calm. Palm trees that flex in high winds usually survive storms without damage while more rigid trees that resist the power of the wind fall down or are uprooted. For students, flexibility is the capacity to shift from one thought pattern to another as demonstrated by individuals whose perceptions are not restricted to their history, traditions or familiar social restraints. The reason that flexibility is such a valuable asset is because it promotes cognitive and emotional adaptation. In contrast, being a rigid thinker is a liability because it relies on ineffective ways of coping with unfamiliar situations (Cheng & Cheung, 2005).

Remaining calm is also important for managing uncertainty because this attitude enables people to control the intensity of their negative emotions such as anxiety, fear, sadness, rage, helplessness, cynicism, and the feeling that one has no viable future (Maclem, 2008). Unless these emotions are under control, they restrict critical thinking and inhibit the ability to process new information in an organized fashion. The advantage of staying calm when confronted by uncertain events is that a person remains able to see the broader range of options and choices that are relevant in producing better decisions. Staying calm has the effect of subordinating the emotional brain so the executive logical brain can rationally weigh facts and decide a sensible plan of action. A source of helpful articles and guidelines for teenagers in dealing with anxiety and stress is available at Teen Help http://teenhelp.com.

Stress and Status Hierarchy

Robert Sapolsky, Professor of biology and neurology at Stanford University, has carried out creative research on the effects of stress. His findings contradict intuitive expectations that high status is accompanied by greater levels of stress. The customary assumption has been that the CEO of a company or the principal of a school must deal with more stress than is experienced by teachers and staff whose efforts are supervised by the administration. Sapolsky's (2004) long term studies of baboons discovered that increased plaque in blood vessels, more rapid heart rates, and higher blood pressure characterized lower ranking members of troops while baboons at the top of the hierarchy, those having control over others and making their own decisions experienced the least hypertension and evidence of stress hormone. In effect, the lower the rank of baboons, the higher their risk for heart attack, physical disability, and earlier death.

Results of Sapolsky's primate studies are reinforced by the Whitehall research led by Michael Marmot, Professor of epidemiology and his colleagues at University College in London (Marmot, Ferrie, Shipley, Stansfeld, & Smith, 2003). They tracked 28,000 British Civil Service over a period of 40 years. Everyone employed by the British Civil Service is assigned a rank that identifies their relative standing within the status hierarchy. They all have job stability and each worker enjoys equal access to the same health care system operated by the government. Results indicated that the employees with high status were far less likely to present elevated levels of stress and cholesterol. In addition, they had cleaner arteries, fewer heart attacks, and a lower index of disability than their civil servant colleagues whose rank in the status hierarchy was beneath their own.

Finding ways to prevent people from getting stuck in social subordination conditions that adversely affect their physical and mental health relates to another key observation from Sapolsky (2004). When he returned to Africa on one of his annual visits to assess baboons, he found that the most dominant males had recently died of diseases acquired from scavenging garbage dumps. Departure of these high status members fundamentally altered the dynamic that governed the remaining society. The fewer numbers of aggressive males and greater numbers of socially affiliative females created a new orientation that gave highest priority to congenial interaction. Thus, within a single generation, the way baboons treated one another was transformed from a strict reliance on status hierarchy to a mutual support system that took the form of respectful relationships devoid of aggressive intimidation (Sapolsky, 2004).

These outcomes which show that improvement of the social environment can improve physical health have implications for schools as well as animal troops and civil servants. Principals face daily challenges in their management tasks related to students, teachers, staff, parents, boards of education, and the community. Teachers also encounter extensive demands that often include taking some tasks home for completion at night. Students are the lowest status group in the school hierarchy. They often face stresses that adults are unaware of and tend to underestimate but have the power to minimize adverse conditions producing the stress. Establishing a socially responsive environment in which everyone feels respected, has access to help when needed, and are assured that their views about constructive change will be considered can do much to reduce the stress of being part of the school community (Blum, 2005; P. Strom & Strom, 2008).

Worries of Adolescents

Adolescents are daily exposed to media messages that can be worrisome. Some degree of worry is normal but the likelihood of anxiety or depression increases with the perceived number of worries. Studies undertaken to improve understanding about how worry influences mental and physical health have focused primarily on adults. This narrow focus is unfortunate, considering that excessive worry is frequently reported by adolescents and that adult patients suffering excessive worry usually associate the start of their disorder with adolescence (Brown, Teufel, Birch, & Kancheria, 2006).

The common advice adolescents give friends is "don't worry." Excessive worry can block critical thinking and preoccupy individuals to such an extent that they are unable to pay attention to daily responsibilities. There can be a positive side of worry too. Worries act as a rehearsal for danger by causing us to concentrate on particular problems that we might otherwise ignore and motivate us to seek solutions in advance (Leahy, 2005). Some people seem more able to benefit from focused attention that worries present because they are able to switch off the process and turn away from their worries when it is time to attend to other obligations. People unable to snap out of it and instead remain fixed on their worries do so at considerable cost to their performance at school, home or work (Gosselin, Langlois, Freeston, & Ladouceur, 2007).

Everyone finds it difficult to remain confident when they are confronted by too much uncertainty. During the past decade there has been a significant loss of predictability. As a result, some people try to retain some degree of predictability in their lives to avoid being overwhelmed by uncertainty. Some ways to attain predictability include a rigid schedule that guarantees particular events will happen when expected, being guided by values that ensure consistency of behavior, holding on to unyielding customs and beliefs, and providing relatives favorable feedback regardless of their behavior to reinforce self-confidence.

There is a protective mechanism that adolescents can learn to rely on to prevent excessive worry. The term described earlier, locus of control, refers to the way people perceive the forces that shape their destiny. Those with an internal locus of control believe that they can govern the direction and momentum of their lives. An opposite outlook is held by persons having an external locus of control. They believe that luck and influence of powerful people are the reasons why things happen. Therefore, no matter what they might try to do, their efforts would have little effect. For them, the rewards of life are independent of personal actions. Adolescents who look at life through the lens of an extreme external locus of control run the risk of becoming cynical and alienated because they feel powerless and suppose it is futile to spend time and energy struggling to reach goals that are unattainable (Brown, Higgins, & Paulsen, 2003).

There has been a long-standing search for methods to acquire the capacity of extracting mental benefit from worry while avoiding the hazards associated with it. For example, disappointment and sadness motivated by worry are low arousal states more likely to trigger withdrawal than perseverance. On the other hand, responding to worry by participating in physical exercise generates a high arousal state incompatible with feeling down. Conversely, high-energy negative moods like anger are better dealt with by participating in relaxation and reflection activities. Adaptation calls for shifting to a state of arousal that can terminate the destructive cycle of a dominating negative mood (Darst & Pangrazi, 2008).

A *confidant* is a trusted person with whom personal matters are discussed. A survey of 1,000 adolescents found that those who chose parents to listen to their concerns were much less inclined to worry about being liked by classmates, school failure, their occupational future, and relationships with friends than teenagers who chose non-family listeners such as peers, Internet sources or teachers (Brown, Teufel, Birch, & Kancheria, 2006). Surveys of 10–18 year olds are consistent in identifying the following most prevalent worries (Johnson, Duffett, & Ott, 2005).

(1) The number one worry of adolescents is school performance, particularly doing well on state required tests and getting ready for a career. Relatives should be pleased that teenagers give high priority to their studies. Most students want relatives to be proud of them. However, many report that their parents expect them to perform better than classmates even if they lack superior abilities. Pressures to meet unreasonable expectations lead to unnecessary stress. Family members should regularly discuss goals they have for one another and amend them when warranted.

(2) The worry that adolescents rank second is physical appearance. Most adolescents are preoccupied by how their peers see them. A survey of 700 adolescents from five urban high schools sought to identify the personal exclusion rules they felt were fair to reject someone else. Findings indicated that perceived unattractiveness is the most prevalent reason for exclusion (Leets & Sunwolf, 2005; Sunwolf & Leets, 2003, 2004). This is one reason teenagers are so quick to adopt the new clothing styles of their peers. Parents sometimes trivialize clothing fads claiming they are expensive, encourage conformity, and do not matter in the long run. A more sensible response is to realize that external conformity of dress style does not mean a student lacks individuality or can be pressured to conform in other aspects of behavior.

(3) The third most common worry relates to popularity. Boys and girls want to become popular, an ambition that peaks in seventh grade (Rimm, 2005). It is wise to accept this desire instead of belittling the interest in being well thought of by peers (Hamm & Faircloth, 2005). The wish for peer approval does not signal an end to parent influence. The duration of parent influence is as long or short as an individual parent's willingness to encourage personal development. Adolescents also need to realize their age group tends to focus more on benefits than costs of risky behavior and makes more high risk decisions when in peer groups than alone. Consequently, there may be times when popularity should be set aside in favor of discouraging group intentions or walking away from participation.

(4) "I worry that my parents might get divorced or they could die." These worries are seldom expressed to parents (Fine & Harvey, 2005). Parents should anticipate these fears and describe preparations they have made in the event of their untimely death. "If your Dad and I died, Aunt Joyce has agreed to be your guardian. We know she would raise you in the way we feel is best. Each year we put money in an insurance policy for your college tuition." Part of a teen's concerns deal with how his or her future would be in jeopardy. Talking about it is helpful and reassuring.

(5) Students also worry about how their friends treat them. This concern reaches a peak in eighth grade and is greater among youth who are gay (Mason, 2007). The meaning of friendship and how to maintain good relationships without compromising one's values is a topic that many students wish would be discussed more often in their family. Romantic relationships are a problem for those who may break up or are mistreated by their dating partner. Parents who are willing to dialogue about these concerns are respected because it demonstrates that they realize complications that must be taken into account.

In summary, four of the five most often reported fears of adolescents implicate peers. During middle school and high school, peer influence increases and parental influence declines. Still, parent influence continues to be more powerful than peers at every level from fifth through ninth grade. Most teenagers continue to look to their parents for guidance even though Mom and Dad may suppose that because they are no longer the only source of counseling, their advice is not taken seriously (McGue, Elkins, Walden, & Iacono, 2005).

The study of adolescent fears and worries also reveals that many want to talk about their concerns with adults who are important to them. All parents and teachers should be accessible, ready to listen, and respond to issues youth want to discuss. Talking is an effective way to relieve stress because it causes us to feel that we are not alone and enables us to organize our thoughts. Whereas talking to oneself often increases stress, talking to someone else can usually reduce stress. Finally, when teachers are creative thinkers, interaction helps adolescents become aware of more alternatives.

Stress and Depression

The common sources of stress adolescents identify suggest that their concerns cover life as a whole instead of only particular problems (Blonna, 2006; Greenberg, 2006). Reported stresses are often related to:

1. Conflict with parents, teachers, or friends

2. Rejection from classmates or felt rejection
3. Anxiety concerns about abuse from bullies
4. Body image (pimples, obesity, thinness)
5. Dating (asking someone and being asked)
6. Understanding subjects taught in school
7. Sexuality (becoming involved or waiting)
8. Moving (new school, neighborhood or town)
9. Being the object of prejudice from classmates
10. Wearing the same clothes fashions as peers
11. Breaking up with a girlfriend or a boyfriend
12. Fears about possible international terrorism
13. Excessive homework from multiple teachers
14. Uncertainty over the choice of an occupation
15. Taking illegal drugs and smoking cigarettes
16. Feeling bored and lacking a sense of purpose
17. Having a continually over-scheduled calendar
18. Not getting enough sleep on school nights

The symptoms of adolescent stress that usually claim attention of teachers and parents are aggressive behavior, destruction of property, bullying, stealing, and other anti-social conduct (Larson & Lochman, 2005). However, mental health professionals have found that these are not the primary symptoms of stress. Such overt behaviors, bothersome as they are, inform others that the perpetrators feel stressed and need help. They may be threatened or feel overburdened but continue to struggle, still trying and with assistance may overcome stress.

The more significant symptoms of stress are depression, withdrawal, and resignation. Students who exhibit these behaviors have quit. Depression is one of the most serious threats to adolescent mental health (Kramer, 2005). It is not just a matter of being moody or having to live within difficult environments, but that they have given up hope and therefore no longer show persistence in trying to adjust. Signs of extreme withdrawal is observed when students take illegal drugs, run away from home, skip school, drop out, or commit suicide (Zuckerbrot, Maxon, Pagar, Davies, Fisher, & Shaffer, 2007). The School Mental Health Center Project at UCLA helps students, teachers, and parents deal with stress—http://smhp.psych.ucla.edu/.

When students transition from childhood to adolescence, the conditions of autonomy change. Even though adults continue to sometimes intervene for minimizing stress, teens are increasingly expected to deal with issues of stress on their own (Barnes, Bauza, & Treiber, 2003). Handling this responsibility can be promoted by discussions in middle school and high school classrooms. Students can verbalize problems, state their personal views, and hear solutions that have worked for others. Some guidelines for teachers are:

1. Every student should have a chance to contribute to the discussion even when the person is not a fluent speaker or someone who does not boldly take the risk of self-disclosure.
2. Situations in which students have actual experience and resulted in pleasant or unpleasant emotional reactions are better topics than general issues over which youth lack control.
3. The recommended size of a discussion group is three to six members so everyone has an opportunity for participation.
4. Teachers should realize that they are not the decision makers or summarizers. Their role is to ensure that everyone in groups has a chance to speak and be heard.

Most students adapt to stressors but some of them become overwhelmed. The American Academy of Child and Adolescent Psychiatry estimates that 5% of all students, three million individuals, suffer from significant depression (Kramer, 2005). Depression has no single cause and is not just a state of mind that people should be encouraged to dismiss or ignore. When certain chemicals in the brain such as serotonin and dopamine are out of balance, depression can take over and physicians then prescribe antidepressants to bring the chemicals back into balance. Depression is generally misunderstood (Marshall, Zuroff, McBride & Bagby, 2008).

Despite fairly equal gender rates of depression in childhood, rates change in adolescence as girls become twice as likely to suffer (Rudman & Glick, 2008). The higher risk for females is attributed partly to hormonal changes of puberty, menstruation, menopause, and pregnancy. Fortunately, depression is responsive to intervention during early adolescence and can prevent chronic and severe depression later on in early adulthood. Nevertheless, even though effective treatment is available, less than one-third of adolescents trying to cope with this debilitating condition get care (Zuckerbrot, Maxon, Pagar, Davies, Fisher, & Shaffer, 2007).

Clinical depression, a persistent sad or irritable mood, is the most frequent mental illness among teenagers. Teachers and parents should be observant to detect depression that is shown by one or more of the following signs (Epstein, 2007):

1. difficulty concentrating
2. drop in school grades
3. misconduct problems
4. sleep changes leading to fatigue or loss of energy
5. anti-social or delinquent behavior leading to isolation
6. self-impression of helplessness, worthlessness or guilt
7. continuous feelings of sadness
8. announcement of suicidal thoughts
9. extreme sensitivity to rejection or failure
10. low self-esteem and lack of confidence
11. eating problems shown by appetite or weight change
12. loss of enjoyment for previously pleasurable activities

Depressed students are more likely than classmates to engage in high risk behaviors like drinking, drug taking, driving drunk, and early sexual involvement (MacPhee & Andrews, 2006).

One of the dangers of being preoccupied with problems of the present is the inability to place these difficulties into a longer time perspective. When people cannot disengage from current difficulties, some of them become depressed and conclude that taking their own life appears to be the only option (Holmes & Holmes, 2005). During periods of depression, it can be motivating to look back on achievements of the past to restore self-confidence and support continued effort. Adolescents need to think about the range of possible consequences of disappointing events in a more extended time frame involving the future than just the pain of the moment. Billy Joel wrote a song for adolescents in distress, especially those contemplating suicide. The lyrics for "You're only human" illustrate how looking at events from a perspective that includes a hopeful future can enable adolescents to catch their breath and face the world again.

Each year 5,000 adolescents take their own lives, making *suicide* the third leading cause of death among youth (Bisconer & Gross, 2007). Males account for 80% of suicide completions. Gender difference in self-destruction are perplexing because females are more often diagnosed with depression and try to take their lives three times more often than do males. However, while females complete only one in 25 attempts, males complete 1 in 3. The most common underlying disorder is depression; 30% to 70% of suicide victims suffer from major depression or bipolar (manic-depressive) disorder. Adolescent males more often express their depression by aggression, irritability, anger, and impulsiveness whereas forecast behaviors among female suicides are helplessness, hopelessness, and sadness. The adolescent suicide rate differs by a factor of 20 between the highest risk group (American Indian/Alaska Native males) and the lowest risk group (African American females) (Goldston, Molock, Whitback, Murakami, Zayas, & Hall, 2008). Guns account for nearly 70% of self-inflicted deaths. Households in which there are guns have an incidence of suicide that is five times greater than homes where no guns are available. It seems that restricting access to weapons could significantly reduce suicide among adolescents (Rutter & Behrendt, 2004).

Family breakdown is the primary source of stress that leads to self-destruction. Over 70% of the youth that attempt suicide live in single parent families (Connor & Rueter, 2006). Sexual abuse and intercourse are also factors closely associated with adolescent suicide. A high positive correlation exists between girls who have been sexually mistreated and those who attempt to take their own life. Deep depression can sometimes follow the breakup of a romance, especially if the couple has been sexually active. Poor self-esteem, drug dependence, absence of religious beliefs and atypical gender preference are also associated with suicidal behavior and these problems are frequently traced to the family (Collins, 2003).

At every age, people who suffer sustained feelings of depression and hopelessness are more likely to think about suicide. In most cases they attempt to describe their feelings and need for professional help. Although 80% of adolescents who consider suicide communicate their intention to relatives or other key persons in their life (see http://www.suicidology.org). Unfortunately, this dangerous signal of desperation often goes unrecognized or is not taken seriously (Goldston, Molock, Whitback, Murakami, Zayas, & Hall, 2008). The Teen Suicide Web site provides information about warning signs for suicide and ways to help at http://www.http://www.teensuicide.us/articles2.html.

EMOTIONAL INTELLIGENCE

During the past decade there has been a great increase in studies of emotional growth and dysfunction. Magnetic resonance imaging (MRI), techniques have made visible how regions of the brain act in conjunction with particular cognitive tasks and affective states. The revelation of this neurobiological information is providing insight about conditions that facilitate mental health and interfere with adjustment. This research stream has been influential in enlarging the scope of curriculum to ensure that students gain coping skills that are necessary for a complicated environment. Richard Davidson, neuroscientist at the University of Wisconsin explains that social-emotional learning changes the brain. To view and hear his perspective, visit http://edutopia.org/richard-davidson-sel-brain-video.

Theories of learning do not explain why some people appear to possess a map for living well, why students who have high IQs seldom become wealthy adults, why we feel attraction to certain individuals right away and find others hard to trust, and why some people can withstand adversity and remain resilient while others fall apart when exposed to even the slightest pressure. Psychologist Daniel Goleman (2005, 2006) maintains that the answer relates to emotional intelligence, an ability to validly reason with emotions and rely on emotions to enhance thought. Specifically, *emotional intelligence* consists of self-control, empathy, mood management, self-awareness, and capacity for self-motivation. Goleman (2006) has illustrated how this realm of achievement has been overlooked and should be included in the curriculum to support student adjustment. Helping adolescents acquire emotional intelligence can contribute to their maturity and improve quality of relationships. An interview with Goleman regarding the importance of emotional intelligence is at http://www.edutopia.org. This section examines some components of emotional intelligence that support success such as patience, hope, and the ability to arrange for relaxation.

Patience and Learning to Wait

Some elements of emotional intelligence are examined to demonstrate why they deserve attention in the classroom. The public worries that behaviors which depend on self-control, like willingness to delay gratification and ability to show patience, are in decline. The pressure to maintain an over-scheduled and hurried lifestyle can cause people to abandon their capacity for being able to cope with frustrating situations requiring impulse control (Williams & Williams, 2006).

The need to support development of self-control is illustrated by a long-term research project that began in the 1970s at Stanford University Laboratory School. Walter Mischel, who later became President of the American Psychological Association, conducted the experiment. Mischel met with a preschool class at Stanford whose parents were on the faculty or members of the staff. The challenge he gave to the 4-year-olds was defined in this way,

> If you boys and girls wait until I (the experimenter) go to the school office and come back, you will be given two marshmallows to eat. If you cannot wait until I get back, come to the front of the room and you can take one marshmallow from off the teacher's desk.

This task presented the lure of enjoying an immediate reward or choosing self-restraint to gain a greater reward later. The experimenter left for 15 minutes. This period of time probably seemed long for two-thirds of the class members who delayed gratification by covering their eyes so they would not look at the marshmallows, making up fantasy games to distract themselves, singing songs or staring at trees outside the window. In contrast, one third of the children could not wait for the return of the experimenter so they came forward to claim their reward of one marshmallow (Mischel, 1974).

The significance of emotional differences among these children was not fully evident until the follow up study took place 14 years later (Mischel, Schoda, & Peake, 1988). By then the students were adolescents almost through high school. Some dramatic distinctions were reported between the students who, years earlier, had been able to resist temptation and classmates who showed no inclination to be patient, wait, and demonstrate self-control. Those who got two marshmallows for their willingness to delay gratification had grown to be more socially competent, more self-assertive, and more able to deal with the frustrations of daily life. They were less prone to get upset when faced with unanticipated problems and gave no signs of disorganization when subjected to peer pressure. Teachers saw them as more self-reliant, confident, and trustworthy, a person who could be counted on to assume initiative in situations presenting uncertainty, and able to delay gratification in pursuit of their goals.

These favorable attributes were observed less often in adolescents who, years earlier, settled for one marshmallow immediately (Mischel, Schoda, & Peake, 1988). This group was more often described as stubborn and indecisive, easily upset in situations involving frustration, likely to regress or withdraw if presented with stress, prone to jealousy, ever ready to complain that they were being treated unfairly or shortchanged, and inclined to provoke arguments by showing a quick temper. In effect, even by late adolescence, they had yet to acquire competence in self-control. The ability to postpone satisfaction by persevering to achieve a longer-term goal is a fundamental ingredient for success in situations that range from staying on a diet to completing all the requirements for a high school diploma.

Besides being more able to manage demands associated with daily living, children who waited patiently at age four differed as adolescents in other ways that contribute to academic achievement. In their parents' estimate, they were more able to put their ideas and feelings into words, listen to the logic of others, apply reasoning, concentrate, plan goals, evaluate personal progress, and display a zest for learning. Further, they performed better on the Scholastic Aptitude Test (SAT), a measure commonly required for admission to college. The one-third of children who most quickly came forward to obtain a marshmallow at age 4 had an average verbal score of 524 and 528 quantitative (mathematics) score. In comparison, the one-third of boys and girls who waited longest for a reward had scores of 610 and 652, a total difference of 210 points. Marshmallow results for delay of gratification at age four were twice as powerful a predictor of student SAT scores in adolescence as their IQ scores at age four. This means that the self- imposed ability to deny impulses and delay gratification by persevering toward achieving a longer-term self-chosen goal has a significant impact on academic achievement (Miscel, Shoda, & Ayduk, 2007). Conversely, lack of self-control in childhood has often been identified as a powerful predictor of delinquent behavior (Agnew, 2007).

One reason that children have difficulty making choices requiring them to sacrifice short-term pleasure for longer-term gain is that the patience involved with anticipation is less necessary. Instead, for example, television programs can be recorded using TiVo and retrieved later. The experience of *anticipation*, being patient and willing to wait for rewards, has application in all sectors of life from studying, moving toward a long term career goal, and putting off a desired purchase until enough money has been saved to pay for it. Individuals who shun anticipation see little reason for planning to get the things they want because many products can often be obtained immediately, enjoyed, and paid for later. Parents are the main models for lessons in this context (Sampson, 2007). A study of 600 male and female adolescents explored the relationship between emotional intelligence and impulse buying. The results showed that high emotional intelligence students were much less likely to engage in impulsive buying than peers with low emotional intelligence (Lin & Chuang, 2005). Fourteen states require a course in money management for high school graduation. The rationale is that the obligation of schools does not end with preparing students to make money; they must also be taught to manage their personal finances (Chu, 2007).

Impact of Hope and Optimism

The mythical story of Pandora is about a Greek Princess who receives a mysterious box as a gift from the gods who envied her beauty. She was warned that the box must never be opened. Before long curiosity got the best of Pandora so she decided to raise the lid and peek inside. The penalty for her disobedience was an immediate release of terrible conditions that included diseases, insanity, and depression. Because one of the gods was sympathetic toward Pandora, she was permitted to close the box just before hope, the emotion that enables people to endure hardship, would have disappeared.

Research reveals that hope has a more important influence on motivation and achievement than is generally supposed (Snyder, 2000). Freshmen from the University of Kansas responded to this hypothetical situation:

> Your goal was to earn a B in a course. However, when the first examination is returned, counting for 30% of the final, the grade was a D. One week has gone by since the bad news so it is time to decide what should be done.

The students also completed a measure to assess levels of hope (Snyder, 2000). Those showing high levels of hope reassured themselves that they could perform better, resolved to spend more time studying, and planned ways to do better next time. Persons with moderate hope levels also thought about what they could do to improve their grade but showed less determination to follow through. Those that revealed the least hope appeared to be resigned to doing poorly in the course. After the semester ended, student actual levels of achievement in all their classes were compared to hope levels. Hope was found to be a better predictor of first semester grades in college than SAT scores. Researchers concluded that, when students of equal mental ability are compared in achievement, hope is what sets them apart.

Optimism is another element of emotional intelligence that can influence academic achievement (Seligman, 2006). The way people explain to themselves their failures and successes can impact how they deal with unexpected problems. An *optimistic self-explanatory style* enables a person to see failure as a temporary setback, an outcome they have the power to change by increasing study time and paying attention to teacher presentations. A *pessimistic self-explanatory style* causes one to believe that the reasons for their failure reflect personal shortcomings over which they have no control and should accept instead of pursuing futile attempts to do better. Martin Seligman, Professor of Psychology at University of Pennsylvania, found that the scores of 500 college freshmen on a measure of optimism were a better predictor of first-year grades in higher education than were their marks from high school or SAT scores. Peterson and Seligman (2004) explain that college admissions tests identify knowledge while self-explanatory styles of optimism and pessimism ways of interpreting events identify the students likely to quit and those that persist to overcome difficulties. An important thing to know about a person is how s/he will act when faced with difficulties. Optimism is an attitude that can be learned and leads to *self-efficacy*, the belief that one has the capacity to meet whatever challenges they are likely to encounter (Margolis & McCabe, 2006).

Goleman (2005, 2006) maintains that students need guidance to acquire self-regulation, manage anger, resolve conflict, acquire empathy, and social skills needed to become mature adults. These characteristics, which do much to enrich the quality of life, do not occur naturally but require continuous encouragement, guidance, and support. Similarly, the limitations of intelligence test scores as a predictor of school success should become more widely understood. Such scores may in fact have less impact than non-intellectual qualities that make up emotional intelligence. Education can become more beneficial by adopting a dual emphasis on mental intelligence and emotional intelligence. Students like Michael Guggenheim can provide hope for one another too. He is a sixth grader with dysgraphia, a disorder that makes the simple act of writing painful. After Michael began using a laptop, he decided to share his technology knowledge with homeless kids. His program is called Showing People Learning and Technology, SPLAT. Check out his story at http://www.youtube.com [search: Michael Guggenheim].

Meditation and Relaxation

Stress is an aspect of everyday life so students should be taught suitable ways to look at the pressures they face. Stress can be partly controlled by learning to relax. *Meditation,* to empty the mind of thoughts and to relax, has been confirmed as an effective method of stress reduction (Wallace, 2007). A generation ago reports about effects of meditation were anecdotal. Since then many experiments have been conducted to assess the influence of meditation. In addition, meditation has been explored with employee training at American Telephone and Telegraph, Connecticut General, Blue Cross Blue Shield, Armed Forces, and Health Maintenance Organizations in wellness education programs. In these settings it has been found that measurable changes occur in heartbeat, blood pressure, lactate levels, and muscle tension. Meditation relieves tension, helps to control stress, lowers blood pressure, and improves physical and emotional health. Typically meditators described an enhanced sense of well being, reduced anxiety, improved perception, and lower rates of illegal drug and alcohol abuse.

Neuroscientist Andrew Newberg (2000) from the University of Pennsylvania scanned the brains of eight highly skilled meditators from the Tibetan Buddhist School to identify cognitive changes during this activity. Following injection of a radioactive substance that attaches to red blood cells, the 'tagged' blood briefly leaves a trace that can be detected by the imaging machine. Active brain waves reflect more blood than others because neural activity is fuelled by blood borne oxygen. Single photon emission computed tomography (SPECT) identifies brain areas that are working hardest by showing concentrations of the radioactive marker. These scans reveal different patterns than are typical in a normal state of mind. Some differences included unusually prolonged and intense concentration, reduced metabolism, less awareness of distractions, and up to 20% greater frontal lobe activity (Newberg & Waldman, 2006).

Can short periods of solitude and reflection become a routine part of the daily schedule for students? Such an arrangement would seem to be particularly important for adolescents whose relatives and surrogates over-schedule their lives so they lack opportunities to participate in reflection. It is ironic that, as most people have abandoned the traditional pattern of setting aside one day a week for relaxation, research is affirming the restorative power that can come from meditation (Wallace, 2007).

The implications for including meditation in secondary school and higher education has been largely overlooked. If students could learn to alter their physiological responses through meditation, they might be able to prevent stress from interfering with the learning process. This is a better option than excessive reliance on caffeine, drugs, alcohol or cigarettes for coping with the pressures associated with daily life. Moreover, behavior problems could be dealt with in more constructive ways by encouraging misbehaving students to withdraw for a time, relax, and find more healthy ways of responding to difficulties that are inherent in modern living (Wallace, 2007).

Researchers at the Medical College of Georgia wanted to determine how negative student behavior at school might be influenced through exposure to mediation (Barnes, Bauza, & Treiber, 2003). The 677 male and female Black students from two inner-city high schools were screened on three separate occasions for blood pressure. Then, 45 were declared eligible based on systolic rates above the 85th percentile with respect to age, gender, and height. These 15–18-year-olds were assigned to a meditation orientation or to a health education control group for 1 year. Boys and girls in the meditation group met 15 minutes every day and practiced twice daily at home on weekends. Members of the health education control group attended daily sessions at school focused on lifestyle education.

A comparison of pretest and posttest data after four months of intervention found that the meditation group showed a significant decrease in school absences as compared to the control group. The meditation group also recorded a significant decline in number of school rule infractions while breaking the rules increased in the control group. Number of suspension days for misconduct also declined in the meditation group by 83% while the control group recorded an increase in suspension time.

Anger management was also more effective for the meditators. These outcomes encourage educators to consider stress reduction as a powerful strategy for improving behavior of adolescents (Barnes, Bauza, & Treiber, 2003).

Learning to relax is an aspect of lifestyle that more parents should model for coping with stress. Parents generally overestimate their influence in this context. To offer credible advice on stress, a person must be perceived as demonstrating this capacity in their life. One method is to occasionally retreat from daily tasks to recover a sense of perspective. A study of White ($N = 537$) and Black adolescents ($N = 396$) found that a majority saw their parents as ineffective in teaching them to cope with daily stress. It is troubling that one of the lowest self-ratings reported by White ($N = 391$) and Black ($N = 271$) mothers (60th out of 60 items) was their difficulty arranging leisure time for themselves. Adolescents also rated lack of maternal leisure as 57th out of 60. Many mothers suffer from the stress of multiple responsibilities that include taking care of children and a husband, satisfying an employer, managing a household, and perhaps giving care for aging parents. It is not surprising that youth conclude that, if my parent cannot arrange personal leisure as a way to deal with stress, she cannot teach me (P. Strom, Van Marche, Beckert, Strom, Strom, & Griswold, 2003; R. Strom, Dohrmann et al., 2002).

Black ($N = 102$) and White ($N = 126$) fathers of adolescents resembled the mothers in reporting that their greatest difficulty was also arranging leisure time for themselves. This inability to schedule free time is bound to influence parenting. Fathers do not accept as much responsibility as mothers do for childcare and guidance. It is improbable that a father could teach his children to deal with multiple demands on their time when he is unable to set aside time for his own personal renewal. Living with over-choice, feeling hurried, and sensing a lack of control over events is an increasingly common complaint in society. Fathers and mothers must deal with this problem or they cannot effectively teach children how to manage time. When students conclude that parents cannot teach lessons that they have yet to learn themselves, sources outside the family become the healthy or unhealthy models that teens choose to emulate (R. Strom, Amukamara et al., 2000; R. Strom, Beckert, Strom, Strom, & Griswold, 2002).

Voices of Adolescents

Adolescence is the stage of development when youth try to accomplish important tasks that have lifelong implications. They search for a sense of identity, meaning, and purpose, assert independence and autonomy, choose values to guide their behavior, define integrity and character, acquire competence in skills for employment, reflect on choice of an occupation, make an effort to be perceived as appealing to persons they like, and get along with peers and adults in positions of authority. In combination, these tasks can present considerable stress.

Some adults are inclined to tell anyone when their stress results in frustration. In contrast, teenagers sometimes speak only to others from their own age about distress they endure (Girod, Pardales, Cavanaugh, & Wadsworth, 2005). This reluctance to confide in adults is usually based on the belief that self- disclosure reinforces their dependence, a condition they prefer to deny. The decision to withhold information about stress often means that teachers and parents are unaware of obstacles that can undermine student health and well being. In these situations, adults are unable to recommend suitable alternatives for consideration or take initiatives to reduce stresses over which they have control (Fleming, 2005).

Instead of a guessing game where adults must directly observe or intuit things that bother teenagers, a better choice is to administer anonymous polls that make known information without divulging personal identity. The poll for this chapter is School Stress (Exercise 12.1) and intended to assess the stress felt by students at the school where you work. You can be better informed about their views of teacher and parent expectations for behavior, homework, grades, and over scheduling. Students should feel comfortable reporting the pressures they feel to cheat, get involved with sex, and take drugs. Stress related to body image, fashion, peer relations, romantic connections, encounters with bullies and experiences in extracurricular activities can be assessed. Teachers should identify excessive stresses that schools might reduce and implications for frustrations students must deal with constructively.

FAMILY AND SCHOOL CHALLENGES

There is increasing awareness that, in a technological environment, adolescents are being exposed to significant risks and dangers unrelated to the configuration of their family, amount of household income or ethnic background. This contradicts the traditional view that only certain types of readily identified families are exposed to limitations which require external support to succeed while all other families should be able and expected to take care of themselves without societal support. Specifically, single parents and households with low incomes have been identified as those whose children are considered at-risk. This has been the guiding premise of compensatory education programs operated by the government since they began in the 1960s. Since that time the environment has undergone enormous change. Nevertheless, the practice of using narrow criteria continues to mean that only poor and nonnuclear families are considered to need help. The fact is that most parents are neither poor nor single but commonly face challenges which exceed their ability to respond in an effective way. Still, they are led to feel that it is inappropriate to seek or receive external support.

A more informed view recognizes that low income households can also be resilient and the possession of economic surplus does not always prevent family dysfunction or protect children from trouble. The assumption that families with similar configurations are uniform in the challenges they face does not accurately reflect variation in dynamics among single, blended, nuclear, and extended families. Educators should understand that family structure and income are less influential factors in adolescent development than are parent behavior and access to support from the community. Community efforts to protect adolescents should include families previously regarded as low risk. This paradigm shift is likely to be opposed by those who believe that, except for the poor and minorities, all other families should take care of themselves. Such impressions can be expected to decline as awareness grows about the emerging concept of developmental assets that considers risk and protective features in identifying optimal conditions for adolescent growth.

Developmental Assets

Morbidity rates refer to the incidence of illness or disease per year according to specific factors such as environment, age, gender, or ethnicity. One reason that rates of morbidity are lower in technological societies is a common practice of protecting children by immunizing them (Garrett, 2007). In a similar way, an emerging concept known as developmental assets provides community resources to support healthy choices that can influence student success and respect for others while offering protection from exposure to dangers of drugs, violence, sexual activity, abuse, and academic failure (Rose, 2006). Drawing on many studies of risk and resiliency, augmented with survey responses from over 200,000 students from Grades 6–12, the Search Institute in Minneapolis, Minnesota identified eight areas of human development grouped into forty developmental assets that generalize across gender, race/ethnicity, geography and community size (Benson, 2007). The percentage of students in Grades 6–12 that experience each of these assets appears on the Institute Web site at http://www.search-institute.org/research/assets.

The concept of asset-building calls on socializing systems within communities to actualize their enormous capacity to promote strengths. Attainment of this goal requires a greater balance of two paradigms so concerns about reducing deficits and building assets proceed together with equal enthusiasm. This shift is more likely to occur when more of the public recognizes that deficit reduction and asset building depend on different resources and processes (Lerner & Benson, 2003). In applying the deficit paradigm, interventions to decrease substance abuse, school dropout, teenage pregnancy, bullying, and gang formation are devised and monitored by professionals acting to implement priorities that are set out by the federal and state government or private foundations. In these initiatives, "top down" changes, supported by external funding, focus only on helping youth from low income or minority families (Minuchin, Colapinto, & Minuchin, 2007).

In contrast, the developmental assets paradigm that mobilizes the capacity of communities to nurture strengths places everyone in the socializing systems of family, school, neighborhood, youth organizations, and religious institutions at the hub of action. The guiding strategy for this approach includes far more emphasis on collective efficacy, social trust, social capital, a shared vision of helping youth to thrive, and greater commitment than comes from the energy generated by funding or government policy (Putnam, 2000, 2004; Putnam & Feldstein, 2003). The developmental assets strategy produces change from the "bottom up" by focusing on everyone working together and celebrating the potential to contribute to adolescent growth. In these initiatives, community efforts to protect teenagers include all families, including those previously thought to be at low risk. Then too, progress is more likely to be sustained than is usual with the deficit model where intervention efforts often cease with the termination of external funding (Hymowitz, 2006; Levine, 2006).

The attitude shift needed to merge the deficit paradigm and the developmental assets paradigm may be opposed by individuals and organizations which assume that, except for single parents and others who are poor, families should take care of themselves without external help from their community. This resistance seems likely to fade as public awareness grows about the developmental assets approach that takes into account risk and protective factors to identify optimal conditions for growing up (Benson, Scales, Hamilton, & Sesma, 2006).

Reliance on External Assets

Table 12.1 describes a taxonomy of developmental assets for adolescents. These include kinds of relationships, social experiences, nature of environments, and patterns of interaction that enhance well-being and for which every community is able to exert considerable control. The assets call for involvement of traditional socializing systems like families, neighborhoods, schools, congregations, and youth organizations. The goal is to mobilize asset building in as many environmental settings as possible. This broader orientation transforms the scope of accountability so that parents and schools do not stand alone in providing the support necessary to help children grow up today (Search Institute, 2006).

Twenty developmental assets that all youth should be able to depend upon involve external resources. One category called *Support Assets* includes care, attention, listening, encouragement, and guidance given by relatives, teachers, mentors, neighbors, and other surrogates. A second category, *Empowerment Assets*, originates from recognition by youth that they are valued by adults and encouraged to begin making their unique contribution to the community. Before teenagers are prepared to help others, they need to feel safe at school and in their neighborhood. *Boundaries and Expectations Assets* exist when parents and teachers explain rules of behavior and consequences that will follow when conduct is judged as being out of bounds. Modeling positive behavior and having high expectations for student academic performance is a responsibility of adults, friends, and classmates. *Constructive Use of Time Assets* depends on opportunities for students to engage in activities such as sports, the arts, clubs, religious and congregational programs and quality time at home that collectively enrich perspective, build character, and nourish the development of wholesome friendships.

Importance of Internal Assets

The other 20 developmental assets are internal and should be recognized by students as their responsibility. The *Commitment to Learning Assets* begin with motivation to pay attention in class, perform well, complete academic assignments, care about school, and schedule time to read for pleasure. *Positive Values Assets* require that students decide on personal direction that should include attributes such as honesty, empathy, a willingness to defend the rights of others, and self restraint. Application of these values prevent cheating, bystander apathy, sexual experimentation, substance abuse, and indifference to the welfare of others. *Social Competencies Assets* include assets to support formation of friendships and ability to get along. These assets can help adolescents refuse to get involved with unsafe activities motivated by peer pressure, and bring peaceful solutions to disputes. *Positive Identity Assets* derive from an internal locus of control, having a sense of purpose, and relying on an optimistic attitude in anticipating the future.

The greater the number of developmental assets that an adolescent can rely on, the more likely s/he is to become a healthy, caring, and responsible adult. For promoting positive attitudes and behaviors considered to be thriving indicators, the proportion of students reporting 0–10 assets who identify success in school is 9%, helping friends or neighbors one or more hours a week is 62%, places high value on getting to know

Table 12.1. Forty Developmental Assets for Adolescents (Ages 12–18)*

Search Institute® has identified the following building blocks of healthy development—known as Developmental Assets®—that help young people grow up healthy, caring, and responsible.

EXTERNAL ASSETS

Support	1. Family support—Family life provides high levels of love and support.
	2. Positive family communication—Young person and her or his parent(s) communicate positively, and young person is willing to seek advice and counsel from parents.
	3. Other adult relationships—Young person receives support from three or more nonparent adults.
	4. Caring neighborhood—Young person experiences caring neighbors.
	5. Caring school climate—School provides a caring, encouraging environment.
	6. Parent involvement in schooling—Parent(s) are actively involved in helping young person succeed in school.
Empowerment	7. Community values youth—Young person perceives that adults in the community value youth.
	8. Youth as resources—Young people are given useful roles in the community.
	9. Service to others—Young person serves in the community one hour or more per week.
	10. Safety—Young person feels safe at home, school, and in the neighborhood.
Boundaries & Expectations	11. Family boundaries—Family has clear rules and consequences and monitors the young person's whereabouts.
	12. School Boundaries—School provides clear rules and consequences.
	13. Neighborhood boundaries—Neighbors take responsibility for monitoring young people's behavior.
	14. Adult role models—Parent(s) and other adults model positive, responsible behavior.
	15. Positive peer influence—Young person's best friends model responsible behavior.
	16. High expectations—Both parent(s) and teachers encourage the young person to do well.

Table continues on next page.

Table 12.1. Continued

Constructive Use of Time	17. Creative activities—Young person spends three or more hours per week in lessons or practice in music, theater, or other arts.
	18. Youth programs—Young person spends three or more hours per week in sports, clubs, or organizations at school and/or in the community.
	19. Religious community—Young person spends one or more hours per week in activities in a religious institution.
	20. Time at home—Young person is out with friends "with nothing special to do" two or fewer nights per week.

INTERNAL ASSETS

Commitment to Learning	21. Achievement Motivation—Young person is motivated to do well in school.
	22. School Engagement—Young person is actively engaged in learning.
	23. Homework—Young person reports doing at least one hour of homework every school day.
	24. Bonding to school—Young person cares about her or his school.
	25. Reading for Pleasure—Young person reads for pleasure three or more hours per week.
Positive Values	26. Caring—Young person places high value on helping other people.
	27. Equality and social justice—Young person places high value on promoting equality and reducing hunger and poverty.
	28. Integrity—Young person acts on convictions and stands up for her or his beliefs.
	29. Honesty—Young person "tells the truth even when it is not easy."
	30. Responsibility—Young person accepts and takes personal responsibility.
	31. Restraint—Young person believes it is important not to be sexually active or to use alcohol or other drugs.
Social Competencies	32. Planning and decision making—Young person knows how to plan ahead and make choices.
	33. Interpersonal Competence—Young person has empathy, sensitivity, and friendship skills.

Table continues on next page.

34. Cultural Competence—Young person has knowledge of and comfort with people of different cultural/racial/ethnic backgrounds.

35. Resistance skills—Young person can resist negative peer pressure and dangerous situations.

36. Peaceful conflict resolution—Young person seeks to resolve conflict nonviolently.

Positive Identity

37. Personal power—Young person feels he or she has control over "things that happen to me."

38. Self-esteem—Young person reports having a high self-esteem.

39. Sense of purpose—Young person reports that "my life has a purpose."

40. Positive view of personal future—Young person is optimistic about her or his personal future.

people of other racial and ethnic groups diversity is 39%, pays attention to healthy nutrition and exercise is 27%, avoids doing things that are dangerous is 9%, saves money for something special rather than spending it all right away is 27%, and does not give up when things get difficult is 56%. In comparison, the percentage of students who report 31 to 40 assets and indicate success at school is 54%, helping friends or neighbors one or more hours a week is 96%, places high value on getting to know people of other racial and ethnic groups is 89%, pays attention to healthy nutrition and exercise is 88%, avoids doing things that are dangerous is 44%, saves money for something special rather than spending it all right away is 72%, and does not give up when things get difficult 86% (Search Institute, 2006).

Having more assets can also protect students from making harmful or unhealthy choices. The proportion of students declaring 0–10 assets and reporting problems with alcohol use was 45%, illicit drugs 38%, sexual activity 34%, tobacco 22%, anti-social behavior like shoftlifting or vandalism 47%, violence 62%, depression 44%, and school problems including absenteeism or low grades 44%. In comparison, the percentage of students declaring 31 to 40 assets that reported problems with alcohol use was 3%, illicit drugs 1%, sexual activity 3%, tobacco 0%, anti-social behavior such as shoftlifting or vandalism 1%, violence 6%, depression 5%, and school problems including absenteeism or low grades 4%. The Search Institute Web site at http://www.search-institute.org/content/40-develop-mental-assets-adolescents-ages-12-18 describes how to take action related to each of 40 assets. The significant effect of developmental assets under-scores the need for community organizations and individual volunteers to join teachers and parents in providing the support youth need to become successful adults (Benson, 2007).

Self-Esteem and Confidence

More articles and books have been written about the topic of *self-esteem,* confidence in one's overall worth as an individual, than all other aspects of development. Authors identify self-esteem as the cause for a range of behaviors from why people succeed or fail in finding happiness to suffer-ing depression. A prevalent assertion contends that self-esteem is essen-tial but so fragile that it may be necessary to set common sense aside when responding to this concern (Baumeister, Campbell, Krueger, & Vohs, 2005). Some teachers believe that telling students the truth about their inadequate performance might be unwise. The premise is that when some students are given truthful feedback, it could erode their level of self-con-fidence on which achievement depends. (V. Johnson, 2003).

A high school senior looked back on his studies and expressed an oppo-site view, "I thought I was supposed to accomplish something before I was expected to become proud of myself." This view is shared by Thomas Sow-ell (2007), economist of the Hoover Institute at Stanford University, who maintains that school practices are permeated with an inaccurate assump-tion that self-esteem should precede academic achievement, rather than the other way around. The assumption that boosting self-esteem will pro-duce benefit is not supported by evidence. Self-esteem is a by-product, flowing from attainment based on hard work and achieving personal goals. Educators should recognize that self-esteem cannot be conveyed to stu-dents as a way to improve their performance (Kohn, 2006).

Parents are the most powerful influence on child self-esteem. When asked to rank a list of qualities that they want their children to acquire, self-esteem ranks first, ahead of other characteristics like intelligence and good looks. The explanation parents give for their choice is that people who feel worthy and confident are more likely to build satisfying relation-ships, accept challenges, and attain the occupational success that awaits those willing to adapt and grow (Clarke-Stewart & Dunn, 2006). *Self-concept* defines how individuals see themselves as being capable or inept, accepted or rejected, intelligent or dull. Persons with a favorable self-concept can make plans, look forward to the future, and find satisfaction in most sectors of life. They express confidence, optimism, and are willing to defend ideas. When facing difficulties, those with high self-esteem draw on positive experiences or the past. As adolescents become more independent, their sense of self-worth motivates constructive behavior (Apter, 2006). For these reasons, self-esteem and emotional development go together.

Adolescents with low self-esteem tend to report feelings of being unworthy, inadequate, unaccepted, and isolated. They experience greater uncertainty, anxiety, and depression. From time to time, everyone copes with such feelings, and self-esteem is generally at its lowest point in adolescence. However, when disappointment and lack of confidence become a daily condition, the future is more likely to include poor health, criminal behavior, and limited economic prospects (Trzesniewski, Donnellan, Moffitt, Robins, Poulton, & Caspi, 2006).

There is reason for caution in interpreting assertions that link gender and self-esteem in adolescence. Janet Hyde (2005) at the University of Wisconsin conducted a meta-analyses of 46 studies of gender conducted over twenty years. Her overall conclusion was that the gender gap has been grossly exaggerated by well-intentioned advocates misrepresenting girls as having more problems with self-concept than boys. Instead, the meager distinctions found suggest teenage males and females are more similar than different in the way they see themselves.

Why has the popular message about girls and self-esteem been contrary to evidence? Hyde (2005) speculates that claims of enormous gender differences as presented in popular books like John Gray's (1992) *Men Are From Mars, Women Are From Venus* were accepted as the norm as demonstrated by sales of 30 million books. Deborah Tannen's (1991) *You Just Don't Understand: Women and Men in Conversations* supported the gender differences disadvantage, and remained on *The New York Times* best-seller list for 4 years. Similarly, Carol Gilligan's (1982) *In a Different Voice* described her distinction in the moral outlook adopted by men and women. Mary Pipher's (2005) *Reviving Ophelia: Saving the Selves of Adolescent Girls* provided accounts about self-esteem problems of girls accepted as being normative although written by a clinician interacting with a small sample not representative of adolescents in general (Chafetz, 2006).

More recently, a different picture began to emerge (Meyer, 2008). Dan Kindlon's (2006) *Alpha Girls: Understanding the New American Girl and How She is Changing the World* presents a positive image of girls destined to become leaders, talented, motivated, and confident. Kindlon's team at Harvard interviewed 900 girls and boys in Grades 6–12 across the country. He concluded that contemporary girls are reaping the full benefits of the women's movement and present a new sense of possibility and psychological emancipation. A reality check by the National Center of

Education Statistics confirmed that in a single generation the proportion of degrees earned by men and women has reversed. Sixty percent of bachelors degrees in 1970 were earned by men and 40% by women. Currently, women earn 60% of bachelor's and master's degrees and this difference is maintained across ethnic groups including Whites (59%), Blacks (68%), Hispanics (63%), Asians (57%), and Native Americans (63%) (Knapp, Kelly-Reid, Whitmore, & Miller, 2006).

The following suggestions can enhance self-esteem for adolescent girls and boys.

(1) Adults who are optimistic, trusting, creative, caring, and observant provide a powerful example of how these qualities contribute to adjustment. The National Educational Longitudinal study of 17,000 adolescents determined that consistent parent monitoring of youth activities predicted greater self-esteem and lower risk behaviors (Parker & Benson, 2004).

(2) Arrange time for listening to adolescents and doing things together. This commitment conveys the message that being with the teenager is viewed as an important use of time, requiring full attention and a respect for confidentiality. The readiness of teens to self-disclose is often related to readiness of adults to listen and suggest helpful nonjudgmental alternatives.

(3) Become familiar with the teenager's daily schedule. By scrutinizing the scope of demands placed on a youngster, it is possible to modify them, thereby limiting stress while also teaching planning skills of time management. Research has determined that greater maternal knowledge of student activities results in less over-scheduling and lower rates of juvenile delinquency (Waizenhofer, Buchanan, & Jackson-Newsom, 2004).

(4) Encourage youth to reflect on personality goals they aspire to attain. In the classroom students are obliged to pursue goals that are set for them by others. Still, they are most proud when the goals they set for themselves are reached. Acknowledge that identity is the major task of adolescence, deciding the kind of person to become, and personality remains a key to identity and success through life.

(5) Standing up for classmates who are subjected to abuse can be a criterion for thinking well of oneself. When the safety and well-being of classmates is ignored as related to personal responsibility, high self-esteem is unwarranted.

(6) Teach healthy criteria for constructive peer and self-evaluation. This ability can lead students to become self-critical, an essential asset for deciding to change behavior and knowing the direction for growth.

(7) Teachers contribute to self-esteem by trusting students to work in teams which can support the interdependence attributes needed for group

planning, create a sense of belonging and trust, and practice interpersonal skills to meet expectation in the workplace, home and community.

(8) Students should be able to refuse peer pressure to get involved with activities that could be dangerous. The courage to challenge peer opinions deserves recognition as a powerful resource for others.

(9) Schools give awards for academic and athletic competence. Brainstorming by the faculty and students can identify additional types of awards that recognize commendable behavior reflecting social maturity.

(10) Invite students during class discussion to share observations they have of class members demonstrating mature conduct. Students prize recognition from their peers but seldom hear favorable remarks about themselves within a cooperative group forum.

(11) Self-evaluation can focus on responsibilities of being a good student like preparing for class, getting along at school, finishing assignments on time, and learning at home. Parents and teachers can confirm or challenge conclusions a student has about self. Grades are not given for study habits but students should recognize these habits make a difference in success.

Inflated Self-Esteem

There are school programs that focus on building student self-esteem but helping individuals with inflated self-esteem is uncommon (Dunning, Health, & Suls, 2004). Some of the negative words used to describe these students include egotistical, narcissistic, conceited, arrogant, vain, and smug. When Casius Clay, later called Muhammad Ali, was heavyweight boxing champion of the world, he declared, "When you are as great as I am, it is hard to be humble." Perhaps someone with Ali's accomplishments was entitled to such comments. However, his self-observation urges a related question. How can students with inflated self-concepts learn to assess themselves more accurately? The following possibilities are suggested.

1. Pair them with another student who has superior abilities but does not insist on recognition, whether s/he has greater intellectual, social, physical or interpersonal skills.

2. Recommend movies or literature to help a student identify protagonists or in non-fiction, real people who, although accomplished, have managed to develop a sense of humility and graciousness.

3. Involve the whole class in a self-evaluation of academic and social growth and have them read their conclusions aloud. Then, solicit

written feedback from classmates to reinforce or challenge personal impressions.

4.   Give assignments for the students at the level that they imagine themselves to be so they can come to recognize that they have yet to reach the imagined level.

5.   Place them in a discussion group with others that have inflated self-concepts and obligate each person to recognize the contributions made by other members.

6.   Provide specific constructive criticism of their products so they can adopt more appropriate criteria for judging their work.

7.   Assign exercises that include failure so students can learn from their mistakes while recognizing that they have limitations like everyone else.

8.   Hold the student's work for several days and then ask her/him to evaluate and edit the material. This is a way to recognize flaws and temporal distance can help flaws to be more easily detected.

9.   Ask the students to identify a movie character, musician, sports star or celebrity they admire and describe how their behavior resembles the identified hero(ine).

10.   Have students provide oral reports about their service to the community and tell how performing these tasks have influenced their thinking about themselves.

11.   Ask students to describe a well-known person they consider "over the top" in having an inflated self-concept. What behavior changes do they suggest the celebrity consider?

12.   Have students re-do assignments that are not up to minimal class standard or abilities of the individual.

13.   Meet with a student privately to explain behaviors that are of concern to the teacher or classmates.

14.   Display class results on projects and test scores for everyone to observe with IDs disguised.

15.   Invite members of the class to identify in writing what they see as their personal weaknesses and qualities they would like to attain. Give feedback in group terms but note the ability of inflated students to detect their weak points.

Staying Home for College

While anecdotal evidence abounds, there is scant literature regarding what college students and parents with whom they live can do to attain greater mutual support, reciprocal learning, and harmony (Seiffge-Krenke, 2006). To increase awareness of the possibilities, community college freshmen still living at home and one or both of their parents were interviewed. The sample of 166 students (87 men and 79 women) and 218 of their parents (127 mothers and 91 fathers) were from culturally diverse, low and middle-income backgrounds. The generations were interviewed separately so they were not present to hear or bias responses of one another. These interviews centered on (1) difficulties that college students experience while living with parents, (2) problems encountered by parents whose children live at home while they go to college, (3) possible benefits for college students who reside with their parents, and (4) possible benefits for parents whose college age children remain at home. Generational findings are summarized with implications of related studies (P. Strom & Strom, 2005b).

(1) *Difficulties college students experience when they live with parents.* The most common complaint was lack of privacy, being denied the freedom of personal space enjoyed by peers living by themselves in an apartment or dormitory (Thurber & Walton, & the Council on School Health, 2007). Financial dependence on parents was often accompanied by frustration and ambivalence in making self-comparisons with fully employed friends whose job provided enough income to take care of themselves. One college freshman expressed his frustration this way, "It's bad enough my parents have to give me money but, to make matters worse, we have to live together." The consistency of these observations urge the conclusion that economic independence should cease to be a condition for acceptance of daughters and sons as young adults. Parents who recognize college-age daughters and sons as grownups are more likely to stop treating them as though they were still children. The assumption that students entering college immediately after high school have yet to attain adulthood is reinforced in families where parents do all the chores instead of insisting that everyone assume some responsibilities.

Living at home usually means more arguments over a longer period of time than in the past. Disputes center on sharing the car, excessive phone expenses, use of a bathroom, contents of the refrigerator and accommodating different schedules. Because parents are the homeowners, they may suppose it is acceptable to establish rules without discussion. In the extreme, this policy-making takes the form of arbitrary statements like "as long as you live in my house, you must follow my rules." Listening to loud music or watching television programs which relatives dislike can be troublesome. Taking a girlfriend or boyfriend into the bedroom and closing the door or having friends over for a party requires negotiation. Young men and women often feel they are unable to actually test their limits while they stay at home because there are so few opportunities for them to be responsible for self-care (Apter, 2006).

(2) *Difficulties parents experience when young adult college students stay at home.* Parents of college students living with them identified additional concerns. The lengthy education needed for a career means the duration of parent responsibility for economic support must go beyond previous norms. Otherwise, parents are bound to struggle with doubts about their own success. Some suppose that, if children are still living at home and do not have a full time job by age 25 or 30, their attempt to raise an independent child has failed. There are also parents inclined to make comparisons between what they were doing at the present age of young adult children. One mother said, "When I was your age, I was married, had two children and was working full-time." A more suitable response is to recognize the reality of a more skilled labor market and consequent delay in the age at which people start work, get married and have children (Danziger & Rouse, 2007).

The expectation of having to continue a financially supportive role over a longer time disappoints some parents because it contradicts plans they made earlier to be free of clutter, noise, and disruption when adolescents became old enough to move out. As one father reflected,

> This was to be the time when my wife and I could rediscover each other, remodel our child's bedroom into a comfortable study, have constant access to our car, telephone, and bathroom, take the basketball hoop down from the garage, plant a garden, walk around the house naked if we want to, and spend more money on ourselves instead of putting the children first.

There is no maturity without obligation. Parents should learn to relate to college-age children as adults and, if they failed to do so earlier, train them to assume responsibilities that make life easier for others sharing the same residence. The importance of this achievement is difficult to overstate. Parents are generally agreed that teenagers should have chores. Therefore, division of labor has improved in homes where sons carry out tasks once assigned to girls only. Paula, a middle-aged mother, applauds this shift,

> When I was growing up, kids in my family all had chores. The boys took care of the lawn and other outside jobs. My mother tried to assign my brothers inside tasks like doing dishes which they considered women's work. The boys would bribe their sisters and said that they would give us part of their allowance if we just would do the dishes for them. At this time, my brothers still owe me $825,000. None of them paid their debt.

Allowing youth to ignore their obligations toward family members means that they are being poorly prepared for independent living as well as living with roommates or spouses. Parents acknowledge this shortcoming much more often in relation to sons than daughters.

Parents of college students admitted uncertainty about whether their child has become a grownup. Some gave confusing excuses for why the younger relative could not yet be expected to do his laundry, help shop for groceries, mow the lawn, clean the toilet, or perform other chores. There were also parents who felt insulted by being told they have old fashioned ideas while their college-student children, who advocated equality throughout the world, cannot recognize what that means in terms of sharing chores and taking into account the needs of loved ones with whom they live. In a similar manner, a minority of parents regretted their loss of authority and interpreted oppositional ideas from children as evidence of disrespect. When parents find themselves opposing one another over what to expect of their adult child or how to present a united front, the marriage can sometimes suffer as both partners endure emotional strain.

(3) *Possible benefits for college students living at home with parents.* Students uniformly identified economic advantages they enjoy. Staying at home often means avoiding rent and not having to purchase groceries. These benefits make a great difference in being able to go to college and graduate within a reasonable amount period. Other advantages include getting more sleep and having less late night distractions than students living in a dormitory. For some students, particularly young men, this can also be a final opportunity to acquire healthy attitudes and habits that reflect empathy and sharing rather than unfair expectations that a girlfriend or spouse will take their mother's place in doing everything for them. More parents must do a better job in preparing daughters and sons, raising their expectations in pre-adolescence to do household chores for purposes of self-sufficiency and/or living in a successful relationship. Then too, the examples that parents provide in handling daily frustrations, setbacks, and failures of adulthood are often more carefully observed by college students than when they were in high school.

Students in college have a more demanding schedule than high school students. Their obligations typically include attending classes, doing assignments, fulfilling tasks for their employer and hanging out with friends. The majority of community college students work 20 or more hours a week (O'Toole & Lawler, 2006). In combination, their obligations may leave less time for family interaction than at an earlier age. This opportunity may not seem as important to them because they no longer require supervision from their parents.

(4) *Benefits for parents when adult children continue living at home.* Getting to know children as young adults means learning more about their goals, values, and concerns as individuals and becoming better informed about the prevailing concepts and views that reflect the norms of their generation. Knowing the fears, worries, priorities, and disappointments of young adults can motivate parents to start treating them as grownups. Parents who make it known that they prize the chance to learn from their children have much to gain. When both parties are growth-oriented and willing to learn from each other, they can solicit feedback about their progress in reaching the goals chosen for personal success. When the parent-child relationship based upon hierarchical authority is augmented with greater friendship, both parties are more inclined to look to one another for advice.

Some mothers and fathers do not want to listen to the complaints of young adult children regarding the demands of school, teachers, or the rigors of being a student. These parents often forfeit the role of confidante by reacting with comments that shut down conversation, such as, "You are really lucky to be able to go to school. I never had that opportunity." A more reasonable response is stimulated by a recognition that the stresses experienced at school, with peers, and in the workplace today need to be shared with someone. As a rule, people choose to rely on a trusted relative or friend who listens to them without being judgmental. This circumstance presents parents with possibilities to offer feedback on behavior of the younger relative and suggest alternative ways to consider in dealing with daily dilemmas. Such conversations are motivating and can occur far more often with young adults than with adolescents. In effect, parents whose children remain at home while attending college have a greater amount of time to affect life skill considerations and young adults are in many cases more ready at their age to learn these things (Berns, 2005).

SUMMARY

Influence of Stress

Teachers should observe students for differences in how they respond to stress. Encouraging an internal locus of control motivates confidence, persistence and resilience. Schools that recruit mentors for students provide models that can share healthy ways of interpreting events and managing stress. Teachers can minimize uncertainty by providing easily understood goals for lessons, clear directions for assignments, encouraging the exploration of possibilities and likely consequences before making decisions, and being flexible instead of rigid. Most student worries involve peers, a situation that urges teachers to facilitate constructive group norms. When students show signs of depression, they should be referred to the school counselor.

Emotional Intelligence

Everyone needs patience, self-control, hope, optimism, internal locus of control, and a willingness to delay gratification. The importance of these attributes is reflected by their favorable effect on relationships, mental health, persistence, and attainment of ambitions. Teachers can monitor behavior and give feedback to students on progress in this realm of achievement. As stress levels for all age groups continue to rise, it is important to help students understand that they can modify their hurried lifestyle. Meditation is effective to reduce blood pressure, restore balance, and achieve a sense of calm. Research with high school students underscores the benefits meditation has on being able to focus, maintain concentration, exclude distractions, and reduce the likelihood of taking drugs or alcohol. Parents and teachers should strive to be better models of solitude and reflection, and refusing an over-scheduled lifestyle.

Family and School Challenges

The assumption that efforts to prevent risks for adolescents should focus on family structure or income is being replaced with awareness that the current societal environment poses risks for families of every background, regardless of ethnicity and socioeconomic level. When students are able to depend on more external and internal developmental assets, the chances of becoming healthy, caring and responsible adults improve. Parents and teachers who recognize that self-esteem is a by-product of achievement based on hard work define their task as encouraging persistence and renewed effort following failure. In this way, student self-concept is drawn from competence rather than from gratuitous praise. Staying at home while going to college is a financial necessity for many students. This situation is more promising when both generations know about difficulties perceived by the other party and mutually resolve to learn from each another.

CLASSROOM APPLICATIONS

1. Helping students acquire an internal locus of control should be a teacher goal. This outlook on life has a favorable impact on motivation for learning, adjustment, and autonomy when adolescents realize that what happens to them is usually a result of their choices.

2. Teachers should remind students that everyone must deal with stress each day. An important aspect of coping is to view difficult tasks and failures as obstacles that can be overcome by working hard, remaining persistent, and accessing tutors.

3. The potential resilience of students can be actualized by opportunities to have mentors from the world of work. These out-of-school educators have overcome adversity themselves. Most students that imitate mentors make greater progress than occurs when their lessons about life are limited to the school curriculum.

4. Recognize the relationship between stress and creativity. Some qualities that students need to surmount anxiety, uncertainty, and stress are nurtured when teachers honor creativity. Students with creative abilities are more able to accept uncertainty, tolerate ambiguity, see things in new ways, demonstrate flexibility, and recognize possibilities in unfamiliar situations.

5. Depression and withdrawal are dangerous symptoms that signal the need for counseling. These students have quit, given up hope, and demonstrate withdrawal by skipping classes, taking illegal drugs, dropping out, or talking about suicide. Prompt referral to parents and the school counselor is the proper way for teachers to respond.

6. The greatest worry of adolescents involves school performance. Faculties can examine stresses that the institution imposes to find out if practices and policies should be revised. By using online collaborative scheduling, teachers can become aware of the assignments and deadlines students have in other courses. Working together, the faculty can coordinate the timing for major projects and tests to prevent overload.

7. Patience, learning to wait, hope, optimism and taking time for relaxation are elements of emotional intelligence. These attitudes and corresponding skills are not part of a curriculum but should be modeled by teachers. Similarly, parents should illustrate stress reduction at home by arranging their schedule to include time for relaxation.

8.   Educators should make parents aware that collaboration with the school can support student emotional development. This orientation should make known that a growing number of students cannot manage frustration, resort to anger as a response to difficulties, and interfere with the learning of others. A whole school approach creates healthy peer norms for influencing student behavior.

9.   The concept of developmental assets should be understood by the community so that relevant sources of support assume their role. This approach recognizes that families and schools alone cannot adequately respond to the broad range of problems adolescents face in the current environment. Community organizations, groups, and volunteers are assets that more students should be able to depend on.

10.   The self-esteem of students ought to be based on achievements instead of seen as a way to motivate achievement that has yet to occur. This goal can be met by teachers who set high expectations, let students know they consider them capable of doing the work, monitor progress, detect mistakes, arrange tutoring, encourage diligence, recognize gains, and listen to concerns.

11.   Faculty models should be augmented by the example of retired or senior volunteers who provide assistance in class. The life lessons such individuals can provide about goal-setting, understanding what is required for success at work, respecting dignity of peers, and standing up for the rights of others can support emotional development.

FOR REFLECTION

1.   What are some things adolescents worry about in relation to their school?

2.   Identify some of the uncertainties that are experienced by most teenagers.

3.   What steps should faculty take to introduce student meditation in high school?

4.   What are some gender differences in stresses that occur during adolescence?

5.   What are some methods that can help students avoid being over-scheduled?

6.   In what aspects of teaching do you find yourself showing the least patience?

7. What are the things that you worry about most in fulfilling your teaching role?

8. How should schools respond to students that are unable to handle frustration?

9. Identify the internal developmental assets you think require the most attention.

10. What advice would you give seniors on staying home while going to college?

11. What have been your observations of students who show excessive self-esteem?

12. What practices should parents and teachers rely on for promoting self-esteem?

KEY TERMS

Anticipation
Anxiety
Clinical Depression
Confidant
Developmental Assets
Distress
Emotional Intelligence
Eustress
External Locus of Control
Internal locus of control
Meditation
Mentor
Morbidity Rates
Optimistic Self-Explanatory Style
Pessimistic Self-Explanatory Style
Resilience
Self-Concept
Self-Efficacy
Self-Esteem
Stress
Suicide
Worries

VISIT THESE WEB SITES

Link to these sites at http://www.infoagepub.com/strom-adolescents

Ann Masten, Children Who Overcome Adversity to Succeed in Life
http://www.extension.umn.edu/distribution/familydevelopment/
components/7565_06.html

Computer Clubhouse,
Museum of Science and Massachusetts Institute of Technology
http://www.computerclubhouse.org

Richard Davidson, The Heart-Brain Connection:
The Neuroscience of Social, Emotional, and Academic Learning
http://edutopia.org/richard-davidson-sel-brain-video

Focus Adolescent Services, Anxiety and Anxiety Disorders
http://www.focusas.com/Stress.html

School Mental Health Project, UCLA
http://smhp.psych.ucla.edu/

Search Institute, Assets Research
http://www.search-institute.org/research/assets

Search Institute, Forty Developmental Assets for Adolescents
http://www.search-institute.org/content/40-developmental-assets-
adolescents-ages-12-18

Social and Emotional Learning in Schools,
Daniel Goleman Video Interview http://www.edutopia.org

Teen Help, Depression, Stress and Suicide http://teenhelp.com

Teen Suicide http://www.teensuicide.us/articles2.html

YouTube, Michael Guggenheim, A Boy Empowered
http://www.youtube.com

EXERCISES AND ROLES

Exercise 12.01: School Stress Poll

Role: Voter
The purpose of this poll is to find out how students feel about stress they experience at your school. Stress happens whenever you feel pressure. Some stress helps you perform better. However, too much stress can

limit learning and negatively impact health. Teachers and parents can be more helpful when they are aware of the issues that are causing your stress.

Directions: For each item, select the answer that shows how you feel. Your responses are anonymous and may be combined with those of other students at your school in a report to students, faculty, and parents.

1. Teacher expectations about behavior

   (a) It is not a source of stress for me.
   (b) I am able to manage it well.
   (c) I have difficulty managing it.
   (d) I am unable to manage it.

2. Teacher expectations about grades

   (a) It is not a source of stress for me.
   (b) I am able to manage it well.
   (c) I have difficulty managing it.
   (d) I am unable to manage it.

3. School expectations for homework

   (a) It is not a source of stress for me.
   (b) I am able to manage it well.
   (c) I have difficulty managing it.
   (d) I am unable to manage it.

4. Speaking in front of classmates

   (a) It is not a source of stress for me.
   (b) I am able to manage it well.
   (c) I have difficulty managing it.
   (d) I am unable to manage it.

5. Being able to get good grades

   (a) It is not a source of stress for me.
   (b) I am able to manage it well.
   (c) I have difficulty managing it.
   (d) I am unable to manage it.

6. Pressure to cheat in school

    (a) It is not a source of stress for me.
    (b) I am able to manage it well.
    (c) I have difficulty managing it.
    (d) I am unable to manage it.

7. Parent expectations about behavior

    (a) It is not a source of stress for me.
    (b) I am able to manage it well.
    (c) I have difficulty managing it.
    (d) I am unable to manage it.

8. Parent expectations about grades

    (a) It is not a source of stress for me.
    (b) I am able to manage it well.
    (c) I have difficulty managing it.
    (d) I am unable to manage it.

9. Lack of time for studying

    (a) It is not a source of stress for me.
    (b) I am able to manage it well.
    (c) I have difficulty managing it.
    (d) I am unable to manage it.

10. Relationships with classmates

    (a) It is not a source of stress for me.
    (b) I am able to manage it well.
    (c) I have difficulty managing it.
    (d) I am unable to manage it.

11. Romantic relationships

    (a) It is not a source of stress for me.
    (b) I am able to manage it well.
    (c) I have difficulty managing it.
    (d) I am unable to manage it.

12.   Extracurricular activities (sports, band, clubs)

    (a)   It is not a source of stress for me.
    (b)   I am able to manage it well.
    (c)   I have difficulty managing it.
    (d)   I am unable to manage it.

13.   Uncertainty over career and job choice

    (a)   It is not a source of stress for me.
    (b)   I am able to manage it well.
    (c)   I have difficulty managing it.
    (d)   I am unable to manage it.

14.   Being overscheduled with too much to do

    (a)   It is not a source of stress for me.
    (b)   I am able to manage it well.
    (c)   I have difficulty managing it.
    (d)   I am unable to manage it.

15.   My appearance and how I look to others

    (a)   It is not a source of stress for me.
    (b)   I am able to manage it well.
    (c)   I have difficulty managing it.
    (d)   I am unable to manage it.

16.   Need to dress like others in the group

    (a)   It is not a source of stress for me.
    (b)   I am able to manage it well.
    (c)   I have difficulty managing it.
    (d)   I am unable to manage it.

17.   Feeling pressure from others to have sex

    (a)   It is not a source of stress for me.
    (b)   I am able to manage it well.
    (c)   I have difficulty managing it.
    (d)   I am unable to manage it.

18. Peer pressure about drugs and alcohol

   (a) It is not a source of stress for me.
   (b) I am able to manage it well.
   (c) I have difficulty managing it.
   (d) I am unable to manage it.

19. Dealing with bullies and gangs

   (a) It is not a source of stress for me.
   (b) I am able to manage it well.
   (c) I have difficulty managing it.
   (d) I am unable to manage it.

20. Teacher compares my work to a sibling

   (a) It is not a source of stress for me.
   (b) I am able to manage it well.
   (c) I have difficulty managing it.
   (d) I am unable to manage it.

Select your grade level, gender, ethnicity, and age.

My grade level is 5 6 7 8 9 10 11 12
My gender is female male
My ethnicity is Asian Black Hispanic Native American White Other
My age is 10 11 12 13 14 15 16 17 18 19

Exercise 12.02: Reflections on Coping

Role: Generational Reporter
Interview one or more adolescents. Tell them they will not be identified but find out their age and gender.

1. What are some of the signals that tell you that too much stress is happening?
2. What are the best methods you rely on to gain relief from daily pressures?
3. What are your views about the use of meditation to support stress reduction?

4. How often do you feel stress because of falling behind in your schedule?

5. Why do you suppose some people can handle their stress better than others?

6. In what ways do you stress your classmates at school? teachers? relatives?

Exercise 12.03: Special Education

Role: Challenger

Interview a parent or a teacher of special needs children to find out:

1. Stresses that the adult experiences in meeting needs of children.
2. Unique stresses felt by special education students.
3. How regular students and their parents could help ease these stresses.

Exercise 12.04: Diversity of Family Concerns

Role: Web Site Search

Differences in student outlook, motivation and achievement are often attributed to variance in cultural background. In a similar way, differences in household structure can impact student behavior. Parents from single and blended families have been the focus of many studies to identify challenges they struggle with and find ways to help them. When teachers are informed about common concerns of families from varied household structures, they can be more constructive in responding to needs. Have team members choose blended or single households to research on the Web. Then bring materials to share in class that portray prominent concerns of blended and single parent households.

Exercise 12.05: Entitlement for Higher Education

Make two lists. In one list describe some advantages you see if entitlement to higher education is enacted by legislators. In the other list, identify some disadvantages that might accompany entitlement to higher education.

Exercise 12.06: The Stress of Teaching

Role: Evaluator
There is agreement that teaching is an important profession and one that includes a considerable amount of stress.

1. Describe factors that make teaching in middle school and high school stressful.
2. Suggest some possible ways to reduce the amount of stress felt by educators.

Exercise 12.07: Schools and Emotional Development

Role: Evaluator
Adolescents from all ethnic and income groups report that their parents do a poor job of helping them learn how to manage stresses of daily life. Assume that schools might soon be obligated to provide instruction related to stress and emotional development. What are some ways teachers can help students adjust to an increasingly hurried and dangerous environment? Provide explanations for each recommendation.

Exercise 12.08: Modify Norms

Role: Evaluator
Middle school and high school teachers sometimes observe inappropriate attitudes/behaviors that can undermine growth and well being for students. Prepare two corresponding lists. In the list on the left, identify five student attitudes/behaviors that are inappropriate for school. In the corresponding list on the right, identify the replacement attitudes or behaviors that are more appropriate.

Inappropriate Attitudes or Behaviors	Appropriate Attitudes or Behaviors

Exercise 12.09: Resilience and Intervention

Describe one or two situations that you have observed where intervention by adults has prevented adolescents from learning how to manage disappointment or cope with failure.

Exercise 12.10: Adolescent Expectations of Adults

Role: Improviser

This course has emphasized appropriate expectations for adolescents as a basis for the detection of learning needs, assessment of progress, and recognition of success. View this dynamic from the adolescent vantage. Develop a list of six expectations that teenagers should have for people (teachers and parents) who guide and supervise them.

REFERENCES

Aaronson, E. (1978). *The jigsaw classroom*. Beverly Hills, CA: SAGE.

Action for Healthy Kids. (2006). *About us*. Retrieved June 20, 2008, from http://www.actionforhealthykids.org/about.php

Adams, D., & Hamm, M. (2006). *Redefining education in the twenty-first century: Shaping collaborative learning in the age of information*. Springfield, IL: Charles C. Thomas.

Adams, D., & Hamm, M. (2006). *Media and literacy: Learning in the information age*. Springfield, IL: Charles C. Thomas.

Adams, G., Biernal, M., Branscombe, N., Crandall, C., & Wrightsman, L. (Eds.). (2008). *Commemorating Brown: The social psychology of racism and discrimination*. Washington, DC: American Psychological Association.

Agatston, P., Kowalski, R., & Limber, S. (2007, December). Students' perceptions on cyber bullying. *Journal of Adolescent Health, 41*(6), S59–S60

Agliata, A., Tantleff-Dunn, S., & Renk, K. (2007, January). Interpretation of teasing during early adolescence. *Journal of Clinical Psychology, 63*(1), 23–30.

Agnew, R. (2007). *Juvenile delinquency: Causes and control*. New York: Oxford University Press.

Aikin, W. (1942). *The story of the eight-year study*. New York: Harper & Row.

Albert, B. (2006, January/February). Sex and young adolescents. *Principal, 85*(3), 60.

Alderman, M. (2004). *Motivation for achievement: Possibilities for teaching and learning*. Mahwah, NJ: Erlbaum.

Aldwin, C. (2007). *Stress, coping and development*. New York: Guilford.

Alexander, P. (2005). *Psychology in learning and instruction*. Upper Saddle River, NJ: Prentice-Hall.

Alford, S. (2003). Science and Success: *Sex Education and Other Programs that Work to Prevent Teen Pregnancy, HIV & Sexually Transmitted Infections*. Washington, DC: Advocates for Youth.

Allen, I., & Seaman, J. (2007). *Online nation: Five years of growth in online learning*. Needham, MA: Sloan Consortium. Retrieved April 18, 2008, from http://www.sloan-c.org/publications/survey/pdf/online_nation.pdf

Allen, J. (2005, May/June). Grades as valid measures of academic achievement of classroom learning. *Middle School Journal, 78*(5), 218–223.

Allensworth, E., & Easton, J. (2007, July). *What matters for staying on-track and graduating in Chicago public high schools*. Chicago: Consortium on Chicago School Research.

Altbach, P., Berdahl, R., & Gumport, P. (2005). *American higher education in the 21st Century*. Baltimore, MD: Johns Hopkins Press.

Anagnostopoulos, D. (2005, Spring). Real students and true demotes. *American Educational Research Journal, 43*(1), 5–42.

Anderman, E., & Murdock, T. (2006). *Psychology of academic cheating*. San Diego: Academic Press.

Anderson, D., Lucas, K., & Ginns, I. (2003). Theoretical perspectives on learning in an informal setting. *Journal of Research in Science Teaching, 40*(2), 177–199.

Anderson, L., Krathwohl, D., Airasian, P., & Cruickshank, K. (2000). *A taxonomy for learning, teaching, and assessing: A revision of Bloom's taxonomy of educational objectives.* Boston: Allyn & Bacon.

Anderson, N. (2008, November). Our duty to an overweight generation. *Monitor on Psychology, 39*(10), 5.

Anfara, V. (2006, January). The evidence for the core curriculum—past and present. *Middle School Journal, 37*(3), 48–54.

Apted, M. (2007). *49 Up.* Retrieved April 30, 2008, from Public Broadcasting System http://www.pbs.org/pov/pov2007/49up/about.html

Apter, T. (2001). *The myth of maturity: What teenagers need from parents to become adults.* New York: Norton.

Apter, T. (2006, April). Resolving the confidence crisis. *Educational Leadership, 63*(7), 42–46.

Armstrong, S. (2001, September). Turning the tables – students teach teachers. Retrieved January 2, 2009, from *Edutopia* http://www.glef.org

Asby, E. (2005). *Puberty survival guide for girls.* Lincoln, NB: iUniverse.

Asher, N. (2007, March). Made in the (multicultural) U.S.A.: Unpacking tensions of race, culture, gender, and sexuality in education. *Educational Researcher, 38*(2), 65–73.

Assor, A., Kaplan, H., & Roth, G. (2002, June). Choice is good, but relevance is excellent: Autonomy-enhancing and suppressing teacher behaviors predicting students' engagement in schoolwork. *British Journal of Educational Psychology, 72*(2), 261–278.

Assuras, T. (2004). *Scared of cyber-bullies?* New York: CBS News. Retrieved January 2, 2009, from www.cbsnews.com/stories/2004/05/11/earlyshow/living/parenting/main616717.shtml

Ausubel, D. (1968). *Educational psychology: A cognitive view.* New York: Holt Rinehart & Winston.

Axtman, K. (2005, January 11). When tests' cheaters are the teachers. *The Christian Science Monitor.* Retrieved January 2, 2009, from www.csmonitor.com/2005/0111/p01s03-ussc.html

Bachman, J., O'Malley, P., Schulenberg, J., Johnson, L., Freedman-Doan, P., & Messersmith, E. (2007). *The education-drug use connection: How successes and failures in school relate to adolescent smoking, drinking, drug use, and delinquency.* Mahwah, NJ: Erlbaum.

Baddeley, A. (1997). *Human memory: Theory and practice.* New York: Psychology Press.

Baddeley, A. (1999). *Essentials of human memory.* New York: Psychology Press.

Baker, D., & LeTendre, G. (2005). *National differences, global similarities: World culture and the future of schooling.* Stanford, CA: Stanford University Press.

Balcetis, E., & Dunning, D. (2006). See what you want to see: Motivational influences on visual perception. *Journal of Personality and Social Psychology, 91*(4), 612–625.

Baldwin, J., Falkner, S., Hecht, M., & Lindsley, S. (2006). *Redefining culture.* Mahwah, NJ: Erlbaum.

Ball, A. (2006). *Multicultural strategies for education and social change.* New York: Teachers College Press.

Bandura, A. (1977). *Social learning theory.* Morristown, NJ: General Learning Press.

Bandura, A. (1989). Regulation of cognitive processes through perceived self-efficacy. *Developmental Psychology, 25,* 729–735.

Bandura, A. (1997). *Self-efficacy: The exercise of control.* New York: W. H. Freeman.

Bandura, A. (2004). Swimming against the mainstream: The early years from chilly tributary to transformative mainstream. *Behavior Research and Theory, 42,* 613–630.

Bandura, A., Ross, D., & Ross, S. (1963). Imitation of film-mediated aggressive models. *Journal of Abnormal Psychology, 66,* 3–11.

Barker, J., & Erickson, S. (2005). *Five regions of the future: Preparing your business for tomorrow's technological revolution.* New York: Basic Penguin.

Barlow, D. (2005, September). "Abstinence-only" and hooking up: Two risky choices. *The Education Digest, 71*(1) 63–67.

Barnes, V., Bauza, L., & Treiber, F. (2003). Impact of stress reduction on negative school behaviors in adolescents. *Health and Quality of Life Outcomes, 1*(1), 10.

Barron, F., Montuori, A., & Barron, A. (Eds.). (1997). *Creators on creating: Awakening and cultivating the imaginative mind.* New York: Jeremy P. Tarcher/Penguin.

Barry, A. (1997). *Visual intelligence.* Albany, NY: State University of New York Press.

Barth, R. (2006, March). Improving relationships within the schoolhouse. *Educational Leadership, 63*(6), 8–13.

Bauer, S., & Wise, J. (2004). *The well-trained mind: A guide to classical education at home.* New York: W. W. Norton.

Baum, S., Viens, J., & Slatin, B. (2005). *Multiple intelligences in the classroom.* New York: Teachers College Press.

Baumeister, R. (2005). *The cultural animal: Human nature, meaning, and social life.* New York: Oxford University Press.

Baumeister, R., Campbell, J., Krueger, J., & Vohs, K. (2003, May). Does high self-esteem cause better performance, interpersonal success, happiness or healthier lifestyle? *Psychological Science in the Public Interest, 4,* 1–2.

Baumeister, R., Campbell, J., Krueger, J., & Vohs, K. (2005, January). Exploding the self-esteem myth. *Scientific American,* 84–91.

Baumeister, R., & Tice, D. (1995). *Losing control: How and why people fail at self-regulation.* Orlando, FL: Academic Press.

Beachum, F., & McCray, C. (2005, Summer). Changes and transformations in the philosophy of character education in the 20th century). *Essays in Education, 14,* 1–7.

Beets, M., Pitetti, K., & Cardinal, B. (2005, December). Progressive aerobic cardiovascular endurance run and body mass index among an ethnically diverse sample of 10–15 year olds. *Research Quarterly for Exercise and Sport, 76*(4), 389–397.

Beghetto, R. (2005, Spring). Does assessment kill creativity? *The Educational Forum, 69*(3), 254–263.

Benedict, J. (2001). *Without reservation: The making of America's most powerful Indian tribe and Foxwoods, the world's largest casino.* New York: HarperCollins.

Bennis, W., & Biederman, P. (1997). *Organizing genius: The secrets of creative collaboration*. Reading, MA: Addison-Wesley.

Benson, P. (2007). Developmental assets: An overview of theory, research and practice. In R. Simbereisen & R. Lerner (Eds.), *Approaches to positive youth development* (pp. 33–58). Thousand Oaks, CA: SAGE.

Benson, P., & Lerner, R. (2005). *Developmental assets and asset-building communities: Implications for research, policy and practice*. New York: Springer.

Benson, P., Scales, P., Hamilton, S., & Sesma, A. (2006). Positive youth development: Theory, research and applications. In W. Damon & R. Lerner (Eds.), *Handbook of child psychology* (6th ed., Vol. 1, pp. 894–941). New York: Wiley.

Beran, T., & Shapiro, B. (2005). Evaluation of an anti-bullying program: Student reports of knowledge and confidence on manage bullying. *Canadian Journal of Education*, 28(4), 700–717.

Bergh, S., & Erling, A. (2005, Summer). *Adolescent identity formation: A Swedish study of identity status using the EOM-EIS-II*. *Adolescence*, 40(158), 377–396.

Berkowitz, E., & Cicchelli, T. (2004, November). Metacognitive strategy use in reading of gifted high achieving and gifted underachieving middle school students in New York City. *Education and Urban Society*, 37(1), 37–57.

Berkowitz, M., & Bier, M. (2005, September). Character education: Parents as partners. *Educational Leadership*, 63(1), 64–69.

Berns, G. (2005). *Satisfaction*. New York: Henry Holt.

Berry, J., Phinney, J., Sam, D., & Vedder, P. (2006). *Immigrant youth in cultural transition*. Mahwah, NJ: Erlbaum.

Best, S., & Radcliff, B. (Eds.). (2005). *Polling America: An encyclopedia of public opinion*. Westport, CT: Greenwood.

Bianco, J. (2005, April/May). A call for compassion. *Momentum (Washington, DC)*, 36(2), 38, 40.

Bielick, S. (2008, December). *1.5 Million homeschooled students in the United States in 2007*. Washington, DC: National Center for Education Statistics, Institute of Education Sciences, NCES 2009-030.

Binet, A. (1905). New methods for the diagnosis of the intellectual level of subnormals. *L'Année Psychologique*, 12, 191–244. Retrieved April 1, 2007, from Classics in the History of Psychology http://psychclassics.yorku.ca/Binet/binet1.htm

Bisconer, S., & Gross, D. (2007, April). Assessment of suicide risk in a psychiatric hospital. *Professional Psychology: Research and Practice*, 38(2), 143–149.

Black, S. (2005). Listening to students. *American School Board Journal*, 192(11), 39–41.

Black, S. (2006, October). The power of caring to help kids adjust and achieve is now documented. *American School Board Journal*, 193, 46–49.

Blackhurst, R. (2008, June 22). A class apart. *Financial Times*, 1–2.

Block, J. (Ed.) (1971). *Mastery learning: Theory and practice*. New York: Holt, Rinehart & Winston.

Block, P. (2008). *Community: The structure of belonging*. San Francisco: Berrett-Koehler.

Blonna, R. (2006). *Coping with stress in a changing world*. New York: McGraw-Hill.

Bloom, B. (1976). *Human characteristics and school learning.* New York: McGraw-Hill.

Bloom, B., Englehart, M., Furst, E., Hill, W., & Krathwohl, D. (Eds.). (1956). *Taxonomy of educational objectives: The classification of educational goals, Handbook I: Cognitive Domain.* New York: McKay.

Blum, R. (2005). A case for school connectedness. *Educational Leadership, 62*(7), 16–20.

Blum, R., & Mmari, R. (2006). *Risk and protective factors affecting adolescent reproductive health in developing countries: An analysis of adolescent sexual and reproductive health literature from around the world summary.* Geneva, Switzerland: World Health Organization.

Blumberg, H., Hare, A., & Costin, A. (2006). *Peace psychology.* New York: Cambridge University Press.

Blumenfeld, P., Marx, R., & Harris, C. (2006). Learning environments. In K. Rnninger & I. Siegel (Eds.), Handbook of child psycholoty (6th ed., Vol. 4, pp. 297–342). New York: Wiley.

Bogle, K. (2008). *Hooking up: Sex, dating and relationships on campus.* New York: New York University Press.

Bon, S., Faircloth, S., & Chapple, J. (2005, Summer). Thirty years of providing services for children with disabilities: Implications for secondary education. *American Secondary Education, 33*(3), 3–5.

Bonanno, G. (2004). Loss, trauma, and human resilience: Have we underestimated the human capacity to thrive after extremely aversive events? *American Psychologist, 59,* 20–28.

Bonner, F. (2005, Spring). Transitions in the development of giftedness. *Gifted Child Today, 28*(2), 19–25.

Bosacki, S., Marini, Z., & Dane, A. (2006, June). Voices from the classroom: Pictorial and narrative representations of children's bully experiences. *Journal of Moral Education, 35*(2), 231–245.

Bouchey, H., & Furman, W. (2005). Dating and romantic experiences in adolescence. In M. Berzonsky & G. Adams (Eds.), *The Blackwell Handbook of Adolescence* (pp. 313–329). Oxford, England: Blackwell.

Boudett, K., & Steele, J. (Eds.) (2007). *Data wise in action: Stories of schools using data to improve teaching and learning.* Cambridge, MA: Harvard University Press.

Bourke, J. (2006). *Fear, a cultural history.* London: Shoemaker & Hoard.

Boutelle, M. (2008, February). Uniforms: Are they a good fit? *The Education Digest, 73*(6), 34–37.

Bowker, A. (2004). Predicting friendship stability during early adolescence. *The Journal of Early Adolescence, 24*(2), 85–112.

Bowkett, S. (2005). *One hundred ideas for teaching creativity.* New York: Continuum.

Boyle-Baise, M., & Binford, P. (2005, Spring). The Banneker History Project: Historic investigation of a once-segregation school. *The Educational Forum, 69*(3), 305–314.

Bozick, R. (2006, February). Precocious behaviors in early adolescence: Employment and the transition to first sexual intercourse. *The Journal of Early Adolescence, 26,* 60–86.

Braswell, S. (2006). *American Meth: A history of the methamphetamine epidemic*. Lincoln, NB: iUniverse.

Brewster, K., & Tillman, K. (2008, April). Who's doing it? Patterns and predictors of youths' oral sexual experiences. *Journal of Adolescent Health*, *42*(1), 73–80.

Bridgeland, J., Dilulio, J., & Morison, K. (2006). *The silent epidemic: Perspectives of high school dropouts*. Washington, DC: Civic Enterprises with Peter D. Hart Research Associates for Bill and Melinda Gates Foundation.

Bridgeland, J., Dilulio, J., Streeter, R., & Mason, J. (2008, October). *One dream, two realities: Perspectives of parents on America's high schools*. Washington, DC: Civic Enterprises.

Brier, N. (2007). *Motivating children and adolescents for academic success: A parent involvement program*. Champaign, IL: Research Press.

Brockmole, J. (Ed.). (2008). *The visual world of memory*. New York: Psychology Press.

Bronfenbrenner, U., & Morris, P. (2006). The bioecological model of human development. In R. Lerner (Eds.), *Handbook of child psychology* (6th ed., Vol. 1, pp. 793–828). New York: Wiley.

Brown, B., & Klute, C. (2005). Friendship, cliques, and crowds. In M. Berzonsky & G. Adams (Eds.), *The Blackwell Handbook of Adolescence* (pp. 330–349). Oxford, England: Blackwell.

Brown, D. (2006, March/April). Young adolescents: Different learners, difference strategies. *Principal*, *85*(4), 68–69.

Brown, K., Anfara, V., & Roney, K. (2004, August). Student achievement in high performing, suburban middle schools and low performing, urban middle schools: Plausible explanations for the differences. *Education and Urban Society*, *36*(4), 428, 456.

Brown, M., Higgins, K., & Paulsen, K. (2003, September). Adolescent alienation: What is it and what can educators do about it? *Intervention in School and Clinic*, *39*(1), 3–9.

Brown, S., Teufel, J., Birch, D., & Kancheria, V. (2006, October). Gender, age and behavior differences in early adolescent worry. *Journal of School Health*, *76*(8), 430–438.

Brown, W., & Snyder, W. (2008). *Cocaine, crack, and kids*. Tallahassee, FL: William Gladden Press.

Brückner, H., & Bearman, P. (2005). After the promise: The STD consequences of adolescent virginity pledges. *Journal of Adolescent Health*, *36*, 271–278.

Brumberg, J. (1997). *The body project: An intimate history of American girls*. New York: Random House.

Bubb, S. (2006, January 13). Bully for you. *The Times Educational Supplement*, pp. 32–33.

Buckingham, D., & Willett, R. (2006). *Digital generations: Children, young people, and the new media*. Mahwah, NJ: Erlbaum.

Buki, L., Ma, T., Strom, R., & Strom, S. (2003). Chinese immigrant mothers of adolescents: Self-perceptions of acculturation effects on parenting. *Cultural Diversity and Ethnic Minority Psychology*, *9*(2), 127–140.

Burcet, J. (2004). *Burcet's leap communication hypothesis*. Retrieved October 20, 2008, from http://www.burcet.net/jbl/vers_english/paradigms/leaps/map_leaps.htm

Burns, E. (2005, March 11). Bully off. *The Times Educational Supplement*, pp. 11–12.

Burns, E. (2007). *The essential special education guide for the regular education teacher.* Springfield, IL: Charles Thomas.

Burns, M. (December 2005/January 2006). Tools for the mind. *Educational Leadership, 63*(4), 48–53.

Butler, R., & Green, D. (2008). *The child within: Taking the young person's perspective by analyzing personal construct theory.* New York: Wiley.

Buxton, C. (2005, May). Creating a culture of academic success in an urban science and math magnet high school. *Science Education, 89*(3), 392–417.

Cacioppo, J., Visser, P., & Pickett, C. (Eds.). (2006). *Social neuroscience: People thinking about thinking people.* Cambridge, MA: MIT Press.

Callahan, D. (2004). *The cheating culture: Why more Americans are doing wrong to get ahead.* New York: Harcourt.

Calvin, W. (2004). *A brief history of the mind: From apes to intellect and beyond.* New York: Oxford University Press.

Campbell, J. (2004). *Pathways to bliss: Mythology and personal transformation.* Novata, CA: New World Library.

Canton, J. (2006). *The extreme future: Trends that will reshape the world for the next 5, 10 and 20 years.* New York: Dutton.

Capeheart, L., & Milovanovic, D. (2007). *Social Justice theories.* Piscataway, NJ: Rutgers University Press.

Caplan, N., Choy, M., & Whitemore, J. (1996). *Children of the boat people.* Ann Arbor: University of Michigan Press.

Cappo, J. (2005). *The future of advertising: New media, new clients, new consumers in the post-television age.* New York: McGraw-Hill.

Cardoso, P. (Director). (2002). *Real women have curves* [Motion picture]. United States: HBO Independent Productions.

Carnell, L. (2005, March 11). How to beat 'em. *The Times Educational Supplement, Difficult Years supp*, pp. 12–14.

Carpenter, D., Flowers, N., & Mertens, S. (2004). High expectations for every student. *Middle School Journal, 35*(5), 64–69.

Carr, D. (2005, June). On the contribution of literature and the arts to the educational cultivation of moral virtue, feeling and emotion. *Journal of Moral Education, 34*(2), 137–151.

Carr, N. (2006, April). New rules of engagement. *American School Board Journal, 193*(4), 66–68.

Carreon, G., Drake, C., & Barton, A. (2005, Fall). The importance of presence: Immigrant parents' school engagement experience. *American Educational Research Journal, 42*(3), 465–498.

Carroll, J. (1963). A model of school learning. *Teachers College Record, 64*(8), 723–733.

Carroll, L. (2004). *Alice in Wonderland.* New York: Gramercy. (Original work published 1865)

Carskadon, M. (1990). Patterns of sleep and sleepiness in adolescents. *Pediatrician, 17*(1), 5–12.

Carskadon, M. (2002). *Adolescent sleep patterns: Biological, social, and psychological influences.* New York: Cambridge University Press.

Carskadon, M. (2005, Summer). Sleepiness in teens. *Sleepmatters*, 7(3), 1–4. Retrieved September 7, 2006, from National Sleep Foundation, http://www.sleepfoundation.org/hottopics/index.php?secid=18&id=283

Carskadon, M., Acebo, C., & Jenni, O. (2004). Regulation of adolescent sleep: Implications for behavior. *Annals of the New York Academy of Sciences, 1021*, 276–291.

Carter, B., & Spencer, V. (2006). The fear factor: Bullying and students with disabilities. *International Journal of Special Education, 21*(1), 11–23.

Carter, J. (2005). *Our endangered values: America's moral crisis*. New York: Simon & Schuster.

Carter, L. (2004). *The anger trap*. San Francisco: Jossey-Bass.

Casazza, K., & Ciccazzo, M. (2006, February). Improving the dietary patterns of adolescents using a computer-based approach. *Journal of School Health, 76*(2), 43–36.

Cattell, R. (1987). *Intelligence: Its structure, growth and action*. New York: Elsevier.

Cavanaugh, C., Gillan, K., Kromrey, J., Hess, M., & Blomeyer, R. (2004, October). *The effects of distance education on K–12 outcomes: A meta-analysis*. Naperville, IL: Learning Point Associates.

Ceci, S., & Papierno, P. (2005, March). The rhetoric and reality of gap closing. *American Psychologist, 60*(2), 149–160.

Centers for Disease Control and Prevention (2005). *Teen opinions on smoking survey*. Atlanta, GA: Centers for Disease Control and Prevention. Retrieved January 21, 2007, from http://www.cdc.gov

Centers for Disease Control and Prevention. (2006, June 9). *Youth risk behavior surveillance—United States, 2005*. Surveillance Summaries, *Morbidity and Mortality Weekly Report*, 55 (No. SS-5). Retrieved January 5, 2009, from http://www.cdc.gov/mmwr/PDF/SS/SS5505.pdf

Centers for Disease Control and Prevention. (2009). *Youth and tobacco use*. Retrieved April 12, 2008, from http://www.cdc.gov/tobacco/data-statistics/fact_sheets/youth_data/youth_tobacco.htm.

Centers for Disease Control and Prevention (2008). *About BMI for children and teens*. Retrieved June 25, 2008, from http://www.cdc.gov

Chadsey, J., & Han, K. (2005, November/December). Friendship facilitation strategies: What do students in middle schools tell us? *Teaching Exceptional Children, 38*(2), 52–57.

Chafetz, J. (2006). *Handbook of the sociology of gender*. New York: Springer.

Chao, E. (2006). *Occupational outlook handbook for 2006–2007*. Indianapolis, IN: Jist Works.

Chavez, M., & Insel, T. (2007, April). Eating disorders: National Institute of Mental Health's perspective. *American Psychologist, 62*(3), 159–166.

Chemelynski, C. (2006, July 18). When mean girls turn to female violence. *School Board News*, 8.

Chen, C., Kasof, J., Himsel, A., Dmitrieva, J., Dong, Q., & Xue, G. (2005). Effects of explicit instruction to "Be creative" across domains and cultures. *The Journal of Creative Behavior, 39*(2), 89–110.

Chen, J., & Gardner, H. (2005). Assessment based on multiple-intelligences theory. In D. P. Flanagan & P. Harrison (Eds.), *Contemporary intellectual assessment: Theories, tests, and issues.* New York: Guilford Press.

Cheng, C., & Cheung, M. (2005). Cognitive processes underlying coping flexibility: Differentiation and integration. *Journal of Personality, 73,* 859–886.

Chicago Public Schools (2005). School dropout withfrawal from. retrieved November 1, 2008, from http://clear.cps.k12.il.us/AboutCPS/Departments/Dropout%5FPrevention%5FRecovery.consent.html

Children's Internet Protection Act, Pub.L. 106–554, Title XVII, Sec. 1701, 114 Stat. 2763A–336 (2000).

Children's Partnership (2005). *Online content for low-income and underserved Americans: The digital divide's new frontier/A strategic audit of activities and opportunities.* Santa Monica, CA: Author. Retrieved April 19, 2008, from http://www.childrenspartnership.org

Chiu, C., & Hong, Y. (2006). *Social culture of psychology.* New York: Psychology Press.

Christie, C., Jolivette, K., & Nelson, M. (2005). Breaking the school to prison pipeline: Identifying school risk and protective factors for youth delinquency. *Exceptionality, 13*(2), 69–88.

Chu, J. (2005, Spring). Adolescent boys' friendships and peer group culture. *New Directions for Child and Adolescent Development, 107,* 7–22.

Chu, K. (2007, January 2). High schools teach more kids basics in Finance 101. *USA Today,* 1b.

City, E. (2008). *Resourceful leadership tradeoffs and tough decisions on the road to school improvement.* Cambridge, MA: Harvard University Press.

Cizek, G., & Burg, S. (2006). *Addressing test anxiety in a high-stakes environment.* Thousand Oaks, CA: Corwin Press.

Clark, J. M., & Paivio, A. (1991, September). Dual coding theory and education. *Educational Psychology Review, 3*(3), 149–210.

Clark, K. (1963). Educational stimulation of racially disadvantaged children. In A. Harry Passow (Ed.), *Education in depressed areas* (pp. 142–162). New York: Teachers College Columbia University.

Clarke-Stewart, A., & Dunn, J. (2006). *Families count: Effects on child and adolescent development.* New York: Cambridge University Press.

Clyde, W., & Delohery, A. (2005). *Using technology in teaching.* New Haven, CT: Yale University Press.

Cocca, C. (2004). *Jailbait: The politics of statutory rape.* Albany, NY: State University of New York Press.

Cohen, A., & Wellman, C. (2008). *Contemporary debates in applied ethics.* New York: Wiley-Blackwell

Cohen, L. (2000). *Research methods in education.* New York: Routledge.

Coiro, J., Knobel M., Lankshear, C., & Leu, D. (2008). *Handbook of research on new literacies.* Mahwah, NJ: Erlbaum

Cole, J. (2008). *Seventh annual Internet study of Internet use by children.* Los Angeles, CA: University of Southern California Center for the Digital Future.

Collins, H. T. (2006, March). Global learning. *American School Board Journal, 193*(3), 27–28.

Collins, W. (2003). More than myth: The developmental significance of romantic relationships during adolescence. *Journal of Research on Adolescence, 13,* 1–24.

Coloroso, B. (2004). *The bully, the bullied and the bystander: From preschool to high school—How parents and teachers can help break the cycle of violence.* New York: Harper Collins.

Coloroso, B. (2005, April). A bully's bystanders are never innocent. *The Education Digest, 70*(8), 49–51.

Coltheart, M. (2004). Brain imaging, connectionism and cognitive neuropsychology. *Cognitive Neuropsychology, 21,* 21–26.

Columbo, M., & Columbo, P. (2007, September). Using blogs to improve differentiated instruction. *Phi Delta Kappan, 89,* 60–63.

Combrinck-Graham, L. (Ed.). (2006). *Children in family contexts* (2nd ed.). New York: Guilford.

Congressional Record (2005, December 18). *House Bill Resolution 483 on Teen dating and violence awareness and prevention week,* February 6, 2006, p. H12214.

Connor, J., & Rueter, M. (2006 March). Parent-child relationships as systems of support for adolescent suicidality. *Journal of Family Psychology, 20*(1), 143–155.

Consumer Product Safety Commission. (2007). *A parents' guide to preventing inhalant abuse.* Washington, DC: The Commission, CPSC Document #389. Retrieved July 20, 2008, from http://www.cpsc.gov/CPSCPUB/PUBS/389.html

Coontz, S. (2000). *The way we never were: American families and the nostalgia trap.* New York: Basic books.

Cosby, B., & Poussaint, A. (2007). *Come on, people: On the path from victims to victors.* Dallas, TX: Thomas Nelson.

Costin, C. (2006). *The eating disorders sourcebook.* New York: McGraw-Hill.

Cote, J. (2000). *Arrested adulthood: The changing nature of maturity and identity in the late modern world.* New York: New York University Press.

Covey, H. (2003). *Street gangs throughout the world.* Springfield, IL: Charles C. Thomas.

Covington, M., & Mueller, K. (2001, June). Intrinsic versus extrinsic motivation: An approach/avoidance reformulation. *Educational Psychology Review, 13*(2), 157–176.

Covington, R. (2001, October). Forever young. *Smithsonian, 32*(7), 70–76.

Cowan, N., Naveh-Benjamin, M., Kilb, A., & Sautts, S. (2006, November). Lifespan development of visual working memory. *Developmental Psychology, 42*(6), 1089–1102.

Craft, A. (2005). *Creativity in schools: Tensions and dilemmas.* London: Routledge.

Cropley, A. (2003). *Creativity and education and learning.* London: Kogan Page.

Crosnoe, R. (2006, January). The connection between academic failure and adolescent drinking in secondary school. *Sociology of Education, 79*(1), 44–60.

Crothers, L., Field, J., & Kolbert, J. (2005, Summer). Navigating power, control, and being nice: Aggression in adolescent girls' friendships. *Journal of Counseling & Development, 83*(3), 349–354.

Crouhy, M., Galia, D., & Mark, R. (2005). *The essentials of risk management.* New York: McGraw-Hill.

Crouter, A., & Booth, A. (Eds.). (2006). *Romance and sex in adolescence and emerging adulthood: Risks and opportunities.* Mahwah, NJ: Erlbaum.

Cukras, G. (2006, Winter). The investigation of study strategies that maximize learning for underprepared students. *College Teaching, 54*(1), 194–197.

Cushman, K. (2006, March). Respecting high schoolers as partners, not inferiors. *The Education Digest, 71*(7), 8–14.

Daley, B., & Wood, M. (2006). *Computers are your future.* Upper Saddle River, NJ: Prentice-Hall.

Daley, R. (2006). *Investment to transform 50 Chicago high schools to ensure students are prepared for success.* Retrieved May 29, 2007, from the Gates Foundation http://www.gatesfoundation.org

Dallam, M. (1917). Is the study of Latin advantageous to the study of English? *Educational Review, 54,* 500–503.

Dalton, S. (2008). *Five standards for effective teaching: How to succeed with all learners. Grades K–8.* San Francisco: Jossey-Bass.

Damasio, A. (2003). *Looking for Spinoza: Joy, sorrow and the feeling brain.* New York: Harcourt.

Dan, L. (2005, December 14). Essay plagiarists to be kicked out of school. *China Daily.* Retrieved November 1, 2008, from www.chinadaily.com.cn/english/doc/2005-12/14/content_503398.htm

Daniels, E., & Arapostathis, M. (2005, January). What do they really want? Student voices and motivation research. *Urban Education, 40*(1), 34–59.

Daniel, R. (Director). (1987). *Like father, like son* [Motion picture]. United States: Sony Pictures.

Daniels, S. (2006, Spring). The consequences of childhood overweight and obesity. *The Future of Children, 16*(1), 47–67.

Daniels, S., Greer, F., & the Committee on Nutrition (2008, July). Lipid screening and cardiovascular health in childhood: Policy revision of the American Academy of Pediatrics. *Pediatrics, 122*(1), 198–208.

Danzinger, S., & Rouse, C. (Eds.), (2007). *The price of independence: The economics of early adulthood.* New York: Russell Sage Foundation.

Darst, P., & Pangrazi, R. (2008). *Dynamic physical education for secondary school students.* Boston: Benjamin Cummings.

Darwin, C., & Wilson, E. (Ed.). (2005). *From so simple a beginning: Darwin's four great books.* New York: W. W. Norton.

David-Ferdon, C., & Hertz, M. (2007). Electronic media, violence and adolescents: An emerging public health problem. *Journal of Adolescent Health, 41,* S1–S5.

Davidson, A. (2005, March). Spiritual state. *National Geographic, 207*(3), 31.

Davies, H., & Fitzgerald, H. (2007). *Obesity in childhood and adolescence.* Westport CT: Praeger.

Davila, T., Epstein, M., & Shelton, R. (2006). *Making innovation work: How to manage it, measure it, and profit from it.* Upper Saddle River, NJ: Pearson.

Davis, B. G. (2002). *Tools for teaching: Preventing academic dishonesty.* Berkley: University of California. Retrieved December 1, 2008, from http://teaching.berkeley.edu/bgd/prevent.html

de Bono, E. (1998). *Thinking for action.* New York: DK Publishing.

de Bono, E. (1999). *Six thinking hats.* New York: Little Brown.

de Bono, E. (2007). *A beautiful mind.* Nashua, NH: Vermillion.

De Vita, C. (1996 March). The United States at Mid-Decade. *Population Bulletin, 50*(4). Washington, DC: Population Reference Bureau.

Debevec, K., Shih, M., & Kashyap, V. (2006, Spring). Learning strategies and performance in a technology integrated classroom. *Journal of Research on Technology in Education, 38*(3), 293–308.

Delisie, J. (2005, Summer). Where's the courage? *Gifted Child Today, 28*(3), 22–23.

Denison, P. (2005, November 5). Dealing with the bully at the top. *The Times Educational Supplement, 4608*, 30.

Desetta, A. (2005). *The courage to be yourself: True stories by teens about cliques, conflicts, and overcoming peer pressure.* Minneapolis: Free Spirit.

Deutsch, M. (1949a). A theory of cooperation and competition. *Human Relations, 2*(2), 129–152.

Deutsch, M. (1949b). An experimental study of the effects of cooperation on group process. *Human Relations, 2*(3), 199–231.

Diller, J. (2007). *Cultural diversity* (3rd ed.). Belmont, CA: Thomson Higher Education.

Dillon, N. (2006, January). Multiple choice. *American School Board Journal, 193*(1), 22–25.

DiMaria, F. (2006, December). Service learning for a new kind of student. Hispanic Outlook in Higher Education. *The Education Digest, 72*(4), 50–54.

Dimitriadis, G. (2003). *Friendship, cliques, and gangs.* New York: Teachers College Press.

Discovery Education. (2009). *Engage your students with rich video and online teaching resources.* Discovery Education, Evanston, IL. Retrieved January 15, 2009, from http://www.discoveryeducation.com/products/streaming/

Dongdong, S. (2005, September 14). Exam cheaters may face 7 years in jail. *China Daily.* Retrieved November 1, 2008, from http://en1.chinabroadcast.cn/2238/2005-9-14/148@271735.htm

Donlevy, J. (2006). A New Year's Resolution for 2006: Closing the achievement gap. *International Journal of Instructional Media, 33*(1), 1–3.

Dozier, C., Johnston, P., & Rogers, R. (2006). *Critical literacy/critical thinking.* New York: Teachers College Press.

Driscoll, M. (2004). *Psychology of learning for instruction.* Boston: Allyn & Bacon.

Drucker, P. (2005, January). Managing oneself. *Harvard Business Review,* 1–10.

Drucker, P. (2006). *The essential Drucker.* New York: Harper Collins.

Duffett, A., Farkas, S., & Loveless, T. (2008). *High-achieving students in the era of No Child Left Behind.* Washington, DC: Thomas B. Fordham Institute.

Dunning, D., Heath, C., & Suls, J. (2004, December). Flawed self-assessment: Implications for health, education and the workplace. *Psychological Science in the Public Interest, 5*(3), 69–106.

Durkin, S., Paxton, S., & Wertheim, E. (2005, November). How do adolescent girls evaluate body dissatisfaction prevention messages? *Journal of Adolescent Health, 37*(5), 381–390.

Dutton, D. (2007). *The abusive personality: Violence and control in intimate relationships* (2nd ed). New York: Guilford.

Dweck, C., & Repucci, N. (1973). Learned helplessness and reinforcement responsibility in children. *Journal of Personality and Social Psychology, 25*(1), 109–116.

Eastin, M. (2005, February). Teen Internet use: Relating social perceptions and cognitive models to behavior. *CyberPsychology & Behavior, 8*(1), 62–75.

Education of All Handicapped Children Act of 1975, Pub. L. 94–142, 20 USC 1400 (1975).

Easton, J., & Allensworth, E. (2005, July 28). Study provides early indicators of high school dropout risks. *Black Issues in Higher Education*, 8.

Edwards, O., Mumford, V., Shillingford, M., & Serra-Roldan, R. (2007, July). Developmental assets: A prevention framework for students considered at risk. *Children and Schools, 29*(3), 145–153.

Egan, T., & Akdere, M. (2005). Clarifying distance education roles and competencies. *American Journal of Distance Education, 19*(2), 87–103.

Elkind, D. (2006). *The hurried child*. New York: Da Capo Lifelong Books.

Elliot, A. (2008). *Handbook of approach and avoidance motivation*. New York: Psychology Press.

Elliot, A., & Dweck, C. (Eds.). (2005). *Handbook of competence and motivation*. New York: Guilford.

Elliott, D., Menard, S., Elliott, A., Rankin, B., Wilson, K. W., & Huizinga, D. (2006). *Good kids from bad neighborhoods*. New York: Cambridge University Press.

Elliott, M., Shope, J., Raghunathan, T., & Waller, P. (2006, March). Gender differences among young drivers in the association between high-risk driving and substance use/environmental influences. *Journal of Studies on Alcohol, 67*(2), 252–260.

Elmer, B., & Torem, M. (2004). *Coping with uncertainty*. Oakland, CA: New Harbinger.

Endresen, I., & Olweus, D. (2005, May). Participation in power sports and antisocial involvement in preadolescent and adolescent boys. *Journal of Child Psychology and Psychiatry, 46*(5), 468–478.

Englund, M., Egeland, B., & Collins, W. (2008, February 7). Exceptions to high school dropout predictions in a low-income sample: Do adults make a difference? *Journal of Social Issues, 64*(1), 77–94.

Epstein, R. (2007). *The case against adolescents: Rediscovering the adult in every teen*. Sanger, CA: Quill Driver.

Erikson, E. (1968). *Identity: Youth and crisis*. New York: W. W. Norton.

Erikson, E. (1980). *Identity and the life cycle*. New York: W. W. Norton.

Erikson, R., & Tedin, K. (2004). *American pubic opinion: Its origins, content and impact* (7th ed.). Boston: Longman.

Evans, G., & Kim, P. (2007, November). Childhood poverty and health. *Psychological Science, 18*(11), 953–957.

Evans, P., & Wolf, B. (2005, July–August). Collaboration rules. *Harvard Business Review*, 96–104.

Eysenck, M., & Keane, M. (2005). *Cognitive psychology*. Philadelphia: Psychology Press.

Fagenberg, J., Mowery, D., & Nelson, R. (2005). *The Oxford handbook of innovation*. New York: Oxford University Press.

Falk, B., & Blumenreich, M. (2005). *The power of question: A guide to teacher student research*. Portsmouth, NH: Heinemann.

Family Violence Prevention Fund (2006). *Coaching boys into men—what you can do.* Available at http://endabuse.org/cbim

Farah, M. (2000). *The cognitive neuroscience of vision.* Malden, MA: Blackwell.

Farkas, S., Johnson, J., Duffett, A., Wilson, L., & Vine, J. (2002). *A lot easier said than done: Parents talk about raising children in today's America.* New York: State Farm Companies Foundation and Public Agenda.

Fashola, O. (2005). *Educating African-American males.* Thousand Oaks, CA: SAGE.

Fass, S., & Cauthen, N. (2006, December). *Who are America's poor children? The official story.* New York: Columbia University National Center for Children in Poverty. Mailman School of Public Health.

Federal Interagency Forum on Child and Family Statistics (2008). *America's children: Key national indicators of well-being 2008.* Retrieved January 6, 2009, from http://www.childstats.gov

Fein, R., Vossekuil, B., Pollack, W., Borum, R., Modzeleski, & Reddy, M. (2002). *Threat assessment in schools: A guide to managing threatening situations and to creating safe school climates.* Washington, DC: United States Secret Service and United States Department of Education. Retrieved December 5, 2008, from http://www.ustreas.gov/usss/ntac_ssi.shtml

Feinberg, T., & Keenan, J. (Eds.) (2005). *The lost self: Pathologies of the brain and identity.* New York: Oxford University Press.

Feist, J., & Feist, G. (2006). *Theories of personality* (6th edition). New York: McGraw-Hill.

Fields, J. (2008). *Risky lessons: Sex education and social inequity.* Piscataway, NJ: Rutgers University Press.

Fine, M., & Harvey, J. (Eds.). (2005). *Handbook of divorce and relationship dissolution.* Mahwah, NJ: Erlbaum.

Fingerson, L. (2006). *Girls in power: Gender, body and menstruation in adolescence.* Albany, New York: State University of New York Press.

Firlik, K. (2007). *Another day in the frontal lobe.* New York: Random House.

Flanagan, C., Elek-Fisk, E., & Gallay, L. (2004). Friends don't let friends ... or do they? Developmental and gender differences in intervening in friends' alcohol, tobacco and other drug use. *Journal of Drug Education, 34*(4), 351–371.

Fleming, M. (2005). Adolescent autonomy: Desire, achievement and disobeying parents between early and late adolescence. *Australian Journal of Educational and Developmental Psychology, 5,* 1–16.

Florida, R. (2004). *The rise of the creative class.* New York: Basic Books.

Florida, R. (2005). *Cities and the creative class.* New York: Routledge.

Florida, R. (2008). *Who's your city? How the creative economy is making where you live the most important decision of your life.* New York: Basic Books.

Fogel, A., Garvey, A., Hsu, H., & West-Stromming, D. (2006). *Change process in relationships.* New York: Cambridge University Press.

Fogel, S., Nader, R., Cote, K., & Smith, C. (2007, February). Sleep spindles and learning potential. *Behavioral Neuroscience, 121*(1), 1–10.

Forest, K., & Balcetis, E. (2008, February). Teaching students to work well in groups. *Observer, 21*(2), 27–29.

Foshee, V., Bauman, K., Linder, F., Rice, J., & Wilcher, R. (2007, May). Typologies of adolescent dating violence. *Journal of Interpersonal Violence, 22*(5), 498–519.

Fosnot, C. (2005). *Constructivism: Theory, perspectives, & practice*. New York: Teachers College Press.

Francis, P. (Ed.). (2006). *To cherish the life of the world: Selected letters of Margaret Mead*. New York: Perseus Books.

Frank, A. (1986). *The dairy of Anne Frank*. New York: Random House.

Frank, K., Zhao, Y., & Borman, K. (2004, April). Social capital and the diffusion of innovations within organizations: The case of computer technology in schools. *Sociology of Education, 77*(2), 148–171.

Franke, T. M. (2000). Adolescent violent behavior: An analysis across and within racial/ethnic groups. In D. de Anda & R. Becerra, (Eds.), *Violence: Diverse populations and communities* (pp. 47–70). New York: Haworth Press.

Frankenberger, K. (2000, June). Adolescent egocentrism: A comparison among adolescents and adults. *Journal of Adolescence, 23*(3), 343–354.

Franzese, R., Covey, H., & Menard, S. (2006). *Youth gangs*. Springfield, IL: Charles C. Thomas.

French, S., Seidman, E., Allen, L., & Aber, R. (2006, January). The development of ethnic identity during adolescence. *Developmental Psychology, 42*(1), 1–10.

Freud, A. (1969). Adolescence as a developmental disturbance. In G. Caplan & S. Levbovici (Eds.), *Adolescence: Psychosocial perspectives* (pp. 5–10). New York: Basic Books.

Freud, S. (1923). *The ego and the id*. New York: W. W. Norton.

Frey, K., Kirschstein, M., & Snell, J. (2005, May). Reducing playground bullying and supporting beliefs: An experimental trial of the "Steps to Respect" Program. *Developmental Psychology, 41*(3), 479–490.

Frey, N. (2005, November/December). Retention, social promotion, and academic redshirting: What do we know and need to know? *Remedial and Special Education, 26*(6), 332–346.

Friedman, B. (2005). *Web search savvy*. Mahwah, NJ: Erlbaum.

Friedman, T. (2005). *The world is flat: A brief history of the twenty-first century*. New York: Farrar, Strauss & Giroux.

Fromm, E. (1992). *The anatomy of human destructiveness*. New York: Holt.

Furrer, C., & Skinner, E. (2003, March). Sense of relatedness as a factor in children's academic engagement and performance. *Journal of Educational Psychology, 95*(1), 148–162.

Gagné, R., & Medsker, K. (1996). *The conditions of learning*. Fort Worth, TX: Harcourt Brace.

Gais, S., Plihal, W., Wagner, W., & Born, J. (2000, December). Early sleep triggers memory for early visual discrimination tasks. *Nature Neuroscience, 3*(12), 1335–1339.

Galinsky, A., Magee, J., Inesi, M., & Gruenfeld, D. (2006). Power and perspectives not taken. *Psychological Science, 17*(12), 1068–1074.

Gall, J., Gall, M., & Borg, W. (2005). *Applying educational research* (5th ed.). Boston: Allyn & Bacon.

Gallagher, R. (2006). *How to safely explore the cyberdating scene*. Retrieved from Rutgers University Network for Family Life Education http://sexetc.rutgers.edu

Gallup, G. (1940). *The pulse of democracy*. Princeton, NJ: Gallup.

Gallup, G. (2006). *Highly successful Americans.* Princeton, NJ: Gallup.

Galton, F. (1874). *English men and science: Their nature and nurture.* London: Macmillan.

Gandy, C., & Schultz, J. (2007). *Increasing school attendance for K–8 students: A review of research examining effectiveness of truancy prevention programs.* St. Paul, MN: Amherst Wilder Foundation.

Gardner, H. (1983). *Frames of mind: The theory of multiple intelligences.* New York: Basic Books.

Gardner, H. (1996). *Creating minds.* New York: Basic Books.

Gardner, H. (1997, September). Multiple intelligences as a partner in school improvement. *Educational Leadership, 55*(1), 20–22.

Gardner, H. (2003, April 21). *Recounting multiple intelligences.* Paper presented at the meeting of the American Educational Research Association, Chicago. Retrieved April 15, 2008, from http://www.gse.harvard.edu/news/features/gardner10012003.html

Gardner, H. (2004). *Changing minds.* Boston: Harvard Business School.

Gardner, M., & Steinberg, L. (2005). Peer influence on risk taking, risk preference, and risky decision making in adolescence and adulthood. *Developmental Psychology, 41*(4), 625–635.

Gardner, S., & Birley, S. (2008). *Blogging for dummies.* Hoboken, NJ: Wiley.

Garrett, L. (2007, January/February). The challenge of global health. *Foreign Affairs, 86*(1), 14–38.

Geake, J. (2002, August). *Advances in neuroscience.* Keynote address to Australian Association for the Education of the Gifted and Talented, Sydney, Australia.

Geake, J. (2000, January). *On educating the very able in mathematics: A sampling of current empirical research.* Paper presented to the Mathematics 2000 Festival, University of Melbourne, Australia.

Geary, D. (2005). *The origin of mind: Evolution of brain, cognition, and general intelligence.* Washington DC: American Psychological Association.

Gecke, C. (2006, February). The Generation Z connection: Teaching information literacy to the newest net generation. *Teacher Librarian, 33*(3), 19–23.

Gerrard, M., Burhans, A., & Fair, J. (2003). *Effective truancy prevention and intervention.* St. Paul, MN: Wilder Research Center. Retrieved from http://www.wilder.org/research

Getzels, J., & Jackson, P. (1962). *Creativity and intelligence.* New York: Wiley.

Gewertz, C. (2004). Student-designed poll shows teenagers feel lack of adult interest. *Education Week, 24*(10), 6–7.

Gewertz, C. (2006, March 8). High school dropouts say lack of motivation top reason to quit. *Education Week, 25*(26), 1, 14.

Gewertz, C. (2007, August 27). Ninth grade nation. *Education Week, 1,* 14–15.

Ghiselin, B. (1952). *The creative process.* New York: Mentor Books.

Ghiselin, B. (1987). *The creative process.* New York: New American Library.

Giangreco, M. (2007). Extending inclusive opportunities. *Educational Leadership, 64*(5), 34–37.

Gibbs, N. (2005, February 21). Parents behaving badly. *Time, 165*(8), 40–49.

Giedd, J. (2004). *The primal teen: What the new discoveries about the teenage brain tell us about our kids.* New York: Anchor Books.

Giedd, J. (2008, April). The teen brain: Insights from neuroimaging. *Journal of Adolescent Health, 42*(4), 335–343.

Gilbert, S. (2006). Growing toward adulthood. In R. Kelly (Ed.), *Family Doctor: Your essential guide to health and well being* (pp. 255–256). Cleveland, OH: American Academy of Family Physicians.

Gilliand, S. (Ed.) (2008). *Justice, morality, and social responsibility.* Charlotte, NC: Information Age.

Gillies, R. (2007). *Cooperative learning: Integrating theory and practice.* Thousand Oaks, CA: SAGE.

Gilligan, C. (1982). *In a different voice: Psychological theory and women's development.* Cambridge, MA: Harvard University Press.

Gilligan, C., & Brown, L. (1993). *Meeting at the crossroads.* New York: Ballantine.

Gilligan, C., & Roader-Roth, M. (2005). *Trusting what you know: The high stakes of classroom relationships.* San Francisco, CA: Jossey-Bass.

Gilligan, C., Ward, J., & Taylor, J. (Eds.) (1988). *Mapping the moral domain.* Cambridge, MA: Harvard University Press.

Gilman, R., Huebner, E., Furlong, M. (Eds.). (2009). *Handbook of positive psycholgy in schools.* New York: Routledge.

Girod, M., Pardales, M., Cavanaugh, S., & Wadsworth, P. (2005, Spring). By teens for teachers: A descriptive study of adolescences. *American Secondary Education, 33*(2), 4–17.

Glueck, S., & Glueck, E. (1968). *Delinquents and non-delinquents in perspective.* Cambridge, MA: Harvard University Press.

Goldberg, E. (2002). *The executive brain: Frontal lobes and the civilized mind.* New York: Oxford University Press.

Golden, S., Kist, W., & Trehan, M. (2005, December). A teacher's words are tremendously powerful: Stories from the GED scholars initiative. *Phi Delta Kappan, 87*(4), 311–315.

Golding, W. (1954). *Lord of the flies.* New York: Riverhead Books.

Goldsmith, J., & Wu, T. (2006). *Who controls the Internet: Illusions of a borderless world.* New York: Oxford University Press.

Goldstein, S., & Brooks, R. (2005). *Handbook of resilience in children.* New York: Springer.

Goldston, D., Molock, S., Whitback, L., Murakami, J., Zayas, L., & Hall, G. (2008, January). Cultural considerations in adolescent suicide prevention and psychosocial treatment. *American Psychologist, 63*(1), 14–31.

Goleman, D. (2005). *Emotional intelligence.* New York: Bantam.

Goleman, D. (2006). *Social intelligence: The new science of human relationships.* New York: Bantam Books.

Goleman, D., Boyatzis, R., & McKee, A. (2004). *Primal leadership: Realizing the power of emotional intelligence.* Cambridge, MA: Harvard Business School Press.

Goodenow, C., Szalacha, L., & Westheimer, K. (2006, May). School support groups, other school factors, and the safety of sexual minority adolescents. *Psychology in the Schools, 43*(5), 573–589.

Gordon, I. (2004). *Theories of visual perception.* New York: Psychology Press.

Gordon, R. (2006, October). Selective attention during scene perception: Evidence from negative priming. *Memory and Cognition, 34*(7), 1484–1494.

Gosselin, P., Langlois, F., Freeston, M., & Ladouceur (2007). *Cognitive variables related to worry among adolescents: Avoidance strategies and faulty beliefs about worry.* Amsterdam: Elsevier.

Gray, J. (1992). *Men are from mars, women are from venus: A practical guide for improving communication and getting what you want in your relationship.* New York: HarperCollins.

Greenberg, J. (2006). *Comprehensive stress management* (9th ed.). New York: McGraw-Hill.

Greene, R., & Ablon, J. (2006). *Treating explosive kids: The collaborative problem-solving approach.* New York: Guilford.

Greenfield, P., & Yan, Z (2006, May). Children, adolescents, and the Internet: A new field of inquiry in developmental psychology. *Developmental Psychology, 42*(3), 3291–3394.

Greengard, S. (2002, March). Moving forward with reverse mentoring: Sharing the knowledge. *Workforce,* 12–18.

Griffith, S., & Bonsen, J. (2006). *Instructables Step-By-Step Collaboration.* Retrieved from http://www.instructables.com/group/howtoons/

Grill-Spector, K., & Kanwisher, N. (2005, February). Visual recognition. *Psychological Science, 16*(2), 152–160.

Gross, E. (2004 November). Adolescent Internet use: What we expect, what teens report. *Journal of Applied Developmental Psychology, 25*(6), 633–649.

Grzegorek, J., Slaney, R., Franze, S., & Rice, K. (2004). Self-criticism, dependency, self-esteem, and grade point average satisfaction among clusters of perfectionists and nonperfectionists. *Journal of Counseling Psychology, 51*(2), 192–200.

Guilford J. (1950, September). Creativity. *American Psychologist, 5*(9), 444–454

Guilford, J. (1971). *Creativity tests for children: A manual of interpretation.* Orange, CA: Sheridan Psychological Services.

Guilford, J. (1977). *Way beyond the IQ.* Buffalo, NY: Creative Education Foundation.

Guilford, J. (1979). Some incubated thoughts on incubation. *Journal of Creative Behavior, 13*(1), 1–8.

Guilford, J. (1986). *Creative talents: Their nature uses and development.* Buffalo, NY: Bearly.

Guilford, J., & Hoepfner, R. (1971). *The analysis of intelligence.* New York: McGraw-Hill

Gurian, M., & Stevens, K. (2005). *The minds of boys.* San Francisco: Jossey-Bass.

Gurvey, J., Adler, N., & Ellen, J. (2005, December). Factors associated with self-risk perception for sexually transmitted diseases among adolescents. *Sexually Transmitted Diseases, 32*(12), 742–744.

Haag, P. (2000). *Voices of a generation: Teenage girls report about their lives today.* New York: Marlowe.

Haag, P. (2001). *Hostile hallways, teasing and sexual harassment in schools.* Washington, DC: American Association of University Women.

Hakkarainen, K., Palonen, T., Paavola, S., & Lehtinen, E. (Eds.). (2004). *Communities of networked expertise.* San Diego, CA: Academic Press.

Hall, G. S. (1904). *Adolescence: Its psychology and its relation to physiology, anthropology, sociology, sex, crime, religion and education.* New York: D. Appleton.

Hall, K. (2006, February). Using problem-based learning with victims of bullying behavior. *Professional School Counseling, 9*(3), 231–237.

Halloran, C., & Sears, R. (1995). *The gifted group in maturity*. Stanford, CA: Stanford University Press.

Halpern, C., Kaestle, C., & Hallfors, D. (2007). Perceived physical maturity, age of romantic partner, and adolescent risk behaviors. *Prevention Science, 8,* 1–10.

Halpern-Felsher, B., Cornell, J., Kropp, R., & Tschann, J. (2005, April). Oral versus vaginal sex among adolescents: Perceptions, attitudes, and behavior. *Pediatrics, 115*(4), 845–851.

Hamm, J., & Faircloth, B. (2005, Spring). The role of friendship in adolescents' sense of school belonging. *New Directions for Child & Adolescent Development, 107,* 61–78.

Hamm, S., & Smith, G. (2008, June 16). Social cause meets business reality. *Business Week,* 48–57.

Hample, D. (2005). *Arguing: Exchanging reasons face to face*. Mahwah, NJ: Erlbaum.

Handel, M. (2005). *Worker skills and job requirements*. Washington, DC: Economic Policy Institute.

Hardy, K., & Laszloffy, T. (2006). *Teens who hurt: Clinical interventions to break the cycle of adolescent violence*. New York: Guilford.

Hargis, J. (2005). Collaboration, community and project-based learning: Does it still work online? *International Journal of Instructional Media, 32*(2), 157–161.

Hargrove, B., Creagh, M., & Burgess, B. (2002, October). Family interaction patterns as predictors of vocational identity and career decision-making self-efficacy. *Journal of Vocational Behavior, 61*(2), 185–201.

Hargrove, R. (1998). *Mastering the art of creative collaboration*. New York: McGraw-Hill.

Harpine, E. (2008). *Group interventions in schools: Promoting mental health for at-risk children and youth*. New York: Springer.

Harriott, W., & Martin, S. (2004, September/October). Using culturally responsive activities to promote social competence and classroom community. *Teaching Exceptional Children, 37*(1), 48–54.

Harris, J. (1998). *The nurture assumption*. New York: The Free Press.

Harris, J. (2006). *No two alike: Human nature and human individuality*. New York: W. W. Norton.

Harris, R. (2002). *Creative thinking techniques*. Retrieved from Virtual Salt September 4, 2005, http://www.virtualsalt.com/crebook2.htm

Hart, D., Donnelly, T., Youniss, J., & Atkins, R. (2007, March). High school community service as a predictor of adult voting and volunteering. *American Educational Research Journal, 44*(1), 197–219.

Hartshorne, H., & May, M. (1928). *Studies in deceit*. New York: Macmillan.

Hastings, N., & Tracey, M. (2005, March/April). Does media affect learning: Where are we now? *TechTrends, 49*(2), 28–30.

Hauser, D. (2004). *Five Years of abstinence-only-until-marriage education: Assessing the impact* [Title V State Evaluations]. Washington, DC: Advocates for Youth.

Havighurst, R. (1972). *Developmental tasks and education*. New York: David McKay.

Hebert, A., Sallee, E., & Stock, L. (2008). *Service-e-learning*. Charlotte, NC: Information Age.

Hecker, J., & Thorpe, G. (2005). *Introduction to clinical psychology.* Boston: Allyn & Bacon.

Heilman, K. (2005). *Creativity and the brain.* New York: Psychology Press.

Hemmingway, E. (1964). *A moveable feast.* New York: Charles Scribners Sons.

Hendricks, D. (2008, October 11). Palm scans called next steps for Ids. *The Washington Times*, p. 1.

Henkin, R. (2005). *Confronting bullying.* Portsmouth, NH: Heinemann.

Henley, M. (2003). *Teaching self-control.* Bloomington, IN: National Educational Service.

Herrnstein, R., & Murray, C. (1996). *The bell curve: Intelligence and class structure in American Life.* New York: The Free Press.

Hewitt, J. (2004, December). Anti-bullying week. *Child Education, 81*(12), 25.

Hines, A., & Paulson, S. (2006, Winter). Parents' and teachers' perceptions of storm and stress: Relations with parenting and teaching styles. *Adolescence, 41*(164), 597–614.

Hingson, R., Herren, T., & Winter, M. (2006). Age at drinking onset and alcohol dependence. *Archives of Pediatrics & Adolescent Medicine, 160,* 739–746.

Hinz, C. (2006). Healthy eyesight: It's more than a vision. In R. Kelly (Ed.), *Family Doctor: Your essential guide to health and well being* (pp. 32–33). Cleveland, OH: American Academy of Family Physicians.

Hobson, J. (2005, October 26). Sleep is of the brain, by the brain and for the brain. *Nature, 437,* 1254–1256.

Hoffman, E. (2008, May 22). The search for solutions: Getting kids to think about changing exercise and eating habits is one thing: Keeping them on track is another. *The Washington Post.* p. 1.

Hoffman, M. (Director). (2003). *The emperor's club* [Motion Picture]. United States: Universal Studios.

Hofstede, G. (2001). *Culture's consequence: Comparing values, behaviors, institutions, and organizations across nations.* Thousand Oaks, CA: SAGE.

Hollinger, D. (2006, March 17). Race, politics, and the census. *The Chronicle of Higher Education*, pp. B6–B8.

Holloway, J. (2006, January). Model behavior. *Principal Leadership (High School Education), 6*(5), 44–48.

Holmes, R., & Holmes, S. (2005). *Suicide.* Thousand Oaks, CA: SAGE.

Holverstott, J. (2005, September). Promote self-determination in students. *Intervention, 41*(1), 39–41.

Honawar, V. (2005, June 22). Studies cite effects of abstinence programs. *Education Week, 24*(41), 5.

Honore, C. (2005). *In praise of slowness.* New York: Harper.

Horak, R. (2007). *Telecommunications and data communications handbook.* New York: Wiley Interscience.

Horn, J. (1965). *Fluid and crystallized intelligence: A factor analytic study of the structure among primary mental abilities.* PhD Thesis, University of Illinois.

Horn, J., & Cattell, R. (1967). Age differences in fluid and crystallized intelligence. *Acta Psychologica, 26,* 107–129.

Houck, C., Lescano, C., Brown, L., Tolou-Shams, M., Thompson, J., et al. (2006, July). "Islands of Risk": Subgroups of adolescents at risk for HIV. *Journal of Pediatric Psychology, 31*(6), 619–629.

House, G. (2006, April). Closing the "Reality Gap." *American School Board Journal, 193*(4), 57–59.

Hubel, D., & Wiesel, T. (2004). *Brain and visual perception: The story of a 25-Year collaboration.* New York: Oxford University Press.

Huesmann, L. (2007). The impact of electronic media violence: Scientific theory and research. *Journal of Adolescent Health, 41,* S6–S13.

Huhn, C. (2005, November). How many points is this worth? *Educational Leadership, 63*(3), 81–82.

Hull, N., Hoffer, W., & Hoffer, P. (Eds.). (2003). *The abortion rights controversy in America: A legal reader.* Chapel Hill, NC: University of North Carolina Press.

Hunt, T. (Ed.). (2005). *Moral education in America's schools: The continuing challenge.* Charlotte, NC: Information Age.

Hursh, D. (2008). *High stakes testing and the decline of teaching and learning.* Oxford: Rowman & Littlefield.

Hutchins, L. (2004, December). A call for help. *Child Education, 81*(12), 22–23.

Hutchinson, P., Jetten, J., Christian, J., & Haycraft, E. (2006, December). Protecting threatened identity: Sticking with the group by emphasizing ingroup heterogeneity. *Personality and Social Psychology Bulletin, 32*(12), 1620–1632.

Huxley, C., & Grogan, S. (2005, November). Tattooing, piercing, healthy behaviors and health value. *Journal of Health Psychology, 10*(6), 831–841.

Hwang, Y., & Levin, J. (2002, Fall). Examination of middle school students' independent use of a complex mnemonic system. *The Journal of Experimental Education, 71*(1), 25–38.

Hyde, J. (2005, September). The gender similarities hypothesis. *American Psychologist, 60*(6), 581–592.

Hymowitz, K. (2006). *Marriage and caste: Separate and unequal families in a post-marital age.* Chicago: Ivan, R. Dee.

Indiana University (2004). *High School Survey of Student Engagement.* Bloomington, IN: School of Education, Indiana University. Retrieved May 20, 2008, from http://ceep.indiana.edu/hssse/

Individuals with Disabilities Education Act, 20 U.S.C. 1400, Pub. L. 108–446 (2004).

International Society for Technology in Education (2007). *National Education Technology Standards 2007.* Retrieved April 10, 2008 from http://www.iste.org/AM/Template.cfm?Section=NETS

Inzlicht, M., McKay, L., & Aronson, J. (2006, March). Stigma as ego depletion: How being the target of prejudice affects self-control. *Psychological Science, 17*(3), 262–269.

Ito, K., Gizlice, Z., Owen-O'Dowd, J., Foust, E., Leone, P., & Miller, W. (2006, June 30). Parent opinion of sexuality education in a state with mandated abstinence education: Does policy match parental preference? *Journal of Adolescent Health, 30.*

Jackson, A., & Davis, G. (2000). *Turning points 2000: Educating adolescents for the 21st Century.* New York: Columbia University Teachers College Press.

Jackson, L., Von Eye, A., Biocca, F., Barbatsis, G., Zhao, Y., & Fitzgerald, H. (2006). Does home Internet use influence the academic performance of low-income children. *Developmental Psychology, 42*(3), 429–435.

Jacobs, J., & Klaczynski, P. (2005). *The development of judgment and decisionmaking in children and adolescents*. Mahwah, NJ: Erlbaum.

Janson, H. (1986). *History of art*. Englewood Cliffs, NJ: Prentice-Hall.

Jason, L., Pokorny, S., Muldowney, K., & Velez, M. (2005). Youth tobacco sales-to-minors and possession-use purchase laws: A public health controversy. *Journal of Drug Education, 35*(4), 275–290.

Jennings, J., & Rentner, D. (2006). Ten big effects of the No Child Left Behind Act on public schools. *Phi Delta Kappan, 88*(2), 110–113.

Jennings, L., & Likis, L. (2005, March). Meeting a math achievement crisis. *Educational Leadership, 62*(6), 65–68.

Jensen, A. (1998). *The g factor: The science of mental ability*. Westport, CT: Praeger.

Jimerson, S., & Ferguson, P. (2007, September). A longitudinal study of grade retention: Academic and behavioral outcomes of retained students through adolescence. *School Psychology Quarterly, 22*(3), 314–339).

Jimerson, S., Pletcher, S., Graydon, K., Schnurr, B,, Nickerson, A., & Kundert, D. (2006, January). Beyond grade retention and social promotion: Promoting the social and academic competence of students. *Psychology in the Schools, 43*(1), 85–97.

John-Steiner, V. (2000). *Creative collaboration*. New York: Oxford University Press.

Johnson, A. (2005). *A short guide to action research*. Boston: Allyn & Bacon.

Johnson, D. (2002). *The indispensable teacher's guide to computer skills*. Worthington, OH: Linworth.

Johnson, D. (2005–2006, December/January). A vision for the Net Generation. *Learning & Leading with Technology,* 26–27.

Johnson, D., & Brooke, J. (1999, April 22). Portrait of outcasts seeking to stand out. *The New York Times,* pp. 1, 26.

Johnson, D., & Johnson, R. (2003). *Joining together: Group theory and group skills*. Boston: Allyn & Bacon.

Johnson, J., Duffett, A., & Ott, A. (2005). *Life after high school: Young people talk about their hopes and prospects*. New York: Public Agenda. Retrieved from http://www.publicagenda.org

Johnson, M. (Ed.). (2006). *The Cambridge handbook of age and ageing*. New York: Cambridge University Press.

Johnson, P., & Malow-Iroff, M. (2008). *Adolescents and Risk: Making sense of adolescent psychology*. Westport, CT: Praeger.

Johnson, V. (2003). *Grade inflation*. New York: Springer.

Johnston, L., O'Malley, P., Bachman, J., & Schulenberg, J. (2008). *Monitoring the future: National results on adolescent drug use, overview of key findings, 2007*. (NIH Publication No. 08-6418). Bethesda, MD: National Institute on Drug Abuse.

Jones, D. C. (2004, September). Body image among adolescent girls and boys: A longitudinal study. *Developmental Psychology, 40*(5), 823–835).

Josephson, M. (2008, November 30). *2008 Josephson Institute Report Card on the Ethics of American Youth*. Los Angeles, CA: Josephson Institute of Ethics. Retrieved from http://charactercounts.org/programs/reportcard/

Jouriles, E., McDonald, R., Garrido, E., Rosenfeld, D., & Brown, A. (2005, December). Assessing aggression in adolescent romantic relationships: Can we do it better? *Psychological Assessment, 17*(4), 469–475.

Joussemet, M., Koestner, R., Lekes, N., & Houlfort, N. (2004, February). Introducing uninteresting tasks to children: A comparison of the effects of rewards and autonomy support. *Journal of Personality, 72*(1), 139–166.

Kaestle, C., Halpern, C., Miller, W., & Ford, C. (2005). Young age at first sexual intercourse and sexually transmitted infections in adolescents and young adults. *American Journal of Epidemiology, 161*, 774–780.

Kaestle, C., Wiley, M., & Wiley, D. (2002, November/December). Sexual intercourse and the age difference between adolescent females and their romantic partners. *Perspectives on Sexual and Reproductive Health, 34*(6), 304–309.

Kagan, S. (2008). *Cooperative learning*. San Clemente, CA: Kagan Cooperative Learning.

Kahn, J., Huang, B., Gillman, M., Field, A., Austin, B., & Colditz, G. (2008, April). Patterns and determinants of physical activity in U.S. adolescents. *Journal of Adolescent Health, 42*(4), 369–377.

Kaiser Family Foundation (2005a). *Sex on TV: Executive Summary 2005*. Retrieved from the Kaiser Family Foundation, Menlo Park, California, January 20, 2008, from www.kff.org

Kaiser Family Foundation (2005b, March). *Generation M: Media in the lives of 8–18 year-olds—Report (#7251)*. Menlo Park, California: The Foundation.

Kamphaus, R., & Frick, P. (2006). *Clinical assessment of child and adolescent personality and behavior*. New York: Springer.

Kandel, E. (2006). *In search of memory*. New York: W. W. Norton.

Kaplowitz, P. (2004). *Early puberty in girls*. New York: Random House.

Karlin, S. (2007, September). Examining how youth interact online. *School Board News, 27*, 1–8.

Katz, S., & Smith, B. (2006, January). Using contextual teaching and learning in foods and nutrition class. *Journal of Family and Consumer Sciences, 98*(1), 82–84.

Keller, J. (2005a, May). The new tech tutors. *Technology and Learning, 25*(10), 15–17.

Kelly, A., Schochet, T., & Landry, C. (2004). Risk taking and novelty seeking in adolescence: Introduction to Part I. *Annals of the New York Academy of Sciences, 1021*, 27–32.

Kelly, K. (2005 May 10). Driving to early deaths. *U.S. News & World Report, Mysteries of the Teen Years Special Edition*, 51–54.

Kelsey, C., & Kelsey, C. (2007). *Generation MySpace: Helping your teen survive online adolescence*. New York: DeCapo Press.

Kennedy, A. (2006, April). Nation caught in meth's grip. *Counseling Today, 48*(10), 1, 32–34.

Kerner, M. (2005, October). Leisure-time physical activity, sedentary behavior, and physical fitness among adolescents. *Journal of Physical Education, Recreation and Dance, 76*(8), 26–30.

Kim, H., Sherman, D., Ko, D., & Taylor, S. (2006, December). Pursuit of comfort and pursuit of harmony: Culture, relationships, and social support seeking. *Personality and Social Psychology Bulletin, 32*(12), 1595–1607.

Kindlon, D. (2006). *Alpha Girls: Understanding the new American girl and how she is changing the world*. Emmaus, PA: Rodale.

Kindlon, D., & Thompson, M. (2000). *Raising Cain: Protecting the emotional lives of boys*. New York: Ballantine.

King, J., Walpole, C., & Lamon, K. (2007). Surf and turf wars online—Growing implications of Internet gang violence. *Journal of Adolescent Health, 41*, S66–S68.

King, S. (2000). *On writing*. New York: Scribners.

Kirby, D. (2007). *Emerging answers 2007: Research findings on programs to reduce teen pregnancy and sexually transmitted diseases*. Washington, DC: National Campaign to Prevent Teen and Unplanned Pregnancy.

Kirtley, J. (1919). *Half-hour talks on character building by self-made men and women*. New York: A. Hamming.

Kish, C., Sheehan, J., Cole K., Struyk, L., & Kinder, D. (1997). Portfolios in the classroom: A vehicle for developing reflective thinking. *The High School Journal, 80*(4), 254–260.

Kitchen, C. (2007). *Fact and fiction of healthy vision: Eye care for adults and children*. Westport, CT: Praeger.

Klaus, P. (2008). *The hard truth about soft skills: Workplace lessons smart people wish they had learned sooner*. New York: HarperCollins.

Klein, J. D., & Committee on Adolescence (2005). Adolescent pregnancy. *Pediatrics, 116*(1), 281–286.

Klinger, H. (2006). *Why are so many minority students in special education? Understanding race and disability in schools*. New York: Teachers College Press.

Knapp, L., Kelly-Reid, J., Whitmore, R., & Miller, E. (2006). *Postsecondary Institutions in the United States: Fall 2005 and Degrees and Other Awards Conferred*: 2004-05 (NCES 2007-167). United States Department of Education. Washington, DC: National Center for Education Statistics. Retrieved November 24, 2008, from http://nces.ed.gov/pubsearch

Knitzer, J. (2008). *Annual report from the director of the National Center for Children in Poverty*. New York: Columbia University National Center for Children in Poverty, Mailman School of Public Health.

Kobayashi, S. (1986). Theoretical issues concerning superiority of pictures over words and sentences in memory. *Perceptual and Motor Skills, 63*, 783–792.

Kochkin, S. (2005). *Hearing loss: Prevalence of hearing loss*. Retrieved January 21, 2008, from the Better Hearing Institute, http://www.betterhearing.org/hearing_loss/prevalence.cfm

Kogan, S. (2004, February). Disclosing unwanted sexual experiences: Results from a national sample of adolescent women. *Child Abuse & Neglect, 28*(2), 147–165.

Kohlberg, L. (1973). The contribution of developmental psychology to education—examples from moral education. *Educational Psychology, 10*, 2–14.

Kohlberg, L. (1975). The cognitive-developmental approach to moral education. *Phi Delta Kappan, 56*, 670–677.

Kohlberg, L. (1984). *The psychology of moral development*. San Francisco: Harper & Row.

Kohlberg, L. (1987). *Child psychology and childhood education: A cognitive developmental view*. London: Longman.

Kohlberg, L., & Gilligan, C. (1971). The adolescent as a philosopher: The discovery of the self in a postconventional world. *Daedalus, 100*, 1051–1086.

Kohler, P., Manhart, L., & Lafferty, W. (2008, April). Abstinence-only and comprehensive sex education and the initiation of sexual activity and teen pregnancy. *Journal of Adolescent Health, 42*(4), 344–351.

Kohn, A. (2006). *Unconditional parenting: Moving from rewards and punishment to love and reason*. New York: Simon & Schuster.

Kosciw, J., Diaz, E., & Greytak, E. (2008). *The 2007 national school climate survey: The experience of lesbian, gay, bisexual and transgender youth in our nation's schools*. New York: Gay, Lesbian, and Straight Education Network.

Kowalski, R., Limber, S., & Agatston, P. (2008). *Cyberbullying*. Malden, MA: Blackwell.

Kozminsky, E., & Kozminsky, L. (2003). Improving motivation through dialogue. *Educational Leadership, 61*(1), 50–54.

Kozulin, A., Gindis, B., Ageyev, V., Miller, S., Pea, R., Brown, J., & Heath, C. (Eds.). (2003). *Vygotsky's educational theory in cultural context*. Cambridge, MA: Cambridge University Press.

Kramer, P. (2005). *Against depression*. New York: Penguin.

Krathwohl, D. (2002). A revision of Bloom's taxonomy: An overview. *Theory Into Practice, 41*(4), 216–218.

Kraut, R., Brynin, M., & Kiesler, S. (2006). *Computers, phones, and the Internet: Domesticating information technology*. New York: Oxford University Press.

Kroger, J. (2005). *Identity in adolescence: The balance between self and others*. New York: Routledge.

Kuhn, D. (2005). *Education for thinking*. Cambridge, MA: Harvard University Press.

Kuhn, T. (1962). *The structure of scientific revolutions*. Chicago: University of Chicago Press.

Ladd, G. (2005). *Children's peer relationships and social competence: A century of progress*. New Haven, CT: Yale University Press.

Lahey, B., Moffitt, T., & Caspi, A. (Eds.). (2003). *Causes of conduct disorder and juvenile delinquency*. New York: Guilford.

Laino, C. (2008, November 11). *Study shows obese and overweight children have as much plaque buildup as 40 year-olds*. Retrieved January 8, 2009, from Web MD, http://www.webmd.com

Lamarck, J. (1830). *Philosophie zoologique*. Paris, France: G. Balliere.

Lambert, B. (2005, June 28). Long Island school official helped son cheat on test, investigators say. *The New York Times*. Retrieved March 15, 2009, from http://www.nytimes.com/2005/06/28/nyregion/28cheat.html

Lancaster, L., & Stillman, D. (2005). *When generations collide*. New York: Harper Collins.

Langton, J. (2007). *Iced: The crystal meth epidemic*. Toronto, Canada: Key Porter Books.

Larson, J. (2008, January). Angry and aggressive students. *Principal Leadership, 8*, 12–15.

Larson, J., & Lochman, J. (2005). *Helping school children cope with anger*. New York: Guilford.

Larson, R., Wilson, S., Brown, B., Furstenberg, F., & Verma, S. (2002). Changes in adolescents' interpersonal experiences: Are they being prepared for adult relationships in the 21st century? *Journal of Research on Adolescence, 12*(1), 31–68.

Larzo, M., & Poe, S. (2006, March). Adverse consequences of tattoos and body piercings. *Pediatric Annals, 35*(3), 187–192.

Lasky, B., & Karge, B. (2006, March). Meeting the needs of students with disabilities: Experience and confidence of principals. *National Association of Secondary School Principals Bulletin, 90*(1), 19–36.

Lathrop, A., & Foss, K. (2005). *Guiding students from cheating and plagiarism to honest and integrity: Strategies for change*. Englewood, CO: Libraries Unlimited.

Lattimore, R. (2005, July). African American students' perception of their preparation for a high stakes mathematics test. *The Negro Educational Review, 56*(2/3), 135–146.

Laursen, E. (2005, Fall). Rather than fixing kids—build positive peer cultures. *Reclaiming Children and Youth, 14*(3), 137–142.

Lazarus, W., Wainer, L., & Lipper, L. (2005). *Measuring digital opportunity for America's children*. Santa Monica, CA: The Children's Partnership.

Leahy, R. (2005). *The worry cure*. New York: Three Rivers Press.

LeDoux, J. (2002). *Synaptic self: How our brains become who we are*. New York: Viking Press.

Lee, S. (2006,a March/April). The learner center paradigm of instruction and training. *TechTrends, 50*(2), 21–22.

Lee, S. (2006b). *Overcoming crystal Meth addition: An essential guide to getting clean*. New York: Marlowe.

Lee, S., & Olszewski-Kubilius, P. (2005, Winter). Investigation of high school credit and placement for summer coursework taken outside of local schools. *Gifted Child Quarterly, 49*(1), 37–50

Leets, L., & Sunwolf (2005, September). Adolescent rules for social exclusion: When is it fair to exclude someone else? *Journal of Moral Education, 34*(3), 343–362.

Lehman, D., Chiu, C., & Schaller, M. (2004). Psychology and culture. *Annual Review of Psychology, 55*, 684–714.

Leland, B. (2002). *Plagiarism and the Web*. Macomb, IL: Western Illinois University. Retrieved January 4, 2009, from www.wiu.edu/users/mfbhl/wiu/plagiarism.htm

Lenhart, A., & Madden, M. (2007). *Social networking websites and teens: An overview*. Retrieved February 10, 2008, from Pew Internet and American Life Project, Washington, DC, http://www.pewinternet.org

Lenhart, A., Madden, M., & Hitlin, P. (2005, July 27). *Teens and technology: Youth are leading the transition to a fully wired and mobile nation*. Retrieved July 27, 2005, from Pew Internet and American Life Project, Washington DC, http://www.pewinternet.org

Lerner, R., & Benson, P. (2003). *Developmental assets and asset-building communities*. New York: Kluwer.

Lettenberg, H., & Saltzman, H. (2000). A statewide survey of age at first intercourse for adolescent females and age of their male partners relation to other risk behaviors and statutory rape implications, *Archives of Sexual Behavior, 29*(3), 203–215.

Leu, D., Castek, J., Hartman, D., Coiro, J., Henry, L., Kulikowich, J., & Lyver, S. (2005). *Evaluating the development of scientific knowledge and new forms of reading comprehension during online learning.* Final Report to North Central Regional Laboratory/Learning Points Associates. Retrieved April 15, 2008, from http://www.newliteracies.uconn.edu/ncrel_files/FinalNCRELReport.pdf

Levin, D., & Arafeh, S. (2002). *The digital divide: The widening gap between internet-savvy students and their schools.* Washington, DC: Pew Internet and American Life Project. Retireved from http://www.pewinternet.org

Levine, J. (2006). *Mayo Clinic obesity researchers test 'Classroom of the future'.* Retrieved March 14, 2008, from Mayo Clinic http://www.mayoclinic.org/news2006-rst/3278.html

Levine, M. (2006). *The price of privilege: How parental pressures and material advantage are creating a generation of disconnected and unhappy kids.* New York: Harper Collins.

Levine, M. (2006). *The price of privilege.* New York: Harper Collins.

Lewandowski, A. (2005, December 14). What happened to effort? *Education Week, 25*(15), 25–26.

Lewis, A. (2000, May). Listening to adolescents. *Phi Delta Kappan, 81*(9), 643–644.

Liau, A., Khoo, A., & Peng, H. (2005). Factors influencing adolescent engagement in risky Internet behavior. *CyberPsychology & Behavior, 8*(6), 513–520.

Lickona, T. (2004). *Character matters: How to help our children develop good judgment, integrity, and other essential virtues.* New York: Touchstone.

Lillard, D., & DeCicca, P. (2001). Higher standards, more dropout? Evidence within and across time. *Economics of Education Review, 20*(5), 459–473.

Lin, C., & Chuang, S. (2005, Fall). The effect of individual differences on adolescents' impulse buying behavior. *Adolescence, 40*, 581–588.

Lind, L. (1957). *Latin poetry in verse translation.* Boston: Houghton Mifflin.

Linley, P., & Joseph, S. (Eds.) (2004). *Positive psychology in practice.* Hoboken, NJ: Wiley.

Liu, M. (2005). The effect of a hypermedia learning environment on middle school students' motivation, attitudes, and science knowledge. *Computers in the Schools, 22*(3/4), 159–171.

Liungman, C. (2005). *Symbols: Encyclopedia of Western signs and ideograms.* Stockholm, Sweden: HME.

Lloyd, P. (2007). *Creative Center of the Universe.* Retrieved May 18, 2007, from http://www.Gocreate.com

Locke, E. (2002). Setting goals for life and happiness. In C. Synder & S. Lopez (Eds.), *Handbook of positive psychology* (pp. 299–312). New York: Oxford University Press.

Locke, E., & Latham, G. (2002, September). Building a practically useful theory of goalsetting and task motivation: A 35-year odyssey. *American Psychologist, 57*(9), 707–717.

Lodge, J., & Frydenberg, E. (2005, Fall). The role of peer bystanders in school bullying: Positive steps toward promoting peaceful schools. *Theory Into Practice*, 44(4), 329–336.

Love, B. (2005, August). Environment and goals jointly direct category acquisition. *Current Directions in Psychological Science*, 14(4), 195–203.

Loveless, T. (2005). Test-based accountability: The promise and the perils. *Brookings Papers on Education Policy*, 7–45.

Lozito, J., & Mulligan, N. (2006, July). Exploring the role of attention during memory retrieval: Effects of semantic encoding and divided attention. *Memory and Cognition*, 34(5), 986–998.

Lucas, C. (2006). *American higher education*. New York: Palgrave Macmillan.

Lucas, G. (2008). *Teaching communication*. Retrieved March 15, 2008, from The George Lucas Educational Foundation Edutopia http://www.edutopia.org

Ludwig, A. (1995). *The price of greatness: Resolving the creativity and madness controversy*. New York: Guilford Press.

Luterman, D. (Ed.) (2006). *Children with hearing loss*. Sedona, AZ: Auricle Ink Publishers.

Lyst, A., Gabriel, S., O'Shaughnessy, T., Meyers, J., & Meyers, B. (2005). Social validity: Perceptions of Check and Connect with early literacy support. *Journal of School Psychology*, 43(3), 197–218.

Macgill, A. (2007, October 24). *Parent and teenager Internet use*. Pew Internet and American Life Project, retrieved September 1, 2008, from http://www.PewInternet.org

Maciariello, J. (2005, Summer). Peter F. Drucker on a functioning society. *Leader to Leader*, 37, 26–34.

Maclem, G. (2008). *Practitioner's guide to emotional regulation in school-age children*. New York: Springer.

MacPhee, A., & Andrews, J. (2006, Fall). Risk factors for depression in early adolescence. *Adolescence*, 41(163), 435–466.

Madaras, L. (2007a). *What's happening to my body: Book for boys*. New York: Newmarket Press.

Madaras, L. (2007b). *Ready, set, go: What's happening to my body*. New York: Newmarket Press.

Maddi, S. (2002). The story of hardiness: Twenty years of theorizing, research, and practice. *Consulting Psychology Journal*, 54(3), 175–185.

Mahalingam, R. (2006). *Cultural psychology of immigrants*. Mahwah, NJ: Erlbaum.

Mahoney, J., Cairns, B., & Farmer, T. (2003, June). Promoting interpersonal competence and educational success through extracurricular activity participation. *Journal of Educational Psychology*, 95(2), 409–418.

Mahoney, J., Larson, R., & Eccles, J. (2005). *Organized activities as contexts of development*. Mahwah, NJ: Erlbaum.

Males, M., & Chew, K. (1996). The ages of fathers in California adolescent births. *American Journal of Public Health*, 86(4), 565–568.

Mannix, D. (2008). *Social skills for secondary students with special needs*. San Francisco: Jossey-Bass.

Mannix, E., & Neale, M. (2005, October). What difference makes a difference: The promise and reality of diverse teams in organizations. *Psychological Science in the Public Interest*, 6(31), 31–55.

Maras, P. (2007). *Social psychology and education*. New York: Psychology Press.

Marcia, J. (1989). Identity in adolescence. *Journal of Adolescence*, 12, 401–410.

Marcia, J. (1999). Representational thought in ego identity, psychotherapy and psychosocial development theory. In I. Siegel (Ed.), *Development of mental representation: Theories and applications* (pp. 391–414). Mahwah, NJ: Erlbaum.

Marcia, J., & Carpendale, J. (2004). Identity: Does thinking make it so? In C. Lightfoot, C. Lalonde, & M. Chandler (Eds.), *Changing conceptions of psychological life*. Mahwah, NJ: Erlbaum.

Margolis, H., & McCabe, P. (2006, March). Improving self-efficacy and motivation. *Intervention*, 41(4), 218–227.

Marin, B., Coyle, K., Gomez, C., Carvajal, S., & Kirby, D. (2000, December). Older boyfriends and girlfriends increase risk of sexual initiation in young adolescents. *Journal of Adolescent Health*, 27(6), 409–418.

Marmot, M., Ferrie, J., Shipley, M., Stansfeld, S., & Smith, G. (2003). Future uncertainty and socioeconomic inequalities in health: The Whitehall II studies. *Social Science and Medicine*, 57, 637–646.

Marquart, B., Nannini, D., Edwards, R., Stanley, L., & Wayman, J. (2007, Winter). Prevalence of dating violence and victimization. *Adolescence*, 42(168), 1–13.

Marquet, P. (2000). Sleep on it. *Nature Neuroscience*, 3(12), 1235–1236.

Marshall, M., Zuroff, D., McBride, C. & Bagby, M. (2008, March). Self-criticism predicts differential responses to treatment for major depression. *Journal of Clinical Psychology*, 64(3), 231–244.

Marshall, R., Bryant, R., Amsel, L., Suh, J., Cook, J., & Neria, Y. (2007, May/June). The psychology of ongoing threat: Relative risk appraisal, the September 11 attacks, and terrorism-related fears. *The American Psychologist*, 62(4), 271–286.

Martin, G., & Pear, J. (2006). *Behavior modification*. Upper Saddle River, NJ: Prentice-Hall.

Martin, S. (1996). *Picasso at the Lapin Agile*. New York: Samuel French.

Martin, S. (2005, October). Healthy kids make better students. *Monitor on Psychology*, 36(9), 24–26.

Martinez, J., & Porter, W. (2008, March). *Family and community engagement in creating positive school climates*. Presentation to the Summit on School Engagement, National Center for School Engagement, Denver, CO. Retrieved from http://www.schoolengagement.org

Maslow, A. (1968). *Toward a psychology of being*. Princeton, NJ: Van Nostrand Reinhold.

Maslow, A. (1973). *The farther reaches of human nature*. New York: Viking.

Maslow, A. (1987). *Motivation and personality*. New York: Harper Collins.

Maslow, A. (1994). *Religion, values, and peak experiences*. New York: Penguin.

Maslow, A. (1998). *Toward a psychology of being*. New York: Wiley.

Mason, G. (2007). *Spectacle of violence*. New York: Taylor & Francis.

Masten, A. (2000). *Children who overcome adversity to succeed in life*. Retrieved June 20, 2008, from University of Minnesota Extension, http://www.extension.umn.edu/distribution/familydevelopment/components/7565_06.html

Masten, A. (2001, March). Ordinary magic: Resilience processes in development. *The American Psychologist, 56*(3), 227–238.

Masten, A. (2007). Resilience in developing systems: Progress and promise as the fourth wave rises. *Developmental and Psychopathology, 19*, 921–930.

Matthews, J. (2008, March 31). New microphones are bringing crystal-clear changes. *Washington Post*, p. 1.

Maxwell, B., & Reichenbach, R. (2005, September). Imitation, imagination and re-appraisal: Educating the moral emotions. *Journal of Moral Education, 34*(3), 291–307.

Maxwell, K. (2002). Friends: The role of peers across adolescent risk behaviors. *Journal of Youth and Adolescence, 31*(40), 267–277.

Mayer, R. (2003). E. L. Thorndike's enduring contributions to educational psychology. In B. Zimmerman & D. Shunk (Eds.), *Educational Psychology: A century of contributions* (pp. 113–154). Mahwah, NJ: Erlbaum.

Mayo Clinic (2007). *Exercise: 7 benefits of regular physical activity*. Retrieved January 4, 2009, from Mayo Clinic, http://www.mayoclinic.com/health/exercise/HQ01676

Mayr, U., Awh, E., Keele, S., & Posner, M. (2005). *Developing individuality in the human brain*. Washington, DC: American Psychological Association.

McArdle, J. (2007, September). John Horne. *American Psychologist, 62*(6), 596–597.

McCabe, D., & Pavela, G. (2004). Ten [updated] principles of academic integrity. *Change, 36*(3), 10–15.

McCabe, E. (1985, August 1). Creativity. *Vital Speeches of the Day, 51*(2), 628–632.

McCann, M. (2003). *A study of visual intelligence and the influence of a visual enrichment program on measures of IQ and creativity on students nominated as gifted*. Adelaide, South Australia: Unpublished PhD Dissertation at the University of Adelaide.

McClelland, D. (1976). *The achieving society*. New York: Irvington.

McClelland, D. (1987). *Human motivation*. New York: Cambridge University Press.

McClelland, D. (Ed.). (1992). *The development of social maturity*. New York: Irvington.

McCotter, M., Gosselin, F., Sowden, P., & Schyns, P. (2005). The use of visual information in natural scenes. *Visual Cognition, 12*(6), 938–953.

McDougall, W. (1916). *An introduction to social psychology*. London: Methuen.

McGrath, M. (2006). *School bullying: Tools for avoiding harm and liability*. Thousand Oaks, CA: SAGE.

McGue, M., Elkins, I., Walden, B., & Iacono, W. (2005). Perceptions of the parent-child adolescent relationship: A longitudinal investigation. *Developmental Psychology, 41*(6), 971–984.

McGuffey, W. (1989). *McGuffey's Eclectic Readers*. New York: Wiley.

McGuire, S., Klein, D., & Couper, D. (2005). Aging education: A national imperative. *Educational Gerontology, 31*(6), 441–460.

McInerney, D., & Van Etten, S. (Eds.) (2005). *Focus on curriculum: Research on sociocultural influences on motivation and learning*. Charlotte, NC: Information Age.

McKenney, S. (2005, Winter). Technology for curriculum and teacher development. *Journal of Research on Technology in Education*, *38*(2), 167–190.

McKim, R. H. (1980). *Thinking visually: A strategy for problems solving*. Los Angeles: Dale Seymour.

McLuhan, M. (1964). *Understanding media: The extensions of man*. New York: Signet.

McLuhan, M., & Flore, Q., (2005). *The medium is the massage*. Berkeley, CA: Ginko Press.

McNeill, D. (2001). Who killed Yo Hirano? *Tokyo Journal*, *20*(237), 12–16.

Mead, M. (1928). *Coming of age in Samoa: A psychological study of primitive youth for Western civilization*. New York: HarperCollins.

Mead, M. (1930). *Growing up in New Guinea*. New York: William Morrow.

Mead, M. (1978). *Culture and commitment*. New York: Columbia University Press.

Mead, M. (2001). *Coming of age in Samoa: A psychological study of primitive youth for Western civilization*. New York: Harper Collins.

Medina, J. (2008). *Brain rules*. Seattle, WA: Pear Press.

Menard, S. (2002). *Longitudinal research*. Thousand Oaks, CA: SAGE.

Menzies, H. (2005). *Stress and the crisis of modern life*. Vancouver, Canada: Douglas & McIntyre.

Merry, M. (2005). Indoctrination, moral instruction, and nonrational beliefs: A place for autonomy? *Educational Theory*, *55*(4), 399–420.

Merton, R. (1948, Summer). The self-fulfilling prophecy. *Antioch Review*, 193–210.

Messmer, N. (2006, January). Developing powerful student researchers. *Learning and Leading with Technology*, *33*(4), 23–24.

Mettles, S. (2005). *Soldiers to citizens: The G.I. bill and the making of the greatest generation*. New York: Oxford University Press.

Meyer, P. (2008). Learning separately: The case for single sex schools. *Education Next*, *8*(1), 1–7.

Michelozzi, B., Surrell, L., & Cobez, R. (2004). *Coming alive from nine to five in a 24/7 world: A career search handbook for the 21st century*. New York: McGraw-Hill.

Mill, John Stuart (2000). *Autobiography* [1832]. Chestnut Hill, MA: Adamant Media Corp.

Millar, G. (2001). *The Torrance kids at mid-life*. Westport, CT: Greenwood.

Millar, R., & Shevlin, M. (2003, February). Predicting career information-seeking behavior of school pupils using the theory of planned behavior. *Journal of Vocational Behavior*, *62*(1), 26–42.

Miller, G. A. (1956). The magical number seven, plus or minus two: Some limits on our capacity for processing information. *Psychological Review*, *63*, 81–97.

Miller, S., Adsit, K., & Miller, T. (2005, November/December). Evaluating the importance of common components in school-based Web sites. *TechTrends*, *49*(6), 34–41.

Miller, S., & Borowicz, S. (2006). *Why multimodal literacies: Designing bridges to 21st century teaching and learning*. Buffalo, NY: State University of New York Press.

Millis, B. (2005). *Cooperative learning structures*. University of Texas at Austin, Division of Instructional Innovation and Assessment. Retrieved January 6, 2007, from http://www.utexas.edu/academic/diia/research/projects/hewlett/cooperative

Milsom, A., & Gallo, L. (2006, January). Bullying in middle schools: Prevention and intervention. *Middle School Journal, 37*(3), 12–19.

Minuchin, P., Colapinto, J., & Minuchin, S. (2007). *Working with families of the poor* (2nd ed). New York: Guilford.

Mischel, W. (1974). Processes in delay of gratification. In L. Berkowitz (Ed.), *Advances in experimental social psychology* (Vol. 7, pp. 249–292). San Diego: Academic Press.

Mischel, W., Schoda, Y., & Ayduk, O. (2007). *Introduction to personality*. New York: Wiley.

Mischel, W., Schoda, Y., & Peake, P. (1988). The nature of adolescent competencies predicted by preschool delay of gratification. *Journal of Personality and Social Psychology, 34*, 387–696.

Mishna, F., Scarcello, I., & Pepler, D. (2005). Teachers' understanding of bullying. *Canadian Journal of Education, 28*(4), 718–738.

Mitchell, T., Church, T., & Zucker, M. (2008). *Move yourself: The Cooper Clinic medical director's guide to all the healing benefits of exercise*. New York: Wiley.

Mitra, D. (2004, April). The significance of students: Can increasing 'student voice' in schools lead to gains in youth development? *Teachers College Record, 106*(4), 651–688.

Mitra, S. (2003). Minimally invasive education: A progress report on the "Hole-in-the wall" experiments. *British Journal of Educational Technology, 34*(3), 367–371.

Mitra, S. (2005). Self-organizing systems for mass computer literacy. *International Journal of Development Issues, 4*(1), 71–81.

Mitra, S. (2006). *The hole in the wall: Self-organizing systems in education*. New Delhi: Tata-McGraw-Hill.

Moffitt, T., Caspi, A., Rutter, M., & Silva, P. (2008). *Sex differences in antisocial behavior*. New York: Cambridge University Press.

Mohr, D., Townsend, J., & Pritchard, T. (2006, Winter). Rethinking middle school physical education. *The Physical Educator, 63*(1), 18–29.

Monroe, B. (2004). *Crossing the digital divide*. New York: Teachers College Press.

Montgomery, D., & Parks, D. (2007). Counseling the adolescent about tattoos. *Journal of Pediatric Health Care, 15*(1), 14–19.

Montgomery, K., & Wiley, D. (2008). *Building E-Portfolios using PowerPoint: A guide for educators*. Thousand Oaks, CA: SAGE.

Moore, M. (2002). *Bowling for Columbine*. Film released by United Artists, Alliance Artists and Dog eat Dog Films.

Moore, R., & Robillard, A. (2008). *Pluralizing plagiarism: Identities, context, and pedagogies*. Portsmouth, NH: Boynton/Cook.

Moore, S., & Rosenthal, D. (2006). *Sexuality in adolescence*. New York: Psychology Press.

Morrisey, K., & Werner-Wilson, R. (2005, Spring). Relationship between out-of-school activities and positive youth development. *Adolescence, 40*(157), 67–86.

Morrison, H. (1926). *The practice of teaching in the secondary school*. Chicago: University of Chicago Press.

Morrison, J., & Anders, T. (2001). *Interviewing children and adolescents*. New York: Guilford Press.

Morrissey, K., & Werner-Wilson, R. (2005, Spring). Relationship between out-of-school activities and positive youth development. *Adolescence, 40*(157), 67–86.

Morrow, J. (2005, December). Are American children and youth fit? It's time we learned. *Research Quarterly for Exercise & Sport, 76*(4), 377–388.

Morse, A., Anderson, A., & Christenson, S. (2004, February). Promoting school completion. *Principal Leadership, 4*(6), 9–13.

Moscicki, A. (2005, December). Impact of HPV infection in adolescent populations. *Journal of Adolescent Health, 37*(6) (Supplement), 3–9.

Moses, M., & Chang, M. (2006, January/February). Toward a deeper understanding of the diversity rationale. *Educational Researcher, 35*(1), 6–11.

Munger, M. (2003). *The history of psychology.* New York: Oxford University Press.

Mupinga, D. (2005, January/February). Distance education in high schools: Benefits, challenges, and suggestions. *The Clearing House, 78*(3), 105–108.

Murphy, G. (1949). *Historical introduction to modern psychology.* New York: Harcourt, Brace & World.

Murray, A. (2006). *Paradigm found: Leading and managing for positive change.* Novato, CA: New World Library.

National Association of Anorexia, Nervosa and Associated Disorders. (2007). *Eating disorder information and resources.* Retrieved January 2, 2009, from the Association http://www.anad.org

National Association of School Psychologists. (2003). *Position statement on student grade retention and social promotion.* Retrieved July 1, 2008, from http://www.nasponline.org

National Campaign to Prevent Teen and Unplanned Pregnancy. (2003, June). *Where and when teens first have sex.* Retrieved July 20, 2007, from National Campaign to Prevent Teen Pregnancy, Washington, DC, http://www.thenationalcampaign.org

National Campaign to Prevent Teen and Unplanned Pregnancy (2006a, May 3). *One third of sexually experienced teen girls have been pregnant.* Retrieved July 20, 2007, from National Campaign to Prevent Teen Pregnancy, Washington, DC, http://www.thenationalcampaign.org

National Campaign to Prevent Teen and Unplanned Pregnancy (2006b, May). *Parent-child communication about sex and related topics.* Retrieved July 20, 2007, from The National Campaign to Prevent Teen Pregnancy, Washington, DC, http://www.thenationalcampaign.org

National Campaign to Prevent Teen and Unplanned Pregnancy (2008, January). *Latino initiatives.* Retrieved April 15, 2008, from http://www.thenationalcampign.org

National Center for Health Statistics (2006). *Prevalence of overweight among children and adolescents: United States, 2003–2004.* Hyattsville, MD: U.S. Department of Health and Human Services.

National Defense Education Act of 1959, Pub. L. 85-864. US Stat at Large, 72, pp. 1580–1605 (1958).

National Center for Missing & Exploited Children (2008). *What is online enticement of children for sexual acts.* Retrieved June 1, 2008, from http://www.ncmec.org

National Center of Addiction and Substance Abuse (2006). *Annual Report*. New York Columbus University. Retrieved April 15, 2008, from http://www.casacolumbia.org/

National Education Association (1895). Proceedings of the National Council of Education, 1894. St. Paul, MN: Pioneer Press.

National Governors Association Task Force on State High School Graduation Data (2005). *Graduation counts redesigning the American High School*. Washington, DC: National Governors Association.

National Institute for Out-of-School Time (2005). *Links to learning: A curriculum for after school programs*. Wellesley MA: Wellesley College.

National Research Council (2004). *Engaging schools: Fostering high school students' motivation to learn*. Washington, DC: National Academics Press.

National Sleep Foundation (2006a). *2006 Sleep in America poll*. Washington, DC: The Foundation.

National Sleep Foundation (2006b). *Adolescent sleep needs and patterns: Research report and resource guide*. Washington, DC: The Foundation.

Nay, R. (2003). *Taking charge of anger: How to resolve conflict, sustain relationships, and express yourself without losing control*. New York: Guilford Press.

Negroponte, N. (2007). *One laptop per child*. Cambridge, MA: Massachusetts Institute of Technology. Retrieved July 12, 2008, from http://www.laptop.org

Newberg, A. (2000). *Why God won't go away*. New York: Ballantine Books.

Newberg, A., & Waldman, M. (2006). *Why we believe what we believe: Uncovering our biological need for meaning, spirituality, and truth*. New York: Free Press.

Newman, B., Lohman, B., & Newman, P. (2007, Summer). Peer group membership and a sense of belonging: Their relationship to adolescent behavior problems. *Adolescence, 42*(166), 1–23.

Nichols, S. & Berliner, D. (2007). *Collateral Damage: How high stakes testing corrupts American schools*. Cambridge, MA: Harvard University Press.

Nistler, C., Hodgson, H., Nobrega, F., Hodgson, J., Wheatley, R. & Solberg, G. (2006, September). Marijuana and adolescents. *Minnesota Medicine, 89*, 1–7.

No Child Left Behind Act of 2001, Pub. L. No. 107-110. 115 Stat. 1425 (2002).

North American Council for Online Learning (2006, November). *Virtual schools and 21st century skills*. The Council: Vienna, Virginia.

Nucci, L. (2008). *Handbook of moral and character education*. New York: Routledge.

O'Bannon, B., & Judge, S. (2005, Winter). Implementing partnerships across the curriculum with technology. *Journal of Research on Technology in Education, 37*(2), 197–216.

O'Donnell, L, Stueve, A., Simmons, R., Dash, K., Agronick, G., & JeanBaptiste, V. (2006, February). Heterosexual risk behavior among urban young adolescents. *The Journal of Early Adolescence, 26*, 87–109.

O'Toole, J., & Lawler, E. (2006). *The new American workplace*. New York: Palgrave Macmillan.

Ogden, C., Carroll, M., Curtin, L., McDowell, M., Tabak, C., & Flegal, K. (2006). Prevalence of overweight and obesity in the United States, 1999–2004. *Journal of American Medical Association, 295*, 1549–1555.

Ogden, C., Carroll, M., & Flegal, K. (2008). High body mass index for age among US children and adolescents, 2003–2006. *Journal of American Medical Association, 299*(20), 2401–2405.

Okojie, M., & Olinzock, A. (2006). Developing a positive mindset toward the use of technology for classroom instruction. *International Journal of Instructional Media, 33*(1), 33–41.

Oracle Education Foundation (2006). *Students from 11 countries win ThinkQuest competition.* Retrived from http://www.oracle.com/corporate/press/2005_jun/oeftq_win05.html

Orey, M., McClendon, V., & Branch, R. (Eds.) (2006). *Educational media and technology yearbook* (Vol. 31). Englewood, CO: Libraries Unlimited.

Orpinas, P., & Horne, A. (2006). *Bullying prevention: Creating a positive school climate and developing social competence.* Washington, DC: American Psychological Association.

Osborne, A., & Russo, C. (2007). *Special education and the law.* Thousand Oaks, CA: Corwin Press.

Osgood, R. (2007). *The history of special education.* Westport, CT: Praeger.

Otto, L. (2001). Youth perspectives on parental career choice. *Journal of Career Development, 27*(2), 111–118.

Owens, F. (2007). *No speed limit: The highs and lows of meth.* New York: St. Martin's Press.

Paivio, A. (1971). *Imagery and verbal process.* New York: Holt Rinehart & Winston.

Paivio, A. (1990). *Mental representations: A dual coding approach* (2nd ed.). New York: Oxford University Press.

Paivio, A. (1991). Dual coding theory: Retrospect and current status. *Canadian Journal of Psychology, 45,* 255–287.

Paivio, A. (2006). *Mind and its evolution: A dual coding theoretical interpretation.* Mahwah, NJ: Erbaum.

Parker, A., Wilding, E., & Bussey, T. (Eds.) (2002). *The cognitive neuroscience of memory: Encoding and retrieval.* New York: Psychology Press.

Parker, J., & Benson, M. (2004, Fall). Parent-adolescent relations and adolescent functioning: Self-esteem, substance abuse and delinquency. *Adolescence, 39,* 519–530.

Parks, M. (2007). *Personal relationships and personal networks.* Mahwah, NJ: Erlbaum.

Partnership for Drug-Free America (2006). *The Partnership attitude tracking study (PATS): Teens in grades 7 through 12 2005.* Retrieved October 1, 2007, from http://www.drugfreeamerica.org/

Patrick, S. (2008, September 26). Online teaching and learning. *Education Week,* 1–4.

Patrikakou, E., Weissberg, R., Redding, S., & Walberg, H. (2005). *School-family partnerships for children's success.* New York: Teachers College Press.

Paul, J., & Freshman, B. (2006). *Oral sex.* Bothell, WA: Book Publishers Network.

Paulson, A. (2003, December 30). Internet bullying. Boston: *Christian Science Monitor.* Retrieved November 1, 2008, from www.csmonitor.com/2003/1230/p11s01-legn.html

Paxson, C., Donahue, E., Orleans, C., & Grisso, J. (2006). *Childhood overweight and obesity.* Princeton: The Future of Children.

Pedersen, S., & Williams, D. (2004). A comparison of assessment practices and their effects on learning and motivation in a student-centered learning environment. *Journal of Multimedia and Hypermedia, 13*(3), 283–306.

Penrose, R. (2002). *The Emperor's new mind. Concerning computers, minds and the laws of physics.* Oxford, England: Oxford University Press.

Peter, J., Valkenburg, P., & Schouten, A. (2005, October). Developing a model of adolescent friendship formation on the Internet. *CyberPsychology and Behavior, 8*(5), 423–430.

Peterson, C. (2006). *A primer in positive psychology.* New York: Oxford University Press.

Peterson, C., & Seligman, M. (2004). *Character strengths and virtues: A handbook and classification.* New York: Oxford University Press and the American Psychological Association.

Peterson, J., & Ray, K. (2006, Spring). Bullying and the gifted: Victims, perpetrators, prevalence, and effects. *Gifted Child Quarterly, 50*(2), 148–168.

Peterson, N. (2005, Spring). Early 20th century photography of Australian Aboriginal families: Illustrations or evidence. *Visual Anthropology Review, 21*(1 & 2), 11–26.

Pfiefer, K., & Middleman, A. (2006). *American Medical Association Boy's guide to becoming a teen.* San Francisco: Jossey-Bass.

Phye, G., Robinson, D., & Levin, J. (Eds.) (2005). *Empirical methods for evaluating educational interventions.* San Diego: Academic Press.

Piaget, J. (1954). *The construction of reality in the child.* New York: Basic Books.

Piaget, J. (1963). *Origins of intelligence in children.* New York: Norton.

Piaget, J. (1969). *Psychology of intelligence.* New York: Littlefield, Adams.

Piaget, J. (1970). Piaget's theory. In P. Mussen (Ed.), *Carmichael's manual of child psychology* (Vol. 1, pp. 702–732). New York: Wiley.

Pickering, S. (Ed.) (2005). *Working memory and education.* San Diego: Elsevier.

Pink, D. (2008). *A whole new mind: Why right-brainers will rule the future.* New York: Riverside Books.

Pinquart, M., & Silbereisen, R. (2004 Spring). Transmission of values from adolescents to their parents. *Adolescence, 39*(153), 83–100.

Pipher, M. (2005). *Reviving Ophelia: Saving the selves of adolescent girls.* New York: Penguin.

Pippert, W. (2007, November). A career in social psychology: An address by Morton Deutsch. *Psychological Science, 20*(10), 11–12.

Poftak, A. (2005, September). Reform school. *Technology and Learning, 26*(2), 9.

Ponterotto, J., Utsey, S., & Pedersen, P. (2006). *Preventing prejudice: A guide for counselors, educators and parents.* Thousand Oaks: SAGE.

Popham, J. (2007). *America's failing schools: How parents and teachers can cope with No Child Left Behind.* New York: Taylor & Francis.

Posner, M. I. (Ed.) (2004). *Cognitive neuroscience of attention.* New York: Guilford.

Powell, L, Calvin, J., & Calvin, J. (2007). Effective obesity treatments. *American Psychologist, 62*(3), 234–246.

Power, F., Nuzzi, R., Narvaez, D., Lapsley, D., & Hunt, T. (Eds.). (2007). *Moral education.* Westport, CT: Praeger.

Powers, C., Higgins, A., & Kohlberg, L. (1991). *Lawrence Kohlberg's approach to moral education*. New York: Columbia University Press.

Prensky, M. (2008, March). Turning on the lights. *Educational Leadership, 65*(6), 40–45.

Prensky, M. (December 2005/January 2006). Listen to the natives. *Educational Leadership, 63*(4), 8–13.

Prinstein, M., & Dodge, K. (Eds.). (2008). *Understanding peer influence in children and adolescents*. New York: Guilford.

Prinstein, M., Meade, C., & Cohen, G. (2003). Adolescent oral sex, peer popularity, and perceptions of best friends' sexual behavior. *Journal of Pediatric Psychology, 28*(4), 243–249.

Privateer, P. (2006). *Inventing intelligence*. London: Blackwell.

Provenzo, E. (2005). *The Internet and online research for teachers* (3rd ed.). Boston: Allyn & Bacon.

Public Agenda (2004). *Teaching interrupted: Do discipline policies in today's public schools foster the common good?* Retrieved December 3, 2004, from http://www.publicagenda.org

Pulliam, J., & Van Patten, J. (2006). *History of education in America* (8th ed.). Upper Saddle River, NJ: Prentice Hall.

Putnam, R. (2000). *Bowling alone: The collape and revival of American community*. New York: Simon & Schuster.

Putnam, R. (2004). *Democracies in flux: The evolution of social capital in contemporary society*. New York: Oxford University Press.

Putnam, R., & Feldstein, L. (2003). *Better together: Restoring the American community*. New York: Simon & Schuster.

Rachlin, H. (2004). *The science of self-control*. Cambridge, MA: Harvard University Press.

Rachman, S. (2004). *Anxiety*. Andover, NH: Psychology Press.

Rader, L. (2005, January/February). Goal setting for students and teachers: Six steps to success. *The Clearing House, 78*(3), 123–126.

Radvansky, G. (2005). *Human memory*. Boston: Allyn & Bacon.

Raths, L., Harmin, M., & Simon, S. (1966). *Values and teaching*. Columbus, OH: Charles E. Merrill.

Rathus, S., Nevid, J., & Fichner-Rathus, L. (2005). *Human sexuality in a world of diversity*. Boston: Allyn & Bacon.

Ratner, C. (2006). *Cultural psychology*. Mahwah, NJ: Erlbaum.

Raymond, A., & Raymond, S. (2008). *Hard Times at Douglass High: A No Child Left Behind Report Card*. Home Box Office Documentary Films, DVD.

Redd, N. (2007). *Body drama: Real girls, real bodies, real issues, real answers*. New York: Gotham.

Reeb, R. (2006). *Community action research: Benefits to community members and service providers*. New York: Routledge.

Reese, W. (2007). *History, education, and the schools*. New York: Palgrave.

Reeve, J. (2006). Extrinsic rewards and inner motivation. In C. Evertson & C. Weinstein (Eds.), *Handbook of classroom management*. Mahwah, NJ: Erlbaum.

Reiser, B. (2004). Scaffolding complex learning: The mechanisms of structuring and problematicing student work. *The Journal of the Learning Sciences, 13,* 273–304.

Republic of China Ministry of Education (2001). *Creativity education: White paper.* Taipei, Taiwan: Republic of China Ministry of Education.

Reschly, A., & Christenson, S. (2006). School completion. In G. G. Bear & K. M. Minkle (Eds.), *Children's needs: Development, prevention, and intervention* (pp. 103–112). Bethesda, MD: National Association of School Psychologists.

Rescoria, L., & Rosenthal, A. (2004, March). Growth in standardized ability and achievement test scores from 3rd to 10th grade. *Journal of Educational Psychology, 96*(1), 85–96.

Revenaugh, M. (December 2005/January 2006). K–8 virtual schools: A glimpse into the future. *Educational Leadership, 63*(4), 60–64.

Reyna, V., & Farley, F. (2006). Risk and rationality in adolescent decision making: Implications for theory, practice and public policy. *Psychological Science in the Public Interest, 7*(1), 1–50.

Rhodes, J. (2005). A model of youth mentoring. In D. Dubois & M. Karcher (Eds), *Handbook of youth mentoring.* Thousand Oaks, CA: SAGE.

Richardson, J., & Newby, T. (2006). The role of students' cognitive engagement in online learning. *American Journal of Distance Education, 20*(1), 23-37.

Rickover, H. (1959). *Education and freedom.* New York: E. P. Dutton, p. 16.

Rimm, S. (2005). *Growing up too fast.* Emmaus, PA: Rodale.

Ripkin, C., & Woolf, R. (2006). *Parenting young athletes: The Ripkin way.* New York: Penguin.

Rizzo, M., & Brown, J. (2006). *Building character through community service.* Lanham, MD: Rowman & Littlefield.

Roberts, D., Foehr, U., & Rideout, V. (2005, March). *Generation M: Media in the lives of 8–18 year-olds.* Menlo Park, CA: Kaiser Family Foundation. Retrieved April 19, 2008 from http://www.kff.org

Rock, M. (2004, September). Graphic organizers: Tools to build literacy and foster emotional competency. *Intervention, 40*(1), 11–37.

Rodgers, D., & Withrow-Thorton, B. (2005). The effect of instructional media on learner motivation. *International Journal of Instructional Media, 32*(4), 333–342.

Rogers, C. (1961). *On becoming a person.* Boston: Houghton Mifflin.

Roid, G. (2003). *Stanford-Binet Intelligence Scales* (5th ed.). Itasca, IL: Riverside.

Romanowski, M. (2006, January/February). Revisiting the common myths about homeschooling. *The Clearing House, 79*(3), 125–129.

Rose, H. (2006, Winter). Asset-based development for child and youth care. *Reclaiming Children and Youth, 14*(4), 236–240.

Rose, R., & Bloymeyer, R. (2007, November). *Access and equity in online classes and virtual schools.* Washington, DC: North American Council for online learning. Retrieved April 15, 2008, from http://www.nacol.org

Rosen, L. (2007). *Me, MySpace, and I: Parenting the Net generation.* New York: Palgrave Macmillan.

Rosenthal, R. (1963). On the social psychology of the social psychological experiment. *American Scientist, 21,* 268–283.

Rosenthal, R. (2002). Covert communication in classrooms, clinics, courtrooms, and cubicles. *American Psychologist, 57*(11), 839–849.

Rosenthal, R., & Jacobson, L. (1968). *Pygmalion in the classroom: Teacher expectations and pupils' intellectual development.* New York: Holt, Rinehart & Winston.

Roseth, C., Johnson, D., & Johnson, R. (2008, March). Promoting early adolescents' advancement and peer relationships: The effects of cooperative, competitive, and individualistic goal structures. *Psychological Bulletin, 134*(2), 223–246.

Rossman, J. (1964). *Industrial creativity: The psychology of the inventor.* New Hyde Park, NY: University Books.

Rotberg, I. (Ed.) (2004). *Change and tradition in global education reform.* Lanham, MD: Rowman & Littlefield.

Rowling, J. (1999). *Harry Potter and the chamber of secrets.* New York: Arthur A. Levine Books.

Rubin, H., & Rubin, I. (2005). *Qualitative interviewing.* Thousand Oaks, CA: SAGE.

Rubin, K. (Ed.) (2006). *Parenting beliefs, behaviors and parent-child relations: A cross-cultural perspective.* New York: Psychology Press.

Rubin, M. (2006). *Droidmaker: George Lucas and the digital revolution.* Gainesville, FL: Triad.

Rubinstein-Avila, E. (2006). Connecting with Latino learners. *Educational Leadership, 63*(5), 38–43.

Rudman, L., & Glick, P. (2008). *The social psychogy of gender.* New York: Guilford.

Rumberger, R., & Palardy, G. (2005). Test scores, dropout rates, and transfer rates as alternative indicators of high school performance. *American Educational Research Journal, 42*(1), 3–42.

Runco, M. (2006). *Creativity: Theories and themes: Research, development and practice.* San Diego, CA: Academic Press.

Russell, J. (2007). *How children become moral selves: Building character and promoting citizenship in children.* Portland, OR: Sussex Academic Press.

Russo, C. (2004, Summer). A comparative study of creativity and cognitive problem solving strategies of high-IQ and average students. *Gifted Child Quarterly, 48*(3), 179–190.

Rutter, L. (1980). *Changing youth in a changing society.* Cambridge, MA: Harvard University Press

Rutter, L., Graham, P., & Chadwick, F. (1976). Adolescent turmoil: Fact or fiction. *Journal of Child Psychology and Psychiatry, 14*, 35–56.

Rutter, P., & Behrendt, A. (2004, Summer). Adolescent suicide risk: Four psychological factors. *Adolescence, 39*, 295–302.

Sadler, P., & Good, E. (2006). The impact of self and peer-grading on student learning. *Educational Assessment, 11*(1), 1–31.

Sadoski, M., & Paivio, A. (2001). *Imagery and text: A dual coding theory of reading and writing.* Mahwah, NJ: Erlbaum.

Salend, S. (2005). *Creating inclusive classrooms: Effective and reflective practices for all students.* Columbus, OH: Merrill.

Salend, S., & Duhaney, L. (2005, March). Understanding and addressing the disproportionate representation of students of color in special education. *Intervention, 40*(4), 213–220

Salmivalli, C., Kaukiainen, A., & Voeten, M. (2005, September). Anti-bullying intervention: Implementation and outcome. *The British Journal of Educational Psychology, 75*(3), 465–487.

Sampson, R. (2008). Moving to inequality: Neighborhood effects and experiments meet social structure. *American Journal of Sociology, 114,* 189–231.

Sampson, W. (2007). *Race, class, and family intervention: Engaging parents and families for academic success.* Lanham, MD: Rowman & Littlefield.

Santelli, J., Ott, M., Lyon, M., Rogers, J., Summers, D., & Schleifer, R. (2006). Abstinence and abstinence-only education: A review of U.S. policies and programs. *Journal of Adolescent Health, 38*(1), 72–81.

Santo, S. (2005, November/December). Knowledge management: An imperative for schools of education. *Tech Trends: Linking Research and Practice to Improve Learning, 49*(6), 42–49.

Saper, C., Scammell, T., & Lu, J. (2005, October 27). Hypothalamic regulation of sleep and circadian rhythms. *Nature, 437,* 1257–1263.

Sapolsky, R. (2004). *Why zebras don't get ulcers.* New York: Henry Holt & Company.

Saunders, C., & Macnaughton, J. (2005). *Madness and creativity in literature and culture.* New York: Palgrave Macmillan.

Savage, J. (2007). *Teenage: The creation of youth culture.* New York: Penguin.

Sax, L. (2005). *Why gender matters: What parents and teachers need to know about the emerging science of sex differences.* New York: Doubleday.

Schaie, K., & Uhlenberg, P. (2007). *Social structure: Demographic change and well-being of older persons.* New York: Springer.

Schroeder, B., & Wiatt, C. (2005). *The diet for teenagers only.* New York: Harper Collins.

Schultz, E. (2004). *Cultural anthropology.* New York: Oxford University Press.

Schultz, K. (2003). *Listening: A framework for teaching across differences.* New York: Teachers College Press.

Schulz, L., Bennett, P., Ravussin, E., Kidd, J., Kidd, K., Esparza, J., & Valencia, M. (2006). Effects of traditional and western environments on prevalence of type 2 diabetes in Pima Indians in Mexico and the U.S. *Diabetes Care, 29,* 1866–1871.

Schumacher, P., & Queen, J. (2007). *Overcoming obesity in childhood and adolescence: A guide for school leaders.* Thousand Oaks, CA: Corwin Press.

Schunk, D. (2007). *Learning theories: An educational perspective.* Upper Saddle River, NJ: Prentice-Hall.

Schwartz-Shea, P., & Yanow, P. (2006). *Interpretation and method: Empirical research and the interpretative turn.* Armonk, NY: M. E. Sharpe.

Schwartz, B. (2004). *The paradox of choice: Why more is less.* New York: HarperCollins.

Search Institute (2006). *The 40 developmental assets for adolescents ages 12–18.* Minneapolis, MN: The Institute.

Segrin, C., & Flora, J. (2005). *Family communication.* Mahwah, NJ: Erlbaum.

Seidensticker, B. (2006). *Future hype: The myths of technology.* San Francisco: Barrett-Koehler.

Seiffge-Krenke, L. (2006, September). Leaving home or still in the nest: Parent child relationships and psychological health as predictors of different leaving home patterns. *Developmental Psychology, 42*(5), 864–876.

Seligman, M. (2004). *Authentic happiness: Using the new positive psychology to realize your potential for lasting fulfillment.* New York: The Free Press.

Seligman, M. (2006). *Learned optimism: How to change your mind and your life.* New York: Vintage.

Seligman, M. (2007). *The optimistic child.* Boston: Houghton Mifflin.

Selye, H. (1956). *The stress of life.* New York: McGraw-Hill.

Senge, P., Scharmer, C., Jaworski, J., & Flowers, B. (2005). *Presence: An exploration of profound change in people, organizations, and society.* New York: Doubleday.

Shannon, J. (2006). *Adolescent health sourcebook.* Amsterdam: Elsevier.

Sharez-Orozco, M. (2005, November). Rethinking education in the global era. *Phi Delta Kappan, 87*(3), 209–212.

Shearer, C. (2004). Using a multiple intelligence assessment to promote teacher development and student achievement. *Teachers College Record, 106*, 147–162.

Shek, D. (2007, January). A longitudinal study of perceived parental psychological control and psychological well being in Chinese adolescents in Hong Kong. *Journal of Clinical Psychology, 63*(1), 1–22.

Sheldon, K., & King, L. (2001, March). Why positive psychology is necessary. *The American Psychologist, 56*(3), 216–217.

Shepard, R. (1967). Recognition memory for words, sentences, and pictures. *Journal of Verbal Learning and Verbal Behavior, 6*, 156–163.

Shepard, R. (1990). *Mind sights.* New York: Freeman.

Sherif, M. (1958). Superordinate goals in the reduction of intergroup conflict. *American Journal of Sociology, 63*(4), 349–356.

Sherif, M. (1966). *In common predicament: Social psychology of intergroup conflict and cooperation.* Boston: Houghton Mifflin.

Shernoff, D., Csikszentmihalyi, M., Schneider, B., & Shernoff, E. (2003). Student engagement in high school classrooms from the perspective of flow theory. *School Psychology Quarterly, 18*(2), 158–176.

Shirma, M. (2005, June 30). Anabolic steroids and other performance enhancing drugs. *Journal of Alcohol and Drug Education, 49*(2), 89–90.

Siegel, D. (2006a, April). Exercise training in obese children and adolescents. *Journal of Physical Education, Recreation and Dance, 77*(4), 12.

Siegel, D. (2006b, January). The effects of physical activity on the health and well being of youths. *Journal of Physical Education, Recreation and Dance, 77*(1), 11.

Simon, S. (1978). *Values clarification.* New York: Hart.

Simpson, A. (2001). *Raising teens: A synthesis of research and a foundation for action.* Boston: Center for Health Communication, Harvard School of Public Health.

Simpson, R., LaCava, P., & Graner, P. (2004, November). The No Child Left Behind Act: Challenges and implications for educators. *Intervention, 40*(2), 67–75.

Sizer, T. (2004). *Horace's compromise: The dilemma of the American high school.* Boston: Mariner Books.

Skinner, B. F. (1948). *Walden two.* New York: Macmillan.

Skinner, B. F. (1965). *Science and human behavior.* New York: Free Press.

Skinner, B. F. (1971). *Beyond freedom and dignity*. New York: Bantam.

Skinner, B. F. (1976). *About behaviorism*. New York: Vintage.

Skinner, B. F. (1980, November 3). Reward or punishment: Which works better? *U.S. News & World Report*, 79–80.

Skinner, B. F. (1985). *The shaping of a behaviorist: An autobiography*. New York: New York University Press.

Smagorinsky, P., & Taxel, J. (2005). *The discourse of character education: Culture wars in the classroom*. Mahwah, NJ: Erlbaum.

Smith, B., Roderick, M., & Degener, S. (2005, April). Extended learning time and student accountability. *Educational Administration Quarterly, 41*(2), 195–236.

Smith, D. (2008). *Divide or conquer: How great teams turn conflict into strength*. Virginia Beach, VA: Portfolio.

Smith, K., Moriarty, S., Barbatsis, G., & Kenney, K. (Eds.) (2005). *Handbook of visual communication: Theory, methods, and media*. Mahwah, NJ: Erlbaum.

Smith, R. (2005). *Culture and the arts in education*. New York: Teachers College Press.

Snarey, J. (1985). Cross-cultural universality of social-moral development: A critical review of Kohlbergian research. *Psychological Bulletin, 97*(2), 202–232.

Snyder, C., & Lope, S. (Eds.). (2007). *Positive psychology: The scientific and practical exploration of human strengths*. Thousand Oaks, CA: SAGE.

Snyder, C. R. (2000). *Handbook of hope: Theory, measures, and applications*. San Diego: Academic Press.

Solomon, G., & Schrum, L. (2007). *New tools, new schools*. Washington, DC: International Society for Technology in Education.

Somers, C., & Surmann, A. (2005, February). Sources and timing of sex education: Relations with American adolescent sexual attitudes and behavior. *Educational Review, 57*(1), 37–54.

Sommers, C. (2001). *The war against boys: How misguided feminism is harming our young men*. New York: Simon & Schuster.

Sommers, C., & Satel, S. (2005). *One nation under therapy*. New York: St. Martin's Press.

South Texas High School for Health Professions, Mercedes (2005, June). Fulfilling community needs. *Principal Leadership, 5*(10), 28–33.

Sowell, T. (2007). *A conflict of visions*. New York: Basic Books.

Spear-Swerling, L., & Sternberg, R. (1998, January). Curing our epidemic of learning disabilities. *Phi Delta Kappan, 79*, 397–401.

Spearman, C. (1904). "General intelligence," objectively determined and measured. *American Journal of Psychology, 15*, 201–209.

Spellings, M. (2007, January). *Building on results: A blueprint for strengthening the No Child Left Behind Act*. Washington, DC: United States Department of Education.

Spellings, M. (2008, April 25). *U.S. Secretary of Education announces proposed regulations to strength No Child Left Behind*. Washington, DC: United States Department of Education.

Spies, J., Plake, B., & Murphy, L. (2005). *The Mental Measurements Yearbook (16ᵗʰ)*. Lincoln: Buros Institute, University of Nebraska Press.

Spiro, R. (2006, January/February). The new Gutenberg revolution: Radical new learning, thinking, teaching, and training with technology. *Educational Technology, 46*(1), 3–6.

Spurzheim, J. (1883). *Education: Its elementary principles founded on the nature of man.* New York: Fowler & Wells.

Stainburn, S. (2005, November/December). Straight talk. *Teacher Magazine, 17*(3), 36–39.

Standing, L., Conezio, J., & Haber, R. (1970). Perception and memory for pictures: Single trial learning of 2500 visual stimuli. *Psychonomic Science, 19,* 73–74.

Standler, R. B. (2000). *Plagiarism in colleges in USA.* Concord, NH: R. B. Standler. Retrieved from www.rbs2.com/plag.htm

Stanovich, K. (2006). Rationality and the adolescent mind. *Psychological Science in the Public Interest, 7*(1), 1–2.

Starko, A. (2001). *Creativity in the classroom.* Mahwah, NJ: Erlbaum.

Starnes, R. (2005 November). Pushing kids past our low expectations. *The Education Digest, 71*(3), 21–24.

Steele, S. (2006). *White guilt.* New York: HarperCollins.

Stefanakis, E. (2002). *Multiple intelligences and portfolios.* Portsmouth, NH: Heinemann.

Sternberg, R. (Ed.) (2003). *Handbook of creativity.* New York: Cambridge University Press.

Sternberg, R., Jarvin, L., & Grigorenko, E. (2009. *Teaching for wisdom, intelligence, creativity, and success.* Thousand Oak, CA: Corwin Press.

Sternberg, R., & Jordan, J. (Eds.). (2005). *A handbook of wisdom.* New York: Cambridge University Press.

Sternberg, R., & O'Hara, L. (2002). Creativity and intelligence. In R. Sternberg (Ed.), *Handbook of creativity* (pp. 251–272). New York: Cambridge University Press.

Sternberg, R., Roediger, H., & Halpern, D. (Eds.) (2006). *Critical thinking in psychology.* New York: Cambridge University Press.

Sternberg, R., & Subotnik, R. (Eds.) (2006). *Optimizing student success in school with the other 3 Rs: Reasoning, resilience and responsibility.* Charlotte, NC: Information Age.

Stevenson, R. L. (1886). *Strange case of Dr. Jekyll and Mr. Hyde.* New York: Scribners.

Stickgold, R. (1998). Sleep, off-line memory processing. *Trends in Cognitive Science, 2*(12), 484–492.

Stickgold, R. (2005, October 27). Sleep-dependent memory consolidation. *Nature, 437,* 1272–1278.

Stickgold, R., & Hobson, J. (2000, December). Visual learning discrimination learning and post-training sleep. *Nature Neuroscience, 4*(12), 1237–1238.

Stickgold, R., & Luskin, D. (2001, June). Visual discrimination across multiple sections and days. Paper presented at the American Academy of sleep medicine and the Sleep Research Society in Chicago, page A432 of conference proceedings.

Stiggins, R., & Chappius, S. (2005, October). Putting testing in perspective: It's for learning. *Principal Leadership, 6*(2), 16–20.

Storey, J., & Graeme, S. (2005). *Managers of innovation: Insights into making innovation happen*. Malden, MA: Blackwell.

Story, M., Kaphingst, K., & French, S. (2006, Spring). The role of schools in obesity prevention. *The Future of Children, 16*(1), 109–142.

Stout, E., & Frame, M. (2004, December). Body image disorder in adolescent males: Strategies for school counselors. *Professional School Counseling, 8*(2), 176–181.

Stover, D. (2005, December). Climate and culture: Why your school board should pay attention to the attitudes of students and staff. *American School Board Journal, 192*(12), 30–32.

Straker, D. (2008). *Creating minds*. Retrieved from http://www.creatingminds.org

Street, J. F. (2007, March 5). *Mayor John Street inducts new Parent Truant Officers.* http://ework.phila.gov/philagov/news/prelease.asp?id=296

Striegel-Moore, R., & Bulik, C. (2007, April). Risk factors for eating disorders. *American Psychologist, 62*(3), 181–198.

Strom R., & Strom, P. (2002a). Changing the rules: Education for creative thinking. *Journal of Creative Behavior, 36*(3), 183–199.

Strom, P., & Strom, R. (2002b). *Interpersonal Intelligence Inventory*. Bensenville, IL: Scholastic Testing Service.

Strom, P., & Strom, R. (2002c). Overcoming limitations of cooperative learning among community college students. *Community College Journal of Research and Practices, 26*(4), 315–331.

Strom, P., & Strom, R. (2003, Winter). Uniting adolescent support systems for?safe learning environments. *The Educational Forum, 67*, 164–173.

Strom, P., & Strom, R. (2004, Summer). Entitlement: The coming debate in higher education. *The Educational Forum, 68*(4), 325–335.

Strom, P., & Strom, R. (2005a, Fall). Cyberbullying by adolescents: A preliminary assessment. *The Educational Forum, 70*(1), 21–36.

Strom, P., & Strom, R. (2005b). Parent-child relationships in early adulthood: College students living at home. *Community College Journal of Research and Practice, 29*(7), 517–529.

Strom, P., & Strom, R. (2008). Improving American schools: Perceptions of adults and students. In D. McInerney & A. Liem (Eds.), *Teaching and learning: International best practice* (Volume 8 Research on Sociocultural Influences on Motivation and Learning) (pp. 111–132). Charlotte, NC: Information Age.

Strom, P., Strom, R., & Wing, C. (2008, December). Polling students about conditions of learning. *National Association of Secondary Schools Bulletin, 92*(4), 292–304.

Strom, P., & Strom, R. (2009). *Teamwork Skills Inventory*. Bensenville, IL: Scholastic Testing Service.

Strom, P., Van Marche, D., Beckert, T., Strom, R., Strom, S., & Griswold, D. (2003). The success of Caucasian mothers in guiding adolescents. *Adolescence, 38*(151), 501–517.

Strom, R., & Strom, P. (2007). New directions in teaching, learning and assessment. In R. Maclean (Ed.), *Learning and teaching for the twenty-first century* (pp. 115–134). New York: Springer.

Strom, R., Amukamara, H., Strom, S., Beckert, T., Moore, E., Strom, P., et al. (2000). African American fathers: Perceptions of two generations. *Journal of Adolescence, 23,* 513–516.

Strom, R., Beckert, T., Strom, P., Strom, S., & Griswold, D. (2002). Evaluating the success of Caucasian fathers in guiding adolescents. *Adolescence, 37*(145), 131–149.

Strom, R., Dohrmann, J., Strom, P., Griswold, D., Beckert, T., Strom, S., et al. (2002). African American mothers of adolescents: Perceptions of two generations. *Youth and Society, 33*(3), 394–417.

Strom, R., Lee, T., Strom, P., Nakagawa, K., & Beckert, T. (2008, September). Tiawanese grandmothers: Strengths and learning needs as perceived by grandmothers, mothers and granddaughters. *Educational Gerontology, 34*(9), 812–830.

Strom, R., Strom, P., Strom, S., Shen, Y., & Beckert, T. (2004). Black, Hispanic and White American mothers of adolescents: Construction of a national standard. *Adolescence, 39*(156), 669–686.

Strong, R., Silver, H., Perini, M., & Tuculescu, G. (2003, September). Boredom and its opposite. *Educational Leadership, 61*(1), 24–29.

Struyk, R. (2006, September/October). Gangs in our schools. *The Clearing House, 890*(1), 11–13.

Stuart, M., Lieberman, L., & Hand, K. (2006, April). Beliefs about physical activity among children who are visually impaired and their parents. *Journal of Visual Impairment and Blindness, 100*(4), 223–234.

Stuhlman, M., Hamre, B., & Pianta, R. (2002, November). Advancing the teen/teacher connection. *The Education Digest, 68*(3), 15–17.

Subrahmanyam, K., Greenfield, P., & Tynes, B. (2004, November). Constructing sexuality and identity in an online teen chat room. *Journal of Applied Developmental Psychology, 25*(6), 651–666.

Substance Abuse and Mental Health Services Administration (2005). *Overview of findings from the 2004 national survey on drug use and health.* Washington, DC: U.S. Department of Health and Human Services, Substance Abuse and Mental Health Services Administration.

Sun, S., Schubert, C., Liang, R., Roche, A., & Chumlea, W. (2005, November). Is sexual maturity occurring earlier among U.S. children? *Journal of Adolescent Health, 37*(5), 345–355.

Sunstein, B. (2000). *The portfolio standard: How students can show us what they know and are able to do.* Portsmouth, NH: Heinemann.

Sunwolf & Leets, L. (2003). Communication paralysis during peer-group exclusion: Social dynamics that prevent children and adolescents from expressing disagreement. *Journal of Language and Social Psychology, 22,* 355–384.

Sunwolf & Leets, L. (2004, August). Being left out: Rejecting outsiders and commuicating group boundaries in childhood and adolescent peer groups. *Journal of Applied Communication Research, 32*(3), 195–223.

Suzuki, L. (2004, November). The search for peer advice in cyberspace: An examination of online teen bulletin boards about health and sexuality. *Journal of Applied Developmental Psychology, 25*(6), 685–698.

Swami, V., & Furnham, A. (2007). *The psychology of physical attraction*. Clifton, NJ: Psychology Press.

Swann, W., Chang-Schneider, C., & McClarty, K. (2007, February/March). Do people's self-views matter? Self-concept and self-esteem in everyday life. *American Psychologist, 62*(2), 84–94.

Swanson, C. (2008a). *Cities in crisis: A special analytic report on high school graduation*. Bethesda, MD: Editorial Projects in Education with support from America's Promise Alliance and the Bill and Melinda Gates Foundation. Available from http://www.americaspromise.org/

Swanson, C. (2008b, January 10). Grading the states. *Education Week, 27*(18), 36–57.

Swanson, C., & Chaplin, D. (2005). *Counting high school graduates when graduates count: Measuring graduation rates under the high stakes of NCLB*. Washington DC: The Urban Institute.

Swanson, D., Spencer, M., & Peterson, A. (1998). Identity formation in adolescence. In K. Boreman & D. Schneider (Eds.), *The adolescent years: Social influences and educational challenges*. Ninety seventh yearbook of the National Society for the Study of Education, Part I (pp. 18–41). Chicago: National Society for the Study of Education.

Swearer, S., Espelage, D., & Napolitano, S. (2009). *Bullying prevention and intervention: Realistic strategies for scholols*. New York: Guilford.

Sweller, J. (2003). Evolution of human cognitive architecture. In B. Ross (Ed.), *The psychology of learning and motivation* (Vol. 43, pp. 215–266). San Diego: Academic Press.

Tally, B., & Goldenberg, L. (2005, Fall). Fostering historical thinking with digitized primary sources. *Journal of Research on Technology in Education, 38*(1), 1–21.

Tancredi, L. (2005). *Hardwired behavior: What neuroscience reveals about morality*. New York: Cambridge University Press.

Tannen, D. (1991). *You just don't understand: Women and men in conversations*. New York: Ballantine.

Taylor, R. (2005). *Assessment of exceptional students: Educational and Psychological procedures* (7th ed). Boston: Allyn & Bacon.

Temple, P. (2006). *Identity theory*. San Francisco: MacAdam/Cage.

Terman, L. M. (1916). *The measurement of intelligence*. Boston: Houghton Mifflin.

Terman, L. M. (1925). *Mental and physical traits of a thousand gifted children: Genetic studies of genius* (Vol. 1.). Stanford: CA: Stanford University Press.

Terman, L. M., & Oden, M. H. (1947). *The gifted child grows up*. Palo Alto, CA: Stanford University Press.

Terman, L. M., & Oden, M. H. (1959). *Genetic studies of genius: The gifted group at mid-life* (Vol. 5.). Stanford, CA: Stanford University Press.

Tersman, F. (2006). *Moral disagreement*. New York: Cambridge University Press.

Teti, D. (2004). *Handbook of research methods in developmental science*. Oxford: Blackwell.

Theobald, M. (2006). *Increasing student motivation: Strategies for middle and high school teachers*. Thousand Oaks, CA: Corwin.

Thoman, E., & Jolls, T. (2005). *Literacy for the 21st century: An overview and orientation guide to media literacy education*. Center for Media Literacy, Los Angeles. Retrieved April 10, 2008, from www.medialit.org

Thomas-Presswood, T., & Presswood, D. (2008). *Meeting the needs of students and families in poverty*. Baltimore: Paul H. Brookes.

Thomas, A. (2007). *Youth online: Identity and literacy in the digital age*. New York: Peter Lang.

Thomas, G., & Loxley, A. (2007). *Deconstructing special education and constructing inclusion*. New York: Open University Press, McGraw-Hill Education.

Thompson, R. (2006). *Nurturing future generations: Promoting resilience in children and adolescents through social, emotional and cognitive skills*. New York: Brunner-Routledge.

Thorn, A., & Page, M. (2008). *Interactions between short-term and long-term memory in the verbal domain*. New York: Psychology Press.

Thorndike, E. L. (1913). *Educational psychology: The original nature of man*. New York: Teachers College Columbia University.

Thorndike, E. L. (1924). Mental discipline in high school studies. *Journal of Education Psychology, 15*(2), 83–98.

Thorndike, E. L. (1932). *Fundamentals of learning*. New York: Teachers College Columbia University.

Thorndike, R. (2005). *Measurement and evaluation in education*. Columbus, OH: Merrill Education/Prentice-Hall.

Thurber, C., Walton, E., & the Council on School Health (2007, January). Preventing and treating homesickness. *Pediatrics, 119*(1), 192–201.

Thurlow, M., & Wiley, H. (2006). A baseline perspective on disability subgroup reporting. *The Journal of Special Education, 39*(4), 246–264.

Thurstone, L. (1938). Primary mental abilities. *Psychometric Monograph, 1*, 2–10.

Toffler, A. (1970). *Future shock*. New York: Random House.

Toffler, A., & Toffler, H. (2000, February/March). What next? *Civilization*, 51–54.

Toffler, A., & Toffler, H. (2006). *Revolutionary wealth*. New York: Alfred Knopf.

Tolkien, J. R. R. (2003). *The Fellowship of the Ring (The Lord of the Rings, Part 1)*. Boston: Houghton Mifflin.

Tompson, T. (2006, February 7). A look at AP-AOL's homework poll: Demographics. *USA Today*, 1.

Tomsho, R., & Golden, D. (2007, May 12–13). Educating Eric: A troubled student was put into regular classes. Then he killed the principal. *The Wall Street Journal*, pp. A1, 6.

Torrance, E. P. (1965). *Rewarding creative behavior: Experiments in classroom creativity*. Englewood Cliffs, NJ: Prentice-Hall.

Torrance, E. P. (1978). Giftedness in solving future problems. *Journal of Creative Behavior, 12*, 75–89.

Torrance, E. P. (1994). *Creativity: Just wanting to know*. Pretoria, South Africa: Benedic Books.

Torrance, E. P. (1995). *Why fly? A philosophy of creativity*. Norwood, NJ: Ablex.

Torrance, E. P. (Ed.) (2000a). *On the edge and keeping on the edge*. Westport, CT: Greenwood.

Torrance, E. P. (2000b). The millennium: A time for looking forward and looking backward. *The Korean Journal of Thinking and Problem Solving, 10*(1), 5–19.

Torrance, E. P. (2002). *Torrance Tests of Creative Thinking*. Bensenville, IL: Scholastic Testing Service.

Torrance, E. P. (2002). *The Manifesto: A guide to developing a creative career*. Charlotte, NC: Information Age.

Torrance, E. P., & Ziller, R. (1957). *Risk and life experience: Development of a scale for measuring risk-taking tendencies*. Lackland Air Force Base, San Antonio, TX: Research report AFPTRC-TN 57-23-ASTIA Document No. 09826.

Trenholm, C., Devaney, B., Fortson, K., Quay, L., Wheeler, J., & Clark, M. (2007, April*). Impact of four title V, section 510 abstinence education programs*. Princeton, NJ: Mathematica Policy Research Institute.

Trier, J. (2007, February). Cool engagements with You Tube. *Journal of Adolescent and Adult Literacy, 50*(5), 408–412.

Tropp, L., & Pettigrew, T. (2005, December). Relationship between intergroup contact and prejudice among minority and majority status groups. *Psychological Science, 16*(2), 951–957.

Trost, R. (2004). *Computer-assisted brainstorming and the global think tank*. Creative Center of the University. Retrieved November 30, 2004, from http://gocreate.com/Articles/agtt.htm

Trzesniewski, K., Donnellan, M., Moffitt, T., Robins, R., Poulton, R., & Caspi, A. (2006, March). Low self-esteem during adolescence predicts poor health, criminal behavior, and limited economic prospects during adulthood. *Developmental Psychology, 42*(2), 381–390.

Turnbull, A., Turnbull, R., Shank, M., & Smith, S. (2004). *Exceptional lives: Special education in today's schools*. Columbus, OH: Merrill/Prentice-Hall.

Twenge, J. (2006). *Generation me*. New York: Free Press.

Tyson, N. (2006, May). Rules for engaging challenging people. *Principal Leadership, 6*, 8–9.

Udry, R. (2008). *The national longitudinal study of adolescent health*. Carolina Population Center. Retrieved January 2, 2009, from http://www.cpc.unc.edu/projects/addhealth

Umemoto, K. (2006). *The truce: Lessons from an L.A. gang war*. Ithaca, NY: Cornell University Press.

United States Bureau of the Census (2008). *U.S. Interim projections by age, sex, race, and Hispanic origin: 2000–2050*. Retrieved September 25, 2008, from http://www.census.gov/ipc/www/usinterimproj/

United States Department of Agriculture. (2008a). *Steps to a healthier you*. Retrieved January 2, 2009, from http://www.mypyramid.gov

United States Department of Agriculture. (2008b). Center for Nutrition Policy & Promotion. *My pyramid tracker* (OMB 0584-0535). Retrieved January 2, 2009 from http://www.mypyramidtracker.gov

United States Department of Education, National Center for Education Statistics. (2008). *The conditions of education 2008* (NCES 2008–03D, Indicator 23). Retrieved January 5, 2009, from http://www.nces.ed.gov/programs/coe

United States Department of Education. (2008). *Family Policy Compliance Office, Family Educational Rights and Privacy Act.* Retrieved January 2, 2009, from http://www.ed.gov/policy/gen/guid/fpco/ferpa/index.html

United States Department of Health and Human Services. (2008, March 13). *Inhalant use across the adolescent years.* Retrieved from Office of Applied Studies, Substance Abuse and Mental Health Services Administration, June 25, 2008, from at http://oas.samhsa.gov

United States Department of Health and Human Services & National Institutes of Health. (2008). *Go, slow and whoa foods.* Retrieved January 2, 2009, from http://www.nhlbi.nih.gov/health/public/heart/obesity/wecan/live-it/go-slow-whoa.htm

United States Department of Justice. (2008, April 30). *Gangs.* Retrieved December 1, 2008, from U.S. Department of Justice, Office of Community Oriented Policing Services http://www.cops.usdoj.gov/default.asp?item=1593

United States Department of Labor. (2008a). *Occupational outlook handbook, 2008–2009 Edition.* Washington, DC: The Department. Retrieved January 2, 2009, from http://www.bls.gov

United States Department of Labor. (2008b). *Occupational projects and training data, 2008–2009 Edition.* Washington, DC: The Department. Retrieved January 2, 2009, from http://www.bls.gov

University of Texas. (2008). *Distance Education Center: High school courses.* Retrieved July 3, 2008, from http://www.utexas.edu/cee/dec/uths/

Uttal, W. (2005). *Neural theories of mind: Why the mind-brain problems may never be solved.* Mahwah, NJ: Erlbaum.

Vail, K. (2005, September). The world of e-learning. *American School Board Journal, 192*(9), 30–31.

Valdiserri, R. (2004, October). Mapping the roots of HIV/AIDS complacency: Implications for program and policy development. *AIDS Education and Prevention, 16*(5), 426–439.

Valenza, J. (December 2005/January 2006). The virtual library. *Educational Leadership, 63*(4), 54–59.

Vaillant, G. (2003). *Aging well.* Boston: Little Brown.

van Dijk, J. (2005). *The deepening divide: Inequality in the information society.* Thousand Oaks, CA: SAGE.

Van Vugt, M., De Cremer, D., & Janssen, D. (2007, January). Gender differences in cooperation and competition. *Psychological Science, 18*(1), 19–23.

Vangundy, A. (2004). *101 Activities for teaching creativity and problem solving.* New York: Wiley.

Velleman, J. (2005). *Self to self.* New York: Cambridge University Press.

Villa, R., & Thousand, J. (2005). *Creating an inclusive school.* Alexandria, VA: Association for Supervision and Curriculum Development.

Vonderwell, S., & Zachariah, S. (2005, Winter). Factors that influence participation in online learning. *Journal of Research on Technology in Education, 38*(2), 213–230.

Vose, D. (2008). *Risk analysis:* A quantitative guide. New York: Wiley

Vossekuil, B., Fein, R., Reddy, M., Borum, R., & Modzeleski, W. (2002). *The final report and findings of the safe school initiative.* Washington, DC: United States

Secret Service and United States Department of Education. Retrieved January 5, 2004, from http://www.ustreas.gov/usss/ntac_ssi.shtml

Vygotsky, L. (1978). *Mind in society.* Cambridge, MA: Harvard University Press.

Vygotsky, L. (1994). The development of thinking and concept formation in adolescence. In R. Van der Veer & J. Valsiner (Eds.), *The Vygotsky reader* (pp. 185–265). Cambridge, MA: Blackwell.

Vygotsky, L. (1998). The collected works of L. W. Vygotsky. In R. Rieber (Ed.), *Child psychology.* New York: Plenum.

Wahlstrom, K. (2002, December). Changing times: Findings from the first longitudinal study of later high school start times. *National Association of Secondary School Principals Bulletin, 86*(633), 3–21.

Waizenhofer, R., Buchanan, C., & Jackson-Newsom, J. (2004, June). Mothers' and fathers' knowledge of adolescents' daily activities: Its sources and its links with adolescent adjustment. *Journal of Family Psychology, 18*(2), 348–360.

Wallace, B. (2007). *Contemplative science: Where Buddhism and neuroscience converge.* New York: Columbia University Press.

Wallace, M. (2008). *50 Years from today.* Dallas, TX: Thomas Nelson.

Wallach, M., & Kogan, N. (1965). *Modes of thinking in young children of the creativity-intelligence distinction.* New York: Wadsworth.

Wang, R., Bianchi, S., & Raley, S. (2005, December). Teenagers' Internet use and family rules: A research note. *Journal of Marriage and Family, 67*(5), 1249–1258.

Ward, J. (2006). *The student's guide to cognitive neuroscience.* New York: Psychology Press.

Washington State Office of the Attorney General (2006). *Teen dating violence.* Retrieved November 20, 2008, from http://www.atg.wa.gov/page.aspx?id=1968

Washington State Office of the Attorney General (2008). Dating rights and dating responsibilities. Retrieved December 15, 2008, from http://www.atg.wa.gov/page.aspx?id=1968

Waters, M. (Director). (2003). *Freaky friday* [Motion picture]. United States: Buena Vista Pictures.

Watchler, C. (2005, March). Giving up name-calling for a week, or forever. *The Education Digest, 70*(7), 40–44.

Watkins, K. (2006, January). The Google game. *School Library Journal, 52*(1), 52–54.

Watson, J. (1925). *Behaviorism.* New York: W. W. Norton.

Watson, J. (1928). *The ways of behaviorism.* New York: Harper Brothers.

Watson, J. (1930). *Behaviorism.* New York: W. W. Norton.

Watson, J., & Rayner, R. (1920). Conditioned emotional responses. *Journal of Experimental Psychology, 3,* 1–14.

Watson, J., & Rayner, R. (2000). Conditioned emotional responses. *American Psychologist, 55*(3), 313–317.

Watson, J., & Ryan, J. (2007). *Keeping pace with K-12 online learning: A review of state-level policy and practice.* Washington, DC: North American Council for Online Learning.

Way, N., Gingold, R., Rotenberg, M., & Kuriakose, G. (2005). Close friendships among urban, ethnic-minority adolescents. *New Directions for Child and Adolescent Development, 107,* 41-59.

Weber, S., & Dixon, S. (Eds.) (2007). *Growing up online: Young people and digital technologies.* New York: Palgrave Macmillan.

Wehlburg, C. (2008). *Promoting integrated and transformative assessment: A deeper focus on student learning.* San Francisco: Jossey-Bass.

Weiner, B. (1986). *An attributional theory of motivation and emotion.* New York: Springer.

Weiner, B. (1992). *Human motivation: Metaphors, theories, and research.* Newbury Park, CA: SAGE.

Weiner, B. (2005). Motivation from an attributional perspective and the social psychology of perceived competence. In A. Elliot & C. Dweck (Eds.), *Handbook of competence and motivation* (pp. 92-116). New York: Guilford.

Weiner, B. (2006). *Social motivation, justice, and moral emotions.* New York: Taylor & Francis.

Weiner, E. & Brown, A. (2006). *Future think.* Upper Saddle River, NJ: Prentice-Hall.

Wendland, M. (2003, November 17). Cyber-bullies make it tough for kids to leave playground. *Detroit Free Press.* Retrieved December 15, 2008, from http://www.freep.com

Wheeler, T. (2005, January). Slamming in cyberspace. *American School Board Journal, 192*(1), 28-32.

Whitehouse Drug Policy (2008). *Inhalants.* Washington, DC, Executive Office of the President of the United States. Retrieved July 23, 2008, from http://www.whitehousedrugpolicy.gov/drugfact/inhalants/index.html

Whitley, B. E., Jr., & Keith-Spiegel, P. (2002). *Academic dishonesty: An educator's guide.* Mahwah, NJ: Erlbaum.

Whitted, K., & Dupper, D. (2005, July). Best practices for preventing or reducing bullying in schools. *Children & Schools, 27*(3), 167-175

Whittle, C. (2005). *Crash course: Imagining a better future for public education.* New York: Penguin Group.

Wigfield, A., & Eccles, J. (2002). *Development of achievement motivation.* San Diego: Elsevier.

Willard, N. (2006, April). Flame retardant (Cyberbullying). *School Library Journal, 52*(4), 54-56.

Willard, N. (2007) The authority and responsibility of school officials in responding to cyberbullying. *Journal of Adolescent Health, 41,* 564-565.

Willard, N. (2007). *Cyber-safe kids, Cyber-savvy teens: Helping young people learn to use the Internet safely and responsibly.* San Francisco: Jossey-Bass.

Williams, K., & Guerra, N. (2007, December). Prevalence and predictors of Internet bullying. *Journal of Adolescent Health, 41*(6), S14-S21.

Williams, R., & Newton, J. (2006). *Visual communication.* Mahwah, NJ: Erlbaum.

Williams, R., & Williams, V. (2006). *In control no more.* Emmaus, PA: Rodale.

Wilson, G., Grilo, C., & Vitousek, K. (2007, April). Psychological treatment of eating disorders. *American Psychologist, 62*(3), 199-216.

Wineburg, S., Mosborg, S., Porat, D., & Duncan, A. (2007, March). Common belief and the cultural curriculum: An intergenerational study of historical consciousness. *American Educational Research Journal, 44*(1), 40-76.

Wise, B. (2008). *Raising the grade: How high school reform can save our youth and our nation*. San Francisco: Jossey-Bass.

Woessmann, L., & Peterson, P. (2007). *Schools and the equal opportunity problem*. Cambridge, MA. The MIT Press.

Wolak, J., Mitchell, K., & Finkelhor, D. (2007). Does online harassment constitute bullying? An exploration of online harassment by known peers and online-only contacts. *Journal of Adolescent Health, 41*, S31-38

Wolfson, A., & Carskadon, M. (2005). A survey of factors influencing high school start times. *NASSP Bulletin, 89*(642), 47-66

Wormeli, R. (2006, April). Differentiating for tweens. *Educational Leadership, 63*(7), 14-19.

Worthen, M. (2007). Education policy: Implications from the expert panel on electronic media and youth violence. *Journal of Adolescent Health, 41*, S61-S63.

Wright, J., & Cleary, K. (2006, January). Kids in the tutor seat: Building schools' capacity to help struggling readers through a cross-age peer tutoring program. *Psychology in the Schools, 43*(1), 99-107.

Wu, E. (2005, Summer). Factors that contribute to talented performance: A theoretical model from a Chinese perspective. *Gifted Child Quarterly, 49*(3), 231-246.

Yarbrough, R., & Gilman, D. (2006, March). Four days a week. *American School Board Journal, 193*(3), 43-45.

Yaukey, D., Anderton, D., & Lundquist (2007). *Demography: The study of human population*. Portland, OR: Waveland.

Ybarra, M., Diener-West, M., & Leaf, P. (2007). Examining the overlap in Internet harassment and school bullying: Implications for school intervention. *Journal of Adolescent Health, 41*, S42-50

Young, M., & Penhollow, T. (2006, July/August). The impact of abstinence education: What does the research say? *American Journal of Health Education, 37*(4), 194-202.

Yurgelun-Todd, D. (2005). Inside the teenage brain. Retrieved June 3, 2008, from http://www.pbs.org/wgbh/pages/frontline/shows/teenbrain/interviews/todd.html

Zaff, J., & Smerdon, B. (May, 2008). Putting *children front and center: Building coherent social policy for America's children*. Washington, DC: First Focus.

Zemke, R., Raines, C., & Filipczak, B. (2000). *Generations at work: Managing the class of Veterans, Boomers, Xers, and Nexters in your workplace*. New York: Amacom.

Zimmer-Gembeck, M., & Mortimer, J. (2006, Winter). Adolescent work, vocational development, and education. *Review of Educational Research, 76*(4), 537-566.

Zuckerbrot, R., Maxon, L., Pagar, D., Davies, M., Fisher, P., & Shaffer, D. (2007, January). Adolescent depression screening in primary care: Feasibility and acceptability. *Pediatrics, 119*(1), 101-108.

Zullig, K., Ubbes, V., & Pyle, J. (2006, March). Self-reported weight perceptions, dieting behavior, and breakfast eating among high school adolescents. *The Journal of School Health, 76*(3), 87-92.

Zwigoff, T. (Director). (2006). *Art school confidential* [Motion picture]. United States: Sony Pictures.

LaVergne, TN USA
13 October 2009
160762LV00002B/8/P